Romani Dictionary: Kalderash – English
Rromano Alavari: Kalderashitska – Inglezitska

RROMANO ALAVARI
Kalderashitska – Inglezitska

by Ronald Lee

MAGORIA BOOKS
Toronto, 2010

ROMANI DICTIONARY
Kalderash – English

by Ronald Lee

MAGORIA BOOKS
Toronto, 2010

ROMANI DICTIONARY: KALDERASH – ENGLISH
RROMANO ALAVARI: KALDERASHITSKA – INGLEZITSKA

Chief Editor: Aggott Hönsch István

Cover design by Sebestyén.

First Edition

ISBN 978-0-9811626-4-5

Published by MAGORIA BOOKS

www.MagoriaBooks.com

LIBRARY AND ARCHIVES CANADA CATALOGUING IN PUBLICATION

Lee, Ronald, 1934-
Romani dictionary : Kalderash-English / Ronald Lee.

ISBN 978-0-9811626-4-5

1. Kalderash dialect–Dictionaries–English. 2. Kalderash dialect–Grammar. I. Title.

PK2898.L44 2010   491.4'97   C2010-907546-3

Contents

Introduction

This dictionary has been years in the making. For at least thirty it has existed in typewritten form, circulated unbound and in very few copies. Now, as the logical follow-up to his *Learn Romani*, Ronald Lee's dictionary has become accessible to everybody.

Some may question its thus becoming readily available. Romanies themselves are reluctant to share their language with others, for understandable reasons; especially in the past, those in the non-Romani world who have wanted to learn it have almost always had an ulterior motive for doing so, and almost always for their own ends rather than for the benefit of those who own the language. Grammars of Romani on library shelves in Germany are quietly and permanently removed by Sinti there, who have not forgotten what use knowledge of their language was put to during the Nazi period, the *Porrajmos*. One early draft of this dictionary was kept and destroyed by an American Romani woman who feared that it would fall into the wrong hands. Her concern was not unfounded; from her own city a small book entitled *Gypsy Talk: Law Enforcement's Guide to the Secret Language of the American Gypsy* appeared in 1993, written by Detective Dennis Marlock and privately circulated for use by the police. Its intent was "to help police officers interrogate Gypsy suspects." The mistakes in it are legion.

Is the appearance of this dictionary therefore breaking a trust? Not at all. Rather than doing so, it is providing a means of making the extensive lexicon of Romani available to Romani speakers themselves, since it contains words that only the older generations now know. Besides, there are scores of Romani dictionaries available already (the Romani Archives in Texas has over a hundred different ones), though very few of them have been written for English speakers. I am sometimes asked by Romani acquaintances why I teach a course on our history and culture. I tell them that there are scores of books about "Gypsies" available in libraries and from the Internet, and ninety-nine percent of them are written by non-Roma, and almost all of them are unreliable. Some are misleading at best and downright racist at worst, and they are readily accessible by the general public. Ronald Lee, like myself, besides being a Romani man is an academic, and therefore can present information from the inside and challenge existing misinformation.

Like Gjerdman and Ljungberg's masterpiece written nearly half a century ago, this dictionary also presents the Vlax dialect of the Kalderash Roma, that spoken by Ronald Lee's principal informant the late Russell Demitro. But unlike either Gjerdman or Ljungberg, or more recently Boretzky or Igla, Ronald is himself a Romani man and worked for many years alongside Kalderash speakers in the Romani world. Some of his life during that period of his life is documented in his book *Goddam*

Gypsy. His knowledge of their dialect is immense.

The dictionary records the variety of Kalderash Romani that is spoken in North America. It differs surprisingly little from European Kalderash, and is easily intelligible with other Vlax dialects such as those spoken by the Lovara and Machvaya. Together, Vlax constitutes the largest single dialect cluster of all Romani dialect groups, in terms not only of numbers (having perhaps five or six million speakers worldwide) but also geographically, having speakers found on all continents. It is therefore a logical variety of Romani for learners to begin with. Romanies who have lost the language, even native speakers of other dialects, are learning this kind of Romani. It does not purport to be any sort of "international standard," but work elsewhere is in progress on the creation of such a dialect, and Kalderash Vlax is providing its basis.

The day is past when grammars and dictionaries were written by, and for, non-Romani scholars. Since the advent of the Internet, e-mailing and texting have provided the perfect means of communication for a Diaspora people, and has led to an increase in literacy not only in the national language—English in the United States and Canada—but in Romani as well. The orthography employed here is especially suited to English speakers, making use of digraphs such as /ch/, /sh/ and /zh/ rather than /č/, /š/ and /ž/, an orthography now being used in Romani language publications in Hungary and increasingly used in e-mail correspondence, since it requires no suprascript accent marks. This Romani-to-English dictionary, which will in due course be followed by its English-to-Romani companion, is a masterpiece.

Ian Hancock
Director
The Romani Archives and Documentation Center
The University of Texas at Austin
www.radoc.net

References

Boretzky, N. & Birgit Igla, 1994. *Wörterbuch Romani-Deutsch-Englisch.* Wiesbaden: Harrassowitz.

Gjerdman, O. & E. Ljungberg, 1963. *The Language of the Swedish Coppersmith Gipsy Johan Dimitri Taikon.* Uppsala: Lundqvist.

Lee, Ronald , 1971. *Goddam Gypsy.* Montreal: Tundra Books. Now republished as *The Living Fire*, Magoria Books, Toronto, 2009.

Lee, Ronald, 2008. *Learn Romani.* Hatfield: University of Hertfordshire Press.

Chapter 1

How to use this dictionary

Because Kalderash Romani has noun cases and a complicated inflectional structure for adjectives and other modifiers, subject to gender and number in the nominative and the oblique, the dictionary entries have been organized with this in mind. The following synopsis has been created to give a brief overview of the grammatical structure and how to interpret the entries, many of which are accompanied by examples of word usage and idiomatic expressions.

No attempt has been made to provide an in-depth grammatical survey since this dictionary is designed to be used in conjunction with a textbook giving the grammatical rules and how to form the inflexions. These are all clearly explained in the author's previously-published *Learn Romani – Das-Dúma Rromanes* (2005, Hatfield, Hertfordshire UP), an 18-lesson home-study course which can be augmented by other learning tools including Ian Hancock's *A Handbook of Vlax Romani* (1995, Columbus, Slavica Publisher's, Inc.) and the relevant source material listed in Edward Proctor's *Gypsy Dialects* (2008, Hatfield, of Hertfordshire UP). At the time of writing (2008) these three sources are the most useful learning tools for those wishing to learn basic Kalderash Romani.

The dictionary has been created primarily to assist young Roma and others who wish to either learn Kalderash or to improve their knowledge of it, rather than for academic linguists who wish to study Romani "dialects." This need has been and continues to be amply and ably catered to by qualified academic linguists. However, there is almost a total lack of learning tools for laypeople, students and young Roma in High School or college, who in most cases will be unaware of the terminology and structure of modern linguistics or of phonetic systems requiring complicated diacritical marks not found on standard computer keyboards. The dictionary is designed as a computer-friendly, useful learning tool and linguistic terminology has been kept to a minimum. When used, it is explained in simple language and with examples of usage.

1.1 Choice of entries

The basic choice of entries come from the author's own vocabulary plus words and examples recorded from native speakers and from music CDs by native North-American speakers. The basic entries are from the North-American Kalderash dialect

1

spoken in Canada and the US augmented by words recorded by the author from speakers of mutually intelligible Latin-American and European dialects. I have avoided listing words taken from other published works except material written by native speakers such as Mateo Maximoff and other Kalderash Roma. Some of the published works consulted contained entries which I have never heard or recorded and none have been included in order to avoid possible errors in recording, transcription or typographical errors in the original sources.

It must also be realized that all speakers of Romani are at least bilingual if not multilingual. Because of this, many technical terms and modernisms from the non-Romani language spoken are intermixed with Romani, for example in North-American Kalderash; **Tho kotor manrro ánde tósta!** 'Put a piece of bread in the toaster!' Since there is no established Romani word for 'toaster.' the English word 'toaster' is employed but pronounced as if it were a Romani word. Typical could be; **Trobul o mobíli neve** *brake liners,* **zhanes.** 'The car needs a new brake liners, you know.'

In dialects of Kalderash from Europe, European-language borrowings would be employed in this way which can be confusing to English speakers learning Kalderash. Another pitfall exists in the different terminology used in various countries for items like 'cake,' 'pie,' 'cookie,' etc. Many internationally used terms such as 'banana' and 'pizza' are commonly used and inflected into oblique stems in Kalderash because their structure resembles Romani, **bananáki morki,** 'banana skin,' for example. But with a great many English words such as 'microwave' this is impossible. Many, however, are converted into athematic items such as **plondjéri** 'toilet plunger.' or **tróko** 'truck/lorry' and can then be inflected.

Kalderash like other Romani dialects has been a purely orally-transmitted language until recently and it is thus highly idiomatic. Verbs and expressions often cannot be translated literally and must rely on idiomatic constructions or even proverbs. These have been listed where appropriate. Native speakers communicating in Romani verbally, in writing, over the Internet and in publications, are also developing neologisms that are finding their way into the vocabularies of other speakers and these are listed as such in the dictionary (*neolog*). When speaking ones own dialect, these neologisms do not have to be used as much but in cross-dialectal email communication, they are used because the equivalents in the two native dialects of those communicating are different. For meeting, one dialect may have **diwáno** and **kidemos** for 'meeting' but another may not have either or have one of them but with a different meaning. Thus, to be widely understood across inter-dialectal communication, the neologism **mítingo** might be employed.

Finally, while many of the athematic entries (loan words) might seem to be derived from Spanish, they are, in fact, derived from Romanian, since Kalderash dialects have been heavily influenced by this language. A few words which appear in North-American Kalderash have been borrowed from Spanish but do not appear in central/eastern-European dialects of Kalderash. It goes without saying that Spanish loan words will appear in Kalderash and closely-related dialects in Latin America.

1.2   Caveat

Some compilers of basic children's primers, biblical translations, glossaries and even dictionaries in Vlax-Romani dialects similar to Kalderash have inserted thematic words from other Romani dialects not used in Kalderash such as **rukh** 'tree' and **len** 'river.' Others, in their enthusiasm to create a more Indic Romani have even lifted words from Hindi or calqued on Sanskrit to create terms like **bânduk** 'rifle,' **golni** 'ball'(Hindi **goli** 'bullet.') or **wastin** 'elephant' calqued from Sanskrit via Hindi **hathiñ**. One zealot even introduced the word **almári** for 'cupboard,' which is in fact, a Hindi word adopted from Portuguese in their Indian colonies at least 500 years after the ancestors of the Roma had left India! A non-literary living language is not something to be toyed with for one's own amusement like Esperanto by linguistic zealots devoted to "cleansing" it of its non-Indic athematic items. These spurious 'Romani' entries have been avoided in the dictionary since they are not understood by native speakers of Kalderash. A similar attempt at 'linguistic cleansing' was attempted with French in my native province of Quebec in the 1980s by the Provincial *Office de la Langue Française* to rid French Canadian of its anglicisms and colloquialisms. Predictably, this foundered on the reality of the rocks of the tenacity of the spoken language.

1.3   Pronunciation

There is no standard pronunciation of Kalderash Romani that is common to all native speakers in the many countries and regions of countries where Kalderash speech communities are located, any more than there is a standard pronunciation of colloquial English throughout the English-speaking world. Pronunciation, especially of vowels, differs because of migrations, isolation in specific regions by some groups, influences from the surrounding non-Romani language(s) spoken by the speakers and other factors. The pronunciation given in the following guide is that used by the author. If the subject of the dictionary had been limited a specific dialect spoken in a specific geographical area, say, Bucharest, Romania, or Toronto, Canada, a definite set of rules for pronunciation might apply. However, the purpose of this dictionary, like the author's previous *Learn Romani*, is to create a tool that will be useful both in Europe, the Americas and anywhere else Kalderash-Romani is spoken.

The phonetic system employed in this dictionary is that used for the author's previously-published *Learn Romani* course for which this dictionary is compatible and the author has been using it since the 1960s with many other Romani speakers, in personal correspondence, and in published works. The entries in the dictionary come from the following sources; North-American Kalderash, which is spoken in Canada, the US and Latin America, augmented by words from mutually-intelligible European Kalderash dialects which the author assimilated while interacting with European Romani immigrants both socially and officially as a member of the Roma Community Centre in Toronto from 1997 to 2008. It is augmented by words encountered in email correspondence with native speakers in the US, Latin America and Europe. The entries thus represent a wide spectrum of Kalderash which would be understood throughout the Americas and in Europe by native speakers as the author has found it to be.

The phonetic system is based on English and designed for English speakers. This way, it avoids the use of consonants such as > j < for > y > which are confusing to speakers of English, Spanish and French in the Americas and also the use of unfamiliar diacritical marks employed in Romani phonetic systems based on European languages which would require either special fonts or foreign-language keyboards. The author's phonetic system has been successfully used by Romani speakers in Canada and the US who need to write Romani on a standard computer keyboard without the hassle of non-existent symbols. It was also used for the Kalderash Romani which appeared in the Roma Community Centre magazine, *Romano Lil*. The stress accents and other indicators employed in this phonetic system do not have to be used by native speakers. They have been used to assist the student to pronounce the dictionary entries and Examples of sentences. The phonetics have been designed with usability and practicality in mind. A teenage Romani student in high school in North America needs to be able to write Romani on a computer without needing special fonts or foreign keyboards while publishers producing material in Romani can well afford to do without cost-augmenting and unnecessary encumbrances that might inhibit publication. The accents and stress indicators used for this dictionary at the time of writing were available on Microsoft Word United States – International Keyboard and are usually available in other default options on most computers. As already stated, they do not need to be used by native speakers.

It is impossible to give all the variations of sounds that might be encountered from Kalderash speakers across the world. Those interested in this area should consult the following: *A Handbook of Vlax Romani*, by Ian Hancock, Slavica Publishers, Inc., 1995, which is listed in the bibliography of useful sources and the applicable audio sources outlined in *Gypsy Dialects* by Edward Proctor which is also listed un the bibliography.

The following pronunciation guide, designed for this phonetic system, will enable the student to pronounce Kalderash Romani and to understand it when it is spoken if he or she follows the guidelines indicated.

Vowels

French and Spanish words are given as Examples of pronunciation where feasible to assist bilingual French speakers in Canada and bilingual Spanish speakers in the US and Canada.

a   More like Spanish '*mañana*' but the < a > in English father is close. A is longer when it is stressed than when it is not. Example; **Zha**! 'Go!' and **shurya** 'cutlery.'

â   A very short form of the above < a > sound as in English 'bat.' Example; **âmpochíl** 'arbitrate.'

ã   The < aw > sound as in English 'awful'. Example; **kwãsa** 'scythe.'

e   As in French '*allé*' or the < -ai- > sound in English 'pain.' Examples; **rakle** 'non-Romani boys, **bakre** 'sheep.'

In some Kalderash dialects, especially in France and North America, the final < -e > in the dative case is shortened and sounds more like < û > is in **mángû** for **mánge** or **raklèskû** for **raklêske.**

ê   Between the < e > in English 'bed' and Spanish '*huevo*.' Examples; **amên** 'us' **mênshiya** 'ball.' Some speakers pronounce this as a schwa sound which does not exist in English in which case **kher** 'house' sounds something like **khûr**.

i   Like the < ee > sound in English 'seem.' Examples; **iv** 'snow' or **rakli** 'non-Romani girl.'

î   Close to the < i > sound in English 'tin.' Example; **tînzhíri** 'frying pan, skillet.'

o   A long < o > something like English 'home' or French '*eau*.' Example; **raklo** 'non-Romani boy.'

ô   Close to English sound in got, or Spanish '*hombre*.' Example; **ôblo** 'round.' In American Kalderash, many speakers pronounce the < ô > as < â > because of the influence of American pronunciation of English. Thus **shôto** 'big shot' becomes **shâto** just like American English 'hot' is often pronounced 'hat' by Americans. This should be avoided with European speakers.

u   A long < oo > sound as in English 'you.' Spanish '*luna*' or French 'vous.' Example; **tu** 'you' **manush** 'male person, human being, elderly man.'

û   A very short vowel sound something like the < u > in English 'under.' It is a centralised and unrounded vowel sometimes represented in Romani by < ï > or < ü > with an umlaut as a diacritic. Examples; **zûn (zün)** 'saddle,' **atvtsûn (avtsïn)** 'steel.' The English < u > as in 'under' can be used in the meantime. See also Hancock, I., 1995 p.45, **rrïnza** 'chitterlings.'

y   When < y > used in this alphabet as a 'glide' or 'semi-vowel' it is a short < y > sound which often replaces the terminal long < ee > sound in words like **bakri** 'ewe' or **sapní** 'female snake' when these singular nouns become plurals as in **bakrya** and **sapnya** and in their oblique declensions such as **bakryánsa** and **sapnyánsa**.

    In English, with words ending in < ia >, the pronunciation convention is to pronounced words like Maria as if it were written < **Maríya** > ignoring the obvious glide in the actual pronunciation. In the dictionary, Romani words like **síniya** 'chair' do not use the English convention of < **sínia** > but include the < y > as a glide to properly represent the phonetics of Kalderash since the alphabet used in the dictionary is totally phonetic and cannot employ English non-phonetic spelling conventions. When < y > is used as a consonant as in < **yalovítsa** > 'sterile women or female animal' it has the English value of < y > as in 'yellow.' When it immediately follows a consonant, it is a glide as in **grasnya** 'mares.' When used between two vowels it has the linking value of a glide as in the name Maria but written as Mariya to indicate the linking glide as in **síniya** 'table.'

Vowel Stress

Kalderash Romani and Vlax-Romani dialects in general normally place the stress on the last vowel in the word as in **baxtalo** 'lucky' or **wudar** 'door'. No stress indicators will be shown for these entries. When the stress falls on any vowel other than the last, it will be indicated as follows: **láda** 'trunk, chest,'(stress on the first vowel) **masári** 'butcher' (stress on the second vowel), **barvalo** 'rich' where the stress falls on the third or last vowel and which does not need to be indicated. Stress position can change depending on where the word appears in a sentence. We can have a sentences like: **Wo si manush barvalo** 'He is a wealthy man,' (stress on last vowel, **barvaló**) or **O bárvalo manush mulo** 'The wealthy man died.' (In this second Example; the stress in < **bárvalo** > is on the first vowel not the last. The sentences which accompany many of the entries will show how this occurs in speech patterns.

When the diacritics **â, ã, ê, î, ô, û,** are used to indicate vowel sound, the stress accents will be indicated, even if the stress falls on the last vowel as in **mômêlí** 'candle' unless the vowel marked with the pronunciation mark is to be stressed. Examples; **mênshiya** 'ball' (stress falls on the first vowel), **pônyáva** 'carpet,' (stress falls on the second vowel of the word and **drômorró** 'small, narrow road.' (stress falls on the third or last vowel). In a very few words, all vowels in the word may be **â, ã, ê, î, ô,** or **û,** and in this case, the vowel to be stressed will appear not with the accent < ^ > but with the French grave accent < ` > . Example; **vôrdòn** 'caravan' where both vowels are pronounced < ô >.

Falling Diphthongs

ai   Similar to the sound of English 'high' or 'rye.' Example; **nai** 'finger.' When the nominative noun **nai** has a case ending added to it the diphthong usually becomes < **aiy-** > with the case ending added . Example; **naiyêsa** 'with the finger.' The < **y** > is a glide between the diphthong and the added case ending. Note: Case endings are covered in the grammatical synopsis of this dictionary.

ei   Rarely used, mainly as an interjection (Hey, watch out!) or in songs. It sounds like the < **ey** > in English 'hey!' without the < **h** >. Example; **Éi, shavále!** 'Hey, Romani boys!'

oi   Close to the sound of English 'oyster' or 'boy.' Example; **gunoi.** 'rubbish.' When words with this sound have case endings added the < **oi** > becomes < **oiy-** > with the case ending added. Example; **gunoiyêsa** 'with the garbage.'

ui   Not a sound used in English. It is like the < **ouille** > in french *rartatouille*. Example **sapui** 'soap.' As with < **ai** > and < **oi** >, < **ui** > becomes < **uiy-** >: when the nominative takes a case ending in the oblique. Example: **sapuiyêsa** 'with the soap.'

Note: In words like **shey** 'Romani girl, daughter,' and **dey** 'mother' there is a slight < **-y** > sound after the < **-e** >. This is not a diphthong.

Rising Diphthongs

ya   Typical in plural endings of feminine nouns. **Gazhya** 'non-Romani women,' or **fyal** 'type.'

yi   Typically in **rroiyi** 'spoon'

yo   Typical in passive and athematic verb conjugations. **Baryol** 'He/she grows bigger.'

Stress of Diphthongs

When diphthongs are stressed, the stress is shown on the first letter of the double vowel but the double vowel is stressed as a single sound. Example; **cháiniko** (*chái*-niko), 'tea pot.' When not stressed, no stress mark appears. Example; **raikano** (rai-*kanó*) 'elegant,' where stress falls on the last or final vowel.

Consonants

b   Close to English < b > Examples; **beshel** 'he/she sits' and **basmáli** 'shawl'.

c   Not used. in this phonetic system except in < ch >. In Europe, many Romani phonetic systems use this sound to represent the < ts > sound as in 'itself.' of this phonetic system.

ch   A hard < ch > sound not like English . 'cheer' but more like 'chatter' as in **chiriklo** 'male bird.' There are actually two < ch > sounds in Kalderash Romani, one < chh > is more aspirated than the other. (See Hancock, I, p. 39). Many Kalderash sub-dialects change this aspirated < chh > sounds to a < sh > sound. In the dictionary the alternate < chh > sound is not used. Instead, it appears as < sh > which is common in North-American Kalderash and in many European Kalderash and related dialects. So what will be '**chhavo**' or '**chhav**' (Romani boy) in some European dialects will be written as '**shavo**' or '**shav**' in the dictionary. See < sh > following in this pronunciation guide.

d   A dental < d > as in French or Spanish with the tongue touching the back of the top teeth. Examples; **dav** 'I give' **diwáno** 'meeting, discussion.'

dj   Close to the < j > sound of English 'Jack.' Examples; **djédjêsh** 'train' **djéla** 'thing, matter' **djungalo** 'ugly.' Some speakers pronounce this sound more like a < dy > as in < dyéla > for **djéla** while with others, it is closer to a < dzh > sound.

f   Close to English. Examples; **fárba** 'paint, ' **fakalêtso** 'rolling pin.'

g   Hard < g > as in English 'got'. Examples; **gitára** 'guitar,' **galav** 'saddle bag'. In this phonetic system, this sound should never be pronounced as in English 'George.' (see < dj > preceding)

h   Like English < h > in hammer. Example; **harmasári** 'stallion.'

j   Not used in this phonetic system except in combination with < d > in < dj >. In European-Romani phonetic systems, the < j > is often used to represent the consonant < y > as in 'yellow.' .

k   Close to the English sound in 'cat.' A hard < k > sound, not like English 'kismet.' Example; **kukurúzo** 'Indian corn'.

kh   An aspirated < k > sound like the < kh > in wor**kh**orse. Examples; **kher** 'house' or **khaini** 'chicken.'

l   Closer to the English < l > in 'glue' than in 'lend.' Examples; **lav** 'I take,'. **alav** 'word.'

ly   This is actually a single sound in Romani. Example; **raklya** 'non-Romani girls.' It is close to the < ll > in Castilian Spanish as in '*llamar*' or the <gl > in Italian '*voglio*.' Standard Canadian/American English < li > in 'valiant" or 'Valium' is close.

m   English value as in 'mother.' Examples; **mobíli** 'automobile' **mômêlí** 'candle.'

n   English < n > can be used here but in Romani, it is usually a dental sound with the tongue touching the upper front teeth. Examples; **kána** 'when' **nanári** 'pineapple.'

In some Kalderash dialects. especially in North America, the <-n > is sometimes dropped in words like **rani** or **Rromani** which become **raiyi** 'lady' and **Rromayi** as in **Rromayi buki** 'Romani business.'

ng   when < n > and < g > appear together in a Romani word, they are pronounced as in English 'mango' and never like two words as in 'man go.' Examples; **bangyarev** 'I bend,' **lêngo** 'theirs,' **bêng** 'devil.'

ny   When < n > is followed by the glide or semi-vowel < y > it becomes one sound like the Spanish < ñ > in *'mañana'* or the < ny > in English 'canyon.' Examples; **sapnya** 'female snakes,' (plural of **sapni**).

p   Like English < p > in 'spot.' Examples; **pái** 'water' and **papírya** 'documents.' It must be born in mind that < p > in English, has more of an aspirate sound that it has in Kalderash, French or Spanish.

ph   An aspirated < ph > Do not pronounce it as an < f > as in English 'phone.' This < ph > sound in Romani is close to the English sound in 'hap**h**azard.' Examples; **phúrdav** 'I blow' and **phurt** 'footbridge.'

q   Not used

r   Close to Spanish < r > as in 'Pedro,' and made with the top of the tongue. The < r > must be clearly heard, not slurred or drawled as is common in American, Canadian and British English. Examples; **rai** 'gentleman' **ródav** I seek, search.' Many American Roma, whose Romani is influenced by American sounds, when writing words like **bari** on Internet chat lines, write this as > **badi**.< because of the tapped < r > in American English. Example; **Woy see badi koodva.** for **Woi si bári kúrva.** ' She is a real bitch.' Many non-Romani speakers often hear this < r > as English < l > and thus hear **'zalzáilo'** for Kalderash **zalzáiro** 'acid.'

rr   In some Kalderash dialects, for Example; in Canada , the US and parts of Latin America, in France and other countries of Europe, the Kalderash < rr > is pronounced from the throat (a guttural) like German *'roust'* or the Continental French < r > as in *'rendez-vous.'* It should sound like an uvular < rr > made when a person gargles. .Examples; **Rrom** 'Romani man, or 'husband.' **Rromni,** 'Romani woman or wife.' **rrai** 'switch, can' **burr** 'bush, thicket.' Ask a native speaker to say **rai** 'gentleman' and **rrai** 'cane/switch' for the differences in sound.

In North America and in some western European Kalderash dialects, the guttural < rr > can affect the vowels < e >, < i > and to a lesser extent, < û >, when they immediately follow the < rr >. In this case, **múrre** 'mine' becomes **múrrü**, **sheyorri** 'young girl' becomes **sheyorrü** or **shyórrü** and **bizerrûwo** 'embroidery' becomes **bizerrüwo**. *See also* < û > in the vowel section preceding this section for explanation of < ü > **and** < ï > which do not appear in the dictionary. Those learning Romani do not have to use these sounds since European Roma who do not use them are perfectly understood by speakers of American Kalderash who do use them. They, in turn, however, may have difficulty understanding native speakers of North-American Kalderash who often say **shyorrï** for European-Kalderash **sheyorri** 'young girl.'

In some other Kalderash and Vlax-Romani dialects the < **rr** > sound is often retroflexed or trilled. The < **rr** > must be clearly heard and not slurred. It is not the same sound as < **r** > given above in this alphabet which is a different sound. (See Hancock, I, 1995, p.9/10. For beginners, a clearly pronounced < **r** > will do for both sounds until they can hear these sounds from native speakers or from a cassette or CD. In Britain, the Scottish < **r** > sound, while not exactly the Romani sound, would be better than the standard drawled or slurred English < **r** > as in 'Robert.' Examples; **rroiyi** 'spoon' **rrátsa** 'duck.'

s   Similar to English < **s** > in 'sea.' This is never slurred to become a < **z** > sound as it is in English, for Example; the final < **s** > in 'strangers,' or the < **s** > in 'business.' Examples; **sim** 'I am,' **sap**, 'male snake,' **skamin** 'chair.'

sh   The English sound as in 'shears' will be close enough. There are at least two different < **sh** > sounds in Romani, one as in **shêl** 'one hundred' and **shîl** meaning 'cold, flue.' In **shêl** meaning one hundred, the tongue is forward on the palate but in **shîl,** meaning 'cold or 'flue,' it is curled backwards towards the throat. Beginners can ignore this difference until they become familiar with the sounds from native speakers or recordings. Many European speakers often pronounce the sound as they do the > **sh** > sound in the non-Romani language they also speak. Examples; **shib** 'tongue, language' **shoro** 'head' **shoshoi** 'male rabbit.' The slight differences in sound will not prevent the student from being understood or to understand spoken Romani.

t   A dental < **t** > sound and unaspirated (without the puff of air) like the English < **t** > in 'top.' But in Romani, the tongue should touch the back of the upper front teeth. Examples; **tu** 'you' and **tudkála** 'coal tar.'

th   An aspirated dental < **t** > sound suggesting a puff of air after the < **t** > something like the combination < **th** > in English 'hothouse'. This sound should never be pronounced like < **th** > in English 'think' or as in **thud** meaning a loud noise. The < **th** > sound as in English 'think.' does not exist in Romani ands many speakers pronounce English 'them' as 'dem.' Examples; **thud** 'milk,' **thuv** 'smoke' and **thagar** 'ruler.'

ts   This is a single sound in Romani like the < **ts** > in English 'itself' or in Italian '*pizza*.' Examples; **tsêra** 'tent,' **tsigára** 'cigarette,' and **tsirratsítsa** 'pittance.'

v   This is a troublesome sound in Romani. Some 'authorities' on Romani admit to only one sound for what I have listed as a separate < **v** > and < **w**. In my opinion, this is not justified by what I have been hearing for decades from native speakers from many countries and regions.

Kalderash < **v** > is not a hard < **v** > like English 'volatile' but between English < **v** > and < **w** >, a softer < **v** > than in English. Not all Kalderash speakers pronounce it the same. With some, especially in the former Yugoslavia and in Hungary, a definite < **v** > can be clearly heard due to phonetic osmosis from the host-culture language as in **voliv** 'I love,' and '**vorbiv**,' 'I talk.' In Romanian Kalderash and among many North-American and French

Kalderash speakers, the same words sounds like '**woliw**' or even '**ualiw**,' and '**worbiv**.' This become evident when native speakers pronounce the final < v > in the first person singular of verbs, for example, **beshav** 'I reside' which often sounds like '**besháw**,' or **zhav** 'I go" which sounds like '**zhao**' with a diphthong as in Italian *ciao*.

When a word is regularly pronounced with a < v > sound, it will be indicated. Examples; **vorrúto** 'disgusting' or **vádra** 'bucket.' In the dictionary, I have used both < v > and < w > depending on how I most often hear the sound from speakers with whom I interact and how I normally pronounce the word in question.

w See entry for < v > above. When a word is almost always pronounced with the English value for < w > it will be indicated by this sound. Examples; **wudar** 'door' and **wúlitsa** 'street.'

x A sound from the throat (guttural) like the < ch > in Scottish 'loch.,' Spanish '*justicia*' or German '*Achtung*.' Examples; **xas** 'we eat,' **xoxavel** 'He is lying.'

y Pronounced like English 'yellow' when it is used as a consonant. Examples; **Yádo** 'Hades' and **yalakráno** 'scorpion.' See < y > under vowels for further explanation.

z Like English 'zeppelin.' Examples; **zalzáiro** 'acid' and **zumin** 'soup.'

zh This sound is like the < zh > in 'Doctor. Zhivago.' It exists in English but is shown by different letters, for Example; the < z > in 'azure ' or the < s > in 'pleasure.' Examples; **zhav** 'I go,' **zhanav** 'I know.' French < j > as in '*Jean*.'

1.4 Thematic and athematic items

These two terms may not be clear to those those not familiar with their meanings when applied to Romani. The following brief description is included. to clarify this.

Thematic items. This applies to all words brought by the ancestors of the Roma from India plus words acquired from non-Indic languages outside of India on their migration westwards to and during their lengthy stay in Anatolia in the Seljuk Sultanate of Rum and in the Asiatic Byzantine Empire after their arrival in Anatolia in the 12th century CE if not by the late 11th century CE. This thematic battery includes words of Persian, Armenian and Byzantine Greek origin plus a smattering of terms from other contact languages during the migration to and during the stay in Anatolia such as *mangin* 'treasure' directly or indirectly from Mongolian. All **thematic** words follow a basic set of grammatical rules which are generally predictable though not always strictly followed by all speakers of modern Kalderash.

Athematic items. This applies to those words (loan words) acquired by the migrating Romani groups after the various groups left Anatolia and crossed the Bosphorous by the early 14th century CE, entered the Balkans with the Ottoman Turks or on their own and slowly spread out in small groups until they appeared in central/western Europe in the early 15th century CE. Many groups, of course, remained, in the Balkans which has always had the largest concentration of Roma and where sedentary communities of Roma became established by at least the early 14th century. Later loan words adopted in various Balkan countries and elsewhere in Europe are not always the same in the various Romani dialects in Europe and by extension, in the Americas and elsewhere.

Romani has been described as a "Balkanized-Indian language" and while there is a common core of early Balkan borrowings from various languages that appear in the diverse recorded Romani dialects from Wales to eastern Russia, there are also batteries of words picked up by localized groups which remained or were forced to remain, in specific linguistic areas and now, by emigration, in the Americas. Kalderash is an example of one of these, a number of very closely-related and mutually intelligible dialects which evolved in an area where the surrounding population spoke Romanian during the period of Romani slavery in the Principalities of Moldavia and Wallachia and in Transylvania. It is a member of the Vlax-Romani group of closely-related dialects which include the dialects spoken by the *Lovari, Machwáya, Churári, Mashári and Tsolári* all of which are basically mutually intelligible to native speakers.

All these dialects evolved in Wallachia and Moldavia (which were then Ottoman vassal states) and Transylvania and were heavily influenced by Rumanian and to a lesser extent by Hungarian, modern Greek and Serbian, languages which were often spoken by the nobility and landowners who owned Romani slaves from the 14th century CE to 1864 when they were emancipated, and by the serfs and villagers in certain regions of Wallachia and Moldavia. Many groups, including speakers of Kalderash, then left the regions of former slavery and moved south into the southern Balkans, west into central and western Europe and east into Tsarist Russia. There, later athematic items were adopted. By the late 19th century they had spread to the Americas where they and other Vlax-Romani speaking groups constitute the most numerous indigenous Romani population. Today, the major long-established dialects spoken in the Americas are Vlax-Romani dialects, mainly *Kalderashitska* and *Machvanítska*.

Because of this dispersal of the various Romani groups, **athematic** items appear in one dialect and not in another making mutual communication difficult. Kalderash and related groups, who were mostly nomadic and even today, are mobile, tend to retain a high degree of commonality because of frequent movement between countries and through intermarriage where the only common language is Kalderash Romani. However, differing **athematic** items and different pronunciations of the same words appear in the various related dialects. With today's Internet, mass communication has created a growing number of educated Roma who are using a Vlax-based Romani as a means of international communication over the Internet which is having a leveling effect on such people. The availability of music CDs from many countries in different Romani dialects also contributes to this levelling effect. among Romani speakers in general.

1.5   Explanation of the entries

Nouns: All nouns are listed with their gender shown as *nm* or *nf*. Plural nouns like **love** 'money,' or **tsáliya** 'clothes' are entered as *nm/pl* or *nf/pl*.

Many masculine nouns have feminine inflexions such as **bakro** 'ram' and **bakri** 'ewe.' In such cases, the masculine entry is listed in the dictionary and the feminine inflection is included after the main entry. Since every animate noun would have to be entered twice to include both genders if entered separately, this has been done to keep the number of entries to a workable minimum. Some important feminine nouns derived from their masculine variants have been included separately such as **Rromni** 'Romani woman/wife' or **sapní** 'female snake' which also has the meaning of 'viper.'

Adjectives are listed as *adj*. They are given in their nominative masculine singular declension unless they apply only to the feminine gender such as **phari** 'pregnant.' An entry like **barvalo** *adj* rich, would apply only to masculine nouns in the nominative singular. **O Rrom si barvalo.** 'The man is rich,.' But it would be declined in the feminine when used with a feminine noun as follows, **E Rromni si barvali** 'The woman is rich.' It would also have a nominative common plural in **barvale** plus oblique masculine and feminine singulars and a common plural. The necessary tables are given later in this section.

Adjectives with the < **bi-** > prefix. Only the most commonly-used and important of these are listed as entries. Almost any adjective can take this prefix to give the opposite meaning such as **bi-baxtalo** 'unlucky' from **baxtalo** 'lucky' or **bi-gêtimé** 'unready.'

Genitive adjectives: Almost any abstract noun ending in < **-mos** > can create its own genitive adjective from its oblique stem in **(-más)** and perhaps a thousand or more would have to be listed. Only some of the most commonly used are included. Example: **mudarel** 'he/she kills' gives the abstract noun of **mudarimos** which becomes **mudarimas-** in the oblique stem (accusative case) and forms its genitive case in **mudarimásko** 'murderous, lethal,' which is the genitive case and also the genitive adjective.

Adverbs are listed as *adv*. All those which have their own identify as adverbs such as **andre, mishto, opral, wórta**, etc are listed. Only a few of the most commonly-used adverbs derived or inflected from adjectives are included. The basic rules for forming adverbs are given in this synopsis and a more extensive coverage appears in *Learn Romani*. Some commonly used adverbial phrases are also included and listed as *adv/phr*

All other entries: Their indicators are alphabetized in the list of abbreviations.

Punctuation and diacritical marks

. period

    Between and at the end of Romani and English sentences given as examples: **Kerav buki ándo fóro.** I work in the city.

; semicolon

    Example(s) using the immediately preceding entry. **xal** *vt/i* eat; **Me xav.** I am eating.

: colon

    derived from the main dictionary entry or the immediately preceding entry. Example, **baxtalo,** *adj* lucky, fortunate: *nm* lucky man: *nf* **baxtali** lucky woman. Examples include, a substantive derived from an adjective such as **baxtalo**, a diminutive derived from the main or preceding entry , a feminine form of the masculine entry, such as **sapni** from **sap** 'snake'

, comma

    another meaning of the entry: **baro** *adj* big, important

/ stroke

and/or: **arman/amran** *nf* oath. **Nashavel** *vt* cause or make to flee/race/run.

~ swung dash

main entry. Example, **kerel** *vt/i* do, make: ~ love make money: ~ **mui** make noise.

( ) parentheses

a) when used in an English translation of a Romany sentence, it indicates a word to be understood but not used in the Romani sentence. **Chi zhanav te kerav.** I don't know how to do (it). **b)** to set apart different meanings of a word. **Xal 1)** eat **2)** devour **3)** erode, **4)** wear out. **c)** To indicate English sentences in regular or italic which give explanations of the meanings or other explanatory information about the entry. Example; **kukashtára** 'toilet'. (*not used in polite conversation/before women*)

Abbreviations

abl ablative case

acc accusative case

alt alternative/alternate

adj adjective

adv adverb

adv/phr adverbial phrase

Am North American. Entries used in Canada and USA derived from English, Spanish or some other source and not generally known or used in Europe and Kalderash words I have not heard from native speakers from Europe such as **pozhárniko** 'fireman,' for more commonly used European **pompéri**.

Anat Anatomical

arch archaic

art article

aux auxiliary

Can words used in Canada but could be known by American Kalderash speakers. Not usually used by European speakers.

comp/adj compound adjective such as **bange-wastêsko** left-handed.

comp compound

cond conditional

conj conjunction

cont contraction

Cul Culinary

dat dative case

decl declension

def/art definite article

def/v defective verb such as **trobul** 'need' or **mol** 'it is worth' which generally exists only in the third *psn* in North America although fully-conjugated forms can also be heard from some speakers. Example, **molyov, molyos, molyol,** etc.

dem demonstrative

dim diminutive

Eng English

esp especially

Eur Words used in Europe but not generally heard from native speakers in Canada and US. Some are being re-introduced by newcomers from Europe and through, music CDs from Europe, the Internet, intermarriage and social interaction.

exclam exclamation

exp explanation

f feminine

fig figurative/figuratively

imp imperative

Folk Folklore

Fr French

fr from

fut future
gen genitive
id idiom/idiomatic
indef indefinite
inst instrumental case
interj interjection
interrog interrogative
Lang language
lit literally
m masculine
Mil Military
Mus Music
n noun
nf feminine noun
nm masculine noun
neolog neologism
nom nominative
ns nouns
num numeral
obl oblique: An inflected declension of the
   of the nominative case of the word to
   an inflected case form as a main entry
   or as a definition of an entry.
oft often
pst past tense
part participle, particle
phr phrase
pl plural
pls plurals
poss possessive
pp past participle

pp/adj past participle and adjective
pref prefix
prep preposition/prepositional case
pres present
priv privative
prod productive
pron pronoun
psn person
psns persons/people
qv which see/refer to this under this listing
refl reflexive
s singular
sl slang
smbdy somebody
smth something
suff suffix
Sp Spanish
tnse tense
us usually
v verb
v/refl reflexive verb
var variant form of/variant of
vi intransitive verb
vlg vulgar
voc vocative case
vt transitive verb
vt/i verb which can be transitive or intransitive
Zod Zodiac

Chapter 2

Romani grammar

2.1   Nominative and Oblique

Nominative

The nominative is the form of the noun, adjective and pronoun as it appears in the dictionary.

gurumni *nf*	cow
kon *pron*	who
lolo *adj*	red
love *nm/pl*	money
makh *nf*	fly
murro *pron*	my, mine
kon *pron/interrog*	who
parno *adj*	white
síniya *nf*	table
tsáliya *nf/pl*	clothes
wárekon *pron*	somebody

The nominative of nouns serves as the subject of the sentence. Both **grast** and **síniya** (below) are in the nominative case. The nominative adjective describes the nominative noun subject to gender and number. The nominative pronoun must be inflected like other nouns when used in the oblique.

O parno grast xal char.	The white horse is eating grass.
E loli síniya si shukar.	The red table is attractive.
Kon akharel?	Who is calling?

The Accusative case or The Oblique Stem

The oblique is when the nominative noun is inflected into one of its case forms. This inflection also affects all modifying adjectives, personal pronouns, definite articles or other modifiers.

Animate Nouns

The accusative case of nouns is also called the oblique stem. If the noun in the accusative position in the sentence defines an animate (living person, animal or a supernatural being) it then takes the accusative case which also serves as the oblique stem and is declined for gender and number. If the noun is inanimate like a table, its accusative case is not used as such but is used as the oblique stem like the accusative case of animate nouns as shown in the following:

Kindem parne grastes.	I bought a white horse.
	*Here **grastes** is in the accusative case of **grast** and thus is the oblique stem.*
Kindem parne gasten.	I bought white horses.
Kindem parnya grasnya.	I bought a white mare.
Kindem parne grasnyan.	I bought white mares.
Kas akhardyan?	Whom did you call?

Inanimate Nouns

If the noun in the accusative position is inanimate, like a chair, the nominative does not change when it becomes the accusative/oblique stem. Inanimate nouns in Romani grammar are objects like trees, rocks and most insects which have only one gender in Romani, such as **makh** 'fly' are included in this category. When animates like lambs or fish are killed and cooked, they become inanimates. Thus **astaráv mashen** 'I catch (live) fish,' and **Pekel mashe** 'she is cooking (dead) fish.'

Phaglas o lolo skamin.	He/she broke the red chair.
Phaglas e loli síniya .	He/she broke the red table.
Kindyam lole skamina.	We bought red chairs.
Kindyam lole síniyi.	We bought red tables.

The nominative cannot be used with the other case forms and must be inflected even if the noun is inanimate.

Golótar la lólya siniyása ándo vôrdòn.
He departed with the red table in (his) van.
*Here **síniya** is in the instrumental case form.*

2.2   Noun Case Forms

Masculine Thematic and Athematic

All families of nouns, both **thematic** and **athematic**, are given in the author's previously-published *Learn Romani*. This also gives the English meanings of the case forms and how they are used.

Type 1. Animate thematic nouns ending in a consonant.
The accusative serves as the oblique stem for animate nouns.

phral   brother   ANIMATE NOUN

CASE NAME	SING.	PL.
nominative	**phral**	**phrala**
accusative	**phralês**	**phralên**
instrumental	**phralêsa**	**phralênsa**
ablative	**phralêstar**	**phralêndar**
prepositional	**phralêste**	**phralênde**
dative	**phralêske**	**phralênge**
genitive	**phralêsko**	**phralêngo**
vocative	**phrála**	**phralále**

Type 2. Animate thematic nouns ending in a vowel.

raklo   non-Romani boy   ANIMATE NOUN

CASE NAME	SING.	PL.
nominative	**raklo**	**rakle**
accusative	**raklês**	**raklên**
instrumental	**raklêsa**	**raklênsa**
ablative	**raklêstar**	**raklêndar**
prepositional	**raklêste**	**raklênde**
dative	**raklêske**	**raklênge**
genitive	**raklêsko**	**raklêngo**
vocative	**rakléya**	**raklále**

Type 3. Inanimate thematic nouns ending in a consonant.

tover   ax   INANIMATE NOUN

CASE NAME	SING.	PL.
nominative	**tover**	**tovera**
accusative	**tover**	**tovera**
instrumental	**toverésa**	**toverênsa**
ablative	**toverêstar**	**tovarêndar**
prepositional	**toverêste**	**toverênde**
dative	**toverêske**	**toverênge**
genitive	**toverêsko**	**toverêngo**
vocative	**toveréya**	**toverále***

As can be seen from the foregoing, it is only necessary to learn the nominative and the accusative (oblique stem) of animate nouns since all other cases except the vocative can easily be formed from the accusative if the rules are known or consulted.

*The vocative is normally used mainly with people's names, with family and friends. In more formal speech, in prayer, benedictions and other solemn invocations, it can include God, saints and other supernatural entities. In folktales, poems and songs, it is sometimes used with animals, demons and mythological characters or even trees or flowers. It is given here simple to show how it would be formed if needed.

Feminine Thematic and Athematic nouns

The accusative serves as the oblique stem for feminine thematic nouns.

The majority of nouns denoting female persons and animals end in a consonant or the vowel < i >. Vocatives of inanimate feminine nouns and of minor insects are seldom inflected to the vocative. Some feminine animates have unpredictable oblique stems such as **dey** 'mother' which has **da** and **shey** 'daughter' which has **sha**.

Type 1. Feminine nouns ending in a consonant.

drakh   grape   INANIMATE NOUN

CASE NAME	SING.	PL.
nominative	**drakh**	**drakha**
accusative	**drakh**	**drakha**
instrumental	**drakhása**	**drakhánsa**
ablative	**drakhátar**	**drakhándar**
prepositional	**drakháte**	**drakhánde**
dative	**drakháke**	**drakhánge**
genitive	**drakháko**	**drakhángo**
vocative (if needed)	**drakhíyo**	**drakhále**

Type 2. Thematic feminine nouns ending in a vowel.

rakli   non-Romani girl   ANIMATE NOUN

CASE NAME	SING.	PL.
nominative	**rakli**	**raklya**
accusative	**raklya**	**raklyan**
instrumental	**raklyása**	**raklyánsa**
ablative	**raklyátar**	**raklyándar**
prepositional	**raklyáte**	**raklyánde**
dative	**raklyáke**	**raklyánge**
genitive	**raklyáko**	**raklyángo**
vocative	**raklíyo**	**raklyále**

Athematic Noun Cases

Athematic noun cases follow the same basic inflectional structure as **thematic** noun cases except that they have many variant families which exhibit root inflection and other minor differences which need to be studied in detail in *Learn Romani* or in Hancock's *A Handbook of Vlax Romani*.

Sample 1. Masculine nouns ending in a vowel.
This is the largest family of **athematic** masculine nouns
and it is still being augmented by new additions. There
are many other families which have their own rules for
inflection and these must be studied in detail in *Learn
Romani* or elsewhere.

wáso   dish   INANIMATE NOUN

CASE NAME	SING.	PL.
nominative	**wáso**	**wásurya**
accusative	**wasós-**	**wasonên-***
instrumental	**wasósa**	**wasonênsa**
ablative	**wasóstar**	**wasonêndar**
prepositional	**wasóste**	**wasonênde**
dative	**wasóske**	**wasonênge**
genitive	**wasósko**	**wasonêngo**
vocative	—	—

Pharradyas o wáso.   He/she broke the dish.
Xaladem le wásurya.   I washed the dishes.

Sample 2. Masculine abstract nouns in < **-mos** >.
While the termination < **-mos** > is thematic (from Byzantine
Greek), the root element of the noun can be either **thematic**
as in **marimos** 'fight' or **athematic** as in **volimos** 'love.'

volimos   love   INANIMATE NOUN

CASE NAME	SING.	PL.
nominative	**volimos**	**volimáta**
accusative	**volimas-**	**volimatan-**
instrumental	**volimása**	**volimatánsa**
ablative	**volimátar**	**volimatándar**
prepositional	**volimáte**	**volimatánde**
dative	**volimáke**	**volimatánge**
genitive	**volimásko**	**volimatángo**
vocative	—	—

---

*Since 'dish' is inanimate, these two forms are the oblique stems and would not be used as accusative
nouns. Instead, the nominative forms would serve as the accusatives.

Sample 3. Feminine athematic nouns ending in a vowel.
This is the largest family of athematic feminine nouns and it is
still being augmented by new additions.

motúra   broom   INANIMATE NOUN

CASE NAME	SING.	PL.
nominative	motúra	motúri
accusative	moturá-*	moturán-*
instrumental	moturása	moturánsa
ablative	moturátar	moturándar
prepositional	maturáte	moturánde
dative	moturáke	moturánge
genitive	moturáko	moturángo
vocative	—	—

Kindem motúra.   I bought a broom. *(Nominative as accusative.)*
but:
Kindem harmasariyes.[†] I bought a stallion.

Some feminine nouns ending in < -a > refer to masculine genders such as **gázda**
'boss' and **katána** 'soldier.' While these should be inflected the same as any other
feminine noun ending in < -a > , the tendency of many speakers is to treat them as
masculine and say **o gázda** instead of **e gázda** and **gazdêsko** in the genitive instead
of **gazdáko**.

How to identify thematic and athematic words

Thematic. In singular nouns and adjectives of more than one syllable the stress falls
on the last vowel in the word. No stress accent is shown because this is the normal
position of stress in thematic words. This is how they are shown in the dictionary
entries.

bakro	*nm*	ram, male sheep
bokhalo	*adj*	hungry
chachiwalo	*adj*	truthful, just
petalo	*nm*	horseshoe
rakli	*nf*	non-Romani girl
wudar	*nm*	door, doorway

Athematic. In nouns and adjectives the stress never falls on the final vowel of the
word except in a few rare instances which are easily identified from their entries in
the dictionary, for example, **alxire** *nm* 'pope.'

diligátsiya	*nf*	delegation
filástra	*nf*	window
gálbeno	*adj*	yellow

---

*Oblique stems since 'broom' is an inanimate noun.
[†]*The accusative of* **harmasári** *nm is used here since stallion is an animate noun.*

galbenichóso	adj	yellowish
mênshiya	nf	ball
murtáno	nm	tomcat
ôblo	adj	round

Nouns with one vowel. Entries with only one syllable ending in a consonant can be masculine or feminine. The following are typical and are all **thematic.**

bal	nm/pl	hair
drakh	nf	grape
dukh	nf	pain
kak	nm	uncle
kan	nm	ear
khul	nm	excrement
likh	nf	nit
lil	nm	letter
lim	nf	mucus
nakh	nm	nose
pakh	nf	wing
phal	nf	plank
shib	nf	tongue/language
yag	nf	fire
yakh	nf	eye

Nouns ending in < **-mos** > are always masculine.*

barimos	nm	greatness, size
ansurimos	nm	marriage (of a man)

Gender of Nouns

There are only two genders, masculine and feminine. There is no neuter gender. Thus inanimate objects must be masculine or feminine.

anrro	nm	egg
drom	nm	road
gono	nm	bag
lim	nf	mucus
skamin	nm	chair
snat	nf	warning
yag	nf	fire

---

*This has an alternate form in < **-pe** > which replaces or co-exists with < **-mos** > in some Kalderash dialects which would give **ansuripe** for **ansurimos**. The inflected forms of < **-pe** > remain the same in Kalderash but not in non-Kalderash Romani dialects such as the *Yerli/Arlides* cluster in the South Balkans.

baripe	nm	greatness, size
maripe	nm	fighting, war

Many masculine nouns representing people or animals can also have a female form as shown in the following:

balo	*nm*	male pig	**bali**	*nf*	sow
buzno	*nm*	male goat	**buzni**	*nf*	nanny goat
choxãnó	*nm*	ghost	**choxãní**	*nf*	female ghost

but:

guruv	*nm*	bull	**gurumni**	*nf*	cow
zhukel	*nm*	male dog	**zhukli**	*nf*	bitch
grast	*nm*	gelding	**grasni**	*nf*	mare

The above three are subject to root inflection and thus require two separate entries.

Gender and Definite Article

The definite article must reflect the gender of the subject to which it refers It is important to remember that people and most living things must be defined by gender. In English, for example, the word 'horse' can refer to a male or a female horse as in 'I bought another horse.' In Romani, the horse in question, like most other large animals, would have to be defined by gender when this is known to the speaker.*

The Definite Article

MASC. NOMINATIVE SING.		FEM. NOMINATIVE SING.	
o grast	the male horse	**e grasni**	the mare
o balo	the male pig	**e bali**	the sow
o birtash	the male bar-tender	**e birtáshka**	the female bar-tender

The definite article is used with the names of people and often with other proper nouns.

Me sim o Zlácho.	I am Zlacho.
O Zlácho avel.	Zlacho is coming.
O Zlácho thai o Yóno aven.	Zlacho and Yono are coming.
O súmnakai si kuch.	Gold is expensive.
O Del kam-del!	God will provide!

The plural form for mixed genders is always the masculine plural which serves as a common plural.

le grasta	the male horses
le grasnya	the mares
kindyam grastên	we bought horses (all male/mixed geldings and mares)

---

*grast *nm* implies a gelded horse. Stallion or stud horse is **xarmasári.** *nm*

kindyam grasnyan	we bought mares
le Rroma	The Romani men or
	the Romani men and women
le Rromnya	The Romani women

The Plural Oblique Definite Article

| MASC. SING. OBLIQUE | FEM. SING. OBLIQUE |
| **le grastês**   the gelding | **la grasnya**   the mare |

| MASC. PL. OBLIQUE | FEM. PL. OBLIQUE |
| **Le grastên** the geldings | **le grasnyan** the mares |

Sometimes the plural definite article is elided to **l'**:

Phirélas pa l' gava.
He was traveling through the rural towns.

Indefinite Article

There is no indefinite article other than the numeral **'yekh'** or **'ekh,'** which means 'one.' This is often used in folktales, stories and narrations of past events but less often in daily conversation. In regular speech, the indefinite article is usually omitted:

Si ma grast.	I have a horse.
Ródel kher.	He is looking for a house.
De mánge kotor manrro!	Give me a piece of bread!

but:

Sas ekh bárvalo Rrom kai zhanglem ánde Kalifórniya...
There was a rich Rom I knew in California...

Yekh zhukel nashti kándel do xulan.
A dog cannot obey two masters.

The English word 'It'

The English word 'it' must be translated as **lês** 'he' or **la** 'she' in Kalderash so it is necessary to know the gender of what the word the 'it' references.

Where is your car?	**Kai tíro mobíli?**
I sold it.	**Bikindem lês.** (**mobíli** is *nm*)
Throw me the ball!	**Shúde mánge e mênshiya!**
Here! Catch it!	**Ále! Astar la!** (**mênshiya** is *nf*)

The English word 'them'

'Them' is the same word as the personal pronoun **'lên'** which does not change for gender. In conversations, **lên** is often contracted to **le** as in **Dikhlem le** 'I saw them.'

Have you seen my brothers?	**Dikhlan múrre phralên?**
I haven't seen them.	**Chi dikhlem lên/le.**
Where are your rings?	**Kai tire angushtrya?**
I sold them.	**Bikindem lên/le.**

Compound nouns

There are both **thematic** and **athematic** compound nouns and others which are a mixture of both in their compound elements.

mulêngo-kher *comp/nm*   mortuary
Both elements are **thematic**

mobilêski-shûna *comp/nf*   automobile tire
Both elements are **athematic**

kále-shtákli *comp/nf/pl*   sunglasses
First element **thematic** second element **athematic**

Noun Plurals

These must be studied in *Learn Romani* or one of the other recommended sources. While thematic nouns have more predictable plurals (excepting root inflection), athematic nouns have multiple families and exceptions within these families.

Thematic noun plurals

SING.   PL.
masculine nouns ending in the vowel <-o >
  raklo   **rakle**   non-Romani boy

SING.   PL.
masculine nouns ending in a consonant
  wudar   **wudara**   door

feminine nouns ending in the vowel < - i >
  rakli   **raklya**   non-Romani girl

feminine nouns ending in a consonant
  drakh   **drakha**   grape

Exceptions to these rules are given in the dictionary following the singular entry.

Irregular Noun Plurals

Some nouns, both thematic and athematic have irregular and unpredictable plurals. These are given in the dictionary. Plurals that are predictable from the rules given above and in *Learn Romani* are not listed in the dictionary.

SING.	PL.
dáta *nf* time	**dêtsi**
firánga *nf* curtain	**firênzhi**
rráta *nf* wheel	**rróti**
várga *nf* stripe	**vêrzhi**
zhukel *nm* dog	**zhukla** (root inflection)

Noun singulars which also serve as plurals.

Some nouns, mainly **thematic**, have the same form for singular and plural in the nominative singular and plural in general conversation but this practice is not standard among all speakers like 'fish' and 'sheep' are both singulars and common plurals among English speakers.

dand *nm*	tooth and teeth
grast *nm*	horse and horses

Avél hergéla grast.	A herd of horses is approaching.

When these nominative nouns are inflected to the oblique, they are declined in their plural forms. when the oblique plural is required.

He came with his horse.	**Avilo pêske grastêsa.**
He came with his horses.	**Avilo pêske grastênsa.**

Compound Noun Plurals

In compound nouns, plurals are not usually given in the dictionary. It is important to remember that both elements of the compound must be plural.

SING.		PL.
perimáski-cheran (thematic)	falling star	**perimáske-chera**
snatáko-sámno (athematic)	danger signal	**snatáke-sámnurya**

2.3   The Adjective and stress

Thematic adjectives

No stress indicators are shown for thematic entries. But be aware that the stress can change depending on the position of the adjective in any given sentence.

baro	*adj*	big, great, large
barvalo	*adj*	rich, wealthy

Athematic Adjectives

Athematic adjectives will have their stress elsewhere but never on the last vowel of the entry.

drágo	*adj*	beloved, dear
legálno	*adj*	legal
Inglezítsko	*adj*	English

Stress of adjectives in conversation

The stress of **thematic** adjectives always falls on the last vowel of the adjective in the main entries which is how it is usually pronounced. This is outlined in the section on phonetics. In regular speech, however, the stress of **thematic** adjectives can change position and we can have **Barvalo si, kodo Rrom** 'He is wealthy, that man,' or **Wo si bárvalo Rrom.** 'He is a wealthy Rom.'

One rule, which has been given by some authorities, is that when the **thematic** adjective is descriptive and precedes the noun, it is not stressed on the final vowel but when it is in apposition (after the noun) it is always stressed on the final vowel. In practice, however, this rule is not universally followed by native speakers who usually place the stress in the first or last vowel of the adjective when it is descriptive but universally on the final vowel when it is in apposition.

DESCRIPTIVE ADJECTIVE		ADJECTIVE IN APPOSITION
o bókhalo grast	the hungry gelding	**o grast bokhalo**
e bókhali grasni	the hungry mare	**e grasni bokhali**

Hêrmêntíl-pe o bókhalo grast.
The hungry horse is neighing.

Mangel khas o grast bokhalo.
The hungry horse wants hay.

Pravardem le bokhale grastes.
I fed the hungry horse.

In examples using the case form, the adjectives takes the stress on the last or final vowel.

More conservative speakers may also use the following construction using the post-nominal adjective. See also Hancock, p. 75.

Pravardem le grastes, le bokhales.
I fed the horse, the hungry one.

Dem-dúma le Rromêsa, le bokhalêsa.
I spoke with the Rom, with the hungry one.

Thematic adjectives in the dictionary

All adjectives are given in the masculine nominative singular unless they apply only to the feminine gender such as **phari** 'pregnant'.

pharo	*adj*	difficult, heavy
phari	*adj*	pregnant

All adjectives must be inflected for gender and number in the nominative and inflected to its corresponding oblique forms when used in the oblique with inflected nouns.

	NOMINATIVE
baro Rrom	important Romani man
bari Rromni	important Romani woman
bare Rroma	important Romani people (men and women)
bare Rromnya	important Romani women

	OBLIQUE
le bare Rromêsa	with the important Romani man
la barya Rromnyása	with the important Romani woman
le bare Rromênsa	with the important Romani men*
le bare Rromnyánsa	with the important Romani women

Thematic and **athematic** adjectives which do not end in a vowel do not change for gender in the nominative but they do when inflected to modify nouns in the oblique. There are only a few of these such as **kuch** 'expensive,' **ivand** 'raw' and 'shukar 'beautiful/handsome.'

	NOMINATIVE
THEMATIC EXAMPLE	
shukar	beautiful, handsome
o shukar grast	beautiful gelding (*nm*)
e shukar grasni	beautiful mare (*nf*)
le shukar grasta	beautiful geldings (*nm/pl*)
le shukar grasnya	beautiful mares (*nf/pl*)

	OBLIQUE
le shukare grastêsa	with the beautiful gelding
la shukarya grasnyása	with the beautiful mare

---

*The plural form for a mixed gender group is always the masculine form.

le shukare grastênsa   with the beautiful horses
                              (both genders or all male)
le shukare grasnyánsa   with the beautiful mares

Athematic adjectives in the dictionary

Main entries for singular **athematic** adjectives ending in a vowel are also given in the masculine nominative but in their case, there is no change when used to modify feminine nouns in the nominative singular.

drágo rrom   beloved husband
drágo rromni   beloved wife

Athematic adjectives can be easily identified in the main entries because their stress never falls on the last or ultimate vowel of the adjective as it does for **thematic** adjective entries, *ex:* **mûndro** 'wonderful'(*athematic*) and **barvalo** 'rich, wealthy.' (*thematic*). Athematic adjectives differ greatly from **thematic** adjectives since they belong to families which have their own rules for nominative and oblique declensions. They are all covered in detail in the author's *Learn Romani* and in Ian Hancock's *A Handbook of Vlax-Romani.*

NOMINATIVE

mûndro   wonderful

MASC. SING.	FEM. SING	MASC. PL.	FEM. PLUR.
mûndro	**mûndro**	**mûndri**	**mûndri**

lúngo   long

MASC. SING.	FEM. SING	MASC. PL.	FEM. PLUR.
lúngo	**lúngo**	**lúndji**	**lúndji**

OBLIQUE

mûndrone	**mûndronya**	**mûndrone**	**mûndrone**
lúngone	**lúngonya**	**lúngone**	**lúngone**

ATHEMATIC EXAMPLE

prósto   common, ordinary

NOMINATIVE

o prósto gazho	the common man
e prósto gazhi	the common woman
le prósti gazhe	the common men
le prósti gazhya	the common women

OBLIQUE

le próstone gazhésa	with the common man
la próstonya gazhyása	with the common woman
le próstone gazhênsa	with the common men
le próstone gazhyánsa	with the common women

The declensions given here are the most common but there are also other families with differing forms and root inflection which are outlined in *Learn Romani.*

Adjectives with the suffix < -ichóso >

The productive suffix < **ichóso** > can be added to both thematic and athematic adjectives to change the meaning slightly like the < **-ish** > in English 'reddish.'

> *adj.* **lolo**   'red'   → **lolichóso**   'reddish'
>   thematic root

> *adj.* **gálbeno** 'yellow' → **galbenichóso** 'yellowish'
>   athematic root

NOMINATIVE

MASC. SING.	FEM. SING.	MASC. PL.	FEM. PL.
lolichóso	**lolichóso**	**lolichósone**	**lolichósone**

OBLIQUE

MASC. SING.	FEM. SING.	MASC. PL.	FEM. PL.
lolichósone	**lolichósonya**	**lolichósone**	**lolichósone**

Adjectives can become nouns

Adjectives and past participles of verbs, which also serve as adjectives, can have nominalized forms and thus become nouns as in Spanish *el hombre rico* 'the rich man or *el rico* 'the rich man.' They are then subject to gender and number in the nominative and the oblique.

	ADJ.	DERIVED NOUNS		PLURAL
rich	**barvalo**	**barvalo**	rich man	**barvale**
		barvali	rich woman	**barvalya**
dead	**mulo**	**mulo**	dead man	**mule**
		muli	dead woman	**mulya**

Genitive adjectives

Genitive adjectives are derived from the genitive case forms of nouns which are used to show possession. For example, John's hat would be **le Yankóski stagi** 'the Yanko's hat' and Mary's hat would be **la Maráki stagi** 'The Mary's hat' and the life of the Roma would be **le Rromêngo tráyo** 'The life belonging to the Roma.' When used in this way, the genitive case is a noun case implying possession. However, any noun can be inflected into the genitive case giving the following: type of examples of the genitive case used as an adjective. When used as an adjective, it must follow the rules of **thematic** adjectives for gender and number in the nominative and the oblique even if the root element is athematic because the case ending must be considered thematic.

ENG.	KALD.	GEN. NOUN	USE AS A GEN. NOUN
male cat	**murtáno**	**murtanósko**	**le murtanósko wáso** the cat's bowl
"	"	"	**le murtanóski pori** the male cat's tail
female cat	**mútsa**	**mutsáko**	**la mutsáko wáso** the female cat's bowl
"	"	"	**la mutsáki pori** the female cat's tail
male cats	**murtáya**	**murtanêngo**	**le murtanênge wásurya** the male cats' bowls
female cats	**mútsi**	**mutsángo**	**le mutsánge wásurya** the female cats' bowls

but:

ENG.	KALD.	GEN. ADJ.	USE AS A GEN. ADJ.
glass	**stákla**	**stakláko**	**o stakláko wáso** the glass bowl
"	"	"	**e stakláki filástra** the glass window
death	**merimos**	**merimásko**	**o merimásko Rrom** the dying Romani man
"	"	"	**e merimáski Rromni** the dying Romani woman

Compound adjectives using the genitive adjective

These are common in **Kalderash** and are composed of a descriptive adjectives such as **lasho** 'good' and a genitive adjective **xamásko** 'of or pertaining to eating' to create **lashé-xamásko** 'good to eat or delicious' which are formed from abstract nouns in < **-mos** >, a masculine productive suffix.

xamos *nm*   act of eating/eating
xamás-   singular accusative/oblique stem
xamásko   genitive adjective

In compound adjectives of this type, the descriptive adjective must be in the masculine oblique singular because it modifies a masculine noun in < **-mos** > while the second element, the genitive adjective, is declined for gender and number in the nominative and the oblique. All dictionary entries of these compound adjectives are given in the nominative masculine singular.

Nominative

lashé-xamásko	delicious, good to eat
lashé-xamásko shônko	delicious ham
lashé-xamáski múra	delicious berry
lashé-xamáske múri	delicious berries

Past participles as adjectives

The past participles of both **thematic** and **athematic** verbs can be used as adjectives. Those derived from **thematic** verbs must follow the rules for **thematic** adjectives for gender and number in the nominative and the oblique. Those derived from **athematic** verbs have only one form which does not change for gender, number in the nominative or the oblique.

Thematic past participles

mulo	dead
mulo zhukel	dead male dog
muli zhukli	dead bitch
mule zhukle	dead male dogs
mule zhukla	dead bitches

Past participles as nouns

Since they serve the function as adjectives, past participles can also be nominalized and serve as nouns when applicable. When used as nouns, they are subject to gender and number in the nominative and the oblique.

PAST PARTICIPLE		AS A MASCULINE NOUN
dukhado	injured	male patient
mudardo	murdered	male murder victim
mulo	dead	male corpse
nashlo	fled	male fugitive

PAST PARTICIPLE		AS A FEMININE NOUN
dukhadi	injured	female patient
mudardi	murdered	female murder victim
muli	dead	dead woman
nashli	fled	female fugitive

Athematic past participles

These have only one form in North-American Kalderash which does not change for gender or number and have no oblique declensions. In some European dialects they do have these. (see Hancock pp. 19-20)

marime	contaminated	
marime ponyáva	contaminated carpet	with *nf*

marime rroiya	contaminated spoons	with *nf/pl*
marime vôrdòn	contaminated wagon	with *nm*
marime wásurya	contaminated dishes	with *nm/pl*
farbome	painted	
farbome wudar	painted door	with *nm*
farbome síniya	painted table	with *nf*
farbome wusht	made-up lips	with *nm/pl*

The particle bi- used with adjectives

The particle **bi-** in **Kalderash** means 'without' and can be used by itself as follows. **Golótar bi lêski raxámi.** 'He left without his jacket.'

When prefixed to an adjective it can change the word to create the opposite meaning. This is the equivalent of English prefixes such as dis- in dishonest or un- in unclean. Adjectives so modified must still follow the rules of other adjectives for gender and number in the nominative and the oblique.

ADJ.	ENG.	WITH BI-PREFIX	ENG.
chacho	true	bi-chacho	untrue
farbome	painted	bi-farbome	unpainted
lasho	good	bi-lasho	bad
merimásko	mortal	bi-merimásko	immortal
pakyailo	believed	bi-pakyailo	disbelieved
pharrado	broken	bi-pharrado	unbroken
vulime	wrapped up	bi-vulime	unwrapped
wuzho	clean	bi-wuzho	unclean

Since **bi-** can be prefixed to adjectives and past participles to change the meaning, only the most common and important are listed in the dictionary in order to keep entries to a minimum.

The use of **bi-** when prefixed to genitive adjectives is also very important in Romani since these can translate many English constructions which cannot otherwise be translated.

EXAMPLE
Bi-lovênge sámas kána areslam ándo fóro.
We had no money when we arrived in the city.

Bi-tserênge sas ándo kodo kámpo.
They had no tents in that camp.

Bi-tserêngo 'without tents' *pl/gen/adj* of **tséra** *nf* 'tent.'

This family of adjectives is also important since it serves as the negative of the instrumental case.

| xabenêsa | with food |
| bi-xabenêsko | without food (foodless) |

Dyas amênge sláva bute xabenêsa
We gave ourselves a feast with a lot of food.

O marimos meklas amên bi-xabenêsko
The war left us without food.

Adverbs

Thematic adjectives drop the final vowel and add < **-es** >

ADJECTIVE		ADVERB
baxtalo	lucky	**baxtales**

Thematic adjectives that end with a consonant simply add < **-es** >

ADJECTIVE		ADVERB
shukar	beautiful	**shukares**

Athematic adjectives ending in a vowel add < **-nes** > to their nominative singular form which appears as the main entry.

ADJECTIVE		ADVERB
drágo	darling, dear	**drágones**
yéftino	cheap	**yéftinones**

Those ending in a consonant take < **-ones** >

ADJECTIVE		ADVERB
kuch	expensive	**kuchones**

Some adverbs, both **thematic** and **athematic** exist as adverbs in their own right or if **athematic**, often keep the same form as both adjectives and adverbs. This rule can vary greatly among native speakers and groups of speakers. Those in my dialect are listed in the dictionary.

fúgo	*adj/adv*	quick, quickly
mishto	*adv*	fine, well
wórta	*adj/adv*	right, correctly

Adverbs are often formed by employing inflected nouns in the oblique which can include many with the prefix < **bi-** >

zor *nf*	power, strength
zorása	with power/strength, instrumental case of **zor**

Del-dúma zorása.
He/she speaks with power/convincingly.

bi-zoráko without having power/strength/unconvincingly, genitive case of 'zor' with prefix < **bi-** >

Del-dúma bi-zoráko.
He speaks without power/strength/unconvincingly.

2.4   Numerals

The cardinal and ordinal numerals appear in the dictionary. The rules for declining numerals are given in *Learn Romani* and in Hancock. What should be born in mind is that Kalderash numerals can be nominalized (take noun forms) like thematic adjectives and possessive pronouns. They are then declined for gender and number in the nominative and the oblique.

NOMINATIVE
Three (men) are singing.	**Trin gilaban.**
Three (women) are singing.	**Trin gilaban.**

OBLIQUE
I heard three (men) singing.	**Ashundem trinen te gilaban.**
I heard three (women) singing.	**Ashundem trinan te gilaban.**
I came with three (men).	**Avilem trinênsa.**
I came with three (women).	**Avilem trinánsa.**

trinorre	three little children of mixed gender or all male gender
trinorrya	three little female children

OBLIQUE
Ansurimé-lo trinorrênsa.
He is married with three sons or mixed gender children.

Ansurimé-lo trinorryánsa.
He is married with three little daughters.

2.5   Conjunctions and prepositions

These are all included in the dictionary and most are accompanied by examples of usage. Some are multifunctional and others are compounds.

It is important to bear in mind that common English prepositions like 'by,' 'from,' 'to' and 'with' are most often translated into Kalderash by noun cases (postpositions). For example, 'with the horses' would be **le grastênsa** 'the horses-with,' and 'from the town' as **le gavêstar** 'the town-from.'

2.6   Verbs

It is vitally important to understand that here is no infinitive of the verb in Kalderash Romani. All verb entries are given in the third person singular conjugation which is a common practice in Romani linguistics. The past participle/adjective is also listed.

This serves as an aid in identifying which verb family an entry belongs to and allows the past tense to be formed.

EXAMPLES OF DICTIONARY ENTRIES

sikavel	*vt*	he/she teaches	*pp/adj*	**sikado**
gilabal	*vt/i*	he/she sings	*pp/adj*	**gilabado**
volil	*vt*	he/she loves	*pp/adj*	**volime**
farbol	*vt*	he/she paints	*pp/adj*	**farbome**

All other tenses, excluding the imperative singular and plural for thematic verbs can be formed from the present indicative and past tense. In many cases, the entry contains an example of the past and other tenses in the sentences. The rules for all verb conjugations can be found in *Learn Romani*. Most verbs have more than one meaning and the dictionary should be consulted to determine these. The past participle/adjective is always listed in the dictionary and this, minus its final vowel gives the root or stem of the of the past tense for most verbs.

Example:
phabardo *pp/adj* burned **phabardem** I burned,
1st person
past tense

Verb Entries

Transitive verbs shown by *vt*:

phabarel *vt*   he/she burns/incinerates

Intransitive verbs shown by *vi*:

sovel *vi*   he/she sleeps

Transitive or **intransitive** shown by *vt/i*:

zhanel *vt/i*   he/she knows

Primary verbs

This is the most difficult family to deal with because of the unpredictability of their past tense conjugations, root inflection and other factors. For this dialect, they are best studied in detail in *Learn Romani*. They include both transitive and intransitive verbs while many are absoluite transitives and are indicated in the dictionary by *vt/i*.

Sample 1
dikhel *vt/i* see: *pp/adj* **dikhlo***

PRESENT INDICATIVE		PAST TENSE	
dikhav	I see	**dikhlem**	I saw
dikhes	you see	**dikhlan**	you saw
dikhel	he/she sees	**dikhlas**	he/she saw
dikhas	we see	**dikhlam**	we saw
dikhen	you see	**dikhlan/dikhlen**	you saw
dikhen	they see	**dikhle**	they saw

IMPERATIVE TENSE
sing. **dikh**   pl. **dikhen**

Sample 2
avel *vi* come: *pp/adj* **avilo**

PRESENT INDICATIVE		PAST TENSE	
avav	I come	**avilem**	I came
aves	you come	**avilan**	you came
avel	he/she comes	**avilo**	he came
		avili	she came[†]
avas	we come	**avilam**	we came
aven	you come	**avilan**	you came
aven	they come	**avile**	they came

IMPERATIVE TENSE
sing. **av** pl. **aven**

Sample 3
gilabal *vt/i* sing: *pp/adj* **gilabado**

PRESENT TENSE		PAST TENSE	
gilabav	I sing	**gilabadem**	I sang
gilabas	you sing	**gilabadyan**	you sang
gilabal[‡]	he/she sings	**gilabadyas**	he/she sang
gilabas	we sing	**gilabadyam**	we sang
gilaban[‡]	you sing	**gilabadyan**	you sang
gilaban[‡]	they sing	**gilabade**	they sang

IMPERATIVE TENSE
sing. **gilaba** pl. **gilaban**

In verbs of this type in < -al > the imperative singular does not end in a consonant but takes an extra vowel < -a >. Some others like this are:

---

*Note how the *pp/adj* gives the stem of the past tense.

[†]Some primary verbs end in a vowel like **avilo/avili** and thus have separate forms for masculine and feminine nouns.

[‡]In verbs of this type, the third person singular and plurals and the second person plural in < –al > and < –an > differ from the majority of other primary verbs with < –el > and < –en >

EXAMPLES: SING.   PL.

asal	laugh	**asa**	**asan**
azbal	touch	**azba**	**azban**
bilal	melt	**bila**	**bilan**
daral	fear	**dara**	**daran**
izdral	tremble	**izdra**	**izdran**
mêrzál	envy	**mêrzá**	**mêrzán**
pakyal	believe	**pakya**	**pakyan**

AND < **-AL** > VERBS WITH ONE SYLLABLE.

xal	eat	**xa**	**xan**
zhal	go	**zha**	**zhan**

Sample 4
zhanel *vt/i* know *pp/adj* **zhanglo**

Verbs of this type undergo root inflection between the present indicative and the past tense.

PRESENT INDICATIVE		PAST TENSE	
zhanav	I know	**zhanglem**	I knew
zhanes	you know	**zhanglan**	you knew
zhanel	he/she knows	**zhanglas**	he/she knew
zhanas	we know	**zhanglam**	we knew
zhanen	you know	**zhanglan**	you knew
zhanen	they know	**zhangle**	they knew

IMPERATIVE TENSE
sing. **zhan** pl. **zhanen**

Sample 5
kídel *vt/i* collect: *pp/adj* **kidino**

PRESENT INDICATIVE		PAST TENSE	
kídav	I collect	**kídem**	I collected
kídes	you collect	**kídan**	you collected
kídel	he/she collects	**kídas**	he/she collected
kídas	we collect	**kídam**	we collected
kíden	you collect	**kídan**	you collected
kíden	they collect	**kídine**	they collected

IMPERATIVE TENSE
sing. **kíde** pl. **kíden**

Verbs of this type differ from the previous samples in the following:

1. The stress falls on the first vowel in the word, not on the last.

2. The past participle serves only as the stem of the third person plural. For other past tense conjugations the < -ino > is deleted and the remaining < kíd- > becomes the stem.

Others verbs with imperatives like this are **anklel** 'climb,' **del** 'give,' **kándel** 'obey,' **khándel** 'smell,' **shpídel** 'push,' **shúdel** 'throw,' **wúshtel** 'rise,' and **xútel** 'jump.' Not all of these are stressed on the first vowel in the other tenses. One exception in the imperative is **húlel** *vi*, 'descend.'

IMPERATIVE		SING.	PL.
shúdel *vt*	throw	**shúde**	**shúden**
but:			
húlel	descend	**húli**	**húlen**

Causative and Denominative verbs.

These verbs are far more predictable and much easier to deal with. They are formed from adjectives, primary verbs and nouns. They are transitive but some speakers sometimes use them as transitive absolutes (without an object).

Sample 1
sikavel *vt* teach: *pp/adj* **sikado**

PRESENT INDICATIVE		PAST TENSE	
sikavav	I teach	**sikadem**	I taught
sikaves	you teach	**sikadyan**	you taught
sikavel	he/she teaches	**sikadyas**	he/she taught
sikavas	we teach	**sikadyam**	we taught
sikaven	you teach	**sikadyan**	you taught
sikaven	they teach	**sikade**	they taught

IMPERATIVE TENSE
sing. **sikav**   pl. **sikaven**

Sample 2
kalyarel *vt* make black/blacken *pp/adj* **kalyardo**

PRESENT INDICATIVE		PAST TENSE	
kalyarav	I blacken	**kalyardem**	I blackened
kalyares	you blacken	**kalyardyan**	you blackened
kalyarel	he/she blackens	**kalyardyas**	he/she blackened
kalyaras	we blacken	**kalyardyam**	we blackened
kalyaren	you blacken	**kalyardyan**	you blackened
kalyaren	they blacken	**kalyarde**	they blackened

IMPERATIVE TENSE
sing. **kalyar**   pl. **kalyaren**

Thematic Passive and Inchoative verbs

These verbs are intransitive and are formed from adjectives and the past participles of verbs. They express the same thing as English verbs with 'be,' 'become' and 'get.' They can have other functions which will be seen in the English translations in the dictionary and in *Learn Romani*.

Verbs like this have two forms of the present indicative. The long form is used more in Europe and the short form is more commonly heard in North America. Both forms are universally understood.

Sample 1 from **thulo** *adj* fat
thulyávol *vi* become/get fat: *pp/adj* **thulilo**

PRESENT INDICATIVE			PAST TENSE	
LONG FORM	SHORT FORM			
thulyávov	**thulyov**	I get fat	**thulilem**	I got fat
thulyávos	**thulyos**	you get fat	**thulilan**	you got fat
thulyávol	**thulyol**	he/she gets fat	**thulilo**	he got fat*
			thulili	she got fat*
thulyávos	**thulyos**	we get fat	**thulilam**	we got fat
thulyávon	**thulyon**	you get fat	**thulilan**	you got fat
thulyávon	**thulyon**	they get fat	**thulile**	they got fat

IMPERATIVE TENSE
sing. **thulyo**   pl. **thulyon**

Note that the stress is not necessarily always on the final vowel in passive and inchoative verbs. It is important to watch for the changes in stress in verb conjugations and tenses. The stress falls on the second vowel in **mudárdyol** but on the last or ultimate vowel in **mudardilo** and on the second vowel of the 1st psn past tense.

Sample 2 from **mudardo** *adj* killed, murdered
mudárdyol *vi* be/get killed/murdered: *pp/adj* **mudardilo**
mudárdilem I got killed

PRESENT INDICATIVE			PAST TENSE
LONG FORM	SHORT FORM		
mudárdyovav	**mudárdyov**	I get killed	**mudárdilem**
mudárdyoves	**mudárdyos**	you get killed	**mudárdilan**
mudárdyovel	**mudárdyol**	he gets killed	**mudárdilo**
		she got killed	**mudárdili**[†]
mudárdyovas	**mudárdyos**	we get killed	**mudárdilam**
mudárdyoven	**mudárdyon**	you get killed	**mudárdilan**
mudárdyoven	**mudárdyon**	they get killed	**mudárdile**

IMPERATIVE TENSE
sing. **mudárdyo**   pl. **mudárdyon**

---

*Inchoative and passive verbs always have different masculine and feminine forms of the third person singular in the past tense to indicate gender.
[†]Feminine 3rd *psn* sing past tense

Absolute Transitive verbs

Occasionally a **thematic** verb can be used as an absolute transitive (without an object) by some native speakers.

> **O kham phabarel.**   'The sun is shining.'

This sentence has no object even though the verb is transitive. It actually means 'The sun is burning *smthg*.' This usage is rare in Kalderash in the Americas and can be attributed to the speech patterns of some speakers. It is colloquial use of a transitive verb. Grammatically, the sentence should be **O kham phabol.** 'The sun burns.' **Phabol** is the intransitive form of the verb.

Other tenses

These need to be studied from a textbook such as *Learn Romani* where they are all explained in detail with examples of usage. Other sources for Kalderash can be found in Hancock and in *Gypsy Dialects* by Edward Proctor. It is important to find sources for the exact dialect of Kalderash one wishes to learn but unfortunately, some of these are lacking.

Future tense

As in English, the present indicative can serve to express the future tense.

> **Zhav tehára**.   I am going tomorrow.

An emphatic future is formed with the prefix **kam-** which can be attached to any present indicative conjugation.

> **Kam-zhav tehára!**   I shall go tomorrow!

Conditional tense

A conditional tense can be formed with the prefix **kámas-** which can also be prefixed to any conjugated tense of any verb.

> **Kámas-zhav te sas man love.**
> I would go if I had money.

> **Kámas-gêlèm te sas man love.**
> I would have gone if I had money.

Past continuous/Imperfect

This is the present indicative with the addition of < **-as** >.

> **Zhávas kothe kána símas terno.**
> I used to go there when I was young.

Pluperfect or Past Perfect

This is the past tense with the addition of <-as > or < –sas > as required.

EXAMPLES:

gêlèm   I went   **gêlèmas**   I had gone

Te gêlémas kámas-dikhlem lês.
If I had gone I would have seen him.

avilo   he came   **avilósas**   he had come
avili   she came   **avilísas**   she had come

Reflexive thematic verbs

Thematic Romani verbs become reflexive by combining the conjugated verb with the appropriate personal pronoun in the accusative case. Reflexive verbs are indicated in the main entries by *v/refl*.

xalavel *vt* wash
xalavél-pe *v/refl* he/she washes himself/herself

PRESENT INDICATIVE		USUALLY PRONOUNCED
xalaváv-man	I wash myself	**xalavá-ma**
xalavés-tut	you wash yourself	**xalavés-tu**
xalavél-pês	he/she washes himself/herself	**xalavél-pe**
xalavás-amên	we wash ourselves	**xalavás-ame**
xalavén-tumên	you wash yourselves	**xalavén-tume**
xalavén-pên	they wash themselves	**xalavén-pe**

The usually pronounced form is what appears in the dictionary listings because the first column examples are used in more formal speech by elders and the usually-pronounced form by younger speakers and in general conversation by everybody.

xalavel *vt* wash
xalavél-pe *v/refl* he/she washes himself/herself

PAST TENSE		USUALLY PRONOUNCED
xaladém-man	I washed myself	**xaladé-ma**
xaladyán-tut	you washed yourself	**xaladyán-tu**
xaladyás-pes	he/she washed himself/herself	**xaladyá-pe**
xaladyám-amên	we washed ourselves	**xaladyám-ame**
xaladyán-tumên	you washed yourselves	**xaladyán-tume**
xaladé-pên	they washed themselves	**xaladé-pe**

Compound Verbs

Compound verbs are usually composed of a **thematic** verb and a **thematic** or **athematic** noun.

del dab *comp/vt*   give blow, hit, swat

In separable compound verbs of this type, the two elements can remain together or be separated.

Dem dab lês.
I hit him.

or:

Dem lês dab ándo mui.
I struck him a blow in the mouth.

but:

chumi-del usually written as **chumídel**
vt kiss, the two elements cannot be separated
Chumídem la pe l' wusht.
I kissed her on the lips.

The ablative suffix < -tar >

The ablative suffix < **-tar** > is suffixed to certain verbs to change the meaning or to indicate ablative motion or condition.

zhal	he/she goes	**zháltar**	he/she departs
golo	he went	**golótar**	he departed
goli	she went	**golítar**	she departed
gole	they went	**golêntar**	they departed*
merel	he/she is dying	**meréltar**	he/she is passing away

Athematic Verbs

Athematic verbs are much easier to deal with than **thematic** verbs because there are only two basic families both of which are completely predictable in their conjugations.

The < -il > family

This is the largest group and is still being added to by modern speakers. In North-American Kalderash it is the conjugation given to English loan verbs (**athematic** items) for example **dompil** 'dump' and **minil** 'mean' from North-American English.

---

*When a verb conjugation such as **gêlé** ends in the vowel < **-e**) in the 3rd psn past tense, it often takes the conjugation < **-êntar**) as the ablative suffix. Example; **gêlé** 'they went,' becomes **gêlèntar**, 'they departed,' while **gêló** 'he went'simply adds < **-tar** > to become **gêlótar**.

The < -ol > family

This group consists of **athematic** verbs that have been created in the past but this conjugations seems to be no longer productive in North America. Typical are **farbol** 'paint' and **krutsol** 'economize.'

Transitive athematic verbs

1) **dubil** *vt* win: *pp/adj* **dubime**
2) **farbol** paint: *pp/adj* **farbome**

PRESENT INDICATIVE

LONG FORM	SHORT FORM	LONG FORM	SHORT FORM
dubisarav	dubív	farbosarav	farbov
dubisares	dubis	farbosares	farbos
dubisarel	dubil	farbosarel	farbol
dubisaras	dubis	farbosaras	farbos
dubisaren	dubin	farbosaren	farbon
dubisaren	dubin	farbosaren	farbon

IMPERATIVE TENSE

SING. & PL.	SING. & PL.
dubisar	farbosar

PAST TENSE

dubisardem	farbosardem
dubisardyan	farbosardyan
dubisardyas/dubisardya	farbosardyas/farbosardya
dubisardyam	farbosardyam
dubisardyan	farbosardyan
dubisarde	farbosarde

PAST PARTICIPLE / ADJECTIVES

dubisardo*	dubime	farbosardo*	farbome

The English 'be,' 'become,' 'get' and 'make.'

Where English employs the words 'be,' 'become' and 'get' with adjectives and past participles of verbs, as in to 'be happy,' 'get hungry.' or 'become lonely,' Kalderash **thematic** verbs employ the passive and inchoative form of the verb. These forms appear in the dictionary as intransitive verbs indicated by *vi.*

makyol *vi*	get/become intoxicated/drunk
makyárdyol *vi*	be made drunk (by *smbdy* or *smthg*)
mudárdyol *vi*	be/get murdered/killed

---

*This form of the past participle/adjective is inflected for gender and number in the nominative and in the oblique. It is seldom used in North-American Kalderash but is common in Europe.

EXAMPLES:
Mai baryol gês-gêsèstar.
He/she gets bigger day by day.

Makilo ánde sláva.
He got drunk during the feast.

Makyárdilo la rrakyátar.
He became intoxicated by the whisky.

Mudárdilo ándo marimos.
He was killed during the war.

Phurilótar thai diláilo.
He became old and senile.

Phurilítar thai diláili.
She became old and senile.

Intransitive athematic verbs

The reflexive form of the athematic usually serves as both the reflexive and the passive verb in North-American and some other dialects of Kalderash. Thus **ansuríl-pe** can mean both he marries as a reflexive verb, (*Sp Se casa.*) and **Mangel te ansuríl-pe** 'He wants to get married (*Sp Quiere casarse.*) as a passive verb. European a Kalderash dialects, on the other hand, often employ a separate intransitive formation in **ansurisávol/moritisávol**.

dubíl-pe	he/she wins/is winning
farból-pe	he/she is painting himself/herself
	he/she is being painted

Reflexive Athematic Verbs

PRESENT INDICATIVE

LONG FORM	SHORT FORM
dubisaráv-man	dubí-ma
dubisarés-tut	dubís-tu
dubisarél-pês	dubíl-pe
dubisarás-amên	dubís-ame
dubisarén-tumên	dubín-tume
dubisarén-pên	dubín-pe

LONG FORM	SHORT FORM
farbosaráv-man	farbó-ma
farbosarés-tut	farbós-tu
farbosarél-pês	farból-pe
farbosarás-amên	farbós-ame
farbosarén-tumên	farbón-tume
farbosarén-pên	farbón-pe

PAST TENSE
There is only one form for the reflexive past tense.

dubisáilem	I won
dubisáilan	you won
dubisáilo	he won
dubisáili	she won
dubisáilam	we won
dubisáilan	you won
dubisáile	they won

farbosáilem	I got painted
farbosáilan	you got painted
farbosáilo	he got painted
farbosáili	she got painted
farbosáilam	we got painted
farbosáilan	you got painted
farbosáile	they got painted

Passive Athematic Verbs

With **athematic** verbs, the reflexive form of the verb is usually employed to express '
be,' 'become' and 'get,' in North-American Kalderash. However, a passive verb form
can also be employed to express this but this is more common in European Kalderash.
Both forms are mutually intelligible to native speakers.

REFLEXIVE VERB	PASSIVE VERB	
ansuchí-ma	**ansuchisávov**	I am becoming confused
ansurisáilo	**ansurisaváilo**	he got married
moritisáili	**moritisaváili**	she got married
ôblol-pe	**ôblosávol**	it is becoming round
tristól-pe	**tristosávol.**	he/she is becoming sad
tavalíl-pe	**tavalisávol**	it is rolling

EXAMPLE:
ansurisávol be married (*for a man only*)

PRESENT INDICATIVE

ansurisávov	I become married
ansurisávos	you become married
ansurisávol	he becomes married
ansurisávos	we become married
ansurisávon	they become married
ansurisávon	they become married

PAST TENSE

ansurisaváilem	I became married
ansurisaváilan	you became married
ansurisaváilo*	he became married
moritisaváili*	she got married
ansurisaváilam	we became married
ansurisaváilan	you became married
ansurisaváile	they became married

IMPERATIVE TENSE

SING.	PL.
asurisávo	**ansurisávon**

Note: For a more detailed explanation of athematic passive verbs see Hancock's *A Handbook of Vlax Romani* pp 120 & 125-6

The Present Participle

The present participle is no longer productive in North-American Kalderash although some fossilized examples appear in use by native speakers. It is alive and productive among some European Kalderash speech communities. It can be recognized by its endings in < -**andoi** > and < -**indoi** >

zhándoi   going

Wo xálas zhándoi
He was eating while going/departing.

Béshindoi pásha la yagáte, ashundem le ruva ándo wêrsh.
Sitting beside the fire, I heard the wolves in the forest.

2.7   Verbals

Expressing the infinitive of the verb

There is no infinitive of the verb in Kalderash. The particle '**te**, ' which is used to introduce optative and subjunctive sentences, is regularly used as follows:

I go.	**Zhav.**	I want to go.	**Mangav te zhav.**	
You go.	**Zhas.**	You want to go.	**Manges te zhas.**	
He/she goes.	**Zhal.**	He/she wants to go.	**Mangel te zhal.**	
We go.	**Zhas.**	We want to go.	**Mangas te zhas.**	
You go.	**Zhan.**	You want to go.	**Mangen te zhan.**†	
They go.	**Zhan.**	They want to go.	**Mangen te zhan.**†	

Literally, the above means 'I want that I go,' 'you want that you go,' and so on.

---

*We cannot have **ansurisaváili** because there is a different verb for women in **moritisaváili** 'she became married' from **moritil** *vt* to marry off (a daughter).

†When the meaning is not clear, confusion is avoided by employing the nominative personal pronouns: **Tume mangen te zhan.**   You want to go.   **Won mangen te zhan.**   They want to go.

When 'te' is placed between two conjugated verbs in the present indicative in any person, singular or plural, the verb following 'te' serves the same function as the infinitive in English even though conjugated verbs so used are really in the subjunctive mood in Kalderash. For example, the subjunctive tenses, *Je veux qu'il fasse* in French, or *Quiero que lo haga,* in Spanish, translate as **mangav te kerel,** 'I want him/her to do so,' in Kalderash.

SAMPLES:
Mangel te gilabav.
He/she wants me to sing.

Manges te kines lês/la.
Do you want to buy it? (**lês** *nm*/**la** *nf* 'it')

Xav te sastyovav.
I eat to be healthy.

Chi mangel te zhal.
He/she doesn't want to go.

Mangen te aven túsa.
They want to come with you.

The other verbals of English are similarly expressed. The conjugated verb preceding 'te' can be in any tense, person, number but the conjugated verb following it, if there is one, must be in the present indicative. But as shown in the following, the preceding verb can be separated from 'te' by a personal pronoun or some other word or words when used instead of the defunct participle in North-American Kalderash.

Ashundem la te gilabal.
I heard her singing.

Ashunávas lên te gilaban.
I was listening to them singing.

Dikhlem la te pekel.
I saw her cooking.

Kam-dikhav lês te kerel.
I shall watch him doing it.

Dikhlam e barí-kangiri te phabol.
We watched the cathedral burning.

Note in the above that there is a compound noun between the two verbs.

Dikhlas la te khelél-pe.
He saw her dance/dancing.

Dikhlas pêske dades te merel.
He watched his father die.

Note in the above sentence, the inflected reflexive genitive pronoun **pêske** 'his own' and **dades** 'father' come between the two verbs.

Te bashavav e gitára si múrri plácha.
Playing the guitar is my pleasure.

Here the present indicative followed by '**te**' serves the same function as a noun participle in English and there is no second verb following '**te**.'

Te khelél-pe pe l' grasten si pêski mártiya.
Gambling on the horses is his nemesis.

Te del o Del amênge baxt!
May God grant us good fortune!

The above shows the use of '**te**' to introduce optative statements.

The particle < ke >

This is used to introduce a dependent clause.

Zhanglem ke xoxavélas.
I knew that he/she was lying.

The negative particles

1. **chi**   This is used as the negative particle.
   Chi zhav.   I am not going.
   Chi zhanel.   He doesn't know.

2. **na**   This is used with the imperative.
   Na ker kadya!   Don't do that!

   IT IS ALSO USED AS FOLLOWS:
   Mothodem lêske te na kerel.
   I told him not to do it.

   Te del o Del te na merel!
   May God grant that he does not die!

3. It is also the word for '**no**' in answer to a question
   Zhas kai sláva?   Are you going to the feast?
   Na!   No!

4. **níchi**   no, none, not, nothing & *id*
    Sa zhan kai sláva hai me níchi.
    They are all going to the feast and I'm not.

Verb Auxilliaries

Kalderash has a number of what are called verb auxilliaries in English some of which
are actually defective verbs in Klderash which exist in some dialects only in the
present and past tenses. Their dictionary entries give examples of their usage.

1. **Móra**   had better, must, need to, should
    Móra te zhas akana.
    We should go now. (We should that we go now.)

    Móra te ashunes so mothol.
    You had better heed what he says.

    Kon si te phenel o chachimos, móra te thol yekh punrro ánde bakháli.
    He is is about to tell the truth had better place one foot in the stirrup.

2. **músai**   must
    Músai te zhas akana!   You must go immediately!

3. **shai**   able to, can
    Shai zhav.   I am able to go
    Shai keres?   Can you do it?

4. **shai-vi**   maybe, perhaps
    Shai-vi te na avel.   Perhaps he isn't coming.

5. **nashti**   cannot, not able
    Nashti zhav.   I can't go.

6. **nashti**   with conjugations of the verb 'to be'
              in the *3rd psn sing*
    Nashti sas mánge te zhav.   I was not able to go.

    Nashti avel mánge te zhav. I will not be able to go.

7. **trobul**   need, ought, should
    Trobul te zhav akana.   I need to go now.

    Trobúlas te zhav araki.   I needed to go yesterday.

The Verb 'to be' and 'to become'

The verb 'to be' has the following forms in the present and past tenses. All other tenses are the same as the verb **avel** 'to come/become.'

PRESENT INDICATIVE		PAST	
I am	**sim**	I was/used to be	**símas**
you are	**san**	You were/used to be	**sánas**
he/she is	**si**	He/she was/used to be	**sas**
we are	**sam**	We were/used to be	**sámas**
you are	**san**	You were/used to be	**sánas**
they are	**si**	They were/used to be	**sas**
it is	**si**	It was/used to be	**sas**
there is/are	**si**	There was/were/used to be	**sas**

The Enclitics

The present tense of the verb to be is sometimes replaced by the following enclitics in short sentences and replies to questions.

-lo	he is
-la	she is
-le	they are

These are joined to the adjective or preposition as follows:

Baré-le.	They are large.
Barí-la.	She/it is big. (if referring to a feminine noun)
Baró-lo.	He/it is big. (if referring to a masculine noun)
Bokhalí-la.	She's hungry.
Dilé-le.	They are crazy.
Mató-lo.	He's drunk.
Opré-lo.	He's upstairs.
Telé-la.	She's downstairs.

They are often used with interrogatives. Note that the verb to be is not always used in these types of sentences.

Kai o Fránki?	Where is Frank?
Opré-lo.	He's upstairs.
Kai e Mára?	Where is Mary?
Avrí-la.	She's outside.

Kai tire gláti?	Where are your children?
Kheré-le.	They are at home.

Kai-lo?	Where is it? (if referring to a masculine noun)
Kai-la?	Where is it? (if referring to a feminine noun)
Kai-le?	Where are they?

Personal Pronouns

NOMINATIVE		ACCUSATIVE	
I	me	me	man & ma*
you	tu	you	tut & tu*
he	wo	him	lês
she	woi	her	la
we	ame	us	amên & ame*
you	tume	you	tumên & tume*
they	won	them	lên & le*

Note: 'It' is either **lês** ' he' or **la** 'she' depending on the gender of the noun to which it refers. There is no neuter gender.

THE FOLLOWING SHOULD ALSO BE NOTED:

himself	pês & pe*
herself	pês & pe*
itself	pês & pe*
themselves	pên & pe*

INSTRUMENTAL	ABLATIVE	PREPOSITIONAL
mánsa	mándar	mánde
túsa	tútar	túte
lêsa	lêstar	lêste
lása	látar	láte
pêsa	pêstar	pêste
amênsa	amêndar	amênde
tumênsa	tumêndar	tumênde
lênsa	lêndar	lênde
pênsa	pêndar	pênde

DATIVE	GENITIVE
mánge	murro & mo†
túke	tiro & tyo†
lêske	lêsko
láke	láko
pêske	pêsko/páko‡
amênge	amaro
tumênge	tumaro
lênge	lêngo
pênge	pêngo

The possessive personal pronoun behaves like an adjective and is declined for gender and number in the nominative and in the oblique. When it precedes the

---

*These are the truncated forms often used in daily speech to replace the preceding longer form. The longer form is the oblique stem.

†Truncated forms used in daily speech.

‡The word **páko** 'her own' is influenced by **láko**.

noun, the stress usually falls on the first vowel of the long form when two forms exist. When it is in apposition, the stress falls on the final vowels in **murro, tiro, amaro** and **tumaro** but never of **lêsko, láko, pêsko, páko, lêngo** or **pêngo**. However, it must be born in mind that Kalderash has a rising and falling intonation pattern that is followed by native speakers whose speech habits are not governed by strict grammatical rules. No hard and fast rules can be given for possessive personal pronoun stress in the nominative and oblique.

NOMINATIVE
my house	**múrro kher** *nm*
my apple	**mûrri phabai** *nf*
my money	**mûrre love** *nm/pl*
my clothing	**múrre tsáliya** *nf/pl*

OBLIQUE
with my house	**murre kherêsa**
with my apple	**murra phabása**
with my money	**murre lovênsa**
with my clothing	**murre tsalyánsa**

The nominalized pronouns

In Kalderash, the possessive personal pronoun/pronominal adjective can become a nominal pronoun. It can then be inflected to the oblique and like other nominalized adjectives, it is then subject to gender and number. This process is complicated and difficult to work with since the gender and number of the subject(s) referred to must be clearly understood. This usage is fully explained in more detail in the author's *Learn Romani*.

Paradigm of the Pronominal Adjective Oblique stem

	MASC. SING.	FEM. SING.	MASC. PL.	FEM. PL.
my	murrês-	murrá-	murrên-	murrán-
your/yours	tirês-	tirá-	tirên-	tirán-
his	lêskorrès-	lêskorrá-	lêskorrèn-	lêskorrán-
his own	pêskorrès-	pêskorrá-	pêskorrèn-	pêskorrán-
her/hers	lakorrês-	lakorrá-	lakorrên-	lakorrán-
her own	pakorrês-	pakorrá-	pakorrên-	pakorrán-
our/ours	amarês-	amará-	amarên-	amarán-
your/yours	tumarês-	tumará-	tumarên-	tumarán-
their/theirs	lêngorrès-	lêngorrá-	lêngorrèn-	lêngorrán-
their own	pêngorrès-	pêngorrá-	pêngorrèn-	pêngorrán-

1. I danced with his wife and he danced *with mine.*
   Me kheldém-ma lêska rromnyása thai wo kheldyás-pe *murrása.*

Here, **murrása** refers to a feminine singular noun.

2. He sold his house so I don't know what to do *with mine*.
   Bikindyas pêsko kher ap chi zhanav so te kerav *murrêsa*.

   Here **kher** is a masculine noun so **murrês-** must be inflected to
   the masculine singular instrumental.

3. I ate my apple. What did you do *with yours*?
   Xalem murri phabai. So kerdyan *tirása*?

   Here, **phabai** 'apple' is a feminine singular noun so we have
   tirása 'with yours.'

4. You ate your apple, now you want one *of mine*.
   Xalyan tiri phabai, akana manges yekha *murrándar*.

   Here **phabái** is a feminine noun so **murrán-** must be inflected
   to the feminine plural ablative to fit with **phaba** 'apples' feminine
   plural noun.

5. I spent my money, I don't know what he did *with his*.
   Xalem múrre love, chi zhanav so kerdyas *pêskorrènsa*.

   Here, 'with his' is what must be declined. Since it refers to
   money, which is a masculine noun plural, it would be
   < **pêskorrèn-** > inflected to its instrumental masculine noun
   plural form of **pêskorrènsa**.

6. **Won dine-dúma lênge barésa thai ame dyam-dúma *amarêsa*.**
   They consulted with their leader and we consulted *with ours*.

   Here **amarésa** refers to a masculine singular noun.

7. He is one *of our* Roma.
   Wo si Rrom *amarêndar*.

   This is literally: He is a Romani man from ours, meaning our
   people. Here **amarêndar** refers to one of many people
   and the plural nominalized form must be employed.

Nominalized demonstrative pronouns

Demonstrative pronouns are also nominalized in Kalderash and take the meanings
of 'this man,' 'that woman,' or 'these other men.'

NOMINATIVE			OBLIQUE	
MASCULINE		FEMININE	MASCULINE	FEMININE
kako	this	kakya	kakales	kakalan
kodo	that	kodya	kodoles	kodolan
kuko	yonder	kukya	kukoles	kukolan
kolaver	that other	kolavrya	kolavres	kolavryan
kakale	these	kakala	kakalen	kakalan
kodole	those	kodola	kodolen	kodolan
kukole	yonder	kukola	kukolen	kokolan

EXAMPLES OF USAGE:
Who is this man?
Kon si kako?

Do you know this man?
Zhanes kakales?

These men are my relatives.
Kakale si múrre nyámurya.

Who are those men over by the door?
Kon si kodole pashál o wudar?

Who is that man way over there?
Kon si kuko?

Who are these women?
Kon si kakala?

I told one of those man.
Mothodem yekhe kodolêndar.

Who is that lady?
Kon si kukya?

She came with these women.
Avili kakalánsa.

It was one of those women.
Yekha kodolándar sas.

He works with that other man.
Kerel buki kolavrêsa.

She left with that other woman.
Gêlítar kolavryása.

It belongs to that man.
Kodolêsko si.

It belongs to this woman.
Kakaláko si.

How to express 'to have'

There is no verb to have in Kalderash Romani. Instead, the third person singular and plural of the verb 'to be' in its appropriate tense are combined with the accusative personal pronouns as follows:

si man it is/there is to me   **Si-man kher.** I have a house.

PRESENT TENSE	USUALLY PRONOUNCED AS		EQUIVALENT OF
si man	si ma	there is/it is to me	I have
si tut	si tu	there is/it is to you	You have
si lês	si le	there is/it is to him	He has
si la	si la	there is/it is to her	She has
si amên	si ame	there is/it is to us	We have
si tumên	si tume	there is/it is to you	You have
si lên	si le	there is/it is to them	They have

PAST TENSE		
sas man	sas ma	I had/used to have
sas tut	sas tu	You had/used to have
sas lês	sas le	He had/used to have
sas la	sas la	She had/used to have
sas amên	sas ame	We had/used to have
sas tumên	sas tume	You had/used to have
sas lên	sas le	They had/used to have

All other tenses are formed from **avel** 'to be, become.'

IMPERATIVE TENSE
SING. **av**   PL. **aven**

FUTURE TENSE		
avel man	I will have	avel ma
avel tut	You will have	avel tu
avel lês	He will have	avel lês
avel la	She will have	avel la
avel amên	We will have	avel ame
avel tumên	You will have	avel tume
avel lên	They will have	avel le

The foregoing applies to possession of one item. The plural form is in **aven.**

Aven ma love.
I will have money.

Aven la tsáliya.
She will have clothes.

Aven le but shaven.
They will have many children.

The prefix < **kam-** > can also be used with **avel** and **aven** to imply the emphatic future.

Kam-avel man atwéto tehára.
I shall have a reply tomorrow.

Te del o Del te kam-aven ma love!
May God grant that I shall have money!

CONDITIONAL TENSE
kámas-avel man (if thing possessed is *nm* or *nf* singular)
kámas-aven man (if thing possessed is *nm/nf/pl*)

EXAMPLES:
Kámas-avel man kher te sas man love.
I would have a house if I had money.

Kámas-aven man love te kerávas buki.
I would have money if I had been working.

PLUPERFACT
aviló-sas man I had had (if thing possessed is *nm/s*)
avilí-sas man I had had (if thing possessed is nf/s)
avilé-sas man I had had (if thing possessed is *nm/nf/pl*)

EXAMPLES:
In the following examples "**te**" has the meaning of 'if.'

Te aviló-sas ma mobíli, chi avilémas po tréno.
If I had had a car, I would not have come on the train.

Te avilí-sas ma dukh, golémas ka o dóftoro.
If I had had pain, I would have gone to the doctor.

Te avilé-sas lês love, kámas-kindyas la.
If he had had money he would have bought it.

THE INFINITIVE
The conjugated verb tense is used with the particle '**te**' to form the infinitive and optative mood.

INFINITIVE MOOD
Mangav te avél man kher.   I want to have a house.

Mangel te aven la shukar tsáliya.   She wants to have nice clothes.

OPTATIVE MOOD
Te avel man baxt!   May I have good fortune!

Te aven man love!   May I have money!

Negation

To express the negative, the following forms are employed,

nai	it is not	**Nai murro.**	It is not mine.
manai	there is no/not	**Manai love.**	There is no money.
nas	there was not	**Nas múrro.**	It was not mine.
manas	There was no, none.	**Manas xabe.**	There was no food.

PRESENT TENSE
Nai man grast.
It is not to me a horse/I do not have a horse.
Nai tut phabai.
You do not have an apple?/Don't you have an apple?

Nai lês kher.
He does not have a house?/Doesn't he have a house?

Nai lês love.
He has no money?/Doesn't he have money?

Nai la baxt.
She has no luck.

Nai amên mobíli.
We have no automobile.

Nai lên gláti.
They have no children.

PAST TENSE
Nas man grast.
I had no horse./I did not have a horse.

Nas tut phabai.
You did not have an apple.

The tenses created from < **avel** > take **chi** in the negative

Chi avel man grast.
I will not have a horse.

The infinitive and subjunctive forms are negated with < **na** > like other verbs.

Te del o Del te na avel.
May God grant that he doesn't arrive!

Gîndívas man ke na avelas man baxt.
I thought that I would not receive luck.

Alternative forms of how to express possession

There are slightly differing forms of the above in use by various groups of speakers and individuals. With some, we have the following which replaces the accusative pronoun with the prepositional pronoun.

PRESENT TENSE		PAST TENSE	
mánde si	I have	**mánde sas**	I had
túte si	you have	**túte sas**	you had
lêste si	he has	**lêste sas**	he had
láte si	she has	**láte sas**	she had
amênde si	we have	**amênde sas**	we had
tumênde si	you have	**tumênde sas**	you had
lênde si	they have	**lênde sas**	they had

The other tenses follow like those outlined for the accusative.
Avél mánde baxt.
I will have luck.

Kam-avel lêste baxt.
He will have luck.

Avilí-sas láte baxt.
She would have had luck.

Further Examples

In sentences such as 'The man has a hat .'the patterns is as follows:

O mursh si lês stagi.
The man has a hat.

This translates literally as: 'The man, it is to him, hat.'

MORE EXAMPLES:

The Rom has a white horse
O Rrom si lês párno grast.

The Rom has no horse.
O Rrom nai lês grast.

My brother has no money.
Múrro phral nai lês love.

My sister will have food.
Múrri phey kam-avel la xabe.

John has no money.
O Yánko nai lês love.

Mary will have money.
E Mára, kam-aven la love.

The horse had no food.
O grast nas lês xabe.

If Steve had had money he would have bought the car.
Te avilé-sas lês love, o Stevo, kamás-kindyas o mobíli.

Word Order

Unlike English, there is no standard word order or sentence construction in Kalderash Romani because of the noun cases. The following should help make this clear.

1. **O Rrom zhal ka o washári te bikinel pêske grastês.**
   The Romani man is going to the horse fair to sell his horse.

The above is how this would normally be said in North-American Kalderash where Romani is more influenced by English word order. It could just as easily be expressed as follows:

2. **Te bikinel pêske grastês, o Rrom zhal ka o washári.**
   This would be more likely in central/eastern Europe.

or

3. **Ka o washári, zhal o Rrom te bikinel pêske grastês.**
   This might appear in poetry

or

4. **Zhal o Rrom ka o washári te bikinel pêske grastês?**
   More likely when asking a question.

or

5. **Pêske grastês te bikinel, zhal o Rrom ka o washári.**
   Likely in a folk tale.

or

6. **Ka l' washariyêste zhála o Rrom pêske grastês te bikinéla.**
   In Rhetorical Romani.*

---

*Rhetorical Romani, a flowery, ornate form of Kalderash used by elders and during formal events such as the *Kris Romani* (Romani Tribunal) or in benedictions, invocations, folk tales, etc. It is described with examples of use in *Learn Romani.*

Chapter 3

Recommended books and other learning tools

Learn Romani – Das-Dúma Rromanes (**Lee, Ronald, 2005, Hatfield, Hertfordshire UP**)

This dictionary is designed to be compatible with the author's home-study textbook now in its second printing (2008). It uses the same phonetic system as this dictionary.

A Handbook of Vlax Romani (**Hancock, Ian, 1995, Columbus, Ohio, Slavica Publishers, Inc.)**

To date, this is the best source available on the grammatical structure of the Vlax-Romani dialects which include Kalderash. It is not designed for a specific dialect but as an overview of a range of closely-related dialects sharing a basic common vocabulary and grammatical structure. Hancock uses a phonetic system similar to that used in *Learn Romani* and in this dictionary but with some variations which will need to be taken into account. It would be invaluable for those planning to use Kalderash in Europe since it lists variations and grammatical forms unique to specific dialects in differing Vlax-Romani dialects.

Gypsy Dialects **(Proctor, Edward, 2008, Hatfield, Hertfordshire UP)**

This bibliography of learning tools from books to audio and video sources is invaluable to anyone learning Romani. The particular dialect references are clearly indicated and will be kept up to date as future learning tools appear (see chapter 10). Unfortunately, some of the excellent sources listed are for works that are now out of print and difficult or impossible to obtain although most can be found through interlibrary loan and in major public and university libraries.

Dictionnaire Tsigane-Français: dialecte kalderash **(Calvet, Georges, 2009, L'Ashiatèque, Paris)**

This is excellent for French-speaking readers and can be used in conjunction with the audio course by Père André Barthélémy listed below.

Rromano Alavari, Kalderash–English Dictionary (Lee, Ronald, 2010, Magoria Books, Toronto)

Scheduled for publication in December, 2010.

Rromano Alavari, English–Kalderash Dictionary (Lee, Ronald, 2011, Magoria Books, Toronto)

Scheduled for publication in 2011.

Vroem VZW (Père André Barthélémy)

This is an audio course consisting of 70 audio recordings of approximately 2 minutes in Kalderash Romani with an accompanying PDF that includes both the Romani text and the French translations. It is currently available from Belgium, at a cost of 40 Euros. Order from: vroem@vroemvzw.be

RomaniDictionary.com (http://www.romanidictionary.com/)

Magoria Books is currently developing this website with an intended focus on its upcoming dictionaries and other learning tools for Kalderash and other Romani dialects, including materials relating to Ronald Lee's Kalderash-English dictionary, Hedina Sijerčić's planned Gurbeti-Romani dictionary, and other Romani-focused publications.

Romlex (http://romani.uni-graz.at/romlex/)

This is an Internet lexical data base for many dialects of Romani including Kalderash and which gives automatic translations to or from English and several other major languages. Unfortunately, it also includes many dialects of Kalderash under one heading, giving the impression to the uninitiated that this is a single, homogeneous or universal dialect. While this may be true for native speakers, for someone unfamiliar with Romani and beginning to learn a specific dialect of Kalderash it has the following pitfalls which the student should be aware of.

1. No stress indicators are used making it difficult to pronounce the words properly and the diacritical marks used to indicate pronunciation cannot be reproduced on a standard computer keyboard thus requiring the hassle of special fonts for the student.

2. Since this is a data base, not a dictionary, a large number of possible entries that could have been included are missing. Furthermore, a data base, by its very nature, cannot contain a large number of idiomatic expressions.

3. Varying versions of the same word with differing forms and pronunciation from diverse Kalderash dialectal groups and published works from Swedish to Russian and Romanian Kalderash are listed. If one enters the noun 'work' for instance, three Romani words appear as follows; **buchi, buki** and **buti** or if 'make drunk' is entered, two forms will appear **makyarel** and **matyarel**

(another possible entry, **machyarel**, widely used in French Kalderash and in **Machwanítska** is not listed). Again, distorted and truncated forms of words used by some speakers or by informants who might have been suffering from asthma are included along with the widespread traditionally used forms. Taking the transitive verb 'to comb' which also means to 'divide' we find **hulavel** which I have found to be the traditional form from both native speakers in the Americas (often **ulavel** in Latin America) and from Europe, Romlex also lists **fulavel** and **vulavel,** variants which I doubt would even be widely understood by native speakers if not clear from the rest of the sentence. Some entries from specific Kalderash dialects, say from Sweden or Russia, would not be understood by native speakers of other dialects .The problem for the student would be to somehow divine which one of the entries belonged in the dialect he or she was learning and which entry would be the most widespread variant most likely to be heard and understood from and by native speakers.

The following should make this clear:

'She was selling flowers in the market place all day.'

North-American Kalderash

Bikinélas lulugya ándo pasári sórro ges.

French Kalderash

Bichinélas luludjya ándo pyátso sórro dyes.

To construct this sentence relying on Romlex for unknown words could result in a bizarre construction something like the following:

Bichinelas luludya ándo bazári (–?) dyes.

This is nobody's dialect but would probably be understood by native speakers if the missing expression 'all day' not listed in Romlex was already known to the student.

Barring these failings as beginner learning tool for the student, **Romlex** is an excellent source for academics or anyone who has done the basic groundwork and who doing more advanced studies in Romani linguistics and for assistance in translating the dialects included in its data base.

Kalderash – English Dictionary

A

ába *adv* already, hardly, yet *var of* **yába** *qv*
abazhúra *nf* lampshade
abíya *nf* abbey
abiyado/abyado *nm* newly-married groom:
  nf **abiyadi**: *nm/pl* **abiyade**
  recently-married couple
abiyash *nm* abbot: *nf* **abiyáshka** prioress
abiyav/abyav *nm* marriage, wedding,
  wedding party/reception
abiyavêsko *gen/adj* marriage, nuptial;
  abiyavêsko-khelimos wedding dance *see
  also* **kólo** *nm*
Abrílo *nm* April
Abrílone *adv* in April
Adámo *nm* Adam (*see also* **Dámo**)
adaptóri *nm* adaptor, adaptor plug
adînko/adênko *adj/adv* deep, *see also*
  dur-tele *adv*
adînkomós *nm* depth
adînkonès *adv* deeply
adjénda *nf* agenda
adjénto *nm* male agent: *nf* **adjentáika** *see
  also* **yagánto** *nm*
adjéntsiya *nf* agency (*Eur*)
adjudikatóri *nm* adjudicator: *nf*
  adjudikatórka (*Can*) **Note:**
  Adjudicators make decisions in refugee
  claims at the Canadian Immigration and
  Refugee Board (IRB) after reviewing the
  case and conducting an in camera hearing
  with the claimant and his/her legal
  counsel.
administratóri *nm* administrator: *nf*
  administratórka
administrátsiya *nf* administration
admirálo *nm* admiral (*Mil*)

ádo *nm* advertisement (*Am*); **Thodem o
  ádo ánde hêrtíya**. I placed the ad in the
  paper.
adoptil *vt* **1)** adopt: *pp/adj* **adoptime 2)**
  v/refl **adoptíl-pe** be adopted; **Adoptisáilo
  Gazhêndar**. He was adopted by
  non-Roma.
adoptimos *nm* adoption
adréso *nm* address; **adréso-poshtáko**
  postal/mailing address
advertaizil *vt* **1)** advertise: *pp/adj*
  advertzaizime (*Am*) **2)** *v/refl*
  advertaizíl-pe be advertised**; Chi mai
  bikíndyon le mobílya te na
  advertaizín-pe ánde l' hêrtíyi**. The cars
  will never sell if they are not advertised in
  the papers.
afidévito *nm* affidavit: *pl* **afidévitsi**
afirmátsiya *nf* affirmation, oath of
  affirmation *see also* **solax** *nf*
afísha *nf* poster, wall poster (*Eur*)
Áfrichi *nf/pl* Africa, Africas; **Manai but
  Rroma ánde l' Áfrichi**. There are not
  many Roma in the Africas/African
  countries.
Áfrika *nf* Africa
Afrikáko *gen/adj* of Africa, African
Afrikanítska *nf* African language (*Swahili,
  Somali, etc*): *pl* **Afrikanítski**
Afrikanítsko *adj* African
Afrikáno/Afrikánto *nm* African**: *nf*
  Afrikánka
ages *adv* **1)** today **2)** *nm* today
agesésko *gen/adj* today's
agesuno *adj* current, daily, up-to-date
ágila *nf* eagle (*Am from Sp*)
agor *nm* conclusion, end

agoral/agora *prep* from the edge/end (*of*); **Pelo agoral e síniya.** It fell from/off the edge of the table. **Avilo agoral e líniya.** He came from the end of the line.

agore *prep* to the end/edge (*of*), up to/as far as the end (*of*); **Gêlèm agore e líniya.** I went to the end of the line

agorêste *prep* at/to the end, towards the end

agorimáste *prep* at/to the end; **Das-ame sláva ka l' agorimáste le bershêstar.** We will have a feast at the end of the year.

agorimos *nm* 1) conclusion, end, termination 2) destination

agoruno *adj* 1) end, last (*in line*) 2) outside (*edge*), marginal 3) last man: *nf* **agoruni**

agorutno *adj var of* **agoruno** *adj qv*

agrikultúra *nf* agriculture, farming

ai *conj* and, also, and so, so, *var of* **hai** *qv*; **Mothodyas mánge te zhávtar ai gêlémtar.** He told me to leave, and I left. **Tu ai me shai zhas tehára.** You and I can go tomorrow.

Ái! *interj* Oh!, Alas!; **Ái, Dévla!** Oh God!

áiso *nm* icecube

áka *exclam/adv* Here!, Behold!; **Rromále, áka avel O Stévo!** Behold, Roma, here comes Steve!

akadémiko *nm/neolog* academic: *pl* **akadémichi**: *nf* **akademikútsa**

akademikósko/akademichêngo *gen/adj/neolog* academic

akademíya *nf* academy

akana *adv* now, at this instant, immediately, right now, right away; **Si akana pansh bersh ke beshas ándo fóro.** It is now five years that we have lived/we live in the city.

akana thai pórma *adv/phr* now and then, occasionally

akanak *adv* now, at this instant; *Eur var of* **akana** *qv*

akanash *adv* by and by, right away, soon, very soon, presently, in a short time

akána-sig *adv* soon, very soon, presently, not long from now, by and by

akanutnes *adv* currently, presently

akanutno *adj* contemporary, current, present

akaring/karing *prep* toward/towards, this way, by here/by this way, over here, by this way; **Nashlótar akaring o wêrsh.** He ran off towards the forest.

akatála *exclam/adv* us with *nom/prons* Behold! **Akatála-me, Rromále, areslem!** Behold me, Roma, I have arrived! **Akatála-wo, o dilo, dikh so kerel!** Behold him, the fool, look at what he's doing! **Akatála-woi, sar khelél-pe!** Behold her, how she dances!

akathar *adv* from here

akathe *adv* here (*Eur*)

akhardo *pp/adj* called, invited, summoned

akhárdyol *vi* 1) be summoned, called, invited: *pp/adj* **akhardilo**; ~ **ánde kris** be indicted; **Akhárdilem ánde kris.** I have been indicted. 2) be named

akharel *vt/i* 1) call, invite, summon: *pp/adj* **akhardo** 2) call, name 3) *vt/phr* ~ **ánde kris** indict, summon to appear at a trial 4) *comp/vi* ~ **kris** call for a trial 5) *v/refl* **akharél-pe** be named, called; **Sar akharél-pe?** How does he call himself/what is he called?

akharimásko-lil *comp/nm* letter of invitation, subpoena, summons

akharimásko-sámno *comp/nm/neolog* exclamation point

akharimos *nm* 1) appeal, call, invitation 2) summons

akhor *nm* 1) nut 2) stye (*in eye*)

akhorin *nf* nut bush/tree

áko *conj* if; If he has enough money, he can buy the car. **Áko si lês dósta love, shai kinel o mobíli.**

akompanimos *nm* accompaniment (*Mus*)

akompanyash *nm* accompanist (*Mus*): *nf* **akompanyáshka**

akórdo *nm* agreement, accord (*Eur*); **Sim de akórdo túsa.** I agree/am in agreement with you.

aksidênto *mn* accident: *adv/phr* **po aksidênto** by accident, accidentally

aktivísmo *nm* activism

aktivísta *nm/nf* activist

ákto *nm* **1)** act (*play*) **2)** act of law, Bill, deed, order, statute, law in force, court order

ákto-krisáko *comp/nm* court order

aktóri *nm* actor, film star: *nf* **aktórka** actress, film star

áktsiya *nf* action, initiative

akushádyol *vi* be cussed out, insulted, sworn at/vilified: *pp/adj* **akushadilo**; **Akushádilem.** I was insulted, cussed out, vilified, put down.

akushavel *vt* cause/instigate *smbdy* to be berated/cursed/insulted/profaned/cussed out/verbally castigated: *pp/adj* **akushado**

akushel *vt* **1)** blaspheme, profane, swear at, use foul language: *pp/adj* **akushlino**; **Akushav tumáre Devlên.** I blaspheme your gods/I curse everything you hold dear(*insult*). **2)** berate, chastise verbally, cuss out, scold, reprimand, vilify **3)** *v/refl* **akushén-pe** swear at each other/one another; **Akushliné-pe thai mardé-pe.** They cussed each other out and came to blows/fought each other. **Ashundem le te akushén-pe.** I heard them cussing each other out.

akushimásko *gen/adj* blasphemous, insulting

akushimos *nm* **1)** swearing, cussing, exchange of insults **2)** blasphemy

akushlino *pp/adj* blasphemed, cussed out, scolded, vilified

al *vi cont of* **avel** *vt/i* **1)** become **2)** come; **Chi mangel te al.** He doesn't want to become/come.

alabástra *nf* alabaster

alabastráko *gen/adj* made of alabaster

alárma *nf* **1)** alarm, burglar alarm, fire alarm **2)** *comp/vt/i* **del ~** give alarm; *comp/vt/i* **3)** *comp/vi* **lel ~** take alarm

alav *nm* word (*Eur*) *see more common* **swáto** *nm*

alavári *nm/neolog* **1)** dictionary **2)** lexicon

Albanézo *nm* Albanian man: *nf* **Albanezáika**

Albanítska *nf* Albanian (*Lang*)

Albanítsko *adj* Albanian

albiyátsa *nf* glaucoma; **Si lês albiyátsa.** He has glaucoma.

albiyátsi *nf/pl* cataracts

alduwil *vt* bless: *pp/adj* **alduwime** (*Eur*); **Alduwisar tut!** Bless you!

alduwimos *nm* blessing (*Eur*)

ãle *v/imp/s* **1)** Here!; **Ãle, le tsîrrá xabe ke but si-ma!** Here, take a little food because I have a lot! **2)** *v/imp/pl* **ãlen**; **Ãlen, Shavále, dósta si!** Here, boys, there's enough of it! (*to go around, food, beer, etc*).

Alemánya *nf* Germany *see also* **Nyampsíya** *nf and* **Nyámpso** *nm*

Alemanyáko *gen/adj* of Germany, German

alfabéto *nm* alphabet; **Chi zhanel lêsko alfabéto.** He doesn't know his alphabet/He is illiterate. **Nai amên afabéto Rromano.** We have no Romani alphabet.

-ali *prod suff* added to cardinal number roots to form feminine nouns indicating number one, number two, number fifty, etc; **yekhali** number one, **duwali** number two, **pindali** number fifty

almanáko *nm* almanac

almándo *nm* almond (*nut*)

alo! *interj* hello! (*usually on the telephone*)

alokátsiya *nf* allocation

alol/alosarel *vt* **1)** choose, pick, pick and choose, select: *pp/adj* **alome/alosardo**; **Alosar túke sogodi kai plachal tut.** Choose for yourself whichever one pleases you. **2)** elect; **Alosarde pênge prizidênto.** They elected themselves a president. **3)** prefer **4)** sort, sort out **5)** *v/refl* **a)** **alól-pe/alosarél-pe** appoint/elect oneself, choose oneself, nominate oneself, select oneself **b)** be chosen/favoured/preferred/selected **c)** be nominated, elected **d)** be appointed by consensus **e)** be sorted out, sort itself/themselves out; **Mek te alón-pe!** Let them sort it out!

Álom ! *interj* used in Hungarian Vlax-Romani songs as in; **Álom! Álom!**

Nai na nai! This is a nonsensical insert like tra-la-la in English songs.

alomáski-lísta *comp/nf* election list/slate

alomáta *nm/pl* choices, selections, list of meals on a menu

alome *pp/adj* 1) chosen, picked, selected 2) elected 3) favorite, favoured 4) preferred

alomos *nm* 1) choice, favorite, preference, option, selection 2) election

alosardo *nm* 1) chosen one, man chosen, favoured, elected: *nf* **alosardi**

alosarimos *nm* election, selection

alotóri *nm* elector, voter: **alotórka** *nf*

alserída *nf* ulcer

alseridil *vt* 1) create an ulcer, ulcerate: *pp/adj* **alseridime** 2) *v/refl* **alseridíl-pe** become ulcerated, develop an ulcer/ulcers

altári/altéri *nm* altar

alúmino *nm* aluminum

aluminósko *gen/adj* made of aluminum

Alxeríya *nf* Algeria

Alxire *nm* Pope: *pl* **Alxireyi**

amal *nm* male friend (*Eur*): *nf* **amalin/amalni**

amalano *adj* cordial, friendly (*Eur*)

amalipe/amalimos *nm* friendship (*Eur*)

amaro *pron/poss & nominalized pron* our, ours; **Amáro kher si.** This is our house. **Rrom amarêndar si.** He is one of our Roma.

amatóri *nm* amateur: *nf* **amatórka**

ambasáda *nf* embassy

ambasadóri *nm* ambassador

amblado *pp/adj* hung, hanged, suspended

ambládyol *vi* 1) be hanged, executed by hanging: *pp/adj* **ambladilo** 2) be dangled/hung/ suspended

amblal *nf* torch, firebrand, flambeau; **Dyam-yag le amblala te ródas la ándo têmnomós**. We lit torches to find her in the darkness.

amblavel *vt/i* 1) hang, execute by hanging: *pp/adj* **amblado**; **Amblade lês katar o kasht.** They hanged him from a tree. 2) dangle, hang, hang up, suspend; **Ambladyas pêsko kopúto.** He hung up his coat. **Ambladyas o patréto po zudo.**

He hung the picture on the wall. 3) depend on 4) *v/refl* **amblavél-pe** hang oneself, commit suicide by hanging oneself; **Ambladyás-pe ándo wêrsh.** He hanged himself in the forest.

amblayimásko-kasht *comp/nm* gallows

amblayimos *nm* 1) hanging, execution by hanging 2) suspension

amblayitóri *nm* 1) hangman 2) hanger, clothes' hanger

amboldári *nm* 1) tap, tap and wrench combination (*tool for forming a threaded screw hole*) 2) Spanish windlass

ambóldel *vt/i* 1) gyrate, orbit, pirouette, revolve, rotate, screw (*cap*), spin, turn, turn/twist around: *pp/adj* **amboldino** 2) give back, return, reverse, turn around, turn back; **Sóstar ambóldes?** Why are your turning around/back? **Amboldem o cháso.** I turned the clock back. **Amboldem o mobíli.** I reversed the car. **Amboldyas pêske swáturya.** He changed his testimony/reversed what he/she had said previously. **Ambóldes múrre swáturya.** You are twisting my words around 3) give back, reciprocate 4) push back, recoil 5) *comp/vt/i* ~ **pálpale** a) retrace one's steps, turn back again b) bounce back, come back, rebound; **Láko arman amboldyas pálpale láte.** Her curse rebounded back to her. 6) *v/refl* **ambóldel-pe** give back, go back, return, turn oneself around, reverse one's direction, revolve, spin around, turn, orbit, be orbiting, be reciprocated; **Amboldisáwo hai dikh pála túte!** Turn around and look behind you!

amboldil *vt* 1) reverse, turn *smth* around: *pp/adj* **amboldime**; **Amboldisar o mobíli te zhas pálpale!** Turn the car around so we can go back! 2) churn, turn; **Amboldinisáilo lêsko gi.** His stomach turned. 3) *v/refl* **amboldíl-pe** turn oneself around; **Amboldisár-tut te dikhes kon si pála túte!** Turn around so you can see who is behind you!

amboldimáski-púshka *comp/nf* **1)** revolver **2)** Gatling gun, minigun

amboldimásko *gen/adj* rotating, revolving, spinning

amboldimásko-wudár *comp/nm* **1)** revolving door **2)** revolving refugee claims (*Can*)

amboldimos *nm* **1)** about face, pirouette, reversal, rotation, turn over, turn around **2)** recoil

amboldino *pp/adj* **1)** inside out, backwards, back-to-front, turned around, reversed **2)** inverted, rolled over, turned over, upside down

ambolditóri *nm* **1)** swivel table/plate, turntable **2)** weather vane

âmbréla *nf* umbrella

ambrol *nm* pear

ambrolin *nf* pear tree

ambulántsiya *nf* ambulance

ame *pron/nom* we & *pron/acc* us, ouselves (*cont of* **amên** *qv*)

amên *pron/acc/pl* us, ourselves

amên sya *pron/pl/acc* all of us, us all; **Dosharel amên sya,** He blames us all.

amênde *pron/prep* to us, to our place; **Chi mai avel amênde.** He never comes around any more.

Amérika *nf* **1)** United States of America **2)** America (*continent*): *nf/pl* **Américhi** (*the*) Americas, all countries on the American continent.

Amerikáko 1) *gen/adj* of America/USA; **tiléri-Amerikáke** American dollars **2)** native to America/USA; **Rrom Amerikácha** American Roma

Amerikanítska *nf* American English (*Lang*)

Amerikanítsko *adj* American; **Amerikanítsko televízhono** American television

Amerikanitskones *adv* like the Americans, in the American way, in the American "language."

Amerikáno *nm* male American/American man: *nf* **Amerikánka**

amilai *adv* this summer

Ámin! *interj* Amen!

amíra *nf* **1)** oath, vow **2)** curse (*Am*) *var of* **arman** *qv*

amnári *nm* **1)** tinder box **2)** flintlock mechanism to start a fire **3)** cigarette lighter

amplafikatóri *nm* amplifier, speaker box (*Mus*)

ámplo *nm* amplifier, speaker box (*Mus*)

ámpo *nm* amp

âmpochíl *vt* **1)** reach an understanding/agreement/compromise, reconcile, settle (*dispute*), arrange (*compromise*): *pp/adj* **âmpochimé 2)** arbitrate **3)** *v/refl* **âmpochíl-pe** reconcile oneself, be reconciled, reach a compromise/agreement/amicable solution, arbitrate

âmpochimós *nm* agreement, arbitration, compromise, reconciliation

âmpochitóri *nm* arbitrator

amporádji *nm/pl* amperage

ampuyil *vt* **1)** breed (*animals*): *pp/adj* **ampuyime 2)** *v/refl* **ampuyíl-pe** breed, mate

ampuyimos *nm* **1)** breeding/mating of animals **2)** young born of animal mating, litter, brood, offspring

ampuyitóri *nm* breeder of animals: *nf* **ampuyitórka**

amran *nm see* **arman** *nm*

amrandel *vt* **1)** curse, damn: *pp/adj* **amrandino 2) amrandel-pe** curse/damn oneself

amunátsiya *nf* ammunition

amuzil *vt* **1)** amuse, entertain: *pp/adj* **amuzime 2)** *v/refl* **amuzíl-pe** amuse oneself

amuzimos *nm* amusement, entertainment

Amyúla *nf* a A mythical country in Canadian/American Romani folktales where the Roma are claimed to have originated. The capital is called **Rusalíno** which might be connected etymologically with Jerusalem in folklore.

an *prep* in, to *see* **ándo/ánde**; **Phendem lês wórta an lêsko mui.** I told him straight to/in his face.

anasétiko *nm* 1) anesthetic 2) *comp/vt* **del ~** anesthetize

anav *nm* name

anavyárdyol *vi* be given a name, be named: *pp/adj* **anavyardilo**

anavyarel *vt* 1) call, give a name to, name: *pp/adj* **anavyardo** 2) *v/refl* **anavyarél-pe** name oneself

anavyarimos *nm* ceremony of naming a child, naming

anchépo *nm/arch* camphor, smelling salts

ánd êkh dáta *adv/phr* all of a sudden, immediately, right away, suddenly (*Am*); **Peló pe mánde ánd êkh dáta kon sas.** I suddenly realized who he was. **Músai te zhas ánd êkh dáta.** We must leave immediately.

ánd êkh than *adv/phr* all at once, together, united (*Am*); **Pálpale ánd-êkh-than-le.** They are (*back*) together. **Músai te beshas ánd ekh tan ánde kakya buki.** We must stand united in this issue. **Mai ekh dáta ánd-ekh-than-le.** They are back together again.

and *prep* in, into (*us when it is not followed by a def art*); **Lêm la ánd angáli.** I took her in (an) embrace/I embraced her.

ánda e pêrvina *adv/phr* from the beginning

ánda e pêrvina zhi-ka o gor *adv/phr* from beginning to end

ánda godya *conj* because of that, for that reason, that's why

ánda kakya *conj* because of this, for this reason, this is why

ánda *prep/conj* 1) about, from, concerning, out of, because of, due to, surrounding, through, for; **Avilo ánda o wêrsh.** He came out of the forest. **Ánda láte me meráva.** Because of her, I am dying. **Ánda gadya buki sa le Rroma xan-pe.** Because of that business, all the Roma are arguing. **Shéyo! Ánda túte me meráva.** Oh Romani girl! Because of you I am dying/dying for love of you. (*Can Kalderash song*) 2) of; **Yekh ánda l' Rrom Vankoveréshti mothodyas ma.** One of the Vancouver Roma told me. **Dyas mánge do-pash ánda l' love.** He gave me half of the money. **Note**: Used in this way, **ánda** can replace the use of the ablative case as in; **Dyás mánge do-pash le lovêndar.** He gave me half of the money.

ánda sóste *comp/adv* about what, from what, for what reason, why; **Ánda sóste mangel te dikhel man?** About what does he want to see me?

ándar *Eur var of* **ánda** *prep/conj qv*

ánde *adv/prep* 1) in, inside, into, during *used before feminine nouns and plurals of both genders*; **ánde sóba** in/inside the room, **ánde lênge posukya** into their pockets. **Kheldyás-pe ánde sláva.** She danced during the feast. **Zhal po lóvo ánde l' wêrsh.** He hunts in the forests.

ánde kol gesa *adv/phr* back then, in those days

ánde l' *prep/cont* of **ánde le** *used with pural nouns*; **ánde l' wêrshènde** into the forests; **Ándo marimos, le Rroma garadé-pe ánde l' wêrshènde.** During the war, the Roma hid themselves in the forests.

ánde pêrvina *id/comp/adv* in the beginning, originally, to begin with

ánde phuv *id/prep* into the ground. **Note:** *This idiom is used in many expressions as follows*; **Sovél-pe ánde phuv.** He is sleeping himself to death. **Piyél-pe ánde phuv.** He is drinking himself to death. **Yekh ges, thav lês ánde phuv.** On day I'll put him into the ground/kill him. **Dyas-pe ánde phuv.** He drove himself to death.

ánde saré l' thana *adv/phr* in all places, everywhere

ánde wúrma *adv/phr* 1) at last, at the end, finally, in the end 2) late, towards the end

andesára 1) *nf* evening, dusk, nightfall 2) *adv* **de andesára** since evening; **Chi**

dkhlem lês de andesára. I haven't seen him since the evening.

andívo *nm* chicory, endive

ándo *adv/prep* **1)** during, in, inside, into *used before masculine nouns only*; **ándo wêrsh** in the forest **2)** during; **Ándo marimos, nashti kerásas buki hai bokhalyósas.** During the war, we were not able to work and we were starving. **Dyas ándo kher pa e filástra.** He got into the house through the window.

ándo bírro *adj/phr* in debt, indebted

ándo gado cháso *id/phr* in this hour, at this time, hour of judgement; **Te marel tu o Del ándo gádo cháso!** May God punish you in this hour of judgement!

ándo gláso *adv/phr* in tune; **Tyi gitára nai ándo gláso.** Your guitar is not in tune.

ándo párno ges *adv/phr* in broad daylight, in plain view

ándo rat *id* in the blood, through heredity; **Si amên musíka ándo rat.** We have music in the (our) blood. **Gadya familíya si la turbyála ándo rat.** That family has insanity in the blood/has produced many people who were insane.

ándo sádo *id/prep* in the garden, orchard, courting; **Seráv-man kána sámas ándo sádo.** I remember when we were in the garden/courting.

ándo than *adv/conj* in place of, instead of; **Me zhav ándo lêsko than.** I am going in his place/instead of him. **Ándo than te zhas ages, zhas tehára.** Instead of going today, let's go tomorrow.

ándo wast *adv/phr/id* **1)** in hand, in one's possession, under one's ownership; **Sodya love si tut ándo wast?** How much money do you have in hand/immediately available? **Si lês mobílya ándo wast kai mangel te bikinel.** He has cars in hand that he wants to sell. **Si ánde l' Babêsko wast.** Bob has it in his possession. **2)** *id* responsibility; **Akana si ándo tíro wast.** Now it's in your hands/Now it's up to you/Now it's your responsibility. **3)** in custody; **Ánde l' rángo wast-lo.** He's in

police custody. **4)** *comp/vt/i* **del ~** give into custody, hand over, surrender; **Dyas le love ándo wast.** He handed over the money. **5)** *comp/v/refl* **del-pe ~** give oneself into custody, surrender, turn oneself in

andral *adv/prep* from within/inside, inside, out of; **Ashundem e muzíka andral.** I heard the music from inside. **Avilo andral o kher.** He emerged from inside the house.

andre/andrû *prep/adv* **1)** aboard, in, inside, on board, on the inside; **Háide andre!** Come in/inside! **Si wárekon andre amári organizatsiya kai kerel problémi.** There is somebody inside our organization who is creating problems. **Kon si andre o hãlo?** Who is inside the hall? **Chi zhanav sodya zhene si andre.** I don't know how many people are inside. **2)** aboard, on board. **Wo sas andre, ándo vapóri.** He was on board, in the ship.

andrezhil *vt* **1)** tempt *pp/adj* **andrezhime 2)** *v/refl* **andrezhíl-pe** be tempted, tempt oneself

andrezhimos *nm* temptation

andruno *adj* **1)** internal, inside, inner: *irreg/fem in* **andruwi 2)** insider, inside man: *nf* **andruwi 3)** inside, interior; **o andruno la khangeriyáko** the inside/interior of the church

anel *vt/i* **1)** bring, carry, deliver, fetch, get: *pp/adj* **ando; An mánge pênsilo!** Bring/get me a ballpoint pen! **An mánge pái!** Get me (some) water! **Zha an mánge skára!** Go get me a ladder! **Anas la ándo vôrdòn!** We'll bring it in the station wagon! **O gazho andyas o xabe katar o Chinamáno.** The man has delivered the food from the Chinese restaurant. **2) ~ pai** bring water, irrigate **3)** *v/refl* **anél-pe** look like, resemble, take after; **Anél-pe pêske dades.** He resembles his father. **Pe kãste anél-pe?** Whom does he look like?

angáli *nf* **1)** embrace; **Lyas la ánd angáli.** He took her in an embrace. **2)** lap;

Beshélas pe lêski angláli. She was sitting on his lap. **3) del-pe ánd ~** embrace, hug; **Diné-pe ánd angáli.** They embraced/hugged each other.

angalíya *nf* tobacco pipe

angar do-pash phabardo *nm/phr* coke

angar *nm* coal

angarári *nm* fireman (*on a train*), stoker

angarêngi-tudkála *comp/nf* coal tar

angarêsko /angarêngo *gen/adj/s/pl* coal, related to coal; **bov-angarêngo** coal stove

angár-kashtuno *comp/nm* charcoal

angár-kovlo *comp/nm* bituminous coal

angár-zoralo *comp/nm* anthracite coal

ángelo/ángyelo *nm* angel: *pl* **ánzhelya:** *nf* **angeláika:** *pl* **ánzheláiki**

ángla *prep* before, in front of, ahead of, preceding; **Zha ángla mánde!** Go in front of me/ahead of me! **Ángla mánde dui droma, hai chi zhanav savo te lav.** Before me are two roads, and I don't know which one to take. (*song*)

ángla- *prod/prefix* pre-, *used with adjs*; **ángla-komunísto Ivrópa** pre-communist Europe

anglal 1) *adv/prep* forward, forwards, in the front/forefront, in front of; **Arakhlem les anglál o kher.** I found it in front of the house. **Dikhlan múrro névo mobíli avri anglal o kher?** Did you see my new car outside in front of the house? **Beshlem anglal.** I sat in the front. **2)** up front; **Mangel shel tiléri anglal.** He wants a $100 up front. **3)** *conj* before *with* **mai; Mangav te xav mai anglal katar te zhávtar.** I want to eat before I leave. **3)** *comp/vi* **del ~** get ahead, move ahead/forward(s) **4)** **zhal ~** advance, go ahead, more forward; **Músai te zhas mai anglal ánde amári bukí.** We need to move ahead in out work.

anglal *adv* from the future; **Drabarel anglal.** She predicts from the future.

anglal kai palal *adv* front to back/back to front, backwards, the wrong way round

ángla-marimásko *gen/adj* pre-war (*pre-Second World War*)

ángla-milai *comp/nm* spring, time after winter before the hot summer, spring planting season

ángla-mizméri *nm/adv* before noon, forenoon

angle *adv/prep* **1)** forward, ahead of, *often with* **mai; Zha mai angle mándar!** Go/move more ahead/ahead of me! **Zha angle!** Move ahead!/Advance! **2)** *nf* future, time ahead; **dur ánde angle** far into the future **3)** *adv* **angle** ahead, into the future **4)** *adv* **ánde angle** in the future

Anglézo *nm* Englishman: *nf* **Anglezáika**

Ángliya/Anglíya *nf* England

Angliyáko *gen/adj* of England; **E Emperatyása la Anglyáko.** The Queen of England. **Rrom-Angliyáko** English Rom, a member of the British *Kalderash* population: *pl* **Rrom-Angliyácha**

anglunes *adv* early, firstly, first and foremost, initially, primarily *often with* **mai**

anglunimos *nm* priority

angluno *adj* **1)** first, foremost, front, leading *often with* **mai; Mai mishto si t' aves o mai angluno mashkar le Rromênde neg o mai paluno mashkar le Gazhênde.** It is better to be first among the Roma instead of the last among the non-Roma. (*proverb*) **2)** foremost, important, **o mai angluno** the most important **2)** former; **lêski angluni Rromni** his former wife **3)** *nm* front man. first man, leading man, most important man: *nf* **angluni** front woman, first woman, leading woman

angropash *nm* **1)** gravedigger **2)** funeral director **3)** mortician **4)** *sl psn* who will be the death of *smbdy*; **Kodo Rrom kam-avel múrro angropash.** That man will be the death of me yet.

angropol *vt* **1)** inter, bury **2)** bury/smother engulf (*snowdrift/avalanche*) **3)** *v/refl* bury oneself (in); **Angroposailem ánde bukí.** I buried myself in work.

angropome *pp/adj* buried, interred, laid to rest

angropome zhívindo *comp/adj* buried alive

angropomos *nm* 1) burial, interment 2) funeral

angrushti/angushtri *nf* ring; **angrushtí-sumnakuni** gold ring

angyêliko *adj* angelic

ángyêlo *nm* angel: *pl* **ánzhêlya:** *nf* **angyeláika:** *pl* **anzheláiki**

animos *nm* delivery

anitóri *nm* bearer, bringer

ankaládyol *vi* 1) be delivered (*baby*), come out, emerge: *pp/adj* **ankaladilo** 2) be extracted, removed, rescued, withdrawn 3) be published 4) be exhumed 5) be pulled apart/separated

ankalavel *vt* 1) deliver (*baby*), extract, get out, pull apart/out, remove, separate, take out, draw out (*gun*), withdraw: *pp/adj* **ankalado; Ankaladyas pêski púshka hai dyas yag ánde balwal.** He drew his gun and shot into the air. 2) get *smbdy* out of (*trouble*), preserve, remove, rescue, save, save from destruction; **Ankalavas o mobíli katar o iv.** We'll get the car out of the snow. **Ankaladyas múrro tráyo.** He saved my life. 3) bring out, publish 5) exhume 6) earn (*money*) 7) *v/refl* **ankalavél-pe** get oneself out of, remove oneself, withdraw oneself, rescue/save oneself; **Ankaladém man katar o xamos.** I withdrew myself from the argument. **Nashlémtar te ankalaváv-man.** I fled to save myself.

ankalayimos *nm* 1) delivery (*of a baby*), liberation, rescue, redemption, salvation 2) extraction, removal, withdrawal 3) exhumation 4) publication 5) revelation

ankalayitóri *nm* 1) liberator, redeemer, rescuer, saviour: *nf* **ankalayitórka** 2) publisher

ankerel *vt var of* **ingarel** *qv*

anklel *vt/i* 1) circulate, get around, get out, get up (*after falling*): *pp/adj* **anklisto** 2) emerge, go out, leave; **Ankle avri!** Get out**! Na anklen avri shavorrále!** Don't go outside children! **Anklisto ánda o vôrdòn.** He came out of the wagon. 3) clamber/climb/climb up on, get on/up on, rise up, mount (*horse*); **Anklistem e playing.** I climbed up the mountain. **Anklisto pe sténa.** He got up on the stage. 4) come up, rise up from, emerge; **Ándo milai le tsímburya anklen katar e phuv.** In the spring, the seeds emerge from the earth. 5) ascend, rise, rise up; **O kham anklel.** The sun is rising. 6) turn out, come out; **Anklisto mishto amênge.** It turned out well for us. 7) appear, come out, be published; **Kána anklel godo stóriyo ánde gazéta?** When will that story appear in the magazine?

anklimásko-kher *comp/nm* publishing house

anklimos *nm* 1) ascendance, ascent, climb, departure, rising; **o anklimos le khamêsko** dawn, the sunrise/rising of the sun 2) debut, emergence 3) outcome 4) resurrection 5) ascendency, triumph 5) **upward mobility** 6) edition, printing, publication; **Múrri búkfa anklisti ándo pêsko dúito anklimos.** My book has been published in its second printing.

anklisto *pp/adj* 1) mounted, on horseback 2) arisen/risen, raised, resurrected 3) *nm* mounted man/policeman/soldier, cavalryman; **Avile le rai, le ankliste.** The police came, the mounted ones.

anklitóri *nm* climber, mountaineer: *nf* **anklitórka**

ankolil *vt* 1) corral; **Ankolisardyam le grasten.** We corralled the horses. 2) surround, encircle, orbit 3) detour, deviate, detour, get/go around 4) hedge (*around an issue*) *v/ref* 5) **ankolíl-pe a)** surround oneself (*with*); **Sáyek ankolíl-pe dilênsa.** He **always** surrounds himself with fools. **b)** avoid, circle around, deviate **c)** hedge around; **Ankolin-pe.** They're hedging.

ankolime *pp/adj* 1) corralled 2) encircled, surrounded; **Ankolime símas**

dushmanênsa. I was surrounded by enemies.

ankolimos *nm* 1) corralling 2) encirclement. orbit 3) surroundings 4) detour, deviation

ankólo *nm* circle

anrralo *adj* egg-shaped, oval

anrro *nm* 1) egg 2) eyeball 3) ovary 4) *vlg/sl* testicle *see* **pelo** *nm*

ânspektóri *nm* inspector: *nf* **ânspektórka**

ansuchil *vt* 1) create chaos, complicate, confuse, foul up, mix up: *pp/adj* **ansuchime** 2) entwine, tangle, twirl, twist, wring; **Ansuchisardyas lêski korr.** She wrung its neck. 2) *v/refl* **ansuchíl-pe** become confused/mixed up, become entangled/tangled/entwined/snarled up/fouled; **Ansuchil-pe o shavorro pe l' phaleya.** The little boy is rolling around on the floor.

ansuchimásko *gen/adj* chaotic, confusing, entangling

ansuchime *pp/adj* 1) confused, mixed up 2) entangled, entwined, twisted, tangled; **ansuchimé-lo o shelo.** The rope is tangled.

ansuchimos *nm* 1) chaos, confustion, foul up, mix-up 2) entanglement

ansuril *vt* 1) marry, marry off; **Ansurisadyas pêske shaves ánde lêngi familíya.** He married his son into their family. 2) *v/refl* **ansuríl-pe** get married, marry; **Ansurisáilo.** He got married. **Wo mangel te ansuríl-pe.** He wants to get married. **Pushlas la te ansuril-pe lása.** He asked her if he could marry her. **Note:** *This verb is used ony for men. For women see* **môritíl** *vt*

ansurimásko *gen/adj* marital, marriage (*of a man*); **Si tu gûndo ansurimásko?** Do you have a marriage thoughts/Are you thinking about marriage?

ansurime *pp/adj* married (*man*)

ansurimos *nm* marriage (*of a man*)

anti-Rromanísmo *nm/neolog* discrimination/persecution of Roma, Romaphobia

anti-Tsiganísmo *nm/neolog* Anti-Gypsyism

ântrégo/întrégo *adj/adv* 1) complete, entire, entirely, whole; **Phiradyas e lúmya ântrégo.** He traveled the whole world. **Xalyam o shônko, ântrégo.** We ate the ham, all of it. **Bikindyas le grast, ântrézhi.** He sold the horses, all of them. 2) *nm* all of it, the entire matter/thing

antúnchi *adv* then; **Antúnchi te avel kerdo!** Then let it be so done!

anúmi/anúme *adv* deliberately, on purpose, purposely; **Kerdyas anúmi.** He did (*it*) on purpose.

anzárdyol *vi* 1) become erected, raised, constructed: *pp/adj* **anzardilo** 2) be reached

anzarel *vt* 1) extend, reach, span, stretch: *pp/adj* **anzardo** 2) erect, construct, set up; **Anzardyam le tséri,** We erected the tents 3) lift, hoist, raise (*flag*)

anzarimos *nm* building, construction, hoisting, erection, raising

anzol *vi* extend (*to*), reach, span: *pp/adj* **anzulo**

anzomos *nm* extension, reach, span

ap/apo *conj/prep/imp* after all, anyhow, now, then, so, on, well; **Te trobul te kerel, ap, mek te kérdyol** If it needs to be done, then let it be done. **Ashundem so phendyas ap phendem lêske múrro gûndo.** I heard what he said, then I told/gave him my opinion. **Akushla ma, ap me gêlémtar.** He insulte me, upon that/so, I departed. **Ápo ashun!** Now listen!

aparáta *nf* 1) apparatus, device 2) tool

aparáti *nf/pl* equipment, devices, paraphernalia, tools

apendíchi *nf/pl* 1) appendicitis 2) appendix; **Pelo naswalo, lêske apendíchi, zhanes.** He fell sick, his appendix, you know.

aplikátsiya *nf* application

apostólo *nm* apostle

aprikáta *nf* apricot

aptéka *nf* apothecary, drug store

aptekári apothecary, druggist: *nf* **aptekárka**

apuntaménto *nm* appointment

Arabítska *nf* Arabic (*Lang*)

Arabítsko *adj* Arab; **Arababítsko ponyáva** Arabian carpet

Arábiya *nf* Arabia

Arábo *nm* Arab: *nf* **Arabáika**

arakhadimos *nm* birth, delivery (*of a baby*)

arakhadino *nm* foundling: *nf* **arakhadini**

arakhádyol *vi* **1)** become found, find oneself, turn up (*after being lost*): *pp/adj* **arakhadilo 2)** feel; **Sar arakhádyos?** How do you feel? **3)** be born; **Arakhádilem ánde Kanáda.** I was born/found in Canada. *This is the polite way to say I was born instead of* **biyándilem,** *I was born, which implies all the pollution of birth, and is thus a taboo topic in mixed conversation. See* **byándyol** *vi* **4)** come together, meet **5)** fit (*clothing*) **6)** be found/located/situated

arakhári *nm* defender, guardian, protector

arakhel *vt* **1)** find, discover: *pp/adj* **arakhlo/arakhlino 2)** come across **3)** defend, protect, shelter **4)** be wary, guard, watch over, watch out; **T'arakhes kyo drom!** May you travel safely! **Trobul ame Rrom te arakhel o wudar.** We need a Rom to guard the door. **5)** keep under surveillance, watch; **Le rai sáyek arakhen e ófisa.** The police are always watching the parlour. **6)** *v/refl* **arakhél-pe a)** abstain from, avoid, be careful, be on one's guard, defend oneself, guard oneself, take care, watch over oneself **b)** meet up with, run into; **Arakhlé-ma lêsa ándo Târáno.** I ran into him in Toronto. **c)** behave oneself, comport oneself; **Arakhél-pe pe mishtimáste.** He behaves himself well/He is well behaved **d)** find oneself; **Kána ratilo, arakhlyám-ame xasarde ándo wêrsh.** When night fell, we found ourself lost in the forest.

arakhimáta *nm/pl* evidence, findings

arakhimos 1) *nm* defense, protection, sanctuary **2)** discovery, finding **3)** surveillance **4)** *comp/vt* **del ~** give/provide protection; **Dem lêske arakhimos.** I gave him protection.

araki *nf* **1)** yesterday, last night; **Araki nas baxtali mánge.** Yesterday was not lucky for me. **2)** past (*fig*); **Le Rroméngi araki,** The Romani past (*yesterday*); **Sáyêk del-dúma ánda pêske arakya.** He's always talking about his past (*his yesterdays*). **3)** *adv* last night, yesterday; **Gêlítar araki.** She left yesterday.

arakya *nf/pl* past, yesterdays; **Serel pêske arakya.** He's remembering his yesterdays/past.

arakyára *adv usually with* **de** *as in* **de arakyára** since last night/yesterday; **Símas kathe de arakyára.** I have been here since last night/yesterday.

arakyarel *vt* **1)** store overnight, house/put up overnight, park overnight: *pp/adj* **arakyardo 2)** *v/refl* **arakyarél-pe** stay overnight, pass the night; **Arakhyardyám-ame ándo motéli.** We stayed overnight in a motel.

arakyuno *adj* **1)** from/of yesterday, yesterday's; **Naswalo sas desar e sláva e arakyuni.** He has been sick since yesterday's feast. **2)** last night's

araskápo *nf* horoscope

arasláno *nm* lion, man-eating lion: *nf* **araslánka**

archichéski-shib *comp/nf* tongue of tin, tin icicle (*used in plating copper mixing bowls*); **Bilavas o archíchi hai shorras ánde l' shantsútsurya pe phuv te keras archichêske shiba te hanos le basûni.** We melt the tin and pour it into little trenches on the ground to make strips of tin to plate the basins.

archichêsko *gen/adj* made of tin

archíchi *nm* **1)** tin **2)** solder

ardei *nm* **1)** paprika, pepper **2)** capsicum

ardjentári *nm* silversmith: *nf* **ardjentárka** silversmith's wife

aremil *vt* plate *(with copper)*: *pp/adj*
 aremime *(Eur) see* **hanol** *vt*
aresel *vi* **1)** arrive at, get, get to, make it to, reach: *pp/adj* **areslino**; **Sóma areslo ándo gav kána peli e ryat.** He just made it into town when night fell. **Chi aresas khatênde.** We are not getting anywhere/not going anywhere. **2)** last *(until)*, suffice, **3)** achieve, attain, manage to do
aresimos *nm* **1)** arrival, termination of a trip **2)** remainder **3)** attainment
aríchi *nm* **1)** porcupine **2)** hedgehog: *pl* **aricheyi**
árka *nf* ark; **Árka-Nowêski**, Ark of Noah
Arlítska *nf* Any one of a group of closely-related Non-Vlax Romani dialects spoken in the South Balkans and now in western Europe and the Americas by refugees and immigrants from this region.
Arlítsko *gen/adj* of the Arli Romani group; **Arlítsko Rrom**, a Rom of the Arli group: *nf* **Arlítsko Rromni**
árma *nf* **1)** army *(Mil)* **2)** weapon **3)** **lel-pe ármi** *vi* take up arms, arm oneself
armaiya *nm/pl* damnation
arman/amran *nm* **1)** curse, malediction; **Perel arman pe túte te na mothos o chachimos ánde gadya buki.**You'll bring down a curse on yourself if you don't tell the truth in this matter. **2)** oath, vow **3)** *comp/vt* **del ~** curse, damn, lay a curse; **Motho o chachimos, wórka níchi, dav tu arman!** Tell the truth, or if you don't, I'll lay a curse on you!
armandino/amrandino *comp/pp/adj* cursed, damned, doomed; **Amrandino sas katar e materítsa.** He was cursed/damned from the womb/from birth.
armil *vt* **1)** arm *(with weapons)*: *pp/adj* **armime 2)** *v/refl* **armíl-pe** arm oneself
armoníya *nf* harmony
aropláno *nm* aeroplane, aircraft
árpa *nf* harp *(Mus)*
arpári *nm* harpist: *nf* **arpáika**
árro *nm* flour, grain *var in* **várro/wárro** *qv*

árro-zhováko *comp/nm* oatmeal
arséniko *nm* arsenic
árta *nf* art
artichóka *nf* artichoke *(Am)*
artísta *nm/nf* artist, artistic/creative person, person who takes pride in his/her work; **Me sim artísta. Chi kerav buki djungali.** I am an artist. I don't do ugly work. *(meaning working as a coppersmith in this sentence).* **Note**: In *Kalderash*, artist has more of the French meaning of a person with creative ability and temperament.
artístiko *adj* artistic, creative
artísto *nm var of* **artísta** *nm/nf*
artizána *nf* art, craft, handicraft
artizanáti *nf/pl* handicrafts, hand-crafted items
artrítiko *nm* arthritis, bursitis *(Am) gen/adj* **artritikósko** arthritic
Arxentína *nf* Argentina
Arxentíno *nm* Argentinean man: *nf* **Arxentútsa**
Arxentítsko *adj* from Argentina, Argentinean
arxivil *vt* archive, store in an archive: *pp/adj* **arxivime**
arxivísto *n* archivist: *nf* **arxevísta**
arxívurya *nm/pl* archives
aryat *nf* **1)** tonight **2)** *adv* tonight, this evening
arzhintári *nm* silversmith
asal *vi* **1)** laugh: *pp/adj* **asailo/asanilo**; **Asávas lêstar**. I was laughing at him. **2)** smile; **Asal pe mánde,** She is smiling at me. **Asayas kána ashundyas.** He smiled when he heard (that). **Note: 1)** takes an *abl/n/acc in the acc* when the *acc* is animate while **2)** is used with **pe** as shown in the examples given **3)** ~ **dilivanes**, giggle, smile asininely
asamásko *gen/adj* **1)** amusing, comical, funny, laughable **2)** ridiculous; **Asamáski logódba si kai phendyan.** That's a ridiculous proposal that you made.
asaltil *vt* assault, attack

asaltime *pp/adj* **1**) assaulted, attacked **2**) be ~, **asaltíl-pe** *v/refl*

asálto *nm* assault (*Mil*), attack

asamos *nm* **1**) laugh, laughter, mirth **2**) smile **3**) *comp/vi* **perel ándo** ~ break into laughter, start laughing

asav *nm* **1**) mill, windmill **2**) grinder; **kafáko** ~ coffee grinder

asavári *nm* miller: *nf* **asavárka** miller's wife

asavel *vt* cause to laugh, deride, laugh at, make fun of, mock: *pp/adj* **asado; Asavel ma.** He is mocking me/causing people to laugh at me.

asavêsko-barr *nm* millstone

asayimos *nm* ouburst of laughter

ashado *pp/adj* **1**) detained, held up, stopped, stalled **2**) *nm* detainee: *nf* **ashadi 3**) stranded *psn*

áshado pai *comp/nm* stagnant water

ashádyol *vi* **1**) be silent, cease, remain, stay: *pp/adj* **ashadilo 2**) be detained/dammed/held up/impeded/stopped/stranded; **Ashádilem ándo tráfiko.** I got stuck in the traffic. **Ashádilo ánde imigrátsiya.** He was detained in immigration. **3**) to be ceased/ended; **Ashádile pêske gesa.** His days are ended/over. **4**) catch one's breath, stop to rest, take a break

ashárdyol *vi* **1**) be complimented/lauded/praised: *pp/adj* **ashardilo** (*Eur*) **2**) be flattered

asharel *vt* **1**) compliment, laud, praise: *pp/adj* **ashardo** (*Eur*) **2**) flatter, snow job, suck up to

asharimos *nm* **1**) praise (*Eur*) **2**) flattery, snow job

ashavel *vt* **1**) bring to a stop, detain, halt, make to desist/stop, prevent, put an end to, stop: *pp/adj* **ashado 2**) block up, impede, dam (*river*) **3**) interrupt; **Ashadyas múrre vórbi.** He interrupted my conversation. **4**) avert, prevent **5**) allow/make to remain

ashayimos *nm* **1**) stoppage, blockage, deadlock, gridlock, obstacle **2**) delay, detention

ashel *vt/i* **1**) stand, stay, remain: *pp/adj* **ashilo; Kon ashel avri?** Who is standing outside? **2**) cease/stop doing, desist, end, stop; **Ash kyo mui!** Stop your mouth/shut up! **Ashilo lêsko yilo.** His heart stopped/He died of heart failure. **Ashilo te piyel doháno.** He stopped smoking. **3**) be available, be left, remain, be outstanding/remaining; **Ashilem xolyáriko.** I remained angry. **Chi ashel khánchi.** There's nothing left (*remaining*). **Chi ashel thud ándo frígo.** There's no milk left in the fridge. **Ashel férdi trin ges te das-gáta e buki.** There are only three days remaining/left to complete the work. **Sóde love ashen ándo bánko?** How much money is left in the bank? **4**) stand (*with*), agree (*with*); **Ashav tumênsa pe gadya treyába.** I remain with you/agree with you, on this issue. **5**) stand (*as security for smbdy*); **Ashel mánge ánde kumpaníya.** He will stand for me in the (local) community. **6**) endure, last, remain; stand; **Te ashel mil bersh!** May it (the house) stand for a thousand years! **7**) *comp/vi* ~ **nango** get cleaned out (*in bankruptcy or gambling*) **8**) *comp/vi* ~ **phari** become pregnant, be impregnated

ashimos *nm* break, halt, lull, recess, respite, stop

Áshta! *v/imp* **1**) Hand it over! Show it! Let's see it! **Áshta ke dikhav lês!** Hand it here so I can see it! **2**) Wait! Hang on! **Áshta te arakhav múrre shtákli!** Hang on till I find my glasses!

ashundimos *nm* fame, glory, renown

ashundo *pp/adj* famous, renowned, well-known

ashúndyol *vi* **1**) be heard, be heard about: *pp/adj* **ashundilo; Chi mái ashúndyol kodo swáto.** That word isn't heard/used any more. **2**) be famous/renowned/well known

ashunel *vt/i* **1)** hear: *pp/adj* **ashundo 2)** heed, listen, obey, pay attention (to); **Chi mai ashunel ma.** He/she never pays attention to me. **Ashún-ta mánde!** Listen to me! **3)** overhear **4)** *v/refl* **ashunél-pe** be heard, hear oneself. **Musái te shunél-pe amáro gláso.** Our voice must be heard.

ashunimos *nm* **1)** audience, hearing; **Mangel ashunimos ánde kris.** He wants a hearing in court. **2)** eavesdropping **3)** acoustics

ashunitóri *nm* **1)** eavesdropper, listener: *nf* **ashunitórka 2)** hearing aid

ashunitórya *nm/pl* audience, listeners

ashwar *nf* halter (*for a horse*)

asimilátsiya *nf* assimilation (*Eur*) *see also* **Gazhikanimos** *nm*

asosiyátsa *nf* association

aspariga *nf* single asparagus stalk: *pl* **aspirídji**

aspiratóri *nm* vacuum cleaner (*Eur*)

aspirína *nf* aspirin

áspro *adj* coarse, hard, rough

astáchi *nm* **1)** cast-iron cooking pot, often on three legs **2)** cast iron, pig iron

astachiyêsko *gen/adj* cast iron, made of cast iron

astachuno *adj* **1)** resembling cast iron, having the quality of cast iron; **Si lês astachuno yilo.** He has a heart of cast iron.

astardi *nf* rowel of a spur

astardo *pp/adj* **1)** arrested, captured, detained, seized, trapped **2)** begun/commenced/started **3)** addicted, trapped **4)** *nm* addict, captive, captive wild male animal, prisoner: *nf* **astardi**

astárdyol *vi* **1)** be/become addicted, captured, caught, seized, trapped: *pp/adj* **astárdilo; Astárdilem ándo tráfiko.** I got caught up in the traffic. **2)** be conceived, begin, commence, get started, originate, start; **Astárdili e sláva?** Has the feast started? **Astarárdilem rano ánde diminyátsa.** I got started early in the morning. **3)** becom addicted to *smthg*;

Piyélas parno hai astárdilo. He was using cocaine and he became addicted. **4)** become attached, stick to **5)** become connected/related to by marriage

astarel *vt* **1)** arrest, catch, capture, entrap, get (*understand smthg*), grab, grasp, impound, seize, snatch, trap: *pp/adj* **astardo 2)** attach, fasten, harness/hitch (*horse*), hook up; **Astardyas o grast ka o vôrdòn.** He hitched the horse up to the caravan. **3)** join, put together; **Astardem le dui kotora kasht ánd-êkh-than.** I joined the two pieces of wood together. **4)** catch up to, overtake **5)** begin, commence, start; **Dem-man te astaráv o djuléshi.** I decided to begin the meeting. **6)** engage (*gears*) **7)** make *smbdy* addicted; **Na pi o parno, astarel tu.** Don't take cocaine, it will make you addicted. **8)** *v/refl* **astarél-pe** attach oneself to, cling to, stick to; **Astarél-pe mánsa sar o kléyo.** He sticks to me to me like glue/I can't get rid of him. **9)** palm off, stick *smbdy* with *smth*; **Astardem lês lása.** I palmed it off on him. (*Am*)

astarimos *nm* **1)** capture, entrapment, seizure, trap **2)** attachment, fastening, hitching device **3)** beginning, commencement, start **4)** addiction

astarimós-mashêngo *comp/nm* catching fish, fishing

astarni *nf* catch, trap

astrécha *nf* ostrich: *gen/adj* **astrecháko** belonging to an ostrich; **astrechánge pora** ostrich feathers

aswin/asvin *nf* tear, teardrop: *pl* **aswa/aswaiya**

atarde *adv* hither, here; **Atarde, Rromále!** Here, over here, Roma! **Háiden atarde, shavorrále!** Come over here, children!

ateléri *nm* studio, workshop (*Eur*)

aténtsiya *nf* attention

athavel *see* **hathavel** *vt*

atwéto *nm* **1)** answer, conclusion, decision, reply **2)** resolution, solution **3)** *comp/vt/i* **del ~** answer, give reply, reach a decision

3) *comp/vt/i* **arakhel** ~ find an answer/solution, resolve, solve

áva *adv* yes *see also* **va**

avel *vi* **1)** attend, be coming, come: *pp/adj* **avilo**; **Kon avel?** Who is coming? **Avilem po báso.** I came by bus. **Avilyam ánde kontáina ándo fúndo le vaporiyêsko.** We came in a shipping container in the hold of the ship. **2)** achieve orgasm **3)** ~ with **pe** come down on, descend upon; **Avile le rai pe mánde.** The police came down on me/started to investigate me. **4)** appear, approach **5)** ~ **pála** follow **6)** **pálpale** come back again, be reincarnated **7)** arrive, get here/there; **Avilyam anglál e ryat.** We got there before nightfall. **8)** *v/refl* **avél-pe a)** come due, appear materialize **b)** happen, take place **9)** **avéltar** *vi* come out from, emerge from, exit; **Avilótar katar o wêrsh.** He emerged from the forest. **Katar avilántar?** From where did you exit? **10)** be, become; **Woi avel múrri Rromni.** She will be/become my wife. **Chi zhanav so avéla lênsa kána merávtar.** I don't know what will become of them when I pass on/die. **Note:** *all tenses of the verb to be/to become, except the present indicative and the past tense, are formed from* **avel**; *pres/ind* **Sim baxtalo.** I am lucky. *pst* ; **Símas baxtalo.** I was lucky. *fut* **Kam-avav baxtalo.** I will be lucky. *pst/cont* **Avávas-baxtalo.** I used to be lucky. *pluperfect* **Avilémas baxtalo.** I had been lucky. *cond* **Kámas-avav baxtalo.** I would be lucky. *imp/s* **Av!** *imp/pl* **Aven!**

aver **1)** *pron/adj* **1)** other, another; **Zhas aver ges.** We'll go another day. **2** another male person, somebody else; **Avilo aver.** Another man came. **Volil avres.** She loves another man. **Volil avrya.** He loves another woman. **Mothodyas avrêske.** He told another (man). *see also var* in **khaver** *pron/adj*

avér-fyal *adv/phr* **1)** different, differently **2)** opposite; **Nai so phenel wo, avér-fyal si.** It's not as he says, it's the opposite. **Chi zhanel aver-fyal.** He doesn't know the difference. **3)** *nm* alternative, opposite, something else; **Nai tut avér-fyal.** You have no alternative. **Wo phenel avér-fyál.** He says the opposite. **4)** *adj* another kind of/brand of/ make of; **Mangav te kinav avér-fyal mobíli.** I want to buy another make of car.

avér-fyálo *comp/adj* **1)** alternative, different, opposite: *pl* **avér-fyálurya**; **Godo si avér-fyálo gitára.** That's a different guitar **2)** *nm* difference

avér-kurko/yavér-kurko *comp/adj*; **Avav pe yaver-kurko.** I'll come next week.

avér-nav *comp[/nm* alias

avér-tehára **1)** *comp/nf* the day after tomorrow **2)** *adv* day after tomorrow

avér-than *adv* elsewhere, somewhere else; **Sáyek si po aver than, o Rrom godo.** That man is always somewhere else. He died somewhere else. **Mulo avré-thanêste.**

averutno *adj* another, other

aver-zhênó *n* another person, somebody else: *nf* **aver-zhêni**

Áve-uf! *exclam* Alas! Goodness me! God! Oh God! *(arch)* appears in folktales and recorded from elderly speakers; **"Áve-Uf!" Phênga-woi. "Xoxádilem!"** "Alas!" said she. "I have been deceived!" From *Can Kald folk* **Mûndro Salamon thai e Mártya** Wonderful Solomon and the Angel of Death.

avgin/ovgin *nm* honey

avginalo/ovginalo *adj* honey, sweet like honey

Avgósto *nm* August

Avgóstone *adv* in August

avimos *nm* **1)** arrival, attendance, *(the)* coming; **O dúito avimos le Kristósko** The second coming of Christ **2)** appearance *(at an event)*

ávindoi *v/part* coming, approaching *(Can)* **Note:** **-doi/-índoi** This present-participle

suffix construction is no longer
productive in North-American Kalderash
but some fossilized examples are retained
and can be heard occasionally from some,
usually elderly, speakers or immigrants;
Wo xálas zhándoi. He was eating while
walking away. Others recorded in Canada
are **sóvindoi** 'sleeping' and **gílabandoi**
'singing.' It can also be heard in some
Kalderash and related dialects in Europe
where it is more common, especially in
some Romanian Vlax-Romani dialects.

aviyáko *gen/adj* having to do with
aviation,flying

aviyátsiya *nf* **1)** airforce(*Mil*) **2)** aviation,
flying

aviyóno *nm* aircraft (*Eur*)

avlin *nf* **1)** mansion, manor **2)** castle,
château, palace; **Lêsko kher si chachi
avlin.** His house is a real palace. **3)**
courtyard, patio

avlinash *nm* owner of a large, imposing
house/mansion: *nf* **avlináshka**

avokáto *nm* advocate, attorney, lawyer: *nf*
avokatáika

avrêngo *gen/adj* belonging to others if
nm/pl or mixed *nm/nf/pl & nf/pl*

avrêsko *gen/adj* belonging to another if
nm; **Nai murro, avrêsko si.** It's not
mine, it belongs to somebody else.

avrêste *prep/pron/adv* **1)** to another man **2)**
elsewhere

avré-themêsko *gen/adj* alien, of
another/foreign country; **avré-themêsko
Rrom** Romani man from another country,
foreign Rom: *nf* **avré-themêski Rromni**

avri *nf* **1)** outdoors, outside **2)** *adv*
outdoors, outside; **Zha avri!** Go outside!
Meklem o radyútso avri o kher. I left
the portable radio outside the house.

avruno **1)** *adj* external, exterior, outside,
outer **2)** *nm* outsider, one not of the
in-group, loner: *nf* **avruwi; Woi si
avruwi mashkar le avre Rromnyánde.**
She is an outsider/loner among the other
women. **3)** *nm* another **5)** exterior; **o**

avruno le kherêsko the exterior of the
house

avrya *pron* another (*if nf*) **2)** *nf* another,
another woman; **Yekh Rromni si la trin
shave, avrya si la pansh, but shave si
amare Rromnyánde.** One woman has
three children, another has five, our
women have many children. **Volil avrya.**
He loves another woman. **Mothodyas le
avryánge.** She informed the other
women.

avryáko *gen/adj* belonging to another *if nf*;
Si pêsko shav avryáko. He's his son by
another woman/wife

avryal *adv/prep* from outside, outside, on
the outside; **Ashundem o bashimos
avryal o kher.** I heard the noise from
outside the house. **Avilo andre avryal.**
He came in from outside. **Si lên but
lulugya pe swáko rêgá avryal o kher.**
They have a lot of flowers all around the
outside of the house. **Rrêspisáilo but
gunoi pe phuv avryal lêngo kher.** A lot
of garbage has been scattered on the
ground outside their house. **Wo si Rrom
streyíno, avryal amári kumpaníya.** He
is a a stranger Rom from outside our
community.

avryángo *gen/adj* belonging to others, *if
nf/pl*

avtobáso *nm* autobus, bus (*Eur*)

avtsîn/avtsûn *nm* steel; **avtsîn kai chi mai
ruzheníl-pe** stainless steel/steel that
never rusts

avtsînaló *adj* having the quality of or
resembling steel

avtsînêsko *gen/adj* made of steel

âwérish *adv see* **owérish**

awordal *adv/prep* from over here; **Shai
ashunav la awordal.** I can hear her from
over here. **Háide awordal!** Come over
here!

aworde *adv* over here, this way; **Háiden
aworde Shavále!** Come over here, Boys!
Rromále, aworde! Roma, over here!
Shéyo! Aworde túsa! Girl! Over here
with you/come over here!

awtóri/ãtóri *nm* author: *nf* **awtórka**

azbádyol *vi* **1)** be fondled, touched, caressed: *pp/adj* **azbadilo 2)** be felt up, groped, sexually molested (*Am*)

azbal *vt/i* **1)** caress, feel, fondle, stroke, touch: *pp/adj* **azbado**; **N'azba o bov te na phabarés-tut!** Don't touch the stove, lest you get burned! **2)** affect (*emotionally*), impress **3)** touch upon, have relevance to *smth*; **Chi azbal amári buki.** That has no relevance to our task. **4)** contact (*eletrical/sound system*)

azbayimos 1) *nm* contact, feeling, fondling, impression, touching **2)** groping, sexual molestation *see also* **pipiyimós** *vt*

azbésto *nm* asbestos (*Am*): *gen/adj* **azbestósko** made of asbestos

azbimos *nm* feel, touch

azhukérdyol *vi* be waiting, be kept waiting: *pp/adj* **azhukerdilo**; **Azhukérdilem trin chásurya.** I have been waiting thee hours.

azhukerel *vt/i* **1)** wait, wait for: *pp/adj* **azhukerdo**; **Azhúker!** Wait! **Azhukerav o Stévo.** I am waiting for Steve. **Azhukerásas le gósturya.** We were waiting for the guests. **Azhukerélas trin ges te avel pêsko phral.** He has been waiting three days for his brother to arrive. **Azhukerav avri.** I'll wait outside. **2)** anticipate, expect; **Azhukerav chêko,** I'm waiting for a cheque. **3)** have patience, be patient

azhukerimos *nm* anticipation, expectation, wait, waiting period

azhutil *vt* **1)** aid, assist, help: *pp/adj* **azhutime 2)** *v/refl* **azhutíl-pe** help oneself

azhutimásko *gen/adj* helpful, useful

azhutimos *nm* aid, advice, assistance, help, service, support: *gen/adj* **azhutimásko** helping, supporting; **azhutimásko wast** helping hand

azhutóri *nm* lawyer *see also* **zhutóri** *nm*

azilantíya *nf* political asylum, Convention-refugee status

azilánto *nm* refugee: *nf* **azilantáika** female refugee

azilantomos *nm* refugee status/asylum

azílo *nm* asylum, refugee status; **Mangel azílo.** He wants refugee status/asylum.

azílo-polítiko *comp/nm* political asylum (*Eur*)

Azíya *nf* Asia

Aziyáko *gen/ádj* Asia; **Gazhó-Aziyáko** Asian man: *nf* **Gazhí-Aziyáki** Asian woman.

B

-ba *imp/non-productive suff* retained only in a few fossilized expressions in Canada/US; **Dé-ba**! start! **Zhá-ba**! Go! **Dên-ba, Rromále! Mudaren le po than!** Strike up (*the music*) Boys! Sock it to them/Slay them on the spot!

ba *adv* surely, certainly; **Ba chi**! Certainly not! **Ba ke níchi**! Not at all! (*Eur*) **Ba me chi zhav.** I'm certainly not going. **Zhas tu ba níchi?** Are you going or not?

bába *nf* 1) old woman, grannie 2) elderly witch; **wash-bába** old witch of the forest (*Folk*)

bába yága arch crone or bone woman who lives in the forest based on the Russian folk mythology character (*Folk*)

bábitsa *nf* 1) midwife 2) hailstone

bábitsi 1) hail, hailstones 2) *comp/vi* del ~ hail

babúno *nm* male baboon: *nf* **babunáika**

badil *vt* 1) annoy, bother, disturb, harass, pester: *pp/adj* **badime; Na badisar ma!** Don't bother me! **Rayído! Badin tu l' daba?** Edith! Is the hammering bothering you/Are the blows (from the hammer) bothering you? 2) *v/refl* **badíl-pe** become disturbed, bother oneself, fret about, worry (about); **Na badisar-tut kodolása!** Don't bother yourself with that! **Na badisar-tut!** Don't bother/Never mind! **Chi mai badí-ma kodolênsa.** I never bother with those people.

badimásko *gen/adj* annoying, bothersome

badimos *nm* aggravation, annoyance, botheration, harassment, nuisance

bagázho *nm* 1) baggage, luggage 2) freight: *gen/adj* **bagazhósko** of/for baggage or luggage

bagi *adv & id implying doubt or disbelief* maybe, perhaps, who knows; **Phenel ke avel tehára, bagi.** He says that he'll come tomorrow, but who knows. **Phenel ke mothol o chachimos, bagi.** He says he is telling the truth, perhaps. **Pokinen ma tehára, bagi.** They'll pay me tomorrow, so they say.

bagrémo *nm* holly; **bagremésko kasht** holly tree, **bagreméski múra** holly berry

bai *adv* surely, so; **Katar woi phirel, lulugya bai baryon, Katar woi chi phirel, lulugya bai kernyon.** From where she walks, flowers surely grow, from where she walks not, flowers surely whither. (*from the Am Romani folksong song* Delilah). **Láke yakha si bai bare.** Her eyes are so big.

bai *nf* sleeve (*of a garment*)

baigi *adv/id see* **bagi** *adv & id*

baiyêngo *gen/adj* sleeved, having sleeves

báiyero *nm* amulet, lucky charm: *pl* **báiyerya**

baiyorri *nf* short sleeve

bakalára *nm* codfish

bakháli *nf* stirrup; **Kon si te phenel o chachimos, móra te thol yêkh pûnrró ánde bakháli.** He who is about to tell the truth should place one foot in the stirrup. (*proverb*)

bakhálya *nf/pl* stirrups

bakil *vt* 1) back up (*vehicle*): *pp/adj* **bakime** 2) *v/refl* **bakíl-pe** back up; **Nashti bakí-ma.** I can't back up. (*Am*)

bakrano *gen/adj* relating to lambs/sheep; **Bákrano Ges** Lamb Day, Feast on May 5th in Romania, equivalent to

Hederlezi/Djurdjevdan in the South
Balkans
bakrári *nm* shepherd: *nf* **bakrárka**
shepherd's wife
bakrêski-morki *comp/nm* fleece,
sheepskin
bakri *nf* ewe, female lamb
bakrisho *nm* lamb: *pl* **bakrishe**
bakro *nm* (**1**) male sheep, ram **2**) lamb **3**)
Bakro Aries (*Zod*)
bakro xasardo *comp/nm* lost soul/sheep;
id **Phiravél-pe sar o bakro xasardo.** He
is wandering around in a daze.
bakrorro *nm* lamb
bakrunes *adv* like a sheep, like sheep;
Zhan pála lêste bakrunes. They follow
him like sheep.
bakruno *adj* ovine, sheep like, of sheep;
nm **mas-bakruno** mutton
bakryorri *nf* female lamb; **Shinas**
bakryorra kai Santána. We sacrifice
lambs to Saint Ann
bâksa *nf* box, crate, wooden crate
bakshish *nm* **1**) handout **2**) tip, gratuity
bal **1**) *nm* single hair (*Anat*) **2**) *nm/pl* **bal;**
Si la lúndji bal. She has long hair.
Shukar sas, lúngone kale balênsa. She
was beautiful, with long, black hair.
bāla *nf* pool/billiard ball (*Am*)
balai *nf* **1**) tub, washing tub: *pl* **bala 2**)
trough for washing tools/utensils. **3**)
bathtub
balaláika *nf* balalaika
balalo *adj* covered with hair, hairy, hirsute;
Balalo sas. He was covered with hair.
balamo *nm* **1**) shop, store **2**) meat market
(*Eur*)
balano *adj* porcine, from a pig; **mas**
balano pork
báldo *nm* ball, dance party (*Eur*); **báldo**
Rromano Romani ball/dance
baléna *nf* whale
balêngi-pori *comp/nf* ponytail
balêngo *gen/adj* **1**) of hair, related to hair,
possessing hair **2**) relating to pigs;
balêngo phandayimos pig stye, place
where pigs are corralled/kept

bali *nf* **1**) sow **2**) *fig* pig/loose woman
bālíl *vt* **1**) blackball, condemn, drive out,
ostracize: *pp/adj* **bālimé 2**) *v/refl* **bālíl-pe**
become blackballed, blackball oneself,
condemn oneself, ostracize oneself (*Am*)
bālimé *pp/adj* blackballed, condemned,
ostracized (*Am*)
bālimós *nm* blackballing, condemnation,
ostracization (*Am*)
balisho *nm* piglet
balivas *nm var* of **balovas** *qv*
Balkáno *nm* Balkans; **ándo Balkáno** in
the Balkans
balkóno *nm* balcony
balo *nm* **1**) boar, male pig **2** *fig* male pig,
slob, disgusting man **3**) glutton; *nf* **bali;**
Xan sar bale. They eat like pigs/they are
gluttons.
baló-khorro *comp/nm* guinea pig: *pl*
balé-khorre
baló-phuvyáko *comp/nm* groundhog,
mole: *pl* **balé-phuvyáke**
balorro *nm* guinea-pig
balovas/balivas *nm* bacon
bálta *nf* **1**) swamp. marsh, bog, quicksand:
pl **báltsi 2**) pool, pond **3**) swimming pool
baltútsa *nf* puddle
baluchála/bulchála *nf* **1**) inferior food,
junk food, airline/hospital food, slop; **Chi**
xav kakya baluchála. I won't eat this
slop. **2**) *psn* who eats like a hog,
sloppy/slovenly *psn*
baluchil *vt* **1**) gobble, gulp down slop, slop
one's food: *pp/adj* **baluchime 2**) *v/refl*
baluchíl-pe slop one's food; **Baluchíl-pe**
sar a balo. He slops down his food like a
hog.
baluchime *pp/adj* **1**)
badly-dressed/ill-dressed, sloppy **2**)
slovenly
baluchimos *nm* sloppiness, slovenliness
baluwíl-pe *v/refl* **1**) be lingering, linger **2**)
be loafing, loaf, loaf around **3**) get into
mischief
baluwimos *nm* **1**) lingering, loafing **2**)
mischief
baluwitóri *nm* loafer, malingerer

balwal *nf* **1)** wind: *pl* **balwalya/balwala; Lya lês e balwal.** The wind took it/blew it away. **Arakh te na lêl tut e balwal!** Watch out the wind doesn't take you/Be careful you don't catch some fatal disease! **2)** draught **3)** air **4)** oxygen (*as provided for people with breathing problems*); **Nashti phúrdel, de lêske balwal!** He can't breathe, give him oxygen! **5)** breath **6)** stomach gas **6)** *fig* fart; **Nakhlas balwal.** He passed wind. **7)** *vi* **lel ~** breathe, get/take air; **Nashti lel balwal.** He can't breathe. **8)** *id* **Line lês le balwalya hay mulo.** He had a stroke and died.

balwaláki lulugi *comp/nf* dandelion

balwaláko *gen/adj* **1)** of the wind; **o vuzheyimos la balwaláko** the whistling of the wind **2)** pneumatic

balwalalo *adj* breezy, drafty, gusty, windy, windswept

balwalása *adv/nf/inst* with the wind; **Gêló la balwalása.** He went with the wind/took off like the wind.

balwalorri *nf* draught, light wind

balwalyárdyol *vi* to be aired out, fumigated: *pp/adj* **balwalyardilo**

balwalyarel *vt* air, air out, fumigate: *pp/adj* **balwalyardo**

bambóna *nf* candy, sweet: *pl* **bambóni**

bánda *nf* **1)** band (*Mus*) **2)** band, group

bandázho *nm* bandage

bandazhuwil *vt* **1)** apply a bandage, bandage, wrap in a bandage: *pp/adj* **bandazhuwime 2)** *v/refl* **bandazhuwíl-pe** bandage oneself

bandído *nm* bandit, gangster (*Am fr Sp*)

bangé-punrrêngo *gen/adj* bow-legged

banges *adv* **1)** askance, crookedly, in a bent manner, in a deformed/twisted way, in a winding direction; **Kadkar o drom zhal banges.** From here on, the road goes in a winding direction. **Dikhel banges pe mánde.** He's squinting/looking hostilely at me. **2)** ungrammatically; **Del-dúma Rromanes banges.** He speaks Romani in an ungrammatical way. **3)** incorrectly

bangé-yakhêngo *gen/adj* cross-eyed

bangimos *nm* **1)** bend, curve, turn-off/exit (*on a highway*) **2)** abnormality, deformity **3)** lies, twisted facts/information, slanted information **4)** error

bango *adj* **1)** bent, crooked, curved **2)** crippled, deformed, twisted **3)** incorrect, wrong (*opposite of right*); **Lyas o bángo drom.** He took the wrong road.

bangó-pûnrró *nm* club foot

bangyardo 1) *pp/adj* bent, crippled, deformed, twisted **2)** curved **3)** cripple: *nf* **bangyardi**

bangyárdyol *vi* **1)** become bent, crippled, curved, deformed, snarled up, tangled up, twisted out of shape: *pp/adj* **bangyardilo 2)** be accused

bangyarel *vt* **1)** bend, curve, duck, fold, make to lean, twist down: *pp/adj* **bangyardo 2)** cripple, deform, distort; **O Del bangyardyas tu hai shudyas tu pe mánde.** God distorted you and flung you to me.(*said by a wife in anger to her husband*) **3)** turn, turn off (*to*), swerve, veer **4)** accuse **5)** *comp/vt* **~ tele,** bend.down, force down; **Bangyar e kriyánga tele!** Bend the branch down! **6)** *v/refl* **bangyarél-pe** bend oneself/bend over; **Bangyardyás-pe.** He bent down.

bangyarimásko *gen/adj* able to be bent, flexible

bangyarimos *nm* **1)** bending out of shape, foul up/tangle up, deformity, tangle, twisted wreckage **2)** curve in a river/road **3)** accusation

bangyol *vi* **1)** curve, bend/bow down, duck, stoop, hang down, droop down, incline downwards: *pp/adj* **bangilo 2)** buckle, collapse **3)** become downcast **4)** be accused **5)** warp **6)** *list of comp/vt/i* **~ anglal** lean forward(s), **~ inkyal** bend/lean across/over, **~ karing** lean towards, **~ opral** bend upwards, **~ pálpale**, lean backwards, **~ prótivo** lean up against, **~ rêgáte** lean to one side/sideways, **~ tele** bend down, incline downwards, lean down; **Sa l' kriyénzhi**

bangile tele telal o pharimos le ivêsko. The boughs all bend downwards under the weight of the snow.

bánka *nf* 1) banknote, letter of credit, paper money 2) bankroll, poke; **Si ma bánka, nai ma dui, chumidav tut ándo mui.** I have one bankroll, I don't have two, I kiss you on the mouth. (*folk song*)

bankazhívo *nm* banker, bank manager, holder of community funds, treasurer: *nf* **bankazhivútsa**

bankil *vt* bank: *pp/adj* **bankime**

bankimos *nm* banking

bánko/bánka *nm/nf* bank

bánya *nf* 1) bath 2) hot spring

bar *nf* 1) barrier, fence, hedge, low wall; **Beshel pe bar.** He/she is sitting on the fence/not becoming involved in the issue.**Thodine bar po drom.** They set up a roadblock 2) garden (*Eur*)

bára *nf* 1) bar of a saloon/restaurant/hotel 2) bar (*metal bar*), crowbar, power bar

baráka *nf* 1) dormitory, hut, shack, barracks: *pl* **baráchi** 2) building housing inmates in a concentration/detention camp

bárba *nf* beard: *gen/adj* **barbáko** possessing a beard

barbáriya *nf* barber shop

barbúto *nm* 1) male barbarian, uncouth lout, *sl* shitkicker: *nf* **barbáika**, female barbarian, uncouth woman, *sl* female shitkicker 2) catfish (*Can*)

barbyáriya/byarbyáriya *nf* barber shop

barbyéri/byarbyéri *nm* barber

bãrda/bwárda *nf* 1) butcher's cleaver, cleaver, chopper 2) carpenter's adze 3) machete

bardakash brothel keeper: *nf* **bardakáshka** bawd, Madame

bardáko *nm* brothel, house of ill repute; **So si kako parfúmo ánde ófisa, khandel sar o bardáko!** What's all this perfume in the office, it smells like a brothel!

baré-buzhanglo *comp/gen/adj* know-it-all, opinionated, smart-assed

baré-dandêngo *comp/gen/adj* astute, sharp, smart

bárem *adv* at least, the least; **De lêske bárem tsîrra love te kinel xabe!** At least give him a little money to buy food!

baré-môsko *comp/gen/adj* loud-mouthed

baré-pelêngo *comp/gen/adj* well-hung, displaying prominent male genitalia

bares *adv* a lot, enormously, greatly, highly, importantly, to a great extent

baré-vorbáko *comp/gen/adj* eloquent, great talking

baré-yilêsko *comp/gen/adj* generous

bari *nf* 1) wife of a local Romani leader 2) important woman, female leader; **E bari la wushkoláki** The headmistress/principal of a school; **e bari ándo wêlféri** the head woman in the social welfare department

barí-baxt *comp/nf* great success (*in business, etc*)

barí-bi-baxt *comp/nf* great disaster, long run of bad luck

barí-buki *comp/nf* 1) big deal 2) priority 3) important matter

barí-dab *comp/nf* heavy blow, powerful wallop

barí-djéla *comp/nf* big deal, important matter; **Nai bari djéla.** It's not an important matter/It's of no consequence/importance.

barikamos *nm* arrogance, ostentatiousness, pride, vanity

barikanimos *nm* 1) arrogance, haughtiness, ostentatiousness 2) splendour

barikano *adj* 1) arrogant, haughty, ostentatious 2) proud; **Barikano si pêske shavêndar.** He is proud of his sons. 3) *nm* dude, obstentatious man, show off, snob: *nf* **barikani** ostentatious woman, *fig* clothes horse

barí-khangeri *comp/nf* 1) Basilica of Ste. Anne de Beaupré 2) cathederal

barilo *pp/adj* 1) adult, grown up 2) *nm* adult man/young man: *nf* **barili**

bári-lúmiya *comp/nf* greater world, the wide world, whole world; **Phirdas ánde**

bári lúmiya te ródel pêske Rromnya.
He travelled all over the world to find
himself a wife.

barimásko *gen/adj* haughty, ostentatious,
priggish, pig-headed, proud, vain

barimáta *nm/pl* 1) arrogance, haughtiness,
ostentatiousness, vanity; **Thon pênge
barimáta pe pênde.** They behave
ostentatiously/show off/They act like
snobs. 2) *comp/vi* **kerel ~** boast, brag

barimatángo *gen/adj* 1) arrogant, haughty,
ostentatious, priggish, vain 2) proud 3)
disdainful

barimos *nm* 1) area, size, dimensions 2)
arrogance, disdain, haughtiness, pride 3)
ostentatiousness, snobbery 4) importance,
greatness 5) growth 6) development,
growth

barí-papin *comp/nf* swan

Barí-Parashtuvi *comp/nf* Good Friday

bári-yag *comp/nf* big bonfire,
conflagration, inferno, serious fire

bárka *nf* boat. sailing vessel, sailing yacht
(*Eur*)

baro *adj* 1) big, great, large, tall; **bare love**
big monies/a lot of money, **o mai baro**
the biggest/most important 2) head,
important, major; **o rai o baro** chief of
police, head detective 3) loud (*in a
limited sense*); **báro bashimos** loud
clamour, **báro mui** loud mouth, loud
babbling 4) adult, fully grown, mature;
bare manúsha adult people/adults, **shav
o mai baro** eldest son, **shey-bari** mature
girl, eldest, unmarried daughter 4) *nm* big
man, fixer, head man of a territorial
community or traveling group, honcho,
important man, kingpin, leader, territorial
boss; **O Tóma si o baro ándo Chikágo.**
Tom is the honcho in Chicago.

baró-barr *comp/nm* boulder, *fig* huge
impediment

baró-buzhanglo *comp/nm* opinionated
man, Mr. know-it-all, smart ass, wise guy:
nf **barí-buzhangli**, Mrs/Ms know-it-all,
Miss smarty-pants

baró-diklo *comp/nm* large kerchief, shawl
see also **basmáli** *nm*

baró-drom *nm* freeway, highway

baró-gazho *comp/nm* big man, boss,
honcho, important man, man in charge: *nf*
barí-gazhí head woman, woman in
charge

báro-ges/báro-dives *comp/nm* feast day,
holiday (*Eur*)

báro-kar/kar-baro *comp/nm* erect penis,
erection

báro-lazhav *nf* scandal, disgraceful affair

báro-mui *comp/nm/nf* loudmouth,
overly-opinionated man/woman; **Wo si
bi-gogyáko báro-mui.** He is a brainless
loud mouth.

baróno *nm* baron: *nf* **baronáika** baroness,
baron's wife

báro-shâto *comp/nm* big shot, super
honcho (*Am*)

baró-shoro *nm* ignoramus who claims to
know everything, ostentatious lout

bar-phaleyángo *comp/nm* planked fence,
fence made of wooden planks

barr *nm* 1) rock, stone 2) gravestone 3)
monument

barrá-ánde-beshúka *comp/nf* gallstones
(*stones in the bladder*)

barralo *adv* 1) rocky, stony, studded with
stones (*as the bed of a stream*) 2)
cobblestoned

barr-ándo-gi *nm/pl* pendicitis

barrêngo *gen/adj* rocky, made of
rocks/stones; **barrêngi djardína** rock
garden

barrêsko *gen/adj* made of stone

barrol *vt* 1) petrify, turn to stone: *pp/adj*
barrulo 2) **barról-pe** become petrified

barrorre *nm/pl* gravel, pebbles

barrorro *nm* pebble

barrudil *vt* 1) detonate; *pp/adj* **barrudime**
2) explode, blow up 3) *v/refl* **barrudíl-pe**
explode, blow up/hit the roof (*fig*);
**Barrudisáilo múrro dad kána
zhanglas.** My father blew up in anger/hit
the roof when he found out.

barrudimos *nm* blast, detonation. explosion

Barruni *nf* Woman of Stone, a woman whose glance can turn a human being into stone or who can destroy people by draining their essence of life by her gaze (*Folk*)

barruno *adj* stone, constructed of stone; **bírto-barruno** *nm* stone bar, tavern with stone floor and walls

barrúto/barrúdo *nm* **1**) gunpowder **2**) dynamite, explosives

barryárdyol *vi* be turned to stone, become petrified: *pp/adj* **barryardilo**

barryarel *vt* petrify, turn to stone: *pp/adj* **barryardo**

barryarimos *nm* petrification

barvalimos *nm* affluence, prosperity, riches, richness, wealth

barvalo 1) *adj* rich, wealthy **2**) *nm* rich/wealthy man: *nf* **barvali** rich/wealthy woman

barvalyárdyol *vi* become enriched/rich/wealthy: *pp/adj* **barvalyardilo**

barvalyarel *vt* enrich, make rich/wealthy: *pp/adj* **balvalyardo**; **barvalyarel amári kultúra.** It will enrich our culture.

barvalyarimásko *gen/adj* enriching, wealth-creating

barvalyarimos *nm* enrichment

barvávol *vi* become/get rich/enriched: *pp/adj* **barvailo**; **Barváilo ánde América.** He got rich in America.

baryáko *nm* **1**) gardener, landscaper: *pl* **baryáchi** (*Eur*) **2**) flag (*Eur*)

baryárdyol *vi* be brought up/raised from childhood: *pp/adj* **baryardilo**; **Baryádyili le Rromênsa.** She was raised by Roma. **2**) be raised/grown (*crops*) **3**) be/augmented increased

baryarel *vt* **1**) raise (*children*): *pp/adj* **baryardo 2**) grow (*crops*), cultivate **3**) augment, enlarge, increase, expand **4**) make important **5**) develop, enhance **6**) with **mai**: overly enlarge, exaggerate; **Mai baryarel pêske swáturya.** He's

exaggerating his comments. **7**) arouse, inspire; **Baryarel pêngi yag.** He is arouding their enthusiasm.**Baryardyas múrro yilo.** He inspired my soul.

baryarimos *nm* **1**) cultivation **2**) raising of crops, rearing of children

báryo *nm* district of a city, *esp* a Latino district, barrio (*Am fr Sp*): *pl* **bárya**

baryol *vi* **1**) grow, grow up: *pp/adj* **barilo**; **Barilem ánde Kanáda.** I grew up in Canada **2**) become bigger/larger, increase in size; **Mai baryol swáko ges.** He gets bigger every day. **3**) bear (*fruit/nuts*), bloom, blossom, come to fruition, mature **4**) wax (*moon*) **5**) develop **6**) become aroused, inspired; **Barili pêski yag.** His enthuisiasm was aroused.

bása/báso *nf/nm* accompaniment, base (*Mus*)

basári *nm* bass player (*Mus*)

bashadi *nf* musical instrument (*Eur*)

Bashaldo *nm* member of the Hungarian-Romani musician group (*from a status definition among* **Romúngere**): *pl.* **Bashalde:** *nf* **Bashaldútsa** (*Am*)

bashavel *vt/i* **1**) play, play music (*Eur*); **Bashaves?** Do you play music? **Me bashavav Rromanes**. I play in the manner of the Roma (*Romani music*). **2**) bang,/clang/clash together, create a loud noise, honk (*horn*), pound, thump **3**) crack (*a whip*)

bashayimos *nm* **1**) art of playing music, music (*Eur*) **2**) banging, hammering, loud noise, percussion, racket; **Yoi, Dévla, mudarel ma o shoro godo bashayimos!** Oh, God, that racket is killing my head/driving me crazy! **3**) reverberation, sound **4**) **djúngalo ~**, cacophony

bashel *vi* **1**) emit sound, honk (*horn*), make a noise **2**) click, jingle, rattle, ring, tick, tinkle **3**) backfire, bang, clang, peal (*bells*) **4**) burst/explode/go off with a bang: **Bashlo o fushágo.** The firecracker went off with a bang. **5**) bark, meow, roar **Note:** this gloss is widely used to define animal sounds; **O zhukel bashel.** The dog is barking. **O bashno bashlo.** The rooster crowed. **Le gurumnya bashen.** The cattle are mooing. **E mútsa bashel kovles.** The cat is purring. **Le chiriklya bashen.** The birds are chirping. **5)** burst, go bang; **E beshúka bashli.** The balloon burst. **6)** snap (*fingers*)

bashimos *nm* **1)** bang, banging, clanging, click, clicking, pealing ticking **2)** noise, sound **3)** sounds of animal noises, barking, crowing, twittering, etc

bashli/bashni *nf* backfire, bang, click, gunshot, retort, thud; **Ashundem e bashli la pushkáki.** I heard the retort of the gun. **Pharrulo barya bashlyása.** It exploded with a loud bang. **Pelo barya bashlyása.** It fell with a loud crash. **Ashundem e bashli la trigantsyáki la pushkáko.** I heard the click of the loading/cock of the trigger of the gun.

bashno *nm* **1)** rooster **2)** weather cock/vane

basil *vt* **1)** accompany, provide bass rhythm (*Mus*): *pp/adj* **basime; Shavále, basisar ma te mudarav lên!** Boys, accompany me so I can slay them/drive them wild! (*yelled to the band by a lead player*) **2)** base (*smth on*)

basmáli/bazmáli *nm* shawl, long shawl that also covers the head (*worn by traditional Romanian-Romani women*) (*Eur*)

báso *nm* **1)** base guitar/string bass (*Mus*) **2)** accompaniment, base, rhythm (*Mus*) **3)** autobus, bus (*Am*) **4)** traditional fast dance melody played on festive occasions at group events (*Am*)

basûna *nf* **1)** basin **2)** mixing bowl used in bakeries and confectionary factories to mix dough; **Hanosardyam desh-u-pansh basûni ages.** We tin-plated fifteen mixing bowls today.

basûna-harkuni *comp/nm* copper basin

basûnèngo-hanomos *comp/nm* wipe-tinning/tin-plating of mixing bowls

basutno *adj* basic, fundamental

bãta/báta *nf* **1)** bat, baseball bat, club, stick **2)** *nm* bat (*fool*) (*Am*): **Che dílo báta!** What a crazy bat!

batalíya *nf* battle (*Mil*)

batalyáki-níva *nf* battlefield

batalyáko-paraxódo *nm* battleship

batalyóno *nm* battalion (*Mil*)

Báte *nm/voc* Daddy! Dad! **Ashun Báte!** Listen, Dad! **Báte! So sim te kerav?** Dad! What am I supposed to do?

Báterr! *interj* Amen! So be it! So help me God!

bateríya *nf* **1)** battery, car battery **2)** set of drums (*Mus*)

bavalo *adj* rich, well-off (*Am*) see **barvalo** *adj*

baxt *nf* **1)** luck **2)** good karma **3)** prosperity in business, success in an undertaking **4)** blessing, providence **5)** Grace; **Devlêski Baxt** God's Grace **6)** household icons **7)** destiny, fortune, fate; **Sas pêski baxt te merel mai anglal te xal pêsko manrro.** *id* It was his fate to die before eating his bread/living his full lifespan. *id* **Nas ánde múrri baxt.** It wasn't meant to be/It wasn't in my cards. **Sas pêski baxt.** It was his destiny. **8) del ~** bless, give luck, provide good fortune; **Te del o Del amênge baxt!** May God grant us good fortune/May God give us blessings!

baxtalimos *nm* contentment, providence

baxtalo *adj* **1)** blessed, content, fortunate, lucky, providential **2)** *nm* lucky man: *nf* **baxtali** lucky woman

báxtalo-báiyero *comp/nm* amulet, good luck piece, lucky charm

baxtályol *vi* **1)** become lucky, fortunate, prosperous in business: *pp/adj* **baxtalilo** **2)** be blessed, be given good fortune (*by God or a Saint*)

baxtarel *vt* **1)** make lucky, bring luck/prosperity in business: *pp/adj* **baxtardo** **2)** leave inheritance to (*in a will, etc*); **Baxtardya lês lêsko dad.** His father left him an inheritance. **3)** bless, bestow blessing(s)

baxtarimos *nm* **1)** good fortune, luck, prosperity **2)** blessing(s)

Bayash/Beyash *nm/s/pl* **1)** Non-Kalderash Romani groups who do not speak Romani including *Romúngere*, English *Romanichals* and non-Kalderash Roma whose Romani is not mutually comprehensible with *Kalderashítska* (*Am*); **Nai Rrom amarêndar, Bayash si.** They are not our Roma, they are Bayash. **2)** Definitive term for Romanian-speaking Romani groups who have lost Romani (*Eur*): *nf* **Bayáshka/Bayashútsa Note:** North-American *Kalderásha* and *Machváya* tend to call any non-Vlax Roma who are not of their groups *Bayash*. Technically speaking, the genuine **Bayash** are Vlax-Roma who have lost Romani as a group and speak Romanian. In Romania, non-Romani speaking Roma of any group are collectively referred to as **Rrom-Kashtale** *qv*

báyo *nm* **1)** care, misfortune, problem, scrape, trouble; **Che báro báyo!** What a catastrophy! **Na den-tume ándo báyo, shavorrále!** Don't get into trouble, kids! **Dem ándo báyo.** I got into trouble/misfortune. **Dyas mánge báyo.** He caused tragedy for me. **2)** court case (*for kris*)

bayútso *nm* petty crime, trifling offence

bazári *nm* market, marketplace

bázga *nf* pitch, vegetable tar

béda *nf* **1)** scrape, serious trouble, trouble **2)** ill fortune, misfortune; *id* **Béda mánge!** Woe is me! **3)** accusation, crime, criminal offence **4)** *comp/vt* **del ánde ~** ; get (*smbdy*) into trouble; **Dyas ma ánde béda.** He got me into trouble. **5)** *v/refl* **Dél-pe ánde ~** get oneself into trouble; **Shavále! Na den-tume ánde béda!** Boys! Don't get into trouble! **6)** *comp/vi* **mekel ánde ~** leave in the lurch **7)** *comp/vi* **perel ánde ~** fall into trouble, get into trouble

bedash *nm* trouble maker: *nf* **bedáshka**

bélka *nf* squirrel: *pl* **bélchi**

begil *vt* ask, beg, request **:** *pp/adj* **begime** (*Am*)

begimos *nm* request (*Am*)

belchúgo *nm* **1)** hook, gaff, grapnel **2)** clasp, fastener, snap; **treláko-belchúgo**, trailer hitch (*Am*)

béli *nf* **1)** An upright pole that supports the after end of the ridgepole of a *Kalderash* tent. **2)** supporting pole **3)** crutch, oarlock, support

belzûna *nf* blowtorch, propane gas torch, welding torch

bêncho *nm* bench, workbench, park bench (*Am*)

benefíto *nm* benefit; **Kásko benefíto kerdyan?** For whose benefit did you do that?

benevólo *nm* unpaid volunteer: *nf* **benevóli** (*Eur*)

beng/bêng *nm* **1)** devil, Satan; **O beng lyas lês.** The devil took him/He became evil. **O Beng phirel pe phuv.** The devil is walking on the earth/There is evil about/We are surrounded by evil. **Zha ka o beng!** Go to hell/the Devil! **2)** rascal, rogue

bengailo *pp/adj* epileptic: *nm* epileptic: *nf* **bengaili**

bengalo *adj* **1)** demonic, deceitful, devilish, inhuman, evil, wicked; **bengali buki** devilish/evil business **2)** *nm* evil man, human devil: *nf* **bengali 3)** *adj/nm* epileptic: *nf* **Bengali**

bengáwol *vi* **1)** become crazy, go berserk/postal, turn into a demon/devil: *pp/adj* **bengailo; Bengáilo hai pushkisardyas trine zhenen.** He went postal and shot three people. **2)** have a fit, go into fits

bengênde *prep/nm/pl* into devils; **Dyás-pe ánde bengênde.** He had an epileptic fit. **Pelo ánde bengênde.** He fell into an epileptic fit.

bengêski buki *nf* Devil's work/handiwork

bengêski-zhuvli *comp/nf* shrew (*woman*)

bengêsko *gen/adj* **1)** devilish, demonic, demonlike, diabolic, mean, wicked; **Si lês**

bengêski fátsa. He has the face of a devil. **bengêsko-zhukel** hound of hell, devil dog (*Folk*), **Bengêsko than** Devil's domain, hell, **bengêsko grast** rogue horse **2)** mean, ornery; **Che bengêski kriyatúra!** What an ornery critter! (*Am*)

bengimáta *nm/pl* **1)** epilepsy **2)** *comp/vi* **Del-pe ánde ~** suffers from epileptic fits.

bengimos *nm* **1)** atrocity, brutality, deceit, devilment, deviltry, inhumanity, evil **2)** demonic possession **3)** epileptic fit **4)** monstrosity **5)** mischief, roguery; **Che bengimos keren tume, shavorrále?** What mischief are you up to, kids?

bengorro *nm* **1)** demon, evil man, man possessed by the devil or a demon: *nf* **bengorri** female demon, woman possessed by the devil or a demon, wild/devil woman; **Khelél-pe sar e bengorri.** She dances like a woman possessed. **2)** faun, goblin, imp, troll **3)** little rascal/rogue**4)** little devil/rogue; **Múrro shav si bengorro.** My son is a little devil.

bengyarel *vt* annoy, bedevil, drive crazy, pester, place a hex: *pp/adj* **bengyardo**

bengyarimos *nm* deliberate annoyance, devilment/deviltry, pestering

bengyávol *vi* **1)** convulse with/go into fits: *pp/adj* **bengailo 2)** become possessed by demons

bengyayimáta *nm*/pl **1)** convulsions, fits **2)** epileptic fits

bengyayimos *nm* **1)** convulsion **2)** demonic possession

bênuwíl *vt* **1)** suspect: *pp/adj* **bênuwimé 2)** *v/refl* **bênuwíl-pe** have a feeling about/premonition, suspect; **Bênuwí-ma ke wo kerdyas.** I have a feeling that he did (it). **Bênuwisáilem k' avélas amênge bi-baxt.** I had a premonition that we were about to have bad luck.

bênuwimós *nm* hunch, premonition, suspicion

bênzína *nf* **1)** gasoline (*Eur*) **2)** benzene, benzol (*Am*)

berand *nm* **1)** main or ridgepole of a *Kalderash* tent which supports the canvas at its upper apex. **2)** flagpole, any tall pole **3)** ridge beam in a pointed roof **3)** support rod, suspension rod for curtain or shower curtain

berk/brek *nm* breast, bosom (*Anat*) (*Eur*)

berkano *adj* bare-breasted (*Eur*)

bero *nm* **1)** rowboat **2)** canoe (*Can*) **3)** boat (*Eur*)

bêrsh/bersh *nm* **1)** year: *pl* **bêrsh/bêrshá 2)** lifespan, lifetime, years on earth; **Sikilem but ánde múrre bêrsh.** I learned much during my lifetime/years. **3)** *expressions with* **bêrsh**; **o bêrsh te avel** next year, **o bêrsh nakhlo** last year, **de but bêrsh** many years ago, **bêrsh bêrshèstar** year to year, from year to year

bêrshèngo 1) *gen/adj* of years, used to denote age; **Mai bêrshèngo san mándar.** You are older than me (*to a man*). **Panshwardeshé-bêrshèngo si.** He is fifty-years old. **Sóde bêrshèngo san?** How old are you/How many years possess you? **Woi si bish-ta-panshé-bêrshèngi.** She is twenty-five years old. **Wo si shtarwardesh-thai-trine bershêngo.** He is forty-three years old. **2)** *when nominalized;* **Triné-bershêngo si.** He is a three-year-old. **Panshé-bershêngi si.** She is a five-year-old.

bêrshèsko *gen/adj* belonging to one year, yearly, annually; **Yekhé-bershêsko si o khuro.** The colt is a yearling.

beshavel *vt* **1)** make to sit, seat: *pp/adj* **beshado; Beshade le gósturya kai sínya.** They seated the guests at the table. **2)** make to fit in, set; **Beshadem o stîlpo ánde phuv.** I set the post in the ground.

beshel *vt/i* **1)** sit, sit down, be seated: *pp/adj* **beshlo/beshlino 2)** be located, camp, dwell, live, remain, reside, stay; **Kai beshes?** Where are you living/staying? **Beshlas sar kadya trin shon.** It stayed/remained like that for three months. **Nas lês te beshel ap dem**

lês andre. He had nowhere to stay so I put him up. Beshlo pêske kakésa. He stayed with his uncle. 3) seat; O mobíli beshel pansh zhene. The car seats five people. Beshlemlen pe sófta. I seated them on the couch. 4) convene (for a meeting), preside over, sit (on a Board/committee); Sodya zhene beshen po Bórdo akana? How many people are members of the Board now? 5) set (as the sun) O Kham beshlo. The sun has set. 6) be in charge of; Kon beshel pe l' lovênde? Who is in charge of the money? Kon beshel po djuléshi? Who is running/chairing the business meeting? 7) agree, stand, stand with; Beshav túsa pe godo swáto. I stand with you/agree with you on that proposal 8) participate (in); Beshlas ándo diwáno. He participated in the discussion. 9) comp/vi ~ mírno calm down/sit quietly, be quiet 10) comp/vt/i ~ pála reside with, shack up with; Beshlas trin bersh pála Gazhi. He resided with a non-Romani woman for three years. 11) comp/vi ~ pe l' punrrênde remain standing (sitting on one's feet) 13) comp/vi ~ pe rróti be in a wheelchair 14) comp/vi ~ tele sit down, be seated

Beshêntsurya nm/pl saddle makers, Lovari clan that arrived in Canada in the 1970s.

beshimos nm setting, sitting; o beshimos le khamêsko sunset

béshtiya nf 1) female animal/beast 2) immoral woman, fig whore

beshtiyáno nm 1) male beast 2) boor, bottom-feeder, immoral man, slob

beshtiyimos nm bestiality, immorality

beshúka nf 1) bladder (Anat): pl beshútsi 2) abcess 3) bubble, blister 4) balloon

beshúka-phubali comp/nf gall bladder

besuchítsa nf small abcess, little blister, zit

bêtíl vt bet (on horses): pp/adj bêtimé; Sáyek bêtil pe l'grast. He's always betting on the horses. (Am)

beyáto nm 1) boy, lad (Eur): pl beyéchi 2) impudent brat (Am)

bezax nm 1) crime, iniquity, sin, transgression 2) comp/vt kerel ~ commit a sin/commit sin; Kerdyas bari bezax. He committed a great sin. Tíro bezax te avel! Let it/this be your sin! 3) interj Che bezax! How awful! (expression of shock/disgust)

bezaxalimos nm sin, transgression; Trayin ándo bezaxalimos. They are living in sin/in a sinful way of life.

bezaxalo 1) adj offensive, sinful 2) nm culprit, offender, sinful man, sinner, transgressor: nf bezaxali

Bezexa! interj Alas!

bi prep without; Gêlótar bi pêski raxámi. He left without his jacket. Avilo bi pêske love. He came without his money. Note: Bi must be separated from the noun case inflexion to be used this way. He came without money, would be; Avilo bi-lovêngo see bi- in following entry

bi- prod priv/part im-, un-, -less: This is prefixed to many descriptive adjectives, past participle adjectives and adverbs to form their opposites a) adj; lasho good, bi-lasho bad, not good, volime loved, bi-volime unloved, balêngo hairy, possessing hair, bi-balêngo hairless, phanglo tied, bi-phanglo untied b) adv; baxtales luckily, bi-baxtales unluckily, pakivales honorably, respectfully, bi-pakivales dishonourably, disrespectfully. Only those used most often are listed. c) Most descriptive adjectives and past participles with bi- can also become substantives; bi-baxtalo unlucky man, bi-doshwali innocent woman, and are then subject to noun inflexion according to their gender and number; Dem-dúma le bi-baxtalêsa. I spoke to the unlucky man. Ashundem swáturya la bi-doshwalyátar. I listened to testimony from the innocent woman. Maladilem le bi-baxtalêsa. I met with the unlucky people (both genders). Maladilem le bi-baxtalyánsa. I met with the unlucky women.

bi-amaluno *adj* unfriendly (*Eur*)
bi-ansurime *pp/adj* unmarried (*man*)
bi-arakhlo *pp/adj* undiscovered
bi-ashundo *gen/adj* unheard of, unknown
bi-ashunimaskones *adv* inaudibly
bi-ashunumásko *gen/adj* inaudible
bi-azbado *pp/adj* untouched
bi-azhukerdo *pp/adj* unexpected
bi-baiyêngo *gen/adj* sleeveless
bi-balêngo *gen/adj* hairless
bi-balwaláko grast *comp/nm* wheezer (*horse*)
bi-barbáko *gen/adj* clean-shaven, without a beard
bi-baxt *nf* bad luck, bad karma
bi-baxtales *adv* unluckily
bi-baxtalo *adj* **1**) unfortunate, unlucky **2**) *nm* unlucky man: *nf* **bi-baxtali**
bi-báxtalo them *comp/nm* **1**) unlucky country **2**) unlucky people
bibi *nf* **1**) aunt **2**) term of respect for an elderly woman/matriarch
bi-biyandimásko *gen/adj* infertile, sterile
bi-biyando *pp/adj* unborn, yet to be born
Bibíyo *nf/voc* Auntie; **Sar san. Bibíyo?** How are you Auntie? (*Formal address to an older woman*). **Bibíyo! So mai keres?** How are you doing, old lady?
Bíbliya *nf* Bible
Bibliyáko *gen/adj* of the Bible; **Rrom Bibliyáko** Pentecostal Rom, adherent of the Romani Pentecostal Church: *nf* **Rromni Bibliyáki:** *pl* **Rromá-Bibliyácha**
bibliyotéka/bibliyotéko *nf* library (*Eur*)
bi-boldo *adj* **1**) unbaptized, not-baptized **2**) *nm* **Bi-Boldo** Jewish man *nf* **Bi-Boldi**
bi-boryáko *gen/adj* without a bride
bi-brintomásko *gen/adj* non-infectious
bi-bukyáke *nm/nf/pl* **le bi-bukyáke** the unemployed
bi-bukyáko *gen/adj* **1**) unemployed, without work **2**) unemployed man: *nf* **bi-bukyáki**
bi-buzhanglo *adj* inexperienced, innocent, not having the smarts

bi-chachimásko *gen/adj* unjust; **bi-chachimásko ákto** unjust act (*of law*)
bi-chachiwalo *gen/adj* unfair, unjust
bi-chacho *adj* **1**) dishonest **2**) untrue **3**) unjust
bi-chailyardo *pp/adj* unsatiated, unsatisfied
bi-chailyarimásko *gen/adj* insatiable, voracious
bícho *nm* **1**) coach whip, horse whip **2**) coachwhip snake (*Masticophis flagellum*) (*Am*)
bída *nf see* **béda** *nf*
bi-dadêsko *gen/adj* fatherless
bi-dáko *gen/adj* motherless
bi-dandêngo *gen/adj* impotent, ineffective, toothless; **bi-dandêngi kris** ineffective tribunal
bi-daráko *gen/adj* brave, fearless, without fear
bi-darano *adj* unafraid
bi-Devlêsko *gen/adj* atheist; **Manush bi-Devlêsko** Atheist
bi-dikhlo *pp/adj* imaginary, invisible, unseen
bi-dino-gáta *pp/ádj* unfinished
bi-dosháko *gen/adj* innocent, without blame/guilt
bi-doshwali *gen/adj* innocent, chaste, innocent, virgin, without blemish
bi-doshwalo *adj* **1**) innocent guiltless, without blame **2**) *nm* innocent man: *nf* **bi-doshwali,** innocent woman
bi-dukhado *pp/adj* unhurt, uninjured
bi-familyáko *gen/adj* without a family
biftéka *nf* beefsteak
bi-fundósko *adj* unfathomable
bi-futuráko *gen/adj* without a future
bi-gáta *adj* unfinished, incomplete, unready/not ready
bi-gêsko *gen/adj* cruel, heartless, mean
bi-gêtimé *pp/adj* unprepared, unready/not ready
bi-gîndèsko/bi-gûndésko *gen/adj* irresponsible, thoughtless
bi-gîndimásko *adj* unthinkable, yet to be thought of

bi-gîndimé *adj* unimagined, unthought of

bi-gindo *adj* uncounted

bi-gîndósko *gen/adj* impulsive, not well thought out, not well founded, unfounded; **bi-gîndóske xamáta** unfounded arguments

bi-ginimásko *gen/adj* innumerable, uncountable

bi-glasósko *gen/adj/s/nom* voiceless, without representation; *gen/adj/pl/nom* **bi-glasêngo; Ame, le Rroma, sam bi-glasêngo ánde lúmiya.** We the Roma have no representation/voices in the world.

bi-glatêngo *comp/adj* childless

bi-gogyáko *gen/adj* **1)** brainless, careless, carefree, foolhardy, irresponsible, mindless **2)** suffering from Down's syndrome

bi-gorêsko *gen/adj* **1)** endless, without end, without conclusion **2)** without aim, purpose

bi-grastêsko *gen/adj* without a horse; **Rrom bi-grastêsko nai chácho Rrom.** A Rom without a horse is not a true Rom. **Bi-grastêsko sámas.** We were without horses.

bi-grizháko *gen/adj* carefree, without responsibilities

bi-grizhome *pp/adj* uncared for, neglected

bi-hakyarimásko *gen/adj* incomprehensible

bi-hakyarno *gen/adj* unreasonable

bi-hangósko *gen/adj* silently, without a sound

bi-hanome *pp/adj* yet to be plated, unplated

bi-hulado *pp/adj* **1)** disheveled, uncombed; **bi-xúlade bal** disheveled hair **2)** undivided

bi-hulayimásko/bi-huladimásko *gen/adj* indivisible, inseperable, undivided

bi-karshindo *pp/adj* uncircumcised

bi-kásko *pron/gen* without whom

bi-kerdo *adj* **1)** unfinished **2)** undone

bi-khanchêsko *gen/adj* **1)** worthless **2)** destitute **3)** without anything

bi-kherêsko *gen/adj/nom/sing* homeless: *pl* **bi-kherêngo; Kána peli e treséniya, le Rroma ashile bi-kherênge.** When the earthquake struck, the Roma were left homeless/without houses.

bikinel *vt/i* **1)** hawk, peddle, retail, sell: *pp/adj* **bikindo; Bikinel lulugya ánde úlitsa.** She sells flowers in the street. **2)** sell out, betray; **Bikindyas amên le Gazhênde.** He sold us out to the non-Rom **3)** serve; **Chi bikinen bíra kathe.** They don't serve/sell beer here. **4)** *v/refl* sell oneself, sell one's soul; **Kon bikinél-pe le bengêste músai te zhal ándo yádo.** He who sells himself to the devil must go to hell. (*proverb*)

bikíndyol *vi* be sold: *pp/adj* **bikindilo**

bikinimásko *gen/adj* having to do with sales, selling

bikinimos *nm* **1)** buying, hawking, sale **2)** betrayal

bikinitóri *nm* dealer (*in vehicles, etc*), hawker, salesman: *nf* **bikinitórka**

bíko *nm* breeding bull, stud bull

bi-konchináko *gen/adj* endless, without end

bi-krisáko *gen/adj* **1)** disrespecting of the authority of the *Kris-Romani,* not following the laws of the Romani Tribunal **2)** lawless, unlawful, illegal under the rules of the Romani Tribunal

bikyéri *nm* beaker

bilado *pp.adj* **1)** melted, smeltered **2)** thawed **3)** dissipated **4)** vanished.

biládyol *vi* **1)** become dissipated/dissolved/melted/thawed: *pp/adj* **biladilo 2)** become invisible, vanish **3)** be/become assimilated

bilal *vi* **1)** blend into, dissipate, dissolve, fade, fade away, melt, melt away, pale into insignificance, thaw; **O iv bilal.** The snow is thawing: *pp/adj* **bilailo 2)** become invisible, disappear, fade (*into*), vanish; **Bileáilo.** He diappeared/ vanished **3)** dissipate; **Phuter e filástra te bilal o thuv**! Open the window so the smoke can dissipate!. **4)** become assimilated, disappear, merge; **Wúni Rrom biláile mashkar le Gazhênde.** Some Roma have assimilated among the non-Romani population. **5)** become feeble/incapable/incapacitated; **Phurilótar thai biláilo.** He became old and a helpless shadow of his former self. **6)** ~ **ánde balwal** become invisible, dissolve into the wind **6)** be digesting (*food*)

bi-lantsome *pp/adj* unchained, unfettered

bi-lasharimásko *gen/adj* condemned (*property*), fit only for scrap, irreparable, unfixable

bi-lasho *adj* bad, imperfect, not good

bilavayimásko *gen/adj* **1)** having to do with rendering, smelting, melting, melting down, thawing; **bilavayimáski basûna** crucible, **bilavayimásko bov** blast furnace, **bilavayimáski piri** melting pot

bilavayimos *nm* **1)** act of smeltering/melting down/rendering **2)** dissipation, clearing up (*of fog, etc*) **3)** act of making invisible **4)** assimilation

bilavel *vt* **1)** dissolve, smelter, melt down, render: *pp/adj* bilado **2)** thaw, thaw out **3)** dissipate, make insignificant **4)** make to disappear/vanish. **5)** forcibly assimilate **6)** digest (*food*)

bilayimos *nm* **1)** melting down process, rendering, smeltering process, thawing process **2)** disappearance, invisibility, oblivion

bi-lazhano *adj* **1)** brazen, impertinent, shameless **2)** obscene

bi-lazhavêsko *gen/adj* immodest, indecent, shameless, unpardonable

bíldingo *nm* building

biléta *nf* coupon, ticket

bi-lilêngo *gen/adj* illiterate

bilimos *nm* thaw

bi-lindráko *gen/adj* restless, suffering from insomnia, unable to sleep

bi-londo *adj* bland, insipid, tasteless, unspiced

bi-londyárdo *pp/adj* unsalted

bilongil *vt/i* belong: *pp/adj* **bilongime** (*Am*); **Káste bilongil godo mobíli?** Who does that car belong to?

bi-lopuntsime *gen/adj* unhobbled, free to roam, loose, unrestrained

bi-loshano *adj* devastated, distressed, unhappy, upset

bi-lovêngo *gen/adj* broke, without funds/money

bilyardásh *nm* master pool player, poolroom shark (*Am*)

bilyardíya *nf* pool hall, poolroom (*Am*)

bilyárdo *nm* pool table

bilyárdurya *nm/pl* billiards, pool

bilyóno *nm* billion

bi-malado *gen/adj* inappropriate, unbefitting

bi-manglo *pp/adj* not requested, unasked for, unwanted

bi-manushwalo *adj* inhuman

bi-marzome *adj* defrosted, unfrozen

bi-masalo *adj* **1)** herbiforous **2)** *nm* vegetarian: *nf* **bi-masali**

bi-masêsko *gen/adj* without meat, vegetarian; **bi-masêsko xabe,** meatless meal

bi-meklimásko *gen/adj* without permission

bi-merimásko chiriklo *comp/nm* phoenix

bi-merimásko *gen/adj* eternal, immortal, undying

bi-miláko *gen/adj* without pity, merciless

bi-mobilêsko *gen/adj* on foot, without a car (*sing*): **bi-mobilêngo** without cars (*pl*)

bimol *nm* flat (*Mus*) *pl* **bimólurya**; **Si bimol** B flat

bi-moritime *pp/adj* unmarried (*woman*)

bi-nedezhdimásko *gen/adj* desperate, hopeless, without hope

bi-ofisáko *gen/adj* without an office/parlour/place of business; **Nashti drabarel e chorri, bi-ofisáki si.** She can't tell fortunes the poor woman, she is without an office. **Sar shai keras djuléshi bi-ofisáko?** How can we hold a business meeting without an office?

bi-pakiváko *gen/adj* dishonourable, crude, boorish, ill-mannered, without any restraint, scruples or honour, without respect

bi-pakivalo *gen/adj* corrupt, dishonest, disreputable, not respectable, unfaithful, untrustworthy

bi-pako *adj* immature, unripe

bi-pakyayimásko *gen/adj* unbelievable, unbelieving, doubtful

bi-parruyimásko *gen/adj* unchanging, unchangeable, unalterable

bi-pelêngo *gen/adj* 1) without testicles, gelded, neutered (*cat,dog, etc*) 2) *fig* cowardly, gutless, *vlg/sl* without balls (*Sp sin cojones*) 3) impotent

bi -**petalome** *pp/adj* unshod, without horseshoes

bi-phabarimásko *gen/adj* non-inflammable

bi-phanglo *pp/adj* 1) loose, released, untied, untangled, unfettered, unbound 2) unbroken, untrained

bi-phares *adv* 1) easily 2) lightly

bi-pharo *adj* 1) easy 2) light

bi-pharradi *adj* 1) virginal, virgin 2) *nf* chaste girl, virgin

bi-phralêsko without a brother

bi-porêngo *gen/adj* without feathers: *id* **Meyázol khaini bi-porêngi**. He looks like a hen without feathers/like a hopeless case. (*Am*)

bi-poryáko *gen/adj* without a tail; **Murtáno** ~ Manx cat

bi-pravardo *pp/adj* neglected, uncared for, undernourished, unfed

bi-prinjardo *pp/adj* unknown (*not known to anyone*), unrecognized, unrewarded

bi-probáko *gen/adj* without evidence/proof

birévo *nm* man in authority

bip-sonóri *nm* beep on telephone-answering device (*Eur*)

bi-punrrêngo *gen/adj* legless, without legs

bi-punrrêsko *gen/adj* one-legged

bi-pushlo *pp/adj* without asking, without permission, uninvited

bíra *nf* beer, bottle of beer: *pl* **bêri**; **kali bíra** black beer, Guinness, stout

bi-ráno *adj* late, not punctual

birokrátsiya *nf* bureaucracy

birovli *nf* bee, honey bee: *pl* **birovlya**; **bírovli gálbeno** yellow hornet

birovlyêngo-kwíbo beehive

bi-rranglo *adj* 1) in need of a shave, unshaven 2) *nm* unshaven man 3) *fig* bum (*Am*)

bírro *nm* 1) debt 2) tax, toll: *pl* **bírrya**; **ándo bírro** in debt, indebted

bi-Rromêski *gen/adj* without a husband

bi-Rromyáko *gen/adj* single, without a wife; **Sar gîndís te anes shavorren ánde lúmiya bi-Rromnyáko?** How do you expect to bring children into the world without a wife?

birtash *nm* male bartender, saloon keeper: *nf* **birtáshka** female bartender, bar owner's wife

birtashútsa *nf* young barmaid, bartender, tavern owner's daughter

bírto *nm* bar, barroom, beer parlour, pub, saloon, tavern

birútsa *nf* 1) pint of beer 2) bottle of beer. **Pilas trin birútsi.** He drank three bottles of beer.

bi-samáko *gen/adj* 1) careless 2) uncaring

bi-samnósko *gen/adj* without a trace

bi-sasto *adj* unhealthy

bish *nm* 1) twenty 2) twenty (*num*)

bishalel/bishavel *vt/i* send, ship, transfer by wire, mail (*letter, etc*): *pp/adj* **bishaldo**

bishêngi *nf* twenty-dollar bill (*Am*)

bi-sherésko *gen/adj* brainless, headless

bi-shibáko *gen/adj* 1) without a tongue/speech 2) unable to speak; **Rrom bi-shibáko nai Rrom**. A Rom without (Romani) speech is not a (true) Rom. **Chísto Rom san, na Rrom bi-shibáko.** You are a pure Rom, not a tongueless one.

bi-shindo *adj* uncircumcised

bishópo *nm* bishop

bishterdo *pp/adj* forgotten, omitted

bishtérdyol *vi* be/become forgotten, ignored, omitted, left out: *pp/adj* **bishterdilo**; **Yekh ges kam-merav thai**

bishtérdyovav. One day I shall die and be forgotten.

bishterimásko *gen/adj* forgetful, oblivious

bishterimos *nm* **1)** Alzheimer's disease, amnesia, forgetfulness, senility **2)** omission, oversite **3)** oblivion

bíshto *num* twentieth

bishtrel *vt* **1)** forget, ignore, omit: *pp/adj* **bishterdo 2)** *v/refl* **bishtrél-pe** suffer from amnesia, be absent-minded

bi-shukar *adj* ugly

bishwar *adv/num* twenty times; **Bishwar mai baro sas.** It was twenty-times bigger.

bi-sikado *pp/adj* inexperienced, uncouth, uneducated, uncivilized, unfamiliar with, untrained

bisikléta/bisikléto *nf* bicycle

biskócho *nm* biscuit (*Eur*)

bi-suto *adj* sleepless

bi-tango *adj* loose, not tight

bi-themêsko *gen/adj* stateless

bi-tronime *pp/adj* **1)** dethroned **2)** yet to be enthroned

bi-tsalyángo *gen/adj* without clothes

bi-tumime *pp/adj* not yet betrothed

bi-vizáko *gen/adj* without a visa

bi-vorbáko *gen/adj* speechless, tongue tied, without words

bi-vorbángo *gen/adj* lacking vocabulary

bi-vucho *adj* low, short (*in height*)

bi-wastêsko *gen/adj* one-armed; **Zhanes o Spíro, le bi-wastêsko?** Do you know Spiro, the one-armed (man)?

bi-wórta *adj/adj* crooked, uneven

bi-woyáko *gen/adj* dull, insipid, listless, unenthusiastic

bi-wusharado *pp/adj* uncovered, revealed, exposed

bi-wuzdimásko *gen/adj* unreliable, untrustworthy

bi-wuzho *adj* **1)** unclean **2)** impure **3)** non-virginal; **Bi-wuzhi la.** She is a non-virgin. **4)** *nm* devil, Satan

bi-xalado *pp/adj* unwashed

bi-xalo *gen/adj* **1)** uneaten, unconsumed **2)** unused, not worn out/used up; **Si lên tsáliya bi-xale le shavorre?** Have the children any clothes that are not worn out?

bi-xamásko *gen/adj* inedible, uneateable, unfit for consumption

bi-xanzháko *gen/adj* without envy/greed/lust

bi-yakháko *gen/adj* one-eyed

biyandimásko *gen/adj* able to bear young, fertile

biyandimos *nm* birth

biyando *pp/adj* born

byandó-mulo *comp/adj* stillborn

biyándyol *vi* be born: *pp/adj* **biyandilo; O khuro biyándilo araki.** The foal was born last night. *see also* **arakhádyol** *vi* (*for people*)

biyanel *vt* **1)** bear, give birth, bring forth: *pp/adj* **biyando; Chi mai biyandas khurre gadya grasni, yalovítsa si.** The mare never bore foals she is a sterile mare **2)** ~ **frúta** bear fruit.

bi-yertimásko *gen/adj* unforgivable, unpardonable

bi-yertime *pp/adj* unforgiven

bi-yilêsko *gen/adj* heartless, cruel

bizêrrùwo *nm* embroidery, lace, needlework used to decorate clothing: *pl* **bizêrrùwurya**

bi-zhanglo *pp/adj* unknown, unrenowned

biznizmáno *nm* businessman (*Am*): *nf* **biznizmánka; Xlûtro si gadya Rromni, chachi biznizmánka.** She is shrewd that woman, a real businesswoman.

bíznizo *nm* business (*Am*)

bi-zoráko *gen/adj* helpless, ineffective, unconcincingly, without power/strength, wimpish; **Rrom bi-zoráko** Romani wimp

bi-zoralo *adj* weak, puny, feeble

bi-zumado *pp/adj* untested, untried

bi-zûnáko *gen/adj* bareback, without a saddle

blágo *nm* **1)** bliss, blessings; **Blágo kya dáke kai biyandyas tut!** Blessings to your mother who bore you! **2)** ecstasy, joy, spiritual bliss/ecstasy, religious ecstasy

blagostil *vt* 1) create bliss/joy, make happy: *pp/adj* **blagostime** 2) *v/refl* **blagostíl-pe** be living in total bliss, find total happiness

blagostíya *nf* bliss, total happiness; **Trayin ánde chísto blagostíya.** They are living in total/pure happiness/bliss. **Ánde chísto blagostíya si akana.** He is a stranger in Paradise now/He is living in total bliss.

blagostóso *adj* blissful

blagostovil/blagoslovil *vt* 1) bless, consecrate: *pp/adj* **blagostovimé** 2) assent/consent by blessing

blagostovimos *nm* 1) benediction, blessing, communion, consecration 2) assent, consent

blagostóvo 1) blessing 2) assent, consent

blastéri *nm* sand blaster (*Am*)

blastil *vt* sand blast: *pp/adj* blastime (*Am*)

blastimos *nm* sand blasting (*Am*)

blaxári *nm* tinker

blímpo *nm* 1) airship, dirigible (*Am*) 2) *fig* fat man: *nf* **blimpáika**

blína *nf* crepe, pancake

blinítsa *n/f* 1) crêpe 2) omelet (*Am*)

bliznyiáko 1) *adj* twin 2) *nm* twin, look-alike doppelganger: *pl* **bliznyiácha** *nf* **blizniyáika**: *nf/pl* **blizniyáiki** (*Am*), *see also* **zhámeno** *nm*

blokil *vt* avoid, ostracize, shun: *pp/adj* blokime (*Am*)

blôko *nm* 1) city block 2) territory of a reader-advisor in a defined *kumpaníya qv* (*Am*); **Akana ándo Târáno si trin blókurya mashkaral le ófisi.** Now in Toronto, it is three blocks between the parlours (radius of three blocks).

blowil *vt* 1) blow out (*tire*): *pp/adj* **bluwime** 2) *v/refl* **blowíl-pe** blow out, become blown out; **Bluwisáili lêski shûna.** His tire blew out. (*Am*)

blowimos/bluwimos *nm* blow out, flat tire (*Am*)

blúdka *nf* coaster, saucer: *pl* **blúdki/blúdi**

bludkítsa *nf* coaster

bludnítsa *nf* female social outcast, loose woman, prostitute

blûnda *nf* rash, rash from poison ivy: *pl* **blûndi** hives, urticaria

blúza/blúsa *nf* blouse

bob *nm* bean (*in general*)

bóbo *nm* 1) soybean 2) maize

bobríshko *nm* kidney

bógo *nm* plug horse, useless nag

bokála *nm* 1) clay jug, glass jug, jug in general, tankard 2) urn 3) flower pot

bokh *nf* 1) hunger; **bokh e grastuwi** hunger of a horse/sugar diabetes, **bári bokh** famine, starvation, **Lyas lên e bokh.** Hunger seized them/They went into a feeding frenzy. 2) appetite 3) craving, need

bokhalichóso *adj* a little hungry, slightly hungry

bokhalimos *nm* 1) famine, starvation 2) hunger strike

bokhalo *adj* 1) hungry 2) eager for/desperate for; **Bokhalo si te arakhel pêske kher.** He is hungry to find a house for himself/eager to find a house for himself. **Bokhali si te arakhel pêske Rrom.** She is desperate to find herself a husband.

bokháwol *vi* be hungry, get/become hungry, hunger for: *pp/adj* **bokhailo**; **Bokháilem po drom.** I got hungry on the road/while driving.

bokhyárdyol *vi* be caused to starve, be reduced to starvation: *pp/adj* **bokhardilo**

bokhyarel *vt* 1) cause starvation, reduce to starvation, starve: *pp/adj* **bokhyardo** 2) make hungry 3) cause famine 4) create an appetite

bokhyarimos *nm* starvation, famine

bokséri *nm* boxer

bókso *nm* box, cardboard box (*Am*), boxing, boxing match

bóla *nf* 1) ball 2) marble

boldo *pp/adj* baptized, christened

boldyol *vi* 1) be baptized/christened: *pp/adj* **boldilo** 2) be dipped, immersed

bolel *vt* 1) baptize, christen: *pp/adj* **boldo** 2) immerse, dip

bolimos *nm* **1)** baptism, christening **2)** immersion

boltsil *vt* bolt (*door*): *pp/adj* **boltsime** (*Am*)

bóltso *nm* bolt

bómba *nf* **1)** grain; **bómba lond** grain of salt **2)** bomb, missile, shell (*Mil*); **3)** *comp/vt* **Peravel ~** bomb, drop a bomb; **Shudénas granádi hai peravénas bómbi po fóro.** They were shelling and bombing the city.

bómba-atomikáki *comp/nf* atomic bomb/nuclear bomb

bómba-wastêski *nf* hand grenade

bombéri *nm* bomber (*Mil*)

bombil *vt* bomb, shell: *pp/adj* **bombime**

bombimos *nm* air raid, bombing

bompéri *nm* automobile bumper

borbaníya *nf* string bean

borbánzo *nm* chick pea, kidney bean

bórdo *nm* **1)** board, wallboard, paneling **2)** **Bórdo** Board (*of directors*)

Bórdo-Direktóryêngo *nm* Board of Directors

bordyai *nm* **1)** dilapidated shack, hovel: *pl* **bordya 2)** dog kennel **3)** cabin, cottage

bordyáno *nm* shack dweller, squatter living in a makeship shack: *nf* **bordyánka**

bórfa *nf* eggplant (*Solanum melongena*)

borfále *nm* eggplant stew, *Kalderash* stew made with eggplant, beef and other ingredients

bori *nf* **1)** bride **2)** apprentice wife **3)** sister-in-law (*wife of a brother*) **4)** daughter-in-law (*wife of a son*)

bornúto *nm/arch* snuff

bóro *nm* **1)** oak (*wood*) **2)** oak tree

borósko *gen/adj* made of oak

boryáki kunúna *comp/nf* bridal crown

boryáko *gen/adj* bridal

boryorri *nf/dim* **1)** young bride **2)** young married woman **2)** sister-in-law (*brother's wife*) **3)** daughter-in-law (*son's wife*)

boslowil *vt* **1)** bless: *pp/adj* **boslowime; Te boslowil tut o Del.** May God bless you! **2) boslowíl-pe** *v/refl* bless oneself, be blessed

boslowimos *nm* blessing

bov *nm* **1)** oven **2)** stove **3)** furnace **4)** crematorium; **Ándo marimos phabarde le Rromen ánde l' bova.** During the war, they (*the Nazis*) incinerated Roma in the crematoria.

bov-bilavimásko *comp/nm* blast furnace

bov-gasósko *comp/nm* gas stove

bov-ilêktrikósko *comp/nm* electric stove

boyári *nm* boyar, rich land owner

boyárka *nf* **1)** wife of a boyar **2)** woman landowner

bózo bi-baxtalo *comp/nm* ivy

bózo *nm* **1)** shrub **2)** weed

bózurya *nm/pl* **1)** shrubbery, underbrush **2)** weeds

brádo *nm* **1)** fir, spruce (*wood*) **2)** fir or spruce tree

bradósko *gen/adj* made of fir, pine or spruce

bragi *nf* **1)** milking can, also used in Hungarian Vlax-Romani music as a vamping drum **2)** barfly, tramp, woman of immoral conduct

bragi-thudêski *nf* milking can

bragyáko *nm* man of immoral character, rake, womanizer

bragyárka *nm* milkmaid, girl or woman who milks cows

brámnitsa *nf* shoulder yoke for buckets/pails

branil *vt* **1)** object, contest, defend (*by objecting during a trial*): *pp/adj* **branime; Braniv kakale doshimáta.** I contest/defend myself aganst these accusation. **Braniv lêske swáturya.** I object to his statements. **2)** dispute **3)** deny **4)** *v/refl* **a)** object. **braníl-pe; Sóstar braníl-pe?** Why does he object? **Braní-ma.** I object. **b)** defend oneself; **Músai te branís-tu.** You must defend yourself.

branimásko *gen/adj* argumentable, contestable, debatable, defendable; **~ xamos** argument for the defense (*of an accused psn*), debatable argument

branimos *nm* **1)** objection (*of an accused psn*), opposition; **So si lêsko branimos?**

What is his objection? **2)** contestation, defense/explanation (*of an accused psn*) **3)** defense (*of an accused*) **3)** refusal

bráshka *nf* female frog; **Del-duma sar e brashka.** He speaks hoarsely (*like a frog*)

brashkoi *nm* bullfrog: *pl* **brashyoiya**

bravínta *nf* **1)** alcoholic beverages, liquor supply at a gathering/feast/ball **2)** vodka (*Eur*)

bravintári *nm* seller of alcoholic beverages **2)** bootlegger (*Am*)

bravintáriya *nf* **1)** store that sells alcoholic beverages **2)** liquor store

Brávo! *excl* Here, here! Right on! (*Eur*); **Brávo, manúsha!** Right on/Good for you, old man!

brazíra *nf* brassiere (*Am*)

Brazíliya *nf* Brazil

Brazilyáko *gen/adj* of Brazil, from Brazil

Brazilyáno *nm* **Brazilian** *nm*: **Brazilyánka** *nf*

brégo *nm* bank of a river/stream, brink, embankment, shoreline

brêk/bêrk *nm* breast, chest, bosom

breshkelítsa *nf* **1)** film, frog spawn, spittle, scum, green slime on a pond **2)** garbage, slops, pigswill; **balêngi breshkelítsa** pigswill **3)** flotsam **4)** residue, sediment

breshûn *nm* **1)** rain **2)** *vi* **del o ~** rain; **Délas o breshûn sórro ges.** It was raining all day.

breshûndaló/breshûnaló *adj* rainy, wet

breshûndomós *nm* deluge, downpour, rainstorm

breshûnorró *nm* drizzle, light rain

Brey! *excl* Hey, you there!, Hey!, Man!; **Ei, Brey! Kai zhas?** Hey man! Where are you going? **Brey, háide aworde!** Hey, come on over here! **Ashun brey!** Listen, man! Used mainly with young men or between friends, not when addressing middle-aged men or elders. See **Manúsha!, Ráiya!**

brichára *nf* waist belt

brichêski-shib *compl/nf* razor blade

brichíri *nf* rainbow; **wárekai inkyal e brichíri** somewhere over the rainbow

brícho *nm* razor

bríga *nf* care, grief, misfortune, sorrow

brigáda *nf* brigade (*Mil*)

brigáko/brigalo *gen/adj* grieving, sorrowful

brintol *vt* **1)** infect: *pp/adj* **brintome 2)** develop (*boil*), gather (*puss*) **3)** *v/refl* **brintól-pe a)** become contagious, become infected **b)** gather

brintomásko *gen/adj* contagious, infectious

brintomos *nm* contagion, infection

brivdo *pp/adj* **1)** plucked **2)** *fig* ripped off, skinned alive

brívdyol *vi* **1)** be cropped/plucked: *pp/adj* **brivdilo 2)** *fig* be skinned alive, ripped off

brivel *vt* crop, pluck (*chicken*): *pp/adj* **brivdo 2)** rip off, skin *smbdy* alive, swindle

brivimos *nm* **1)** cropping **2)** plucking **2)** rip-off, swindle (*Am*)

brócha *nf* broach (*Am*)

bronkíta *nf* bronchial tube

bronkítsi *nf/pl* bronchitis

brônzo *nm* bronze

bronzósko *gen/adj* made of bronze

brózba *nf* turnip; **brózba-loli** beet, beetroot, **brózba-parni** rutabaga

brozbalo/brozbáko *gen/adj* colour of a turnip, purplish

brúma *nf* **1)** frost, hoarfrost **2)** dew

brumalo *adj* covered with dew, frosty

brumol *vt* **1)** cover with frost: *pp/adj* **brumome 2)** *v/refl* **brumól-pe** become covered with frost

Bruséli *nm* Brussels

brústo *nm* bunch of (*grapes, etc.*), cluster, bouquet (*of flowers*)

bruzhláto *nm* bracelet (*Am*)

brúzho *nm* lump, nugget, ingot; **brúzho súmnakai** gold ingot

bryáva *nf* hinge (*on a door*): *pl* **brévi; Tsirdyas o wudar katar l' brévi.** He tore the door from the hinges.

bryázda *nf* 1) furrow: *pl* **bryézhdi** 2) sod, turf, used to decorate the Easter feast table

búba *nf* beetle, bug

búbitsa *nf* silk worm

buboi *nm* carbuncle, boil: *pl* **buba**

bubóko *nm* duckling, gosling: *pl* **bubóchi:** *nf* **bubóka** female duckling, gosling: *pl* **bubóki**

búchuma *nf* 1) tree stump 2) hub (*of a wheel*)

budáka *nm* pick/pickaxe: *pl* **budácha**

budána *nf* blood pudding (*Eur*)

bufálo *nm* bison, buffalo (*Am*)

bufári/bukfári *nm* 1) wallet 2) pocket book

bûfíl *vt* buff, polish: *pp/adj* **bûfimé** (*Am*) *see* **morrel** *vt*

buflári *nm* 1) extender, extension cord 2) distributor (*of a product/newspaper*)

buflé-dumêngo *comp/gen/adj* broad-shouldered

buflimos *nf* extension, breadth, width

buflo *adj* 1) broad, extensive, far-reaching, vast, wide 2) flat, smooth

buflo felésho *comp/nm* flounce; **fistáno bufle feleshênsa** skirt with flounces

buflo masho *comp/nm* flatfish, flounder

buflyardo *pp/adj* broadened, flattened, dilated, dilitated, distributed, expanded, smoothed, smoothed over, unrolled, widened, made more expansive, publicized.

buflyárdyol *vi* 1) be broadened/widened/ extended/enlarged/broadcast/distributed/ publicized: *pp/adj* **buflyardilo** 2) be dilatated/stretched

buflyarel *vt* 1) broaden, enlarge in area, dilatate, expand, extend in area, spread out, unroll, widen: *pp/adj* **buflyardo** 2) broadcast, distribute, reach out, publicize 3) make flat/smooth 4) stretch 5) ream

buflyarimos *nm* 1) dilatation/dilation, enlargement, expansion, extension, flatness, widening 2) distribution, publication 3) Diaspora; **O Buflyarimos Rromano** The Romani Diaspora

buflyol *vi* 1) be broadast/distributed/publicized: *pp/adj* **buflilo** 2) become wider/broade/more expansive 3) be stretched 4) become flat/smooth

bugni/phugni *nf* pimple, blackhead/pimple/zit

bugnyalo *adj* 1) covered with blackheads/pimples, zit-faced (*Am*) 2) *nm* boy with pimples of his face: *nf* **bugnyali**

bugnyárdyol *vi* become covered with blackheads/pimples: *pp/adj* **bugnyardilo**

bugnyarel *vt* cause blackheads/pimples/zits, cover with pimples: *pp/adj* **bugnyardo**

bugnyol *vi* become covered with pimples: *pp/adj* **bugnilo**

bugóva *nf* bass fiddle (*Eur*)

búka *nf* cheek (*Anat*); **Chumidem la pe búka.** I kissed her on the cheek. **Pher ki búka ánda sos si tut ándo mui.** Fill your cheek from what you have in your mouth (*proverb*).

bukêngi-goy *comp/nf* liverwurst

bukêngo-naswalimos *comp/nm* cirhossis of the liver, liver disease

bukéta *nf* bouquet

búkfa *nf* book, lawbook; **Amári búkfa si ramome ándo chéri.** Our (Romani) lawbook is written in the sky/Our laws are unwritten.

bukfángo-dukyáno *nm* bookstore

bukfári *nm* 1) pocket book 2) wallet (*Am*)

bukfêngi-shkáfa *comp/nf* bookshelf, bookcase

bukfítsa *nf* notebook

buki *nf* 1) work, job of work, employment, handiwork, craft 2) business, type of work 3) thing, object, thing-a-ma-jig, contraption; **Si lês but bukya te mothol túke.** He has a lot if things to tell you. 4) business, matter, issue, deal; **Nai bári buki.** It's not a big deal/It's of no great importance 5) situation; **Djungali buki si.** It's an ugly/bad situation. 6) fact, factor

bukí-djardinêngi *nf* landscaping work

bukí-Gazhikani *comp/nf* non-Romani business

bukí-mobilêngi *nf* autobody work

bukí-Rromani *nf* Romani business/work/trade

búklo *nm* **1)** bota, wooden bottle, wooden container for water: *pl* **búklya 2)** tankard, copper or wooden tankard with tap

buko *nm* liver (*Anat*), *us in pl of* **buke/bukû; Lêske buke si naswale.** His his liver is ailing.

buko *nm* liver, piece of liver *us in pl* **buke/bukû**

bukyáko *gen/adj* of work, having to do with work; **tsáliya-bukyáke** work clothes

Bukyáko Gês *comp/nm* Labour Day

bukyáko lil *comp/nm* work permit

bukyarel *vt* cause to function, get to work, make to function, work: *pp/adj* **bukyardo**

bukyári *nm* craftsman, worker

bukyarimásko *gen/adj* functioning, operating, working

bukyarimásko-markéto *neolog/comp/nm* job/labour market

bukyarimásko-than *comp/nm* work place, working area

bukyarimos *nm* employment, labour, work

bukyárniko *nm* labourer, tradesman, worker, workman: *pl* **bukyárnichi**

bukyáte *prep* at work; **Símas bukyáte sorr o ges.** I was at work all day.

bukyorra *nf/pl* loose ends, odds and ends, small items of adjustment/work to complete a job

bukyorri *nf* **1)** small job, puny job **2)** lousy job, shoddy job; **Che bukyorri kerdyas!** What a lousy job he did!

bul *nf* **1)** backside, posterior, *vlg/sl* ass (*Anat*) **2)** rump (*animal*) **3)** bottom, underside **4)** stern (*of a boat*) **5)** *comp/vt/i* **sikavel e ~** moon, show one's naked behind to *smbdy*

bulabásh/bulibash *nm* leader/representative of a Romani group (*Eur*): *pl* **bulabásha**

buláko *gen/adj* **1)** of the buttocks, posterior/rump; **buláko-naswalimos** piles, **buláki-dukh** pain in the ass **2)** *nm* pederast

buláko-dóftoro *comp/nm* proctologist

bulalo *adj* **1)** having a prominent backside, fat-arsed **2)** flat-bottomed

bul-astachuni *comp/nf* cast-iron backside; **Si lês bul-astachuni.** He is a man who is not influnced by threats of punishment from the **kris-Romani.**

buldozéri *nm* bulldozer

bule *adv/id us as comp/vi with* **del ~ 1)** fornicate **2)** indulge in sexual intercourse (*Am*)

bulguwíl-pe *v/refl* **1)** talk in one's sleep or when delirious **2)** rave

bulguwime *adj* delirious

bulguwimos *nm* delirium, raving

búlka *nf* biscuit, bun, cookie: *pl* **búlchi**

bulnango *comp/adj* bare-assed **2)** *nm* nudist: *nf* **bulnangi**

bumbáko *nm* **1)** cotton **2)** cotton-wool **3)** cotton-candy **4)** wadding

bumbakósko *gen/adj* made of cotton

bumpítsa *nf* small bump (*on a smooth surface*)

búna *nf see* **búnto** *nm*

búnda *nf* **1)** fur coat/jacket **2)** coat, overcoat in general (*Am*); **búnda fárba** coat of paint

bundári *nm* furrier, dealer in fur coats

bûndavúno *nm* gadfly, horse fly (species *tabanidae*) (*Am*): *pl* **bûndavúya**

buntash *nm* agitator, dissenter, instigator, malcontent, protester, shit-disturber, upstart: *nf* **buntáshka**

buntásha *nm/pl* **1)** agitators, protesters, picket line **2)** shit disturbers

búnto *nf* **1)** agitation, dissention, disturbance, riot **2)** bustle, clamour, confusion

buntuyil *vt* **1)** agitate/make agitated, disturb, excite, spook: *pp/adj* **buntuyime; Buntuyisardyas le grasten.** He spooked the horses. **2)** *v/refl* **buntuyíl-pe a)** become agitated/excited, cause

dissent/trouble **b**) riot, disturb the peace;
Buntuyín-pe le gazhe ánde úlitsa. The
people are rioting/creating a public
disturbance in the street. **Na
buntuyisáwo!** Don't get excited!
buntuyimos *nm* **1**) agitation, civil
disturbance, discontent, dissent, riot **2**)
exuberance, tumult
burchelin *nf* birch tree
búrcho *nm* birch (*wood*)
burchol *vt* **1**) crease, crumple, wrinkle:
pp/adj **burchome 2**) *v/refl* **burchól-pe**
become creased/crumpled/wrinkled
burchomos *nm* crease, wrinkle
burgíya *nf* **1**) bit (*for a drill*) **2**) gimlet
burgyash *nm* gimlet sharpener
Burgyéshti *nm/pl* gimlet sharpeners a
Lovari clan that arrived in Canada in the
mid 1970s.
buríko *nm* belly button, navel (*Anat*)
buriyátsa *nf* mushroom: *pl* **buriyêtsi**
buriyátsa-dili *comp/nf* toadstool
buriyátsa-maryáko *nm comp/nm* mussel
búriyo *nm* barrel, keg, wooden cask bound
with iron hoops with a removable lid,
ship cask, tun; *pl* **búriya**
buriyútso *nm* keg, puncheon (*small barrel,
cask*), tap (*wooden cask for beer*)
búro *nm* bush *var of* **burr** *nm*
burr *nm* bush, shrub: *pl* **burra** shrubbery,
forest undergrowth
burr-kanrro *comp/nm* hawthorn bush,
thorn bush
búrrnêx *nf* **1**) handful **2**) hold, grasp **3**) **lel
~** take hold of, grasp, grab
búrsa *nf* **1**) grant (*to an organization*) **2**)
stock exchange/market
bushol *vi* **1**) be called: *pp/adj* **bushlilo**;
Sar bushol kodo? How is that called?
Bushlyas Yóno, láko Rrom. Her
husband was called Yono. **Sar buzhólas
kutári?** What was that fellow called? **2**)
pronounce, say **3**) be
named/called/pronounced; **Sar bushos?**
How are you called/What is your name?
Me bushov, Zlátcho. I am called,
Zlatcho **Areslem ánd êkh fóro,**

Hamiltóno bushol. I arrived in a town ,
it is called Hamilton. **4**) **bushól-pe** call
oneself. **Gyórgi, busháilo.** He called
himself, George.
busht *nf* skewer, spit, spear; **Peklas o mas
pe busht.** He cooked the meat on a spit.
Pusadem le mashes bushtása. I speared
the fish/stabbed it with a fish spear.
bushtyávo *adj* **1**) flabby, bloated, having
puffed cheeks, funny, puffed face **2**) *nm*
person having a funny, bloated face:
bushtyavútsa
busóla *nf* compass (*Eur*)
but 1) *pron* many, much, a lot, a lot of;
Zhanel but paramíchya. He knows
many folk tales. **Si lês but, but love.** He
has a whole lot of money. **Si lês but buki
te kerel.** He has a lot of work to do. **2**)
pron many people, a lot of
people/men/women; **But avile.** Many
attended. **Ashundem godola butêndar.**
I have heard that from a lot of people.
Vorrûtsomé-lo butêndar. He is hated by
a lot of people. **3**) *adv* long, for a long
time; **Beshlas but.** He stayed for a long
time. **Nashti beshav but.** I can't stay
long. **4**) *adv* often (*for* **butivar** *qv*); **Chi
dikav lês but.** I don't see much of
him/see him often. **5**) *adv* much, very,
very much; **Me sim but bokhalo.** I am
very hungry. **Lêske shave si but bare
akana.** His children are very big now. **6**)
nm **o mai ~** the most; **O Yóno si les but
núma o Zlátcho si lês o mai but.** Yono
has a lot but Zlatcho has the most **7**)
adv/phr **~ pála godya** long after that;
Mulo na but pála godya. He died not
long after that.
buté-Gazhyángo *gen/adj* polygamous (*if
non-Rom*)
butêlári *nm* man or youth who collects
empty bottles to cash them in for refund.
butélka/butéla *nf* bottle: *pl* **butélchi**;
butélka thud bottle of milk
buter *adv* more (*with some speakers only*
mai but *qv is more commonly heard*);
Buter ka ekh bêrshèski si e glatútsa

akana. The baby is more than one-year old now.

buté-Rromnyángo *gen/adj* polygamous (*if Rom*)

buté-themêngo *gen/adj/neolog* composed of many countries, multi-national

butíka *nf* 1) boutique 2) wine store

butívar/butíwar *adv* 1) often, many times, on many occasions; **Chi dikhav lês butívar.** I don't often see him. **Dikhlem la te khelél-pe butívar.** I have seen her dance on many, many occasions. 2) usually

butóno *nm* 1) control knob/button (*for appliances*) 2) push button

bútwar *adv* many times *used in comparisons of adjectives/adverbs*; **Lêsko kher si bútwar mai baro murrèstar.** His house is many times bigger than mine. **Múrro mobíli zhal bútwar mai sígo lêskorrèstar.** My car goes many times faster than his (car).

butyarel *vt/i* 1) increase, make more, multiply: *pp/adj* **butyardo** 2) exaggerate, make much to do about, make much of 3) *v/refl* **butyarél-pe** increase; **Pêske grast butyardé-pe ánde hêrgéla.** His horses multiplied themselves into a herd.

butyarimos *nm* 1) increase, multiplication, 2) exaggeration

butyol *vi* increase, multiple, become more: *pp/adj* **butyulo**: *usually with* **mai; Mai butyon pêske love ges-gesèstar;** His wealth increases from day to day.

buzdugáno *nm* 1) bludgeon, club, cudgel 2) ceremonial mace

buzêx *nf* 1) spur 2) goad

buzexal *vt* spur: *pp/adj* **buzexado; "Na buzexa ma," phendyas e grasni," "I-me darav le ruvêndar!"** "Don't spur me," the mare replied, "I too fear the wolves!" (*Folk*). **Buzexálas pêske grastes darátar.** He was spurring his horse out of fear.

buzexil *vt* spur, spur on: *pp/adj* **buzexime**

buzhanel *vt* trick, outsmart: *pp/adj* **buzhanglo; Woi buzhanglas lês.** She outsmarted him. (*Am*)

buzhanglimos *nm* 1) astuteness, cunning, the smarts 2) ability to outsmart *smbdy*

buzhanglo *pp/adj* astute, cunning, sly, tricky

buzharel/buzhyarel *vt* teach how to be cunning, smarten up: *pp/adj* **buzhardo**

buzheril *vt* 1) gossip, spread rumors: *pp/adj* **buzherime** 2) *v/refl* **buzheríl-pe** gossip, be gossiping; **Buzherín-pe ánda lêste.** They are gossiping about him.

buzherimos *nm* gossip, apocrypha. gossip, rumour: *pl* **buzherimáta** hearsay, rumours

buzheritóri *nm* back-stabber, gossiper: *nf* **buzheritórka**

búzho/búzhyo *nm* 1) bundle (*of money*); **Kerdyas búzho love.** He made a bundle of money. (*Am*). 2) bail (*of hay, etc*)

buzno *nm* 1) billy goat, male goat: *nf* **buzni** 2) **Buzno** Capricorn (*Zod*)

buznó-dilo *comp/nm* scapegoat

buznorro *nm* kid, young goat: *nf* **buznyorri** nanny goat

buzukári *nm* bouzouki player (*Mus*)

buzúki *nm* bouzouki (*Mus*) **Note:** In the 1960s, the electrified bouzouki began to replace the violin as a lead instrument in North-American Kalderash folk music and is now commonly used everywhere. It was introduced in Canada in the 1960s by Jimmie Mitchel in Montreal. The top performer in 2006 was *Machváno* Danny Fender of Los Angeles, lead player in the American-Romani group *Band of Gypsies*. Bouzoukis have also appeared in Romani bands in central and western Europe, replacing mandolins and tamburas.

buzuyóko *nm* 1) agrimony, burdock 2) peppermint plant, wild mint 3) basil 4) bay leaf

bwárda *see* **bárda** *nf*

bwãta/báta *nf* 1) bat, stick 2) clapper (*of a bell*), pendulum 3) bat (*mammal*) *see also*

liliyáko *nm* **4)** *nm/f/fig* bat; **Che díli bwãta!** What a crazy bat! (*Am*)
bwãta-chasóski clock pendulum
byaríya *nf* brewery (*Am*)

byárya *nf* beer, bottle of beer: *pl*
  byéri/béri
byerútsa *nf* small beer, pint of beer (*Am*)

CH

chaches *adv* fairly, really, truly; **Chaches dikhlan godya?** Did you really see that?

chaché-wastêsko *comp/adj* right-handed

chachí-buki *nf* fact, reality

chachikano *adj* genuine, real, true

chachimása *nms/inst/adv* with truth, honestly, truthfully; **Motho mánge chachimása.** Tell me truthfully.

chachimásko *gen/adj* **1)** decent, honest, truthful **2)** fair, just, right

chachimáta *nm/pl* **1)** realities, truths **2)** human rights, rights

chachimos *nm* **1)** fairness, honesty, truth **2)** correctness, right **3)** proof **4)** justice, rights **5)** fact, reality **6) chachmos le Devlêsko** God's truth/the true facts (*of a case*)

chachiwalo *adj* fair, just

chacho *adj* **1)** fair, honest, true; **kris chachi** fair trial **2)** correct, factual, right **3)** genuine, real **4)** right (*direction*); **O kher si pe cháchi reg.** The house is on the right side. **5)** *nm* right; **Bangyar ka o chácho!** Turn to the right!

chácho-swáto *id* honestly, really, truly, *id* never was a truer word spoken.

chachunes *adv* genuinely, properly; **Manai but kai den-dúma chachunes e phurani Rromani shib.** There aren't many who speak the old Romani language properly.

chachuno *adj* **1)** genuine, proper, real, true; **Won nai chachune Rroma.** They are not genuine/real Roma. **2)** steadfast **3)** own; **múrro cháchuno phral** my own brother.

chachyarel/chacharel *vt* **1)** clarify, show to be correct, confirm, verify: *pp/adj* **chachyardo 2)** justify, make right, prove to be right/true **3)** *v/refl* **chachyarél-pe** justify oneself, prove oneself innocent (*in court*), prove oneself correct/right

chachyarimos *nm* clarification, confirmation, justification

chái *nm* tea; **chai frutása** tea served with fruit

cháiko *nm* cormorant, gull, kingfisher

chailo *adj* full, satiated

chailyarel *vt* make to eat one's fill, fill/stuff (*with food or drink*), quench, satiate (*smbdy*), slake: *pp/adj* **chailyardo**

chailyol *vi* become satiated/stuffed, filled (*with food or drink*), have one's fill: *pp/adj* **chaililo; Xalem dósta, chaililem.** I have eaten enought, I am satiated. **Chaililo sar o balo.** He stuffed himself like a pig. **Sa xalyam, sa pilyam thai chaililam.** We ate everything, drank everything and became satiated.

cháiniko *nm* teapot: *pl* **cháinichi**

cháiyo *nm* tea, cup of tea, pot of tea

chakal *nm* jackal: *nf* **chakalni**

chalavel *vt* **1)** beat (*rugs*), cuff, slap, spank: *pp/adj* **chalado 2)** punish by slaping/spanking

chalavimos *nm* beating, spanking, slapping around, punishment by spanking

chamb *nf* **1)** rind, crisp skin of cooked meat; **E chamb si lêski mártya.** He is addicted to crisp rind. **2)** scalp (*Anat*)

chambalo *adj* crispy, having a crisp outer skin

chámbel *vt* **1)** chew, munch, ruminate: *pp/adj* **chamblo 2)** gnaw, nibble **3)** eat away at

chambimos/chamblimos *nm* chewing, mastication, munching, rumination

chamudáno/chamudáino *nm* **1)** suitcase, traveling case: *pl* **chamudáya 2)** briefcase, tote bag

châng *nf* **1)** knee (*Anat*) **2)** *comp/vi* **beshel pe l' chângá** kneel down; **Beshlas pe l' chângá te rrûgíl-pe.** He knelt down to pray.

chângorrí *nf* kneecap

chánso *nm* chance, opportunity

cháo! *interj* goodbye! (*us on the telephone*)

chaplado *adj* **1)** batty, feeble-minded, retarded, stricken. **2)** mentally-challenged; **Chaplado godo Rrom.** That Rom is mentally-challenged **3)** *nm* feeble-minded male person: *nf* **chapladi** feeble-minded woman or girl; **Xoxadya la, e chorri chapladi.** He took advantage of her, the poor, feeble-minded girl. **Lazhav si, chaplado Devlêstar o goro.** It's shame, the unfortunate fellow was struck by God/rendered feeble-minded.

chapladó-shonêstar *adj/phr* moonstruck

chapládyol *vi* to be rendered feeble-minded, deprived of one's intelligence, become stricken by God/be a victim of divine punishment: *pp/adj* **chapladilo**

chaplavel *vt* **1)** beat, hit, strike: *pp/adj* **chaplado 2)** inflict injury (*by beating, punishing*)

chaplimos *nm* act of beating, hitting, punishing, striking

char *nf* **1)** grass; **Le grast xan char.** The horses are eating grass. **2)** lawn

charalo *adj* grassy, covered with grass

charánchi *nf* grasshopper, locust, weevil

charanchya/charinchya *nf/pl* swarm/plague of locusts/grasshoppers/weevils

charándash *nm* pencil

charo *nm* **1)** bowl, soup bowl, **2)** dish, plate **3)** wooden bowl/porringer

charrel *vt* **1)** lick; **O ruv charrélas pêske wusht.** The wolf was licking his chops: *pp/adj* **charrdino 2)** suck **3)** *v/refl* **charrél-pe** lick oneself; **Marimé-la e**

mútsa, charrél-pe. A cat is defiled, it licks itself/its own private parts.

charrimásko *gen/adj* suckling; **charrimásko balorro** suckling pig

charrimos *nm* **1)** licking **2)** sucking

charyarel *vt* **1)** graze, pasture, put to graze: *pp/adj* **charyardo**

charyarimos *nm* grazing, grazing area; **Lasho charyarimos le grastêngo si.** It's a good grazing area for the horses.

charyol *vi* **1)** grass over, become overgrown with grass: *pp/adj* **charilo 2)** graze, be grazing; **Charyon le grast.** The horses are grazing.

chasári *nm* maker or repairer of clocks and watches

chasavoi *nm* watch maker

cháso *nm* **1)** hour; **Che cháso si?** What hour/time is it? **2)** o'clock; **Zhas ka l' pansh chásurya.** We'll go at five o'clock. **3)** time; **Che cháso zhástar?** What time are we going? **4)** clock; **O cháso bashlo.** The clock chimed.

chasútso *nm/dim* watch

chávka *nf* **1)** old hen, old fowl with tough meat **2)** old dried out ear of corn (*Am*)

Cháx! *exp of disgust* Yuck!

cháxo *adj* disgusting, yucky; **Che cháxo gazho!** What a disgusting man!

cházhma *nf* **1)** water fountain **2)** hose, hosepipe

che *pron* **1)** what, which; **Che cháso si?** What time is it? **2)** *Interj* What!; **Che bári djúnga!** What an ugly sight, thing or female *psn* or animal! **Che dilimos!** What stupidity!

chêk/chêkh *cont of* **chi êkh,** not one, not a single one

chêk-dáta *adv/phr* at no time, never at any time. (*cont of* **chi-yêkh-dáta**)

chêkèngi-búkfa *comp/nf* chequebook

chêkíl *vt* **1)** check, check up on: *pp/adj* **chêkimé 2) chêkíl-pe** to be checked out/up on

chêkimós *nm* checking, scrutiny

chêkméza *nf* cash box/drawer, till (*at cash register*)

chêko *nm* cheque; **mulo chêko** expired cheque. **Mudardem o chêko.** I cashed the cheque.

chêkùn *nm* 1) cooking fat, fat, lard 2) grease, lubricant, slush 3) rendered tallow

chêkûnaló *adj* 1) fatty, greasy 2) slushed, smeared with fat/lard

chêkûníl *vt* 1) grease, smear with fat/tallow, treat with slush,: *pp/adj* **chêkûnimé** 2) *v/refl* **chêkûníl-pe** smear oneself with fat/grease

chelyédo *nm* family, kin, people, relatives

cheni *nf* earring: *pl* **chenya** (*Eur*)

chentrálno *adj* central; **Chentrálno Ivrópa** Central Europe

chêntro *nm* center, social center (*Eur*); **chêntro komershyálno** mall, shopping center (*Eur*)

chêpêníl *vt var of* **tsêpêníl** *qv* 1) make numb/numbed: *pp/adj* **chêpênimé** 2) make erect, hard/stiff 3) block, create deadlock 4) *v/refl* **chêpêníl-pe a)** become numb/numbed **b)** become stiff/hard **c)** become deadlocked/stalled

chêpênimós *nm* 1) hardness, numbness, stiffness; **chêpênimós ánde korr** stiffness in the neck 2) deadlock, stalemate

chèpêno/chyápeno *adj* 1) numb 2) erect, hard, stiff

chépo *nm* 1) cork, bottle-stopper 2) plug (*sink*) 3) filter (*for cigarette*)

cheran *nf* 1) star: *pl* **chera** 2) comet 3) **cheran kai perel** shooting star

cherángo *gen/adj* relating to the stars

cherchélo *nm* inexpensive item of jewellery, trifle, trinket, toy; **Bikinel cherchélya.** He sells trinkets.

cheréko *nm* side, quarter; ~ **mas** side/quarter of meat

Chergári *nm* Romani Coppermith sub-group historically based around Sarajevo. The word means 'tent-dweller/nomad,' from **chérga**, (*Kalderash* **tséra**) 'tent.'

chéri *nm* 1) heavens, sky 2) Heaven

Cherkáziya *nf* Circassia

Cherkézo *nm* Circassian man: *nf* **Cherkezáika**

chêrko *nm* 1) hoop (*around a barrel*), hoop, rim, metal tire on a wooden wheel 2) brim

chêrkútso *nm* ferrule

chermáno *nm* chairman: *nf* **chermánka** (*Eur*)

chêrniyála *nf* black ink, ink

chêsto *nm* 1) salute (*Mil*) 2) *comp/vt/i* del ~ give salute

chetvérto/chetwérto *nm* quart (*liquid measure*)

Chéxiko *nm* Czech: *nf* **Chexikútsa**

Chexítska *nf* Czech (*language*)

Chexítsko *adj* Czech

Chéxo *nm* 1) Czech Republic 2) former Czechoslovakia

chi 1) *adj/pron* not, neither, not even; **Chi tu wórka me chi zhanas o chachimos.** Neither you nor I know the truth. **Meyázol chudáto, chi mursh wórka zhuvli.** He looks like a freak, neither male nor female. **Chi me wórka chi tu chi zhas.** Neither you nor I will go. **Chi yekh chiriklo nashti te huryal kothe núma tu areslan.** Not even a bird can get up there but you managed to get there. 2) *adv* don't, doesn't, do not; **Chi zhanav.** I don't know. **Chi avel.** He is not coming. **Chi ingarel amáro zakóno.** He doesn't preserve or uphold our law/rules. **Chi kerav túke nasul.** I won't do you (any) harm. 3) *pron* your; **Kai chi phey?** Where is your sister? *var of* **tyi** *qv*

chi mai *adv* never; **Chi mai dikhlem lês.** I never saw him. **Chi mai nerí-ma kána khelá-ma kárti.** I never win when I play cards.

chi mai chi yekh dáta *adv* never once, not even once, not once; **Chi mai mardyas ma, chi mai yekh dáta.** He never beat me, not even once.

chibúko *nm* 1) long-stemmed pipe (*for smoking*) 2) pipe of a hookah

chichárka *nf* cicada

chífo *nm* chief, middle man, 'fixer,' go-between (*Eur*)

chífra *nf* figure, number, letter *(of the alphabet)* (*Eur*)

chik *nf* 1) mud 2) clay 3) guck(*in a sink*), muck, ooze (*on a lake bottom*)

Chikágo *nm* Chicago (*Am*)

chikáko *gen/adj* adobe, made of clay/mud; **chikáke tsígli** adobe bricks

chikalo *adj* muddy, seeped with clay, flecked/splattered with mud

chikat *nm* brow, forehead (*Anat*)

chikatalo *adj* having a prominent forehead

chikáwol *vi* become muddy: *pp/adj* **chikailo**

chikyárdyol *vt* be made to become covered/splattered with mud, become/get covered with clay/guck: *pp/adj* **chikyardilo**

chikyarel *vt* cover/splatter with clay/guck/mud/ooze, make muddy: *pp/adj* **chikyardo**

chikyarimos *nm* mud splatter

Chilimóli *nm* Chile Mole

chi-mai *adv* never, never ever, never even; **Chi mai dikhlem lês.** I never ever saw him. **Chi mai ashundem gadya mai anglal.** I never heard anything like that before.

chimêntéri *nm* cement mixer

chimêntíl *vt* lay cement, cement: *pp/adj* **chimêntimé**

chimêntimós *nm* cementing, laying of cement

chimênto *nm* cement, mortar; bricks and ~ , **shtígli hai chimênto**

Chinamáno *nm* 1) Chinese man: *nf* **Chinamánka** (*Am*) *see also* **Kitáitsa** *nm* 2) Chinese restaurant owner/employee (*Am*); **Akhar o Chinamáno te anel xabe.** Call the Chinese restaurant man to deliver (some) food.

chinesára/tsinesára *nf* evening before a holiday or a feast day

chingar *nf* 1) altercation, brawl, fight 2) argument, controversy, quarrel, squabble, verbal fight; **Sas man chingar lêsa.** I had an argument with him. **So chingar si**

kathe? What's the argument here? 2) family squabble, feud between families

chingarash *nm* argumentative male person, squabbler: *nf* **chingaráshka** *fig* shrew

chingaril *vt* 1) argue, fight verbally, squabble: **chingarime** 2) *v/refl* **chingaríl-pe** argue, brawl, fight, squabble; **Chingarín-pe sórro ges.** They squabble all day. **Chi mangáva te chingarí-ma tumênsa.** I don't want to squabble with you people.

chingarimásko *gen/adj* argumentative, quarrelsome

chingarimos *nm* 1) brawl, fight 2) family dispute, heated exchange of words, infighting, squabble

chinisára *nf* evening before a feast day/holiday

chink *nf* 1) sneeze 2) *comp/vi* **del** ~ sneeze

chípo *nm* chip, French fry

chípurya *nm/pl* chips, French fries (*Am*); **goiyorre thai chípurya** hotdogs and French fries (*Am*)

chirash *nf* cherry: *pl* **chiresh**

chireshelin *nf* cherry tree

chiriklano *adj* avian, birdlike; **gogí-chiriklani** birdbrain (*Am*)

chiriklênsa *id* with the birds, absent-minded, out of it (*Am*) *often with* **beshel; O Gyórgi beshel le chiriklênsa.** George is sitting with the birds/He is not with it/He is out of it. **Le chiriklênsa símas kána phendem godya.** My mind was elsewhere when I said that. **Ashun so mothav túke, kai san, le chiriklênsa?** Listen to what I'm telling you, where are you, with the birds? **Le chiriklênsa si.** He's out to lunch/His mind is totally absent/elsewhere.

chiriklí-mulikani *nf* nightjar (*considered a harbinger of death*)

chirikló-maryáko *nm* seagull, sea bird

chiripíl-pe *v/refl* chirp, twitter: *pp/adj* **chiripime; Chiripín-pe le chiriklé.** The birds are chirping.

chiripimos *nm* chirping, twittering

chiro *pron/var of* **tiro** *qv*

chistérna *nf* cistern, water tank

chísto *adj* clean, complete, pure, genuine, perfect, pure, real, refined, total, unadulterated; **chísto dilo** real schmuck, total fool, **chísto súmnakai** pure gold, **chísti xoxayimáta** pure/total lies

chísto pai *comp/nm* distilled water

chistol *vt* 1) make pure, purify, refine: *pp/adj* **chistome** 2) cleanse of impurities, cleanse of evil/purify spiritually 3) disinfect 4) exorcise 5) *v/refl* **chistól-pe** cleanse oneself of impurities, cleanse oneself spiritually, purify oneself

chistomáta *nm/pl* cleansing agents, disinfectants, purifiers

chistomos *nm* 1) purification, refining process 2) cleansing, spiritual purification with incense 3) disinfection 4) fidelity 5) exorcism

chistoné-ratêsko *comp/adj* pure-blooded, thoroughbred

chitol *vt* 1) read: *pp/adj* **chitome; Chitosardyas búkfa pa l' Rroma.** He read a book about Roma. 2) **chitól-pe** be read, be reading

chitomáta *nm/pl* reading material, text

chitomos *nm* literacy, reading

chivar/chiwar *adv* never, not at any time *see also* **chi mai** *adv*

chívta *nf* 1) band, ribbon, tape 2) cassette tape, recording tape 3) bow, ribbon tied in a bow

chi-yekh/chekh *adv* not one, not even one; **Chi mol chi-yekh tilára.** It's not even worth a dollar.

chi-yekh-dáta *adv/phr* never, never at any time; **Chi mai dikhlem la, chi-yekh dáta.** I never saw her, not even once.

chízma/chísma *nf* high boot, boot: *pl* **chízme** (*Eur*)

chizmári *nm* boot maker (*Eur*)

chizmesára *nf* boots, pair of Hungarian-style, high boots (*Eur*); **Malavel e chizmesára kána khelél-pe.** He strikes the boots when he dances/pounds the floor.

cho/chyo *pron var of* **tyo** *qv*

chobáno *nm* shepherd: *nf* **chobánka** shepherd's wife

choféri *nm* chauffeur, driver

chogni *nf* 1) whip, coach whip, horse/dog whip 2) antenna

chognil *vt* 1) flaggelate, scourge, thrash, whip: *pp/adj* **chognime** 2) bang or clink together, tip (*easter eggs*) 3) bite, peck, sting (*snake*) 4) **chogníl-pe** *v/rfl a)* be whipped **b)** whip oneself, practice self flagellation

chognimos *nm* 1) punishment by whipping, strapping, whipping: *pp/adj* **chognime** 2) banging/clicking/clinking together; **anrrêngo-chognimos** egg-tipping. A *Kalderash* Easter custom of visiting relatives and friends with dyed Easter eggs and banging the visitor's egg against one of the host's eggs for good luck. 3) bite (*snake or insect*), peck, sting 4) flagellation

chóka *nf* choke (*automobile*) (*Am*)

chokanil *vt* 1) hammer, hammer a pattern of beaten copper for decoration: *pp/adj* **chokanime** beaten, hammered 2) engrave, stamp in by hammer

chokanimos *nm* 1) hammering 2) beaten copper pattern

chokáno *nm* hammer: *pl* **chokáya**

chokáno-baro *comp/nm* sledgehammer

chokanútso *nm* 1) small hammer, ball peening hammer, riveting hammer 2) hammer (*of a revolver*)

chokáya *nm/pl* hammers, collection of hammers and formers for coppersmnith work

chokoláta *nf* chocolate, chocolate bar

chokoláti *nf/pl* box of chocolates, chocolates, chocolate candy

chokoláto *adj* chocolate (*color*), **chokolatósko** (*made of ~*)

chokui *nm* 1) ankle 2) wrist

chor *nm* 1) embezzler, grafter, robber, swindler, thief: *nf* **chorni** 2) confidence artist

chorádyol *vi* be robbed/stolen: *pp/adj* **choradilo**; **Káske love chorádile?** Whose money was stolen?

choralo *adj* dishonest, larcenous, thievish, thieving

chorápa *nf* 1) stocking: *pl* **chorápi** 2) sock

chordanes *adv* clandestinely, furtively, secretly, stealthily

chordano *adj* 1) stolen; **chordane kola** stolen goods 2) clandestine, furtive, illicit, secret; **chordano kamimos** illicit love

chordínyol *vi* 1) be robbed/stolen: *pp/adj* **chordinilo**; **Sodya love chordínile?** How much money was stolen? 2) be robbed, mugged; **Chordínili ánde ófisa done bare gazhêndar.** She was mugged in the office by two big (*non-Romani*) men. **Chordínilo o bánko.** The bank was robbed. 3) be embezzled/pilfered

chordo *pp/adj* 1) robbed, stolen 2) abducted, rustled 3) mugged

chórdyol *vi* be robbed/stolen, get stolen *see* **chordínyol** *vi*

chorel *vt/i* 1) steal, swipe: *pp/adj* **chordino/chordo** 2) rob; **Chordyas pêska da.** He robbed his own mother. 3) abduct, rustle 4) mug (*Am*) 5) embezzle, graft, pilfer 6) shoplift

chorikanes *adv* secretly, stealthily, underhandedly

chorikano *adj* 1) secret, stealthy 2) larcenous, light-fingered, thieving

chorimásko *gen/adj* 1) criminal, dishonest 2) thieving

chorimos *nm* embezzlement, hold up, larceny, robbery, stealing, swindling, theft

chor-kumputeryêngo *comp/nm* computer hacker

chorni *nf* 1) female thief/swindler/robber 2) female confidence artist

chorrárdyol *vi* become bankrupt/pauperized/reduced to poverty: *pp/adj* **chorrardilo**

chorrarel *vt* bankrupt, make poor, pauperize, reduce to poverty: *pp/adj* **chorrardo**

chorres *adv* badly, in an inferior way, poorly

chorro *adj* 1) bad, inferior, pathetic, poor (*in quality*), sub-standard 2) hard, difficult, miserable, poor, poverty stricken; **Tsírdas chórro tráyo.** He led a miserable/hard/impoverished life. 3) *nm* indigent/poor man, unfortunate man. wretch: *nf* **chorri**

chorrobíya *nf* oddity, odd/unusual/strange thing, phenomenon, *smth* out of the ordinary, vagary; **Chúda, che chorrobíya!** Strange, what an oddity/strange thing! **Chorrobíya Rromêngi** strange or amusing Romani custom

chorromos/chorrêmós *nm* hardship, need, penury, poverty

chorrorrimos *nm* abject povert

chorrorro *adj* 1) destitute, indigent, miserably poor, poverty-stricken 2) *nm* indigent man, pauper: *nf* **chorrorri** indigent woman, pauper, woman in need

chorrowalo *adj* abjectly poor, destitute, needy, pitifully poor

chorryol *vi* become poor: *pp/adj* **chorrilo**; **Chorrilo thai bi-kherêsko.** He became poor and homeless.

choryal *adv* 1) clandestinely, furtively, on the side/sly, secretively, stealthily; **Kerel love choryal.** He makes money without us knowing about it. 2) in disguise, undercover

choxãlí *nf* herbal potion to repel ghosts

choxãnêski-vyedyáriya *comp/nf* will-o-the-wisp

choxãníl *vt* 1) haunt. 2) spook: *pp/adj* **choxãnimé** 3) *v/refl* **choxãníl-pe** be haunted, become haunted; **Mai palorral katar o mudarimos, choxãnisáilo o kher.** After the murder, the house became haunted.

choxãnimé *pp/adj* haunted; **kher-choxãnimé** haunted house

choxãnimós *nm* haunting, spectral visitation

choxãnó/choxano *nm* **1)** ghost, phantom, spectre/specter: *pl* **choxãné 2)** incubus **3)** demon spirit that can act on its own or by taking posession of a person or animal, shape-shifter **4)** spectral adbuctor/kidnapper: *nf* **choxãní/choxãyí/choxani** female ghost, lamia, succubus

Choxãyángi-ryat *comp/nf* Halloween

chóyo *nm* lipoma, non-malignant tumor

chuchi *nf* **1)** female breast (*Anat*) **2)** nipple, teat/tit **3)** udder **4)** *comp/vi* **del ~** breast feed **5)** *comp/vi* **piyel chuchyátar a)** *vi* drink from the breast **6)** *comp/vt/i* **del chuchyátar** breastfeed

chuchiwali *adj* **1)** big-breasted, bosomy **2)** *nf* **chuchiwali** woman endowed with large breasts

chucho *adj* empty (*probably from Machwanítska see* **nango** *adj*)

chuchya *nf/pl* mammalia, nipples, teats

chuchyáko *gen/adj* of the nipple/teat

chuchyángo *gen/adj* having, exhibiting or possessing breasts/nipples/mammalia/teats/udder; **nangé-chuchyángi khelitórka**, topless dancer

chuchyarel *vt* breast feed: *pp/adj* **chuchyardo**

chuchyátar 1) *adv/nm/abl* from the breast **2)** *comp/vi* **Piyel ~** drink from the breast **3)** *comp/vt* **del ~** breast feed

chuchyol *vi* be breast feeding: *pp/adj* **chuchilo; Chuchyol e gláta.** The baby is still breast feeding.

chúda *id/adj/nf* **1) Chúda!** How odd! How Strange! **Chúda! Che chorrobíya!** Amazing! What vageries! **2)** abnormally, funny, surprisingly; **Meyázol chúda.** It looks funny. **3)** *nf* abnormal *psn*, carnival freak; **Kerdyas o Del ánda lêste chúda**. God made him a freak **4)** *nf* strangeness, peculiarity, *smth* strange or weird **5)** *nf* inexplicable event. miracle

Chúda! *interj* Miraculous! How amazing/odd! How surprising/strange!

chudáto *adj/adv* **1)** abnormal, bizarre, odd/oddly, peculiar, queer, strange, surprising, weird; **Kerdine o kher chudáto.** They built the house abnormally/out of alignment. **Meyázol tsirrá chudáto.** He looks a little weird. **Si lês chudêtsi gîndurya de vrémi.** He has bizarre thoughts at times. **Kerél-pe chudáto.** He is acting strangely. **2)** *nm* miracle, phenomenon, something or somebody very unusual or out of the ordinary **3)** carnival freak: *nf* **chudáta 5)** pervert

chudinil *vt* **1)** amaze, astonish, surprise: *pp/adj* **chudinime 2)** *v/refl* **chudiníl-pe** be amazed/surprised, be flabbergasted, find strange/odd; **Chudinisáilem ánda so phendyas.** I was surprised at what he said/found it strange what he said.

chudinimos *nm* amazement, astonishment, surprise

chugni/chukni *nf* **1)** horsewhip, whip **2)** *comp/vt* **del ~** horsewhip, whip

chugnil *vt* **1)** lash, thrash with a whip, whip: *pp/adj* **chugnime 2)** *v/refl* **chugníl-pe** be thrashed, whipped. *see* **chognil** *vt*

chugúno *nm* **1)** cast iron **2)** pig iron **3)** cast-iron pot on legs

chugunósko *gen/adj* made of cast-iron

chuhurizíl-pe *v/refl* hoot, hoot like an owl or cuckoo

chuhurizimos *nm* hoot, hooting (*of an owl*)

chuhuryáshka *nf* female owl

chuhuryézo *nm* male owl

chukóro *nm* **1)** border, fringe **2)** pom-pom, tassel, toorie: *pl* **chukórya**

chukui *nm* **1)** ankle (*Anat*); **chukui le punrrêsko** ankle of the foot **2)** wrist; **chukui le wastêsko** wrist of the hand **3)** knuckle; **chukui le naiyêsko** *nm* knuckle of the finger, **chukuiya le naiyênge** knuckles of the fingers

chúma *nf* epidemic, plague

chumi *nf* kiss: *pl* **chumya**

chumidel/chumídel *vt* **1)** kiss: *pp/adj* **chumidino; Chumide múrri bul!** Kiss my ass! **2)** *v/refl* **chumidén-pe** be kissing, kiss each other; **Dikhlem le te chumidén-pe palál ándo hãlo.** I saw them kissing in the back of the hall.

chumidemáski-patrin *comp/nf* mistletoe

chumidemos *nm* act of kissing, kissing; **Dikhlem but chumidemáta palal ándo shóyo.** I saw a lot of kissing in the back (*of the theatre*) during the movie.

chumídyol: *vi* be kissed: *pp/adj* **chumidilo; Chi mai chumídilem.** I have never been kissed.

chûmpo/tsûmpo *nm* **1)** leg of an animal or drumstick of a fowl **2)** haunch **3)** junction, joint; **Shindyam la ka o chûmpo kai anklel e kryánga katar o kasht.** We cut it (the branch) at the junction where the branch grows out from the tree.

chunbíra *nf* spruce beer

chungar *nf* drool, saliva, slobber, spit, spittle

chungardel *vt/i* **1)** drool, spit, slobber: *pp/adj* **chungardo 2)** have contempt for, spit on **3)** hiss (*snake*); **O sap chungardas pe mánde.** The snake hissed at me.

chungárdyol *vi* be spat on: *pp/adj* **chungardilo; Márdilem, akushádilem thai chungárdilem.** I was beaten, insulted and spat upon.

chungarimáski piri *comp/nf* spittoon

chúno *nm* boat, rowboat

chúno-motoráko *comp/nm* motorboat: *pl* **chúnurya-motoránge**

chûnrra *nf* braid, pigtail, ponytail; **Khuvel chûnrri.** She braids/weaves braids.

chupágo *nm* traditional *Kalderash* women's blouse worn with the ankle-length **fistáno** *qv*

chuplaflóra *nf* humming bird

chuplil *vt* **1)** gouge, nip, nick, peck, pinch, squeeze (*wood*): *pp/adj* **chuplime 2)** gnaw, nibble **3)** bite (*fish when fishing*) **4)** nip off, trim off

chuplimos *nm* **1)** gouging, peck, pecking, pinch , pinching **2)** gnawing, nibbling

chuplitári *nm* **1)** gouge (*tool*) **2)** woodpecker: *nf* **chuplitárka**

churári *nm* **1)** maker of sieves **2)** gold panner

Churári *nm* Male member of the **Churára,** a Vlax-Romani group: *nf* **Churárka/Churarítsa; Maládilam churarênsa ándo washári.** We met with some Churari at the horsefair.

Churarítska *nf* Churara dialect of Vlax-Romani

Churarítsko *adj* of the Churara

chúro *nm* **1)** sieve, strainer **2)** frame drum **3)** tambourine **4)** strainer formerly used when panning for gold in Wallachia/Moldavia.

chútura *nf* dash, lump, plug (*tobacco*); **chútura-dohanóski** plug of tobacco

chuturútsa *nf/dim* blob, small lump, plug

chuvári *nm* **1)** caretaker, custodian, guardian, janitor, super (*Am*): *nf* **chuvárka 2)** night watchmen

chuvel *vt* place, poke, put: *pp/adj* **chudo/chuto; Chudas o xabe pe síniya.** He/she placed/put the food on the table. (*Eur*)

D

d'aba/dabai *adv* barely, hardly; **Dabai zhanav lês.** I hardly know him.

d'akórdo/de akórdo *adv* in agreement; **Sim d'akórdo lênsa.** I am in agreement with them.

dab *nf* **1)** bang, blow, jab, knock, punch, rap **2)** impact **3)** *comp/vt* **del** ~ bang, hit, impact, punch, strike a blow, slug, touch **4)** *comp/vt* **xal** ~ receive a blow; **Xalyas but daba ándo marimos.** He suffered a lot of punches in the fight. **5) kerel** ~ have an effect, make an impact

dab-mulikani *comp/nf* coup de grace, final straw, mortal blow; *id* **Godo dilo si amári dab mulikani.** That idiot has finished us off/has been the final straw.

daborri *nf* pat, tap

dad/dat *nm* **1)** father *2)* forefather, male ancestor

dada *nm/pl* ancestors, forebears

dadêsko *gen/adj* belonging to a father, paternal

dadêsko-dad *comp/nm* paternal grandfather

daimánta/daimánto *nf* diamond: *pl* **daimántsi**

daimantalo *adj* diamond-shaped, resembling a diamond, shining like a diamond

dáko *gen/adj* maternal; **dáko thud** mothers' milk, **dáki dey** maternal grandmother

dáli/dal *conj* whether; **Chi zhanav dáli me zhav wórka níchi.** I don't know whether I'm going or not.

dámfo *nm* boiler, steam jacket boiler/kettle used in restaurants

Dámo *nm* Adam

damovíko *nm* poltergeist, spook; **Bi-báxtalo khêr si, pherdo damovíkurya.** It's an unlucky house, full of poltergeists.

dand *nm* **1)** tooth *(Anat)*; **Si lên bare dand.** They have big teeth/are very smart, astute. **Trobul âmen avokáto kai si lês bare dand.** We need a very astute lawyer/shark of a lawyer.) **2)** cam, pawl, tooth *(saw)*

dandádyol *vi* get bitten, be bitten: *pp/adj* **dandadilo; Dandádilo zhuklêstar ándo párko.** He got bitten by a dog in the park.

dandalel *vt* **1)** bite, bite into: *pp/adj* **dandaldo; Dandaldyas lês o zhukel.** The dog bit him. **2)** bite/sting **Dandaldyás lês o sap.** The snake stung him.

dandalimos *nm* bite, sting

dandalo *adj* **1)** having big/sharp teeth, toothy **2)** astute, sharp **3)** *nm* male *psn* or animal with prominent teeth: *nf* **dandali 4)** a horse having a tendency to bite humans; **Arakh o grast! Dandalo si.** Watch out for the horse! It's a biter.

dandarel *vt* bite, sting *(snake)*: *pp/adj* **dandardo** *var of* **dandavel** *qv*

dandavel *vt* bite, sting *(snake)*: *pp/adj* **dandado** *var of* **dandalel** *qv*

dandimos *nm* bite, sting

dandwalo *adj* **1)** having sharp teeth, sharp-toothed **2)** an animal inclined to bite without warning; **dandwali mútsa** biting cat **3)** *nm* biter, horse or any animal that bites: *nf* **dandwali**

dand-xoxamne *nm/pl* dentures, set of dentures

Dángo-Ges *comp/nm* Mothers' Day

dar *nf* **1)** apprehension, awe, cowardice, fear, phobia, terror; **Dar lêske te avel.** He is afraid to come. **Dar le Rromênge te zhan kothe.** The Roma are afraid to go there. **2)** ~ *with dative of pronoun or noun* have the feeling/idea, suspect; **Mánge dar ke xoxavel.** I suspect/feel he is lying. **Dar le Rromênge ke nai Rrom pakivalo.** The Roma suspect that he is not an honest man.

darádyol *vi* **1)** cause/make to become alarmed/frightened/scared/terrified: *pp/adj* **daradilo 2)** cause/make to become threatened, be made threatening

daráko *gen/adj* of fear/terror; **kher daráko** house of horrors (*on a carnival*)

daral *vt/i* be afraid, fear, be apprehensive, be terrified: *pp/adj* **darailo; Daral te zhal.** He fears to go/is afraid to go. **Na dara khánchi!** Fear nothing/Don't be afraid! **Daráilo o grast.** The horse became terrified.

darano *adj* **1)** alarming, anxious, awesome, dangerous, intimidating, fearful, frightening, ominous, terrifying **2)** cowardly **3)** *nm* coward: *nf* **darani**

darano suno *nm* nightmare

daravel *vt* **1)** alarm, frighten, give cause to be frightened, scare, terrify: *pp/adj* **darado 2)** intimidate, threaten; **Daravel ma.** He's threatening me. **3)** menace **4)** startle

darayimásko *gen/adj* **1)** alarming, frightening, terrifying; **darayimáski paramíchi** ghost/horror story **2)** menacing

darayimos *nm* **1)** alarm, apprehension, frighfulness, panic **2)** fear, intimidation, terror, threat, menace

darimos *nm* alarm, fear, intimidation, threat

dárro/dáro *nm* **1)** bridal dowry/security: *pl* **dárrya 2)** gift

darruwil *vt* give a present, make a gift/present of: *pp/adj* **darruwime**

daryévo *nm* **1)** river **2) Daryévo** *nm* Danube

Das *nm* Christian Bulgarian: *nf* **Dasni** (*Eur*)

dashbórdo *nm* dashboard (*Am*)

dashtil *vt* **1)** enable, make possible: *pp/adj* **dashtime; Músai te keres sóde dashtis!** You must do as much as you can! **2)** *v/refl* **dashtíl-pe** be able to/manage to; **Kerávas te dashtívas-man.** I would do it if I were able to. **Avel te dashtíl-pe.** She will attend if she is able. **Chi dashtisáilem te arakhav la.** I wasn't able to find it.

Dasikano *adj* **1)** Christian **2)** *nm* Christian Bulgarian: *nf* **Dasikani** (*Eur*)

dáta *nf* date, instant, occasion, time: *pl* **dêtsi; Yertiv tu kakya dáta.** I'll forgive you this time

dáto *nm* detail

datúnchi *adv* since

davúli/daúli *nm* large drum usually played to accompany a **zúrna** (*Eur*)

dazhi *adv* even, even if; **Dazhi me zhav shai-vi te na dikhav lês.** Even if I go, I might not see him. **Chi bashavel ka o báldo dazhi pokines lêske.** He won't play (music) at the dance even if you pay him.

de *part* used with adjectives; **Sóde si de vucho?** How tall is he? **Wo si shov punrre de vucho.** He is six-feet tall. **Woi si pansh hai do-pash punrre de vuchi.** She is five-and-a-half-feet tall. **Vuchó-lo, sar ekh kasht de baro.** It's high, as big/tall as a tree.

de *prep/conj/adv* ago, from, since; **de trin shon** three months ago, **de trin bersh** three years ago: Compound adverbs with **de;** ~ **ages** from today; ~ **akórdo** in agreement; ~ **anglal** from the start/from the front; ~ **antunchára** since then/from then; ~ **antúnchi** since then; ~ **arakyára** since yesterday/last night; ~ **diminyátsa** since morning; ~ **domult** from a long time ago; ~ **dural** from a long way off; ~ **grába** right away; ~ **teharin** from tomorrow, from tomorrow morning

de agesára adv from today (forward)

de akana mai anglal *adv/phr* from now on; **De akana mai anglal, na mai zha le Babêste!** From now on, don't go to Babi's place/visit Babi! **de anglal/d'anglal** *adv* before

de akanára *adv* from now

de arakyára *adv* since yesterday

de atunchára *adv* from then

de diminyátsa *adv* early in the morning, since early in the morning, since the morning

de kanára *adv* since when

de katar *prep* from, beginning/starting from; **De katar o pêrvo Avgósto zhi-ka o déshto Siptímbra, ame zhas ánde vakántsiya.** From the first of August until the 10th of September we are going on vacation.

de kathar adv from this place

de kothar *adv* from that place

de Luwinára *adv* since Monday

de Martsunára *adv* since **Tuesday**

de opral zhi tele *adv/phr* from top to bottom

de Tatradjunára *adv* since Wednesday

de Zhowinára *adv* since Thursday

de Kurkonára adv since Sunday

de Parashtunára *adv* since Friday

de Savotunára *adv* since Saturday

de ternára *adv* since youth; **Bashavélas e gitára de ternára.** He has been playing the guitar since (his) youth.

de vrémi *adv* at times, now and again, on occasion

de vryámya *adv* in time, on time; **Zháltar o djédjêsh de vryámya?** Is the train running on time?

debáta *nf/neolog* debate: *pl* **debêtsi** *see also* **diwano** *nm*

debída *nf* debt, obligation (*Am fr Sp*); **Pokis amári debída.** We honour our debt.

défo *nm* type of tambourine with animal skin and two rows of double bells (*Eur*)

de-fundáko *nm* 1) dive, plunge 2) *v/refl* **dél-pe ~** dive, plunge. *See also* **ka-fundáko** *nm*

defyal *adv* 1) anyway, anyhow, at all, not in the least; **Chi kamav lês defyal.** I don't like it at all. **Me zhav defyal.** I'll go anyway. **Na defyal!** Not at all! **Chi dikhlem la defyal.** I didn't see her at all. 2) *adv* really; **Káko drom si lúngo, defyal lúngo.** This road is long, really long.

deklarátsiya *nf* declaration

deklaril *vt/i* declare, make a declaration: *pp/adj* **deklarime**

dêkúno *nm* deck (*of a house or ship*)

del *vt/i* 1) give, donate, grant, leave (*in a will*): *pp/adj* **dino** 2) provide; **O Del kam-del.** God will provide. 3) hit, kick, strike; **De lês!** Let him have it! **Arakh o grast! Del!** Watch out for the horse! It kicks! 4) spur 5) stab 6) beat (*as heart*) 7) defecate, void 8) *comp/vbs with* **del; 9) ~ ánde/ándo** enter, get into, lead into 10) ~ **ánda e yakh** wink, wink at 11) ~ **ánde phuv** a) strike into the ground (*tent pegs*) b) fall to the ground, crash (*aircraft*), collapse (*bridge*) 12) ~ **ánd angáli** embrace 13) ~ **anglal** a) answer, reply b) get ahead, move forward 14) ~ **andre** a) get in/inside b) let in, put up, allow to share (*dwelling*) c) join, sign up for 15) ~ **ánde lávuta** play the violin 16) ~ **ándo gor** a) succeed, obtain the desired result; b) get even with 17) ~ **ándo póno** become disgusted 18) ~ **arman** curse 19) ~ **atwéto** answer, reply 20) ~ **avri** eject, throw out 21) ~ **bábitsi** hail (*hailstones*) 22) ~ **bakshish** tip, give a handout 23) ~ **balwal** blow wind, create wind (*as a fan*) 24) ~ **bule** a) make love, engage in sexual intercourse b) swindle, rip off (*Am*) 25) ~ **chângá** kneel, kneel down 26) ~ **chink** sneeze 27) ~ **chuchi** breast feed 27) ~ **dab** bump, touch, hit, make contact, strike 28) ~ **drom** a) clear the road, get out of the way b) chase away/out, get rid of 29) ~ **dúma** speak, talk 30) ~ **dúma le mulênsa** speak with the dead, practice spiritualism 31) ~ **gáta** finish, end 32) ~ **gîndo** give thought to, consider 33) ~

glába fine, impose a fine 34) ~ **gogi** realize, bring to mind, remember 35) ~ **gozhni** cuss out, give shit to (*Am*) 36) ~ **inkya** give away 37) ~ **kan** give ear, obey, pay attention 38) ~ **khai** let off an inaudible fart 39) ~ **kham** give sun, shine 40) ~ **khul** cuss out, give shit 41) ~ **kúna** rock (*cradle*) 42) ~ **kwárda** wind (*clock*) 43) ~ **lumína** illuminate 44) ~ **míta** bribe 45) ~ **mui** shout, yell a) face, face up to b) cry out, make noise; 46) ~ **muiyal** capsize, overturn, upset 47) ~ **opral** flow over the top, overflow 48) ~ **opre** raise 49) ~ **pa** come through, come by way of, get through; **Dem pa e filástra.** I got in through the window 50) ~ **pai** hose, water 51) ~ **pakiv** a) honour, respect b) give a feast 52) ~ **pálma** applaud, clap, slap 53) ~ **pálpale** a) back up, reverse b) kick back, rebound, retort, ricochet 54) ~ **pe kiríya**, give on hire, loan, rent 55) ~ **pe strázha** banish, deport, send under guard 56) ~ **po lazhav** seduce, shame 57) ~ **póno** disgust 58) ~ **próbitsa** provide proof/evidence, demonstrate 59) ~ **pûnrró** kick 60) ~ **rat** bleed 61) ~ **rrîl** fart 62) ~ **sherêste** advance, move ahead 63) ~ **shîba** lash punish by whipping 64) ~ **shol** whistle 65) ~ **síniya** prepare a table for guests 66) ~ **shtráfo** fine 67) ~ **shuryása** cut up, slash, stab 68) ~ **skinteyi** shoot/throw off sparks 69) ~ **snat** admonish, warn 70) ~ **solax** give oath, promise, swear (*by*) 71) ~ **spóro** place a bet/wager 72) ~ **suv** inject, give needle 73) ~ **swáto** a) discuss, have discourse, speak b) promise 74) ~ **thuv** emit smoke, smog 75) ~ **trad** admonish, warn 76) ~ **vakimos** lodge a complaint 77) ~ **vraz** weld 78) ~ **wast** a) give hand, shake hands b) help, give a hand 79) ~ **wuzhile:** a) lend, give on loan: b) give on credit 80) ~ **xoli** give anger, affront, aggrevate, enrage, irritate 81) ~ **yag** a) turn on ignition, start (*a vehicle*): b) ignite, set fire to, start a fire c) fire (*gun*) 82) ~ **yag pálpale** backfire 83) ~ **yakh**

notice 84) ~ **yakha** flirt 85) ~ **yakhalo** cast the evil eye 86) ~ **yakhátar** smite by sending the evil eye 87) ~ **rêgáte** get out of the way, remove oneself out of the way 88) ~ **tele: a)** step down, retire, resign; **b)** abase oneself, grovel 89) ~ **vórba** chat, exchange words/ discourse

Del/del *nm* 1) God/god, Supreme Being, Higher Power: *pl* **Dela**; **Te del o Del!** May god grant it so!/I hope so! **Te opril o Del!** May God forbid it! **Ame chi molis ka o Del, molis kai Santána.** We don't pray to God, we pray to Saint Ann. **o Del o baro** the head god/leader of the gods, **O Del o Phurano** The old/ancient God, **O Del o Nevo** The New God.

Del-Kristóso *nm* Jesus Christ

del te kerel *id/phr* have *smthg* done or made

Del Xoraxano *nm* Muslim God, Allah

Delorro *nm* Dear God; **O Delorro kam-del amênge.** Dear God will provide for us.

del-pe *v/refl* 1) begin, commence, get going, start, swing into action; **Dem-man te kerav buki.** I started the work. **Dyás-pe te gilabal.** She started to sing 2) surrender, submit. 3) defecate 4) *comp/vbs with* **del-pe; 5)** ~ **ánde béda** get into trouble 6) ~ **ánde kotorênde** fall to pieces, fall apart 7) ~ **ánde kris** submit to the authority of the Romani tribunal/court 8) ~ **ándo wast** turn oneself in, surrender 9) ~ **ánglal** step forward 10) ~ **barêstar** act haughty, look down on 11) ~ **ándre** implode, collapse in on itself 12) ~ **defundak** dive (*into water*) 13) ~ **dúma** a) speak to oneself; b) hatch a plot, plan mischief usually in the 3rd *psn/pl as in* **Den-pe dúma.** They are plotting *smth* 14) ~ **gogi** remember, be reminded of 15) ~ **lêsa/lása/lênsa** get used to *smth* depending on the gender and number 16) ~ **muiyal** capsize, go belly up, overturn 17) ~ **tele** a) lie down b) alight, descend, land

dêmêribúzo *nm* 1) cocklebur 2) thistle

dentísto *nm* dentist

depanári *nm* 1) corner store, general store (*Can*) 2) *nm* operator of a corner store: *nf* **depanárka**

depénso *nm* expense

depésh *nm* telegram, dispatch, message; *pl* **depéshurya**

derandjil *vt* bother, disturb, disrupt, inconvenience, put out: *pp/adj* **derandjime** (*Eur*)

derándjo *nm* 1) annoyance, botheration, disturbance, inconvenience 2) *vt/i* **kerel ~** bother, disturb; **Kerav túke derándjo?** Am I disturbing you? (*Eur*)

derécho *nm* right (*Am fr Sp*); **Si amáro derécho telal o zakóno.** It is our right under the law.

deréko *nm* 1) log, railway tie 2) pedestal, pillar, wooden vertical or horizontal support

dêrza *nf* rag

dêrzál *vi* become ragged/tattered/torn to rags: *pp/adj* **dêrzailó**; **Lêngi tséra dêrzáili ánde furtúna.** Their tent was torn to rags during the storm.

dêrzaló *adj* 1) patched, ragged, tattered 2) *nm* ragamuffin: *nf* **dêrzalí** 3) *nm* scarecrow

dêrzárdyol *vi* become ripped to shreds, be turned into rags: *pp/adj* **dêrzardiló**

dêrzarél *vt* make ragged/tattered, rip to rags/shreds, reduce to rags and tatters: *pp/adj* **dêrzardó**

dêrzári *nm* rag collector: *nf* **dêrzárka**

dêrzi *nf/pl arch* rags tied to a tree, bush or fence to show those following later which crossroad to take or where to pull into a cart track leading off the road.

desar *conj/adv* 1) since, than, than as, than from; **Desar sóde vryámya san tu kathe?** Since how long are you here? **Kishlo sas desar pêsko ternomos.** He has been thin since his youth. **Mai mishto si te huládyos sar amala desar dushmáya.** It's better we part as friends than as enemies. **Won xan mai mishto desar amári familíya.** They eat better

than our family. 2) *adv/phr* **desar mai anglal** than ever before; **Voliv tut mai but desar mai anglal.** I love you more than ever before. **Meyazólas mai gorde akana desar meyazólas mai anglal.** She looked worse now than (she ever did) before.

desargodi *adv/conj* ever since, since ever; **Sas ma béda desargodi avilem kathe.** I have had trouble ever since I came here.

desetína *nf* acre

desh bersh *comp/nm* decade

desh *num* ten

deshali *nf* number ten, ten in cards

deshêngi *nf* 1) ten-dollar bill (*Am*) 2) ten units of any decimal currency 3) can express age; **Deshêngi si.** She is ten-years-old.

dêshto *nm* stick, walking stick (*Eur*); **Ándo gav bi-zhuklêsko, shai phirel o Rrom bi-deshtêsko.** In a town without even one dog, a Rom can walk without a stick. (*proverb*)

déshto *num* tenth

desh-u-dui *num* twelve

desh-u-dúito *num* twelfth

desh-u-duwares *adv* twelve times

desíl-pe *vi* happen, take place, occur: *pp/adj* **desime** (*Eur*)

desimos/desipe *nm* happening, occurrence

desperáto *adj* desperate (*Eur*)

destinátsiya *nf* destination

destíno *nm* destiny

desya *adv* 1) overly, too, very; **desya but** too much/many. **Desya but mobíliya si ándo fóro, nashti parkis-tu khatênde.** There are too many cars in the city, you can't park anywhere. **Xalyas desya but.** He ate too much. **Pilas desya but mol hai shaglás-pe.** He drank too much wine and threw up. **Desya baró-lo te maládyol ánde láda.** It's too big to fit into the trunk (*of the car*). **Desya nasul godya!** That's really terrible! 2) *pron* **~ but** too many people, too much, too many; **Desya but avile.** Too many people attended.

desya fúgo *adv/phr* as soon/quickly as possible; **Músai te keras wáreso desya fúgo.** We must do something as soon as possible.

detelína *nf* clover

Devel *nm* Divinity, God *var* of **Del** *nm*

Dévla *nm/interj/voc* God! Oh God!

Devláika *nf* Goddess; **Bari Devláika** Great Goddess, Earth Mother

Devléski djéla *comp/nf* 1) Act of God, something of God's doing 2) miracle

Devlêski fátsa *comp/nm* face of God

Devlêski kris *comp/nf* Divine justice, God's judgement

Devlêski sínya *comp/nf* God's table, a feast table to thank God for answering a prayer given by Pentecostal Roma where no alcohol is served and no smoking nor music allowed unlike a **sláva** held by non-Pentecostal Roma honouring a female saint where dancing, music, alcohol and smoking are the norm.

Devlêski wóya *comp/nf* God's will; **Nas le Devlêski wóya.** It wasn't meant to be.

devlêsko dáro *comp/nm* godsend

Devlêsko *gen/adj* 1) belonging to God, of God, Immanculate; **Devlêski buki/Devlêski djéla** Act of God 2) religious, godly

Devlêsko sastimári *comp/nm* faith healer

Devlésko Shav *nm* Son of God, Jesus Christ.

devlikano *adj* devout, divine, godly, religious, pious: *adv* **devlikanes**

dey *nf* mother

Dey-Devlêski *comp/nf* 1) Earth Mother 2) Mother of God/Saint Mary

deyorri *nf* little mother, dear little mother; **shavorrêngi deyorri** dear, sweet little mother of children

didjitálno *adj* digital

diferénsiya *nf* difference *see also* **aver-fyálo** *nm*

diferénto *adj* different

difikultáte *nm* difficulty (*Eur*): *pl* **difikultátya** *see also* **pharimos** *nm*

diftériya *nf* diphtheria

dignitéto *nm/neolog* dignity

dikhel *vt/i* 1) glance at, look at, notice, observe, see, watch: *pp/adj* **dikhlo** 2) watch, keep an eye on *us with* **pe**; **O ruv dikhélas pe láte.** The wolf was watching her. 3) notice; **Chi piyel but o Stévo, dikhlem.** Steve doesn't drink much, (*as*) I have noticed. 4) meet, run into; **Dikhlem lês ánde sláva.** I met him during the celebration/feast 4) ogle, stare, stare at 5) ~ **angle** look forward to 6) ~ **banges.** glance/look at disapprovingly *us with* **pe**; **Dikhélas banges pe mánde.** He was looking at me disapprovingly 7) ~ *with* **pe,** investigate, look into, review 8) **dikhél-pe** *v/refl* a) see each other b) imagine oneself being; **Shai dikhés-tut manginalo?** Can you imagine yourself wealthy? c) check out, take a look around; **Avilem te dikhá-m**a I came to look around.

dikhimos *nm* 1) eyesight, sight, vision 2) glance, look, stare

dikhlo *pp/adj* 1) obvious 2) seen, visible

díkhyol *vi* 1) be seen/noticed/observed: *pp/adj* **dikhilo**; **Chi mai díkhyol, gadya buki.** That thing is no longer seen. 2) be obvious; **Díkhyol ke o Váno dilyáwol.** It is obvious Vano is becoming senile. **Chi preznayin amáre swínti gesa, sar díkhyol.** They don't honour our holidays, that's obvious.

diklo *nm* 1) bandana, kerchief, woman's headscarf

diklorro *nm* handkerchief

dikorátsiya *nf* decoration

diktatóri *nm* dictator (*Eur*)

diktatúra *nf* dictatorship (*Eur*)

dilêngo-kher/kher le dilêngo *comp/nm* asylum

dileno *adj* asinine, silly

Diléya! *nm/voc* Fool!

diligatil *vt* assign, delegate: *pp/adj* **diligatime**

diligáto *nm* delegate: *nf* **diligáta**

diligátsiya *nf* delegation

dilimáta *nm/pl* craziness, nonsense, silliness, stupidity; **Yekh dilo kerel but dile hai but dile keren dilimáta.** One fool creates many fools and many fools create stupidity.

dilimos *nm* **1)** absurdity, ignorance, inanity, silliness, stupidity; **Che dilimos!** What stupidity! **2)** craze, fad, farce **3)** obsession

dilivanes *adv* stupidly, like a fool; **Kerél-pe dilivanes.** He's acting like a fool.

dilivano *adj* foolish, silly, stupid

Dilíyo *nf/voc* Fool!

dilo 1) *adj* absurd, crazy, flakey, foolish, ridiculous, senseless, stupid, silly, innocently stupid; **Diló-lo** He is foolish/He has a few bricks missing **2)** *nm* dummy flake, fool, nut case, silly *psn*, stupid *psn*; **Chísto dilo si.** He is a total fool: *nf* **dili** flake, silly woman, nut case **3)** joker in cards

dilorro *nm* flake, little fool, looney tune, real fool, ridiculous idiot: *nf* **dilyorri**

dilyardo 1) *pp/adj* driven insane, made desperate/frantic **2)** *nm* fanatic: *nm* **dilyardi**

dilyárdyol *vi* be driven crazy: *pp/adj* **dilyardilo**; **Mai-do-gáta dilyárdilem lêstar.** I was almost driven crazy by him. **Ánda láte dilyárdyovav.** I am being driven crazy because of her.

dilyarel *vt* **1)** annoy, pester: *pp/adj* **dilyardo 2)** drive insane, let down, make crazy, make a fool out of, use; **Dilyardyas man.** She deceived me. **3)** confuse, stupefy, mix-up **4)** *v/refl* **dilyarél-pe** act the fool; **Shavorrále, na dilyarén-tume!** Kids, don't act the fool!

dilyarimos *nm* **1)** craziness, foolishness, nonsense, stupidity **2)** annoyance

dilyávol/dilyol *vi* **1)** become crazy, become obsessed about, get crazy, go nuts over: *pp/adj* **dilailo**; **Woi dilyávol ánda l' shukar aktórya po tilivízhono.** She goes crazy over the handsome actors on television. **Diláilo ánda l' bezaxa.** He became obsessed with sin/sinning. **2)**

become forgetful/senile, suffer from Azheimer's disease; **Phurilítar thai diláili.** She grew old and became senile. **3)** become stupefied

dilyorri *nf* little fool, stupid fool

dimáta *nm/pl* donations, gifts, gratuities, hand-outs

diminyátsa *nf* morning

diminyatsáko *gen/adj* tomorrow's

diminyatsára *adv* from (the) morning

dímitsa *nf* hermaphrodite

dimokrasíya *nf* democracy

dimokrátiko *adj* democratic

Dimokráto *nm* democrat: *nf* **Dimokráta**

dimos *nm* donation, gift, offering, present

dímos-ánd-angáli *nf/phr* embrace, hug

dímos-ánda-wast *nm/phr* **1)** surrender **2)** confession **3)** offering of food and water to the deceased three days after death and before the first **pomana**

dímos-bule *comp/nm* **1)** sexual intercourse **2** swindle

dímos-dúma *comp/nm* **1)** conversation, speech, talk **2)** intrigue, plotting

dímos-pálpale *comp/nm* **1)** kick (*of a rifle*), rebound, ricochet **2)** reply, riposte **3)** echo

dímos-po-lazhav *nm/phr* **1)** affront; **pharo dimos-po-lazhav** serious affront **2)** seduction

dinelo *adj* asinine, silly

dino *pp/adj* **1)** given, hit, smitten, struck; **Dino Devlêstar sas.** He has been struck/smitten by God. **2)** *nm* donor: *nf* **dini, 3)** donation, gift

díno-yag *pp/adj* lit, on fire

dinyol *vi* be given/provided: *pp/adj* **dinilo**; **Chi mai dinyovav so mangav.** I am never given what I want. **Dinilo Devlêstar sas.** It was given/provided by God. **Dinilem baxt.** I was given luck.

dipartaménto *nm* department

diplóma *nf* diploma

diplomasíya *nf* diplomacy

diplomátiko *adj* diplomatic

diplomáto *nm* diplomat

dipositil *vt* deposit: *pp/adj* **dipositime** (*Am*)

dipósito *nm* **1)** bank deposit **2)** deposit centre, drop-off centre

dipóto *nm* depotl, drop-off station

dirêkto *adj/adv* direct, directly

direktóri *nm* director; **directóri-egsekutívo** executive director: *nf* **direktórka**

Disímbra *nf* December

Disímbrone *adv* in December

disiplíno *nm* discipline

disízhiya *nf* decision

dísko *nm* **1)** floppy disk, disk **2)** discothèque

dísko-muzíka *comp/nf* disco music (*Eur*)

dískorôk *nm* disco rock, a fusion of disco, rock and Romani rhythm sources performed by Roma in Europe by Romani musicians.(*Eur*)

diskorokíl-pe *v/refl* dance disco rock (*Eur*)

diskotéka *nm* discothèque (*Eur*)

diskriminátsiya *nf* discrimination

diskútsiya *nf* discussion

disponíblo *adj* available (*Eur*)

Ditróya *nf* Detroit (*Am*)

diváno *nm see* **diwáno** *nm*

dividi *nm* DVD

divinil *vt* advise, discuss, negotiate*: pp/adj* **divinime**

divinimos *nm* advice, advising, conversation, talk

divizil *vt* **1)** divide: *pp/adj* **divizime 2)** *v/refl* **divizíl-pe** divide into itself, divide evenly

divizíya *nf* **1)** division (*Mil*) **2)** division (*mathematics*)

divliyarel *vt* make feral/wild: *pp/adj* **divliyardo**

dívliyi zhívini *nf/pl* wild game

dívliyo/dívlyo *adj* **1)** feral, untamed, wild; ~ **buriyátsa** wild mushroom, ~ **mursh** wild man/savage, ~ **mútsa** lynx/wildcat, ~ **rrátsa** wild goose, ~ **than** wilderness, wild place, ~ **tseléri** wild celery, ~ **zhukel** coyote/wild dog

divliyol/divlyol *vi* become wild, go feral, run wild: *pp/adj* **divliyailo**; **Divliyáilo o**

zhukel hai nashlótar. The dog went feral and ran off.

divliyomos *nm* wildness, wild state

dívliyo-mútsa *comp/nf* feral cat, lynx, wildcat

diwanil 1) *vt* converse, negotiate, parley: *pp/adj* **diwanime**; **Diwanin âmpochimós.** They are negotiating an agreement. **2)** *v/ref* **diwaníl-pe** chat informally, debate, hold a meeting, meet to discuss *smth,* parley; **Diwanín-pe ánda gadya buki.** They are discussing that issue.

diwanime *pp/adj* discussed, negotiated

diwáno *nm* **1)** conference, debate, meeting, negotiation, pre-tribunal judicial discussion among Roma to avoid a tribunal court: *pl* **diwáya 2)** discussion, parley, talk

diwanósko *nm* chatty, loquacious, talkative

diyákono *nm* deacon

Diyáspora *nf* Diaspora

diyaz *nm* sharp (*Mus*) *pl* **diyázurya; Re diyaz** D sharp

dîz *nf* castle, fortress

dizáko-túrno *comp/nm* look-out tower of a fortress, watchtower in a fortified zone (*Eur*)

dóba *nf* moment, time, occasion; **Aresli e dóba.** The time has come.

dobáro *nm* brewery

dobúnda *nf* advantage, gain, income, profit; **Che dobúnda lem lêstar?** What profit/advantage did I get from it/What was in it for me?

dobundil *vt* **1)** make profit, profit from, emerge with advantage: *pp/adj* **dobundime 2)** achieve, gain, **3)** succed **4)** *v/refl* **dobundíl-pe** be of advantage, gain, profit; **Dobundívas-man katar godya buki.** I was profiting from that work.

dobundimos *nm* achievement, success

do-fatsángo *gen/adj* two-faced, double-sided

doftoría *nf* doctor's office, medical clinic

dóftoro/dóktoro *nm* medical doctor, physician: *nf* **doftorútsa**

do-gazhyángo *gen/adj* bigamous (*a non-Rom*)

do-gêrbèngo double-humped; **Do-gêrbèngi gûmíla** Bactrian camel

dohanil *vt* 1) smoke (*cigarette, cigar, pipe*): *pp/adj* **dohanime** 2) *v/refl* **dohaníl-pe**

dohanimos *nm* smoking

doháno/doxáno *nm* tobacco; **dohanóski-trushul** tobacco pouch

dokhum *nf* 1) fist. 2) punch, blow with a fist 3) *comp/vt/i* **phandel** ~ clench one's fist; **Phanglas lêski dokhum thai dya lês ándo mui.** He cleched his fist and hit him in the mouth.

dóktoro/dóftoro *nm* medical doctor

dokumentáriyo *nm* documentary (*film*): *pl* **dokumentáriya**

dokumentátsiya *nf* documentation

dokumentil *vt* 1) document, record: *pp/adj* **dokumentime** 2) **dokumentíl-pe** *v/refl* be documented/verified by documents

dokuménto *nm* document

dola *dem/adj* those, *var of* **kodola** *qv* (*used before nf/pl*)

dole *dem/adj* those, *var of* **kodole** *qv* (*used before nm/pls*)

dológo *nm* 1) rein *pl* **dolózhi** 2) **del** ~ give free rein; **De dolózhi le grastes.** Give the horse its head/free rein 3) **tsírdel** ~ rein in, pull up on the reins

dominatóri *nm psn* who rules, ruler: *nf* **dominatórka** domineering women, wife who wears the pants

dominil *vt* dominate, run: *pp/adj* **dominime; O Shándor sáyek dominil le djuléshya.** Shandor always dominates the meetings.

dominimásko *gen/adj* domineering

dôminimós *nm* domination

domolimos *nm* calm. peace, quiet, silence

domólo *adj* calm, peaceful, quiet, silent

do-môngo *gen/adj* hypocritical, two-faced/double-mouthed; **Do-môngo-lo, kodo Rrom.** That man is two-faced.

dômpíl *vt* dispose of, dump: *pp/adj* **dômpimé**

dômpo *nm* 1) dump, garbage dump 2) *fig* substandard housing, dump, hovel, slum (*Am*)

dômpstéri *nm* dumpster (*Am*)

domukh *nf* fist *see also* **dokhum** *nf*

domult *adv* for a long time, a long time ago; **Domult mánde–lo.** I've had it for a long time. **Chi dikhlem la domult.** I haven't seen her for a long time.

domultano *adj* 1) a long time ago, in the ancient past 2) obsolete, outmoded

domúzo *adj* 1) dense, obstinate, persistent, pig-headed, stubborn, thick-headed 2) *nm* dense/thick-headed/stubborn boy or man: *nf* **domuzútsa**

don *pron/acc* the two of them, them both; **Dikhlem le don.** I saw both of them. **Dem-dúma le dónsa.** I spoke with both of them.

dónde *pron/prep* between two, into two parts; **Phaglo dónde.** It broke in two.

dôngo *gen/adj* belonging to the two of them/to both of them, jointly-owned; **Le dôngo si o mobile.** The car is owned by both of them.

do-partyáko *gen/adj* two-part

do-pash *adj/adv* 1) half; **do-pash mulo** half dead, **do-pash peko** half-cooked, medium cooked, **Do–pash Rrom si.** He is half Romani. **do-pash-gazho** transsexual male, **do-pash-gazhi** transsexual female 2) *nf* half; **Áke tiri do-pash.** Here is your half (*of it*).

do-pash drom *adv/phr* halfway, half the way

do-pash nango *adv/phr* half naked, skimpily dressed

do-pash yázno *comp/adj* not clear, opaque

dopashil *vt* 1) divide in half, split into two shares: *pp/adj* **dopashime** 2) *v/refl* **dopashíl-pe** divide itself; **Chi dopashíl-pe wórta.** It won't divide equally into two equal parts/amounts.

dopashin *nf* half; **Shindyas e phabai ánde dopashin.** She sliced the apple in half.

do-pash-ryat *nf/adv* **1**) midnight **2**) *comp/nf* midnight

dópo *nm* **1**) portable anvil **2**) anvil support, *us* a hollow car axle with one wheel-mount sawn off which allows different small anvils or formers with stems to be placed in the open end of the axle and used to rivet handles on pots and pans.

dori galbênsa *comp/nf* strip of ribbon with gold coins attached to decorate female braids

dori *nf* **1**) ribbon, lace **2**) string **3**) fishing line **4**) natal cord

do-rêgáko *gen/adj* double-sided, two-sided

doril *vt* long for, miss, yearn for: *pp/adj* **dorime; Doril pêske familíya.** He misses his family.

dorimos *nm* longing, nostalgia, yearning

dormitóryo *nm* dormitory

doralo *adj* nostalgic

dóro *nm* longing, nostalgia, yearning

do-rromnyángo *gen/adj* bigamous (*if Rom with two Romani wives*)

dorya *nf/pl* bunting

doryávo *nm* river

dosári *nm* dossier, personal file, police file (*Eur*)

dosh *adj* **1**) guilty; **Wo sas dosh** He was guilty **2**) wrong; **Dosh san**. You are wrong.

dosh *nf* **1**) guilt **2**) blame **3**) fault

doshado *nm* guilty party, *psn* found guilty of a crime/offence: *nf* **doshadi**

doshardo *nm psn* accused in a trial, accused, defendant, suspect: *nf* **doshardi**

doshárdyol *vi* be accused/blamed: *pp/adj* **doshardilo; Doshárdilem núma bi-dosháko sím**. I have been accused but I am innocent. **Pansh zhene doshárdile.** Five people have been accused.

dosharel *vt* **1**) accuse, bring/lay charges: *pp/adj* **doshardo 2**) blame

dosharimos *nm* **1**) accusation of guilt **2**) evidence of guilt **3**) blame

doshavel *vt* commit a crime/offence: *pp/adj* **doshado**

do-shibángo *gen/adj* bilingual

doshwalo/doshalo *adj* **1**) at fault, culpable, guilty, responsible; **Chi sim doshwalo.** It's not my fault. **2**) *nm* guilty party, person responsible for *smthg*: *nf* **doshwali**

dósta *adv/pron/interj* ample, enough, plenty, sufficient; **Dósta!** Enough! **Manai dósta.** There isn't enough. **Si tu dósta xabe?** Do you have enough food? **Xalem dósta te chailyarel man**. I have eaten enough to satiate me. **Dósta zhene avile kai sláva**. Plenty of people came to the feast. **Woi si dósta bari te moritíl-pe**. She is big enough to get married. **Dósta bokhalo sim te xav sórro shônko**. I am hungry enough to eat the entire ham. **Si ma dósta buki te kerav**. I have enough work to do.

dostéri *nm* duster (*type of Western, light overcoat/raincoat*) (*Am*)

dostuwil/dostoyil *vt/i* **1**) be sufficient/enough for, last through, suffice for: *pp/adj* **dostuwime** ; **O xabe chi dostuwil e sláva**. The food won't last through the feast. **2**) *v/refl* **dostuwíl-pe** be sufficient, last; **Chi dostuwíl-pe**. It won't be enough.

do-xulángo *gen/adj* belonging to two masters/owners

Dóyka *voc* address to an older matron or elderly woman

drab *nm* drug, herb, chemical

draba *nm/pl* **1**) chemicals for coppersmithing work **2**) herbal remedies

drabarel *vt* **1**) read, give readings, tell fortunes: *pp/adj* **drabardo 2**) apply holistic medicines, heal spiritually **3**) practice herbal medicine and midwifery **4**) *comp/vi* ~ **angle** predict to the future **5**) *comp/vi* ~ **anglal** predict from the future **6**) *comp/vi* ~ **le cheránsa** practice astrology

drabarimásko *gen/adj* having to do with counseling, reading

drabarimásko-mobíli *comp/nm* mobile parlour, usually a van fitted out for readings.

drabarimos *nm* reader-advising, client counseling, divination, psychic reading, telling fortunes; **Drabarimos le wastênsa** palmistry.

drabarni *nf* counselor, psychic, reader-advisor, fortune-teller, herbalist

drabarno *nm* **1)** healer, herbal doctor, *fig* witch doctor **2)** male reader advisor: Traditionally, men never practiced **drabarimos**, which was the major and exclusive female occupation. But recently, in the US and Canada, many Romani men have developed their own form of **drabarimos**, usually offering advice on financial/business investment, astrology, employment counseling, immigration, etc and usually term themselves "professors" or **profesórya**. The husband will open his own office away from his wife's parlour or adjacent to it. He usually works in conjunction with qualified non-Roma such as lawyers, medical doctors, employment agencies, etc.

draborre *nm/pl* cooking/kitchen herbs (*Cul*)

dráfto *nm/neolog* draft, initial draft

drágo *adj* **1)** beloved, darling, dear **2)** *nm* affection, enjoyment, fun, pleasure, preference; *id* **Drágo mánge te gilabav ánde lávuta.** I enjoy playing the fiddle. **Drágo san mánge kadya.** I like/prefer you like that. **Si-man báro drágo túke.** I have great affection for you. **Che drágo!** What pleasure! **3)** *nm* beloved, darling: *nf* **drága; So kames, múrri drága?** What do you want, my darling?

dragóstar *adv/nms/abl* out of affection, willingly

dragostóso *adj* **1)** admirable, affable, charming, endearing nice, sweet; **Wo si dragostóso shavorro.** He's an endearing little fellow. **2)** beloved, dear, esteemed; **Tu san amênge dragostóso.** You are very dear to us. **3)** *adv* affably

drágostya *nf* **1)** admiration, adoration, affection, agapic love, esteem, friendship **2)** passion (*for smthg*); **Le grast si lêske drágostya.** Horses (*horse racing*) are his passion.

dragúno *nm* dragon: *nf* **dragunáika**

drakála *nf* straw mattress

drakh *nf* grape

drakhelin/drakhin *nf/neolog* network

dráma *nf* drama, feature film, play, play acting: *pl* **drémi**

dramátichka *nf* actress, dramatist (*Eur*)

dramátiko *nm* actor: *pl* **dramátichi** (*Eur*)

drámo *nm* dram, ounce

drántsa *nf* toll booth/gate, toll gate, turnpike

drépto *adj* **1)** right **2)** *nm* right, (*under law*): *pl* **drépturya** rights (*Eur*); **Drépturya Manushênge** Human Rights

drépto pe búkfa *nf/phr* copyright

drobroi/dobroi *id* greetings, good day *us used with* **mai; Mai drobroi tu, Káko Stánko!** Good Day to you, Uncle Stanko!

drochin *nf* dew

drochinalo *adj* covered with dew, dewy

drom *nm* **1)** highway, road, roadway, street (*see also* **úlitsa** *nf*) **2)** method, way **3)** *id* journey, travels, trip; **Lasho drom túke/tumênge!** Have a good/safe journey! (**túke**, *for one psn* **tumênge** *for more than one psn*). **Sámas pansh ges po drom.** The trip took five days. **4)** life on the road, traveling life; **Chi zhanélas o drom.** He never knew life on the road. **5)** direction, way **6)** way; **Lem múrro drom.** I went on my way, **Zha tíro drom!** Be on your way! **7)** ~ **tudkalime** paved road **8)** ~ **bi-tudkalime** dirt road **9)** **múlo** ~ cul-de-sac, dead-end road, road going nowhere **10)** *comp/vt* **del** ~ chase away/out, get rid of, dump (*smbdy*)

dromári *nm* commercial traveler, traveling salesman

dromênge Rrom *nm/pl* traveling/nomadic Roma

dromênge-sámnurya *comp/nm* highway signs, route markers, trail signs

dromêske-pátsini *comp/nf* rollerblades, roller-skates

dromêsko suvári *comp/nm* spider (*road sewer*)

dromêsko/dromêngo of the road/of the roads

dromorro *nm* alley, lane, narrow road, small road

drópya *nf* pheasant; **drópya-tsini** quail

drostári *nm* druggist, pharmacist: *nf* **drostárka** woman working in a pharmacy (*Am*)

drósto *nm* drugstore (*Am*)

drûncheníko *nm* 1) yoke of an ox, crossbar of a wagon shaft to which ox harness is attached 2) horse collar 2) type of yoke or bar suspended from horse collars to the outer end of the shaft of the cart or wagon.

drûncheníl *vt* 1) make to jar/jolt/rattle/shake/vibrate: *pp/adj* **drûnchenimé; drûnchenimé-lo** He's all shook up (*Am*) 2) *v/refl* **drûncheníl-pe** rattle, shake, vibrate

drûnchenimós *nm* 1) jolt, rattle, rattling, shaking, vibration 2) turbulence

dubil *vt* 1) achieve, conquer, succeed, win: *pp/adj* **dubime** 2) *v/refl* **dubíl-pe** be successful, pass (*test*), win, win out

dubime *pp/adj* conquered, successful, victorious

dubimos *nm* achievement, conquest, success, victory, winnings

dubitóri *nm* achiever, conqueror, victor, winner: *nf* **dubitórka**

dúcha *nf* shower

duchíl-pe *v/refl* take a shower

dúda *nf* mulberry

dudelin *nf* mulberry bush

dudum *nm* 1) pumpkin 2) gourd

Dudumêngi-Ryat *comp/nf* Halloween (*Can*)

dudumorro *nm* squash, zucchini

dugnimos 1) contamination 2) decomposition, putrification

dugnyailo *pp/adj* 1) contaminated 2) decomposed, putrid, rotten

dugnyal *vi* 1) become contaminated/putrid: *pp/adj* **dugnailo** 2) decompose, go bad, rot (*meat*): **O shônko dugnáilo.** The ham went bad

dugnyála *nf* gut-wrenching stink, nauseous odor, putrid smell, rotting stench

dui 1) *num* two 2) *pron* two people, both *see also* **soldui** *pron*

dui viráma *nm/pl/neolog* colon

dúito *num* 1) second 2) next

Dúito-Marimos *nm* Second World War

dui-war *adv* twice, two times; **Si dui-war mai baro**. It is two times bigger.

duiyali *nf* number two, two in cards

dui-yêkh-fyálo *comp/adj* both the same

duiyorre *nm/pl* two little ones/children: *nf/pl* **duiyorre; Ansurimé-lo, duiyorrênsa.** He's married with two small children.

dukáto *nm* attorney, lawyer: *nf* **dukáika/dukatútsa** (*Am*)

dukh ándo gi *nm/phr* bellyache

dukh ándo shoro *nm/phr* headache

dukh *nf* 1) ache, agony, anguish, hurt, pain; **Xalyas but dukh pêske pûnrrèstar.** He has suffered a lot of pain from his leg. 2) pang (*of hunger*); **dukha bokalimástar** pangs of hunger

dukhado *pp/adj* 1) hurt, injured 2) *nm* injured man, casualty, victim (*if non-fatal*)

dukhádyol *vi* 1) become hurt/injured, become painful, suffer pain: *pp/adj* **dukhadilo; Arakh-tut te na dukhádyos!** Be careful you don't get hurt! 2) be insulted/offended, take offence

dukhal *vt/i* ache, hurt, be hurting/sore: *pp/adj* **dukhailo; Dukhal ma o shoro.** My head aches.

dukhalimos *nm* agony, anguish, pain, suffering

dukhalo *adj* 1) agonizing, full of pain, hurting, painful 2) detrimental

dukhavel *vt* 1) cause pain, hurt, injure: *pp/adj* **dukhado** 2) insult, give offence, offend

dukhayimásko *gen/adj* agonizing, anguished, suffering

dukhayimos *nm* agony, pain, suffering

dukhayitóri *nm* bugbear, pain in the ass, pest, tormentor, (*fig*) torturer: *nf* **dukhayitórka**

dukil *vt* confront: *pp/adj* **dukime** (*Am*)

dukimos *nm* confrontation (*Am*)

dukyáno *nm* 1) shop, store 2) *arch* storefront reader-advisor parlour with living quarters

dukyanzhívo *nm* store owner/keeper, store manager

dum A word without meaning used in folktales, songs and poems to create rhyming sentences as an aid to remembering them; **Katar o brégo. kai dum lel la, thai ándo pái, kai dum thol la.** From the river bank he takes her, and into the water, he places her.(*Folk*)

dúma *nf* 1) speech, talk, common speech, everyday speech; **krisáki-dúma** ornate, flowery speech used in the Romani tribunal of elders 2) *comp/vt/i* **del ~** give talk, speak; **Des-dúma Romanes?** Do you speak like a Rom? 3) *v/refl* **del-pe dúma a)** be spoken about; **Nashti del-pe dúma gadya buki.** That matter is not up for discussion. **b)** hatch *smth,* plot; **Dénas-pe dúma garades.** They were plotting in secret.

dumalo *adj* broad shouldered, having wide shoulders; **Dumalo sim, chi maládyol mánge e raxámi.** I have broad shoulders, the jacket won't fit me.

dumo *nm* back, shoulder; **Símas katána, púshka po dumo.** I was a soldier, (with a) gun on (my) shoulder.

Dunérya *nf* Danube

dúnga *nf* brim, edge, rim

duplikatíl *vt* 1) duplicate: *pp/adj* **duplikatime** 2) *v/refl* **duplikatíl-pe** be duplicated

duplikáto *nm* duplicate

duplikátsiya *nf* duplication

dur *adv* 1) distant, far, far off: *adv/phrs* 2) *comps with* **dur;** ~ **ánde-ryát** far into the

night, until very late 3) ~ **andre** far inside, far into 4) ~ **tele** far down, deep 5) ~ **opre** far up, high up

dural *adv* 1) from afar, from far away; **But Rroma avile, pashal hai dural.** Many Roma came, from nearby and from far away. 2) distant (*in relationship*); **nyámo dural** distant relative, maternal relative

durano *adj* a long way off, distant, far, remote

durikano *adj* distant, far-away, at long range: *adv* **durikanes; Ashundem e muzíka durikanes.** I heard the music far off in the distance.

durimos *nm* distance, endurance, mileage, range; **Sóde si de durimos po galóno?** What's the mileage per gallon (of the car)?

during *adv* far, far away; **Na zhan during, shavorrále!** Don't go far away, children!

durkérdyol *vi* be predicted; *pp/adj* **dukerdilo; Durkérdilo do-mult.** It was predicted a long time ago. (*Eur*)

durkerel *vt* predict, predict the future: *pp/adj* **durkerdo** (*Eur*)

durkerimos *nm* prediction, prophecy (*Eur*)

duruli/turuli *nf* barrel, cask, keg

duryádyol *vi* 1) become distanced, isolated: *pp/adj* **duradilo** 2) be banished, expelled, retired, sent away

duryarel *vt* 1) drive/send/push further away: *pp/adj* **duryardo** 2) remove, take away, put distance between 3) banish, expel, retire, send away 4) remand, move to a later date

duryol *vi* 1) move away from, move/get further away, distance oneself, *us with* **mai**: *pp/adj* **durilo; Mai duryol amênder.** It's getting further away from us. **Mai durilem lêndar.** I got far away from them. **E furtúna mai duryol.** The storm is moving away. 2) be extend, be remanded

dushil *vt* 1) milk (*cow*): *pp/adj* **dushime** 2) draw milk/sustenance from, siphon, sponge off; **Dushil pêski familíya.** He sponges off his family.

dushimos *nm* milking, milking time

dushmanil *vt* **1)** make an enemy/enemies, have enmity for: *pp/adj* **dushmanime 2)** *v/refl* **dushmaníl-pe** hate oneself, be one's (worst) enemy; **Dushmaníl-pe godo Rrom.** That Rom is his own worst enemy.

dushmanítsko *adj* enemy, hostile

dushmanitskones *adv* hostilely, in a hostile manner

dushmaníya *nf* **1)** animosity, antagonism, enmity, hatred, rancor **2)** prejudice **3)** spite

dushmáno *nm* adversary*,* enemy, opponent: *pl* **dushmáya** *nf* **dushmánka**

duwares *adv* twice; **Tsipisáili duwares kána istráili po pávo.** She yelled twice when she slipped on the ice.

dúxo *nm* **1)** soul **2)** spirit **3)** spirit or ghost of a specific *psn*; **O Swînto Dúxo** The Holy Ghost; **Lêski bershêski pomána si gáta akana, anklisto lêsko dúxo ándo Rrayo.** His year-long mourning period is ended now, his soul has ascended into Heaven. **3)** psyche **4)** fragrance, perfume, scent

dúya *nf* berry (*Eur*) *see also* **múra** *nf*

dyárra *nf* teeth of a key

dyéla *nf see* **djéla** *nf*

dyes/djes *nm see* **ges** *nm*

DJ

djakil *vt* **1)** jack up: *pp/adj* **djakime** *(Am)* **2)** *v/refl* **djakíl-pe** be jacked up; **Chi djakíl-pe o mobíli.** The car isn't allowing itself to be raised by the car jack.

djáko *nm* car jack *(Am);* **Lasharel djákurya.** He repairs automobile jacks.

djámena/djámiya *nf* mosque

djángêlo *nm* jungle *(Eur);* **Kerél-pe sar dívliyo mursh katar o djángêlo.** He behaves like a wild man from the jungle/He is unacquainted with civilized behaviour.

Djanuwári *nm* January

Djanuwárone *adv* in January

Djaponézo *nm* Japanese man: *nf* **Djaponezáika** *see also* **Nipóntso** *nm*

djardinash *nm* gardener: *nf* **djardináshka**

djardíno *nf* flower garden, garden

djédjêsh *nm* train; **Zháltar o djédjêsh hai me níchi.** The train is leaving and I'm not/I am being left out of what is happening.

djéla/dyéla *nf* act, affair, deal, deed, thing, object, matter; **Nai bári djéla.** It's not an important matter/big deal. **Kerel djéli malade.** He does foolish acts/deeds.

djeláto *nm* **1)** ice cream *(Eur)* **2)** jelly *(Am)*

djelútsa **1)** little thing/matter, trifling thing/matter **2)** bauble, knickknack, toy

djendjinéri *nm* engine driver, engineer

djenosída *nf* genocide *(Eur)*

djépo *nm* pocket; **Thon sa le love ándo djépo.** The put all the money in (their own) pocket. *(Eur)*

djéti *nm* jetty, landing, pier

djéto *nm* jetliner, jet-propelled aircraft *(Am);* **Huryárdilem po djéto.** I flew in by jetliner.

djikûn/zhikûn *adv/conj* ever since, for, for how long, since, since when; **Chi avilo kónik djikûn me areslem.** Nobody has come here since I arrived.

djinerálno *adj/adv* general/generally

djinerálo *nm* general *(Mil)*

djineratóri *nm* generator

djinerátsiya *nf* generation

djíni *nm/pl* jeans, bluejeans

djípo *nm* jeep *(Am)*

djípsa *nf* gypsum, wallboard *(Am)*

djônkári *nm* junk dealer *(Am)*

djônko *nm* junk, junk automobile *(Am)*

djori *nf* hinny *(mule fathered by a stallion from a female donkey)*

djoro *nm* mule *(mule fathered by a stud donkey from a mare)*

djuléshi *nm* business meeting: *pl* **djuléshya** *(Eur)*

djúli *nf* wood nymph *(Folk);* **Le djúlya farmakuyisarde lês.** The wood nymphs bewitched him.

Djúlone *adv* in July

Djúlyo *nm* July

djúnga *nf* ugly woman/female creature/thing *(if nf);* **bári djúnga** ugly thing/brute, eyesore; **Che bári djúnga!** What an ugly sight!

djúngale-swáturya *comp/nm/pl* vulgarity

djúngali-buki *comp/nf* eyesore

djungalimáta *nm/pl* foul language, obscenities, verbal ugliness

djungalimos *nm* **1)** disorder, disfigurement, ugliness, ugly mess, unsightliness **2)** disgraceful or ugly behaviour/conduct, vulgarity

djungalo *adj* **1)** grotesque, ugly, unsightly **2)** inapproporiate, nasty, off-colour, vulgar; **djúngale vórbi** off-colour comments/remarks **3)** rough (*not smooth*) **4)** littered, messy **5)** dangerous, disturbing. foreboding; **djungalo suno** a disturbing dream **6) djúngale-fármichi** *comp/nf* black/evil magic

djúngalo-swáto *comp/nm* swear word, verbal obscenity, vulgarism

djungárdyol *vi* **1)** become ugly/disfigured/uglified: *pp/adj* **djungardilo 2)** become littered, messy

djungarel *vt* **1)** to make ugly, uglify, ruin (*a job of work*), deface, disfigure, mess up. **2)** make messy, litter with trash, trash up; **Sya djungarde o hãlo le shavorre**, The kids meade a real mess of the hall. **Djungarde o kher**, They trashed the house.

djungáto *nm* ugly man/creature/specimen/thing (*if nm*), eyesore; **Che baro djungáto!** What an ugly behemoth! **O grast sas baro djungáto.** The horse was a great ugly specimen.

djungáwol *vi* become uglified/ugly: *pp/adj* **djungailo**

Djúnone *adv* in June

Djúnyo *nm* June

djuráko *nm* jurist: *nf* **djuráika** *nf*

Djúrdjevdan/Djurdjevdáno *nm* St. George's Day (*May 6th and celebrated by* **Machwáya** *but not* **Kalderash**)

Djurdjevdáne *adv* on St. George's Day

djúri *nm* jury

djurnálo *nm* **1)** journal **2)** newspaper **3)** magazine **4)** diary

E

e *def/art/f* the; **e rakli** the girl; **E rakli avel.** The girl is coming.

Edáno *nm* Eden, Garden of Eden

Ederlézi *nm see* **Hederlézi** *nm*

êdíshono *nm* edition (*Am*)

êditóri *nm* editor (*Am*): *nf* **êditórka** (*Am*)

edítsiya *nf* edition *nf/neolog*

Edjiptáno *nm* Egyptian: *nf* **Edjiptánka**

Edjípto *nm* Egypt

Edjiptósko *gen/adj* Egyptian; **Edjiptóski ponyáva** Egyptian carpet

edukátsiya *nf* education

edukatsyálno *adj* educational

egalitéto *nm/neolog* equity, equality (*Eur*); **egalitéto kulturáko** cultural equality

Eiy ! *adv* Yes! **Eiy, ashunav!** Yes I'm listening. (*Am*). **Ashunes ma?** Are you hearing me? **Eiy.** Yes, I am.

êkh *num* **1)** one *see also* **yêkh 2)** *indef/art* a, an; **Sas hai nas hai shai-vi avel êkh phuro thai êkh phuri**... There was once, and there was not, and there may be again, an old man and an old woman... (*typical beginning of a folktale*). **Note: êkh** and **yêkh** *qv* can be used as an *indef* article in *Kalderash* but it is more usually omitted except in formal or rhetotical speech and in folktales, songs and poems.

êkhé-thanes *adv* together (*Eur*) *see* **ánd-ekh-than** *adv/phr*

ekípa *nf* team (*Eur*)

ekráno *nm* screen, movie screen (*Eur*)

ekspertízo *nm/neolog* expertise

ekspérto *nm* expert

eksplikil *vt* **1)** explain: *pp/adj* **eksplikime 2)** *v/refl* **eksplikíl-pe** explain oneself, explain (*Eur*)

êlifánto/ilifánto *nm* elephant *see also* **worosláno** *nm*

êmayévo *nm* enamel

êmayevósko *gen/adj* made of enamel

êmigránto *nm* emigrant: *nf* **êmigrantáika**

êmigrántsiya *nf* emigration

emísiya *nf* broadcast, emission, program

êmperáto/imperáto *nm* **1)** king **2)** emperor

êmperatóski-rakli *comp/nf* princess (*Am*)

êmperatósko *adj* belonging to a king, royal

êmperatósko-raklo *comp/nm* prince (*Am*)

êmperatsíya *nf* kingdom, empire

êmperatyása *nf* **1)** queen **2)** empress

êmvelópa *nf* envelope, file folder

êndjino *nm* engine (*Am*)

erowína *nf* heroin

-êshti *pron/suff/mf/pl* This is suffixed to the names of founders, totemic animals, ancestral trades, geographical regions, etc, of Vlax-Romani clans; **Mihaiyêshti** People of **Mihai**, **Zurkéshti**, descendents of **Zúrka**, **Bukarêshti** People from Bucharest

-êshto *prod/suff/m/s* indicates a male member of a group; **Grofêshto**, male member of the **Grofêshti** clan: *see* **–êshti** *prod/suff*

-êshtútsa *prod.suff/f/s* indicates a female member of a group; **Minêshtútsa** female member of the **Mineshti** clan: *see* **–êshti** *prod/suff*

espesyálno *adv* especially

Êstikáno *adj* Eastern; **Êstikáno Ivrópa** Eastern Europe (*Eur*)

êstimatíl *vt* estimate: *pp/adj* **êstimatimé**

êstimáto *nm* estimate

Éta! *interj/id* Behold! Look! There it is!; **Éta-lo pe l' phaleya!** There it is, on the floor! **Éta-la! E Mára!** Look! Here is Mary! **Éta-le, le sháturya!** Behold them, the big shots!

etnikálno *adj* ethnic

étniko *nm* ethnicity

Éva/Yéva *nf* Eve; **Adámo thai Yéva** Adam and Eve

evalyuwátsiya *nf* evaluation

evangelísmo *nf* evangelism

evangelísta *nf* evangelist (*Eur*)

Evangéliya/Evangelíya *nf* Gospel (*Eur*)

êvidènsiya *nf* evidence *see also* **próba** *nf*

Evraziyáno *adj* 1) Eurasian 2) *nm* Eurasian man: *nf* **Evraziyánka**

ézero *num/nm* thousand (*Eur*): *pl* **ézera; Trobun lês trin ézera tiléri**. He needs three-thousand dollars.

F

fábrika *nf* factory, plant: *pl* **fábrichi**

fakalêtso *nm* **1)** rolling pin **2)** chump, fall guy, patsy, stooge, sucker **3)** victim **4)** *sl* suit (*minor official or beaurocrat/representative without power who is sent to deliver the official policy/party-line of his superiors*) (*Am*)

faksil *vt* **1)** fax: *pp/adj* **faksime 2)** *v/refl* **faksíl-pe** fax, be faxed

fákso *nm* fax; **Tradav po fákso.** I send by fax.

fákto *nm* fact, detail

faktúra *nf* bill, invoice

fakultéto *nm* faculty

fal *vi/def* **1)** it seems; **fal ma.** it seems to me. **Fal ma ke chi avel.** It seems to me that he is not coming. **Fálas man ke mato sas.** It seemed to me that he was intoxicated. **Sar fal túke?** How does it seem to you? Usually used with the dative case of nouns; **Fálas le Rromêske ke pêsko phral xoxavélas.** It seemed to the man that his brother was lying. **2)** feel; **Fal ma nasul.** I feel sick. **Mánge, fal ma ke xoxovélas.** In my opinion, I feel he was lying.

faláto *nm* germ, grain (*of truth*), iota, kernel, little bit, tiny bit; **Manai yêkh faláto chachimos an pêske vórbi.** There's not a grain of truth in his statements.

falil *vi* seem: *pp/adj* **falime** (*Eur*)

fálka *nf* chin, jaw: *pl* **fálchi**

falkóno *nm* falcon, hawk

fálsheno *adj* false, phony: *adv* **falshenones** falsely

fálsheno fátsa *comp/nf* false identity, misrepresentation

fálshivi-dánd *nm/pl* dentures

fálshivo *adj* artificial, counterfeit, false, phony, prosthetic

familíya *nf* family

familyáko nav *comp/nm* family name, surname

fanári *nm* lamp, lantern, streetlight, traffic light

fanátiko *nm* **1)** fanatic **2)** bigot: *pl* **fanátichi:** *nf* **fanatikútsa 3)** *adv* **sar o ~** fanatically, like a fanatic; **Del-dúma sar o fanátiko.** He speaks like a fanatic.

fánga *nf* **1)** fang **2)** eyetooth (*Am*)

fáno *nm* fan (*Am*)

fantasíya *nf* imagination, fantasy; **Lêsko barvalimos si fantasíya.** His wealth is fantasy.

Faravóno *nm* Pharaoh (*Eur*)

fárba *nf* **1)** paint **2)** dye, colouring, lipstick, make-up **3)** ink; **lóli fárba** red ink

farbári *nm* housepainter, painter

farbol *vt* **1)** paint: *pp/adj* **farbome 2)** colour, dye, stain **3)** cover up, hide the truth through fabrication **4)** *v/refl* **a)** **farból-pe** be painted, apply make-up **b)** be covered up with make-up/paint; **Farból-pe te garavel láko phurimos.** She covers herself with cosmetic goop to hide her age.

farbomos *nm* **1)** painting, paint job **2)** cover up

fárma-katári *nm* male spellbinder, magician, sorcerer, warlock, witch doctor

fárma-katárka *nf* enchantress, spellbinder, weaver of spells/magic, witch

fármako *nm* magic spell, spell

farmakuyil *vt* **1)** bewitch, enchant, cast under a spell, place a spell (on): *pp/adj*

farmakuyíme 2) mystify **3)** *v/refl*
farmakuyíl-pe bewitch oneself, delude
oneself
farmakuyímos *nm* enchantment, magic,
spellbinding, witchcraft
fármichi *nm/pl* magic, sorcery, witchcraft;
Kerel fármichi e phuri. The old lady
practices witchcraft. **Le rai line la pe l'**
fármichi. The police charged her with
witchcraft; **fármichi djungale** *compl/nm*
black/evil magic (*Am*)
farmichil *vt* perform sorcery, work
magic/witchcraft: *pp/adj* **farmichíme**
bewitched, spellbound, beguiled with
spells
fáro *nm* lighthouse: *pl* **fárya** (*Eur*)
Farsikanítska *nf* Persian (*Lang*)
Farsikanítsko *gen/adj* Persian
Farsikáno *nm* Persian *nm*: **Farsikánka** *nf*
Farsíya *nf* Persia (*Iran*)
Fashísmo *nm* Fascism (*Eur*)
Fashísto *adj* **1)** Fascist **2)** *nm* Fascist: *nf*
Fashísta (*Eur*)
fátsa *nf* **1)** façade, front: *pl* **fêtsi 2)** face
(*Anat*); **O manrro si e fátsa l' Devlêski.**
Bread is the face of God (*admonition not
to walk on bread lying on the floor*) **3)** flat
surface; **fátsa sinyáki** table top **4)** colour
5) identity **6)** pattern **7)** appearance,
looks; **Chi kamav lêski fátsa.** I don't
like the look of him. **8)** attitude,
personality **9)** phase **10)** *vt* **del ~** turn face
up, face upwards, face towards; **Dine**
fêtsi pênge dushmáya. They faced their
enemies. **11)** *v/ref* **dél-pe fátsa** face, face
up to *smth*. **Dyas fátsa ka l' pêske**
bezexa. He faced up to his sins.
fatsáko *gen/adj* of the face, facial, surface,
top
fátsa-palal *comp/adv* back to front,
backwards, the wrong way round
fátsiya *nf* fashion; in ~, **ánde fátsiya**
fávula *nf* fable, story
feder *comparative/adv* better *us with* **mai;**
mai feder better, preferable; **Mai feder**
te zhas akana neg te zhas mai palorral.
It's better/preferable we go now than we

go later. *See also more common* **mai**
mishto *comparative/adv*
federátsiya *nf* federation
felésho *nm* **1)** hem **2)** frill, fringe, ruffle **3)**
pleat
féli *nm* **1)** hitch, loop, noose: *pl* **félya 2)**
snare
féliya *nf* slice (*of bread, ham, etc*)
félo *nf* **1)** baffle plate, washer **2)** **félya**
félshero *nm* expert, specialist: *pl* **félsherya:**
nf **fêlsherútsa**
félta *nf* felt
feltáko *gen/adj* made of felt
félya *nf/pl* threaded bolt with matching nut
fénda *nf see* **fendéri** *nm*
fendéri *nm* automobile fender, mudguard;
Wortólas fendérya múrro pápo. My
grandfather used to straighten out
automobile fenders. (*Am*)
féndi *nf/pl* **1)** fenders **2)** repairing of car
bodies and fenders (*Am*)
férdi *adv* barely, except, just, merely, only;
Savorro zhal férdi lêstar. Everybody is
going except him. **Tu san lasho**
shavorro, férdi… You are a good boy,
except… **Pokindem lês e súma férdi**
pansh tilérya. I paid him the amount
except for five dollars. **So ashel te**
keras? What remains to be done? **Férdi**
wúni bukyorra. Merely some loose
ends/small things.
féri *adv* only, just, merely, barely *var of*
férdi *qv*
feril *vt* **1)** defend, guard, preserve, protect,
watch over: *pp/adj* **feríme; Te feril tut o**
Del! May God protect you/watch over
you! **Te feril ame o Del!** God help us! **2)**
prevent; **Te feril o Del.** May God prevent
it! **3)** *v/refl* **feríl-pe** be
guarded/protected/watched over
feríme 1) *pp/adj* defended/protected
against **2)** vaccinated, immune (*to a
disease*)
ferímos *nm* protection (*against*)
fériya *nf* fair: *pl* **féri; Bikinel kola ande l'**
féri pa'l gava. He sells items at the fairs
in the rural areas.

fêrla *nf* nostril (*Anat*)

férma *nm* farm, farmhouse

fermári *nm* farmer: *nf* **fermárka** farmer's wife: *nf* **fermarkútsa** farmer's daughter

féso/fézo *nm* fez

festiválo *nm* festival, pagent, street fair

Fevruwári *nm* February

Fevruwárone *adv* in February

fídesavo *pron/adj* any, any one, any other whichever one; **ándo fídesávo ges** during any other day, **Háide fídesávi vryámya!** Come anytime (you want)! **Le fídesavo túke!** Take whichever one you want!

fidévo *nm* 1) lid 2) top, cover

filástra *nf* 1) window 2) porthole 3) ~ in a computer

filástra-kashtêski *comp/nf* wooden window shutter

filastráke-khosárya *comp/nm/pl* windshield wipers

filatín *nf* 1) mansion 2) chateau 3) castle (*Eur*)

filéro *nm* switchblade knife (*Am fr Pachuco/Sp*): *pl* **filérya**

fílma *nf* film, roll of film

filosoféri *nm* philosopher: *nf* **filosoférka**

filosofíya *nf* philosophy

filtári *nm* quarter (*fraction*)

filtéri *nm* filter

fin *conj* because, if

fína *nf* goddaughter

findjáno *nm* finjan (*Eur*)

fínke *conj* because, if, should, since, on account of (*Eur*); **Fínke avel mánde chi mekav lês andre.** Should he come to my place I won't let him inside.

fíno *nm* godson

firánga *nf* 1) curtain, drape: *pl* **firénzhi** 2) veil, as in **káli firánga**, impenetrable veil of mystery; **Palechíno, muiyangátar, kai si kále firangátar.** Palechina, from your many faces, which are from a dark veil of impenetrable mystery. (*folk song* **Palechino**)

firánga-ducháki *comp/nf* shower curtain

firizil *vt* saw, cut with a saw: *pp/adj* **firizime**

firizimásko *gen/adj* having to do with sawing

firizimásko-asav *comp/nm* sawmill

firizimos *nm* sawing

firízo *nm* saw

fírma *nf* seal, signature

fíro *nm* 1) blade of, blade, petal: *pl* **fírya**; **fíro char** blade of grass. **rozáko fíro** rose petal. 2) fibre, strand, thread 3) filament

fistáno *nm* 1) traditional, ankle-length skirt of Vlax-Romani women 2) fancy dress that can be dry-cleaned 3) dressing gown, gown **Note:** The Romani cleanliness code requires that traditional Romani women must wear a two-piece blouse and skirt which can be washed separately. Fancy, gold-lamé dresses that can be dry cleaned and worn over underclothing are allowed in the US and Canada.

fitili *nm* wick

fláka *nf* fleet (*of ships*)

flanéla *nf* cardigan, sweater

fláshka/flyáshka *nf* flask

fláto *nm* 1) flat (*dwelling*) 2) flat tire (*Am*)

fléchka *nf* 1) dart 2 arrow

flechkítsa *nf* small dart

flínta *nf* 1) flintlock 2) popgun, shotgun 3) *arch* flintlock device for starting a fire

flúyera *nf* 1) flute, cane flute 2) tin whistle, whistle 2) calf of the leg

fluyeril *vt* 1) play the flute/tin whistle: *pp/adj* **fluyerime** 2) *v/refl* **fluyeríl-pe** be whistling, whistle

fluyerimos *nm* playing of the flute

flyáshka/fláshka *nf* 1) flask, bota 2) coquette, flirt

fóka *nf* seal (*Eur*)

fonétichi *nf/neolog* phonetics

fonétiko *adj/neolog* phonetic

fontána *nf* fountain, public water fountain (*Eur*)

forêsko/forósko *gen/adj* belonging to a town/city, urban; **forêske zakóya** urban by-laws

fórma *nf* 1) small, portable anvil with a stem which can be inserted into a **dópo** 2) pattern jig, casting mold, last, shape 3) fettle, physical condition, shape; **ánde láshi fórma** in good form/shape **4)** trick, prank; **Kerdyas fórma pe mánde.** He played a trick on me. **5)** behaviour, form (*Am*); **cháchi fórma** correct behaviour

formáno *nm* foreman, man in charge of a work crew

formáto *nm* format, formation (*Eur*)

fóro *nm* city, large town, market town: *pl* **fórya/fóri**

forósko/forêsko *gen/adj* municipal, of a town or city; **o baro le forósko** mayor of a city/town

forshipáno *nm* pair of horses, two-horse team

forúmo *nm/neolog* discussion group, forum

forútso *nm* small town

fóto *nm* photograph

fotokópiya *nf* **1)** photocopy **2)** *vt/i* **kerel ~** make a photocopy

fraiyil *vt/i* fry: *pp/adj* **fraiyime** (*Am*)

frangoshti *nf* cactus, prickly pear: *pl* **frangoshtya**

fránka *nf* quarter, twenty-five cent piece: *pl* **fránchi** (*Am*)

Fránsiya/Frántsiya *nf* France

Franzuzáko *gen/ádj* of France, French; **Franzuzáko-xabe** French food/cuisine

Franzuzítsa *nf* French girl, young French woman

Franzuzítska *nf* French (*Lang*)

Franzuzítsko *adj* French

Franzúzo *nm* **1)** Frenchman: *nf* **Franzuzáika** Frenchwoman **2)** France; **Golem ándo Franzúzo.** I went to France

fráza *nf/neolog* phrase

fremil *vt* frame (*photos*): *pp/adj* **fremime** (*Am*)

fremimos *nm* **1)** photo framing **2)** framework

fréna *nf* brake: *pl* **fréni** brakes *see also* **lopûnts**

fréno *nm* friend: *nf* **frenáika/frenútsa** (*Am*)

freshkil *vt* **1)** freshen up, make fresh, refresh: *pp/adj* **freshkime 2)** *v/refl* **freshlíl-pe** freshen oneself up

fréshko *adj* fresh

fréto *nm* fret (*Mus*)

frídjo *nm* refrigerator (*Am*)

frígo *nm* refrigerator (*Eur*)

frónto *nm* store-front reader-advisor parlour having a store front with a large window (*Am*)

frúkta *nf* fruit (*Eur*)

frûmêntíl *vt* knead (*dough*): *pp/adj* **frûmêntimé**

frûmêntimós *nm* kneading

frúta *nf* fruit (*Am*)

fryánsa *nf* venereal disease

fryansol *vt* **1)** infect with/spread venereal disease: *pp/adj* **fryamsome 2)** *v/refl* **fryansól-pe** become infected by venereal disease

fryansomos *nm* **1)** spread of venereal disease: *pl* **fryansomáta** venereal diseases

fúga *nf* **1)** escape, flight **2)** hurry **3)** speed

fugása *adv/nf/inst/s* in a hurry, quickly; **Golótar fugása.** He left in a flash.

fúgo *adj/adv* fast, quick, quickly; **Zha mai fúgo!** Drive faster!

fúmo *nm* industrial haze, smoke, smog (*Eur*)

fundáko *nm* **1)** bottom, stock (*of a rifle*) **2)** something that forms the base of something **3)** depth

fundamêntálo *adj* fundamental

fundamêto *nm* foundation, **fundament**

fundániya *nf* **1)** tent cover, main part of a tent covering **2)** body, main part (*of smth*) **3)** back wall of a tent **4)** background

fundatóri *nm* founder: *nf* **fundatórka**

fundátsiya *nm* base, firmament, foundation

fundil *vt* **1)** base (*smthg on*): *pp/adj* **fundime 2)** found **3)** *v/refl* **fundíl-pe** be based on; **Pe sóste fundíl-pe?** What is it based on?

fúndo bottom, base, foundation, pedestal base; **Nashti ingares pai ánde vádra bi-fundóski.** You can't transport water in a bucket with no bottom. (*proverb*) **2)** cargo hold, hold of a ship

funezhil *vt* **1)** cover with soot, make sooty: p*p/adj* **funezhime 2)** *v/refl* **funzehíl-pe** become covered with soot

funezhimos *nm* cleaning out of chimneys/stove canopies

funézhiya *nf* soot

funezhiyári *nm* **1)** *arch* chimney sweep **2)** man who cleans out chimneys and stove canopies for a living

fúrka *nf* fork (*Cul*), fork (*in the road*)

furkéri *nm* hay fork, pitchfork

furtúna *nf* **1)** storm, thunderstorm **2)** **ivêski ~** blizzard, snowstorm

fushágo *nm* **1)** firecracker **2)** bang-bang, whiz-bang, flare, explosive device used in firework displays **3)** flare, railway flare

fushégurya *nm/pl* fireworks display

fusui *nm* bean: *pl* **fusúi**; *The plural in* **fusui** *is commonly heard in Canada & the US for beans*

futbãlo *nm* American football (*Am*)

fûtból *nm* soccer (*Eur*)

fútra *nf* fur/down lining, lining in general, stuffing: *gen/adj* **futráko**

futrári *nm* furrier

futúra *nf* future

futuráko *adj* future

fyal/fyálo *nm* **1)** brand, kind, make (*automobile, etc*), sort; **Che fyal mobíli plachal tu?** What brand of car do you like/pleases you? **Dikhlem but fyálurya grast ándo vashári**. I saw many kinds of horses at the horse fair. **Si but fyálurya Rrom kathe.** There are many kinds of Roma here. **Sa yekh fyálo si.** They are all the same. **2)** diverse; **but fyálurya** a wide diversity

fyúzo *nm* fuse (*electrical*) (*Am*)

G

gabardína *nf* raincoat (*Eur*)

gad *nm* **1**) shirt **2**) woman's blouse; **Nai ma tsóxa, Nai ma gad, Na kinéla múrro dad**. I have no skirt, no blouse, my father won't buy them. (*song*); **gad-shukar** fancy shirt/blouse

gadiki *pron* so many/much; **Si amen gadiki problémi.** We have so many problems. *id* **Gadiki vi-si.** That's all there is.

gadiki de *pron/adj/adv* so many/much, so, just so, exactly so; **Chi mai dikhlem gadiki de zhene.** I have never seen so many/that many people! **Chi sim gadiki de phuro.** I am not *that* old! **gadiki de baro,** just so big, **gadiki de dur** just so far, **Sa gadiki si.** *id* It's all the same.

gadorro *nm* little shirt, garment for a baby: *pl* **gadorre** baby clothes

gadya *adv/id* accordingly, like that, *similarly,* so, that's how/why, thus; **Phendyas gadya.** That's what he said. **Gadya khelél-pe.** That's how she dances.

gagúla *nf* pelican

gáida *nf* bagpipes

galav *nm* saddle bag, traveling bag: *pl* **galave**

gálba *nf* gold coin: *pl* **gálbi**

galbenichóso *adj* yellow ochre, yellowish

galbenil *vt* **1**) make yellow, turn *smthg* yellow: *pp/adj* **galbenime 2**) *v/refl* **galbeníl-pe** catch jaundice

galbenime *pp/adj* pale, pallid

galbeníya *nf* jaundice

gálbeno/gálbono *adj* **1**) yellow **2**) *nm* color yellow or gold

gálbeno-hárkoma *comp/nf* brass

galbenoné-balêngo *comp/gen/adj* blond

galbenûsh *nm* egg yolk

galbenyála *nf* jaundice

gálbi *nf/pl* gold coins, necklace of gold coins

galéra *nf* galley (*vessel*), rowing boat/skiff

galóno *nm* gallon (*Am*)

galúshka *nf* dumpling

gangstéri *nm* gangster, hoodlum, member of a non-Romani criminal organization

gangsterísmo *nm* organized crime, Mafia (*Eur*)

gânsáko *nm* gander

garades *adv* clandestinely, in concealment, secretly

garado *pp/adj* **1**) concealed, hidden; **garade love** hidden money, slush fund **2**) secret **3**) obscure **4**) hooded

garádyol *vi* 1) be/become concealed/hidden, be secret: *pp/adj* **garadilo 2**) be disguised

garantíya *nf* assurance, guarantee

garavel *vt* **1**) conceal, disguise, hide: *pp/adj* **garado 2**) keep hidden, put aside, save/stash away (*money*) **3**) *v/refl* **a**) **garavél-pe** avoid (*the community*), conceal/hide oneself, go into seclusion **b**) hang out, spend one's time; **Kai garavél-pe o mursh kodo?** Where does that guy hang out?

garayimásko than *comp/nm* hiding place, hideaway

garayimáta *nm/pl* **1**) hidden things, secrets **2**) stash

garayimos *nm* **1**) concealment, hiding **2**) secret **3**) secrecy

garázha *nf* filling station, garage (*Am*)

gárda *nf* guard, sentinel, sentry (*Mil*)

gargaril *vt* 1) gargle: *pp/adj* **gargarime 2)** *v/refl* **gargaríl-pe a)** gargle **b)** gurgle

gargarimos *nm* 1) gargling 2) gurgling

gaskéto *nm* gasket *(Am)*

gáso *nm* 1) gasoline 2) gas, natural gas *(Am)* 3) poison gas; **sóba-gasóski** gas chamber

gasol *vt* 1) gas, gas up *(car)*: *pp/adj* **gasome** *(Am)* 2) kill by gassing 3) *v/ref* **gasól-pe** asphyxiate oneself, commit suicide by gassing oneself

gáso-naturálno *comp/nm* natural gas

gasóski-stánsiya *comp/nf* filling/gas station

gasóski-tsáva *comp/nf* gas pipeline

gasósko *gen/adj* relating to gas

gásto *nm* expense, expenditure

gáta *adj/adv* 1) ended, finished, completed, over, ready; **Avél kána wo avéla gáta.** He'll come when he will be finished. 2) *nf* conclusion, end, termination 3) *comp/vt* **del ~** conclude, end, finish, resolve 4) *comp/v/refl* **dél-pe gáta** be finished, get finished; **Phari buki si, chi mai das-ame gáta ages.** It's hard work, we'll never finish it today.

gav *nm* village, small town, town; **báro gav** large village/town, **tsíno gav** small village, **múrro gav** my town *(territory where I work, see* **gava***)*

gava *nm/pl* 1) towns, villages 2) rural route claimed by an itinerant coppersmith Rom; **Ándo milai phirav pa l' gava.** In the summer, I travel through the towns/through my circuit/territory where I have running contracts to do wipe tinning. **múrre gava** my towns/territory. **Kerel buki pa l' gava.** He works throughout the rural area. **Chorel múrre gava.** He's intruding on my territory/towns.

gavári *nm* rural inhabitant, villager: *nf* **gavárka** *(Am)*

gavorro *nm* rural hamlet,village

gavutnikanes *adv* like a local/rural *psn*

gavutnikano *adj* 1) local, rural, of the town 2) resident of a village

gavutno *nm* 1) farmer, peasant: *nf* **gavutni** *(Eur)* 2) villager, rural inhabitant

gázda *nf* boss, owner, proprietor; **gázda la bukyáko** work boss, foreman in charge of a work party

gazderítsa *nf* female mentor/teacher

gazdínka *nf* female manager, lady of the house, matron, owner, proprietress

gazéta *nf* newspaper

gazetári *nm* street newspaper and magazine vendor

Gazhi *nf* 1) Non-Romani woman 2) wife, if non-Romani. 3) woman, if non-Romani. *(see* **Gazho** *for capitalization rule)*; **Chorádili gazhi ánde párka araki,** a (non-Romani) woman was mugged in the park last night. 3) wife, even when Romani. This is used a lot in songs where the male singer will refer to his wife as **múrri gazhi,** but more common in Europe than in Canada/US.

Gazhikanes *adv* like a non-Roma/like the non-Roma, in the non-Romani manner, in a non-Romani language; **Gîndíl-pe Gazhikanes.** He thinks like a non-Rom.

Gazhikaní-buki *comp/nf* non-Romani business, affairs of the non-Roma; **O Kurvimos si Gazhikaní-buki. Nai Rromaní-buki.** Prostitution is non-Romani business, It's not Romani business. **Phandádilo. Hamisáilo ánde Gazhikaní-bukí.** He got arrested. He got mixed up in non-Romani business/crime.

gazhikanil *vt* 1) assimilate: *pp/adj* **gazhikanime 2)** *v/refl* **gazhikaníl-pe** assimilate, become assimilated; **gazhikanisáile.** They assimilated, became assimilated.

Gazhikanimos *nm* assimilation

Gazhikaníya *nf* 1) the culture/world of the non-Roma; **Ame le Rroma, si amên e Rromaníya thai le Gazhe, si lên e Gazhikaníya.** We, the Roma, have the Romani culture and the Gazhe, they have the non-Romani culture. 2) Non-Romani society/societies and its/their rules

Gazhikano *adj* Non-Romani;
Gazhikaní-buki *nf* grunt work,
employment for non-Roma, non-Romani
way/method of doing things; **Gazhinkani
buki gadya, nai Rrómani buki.** That's
the non-Romani way of doing things, It's
not the Romani way.
Gazho *nm* 1) Non-Romani man; **Beshel
pála Gazho.** She's living with a
non-Romani man. 2) husband (*if
non-Romani*) 3) man (*if non-Romani*);
**Kon si kodo gazho kai ashel pashal o
wudar?** Who is that man standing near
the door? **Pokindem le gazhêske le love.**
I paid the man the money. 4) front man;
Wo si amáro Gazho. He is our front
man. (*non-Romani man who fronts for
the **Roma** in renting properties, making
business proposals and representing the
family where landlords, banks, etc, would
otherwise be prejudiced against **Roma***).
Note: This word should be capitalized
when it is used to define **Gazho** as a
proper noun; **Le Rroma thai le Gazhe si
lên pênge hadéturya.** The Roma and the
Non-Roma have their customs.
Otherwise, it should not be capitalized
when used to differenatiate between
Roma and non-Roma; **Mulo gazho ándo
pharrayimos.** A man died in the car
crash. **Kon si kodo gazho?** Who is that
man?
gazhó-phuvyáko *comp/nm* municipal
worker who works underground,
sanitation engineer: *pl* **gazhé-phuvyáke**
(*Am*)
gazhorro *nm* dwarf; **Parnyorri thai le
hifta gazhorre** Snow White and the
Seven Dwarfs: *nf* **gazhorri**
gazhó-sastruno *nm* robot (*metal man*)
(*Am*)
gazhó-skutsome *comp/nm* dude, flashy
dresser, rhinestone cowboy (*Am*)
gazhyángo-dóftoro *comp/nm* gynecologist
gazhyarel *vt* force to assimilate: *pp/adj*
gazhyardo
gazhyarimos *nm* forced assimilation

gêlchi *nf/pl* glands, mumps, glandular
trouble; **gêlchi ándo gortyáno** tonsillitis,
gêlchi ándo nakh adenoids
gêlchíl-pe *v/ref* become glandered: *pp/adj*
gêlchimé
gêlchimé *gen/adj* glandered; **O grast si
gêlchimé.** The horse is glandered.
gêlka *nf* 1) gland: *pl* **gêlchi** 2) goiter 3)
tonsil
gémo *nm* bit (*for a horse harness*)
gêr *nf* 1) eczema, mange 2) scab, scabies
gêraló *adj* 1) mangy 2) scabrous
gêraló-pûnrró *comp/nm* athlete's foot
gêrbáto *adj* hunchbacked: *nm* hunchback:
nf **gêrbáika**
gêrbo *nm* hump
gêrbósko *gen/adj* humped, having a hump
Gêrchiko *nm* Greece
gêrcho *nm* 1) rubber 2)
condom/prophylactic 3) cramp 4)
cartilage. gristle
gêrchól *vt* 1) rubberize: *pp/adj* **gêrchomé**
2) **gêrchól-pe** become cramped, get
cramped, become numb; **Gêrchól-pe
múrro pûnrró.** My foot is becoming
cramped/numb.
gêrchomé *pp/adj* 1) rubberized 2) cramped,
numb
gêrchomós *nm* 1) rubber insulation 2)
cramps, numbness
gêrchòsko *gen/adj* rubber, made of rubber;
gêrchòski-papúsha, rubber dolly,
inflatable rubber doll (*Am*)
gêrí *nf* poor woman, unfortunate woman,
poor wretch; **Xayisáili bokhátar, e gêrí.**
She perished from hunger, the poor
woman.
gêríl *vt* infect with scabies or mange 2)
v/refl **gêríl-pe** become mangy, scabrous
gêrimé *pp/adj* infected with mange/scabies,
mangy, scabby, scabrous
gêrimós *nm* mange, scabies
Gêrkítska *nf* Greek (*Lang*)
Gêrkítsko *adj* Greek
Gêrko *nm* Greek: *nf* **Gerkáika**
ges gesêstar *adv/phr* from day to day

ges/gês *nm* day; *id* **Aver fyal sas ánde múrre gesa.** Things were different in my day.

gesêsko *gen/adj* daily; **gesêski hêrtíya** daily newspaper

gêsívo *nm* thimble

gesol *vi* become daylight, dawn; *pp/adj* **gesulo; Gesólas kána trádilam.** It was dawning when we departed. **Nashlótar o choxãnó kána gesulo.** The phantom fled when dawn broke.

gesutno *adj* daily, day's

gêtíl *vt* **1)** complete, finalize, finish, get ready, make ready, prepare; **Gêtisardém lês te trádel.** I got him ready to leave/depart. **2)** *v/refl* **gêtíl-pe** be/become ready, get ready; **Gêtín-pe, le sheyorra, te zhan kai sláva.** The girls are getting ready to go to the feast. **Zhávtar kána gêtisáilem.** I'll leave when I'm ready. **De mánge vryámya te gêtí-ma!** Give me time to get ready!

gêtimé *pp/adj* finished, completed, prepared, ready

gi *nm* **1)** belly, stomach. **2)** life force, soul, spirit

gichil *vt* **1)** guess, estimate, forecast by guessing, foretell by guessing: *pp/adj* **gichime 2)** solve through guessing or hunches **3)** *v/refl* **gichíl-pe** guess, be guessing; **Zhi zhanel, gichíl-pe.** He doesn't know, he's guessing.

gichimos *nm* estimate, guess. hunch

gichisára *nf* female guesser; **Nai chachí drabarni kadya xoxamni, si gichisára.** She's not a real fortune-teller that phony, she's a guesser.

gichitáriya *nf* riddle, guess, conundrum

gichitóri *nm* master of riddles, good guesser: *nf* **gichitórka**

gído *nm* guidebook, guide (*Eur*)

gilabal vt/i **1)** sing: *pp/adj* **gilabado; Gilaban gilya Rromanes.** They are singing songs in Romani. **Gilabal mishto.** He/she sings well. **2)** ring; **Gilaba o izvóno!** Ring the bell! **Gilaban múrre kan.** My ears are ringing. **3)** play, sound *us* with **ánd-; Gilabal ánde lávuta.** He/she plays the fiddle. **Gilaba ánde gitára!** Play the guitar! **4)** play, sound; **Chi gilabal mishto múrri gitára.** My guitar doesn't sound/play well.

gilabano *adj* singing, song; **chirikló-gilabano** songbird

gilabayimásko *gen/adj* singing, song; **gilabayimáski-chirikli** canary

gilabayimos *nm* singing

gilabayitóri *nm* singer, vocalist: *nf* **gilabayitórka**

gili *nf* **1)** ballad, song **2)** poem, epic ballad set to music

gimnásiya *nf* gymnasium

gimnástiko *nm* **1)** athlete: *nf* **gimnastikútsa 2)** acrobat, gymnast

gimnástiya *nf* athletics gymnastics, physical exercise **4)** comp/vi **kerel ~** do physical exercise, work out

gin *nm* **1)** count, number, **2)** total

gîndáko *nm* beetle, cricket, cockroach, insect

gîndíl *vt/i* **1)** conceive, think, reason, suppose, theorize, understand to be: *pp/adj* **gîndimé; Gindin djúngale gîndurya.** They are thinking ugly thoughts. **Me gîndív ke sim kon gîndís ke san tu!** I have the same allusions as you have. (*lit.* I think that I am who you think you are!) **2)** intend, plan, plan to do; **So gîndís te keres?** What are you planning to do? **3)** suspect; **Kas gîndis chordyas le love?** Whom do you suspect stole the money? **4)** *v/refl* **a) gîndíl-pe** contemplate, be contemplating, think, be thinking; **So gîndís-tu?** What are you thinking? **b)** see oneself, imagine oneself; **Shai gîndís-tu manginalo?** Can you imagine yourself super wealthy? **Nashti gîndí-ma so kerela wo kodole gazhênsa.** I can't imagine what he is doing with those people. **c)** contemplate; **Gîndisáilem pe múrro tráyo.** I contemplated on my life. **d)** intend, plan, be planning to do; **Gîndín-pe wáreso.** They are planning something. **e)** have a

suspicion; **Gîndí-ma kh' wo si o chor.** I
have a suspicion he is the thief. **5)**
comp/vi ~ **te kerel** intend to do, plan to do

gîndimásko *gen/adj* contemplating,
thinking; **e gîndimáski gogi** the thinking
mind

gîndimós *nm* concept, contemplation,
thought

gîndo/gûndo *nm* **1)** assumption,
consideration, feeling, idea, impression,
intention, opinion, plan, theory, thought,
suggestion; **Si tu gîndo ansurimásko?**
Do you have the intention to get married?
Si ma gîndo te kerav. I intend/plan to.
Si ma gîndo te thav anglál tumênde. I
have a suggestion to place before you **2)**
suspicion **3)** consensus, consideration,
decision **4)** *comp/vt/i* **del** ~ give thought
(to), consider; **Músai te das gîndo so
shai keras ánda kakya buki.** We have
to consider what we can do about this
matter. **5)** *comp/vt/i* **del-pe gîndo**
imagine; **Shai des-tu gîndo?** Can you
imagine? **6)** *comp/vt/i* **lel** ~ take thought,
consider, contemplate; **Lávas gîndo
ánda kadya buki.** I have been
considering/comtemplating this issue.

gîndól -pe *v/refl* **a)** have a thought, be
thinking; **So gîndós-tu?** **a)** What are you
thinking/What thoughts are running
through your mind? **b)** be considering,
consider, contemplate, be contemplating,
be considered or thought to be, consider
oneself to be, be deciding

gîndósko *gen/adj* thoughtful, well
founded/thought out

gîndurya *nm/pl* **1)** imagination **2)**
considerations, contemplations

gíndyol *vi* be counted: *pp/adj* **gindilo**

ginel *vt/i* **1)** add, count: *pp/adj* **gindo 2)**
read, interpret (*blueprints*); **Shai gines
plánurya?** Can you read blueprints? **3)** ~
with **pe**; count on, rely on; **Shai gines pe
mánde ánde kakya buki.** You can count
on/rely on me in this matter. **Gín-ta pe
lêste te kerel problémi!** Count on him to
create problems!

ginimos *nm* adding, addition, counting,
interpretation (*of blueprints*)

gípsa *nf* **1)** drywall, wallboard **2)** gypsum,
plaster

gipsáika *nf fem of* **gípso** *nm qv*

gípso *nm* gypsy, Non-Romani traveler,
New-Age gypsy, Irish Traveler/Tinker
(*Am*), **Gípsurya-Gazhikane** New-Age
gypsies, Non-Roma who perform on
Renaissance fairs presenting themselves
as "Gypsies." (*Am*); **Le gípsurya si
Gazhe kai kerén-pe Rrom.** The gypsies
are non-Roma who portray themselves as
Romanies.(*Am*)

gípso-lorízmo *nm/neolog* **1)** "Gypsy Lore"
2) study, classification and definition of
the Romani people by non-Roma

gípso-lorísto *nm/neolog* "Gypsylorist": *nf*
gípso-loráika *nf/neolog*

gitára *nf* guitar; **gitára-Shpanyolítsko**
Spanish guitar, Flamenco guitar,
nylon-string guitar

gitarash *nm* guitarist: *nf* **gitaráshka**

gitarítso *nm/voc* dear guitar, little guitar,
term of affection for a guitar and title of a
table song.

giv *nm* grain, corn, wheat

gízha *nf* eggshell

glába *nf* **1)** fine/penalty, court action,
lawsuit **2)** fine, monetary reimbursement,
especially if ordered by the
Kris-Romani; Dine lês bári glába.
They imposed a big fine on him.

glabil *vt* fine, penalize financially, sue for
financial damages: *pp/adj* **glabime**

gláso *nm* **1)** voice **2)** tune, air, **3)** sound **4)**
representation; **Nai amên gláso ánde
organizátsiya.** We have no
representation in the organization. **5)**
vocal support

gláta *nf* **1)** baby, infant: *pl* **gláti 2)** child
(*Am*); **Si ma pansh gláti.** I have five
children.

glatáko *s/gen/adj* belonging to a newborn
infant, intantile

glatása *nf/inst* with child, pregnant; **Woi si
glatása.** She is with child.

glatêngo *pl/gen/adj* belonging to newborn infants, infantile, infantlike

glatútso *nm* newborn baby boy, infant in arms: *nf* **glatútsa**

gledála *nf* large mirror, vanity mirror, wall mirror

glíma *nf* bright, shiny trinket, glittering bauble

glínda *nf* looking glass, pocket mirror, reflector mirror on a vehicle, rear-view mirror

glindáko *gen/adj* creating a mirror image, reflecting

glóbo *nm* 1) lightbulb 2) globe, sphere

glônto *nm* bullet (*Eur*) *see also* **plûmbo** *nm*

glôntso *nm* mouthful, swallow

godo *pron/dem* that *(illic),* that man

godola *pron/dem/obl* that, those, those people *if nf*

godole *pron/dem/obl* that, those, those people *if nm*

godya *pron/dem* that *(illic),* that woman, that thing *if nf*

gogi *nf* 1) brain/brains, common sense, instinct, intellect, logic, mind, opinion, reason, sanity; **Manges múrri gogi?** Do you want my opinion? **Kon pel drab, xal pêski gogi.** Whoever does drugs, destroys his brains. 2) lesson; **Sikadem lês gogi.** I taught him a lesson. 3) memory 4) *comp/vt* **del ~** remind 5) **thol** be considerate of, think about; **Chi thodyan gogi mánde.** You were not considerate towards me 6) *v/ref* **del-pe ~** consider, think about, reflect; **Dyás-pe gogi so te kerel ánda e buki.** He considered what to do about the matter. **Áshta! Da-ma gogi so te mothav túke.** Hold on! I'm considering what to tell you.

gogyáko *gen/adj* of a mind, cerebral, intellectual

gogyáko-manush *nm* genius, wise man

gogyárdyol *vi* become smartened up/wisened up, be taught a lesson: *pp/adj* **gogyardilo**

gogyarel *vt* 1) make intelligent, smarten/wisen up: *pp/adj* **gogyardo** 2) *v/refl* **gogyarél-pe** make oneself intelligent, wisen up/get the smarts (*Am*)

gogyása *nf/inst* by instinct; **Kerel gogyátar.** He does it by instinct

gogyáte *nf/prep* to one's senses; **Avilo pêske gogyáte.** He came to his senses.

gogyaver *adj* intelligent, logical, sane, wise; **gogyaver Rrom** wise/intellectual Rom

gogyávol *vi* become astute/clever/smart: *pp/adj* **gogyailo**

goi *nf* 1) sausage 2) *vlg/sl* penis 3) suet *for* **khoi** *qv*

goiyorri *nf* frankfurter, hotdog

golféri *nm* golfer

gólfo *nm* golf (*Am*); **golfênge-ruvlya** golf clubs

golobízha/golubízha *nf* artillery shell, cannon ball

golúmbo *nm* dove, pigeon: *nf* **golumbáika**

góma *nf* 1) eraser 2) gum 3) chewing gum

gonil *vt* 1) banish, blackball, chase away/out, cut off from, drive away, exile, expel, force to leave, ostracize: *pp/adj* **gonime; E Kris gonisardya lês.** The Tribunal has blackballed him. **Note:** In Canada and US this verb can be used to indicate somebody who has been declared in violation of the Romani laws of cleanliness or behaviour and has been expelled until reinstated by the Romani Tribunal. 2) *v/refl* **goníl-pe a)** become/get blackballed, blackball oneself **b)** be obliged to leave, become banished/blackballed/expelled

gonime *pp/adj* banished, blackballed, chased away, expelled, ostracized

gonimos *nm* banishment, expulsion from the local Romani community or from one's family.

gonimos-bengorrêngo *comp/nm* exorcism

gono *nm* 1) bag, carry bag, handbag, sack, shopping bag 2) cocoon 3) hood (*over the head*)

gonó-plastikósko *comp/nm* plastic bag: *pl*
goné-plastikóske

gonorro *nm* pouch, small bag; *pl* **gonorre**

gónso *nm* large needle for sewing tent
canvas or tarpaulin

gor *nm* **1)** border, brink, edge, end,
extremity, limit, outer limit, tip; **o gor le
kurkósko** the end of the week **2)** point
(*of a needle, etc*), prong **3)** aim, desire,
direction, focus, intention, endevour, goal,
purpose, quest, target, wish; **Wo dyas
ándo gor.** He reaized his aim
goal/succeeded in his intention. **3)**
appointment **4)** climax, conclusion, end,
finale, outcome, termination **5)** target **6)**
pinnacle

gorchítsa *nf* mustard

gorde *adv* worse *us with* **mái; E Mára
gilabal mai gorde katar e Pavléna.**
Mary sings worse than Pauline.

gorída *nf* **1)** wild grape **2)** chokecherry
(*prunus virginiana*)

górka *nf* gherkin

gormónya/gormoníya *nf* accordion, piano
accordion

gormonyash accordion player: *nf*
gormonyáshka

goro *nm* poor fellow, poor man, poor
wretch: *nf* **gêrí; Te azhutil lês o Del, o
goro!** May God help him, the poor
fellow! **Mulo láko rrom e gêrí.** Her
husband died, the poor thing.

goróxo *nm* green pea, pea

gortyáno *nm* **1)** esophagus, gullet, throat
(*Anat*) **2)** neck *see also* **korr** *nf*

góshto/gústo *adj* impenetrable, dense,
thick; dense forest, **góshto wêrsh**
comp/nm

gostil *vt* **1)** extend hospitality, make
welcome: *pp/adj* **gostime 2)** *v/refl*
gostíl-pe be made welcome, be
welcomed

gostíya *nf* **1)** hospitality **2)** banquet for
invited guests, community banquet

gósto *nm* guest: *nf* **gostáika**

gózba *nf* banquet, feast (*Eur*)

gozhni *nf* dung, manure; **grastêngi gozhni**
horse manure, **gremáda gozhni** pile of
manure, *fig* load of crap (*Am*)

gózhnik *nf* **1)** *sl* stuffing, fripperies **2)**
bullshit, hogwash (*Am*)

gózhnika *nf* glass jar containing bottle
caps, coins and used as a rattle. (*Can*)

gózho *adj* attractive, comely, cute,
handsome (*Eur*)

grába *nf* hurry, haste; **ánde grába** in a
hurry

grabása *adv* hurridly, with haste, **Gêlótar
grabása.** He left with haste/took off like
a bat out of hell. (*Am*)

gradadéto *nm* graduate

gradadil *vt* **1)** graduate: *pp/adj* **gradatime
2) gradadíl-pe** *vt* be graduated, graduate

gradína *nf* **1)** vegetable garden **2)** zoo,
zoological garden (*Eur*)

gradinári *nm* gardener, zoo-keeper: *nf*
gradinárka

grádo *nm* **1)** thermometer **2)** grade, mark **3)**
comp/vi **kerel o ~** make the grade

graduwátsiya *nf* graduation

graféma *nf/neolog* letter (*in spelling*)

gráfo *nm* graph

gramafóno **1)** record player, stereo

gramátika *nf/neolog* grammar,
grammatical structure

grámatno **1)** *adj* grammatical **2)** educated,
schooled **3)** *nm* educated man: *nf*
grámatni

grámo *nm* gram

granáda *nf* bomb, grenade, shell (*Eur*)

gránitsa *nf* border, boundary, frontier

granitsári *nm* customs/immigration officer:
nf **granitsárka**

gráno *nm* grain

grápa *nf* **1)** cavity, gap, hole, pit, dent,
indent, orifice, outlet (*electrical*): *pl*
grópi 2) burrow, den, opening (*to a cave,
tunnel*), warren **3)** foxhole (*Mil*) **4)**
electric outlet, wall plug **5)** loophole,
peep hole

grapítsa *nf* tiny hole: *pl* **gropítsi**

grapítsa-kiyayáki *comp/nf* keyhole

grasni *nf* **1)** mare **2)** battle-ax, domineering/quarrelsome woman

grast kai xinel súmnakai *id* horse that voids gold (*a mythical horse in folklore*); benefactor, Sugar Daddy, **Nashti kines o grast kai xinel súmnakai ándo washári.** You can't buy the horse that voids gold at a horse fair/There are no bargains for sale.

grast *nm* **1)** horse (*gelded*), horse in general: *pl* **grast**; **grast-bukyáko** draught/work horse, **grast-vordonêsko** cart horse **2)** horse races, track; **O Franki si ka l' grast.** Frank is at the racetrack.

grastári *nm* jockey, horseman, rider: *nf* **grastárka**

grastash *nm* groom (*of horses*)

grastêngo *gen/adj/pl* belonging to horses

grastêngo-valóvo *comp/mm* **1)** horse trough, drinking trough for horses

grastêsko *gen/adj/s* belonging to a horse

grastêsko-tsólo ; horse blanket

grast-kashtalo *nm* hobby horse, rocking horse

grastorro *nm* **1)** pony: *nf* **grastorri 2)** dragonfly

grastuno *adj* equine

grêbíl *vt* **1)** urge to hurry, make to hurry, get somebody moving **2)** *v/refl* **grêbíl-pe** get oneself going, hurry, make haste; **Grêbisár-tut!** Hurry up/get moving! **Motho lêske te grêbíl-pe!** Tell him to hurry up!

grêbimé *pp/adj* pressed for time, hurried

grêbimós *nm* hurry, haste

gréda *nf* balk, beam, former, girder, rafter, supporting post/pole: *pl* **grédi** supporting structure

gremáda *nf* **1)** heap, mound, pile, stack: *pl* **gremézhi; gremáda gozhni** heap of manure, **kashtêngi-gremáda** wood pile **2)** pile (*Anat/Am*) **3)** batch

gremézhi *nf/pl* hemorrhoids, piles (*Anat/Am*)

Grésiya *nf* Greece

gréva *nf* strike (*Eur*); **Le gazhe si sáyek ánde vakántsiya vai ánde gréva.** The

non-Roma (*city employees*) are always on vacation or on strike.

gréza *nf* cream of wheat

grífo *nm* **1)** cotter pin, pin, small, round piece of wood or metal **2)** pin of a hand grenade

grímna *nf* bangle, bracelet

grímptso *nm* grasshopper

grípa *nf* influenza

gripíl-pe *v/refl* come down with influenza: *pp/adj* **gripime; Gripimé-lo o Stévo.** Steve came down with the flu. **Gripisáilem hai mai do gáta mulem.** I caught the flu and almost died.

gripime *pp/adj* down/sick with influenza

grípo *nm* suitcase (*Am*)

griyábla *nf* hoe, rake

griyablil *vt* rake: *pp/adj* **griyablime**

griyachóso *adj* disgusting

griyátsa *nf* disgust, nausea; **Griyátsa mánge.** I am disgusted/I find it disgusting.

Griyátsa! **1)** *interj/exp of disgust* Yuck! **2)** *nf* something disgusting: *pl* **grêtsi; Le kokoróchurya si grêtsi.** Cockroaches are disgusting things.

griyatsáko *gen/adj* abhorrent, disgusting/detestable, repulsive

griyatsalo *adj* fastidious, squeamish

griyatsol *vi* **1)** disgust, make disgusting/distasteful/detestable: *pp/adj* **griyatsome 2)** *v/refl* **griyátsól-pe** become disgusting/detestable/repelling; **Griyatsosáile.** They became detestable.

griyatsomásko *gen/adj* disgusting/detestable, off-turning, repelling, soul-sucking, stomach-churning

griyatsome *pp/adj* disgusted, nauseated, repelled

griyatsomos *nm* detestation, disgust, repulsion

grízha *nf* **1)** care, concern, neatness, tidiness

grizhol *vt* **1)** clean up, tidy up, wipe off: *pp/adj* **grizhome 2)** care for, groom (*horses*), nurse **3)** *v/refl* **grizhól-pe**

clean/tidy oneself up, dress to kill, dress up, groom oneself, spruce oneself up

grizhome *pp/adj* clean, neat, spruced up, tidy, well-kept, well-groomed

grizhomos *nm* 1) cleaning up, house cleaning, tidying up 2) neatness, tidiness 3) personal grooming/neatness 4) care, grooming (*of horses*)

grófo *nm* count (*nobleman*): *nf* **grofáika** countess

gropalo *adj* full of holes, pitted with holes

groposhévo *nm* 1) casket, coffin 2) grave (*Eur*)

grûmazári *nm* 1) harness on horse collar to hold cart shafts 2) attachment harness on heavy collar/yoke for a working animal, plough horse, etc. 3) hitching rope

grúntso *nm* kernel

grûnzo *nm* lump, plug; **grúnzo-doháno** plug of tobacco

grúpo 1) circle, group (*of people*) 2) band, group (*Mus*)

grúzha *nf* clod, clutch, clump; **grúzha tórfa** clump of turf

gryázhda *nf* stable: *pl* **gryézhdi**

gryázhdo *nm* barn, grannery, hayloft, silo

gubernáto *nm* government

gubernatóri *nm* governor: *nf* **gubernatórka** child's governess

gubernil *vt* 1) govern: *pp/adj* **gubernime** 2) *v/refl* **guberníl-pe** govern oneself, be governed

gubérniya *nf* *nf* area of government, state

gugles *adv* nicely, sweetly; **Del túke so manges te des lêsa dúma gugles.** You'll get what you want if you talk to him nicely.

guglimáta *nm/pl* sweets, sweetmeats

guglimos *nm* 1) sweet dessert, sweetmeats 2) sweetness 3) icing; **Kindem mariki, guglimása opral**. I bought a cake, with icing on it.

Guglíyo *nf/voc* Sweetie! (*Am*)

guglo *adj* 1) sweet, sweet-tasting 2) fresh (*water*) 3) *nf* **gugli** sweet child/girl, young woman

guglyárdyol *vi* become sweetened up. be made sweet: *pp/adj* **guglyardilo**

guglyarel *vt* 1) sweeten, make sweet: *pp/adj* **guglyardo; Guglyardem lês mitása.** I sweetened him up with a bribe 2) freshen up, make fresh; 3) flatter, sweet talk *smbdy*

guglyarimos *nm* 1) sweetening 2) freshening 3) flattery, snow job

guglyol *vi* become sweet: *pp/adj* **guglilo**

gúgu *nm* bogeyman, ghost, monster (*used with children*); **Zha ka o than hai arakh-tu katar o gúgu!** Go to bed and watch out for the bogeyman! **Arakh o gúgu te na astarel tut!** Watch out the bogeyman doesn't catch you!

guláko *nm* round loaf of bread: *pl* **gulácha**

gúlash *nm* meat stew

gulayil *vt* 1) entertain, treat *smbdy* to a good time: *pp/adj* **gulayime** 2) enjoy, have fun/a good time; **Sa xalyam, sa pilam thai sa gulayisardyam**. We ate, drank and enjoyed everything. 3) *v/refl* **gulayíl-pe** enjoy oneself, be enjoying *smth*, have a good time

gulayimos *nm* enjoyment, entertainment, fun, good time

gulayitóri *nm* hedonist, good-time Charlie (*Am*): *nf* **gulayitórka**

gúlero *nm* 1) collar, collar bone 2) collar of a garment

gumbósho *nm* 1) clasp, pin 2) clothes peg 3) belaying pin, cleat, norman

gumboshútso *nm* pin, safety pin

gumíla *nf* camel

gûmíla/gômíla *nf* 1) hillock, mound 2) camel

gunoi *nm* 1) garbage, trash, rubbish 2) waste material 3) trash can

gunoiyalo *adj* littered with trash; **Gunoiyalo sas o hãlo mai palal katar e sláva**. The hall was littered with trash after the feast.

gunoiyarel *vt* litter with garbage/trash: *pp/adj* **gunoiyardo**

gunoiyári *nm* **1**) garbage collector **2**) bag man, derelict who goes through the garbage cans: *nf* **gunoiyárka** bag lady

gunoiyarimos *nm* litter, littering

gurumni *nf* cow: *pl* **gurumnya** cattle, drove of cattle

gurumníya *nf* cattle yard, stockyard

gurumnyáki púfa *nf* cow pancake, cow flap, cow shit

gurumnyári *nm* cow herdsman, cowboy

guruv *nm* **1**) bull, bullock, ox, steer, *see also* **bíko** *nm* **2**) **Guruv** Taurus (*Zod*); *gen/adj* **guruvêsko**

guruvano *adj* beef, bovine; **mas guruvano** beef, **zumi guruvani** beef stew

guravári *nm* cattle dealer, herdsman of cattle

gusáno *nm* **1**) worm **2**) computer virus

gusenítsa *nf* caterpillar

gúsha *nf* **1**) thyroid gland, thyroid condition **2**) craw, gizzard

gushárka *nf* nanny, nurse

gustil *vt* **1**) taste: *pp/adj* **gustime 2**) *v/refl* **gustíl-pe** taste

gustimos *nm* flavour, taste

gústo *nm* flavour, taste

gustóso *adj* delicious, tasty

gúta *nf* scarlet fever

guzlári *nm* balladeer, minstrel

gyánda *nf* beech nut **2**) chewing gum (*Am*)

gyandelin *nf* beech tree

gyánta *nf* **1**) resin **2**) gum

gyantalo *adj* adhesive, resinous, sticky

gyórtso *nm* **1**) gulp, sip, slug, swig; **Dyas gáta e rrakíya, gyórtso pála gyórtso.** He finished off the whisky, swig after swig. **2**) puff **3**) swallow

H

ha! *adv/interj* **1)** yes! what! yeah! (*Am*) **2)** *adv* yes (*in answer to a question*) *see also* **va** *adv*

haburil *vt* **1)** steam **2)** produce steam, vapor: *pp/adj* **haburime**

háburo *nm* **1)** air, breath **2)** vapor **3)** steam **4)** imaginary person: *nf* **haburáika** *nf*

hadáka *nm* haddock

hadéto *nm* custom, habit, tradition, traditional value; **Amáre hadéturya nai yêkh-fyálo sar le Gazhênge hadéturya.** Our traditional values are not the same as the non-Romani values. (*Am*)

hadéturya *nm/pl* culture, customs, habits, traditions, values (*Am*)

hagíri *nm* stallion, stud horse

hai *conj* and, also, as well as; **Tu hai me zhas**. You and I will go.

hai te na mulo/muli/mule zhi ages, inka trayil/trayin. *id/phr* And if he/she/they is/are not dead, he/she/they still lives/live. Typical ending of a Kalderash folktale.

Háide!/Háidi *interj/imp* Come! Come along! Come on! (*to one psn*): **Haiden!** (*to more than one psn*; **Háide andre!** Get in! (*to one psn*) **Háiden mánsa!** Come with me! (*to more than one psn*)

haiyi *conj* also, and also, too, as well as, including; **Akushlas man haiyi múrro phral.** He insulted me as well as my brother. **Nas férdi le Rroma kai xale miséria, hayi le Gazhe xale.** Not only the Roma suffered misery, the non-Roma also suffered.

hakyardo *pp/adj* **1)** understood **2)** *id.* for sure; **Chi merel bokhátar, hakyardo!** He won't die of hunger, that's for sure!

hakyárdyol *vi* be agreed upon/comprehended/realized/understood: *pp/adj* **hakyardilo**

hakyarel *vt* **1)** comprehend, get the point, realize, understand: *pp/adj* **hakyardo**; **Sargodi hakyares.** However you understand it/Take it as you will. **Hakyares so phenav?** Do you understand what I am saying? **2)** *v/refl* **a)** **hakyarél-pe** come to understand/realize, come to an agreement/understanding. **Hakyarél-pe.** It seems to be/appears to be (*so*). **Hakyarél-pe mishto.** It seems to be OK. **b)** feel, feel about; **So hakyares-tu ánda gadya buki ke chi zhan le shavorre ánde wushkála?** What do you feel about this matter, that the children are not attending school? **c)** have an opinion about; **So hakyarés-tu ánda gadya buki?** What do you make out of this matter?

hakyarimásko *gen/adj* comprehensible, understandable

hakyarimos *nm* **1)** understanding/agreement, comprehension. concept **2)** feeling, opinion **3)** intuition, sensitivity

hakyarno/halyarno *adj* **1)** intuitive, reasonable, sensitive, sensible, understanding. wise **2)** *nm* man with the foregoing qualities: *nf* **hakyarni/halyarni**

hála *nf* dragon (*Folk*)

halavel *vt/i* comprehend, understand: *pp/adj* **halado** (*Am*)

hálmêsh-bálmêsh *compl/nm Kalderash* stew, ragout

hãlo/hálo *nm* banquet hall, large hall, hall

halyarel *vt* **1**) comprehend, experience, make out of, understand: *pp/adj* **halyardo** *var of* **hakyarel** *qv* **2**) feel, sense **3**) *v/refl* **halyarél-pe feel**, feel about, sense, understand; **Halyarávas man ke sas wárekon pála mánde.** I sensed that there was somebody behind me. **Chi halyarel-pe mishto.** He doesn't feel well.

halyarimáta *nm/pl* feelings (*about smthg*)

halyarimos *nm* **1**) agreement, understanding **2**) feeling

hamáko *nm* hammock: *pl* **hamácha**

hamári *nm* maker of harnesses, horse accoutrements and saddles

hambári *nm* pantry extension of a house, storage shed, storeroom

hamil *vt* **1**) blend, fuse, knead, meddle, mix, stir: *pp/adj* **hamime 2**) shuffle (*cards*) **3**) interrupt; **Na hamnisáwo kána me dav-dúma.** Don't interrupt when I am talking **4**) annoy, bother **5**) meddle in, snoop **6**) fraternize, mingle with, hang around with **7**) *v/refl* **hamíl-pe a**) mix in, meddle in; **Hamíl-pe ánde murri buki**. He's meddling in my business. **Na hamisáwo-tut ánde buki!** Don't get involved in the matter! **b**) hang around with, fraternize with, mingle with; **Hamíl-pe le Gazhênsa.** He hangs around with non-Roma **c**) adulterate, fuse together (*Mus*) **d**) be mixed up in, incriminated in, involved in; **Hamisáilo ánde probléma.** He involved himself in the problem. **e**) instigate, interfere

Hamiltóno *nm* Hamilton (*City in Ontario, Canada*)

hamime *pp/adj* **1**) adulterated, alloyed, blended, fused, mixed, mixed together, mixed up, shuffled; **musíka-hamime** fusion music **2**) incriminated/involved (in), mixed up (in)

hamimé-ratêsko *comp/gen/adj* of mixed blood/descent, mongrel

hamimos *nm* **1**) blending, brew, concoction, hodge podge mixture **2**)

fraternization **3**) meddling **4**) fusion **5**) medley **6**) alloy **7**) involvement

hamitóri *nm* **1**) blender, mixer **2**) hanger on, meddler, snooper: *nf* **hamitórka**

hámo *nm* horse collar

hámurya *nm/pl* horse harness

hanamik/xanamik *nm* co-father-in-law, father of son or daugher's spouse: *nf* **hanamíka**: *pl* **hanamícha** co-parents-in-law, father and mother of a son or daughter's spouse

hángo *nm* **1**) melody, tune (*Mus*) **2**) resonance, tone (*quality of sound*), sound (*Mus*); **Tyi gitára si-la lásho hángo.** Your guitar has good tone/sound quality. (*Eur*) **3**) echo

Hâni *nf* Honey! (*Am*); **So keres, Hâni?** What are you doing, Honey?

hanitóri *nm* plater of copper utensils, tinsmith, wipe-tinner

hanol *vt* **1**) plate, plate with tin, wipe-tin **2**) *v/refl* **hanól-pe** be plated, tinned

hanome *pp/adj* plated, wipe-tinned; **hanome sumnakása** gold-plated

hanomos *nm* wipe-tinning, plating of copper bakery mixing bowls with tin, tin smithing

hapníl-pe *v/refl* happen: *pp/adj* **hapnime**; **So hapnisáilo?** What happened? (*Am*)

Harángyelo *nm* Black Angel, Witness from Purgatory (*Folk*)

Harápo/Xarápo *nm* dark-skinned, giant and cannibal ogre in folk tales: *nf* **Harapáika** wife of the **Harápo**

Harapútsa *nf* daughter of the **Harapo**

harávli *nf* **1**) leather (*material*) **2**) leather belt **3**) leather strap/thong, rifle sling, strop, strap for a guitar, handbag strap **4**) pulley drive belt of a compressor, generator **5**) strap; **O wuchitéli dya lês e harávli.** The teacher gave him the strap.

haravlyáko *gen/adj* made of leather

haréma *nf* harem

hárkoma *nf* copper

hárkoma-gálbeno *comp/nm* brass

harkomáko *gen/adj* made of copper

hárkomáko-galbenonya *gen/adj* brass, made of brass

harkomári *nm* coppersmith, copper plater

harkuno *adj* copper, having the look or appearance of copper; **Meyázol hárkoma núma hamimé-lo.** It looks like copper but it's an alloy.

harmasári *nm* 1) stallion 2) *fig* man reputed to have superior sexual prowess, stud 3) *fig* hound dog, womanizer (*Am*); **Kodo phuro harmasári piravél-pe sa le zhuvlyánsa.** That old womanizer flirts with all the women.

harmígo *nm* stallion, stud horse

hárniko 1) *adj* dedicated, hard-working, industrious, motivated, responsible; **Hárnichi Rroma si.** They are industrious Roma. 2) *adj* careful 3) *nm* achiever, hard-working man, industrious man: *nf* **harnikútsa**

harnûvo *nm* 1) canvas, tarpaulin 2) Conestoga wagon, wagon with a tarpaulin top 3) *arch* bow-top Romani caravan 4) canvas roofing 5) canvas top of a convertible

harshûno *nm* yard (*measure*); **trin harshûnurya bumbáko** three yards of cotton

harshûvo *nm* shovel

hârtíya/hêrtíya *nf* 1) paper 2) bill. document 3) toilet paper (*Am*)

harumbash *nm* 1) bandit leader, *us* with **baro** 2) male bandit, hoodlum, outlaw; usually applied to those who commit armed robbery with violence, compared to **chor**, a non-violent thief, pickpocket, shoplifter, etc. The word is often used in *Kalderash* folktales like **Sóde de Dur ka Tómska?** How Far to Tomska? In this folktale, a traveling Kalderash **kumpaníya** was murdered by bandits or **harumbásha**.

harumbashimos *nm* banditry

harumbashíya *nf* banditry, lawlessness

harumbáshka *nf* wife of a bandit leader, female bandit

harumbashútsa *nf* daughter of a bandit leader

harúngo *nm* herring

harzópo *nm* 1) elevator/lift 2) escalator (*Eur*)

hatai *nm/neolog* right: *pl* **hatáya; Rrómane Hatáya** Romani Rights

hatázheno *nm* floor, stage, storey: *pl* **hatázheni** (*Eur*); **O Bíldingo si desh-u-pansh hatázheni de vucho.** The building is fifteen floors high. **hatázheno mai opruno** topmost floor/top floor

hathado *pp/adj* 1) cheated, conned, deceived, swindled 2) *nm* victim of fraud: *nf* **hathadi**

hathádyol *vi* 1) be cheated/conned/deceived/ripped off/swindled: *pp/adj* **hathadilo** 2) be lured (*into smthg*) 3) be misled/mistaken, deceive oneself

hathavel *vt* 1) cheat, con, deceive, defraud, delude, rip off, swindle: *pp/adj* **hathado** 2) lure (*into*) 3) mislead 4) get the better of, outsmart 5) take advantage of, use 6) *v/refl* **hathavél-pe a)** deceive/delude oneself, sell oneself short **b)** mislead oneself, misread (*the signs*)

hathayimos *nm* 1) con shot, deception, duplicity, fraud, rip off, swindle; **Che hathayimos!** What a rip-off! 2) deceit, dishonesty 3) delusion 4) error

hathayitóri *nm* con man, deceiver, dream merchant, fraud, shyster, swindler: *nf* **hathayitórka**

házna *nf* advantage, benefit, profit, use; **Che házna?** What's the use? (*Eur*)

haznáko *gen/adj* advantageous, beneficial, useful

haznil *vt* 1) benefit from, make use of, profit from, use: *pp/adj* **haznime** 2) *v/refl* **hazníl-pe** be advantageous/beneficial, be of use, use

haznimásko *pp/adj* advantageous, useful

haznimos *nm* advantage, benefit, usefulness

Hederlézi/Herdelézi Balkan Romani feast held on May 6 and which is the same date as **Djurdgevdan**, the Feast of Saint George.

helméto *nm* hard hat, helmet (*Am*)

hemisfériya *nm* hemisphere

hêrbári *nm* scavanger

hêrédo *nm* heir: *nf* **hêredáika**

hêrèsh *nf* poll, tax, toll

hêrêshchívo *nm* tax collector, toll collector, ticket collector: *nf* **hêrêshchíva**

hergéla *nf* 1) herd 2) drove, string; **Sas lês hergéla grast pála lêste.** He had a string of horses with him.

hêrkári *nm* archer, Sagittarius (*Zod*)

hêrko *nm* 1) violin bow 2) bow; **hêrko thai súlitsa** bow and arrow

hêrmêntíl-pe *v/refl* bray, grunt, neigh, snort , whinny; **Hêrmentínas-pe le grast.** The horses were whinnying.

hêrmêntimós *nm* neighing, whinnying

hêrmènto *nm* hermit: *nf* **hêrmentáika**

hêrmitánsiya *nf* hermitage

heroi *nm* leg: *pl* **hera** (*Anat*)

hêrtávo *nm* hound, mastiff

hêrtíya/hûrtíya *nf* 1) generic paper, newspaper; **hêrtíya-kukashtaráki** toilet paper (*Am*) 2) bill. contract, document (*Am*) 3) *vt/i phr* **thol ánde hêrtíya** advertise, place in the newspaper

hêrtyáko *gen/adj* made of paper, newspaper; **hêrtyáko riportéri** newspaper reporter *comp/nm*

hifta/ifta *num* seven

hiftali *nf* number seven, seven in cards

hiftapódya *nf* octopus, squid

hiftá-suvya *nf/pl* arcane knowledge, seven needles/secrets, the secrets of some organization; **Zhanel le hiftá-suvya.** He is a member of the Masonic Lodge.

hiftáto *num* seventh

hiftáwardesh *num* seventy

hiftawardeshtáto *num* seventieth

hilyáda/hûlyáda *nf* ton; **hilyáda angar** ton of coal

hímno/ímno *nm* anthem, hymn

himnotaizil/imnotaizil *vt* 1) hypnotize, work as a hypnotist: *pp/adj*

himnotaizime 2) *v/refl* **himnotaizíl-pe** be/become hypnotized

himnotátsiya/imnotátsiya *nf* hypnotism

himnótiko/imnótiko *adj* hypnotic

himnotísto/imnotísto *nm* hypnotist

Hindukítska *nf* Hindi (*Lang*)

Hindukítsko *adj* Hindu, Indian

Hindukíya *nf* Hinduism (*religion*)

Hindúko *nm* Hindu: *nf* **Hindukáika**

hirésho *adj* celebrated, esteemed, famous by reputation

híringo *nm* hearing in court or immigration tribunal (*Can*)

hiriyáno *nm* horseradish

hiriyáno-patrin mustard plant (*Brassica genus Cruciferae*)

híro *nm* 1) news, news of interest to Roma: *pl* **hírya** 2) legend, saga, a story based on actual events or real people including living Roma or Romani ancestors. **Note**: **Hírya** differ from **paramíchya** *qv* since they purportedly refer to factual events while **paramíchya** are fairy tales usually regarded as fiction like *Jack-and-the-Beanstalk* in English.

hírya *nm/pl* 1) reputation (*of a person by accounts of him/her by others*), repute; **Chi mai dikhlem lês núma zhanav lês pe hírya.** I never met him but I know of him by reputation. **kále hírya** bad/evil reputation, **pakivale hírya** excellent reputation 2) fame, reputation, renown 3) apocrypha, hearsay, rumor

históriya/istóriya *nf* history; **Ame, le Rroma, chi zhanas amáre históriya.** We, the Roma, don't know our own history.

historiyásh *nm* historian: *nf* **historiyáshka**

Hitléri *nm* Hitler; **O Hitléri sas amári Mártiya.** Hitler was our Nemesis.

hodenil *vt* 1) rest, put to rest: *pp/adj* **hodenime**; **Te hodinil lês o Del!** May God rest him! 2) relax 3) *v/refl* **hodeníl-pe** rest, rest up, relax, take repose; **Hodení-ma tsîrrá mai anglal te mai keráv buki.** I will rest a little before

I work some more. **Hodeníl-pe o Stánko.**
Stanko is resting/relaxing. **Te hodeníl-pe
ánde pácha!** May he rest in peace! **4)**
take a rest, *with dative case*; **Zhav te
honenív-mánge.** I am going to take a
rest.

hodenimos *nm* rest, relaxation

hódina *nf* **1)** eternal repose/rest **2)** rest,
relaxation **3)** break; **Lem mánge hódina.**
I took a break/rest

hólba *nf* mug, stein

Holokústo *nm* Holocaust.

Hópa! *interj* Hurray! Hurrah!

horézo *nm* rice

horhúna *nf* gorgon

horushpíya *nf* **1)** immorality,
indecent/unacceptable sexual behaviour
2) loose conduct; **Dyás-pe ánde
horushpíya.** He conducted himself
immorally. **3)** prostitution

hotelash *nm* desk clerk: *nf* **hoteláshka**

hotéli *nm* hotel

huladimos *nm* **1)** leave taking, parting,
separation **2)** difference of opinion,
division

hulado *pp/adj* **1)** divided, separated **2)**
combed out, dressed (*hair*) **3)** different
(*in the sense of shared, subdivided*),
various; **Le Rrom ándo káko them
beshen ánde fórurya hulade.** The
Roma in this country live in different
cities.

huládyol *vi* **1)** be separated, be
shared/divided: *pp/adj* **huladilo 2)** be
combed out **3)** leave, part; **Huládilam
sar amala.** We parted as friends.
Xalé-pe thai huládile sar dushmáya.
They argued and departed as enemies.

hulavel *vt* **(1)** divide, divide up, separate,
share **(2)** comb, dress (*hair*): *pp/adj*
hulado 4) *v/refl* **hulavél-pe a)** divide
itself, share himself/herself/itself **b)** be
combed, dressed, comb/dress one's hair

hulayimos *nm* **1)** division, division/sharing
of shares **2)** combing, combing out,
untangling **3)** Apartheid, segregation

hulel *vt/i* **1)** clamber down, climb down,
come down, descend, dismount, get down,
get off, set: *pp/adj* **hulisto; hulisto katar
lêsko grast.** He dismounted from his
horse. **Huli tele!** Descend! Dismount!
Get down! **O kham hulel.** The sun is
setting. **2)** alight, land (*aeroplane*) **3)**
abate, settle down; **Hulel o réko.** The
lake is settling down/becoming calm.

huligáno *nm* hooligan, ruffian: *nf*
**huligánka; Shavále, kerén-tume sar
terne huligáya!** Boys, you are behaving
like young hooligans!

hulimos *nm* **1)** descent **2)** a settling down
3) reduction (*in price*), sale **4) o hulimos
le khamêsko** sundown, sunset

húlpa/vúlpa *nf* fox, vixen

hulyáda *nf* ton: *pl* **hulyédi**, tons, tonnage

hulyándro *nm* born wanderer, drifter,
hobo, footloose vagabond, wanderer: *nf*
hulyandráika

hulyarel *vt* **1)** make to descend, land,
(*aeroplane*): *pp/adj* **hulyardo 2)** depress,
drop, force down, lower, take down;
Hulyardem la katar e filástra. I
lowered it from the window.**O aropláno
hulyardas le rróti.** The aircraft lowered
the undercarriage. **3)** force from a
saddle/unsaddle, unseat; **4)** download
(*from computer*), unload **5)** *v/refl*
hulyarél-pe debase oneself, lower
oneself

hulyarimos *nm* **1)** forced descent, landing
(*aeroplane*) **2)** decrease in price **3)**
lowering **4)** downloading

húlyo *nm* **1)** turkey vulture/buzzard
(*Cathartes aura*) **2)** hawk, chicken hawk

hulyútso *nm* sparrow hawk

humanitárno *adj/neolog* humanitarian

hunavel *vt see* **wunavel** *vt*

hungyal *vi* creak, groan, moan: *pp/adj*
**hungyailo; Hungyan le rróti telal o
pharimos.** The (wagon) wheels are
creaking/groaning under the weight. **Le
phaleya hungyáile telal lêsko
pharimos.** The floor groaned under his
weight (*of a giant in folklore*).

Hungyálas kána sovélas. He was groaning in his sleep/when he was sleeping.

hungyála *nf* creak, groan, moan

hungyayimos *nm* creaking, groaning, moaning

húniya *nf* abyss, chasm, cliff, escarpment, gorge, precipice, ravine, span

hurayimáta *nm/pl* clothing, clothes, garments

hurayimos *nm* 1) clothing, costume, garments, wearing attire 2) act of dressing

hurimos *nm* flight; **ándo hurimos** in flight; **Pushkisardyas e rrátsa ándo hurimos.** He shot the duck in flight.

huryádyol *vi* 1) be dressed, get dressed: *pp/adj* **huryadilo; Hudyádilem te zhav kai sláva.** I got dressed to attend the feast.

huryal *vi* 1) fly, soar, take flight take wing: *pp/adj* **huryailo; Huryal le chiriklênsa.**

He is flying with the birds/His mind is not with us/He is not concentrating/He is out to lunch. (*Am*); **Mek te huryan tire gîndurya!** Let your thoughts take flight/Let your imagination soar. **Huryáile le papina, avel o ivend.** The geese have flown away, winter is approaching. 2) flitter, flutter 3) ~ **inkya** fly away/off; **O chiriklo huryáilo inkya.** The bird flew away/off

huryárdyol *vi* be flown, fly, travel by airliner: *pp/adj* **huryardilo; Huryárdile araki katar o Franzúzo.** They flew in from France yesterday.

huryarel *vt* fly, pilot: *pp/adj* **huryardo**

huryarimos *nm* airline flight, flight

huryavel *vt* 1) clothe, dress, provide with clothing: *pp/adj* **huryado** 2) adorn, deck out, decorate 3) *v/refl* **huryavél-pe** clothe, dress oneself; **Huryavél-pe sar o dilo.** He dresses like a fool.

I

i- *prod pref* also, either, too; **i-me zhav** I too am going. **Sáva kai me xav í-tu xas.** All that I eat, you too will eat. **Ker i-lêske than.** Make room for him too. **I-wo chi zhanel.** He doesn't know either. **Me gelem, i-múrro phral.** I went, also my brother.

-ichóso *prod suff* added to the root of adjectives to modify the meaning. **Lol-**red, gives **lol- + -ichóso** to create **lolichóso** reddish in colour/pink and **kal- + -ichóso** to create **kalichóso** blackish in colour. Adjectives so formed regardless of their root elements are declined like athematic adjectives: *ms/fs* **lolichóso,** *m/s/pl/obl* **lolichósone,** *f/s/obl* **lolichósonya**

idrólichi *nm/pl* hydraulics

idróliko *adj* hydraulic; **indjinéri-idróliko** hydraulic engineer

igalitéto *nm* equality (*Eur*)

igálno *adj* 1) equal, the same 2) *nm* equal, match: *nf* **igalnútsa**; **Arakhlas pêsko igálno.** He has met his match.

ignítsiya *nf* ignition; **De yag e ignítsiya.** Turn on the ignition!

ikóna *nf* icon

ikonáko *nm* icon, statue of a Saint, statue; **Meyázol ikonáko.** She looks like a statue of a Saint.

ikonomíya *nf* economy

ilástiko 1) *nm* elastic band: *pl* **ilástichi** 2) *adj* made of or behaving like elastic, pliable (*Am*)

ilêktrichi *nm/pl* headlights, spotlites, stage lights

ilêktrikásh *nm* electrician

ilêktriko *nm* 1) headlight, spotlite, stage light 2) electricity, hydro power; **Zhal po ilêktriko.** It runs on electricity. **Mulo o iléktriko.** The electric power has gone out. **Mudarde o iléktriko.** They turned off the electricity.

ilêktrikósko *gen/adj* electric

ilêktrobov *nm/neolog* microwave oven

ilêktrolil *nm/neolog* e-mail, e-mail letter; **Tráde lês pe ilêktrolil!** Send it by e-mail!

ilêktropósta *nf/neolog* electronic correspondence/mail

ilifánto *nm* elephant: *nf* **ilifantáika** (*Eur*)

iligálno *adj* illegal

iligalnones *adv* illegally

ílo *nm* diarrhea, dysentery **Note:** *do not confuse with* **yilo** 'heart.'

ilustratívno *adj* illustrated, illustrative; **ilustratívno kníshka** illustrated booklet

imeiylil *vt* email, send by email: *pp/adj* **imeiylime** emailed (*Eur*)

iméiylo *nm* email

imfantríya *nf* infantry (*Mil*)

imigránto *nm* immigrant: *nf* **imigrantáika**

imigrátsiya *nf* immigration, immigration department: *gen/adj* **imigratsyáko**

ímno *nm* 1) hymn 2) anthem

impáche *adv* in peace; **Zha impáche!** Go in peace!

implementuwil *vt/neolog* implement: *pp/adj* **implementuwime**

importánto *adj* important

importántsiya *nf* importance

impósto *nm* income tax, tax (*Eur*)

impresil *vt* 1) impress: *pp/adj* **impresime** 2) **impresíl-pe** *v/refl* (be impressed); **Chi impresisáilem.** I wasn't impressed.

imprésiya *nf* impression
imunitáte/imunitéto *nm* immunity (*Eur*)
imúno *adj* immune
imváziya *nf* invasion
Índiya *nf* India
Indiyáko *gen/adj* Indian, of India;
 Indiyáko pekimos Indian cuisine
Indiyanítska *nf* a North-American Native
 language
Indiyanítsko *adj* Native
 American/Canadian
Indiyáno *nm* Native *psn*: *nf* **Indiyánka:** *pl*
 Indiyáiya Native Canadians/Americans
indjinéri *nm* engineer: *nf* **injinérka**
inegálno *adj* unequal
inegalnones *adv* unequally
informátsiya *nf* information, data
ingárdyol *vi* 1) be carried/carried on/held
 onto/kept/maintained/observed/
 perpetuated/supported: *pp/adj* **ingardilo**
 2) be transported
ingarel/ingerel *vt/i* 1) bear, carry, convey,
 drive, haul, sustain, take, take along, take
 away/there, transport: *pp/adj* **ingardo;**
 Ingardyas la ándo mobíli. He took her
 there in the car 2) hold, hold onto, hold
 up, prop up, support; **Ingaren kris.** They
 are holding a trial. 3) carry on, conserve,
 keep, observe (laws), maintain,
 perpetuate, preserve (*traditions*), retain;
 Ame ingaras amáre hadéturya. We
 keep/maintain our traditions. 4) steer 5)
 hang onto, keep; **Arakhlem la hai
 ingarav la.** I found it and I'll keep it 6)
 v/refl **ingarél-pe** endure, last, remain in
 existence, suffer (*changes*); **Pêske love
 chi ingarén-pe swágdar.** His money
 won't last forever.
ingarimásko *gen/adj* 1) portable 2)
 enduring
ingarimos *nm* 1) transportation 2)
 preservation 3) guidance, steering,
 support
Inglezítska *nf* English (*Lang*)
Inglezítsko *adj* English
Inglezitskones *adv* like the English, in the
 English language

Inglézo *nm* Englishman: *nf* **Inglezáika**
inka/inke *adv* still, yet; **Chi avilo inka.** He
 hasn't arrived yet. **Inka kathé-lo.** He's
 still here.
inkalavel *vt see* **ankalevel** *vt*
inkálka *nf* trespass, trespassing
inkalkil *vt* 1) trespass: *pp/adj* **inkalkime**
inklel *vt/i see* **anklel** *vt/i*
inkya *adv* away, off; **Shúde la inkya!**
 Throw it away!
inkyal *adv/prep* 1) across, over, across
 from, on the other side, through;
 Nakhlem inkyal o drom. I crossed over
 the road. 2) opposite; **Beshélas inkyal
 mándar ánde sláva.** He was sitting
 across from/opposite to me during the
 feast. 3) *comp/vt/i* **zhal** ~ cross over, ford
inkyal e máriya *adv/phr* across the sea,
 overseas
inkyayimos *nm* crossing, ford, fording
 place
inkyorral/inkyorra *adv*
 after/afterwards/later on *us* with **mai;**
 Kam-aven mai inkyorral. They will
 arrive later on.
inspesyálno *adv* especially (*Eur*)
institúto *nm/neolog* institute
institútsiya *nf/neolog* institution
insulátsiya *nf* insulation
intáini/intáina *adv* in vain, for nothing, to
 no avail, to no end, without
 purpose/reason; **Mardyas la intáini.** He
 beat her for no reason.
integril *vt* 1) integrate 2) *v/refl* **integríl-pe**
 become integrated
integrime *pp/adj* integrated
integrimos *nm* integration
intelektuwálno *adj/neolog* intellectual
intelektuwálo *nm/neolog* intellectual: *nf*
 intelektuwálútsa
interezhil *vt* 1) create interest, gain intert,
 interest, make interested: *pp/adj*
 interezhime 2) *v/refl* **interezhíl-pe** be
 interested; **O gazho interezhíl-pe ánde
 amári muzíka.** The non-Romani man is
 interested in our music.

interézhno *adj* **1)** interesting, interested **2)** *nm* enthusiasm, interest; **Si tut interézhno?** Have you any interest? **Manai interézhno ándo kodo prodjékto.** There is no interest in that project. **Ándo kásko interézhno keres gadya?** In whose interest are you doing this? **Nai interézhno te keren khánchi.** They are not interested in doing anything.

Internéto *nm* Internet

Internetóski rêg *comp/nf* Internet site, web site (*Eur*) **Note:** This is a common emerging neologism in Europe where web site seems to be confused with web side by Romani speakers.

Internetósko than *nm* web site

intoleránsiya *nf/neolog* intollerence

întrêgíl *vt* **1)** advance **2)** advance, assault/attack, invade (*Mil*): *pp/adj* **întrêgimé 2)** *v/refl* **întrêgíl-pe** advance/be advancing/assaulting/attacking/invading/moving forward

întrêgimós *nm* **1)** advance, assault, attack, invasion, movement forward, offensive (*Mil*)

investigátsiya *nf* investigation

inya *num* nine

inyali *nf* number nine, nine in cards

inyáto ninth

inyáwardesh *num* ninety: **inyawardeshtáto** ninetieth

ipokrasíya *nf* hypocrisy

ipopotámo *nm* hippopotamus

iril *vt* **1)** give back, retrieve, repossess, return, turn back: *pp/adj* **irime 2)** *v/refl* **iríl-pe** come back, return

irimos *nm* coming back, giving back, retrieval, repossession, return (of)

Islámo *nm* Islam

istóka *nf* breeding stock, livestock

ístra *nf* skid, slide

istral *vi* **1)** glide, skate, skid, slip, slide: *pp/adj* **istrailo; Istráili ánde úlitsa.** She slipped in the street. **2)** *vt/i* ~ **andre** slip in; **Istráili andre pa o wudár paluno.** She slipped in through the back door. **3)**

vt/i ~ **telal** slip under; **Istráilo telal o plapóno.** He slipped under the quilt.

istramos *nm* fall, skid, slip, slide

istrano *adj* slippery

Isús o Krísto/Isukrísto *comp/nm* Jesus Christ

Isúso/Isus *nm* Jesus (*Eur*)

Itáliya *nf* Italy

Italyáko *gen/adj* of Italy

Italyanítska *nf* Italian (*Lang*)

Italyanítsko *adj* Italian

Italyáno *nm* Italian: *nf* **Italyánka**

í-te *conj* even if/should; **Í-te pokines man, chi zhav.** Even if you pay me, I won't go.

itineráryo *nm* itinerary: *pl* **itinerárya**

íto *nm* **1)** spice **2)** generic hot spice

itol *vt* spice (*food*): *pp/adj* **itome**

itome *pp/adj* spiced, spicy

itomos *nm* spicing of food

íturya *nm/pl* hot spices

iv *nm* **1)** snow **2)** *comp/vi* **del o** ~ snow

ivalo *adj* snowy

ivand *adj* crude, raw, uncooked

ivandomos *nm* rawness, in an uncooked state

ivend *nm* winter, wintertime

ivendalo *adj* winter, wintery

ivende *adv* in/during the winter

ivendil *vt* **1)** hole up for the winter, pass the winter: *pp/adj* **ivendime 2)** *v/refl* **ivendíl-pe** pass the winter, winter; **Ivendisáilam ándo Târánto.** We wintered in Toronto.

ivêski-bála *comp/nf* snowball

ivêski-lopáta *comp/nf* snow shovel

ivêski-patrin *comp/nf* snowflake

ivésko *gen/adj* belonging to snow, related to snow

ivêsko-perimos *comp/nm* snowfall

ivêsko-plúgo snow plough

ivóryo *nm* ivory

ivoryósko *gen/adj* made of ivory

Ívro *nm* Euro: *pl* **Ívri** (*currency*) (*Eur*)

Ivrópa *nf* Europe; **Ivrópa ântrégo** the whole of Europe

Ivropáko *gen/adj* of Europe;
  Rrom-Ivropáko Rom from Europe: *pl*
  Rroma-Ivropáke
Ivropanítsko *adj* European
Ivropanítsko-Úniya *comp/nf* European
  Union
Ivropáno *nm* European: *nf* **Ivropánka**
ivya *adv* for nothing, free, gratis; **Dine ame
  andre ivya.** They let us in free.
izdrádyol *vi* **1)** be affected/ impacted on:
  pp/adj **izdradilo 2)** be made to shake,
  tremble
izdral *vi* **1)** dodder, have the shakes, quiver,
  shake, tremble, vibrate: *pp/adj* **izdrailo**;
  Izdrálas darátar, e gêrí. She was
  trembling from fear, poor thing. **Izdral
  phurimástar.** He shakes from cerebral
  palsy. **Izdrálas ánde pêske khereya.** He
  was shaking in his boots. *id* **Kána del
  rrîl, izdral e phuv.** When he farts, the
  earth trembles/He is somebody to worry
  about **2)** be delirious, exhibit stress, suffer
  from stress **3)** chatter (*teeth*)
izdramásko *gen/adj* delirious, hysterical,
  trembling, quivering
izdramos *nm* **1)** delirium, hysteria,
  nervousness, shaking, quivering **2)**
  restlessness **3)** stress
izdrano *adj* agitated, delirious, excited,
  impulsive, nervous, quavering, restless,
  shaking with anticipation or
  apprehension, stressed out, trembling

izdranomos *nm* hypertension, nervous
  energy, restlessness
izdravel *vt* **1)** excite, impact on/make an
  impact, make to shake/tremble/quiver,
  shake up: *pp/adj* **izdrado 2)** create
  mental stress, make nervous, spook,
  stress **3)** make palsied
izdráveno *adj see* **izdrávo** *adj*
izdrávo *adj* healthful, healthy, energetic,
  strong; **Xa mai but, izdrávo si!** Eat
  more, it's good for you!
izdrayimos *nm* **1)** shaking, trembling,
  quivering **2)** cerebral palsy
izdráza *nf* cerebreal palsy
izdrázo *adv* at once, immediately, in a
  flash, right away; **Kána ashundyas o
  nevimos, gêlótar izdrázo.** When he
  heard the news, he left at once. **Biláilo
  izdrázo.** He vanished in a flash.
izelítsa *nm/nf* collaborator, renegade,
  sell-out, traitor
izelitsíya *nf* betrayal, collaboration
izgyárda *nf* **1** locket **2)** woman's necklace,
  us with cameo or gold jewelry attached
ízula/yízula *nf* island
izuláko *gen/adj* insular
izviníl-pe *v/refl* apologize (*Eur*)
izvinimos *nm* apology
izvonésko-sap *comp/nm* rattlesnake (*Am*)
izvóno/izwóno *nm* bell, buzzer, doorbell,
  chime, small gong: *pl* **izvóya**; **Bashlo o
  izvóno.** The bell rang. **Bashav o izvóno!**
  Ring the bell!

K

ka *prep* at, to; **1) ka o fóro** to the city. **ka l' Rromênde** to the Roma; **Dikhlem lês ka o diwáno**. I saw him at the meeting. **Símas ka o Bab sa o pála misméri.** I was at Bob's place all afternoon. **2)** *used with time*; **Aváv ka l' dui ándo mismséri.** I will come at two in the afternoon. **Che cháso si?** What time is it? **Desh ka l' pansh.** Ten to five. **3)** *pron/s* who, that; **Dikhlan le Rrromes ka avilo?** Did you see the man that/who arrived? **Chi zhanav la Rromnya ka beshel kothe.** I don't know the woman who is sitting over there. *See also* **kai** *pron/s/pl*

ka- *prod/pref. Among some **Kalderash** and Vlach-Romani speakers,* **ka -** *is used istead of* **kam-** *qv;* **dikhav** 'I shall see' *gives* **ka-dikhav** 'I shall see'

kabinéta *nf* bathroom, ladies room, washroom, toilet (*Eur*)

kabinéto *nm* cabinet, storage cabinet; **shtakláko kabinéto** cabinet wih glass doors

kabína *nf* cab, car; **kabína pe rráta** cab on a ferris wheel, **kabína po zhútso** cable car.

kábo *nm* **1)** cab of a tractor, truck **2)** taxi (*Am*)

kabúso *nm* caboose of a train (*Am*); *id* **Me trádav o djédjêsh hai tume beshen palal ándo kabúso.** I'll drive the train and you will all sit behind in the caboose/ *id* I am going to run this show all by myself. (*Am*)

kaichi *adv* so; **Kaichi diló-lo ke nashti dikhlel o chachimos.** He is so foolish he can't see the truth.

káda *dem/pron/adj* this, this *psn*/thing (*Eur*) *see also* **kako** *dem/pron/adj*

kadala *dem/pron/adj see* **kakala** *pron*

kadale *dem/pronadj see* **kakale** *pron*

kadáva *dem/pron* this

kadiki/gadiki *adv* **1)** so, so many, so much; **Kadiki but Rroma avile, te chi maládyon sya ánde khangeri.** So many Roma came that they did not all fit inside the church. **2)** this much, this; **kadiki de baro** this big, **kadiki de but** so much, this much *var of* **gadiki** *qv*

kadka *adv* here, over here, right here, in this spot; **Tho lês kadka!** Put it right here!

kadkar *adv* from right here, from this spot, through here; **Kadkar, nai dur.** From here, it's not far.

kado *dem/pron/adj* this *var of more us* **kako** *pron*

kadya *dem/pron/adj/adv* this, so, thus *var of more us* **kakya** *pron*

káfa *nf coffee*; **káli ~** black coffee, **Túrsko ~** Turkish coffee (*Eur*)

kafáki-síniya *comp/nf* coffee table

kafáko-asav *nm* coffee mill, crank operated coffee grinder

kafenáva *nf* coffee shop, café

ka-fundáko *used with* **del-pe**; *v/refl* **dél-pe ~** dive, dive into; **Dyás-pe ka-fundáko ándo pai.** He dived into the water. *see also* **de-fundáko** *nm*

kafundíl-pe *v/refl* dive, dive into, plunge

kafundimos *nm* dive, plunge

kai *adv* where; **Kai zhas?** Where are you going? **Chi zhanav kai beshel.** I don't know where he lives.

kai *conj* **1)** because *var of* **ke** *conj* **2)** and *var of* **thai** *conj*

kai *pron/pl* who, whom, that; **Kodole si le shave kai bashaven ándo spektákulo.** Those are the young men who are playing music in the show. **Arakhlem le love kai xasardem.** I found the money that I lost. **Manai aver Rroma kai si mai xarano vi túte.** There are no other Roma who are as smart as you are.

kaigodi *adv/conj* elsewhere, no matter where, wherever

kak *nm* uncle: *pl* **kákurya**

kak *pron/adj* any, some, no, none; **Nai tut kak buki?** Don't you have any work? **Nai lês kak love.** He has no money. **Nai tut kak love?** Don't you have any money?

káka *nf* baby shit

kakadéra *nf* baby pot, potty; **Tho lês pe kakadéra!** Put him on the potty! **Zhanel te zhal kai kakadéra.** He's toilet-trained.

kakala *dem/pron/acc/adj/s* this *women/things*; **Zhanes kakala?** Do you know this woman? **Avilo kakala Rromnyása.** He arrived with this woman.

kakaláko *pron/gen* belonging to this female person; **E Mára si kakaláki phey.** Mary is this woman's sister.

kakalátar *adv* like this (*if nf*), because of this, from this woman.

kakale *dem/pron/adj* these, these things, these men/people (*of both genders*); **Kakale gazhe avile te farbon o kher.** These men came to paint the house. **Kon si kakale?** Who are these people?

kakalêndar *adv* **1)** like these, like these people, of these, of these people; **Mangel te phiravel tsáliya kakalêndar.** She wants to wear clothes like these. **2)** *conj* because of these/these things/people; **Xalyam but nekázo kakalêndar.** We suffered a lot of aggravation because of these these people.

kakales *pron/acc* this man/thing; **Zhanes kakales?** Do you know this man?

kakalêsko *pron/gen* belonging to this male person; **O Yóno si kakalêsko phral.** John is this man's brother.

kakalêstar *adv* **1)** like this, from this (*if nm*); **Sóde manges kakalêstar?** How much do you want of this/this one? **Mangav aver kakalêstar** I want another (*one*) like this one. **2)** *conj* because of this/this thing/male person or animal **3)** from this man

kakaráchi *nm* **1)** male magpie **2)** male jackdaw/raven: *nf* **kakaráchka**

kakavi *nf* kettle

kakléta *nf* meatball: *pl* **kaklétsi**

kakli *nf* bobbin, flywheel, spindle

kaklil *vt* spin: *pp/adj* **kaklime**

kaklimos *nm* spinning

káklitsa *nf* **1)** loom, spinning wheel **2)** fishing reel

kako **1)** *dem/pron/adj* this (*illic*); **Kako grast si naswalo.** This horse is sick. **2)** *nm* male *psn* animal or masc object; **Kon si kako?** Who is this? (*male psn*). **So si kako?** What;'s this thing?

káko *nm/voc* **1)** uncle **2)** uncle (*fig*) and term of respect for an older man; **Káko Váno** Uncle John **3)** *neolog* **Kako Tóma** Uncle Tom. **Note:** While **Káko** is technically a vocative, there is a tendency to use it as a nominative in titles such as **Káko Stévo,** 'Uncle Steve,' when used to refer to a respected group elder.

kakorro *nm* uncle, dear uncle

kakya *pron/adj/adv* so, thus, this, this thing, this woman; **Kakya shey gilabal mishto.** This girl sings well. **Zhanes kakya?** Do you know this woman?

kakyavári *nm* kettlesmith, maker/repairer of kettles

kakyaváriya *nf* kettle-smith's shop

kála *dem/adj* these (*cont of* **kakala**)

kalanfíra *nf* clove

Kalderári *nm var of* Kalderash

Kalderash *nm* **1)** Coppersmith/Cauldron smith **2)** male member of the **Kalderash** group: *nf* **Kalderashútsa**

Kalderashítska *nf* Kalderash Romani dialect

Kalderashítsko *adj* Kalderash

Kalderútso *nm* young *Kalderash* boy/teenager: *nf* **Kalderútsa**

kale *dem/adj* these (*cont of* **kakale**); **Kale gesa chi mai tradas.** These days we don't travel any more.

kalé-balêngo *comp/gen/adj* brunet

kalendári *nm* calendar

kaleni *nf* blackberry

kales *adv* **1)** tragically, miserably **2)** without documents, quasi legal, surreptitiously, illegally, by the back door, in a round about way; **Chi den amênge papírya te keras buki ápo músai te keras buki kales.** They won't give is work permits so we have to work illegally. **Avile kales ándo them.** They entered the country illegally(*without documents*). **Gêlyám kales.**We traveled illegally (*without documents*). **Te nashti kerav wórta, kerav kales.** If I can't do it the normal way, I'll do it surreptitiously.

kalé-yakhêngo *comp/gen/adj* dark-eyed

káli baxt *nf* tragic fate

káli daimánta *comp/nf* hematite black diamond, Alaska diamond

káli dar *comp/nf* mortal fear/terror

káli firánga *nf* **1)** black curtain, something or *smbdy* inscrutable, unfathomable or mysterious **2)** dark curtain/veil of mystery

Kali Ivrópa Central/Eastern Europe (*Eur*)

Kali Legíya *nf* Black Legion/*Einsatzgruppen*, Gestapo, Nazi SS (*Eur*)

Káli Sára *nf* Saint Sarah (*Eur*), The Black Madonna in the crypt of the church at *Les Saintes Maries de la Mer* in France. Her festival is celebrated on May 24.

kalichóso *adj* blackish in colour, dark-skinned, swarthy

káli-múra *nf* blackberry

kalí-pûnzhaváika *comp/nf* black widow spider, woman seen as a destroyer of men (*Am*)

Kalisfériya *nf* underworld region believed by some *Kalderash*-Romani groups to be a region of darkness, a sea of mud inhabited by reptilian creatures, where the souls of suicide victims and unbaptized children must remain until given Grace by God before they can enter **Rrayo**, the *Kalderash* concept of Heaven or the Afterworld.

kali-yakh *comp/nf* black eye

kalmayil *vt* **1)** calm *smbdy* down: *pp/adj* **kalmayime; Kalmayisar lês!** Calm him down! **2)** *v/refl* **kalmíl-pe** calm oneself down; **Kalmisáwo!** Calm down!

kalo *adj* **1)** black, dark-skinned **2)** dark; **káli ryat** dark night **3)** dreadful, heart-breaking, miserable, pitiable, tragic; **kálo tráyo** miserable/tragic life **4)** marginalized, underground, undocumented; **káli buki** underground economy, **kálo yarmáko** black market **5)** cursed, tragic; **kali gili** tragic song, **kálo kher** tragic/unfortunate/cursed house(*house where smby was murdered or committed suicide*), **kálo lil** letter bearing bad news or news of a tragedy, **kali fátsa** dark/tragic face foreboding of disaster

kalo *nm* spade (*in playing cards*): *pl* **kale; o Túzo kalêngo** the Ace of spades

Kálo Rrom *nm* dark-skinned Rom: *nf* **Káli Rromni**

kaló-kanrro *comp/nm* blackthorn

kaló-liyondári *nm* black panther/leopard

Kalorro *nm* African, African American/Canadian, Black man: *nf* **Kalyorri**

kálo-them *comp/nm* **1)** cursed/tragic/miserable country **2)** cursed/tragic people

kâlpakári *nm* **1)** distiller **2)** moonshiner

kâlpakáriya *nf* brewery, distillery

kâlpáko *nm* **1)** still **2)** vat

kalts/káltsû *nf/pl* trousers; **Kindem nevo zhuto kalts.** I bought a new pair of trousers.

káltsi *nf/pl* britches, slacks, trousers (*Eur*)

kaludjári *nm* monk

kaludjérka *nf* 1) nun 2) prudish/uptight woman

kalugo *adj* 1) black, dark-skinned 2) *nm* Black man: *nf* **Kalugi**

kalyá-morkyáko *comp/gen/adj* dark-skinned

kalyárdyol *vi* 1) be/become blackened/darkened/sun-tanned: *pp/adj* **kalyardilo** 2) be made miserable/tragic

kalyarel *vt* 1) make black/dark, tan: *pp/adj* **kalyardo** 2) blacken (*smbdy's name*) 3) make tragic

kalyol *vi* 1) become black/dark/sun-tanned, turn black: *pp/adj* **kalilo** 2) become blackened, smeared 3) become tragic

kam- *prod/v/pref* shall, will: **Kam-** is prefixed to conjugated verbs in the present tense to create the future tense, shall, will; **Kam-zhav tehára.** I shall go tomorrow. **Kam-kerdyol tehára.** It shall be done tomorrow. **O grast kam-mulyovel teharása.** The horse will have died by tomorrow.

kãma *nf* 1) mane (*horse or lion*) 2) withers

kamado *adj* 1) loved 2) *nm* lover: *nf* **kamadi** lover, sweetheart

kamaflúzha *nf* camouflage

kamafluzhil *vt* 1) camouflage; *pp/adj* **kamafluzhime** 2) **kamafluzhíl-pe** *v/refl*

kámas- *prod/v/pref* prefixed to conjugated verbs to create the conditional mood; **Kámas-kerav.** I would do (it); **Kámas-kerdem**. I would have made/would have done (it). **Kámas-gêlèm araki te zhanglémas te músai sas-mange te zhav.** I would have gone yesterday if I had known that it was necessary for me to go.

kámas-avel *v* it would be; **Kámas-avel mai mishto te zhas akana.** It would be better to go now.

kam-avel *v* he/she/it will be; **Wo kam-avel amáro dushmáno.** He will be/become our enemy.

kam-aven *v* they will be; **Kam-aven ka o djuléshi.** They will be at the meeting. **Kam-aven ma love tehára.** I shall have monet tomorrow.

kámbera *nf* breech, chamber (*of a rifle or field gun*)

kamel *vt/i* 1) desire, want, wish: *pp/adj* **kamlo** 2) love, like 3) make love 4) lend, owe (*money*); **Kamel mánge shel tiléri.** He owes me $100. 5) (*with negative* **chi**) reject; **Chi kamlas.** He rejected it. 6) appreciate; **Chi mai kamel so kerav láke.** She never appreciates what I do for her. 7) *v/refl* **kamél-pe a)** want for oneself, want to possess for oneself; **Dikhlas le grastes hai akana kamél-pe.** He saw the horse and now he wants it for himself. **b)** fall in love, make love **c)** be in love; **Kamén-pe.** They are in love.**c)** make love; **Kamlé-pe.** They made love.

kámera *nf* camera

kamféta *nf* candy: *pl* **kamféti** candies, sweets

kamfitúra *nf* jam, jelly, preserves

kamfóri *nm* camphor

kamfuzil *vt* badmouth, slander: *pp/adj* **kamfuzime**

kamfuzimásko *gen/adj* libelous, slanderous

kamfuzimos *nm* calumny, libel, slander

kamimos *nm* 1) love, desire (*usually erotic*) 2) debt, loan

kamlo *adj* beloved, dear

kampána *nf* 1) large/loud bell, as a church bell 2) large gong or cymbal

kampánya *nf* country, countryside, rural area

kampash *nm* camper, resident of a trailer park: *nf* **kampáshka**

kampína *nf* mobile home, travel trailer (*Eur*)

kámpo *nm* 1) camp, camping ground, trailer park 2) concentration/detention camp (*Eur*)

kampyóno *nm* champion, sports champion (*Eur*): *nf* **kampyóna**

kamyonéri *nm* truck driver (*Eur*)

kamyóno *nm,* truck (*Eur*)

kan 1) *nm* ear (*Anat*): *pl* **kan 2)** eye, eyelet **3)** *comp/vt/i* **del ~** obey, heed; **Chi mai del ma kan.** He never obeys me. **De ma kan!** Heed what I say! **4)** *comp/vi* **lel ~** take heed **5)** *comp/vi* **shúdel ~** ask around, eavesdrop, investigate, make inquiries; **Chi zhanav kai-lo akana núma shudáv kan.** I don't know where he is right now but I'll ask around. **6) thol ~** pay attention.

kána *adv/conj/pron* when, while; **Kána zhas?** When are you going? **Mothav túke kána zhávtar.** I'll tell you when I am leaving. **Pokinav lês kána avel pálpale.** I'll pay him when he returns. **Pelo mulo kána kerélas buki.** He dropped dead while he was working.

Kánada *nf* **1)** Canada (*Am*) **2) Kanáda** *nf* (*Eur*)

Kanadáko *gen/adj* Canadian; **Rrom-Kanadáko** Canadian Rom: *nf* **Romni-Kanadáki:** *nm/pl* **Rrom-Kanadácha** Canadian Roma

kanadéto *nm* candidate *nf* **kanadéta**

Kanadézo *nm* **1)** Canadian: *pl* **Kanadézurya:** *nf* **Kanadáika 2)** Canadian Rom

kanagodi *pron* whenever; **Háide kanagodi plachal tu!** Come whenever you please!

kanalo *adj* **1)** having large ears **2)** *nm* hare: *nf* **kanali**

kanálo *nm* **1)** channel, canal, drain, sewer **2)** TV channel

kándel *vt/i* **1)** follow advice, give heed, listen to, obey, pay attention to, serve: *pp/adj* **kandino**; **Kánglem lêsko mui.** I followed his advice/I did what he told me to do. **Shavorrále! Kánden múrro mui!** Kids! Obey me!/Do as I tell you! **2)** agree with; **Kándes man?** Do you agree with me? **3)** *v/refl* **kándel-pe** be obeyed by *smbdy: see also* **del–kan** *comp/vt/i*

kandelábra *nf* candelabra, chandelier

kandíla *nf* candlestick

kandimos *nm* **1)** attention, heed **2)** obedience **3)** submission

kandino *pp/adj* obedient

kanéla *nf* channel

kanêski-morki *comp/nf* eardrum

kangli/khangli *nf* comb

kanglyarel *vt* comb: *pp/adj* **kanglyardo**

kanglyorri *nf* centipede

kanopíya stove canopy in a restaurant kitchen (*Am*)

kanrralo *adj* prickly, thorny; **masho ~** perch (*fish*)

kanrro *nm* **1)** hawthorn, thorn **2)** stinger (*of bee/wasp*), sting (*bee/wasp*)

kantína *nf* type of bar cum restaurant (*Am from Sp*)

kanvérto *nm* **1)** envelope **2)** dossier, file folder **3)** computer file

kápa *nf* **1)** blanket, coverlet **2)** *arch* shawl *see also* **basmáli** *nm*

kapára *nf* traditional betrothal offering. At the official betrothal ceremony, the father of the boy presents his opposite number a bottle of whisky (**plótska**) to which is attached a headscarf (**diklo**) which envelopes the **kapára,** usually a gold necklace. If the father of the girl accepts this in front of the witnesses, the engagement becomes binding. The girl then wears the **kapára** and the **diklo** at the wedding after she is officially married.

kapéla *nf* **1)** chapel **2)** funeral parlour

kapelmésteri/kapelmáistoro *nm* band leader (*Mus*)

kapélya *nf* baptismal font

kapitalísmo *nm* capitalism, free-enterprise economy (*Eur*)

kapitalísto *nm* capitalist: *pl* **kapitalísti** (*Eur*)

kapitálo *nm* **1)** capital (*city*) **2)** capital (*assets/money*)

kapitáno *nm* captain

káplitsa/kaplítsa *nf* **1)** wall shrine (*shrine on the wall in a Kalderash home with religious icons and other sacred and* *spiritual objects inside, usually painted light blue on the interior*).

kápo *nm* **1)** boss, leader (*Eur*) **2)** kapo in a Nazi concentration camp (*Eur*) **3)** head man in a refugee camp for Roma in Europe (*Eur*) **4)** capotasto (*Mus*)

kaporálo *nm* corporal (*Mil*)

kar *nm* penis (*not used in polite conversation or before women*) (*Anat*)

karabíno *nm* carbine

karalo *adj* **1)** obsessed with sex **2)** sexually aroused (*man or male animal*) **3)** *nm* lecher

karándash *nm* pencil

karáva *nf* **1)** barge, scow (*Am*) **2)** lobster fishing boat (*Eur*) **3)** launch

karavána *nf* **1)** caravan **2)** convoy

karavdi *nf* **1)** lobster **2)** crayfish

kar-baro *comp/nm* erection

karbóno *nm* **1)** carbon **2)** carbon copy

karburéta *nf* carburator

karbúzo/karpúzo *nm* watermelon

kardiyologíya *nf* cardiology

karéto *nm* carat

karfin *nf* **1)** nail: *pl* **karfiya 2)** rivet, stud **3)** cotter pin **4)** firing pin

karfinil *vt* **1)** nail, attach with nails. **2)** apply rivets/studs **3)** crucify **karfinime** *pp/adj* **1)** nailed, attached with nails **2)** rivetted **3)** crucified

karfinorri *nf* carpet tack, push pin, small nail, thumbtack

karing *prep/adv* toward, towards, this way; **Avel karing mánde.** He is coming towards me. **Háide karing!** Come this way! **Thon o shkáfo karing o zudo!** Put the bureau up against the wall!

kariyéra *nf* career

kárlitsa *nf* **1)** wooden platter/tray **2)** cutting board for vegetables

karnivála/karniválo *nf/nm* carnival

karnivalash *nm* **1)** carny, carnival man, shrewd operator, rounder: *nf* **karnivaláshka 2)** concessionaire on a carnival; **Karnivalash sim, chi sim fermári.** I'm a carnival man, I'm not a farmer. **Xlûtro múrri Rromni, sar**

karnivaláshka. My wife is shrewd, like a carnival woman.

Karpátiya *nf* Carpathian region of Eastern Europe

Karpáto *adj* Carpathian; **Rrom-Karpáto** Rom from Transylvania who speaks the Carpathian *Romungeri* dialect of Romani: *nf* **Karpatútsa** *nf*

karpintéri *nm* carpenter, woodworker

karshindo 1) *pp/adj* circumcised **2)** *nm* man who has been circumcised

karshíndyol *v/i* be/become circumcised: *pp/adj* **karshindilo**

karshinel *vt* circumsize: *pp/adj* **karshindo**

karshinimos *nm* circumcision

kárta *nf* **1)** business card **2)** playing card

kárta-bankáki *comp/nm* bank card, Interac card

kárta-kreditóski *comp/nm* credit card

kartóno *nm* cardboard box, carton

kartonósko *gen/adj* made of cardboard

kartúno *nm* cartoon, comic

kartúzo *nm* **1)** cartridge, shotgun shell **2)** cartridge for a printer **3)** cap, detonating cap, firing cap

karuséla *nf* carousel, merry-go-round; **Kruyal, kruyal zhal e karuséla.** Round and round goes the merry-go-round/Life keeps on repeating itself.

kãs/kas *pron/acc* who, whom; **Kãs dikhlan?** Whom did you see? **Kodo si o Rrom kãs me dikhlem kai sláva.** That is the Rom whom I saw at the feast. **Kon akushlas kãs ándo xamos?** Who insulted whom during the argument?

kása *nf* **1)** bank **2)** vault, strongbox **3)** hock shop, pawnshop

kãsa *pron/inst* with whom; **Si kodo o Rrom kãsa gêlyán?** Is that the Rom with whom you went? **Kãsa beshlan kai sláva?** With whom did you sit at the feast? **Chi zhanav kãsa délas-dúma.** I don't know with whom she has been speaking.

kasavêndar *adv* like such, such as those, things like this/that, such things

kasevêstar *adv* like such a thing, so much like, such a; **Kasevêstar dilo si.** He's such a fool.

kasevo *adj/pron* such, such a, so much so; **kasevo lasho grast** such a good horse. **Chi sim kasevo de dilo.** I am not such a fool. **Kasevi si sar e lulugi.** She is so much like a flower.

kasht *nm* 1) tree 2) lumber, wood 3) stand for musical instrument, microphone, music stand 4) coffin; **Dav lês ándo kasht.** I'll put him in his coffin. 5) pulpit, podium 6) mast (*of a ship*), mast (*flagpole*)

kashtalo *adj* 1) having the quality of wood, wooden. 2) *nm* non-Romani-speaking Rom: *nf* **Kashtali** (*Eur*); **Nai chache Rroma. Kashtale si.** They are not real Roma. They are wooden ones.(*Eur*) In Canada/US, **Rrom-Kashtalo** would be **Rrom bi-shibáko:** *nf* **Rromni bi-shibáki:** *pl* **Rrom bi-shibáke**

kashtári *nm* 1) woodsman 2) wood seller 3) forester

kashtêngo shinitóri *comp/nm* tree feller, lumberjack

kasht -kovlo *comp/nm* ash (*tree*)

kasht -mariyáko *comp/nm* driftwood

kashtorro *nm* 1) sapling 2) small tree 3) small block/piece of wood, wooden wedge

kasht-shuko *comp/nm* brushwood, firewood, tinder

kasht-xoxamno *comp/nm* imitation wood, pressed wood

kasht-yagáko *comp/nm* faggots, firewood, kindling wood

kashukimásko *gen/adj* deafening, ear-shattering; **kashukimáski si e muzíka.** The music is deafening/ear-shattering.

kashukimos *nm* deafening noise, deafness

kashuko *adj* 1) deaf; **Nashti bashaves le kashukênge.**You can't play music for the deaf. (*proverb*) 2) *nm* deaf man: *nf* **kashuki**

kashukyárdyol *vi* cause to be deafened, be made deaf: *pp/adj* **kashukyardilo; Kashukyárdilo le barrudimástar.** He was made deaf by the explosion.

kashukyarel *vt* deafen, make deaf: *pp/adj* **kashukyardo**

kashukyol *vi* become deaf: *pp/adj* **kashukilo**

kasíno *nm* casino, gambling casino (*Am*)

kaskéta *nf* 1) peaked cap (*Eur*) 2) baseball cap, golfer's cap

kãsko/kásko *pron/interrog/gen* whose; **Kãsko mobíli chorádilo?** Whose car was stolen? **Chi zhanav kãske shavorre si.** I don't know whose children they are.

kastána *nf* chestnut (*Am*)

kastanáva *nf* chestnut (*Eur*)

kastanelin *nf* chestnut tree

kastanéti *nf/pl* castanets (*Mus*)

kâstománo/kûstománo *nm* client, customer: *nf* **kâstománka** (*Am*)

káta *adv/prep* from; **Push káta lêste!** Ask (*from*) him! *cont of* **katar** *adv/prep qv*

katalógo *nm* catalog

katána *nm/nf* soldier: *pl* **katáya; Thodyás-pe katána.** He joined the army/became a soldier: *nf* **katánka** amazon, female soldier

kataníya *nf* army, armed forces

katáno *nm* soldier *var of* **katána** *qv*

katapúlto *nm* catapult, slingshot

katar o yilo *id/adv/phr* from the heart/in all honesty/sincerely

katar *prep/pron* 1) from where, from wherever; **Katar aves?** From where do you come? **Godo si o stóro katar me kindem le mobilárya**. That is the store from where I bought the furniture. 2) away from, from; **Shavorrále! Zhan katar e yag!** Kids! Get away from the fire! **Avilem katar o fóro.** I came from the city. **Chikáilo katar shorrêste ka pûnrrêste.** He was covered with mud from head to toe. 3) *conj* than; **Mai baro si katar pêsko phral.** He is bigger than his brother. **Bishterdem mai but katar tu zhanes ánda kadya familíya.** I have forgotten more than you know about that family.

katargodi *pron* from wherever

katári *nm* spinner, weaver: *nf* **katárka**

katel *vt/i* **1)** spin: *pp/adj* **katlo 2)** darn, knit, weave **3)** *v/refl* **katél-pe** be darned, knitted, spun

kathar *adv* from here, from right here, this way

katharutno *adj* **1)** from here, from right here **2)** *nm* a man from there: *nf* **katharutni**

kathe *adv* **1)** here (*hic*); **Háide kathe!** Come here! **Kathé-la e Mára?** Is Mary here? **Nai kathé-lo o Péte.** Peter is not here. **2)** *id* **So si kathe?** What's all this about/What's going on here?

katimáski-suv *comp/nf* knitting/darning needle

katimos *nm* darning, knitting, weaving

katíro *nm* mule: *pl* **katírya** (*Eur*)

katlo *nm* yarn, skein

Katóliko *adj* **1)** Catholic; **Rrom Katóliko** Catholic Rom: *pl* **Rroma Katólichi:** *nf* **Romni Katóliko** Catholic Romani woman: *pl* **Rromnya-Katólichi 2)** *nm* Catholic: *nf* **Katoláika**

kats/kátsa *nf/pl* scissors, shears *var of* **katya** *nf/pl* (*Am*)

katúna *nf* large tent, marquee, circus tent (*Eur*)

katya/kats *nf/pl* scissors, shears (*Eur*)

káva *dem/adj* this (*Eur*); **Káva si o chachimos.** This is the truth.

kavaléro *adj* **1)** chivalrous, honourable, principled; **kavaléro Gazho** honorable non-Romani man **2)** *nm* gentleman, honest/honourable man (*Eur*) **3)** knight

kaver *see* **khaver**

kãwáchi *nm* blacksmith, smith

kãwachíya *nf* blacksmithery, forge

káyek *pron var of* **kak** *qv*

kayíl-pe *v/refl* **1)** regret **2)** repent

kayimos *nm* regret, repentence

kâzanári *nm* distiller, moonshiner, man who brews illegal whisky

kâzáno *nm* **1)** large boiler, still **2)** distillery

kazárma *nf* caserne, military barracks/post (*Mil*)

kazéta *nf* cassette tape

kázha *nf* **1)** skin, peel (*apple, etc*): *pl* **kézhi 2)** scab **3)** bark (*on tree*) **4)** shinel *vt*; **~ kézhi** peel (*fruit,vegetables*); **Shindyas kézhi le kolumpírya.** She has peeled the potatoes.

kazhalo *adj* mangey, scabrous

kazom *adv* how many, how much (*Eur*) *see* **sóde** & **sodya** *for Canada/US*

ke *pron* your; **Kai ke phrala?** Where are your brothers?

ke/kê *conj* **1)** because, since, so that/in order to, that; **Nashti zhav kê nai-ma love.** I can't go because I have no money. **Ke manges te zhástar, zhas akana!** Since you want to go, let's go now! **De mánge e próba ke mangav te sikavav la lêste.** Give me the proof because I want to show it to him. **2)** Used to introduce a subordinate clause or an infinitive meaning of the verb when this is a command or a request; **Mangav ke gilabas.** I want you to sing. **3)** that; **Zhanglem kê xoxavélas.** I knew that he was lying. **Note:** Ke is often contracted to a **kh'** or **kû** sound; **Zhanav kh' wo avel.** I know he/she is coming.

kechápa *nf* catsup/ketchup

keflívo *adj* slightly drunk, tipsy

kegol *vi* **1)** clot: *pp/adj* **kegome 2)** **kegól-pe** clot, become clotted

kegomos *nm* clotting

Kêlderásh *nm var of* **Kalderash** *qv*

kêlêrishèngo *gen/adj* beaded; **firánga-kêlêrishèngi** beaded curtain

kêlêrísho *nm* bead, Rosary bead: *pl* **Kêlêríshurya** Rosary

kêltuwíl *vt* **1)** exhaust (*finances*), expend, spend, use up, waste: *pp/adj* **kêltuwimé 2) kêltuwíl-pe** *v/refl*

kêltuwimós *nm* expenditure, expenses, spending

kêltuwitóri *nm* prodigal man: *nf* **kêltuwitórka**

kêltuyála *nf* expense, expenses

kéntro *nm var of* **chéntro** *nm qv*

kénturiya *nf* century

kepol *vt* castrate, geld: *pp/adj* **kepome**

kepóvo *adj* 1) castrated, fixed, gelded;
kepóvo-grast gelding 2) *nm* castrated
man, eunuch, impotent man, gelding

kêr/khêr *nm* boot: *pl* **kêreyá**

kérbo *nm* 1) large, antlered deer 2) moose
(*Can*)

kerchélo *nm* small, cast metal loop on a
pocket watch, medal, etc., to which a
chain can be attached

kerdimáta *nm/pl* manufactured
goods/items, manufactured products

kerdimos *nm* 1) product 2) workmanship

kérdyol *vi* 1) make oneself
become/metamorphose: *pp/adj* **kerdilo**;
Kérdilo vórrutsome. He made himself
hated. **So kérdyos te chi sánas Rrom?**
What would you want to be if you were
not a Rom? **E Mártya kérdili shudemos
thuv.** The Angel of Death
metamorphosed into a puff of
smoke.(*Folk*) 2) pretend to be; **Kérdyol
dilo.** He's pretending to be stupid. 3) to
be born/made; **Kérdilem ánde Kanáda.**
I was born/made in Canada. **Kérdilo o
rédyo ánde Nipóna.** The radio was
produced in Japan. 4) to be
accomplished/done; **So kérdilo?** What
has been accomplished? **Note**: *idioms
with* **kérdyol;** 1) ~ **dilo** *comp/vi* play the
fool 2) ~ **ges** *comp/vi* break day**;
Kérdyolas ges kána gêlèmtar.** Day was
breaking when we departed 3) ~ **kokala**
comp/vi become skin and bones; **Kérdilo
kokala.** He became a bag of bones. 4) ~
mulo *comp/vi* play dead 5) ~
Rrom/Rromni *comp/vi* pretend to be a
Romani man/woman

kerel *vt/i* 1) accomplish, do, make, equal:
pp/adj **kerdino/kerdo; Dévla, so te
kerel?** God, what can be done (about it)?
Dui hai trin keren pansh. Two and
three make/equal five. 2) build, construct
3) happen 4) beget (*children*), create,
form, devise 5) arrange, prepare, set, set

up; **Kerdem síniya.** I prepared a table.
Kerdem kidemos. I arranged a get
together. 6) *comp/vbs with* **kerel**: 7) ~
ánda make out of, turn into 8) ~ **ánda e
yakh** wink 9) ~ **ánda o shoro** nod the
head 10) ~ **béda** commit a crime/ make
trouble 11) ~ **bezax** commit a sin 12) ~
borya exchange brides (*between families*)
13) **Keras borya lênsa.** We exchange
brides with them 14) ~ **bryézhdi** make
furrows 15) ~ **buki** work 16) **châng**
kneel 17) **Kerdyas châng ángla Swînto
Máriya.** He knelt before Saint Mary 18)
~ **dilo ánda** make a fool out of 19) ~
drom get out of the way, move aside 20)
~ **e suv** make the sign of the cross 21) ~
fármichi make magic 22) ~ **gunoi** litter,
make mess 23) ~ **kris** hold a trial 24) ~
mui make a noise,yell 25) ~ **nasul** do
evil, harm. injure 26) ~ **pakyayimos**
foster an illusion/create a belief in 27) ~
pe síla force, overpower, rape 28) ~
phiryása make fun of, mock, play a joke
on, ridicule 29) ~ **sínya** prepare a table
30) ~ **spúma a)** make lather **b)** foam at
the mouth 31) ~ **wortácha** become
friends/partners; **Ame kerdyam
wortácha.** We became business partners
32) **kerél-pe** *v/refl* 1) exert oneself, put
oneself out; **Na mai ker-tu te azhutis
lês!** Don't put yourself out to help him
any more! 2) act like, imitate, pose as,
pretend to be; **Won si Gazhe kai
kerén-pe Rrom.** They are non-Roma
pretending to be Roma/They are bogus
Romani refugee claimants.(*Am*). **Wo si
Gazho kai kerél-pe Rrom.** He's a
wannabe Rom.(*Am*). **Chorre Rroma si
kai kerén-pe barvale.** They are poor
Roma who pretend to be rich. 3) behave;
Kerél-pe sar o dilo. He's behaving like
an idiot.

kerimos *nm* 1) accomplishment, action,
creation, deed, handiwork, exploit,
something accomplished/done/made 2)
action, deed; **Swáko Rrom krisiníl-pe**

pála pêske kerimáta. Each man will be judged by his actions/deeds.

keritóri *nm* creator, maker, manufacturer: *nf* **keritórka**

kerko *adj* 1) bitter, brakish, sour 2) acrimonious 3) embittered 4) resentful

kerkol *vi* 1) become bitter/brackish/sour: *pp/adj* **kerkilo**; **E bíra kerkili.** The beer has become sour 2) become acrimonious 3) become embittered; **Kerkilo pêsko yilo.** His heart became embittered. 4) become resentful

kerkomos *nm* 1) bitterness 2) bile; **kerkomós bukángo** liver bile 3) acrimony 4) resentment

kerkyárdyol *vi* 1) be made bitter/brakish/sour: *pp/adj* **kerkyardyilo** 2) be made acrimonious 3) be embittered 4) be made resentful

kerkyarel *vt* 1) make bitter/sour, make brakish: *pp/adj* **kerkyardo** 2) create acrimony 3) embitter 4) make resentful

kêrlígo *nm* long pole with a hook/boathook/billhook, pruning hook

kêrligútso *nm* small hook

kêrló *nm* 1) edge, brim, rim 2) throat

kermalo *adj* 1) putrid, rotten, infested with maggots/worms 2) infected with a computer virus 3) *fig* crummy (*Am*)

kermo *nm* 1) worm 2) maggot 3) computer virus

kermorro *nm* 1) tiny worm, intestinal worm 2) earwig

kermúso *nm* mouse (*Eur*)

kerno *adj* 1) bad, decayed, putrid, rotten, whithered, wilted 2) fermented

kernyála *nf* 1) decay, rot 2) fermentation

kernyarel *vt* 1) cause to become decayed/rotten, rot: *pp/adj* **kernyardo** 2) cause to ferment

kernyol *vi* 1) become rotten, decay, rot, whither, wilt: *pp/adj* **kernilo; Kernile le lulugya.** The flowers have whithered/wilted 2) ferment

kerráriya *nf* 1) narrow path, track, trail 2) parting in hair

Kerráriya-Solumêngi *comp/nf* Milky Way

kerráriya-viyatsáki *comp/nf* path of life, destiny

kêrtítsa *nf* velvet (*material*)

kêrtitsáko *gen/adj* made of velvet; **kêrtitsáko fistáno** long velvet skirt

kêrzha *nf* 1) crutch 2) *comp/vi* **zhal pe ~** He walks on a crutch/on crutches. 3) *pl* **kêrzhi** stilts

kêsapíya *nf* 1) butcher's shop 2) butchery, slaughter

kêsápo/kâsápo *nm* 1) butcher (*one who kills animals*) 2) knacker, slaughterer

késo *nm* case (*in court*)

kethane *adv* together (*Eur*)

kêtráno *nm* nicotine

kêtrínsa/kêtríntsa *nf* apron

kezáno *nm* boiler (*for distilling*)

kezdil *vt* begin, commence, start: *pp/adj* **kezdime** (*Eur*) 2) *v/refl* **kedjil-pe** be/get started, start

kezdimos *nm* beginning, commencement, start (*Eur*)

kezh *nm* silk

kezhali *nf* 1) spinner of silk webs/spells 2) type of fairy (*Folk*)

kezhlano *adj* silk

ki *pron* your; **Kai ki de?** Where is your mother? *var of* **tyi** *qv*

kibórdo *nm* keyboard (*Mus*), computer keyboard

kícho *nm* 1) hip: *pl* **kíchurya; sane kíchurya** slim hips; **Thulí-la, kichuryánsa sar o grast.** She is fat with hips like a horse. **Phirélas, gláta po kícho.** She was walking, with a baby on her hip. 2) haunch; **O ruv beshélas pe pêske kíchurya.** The wolf was sitting on his haunches.

kídel *vt* 1) assemble, collect, convene, gather, glean, pick, reap: *pp/adj* **kidino** 2) hoard, save (*money*) 3) crush, press, squash, squeeze 4) coil (*rope*), fold up (*bedding*), gather up 5) arrest, pick up 6) harvest 7) round up (*animals*) 8) press, push against; **Kídel pêsko báro nai pe**

filástra. He's pressing his thumb on the window. **9)** *v/refl* **kíden-pe** assemble, congregate, convene, flock together, gather together, huddle together, meet; **Le Rrom kíden-pe ándo hãlo.** The Roma are gathering in the hall. **Kíden-pe avri.** They are congregating outside. **Kíden-pe ánd'ekh tan.** They are crowding/huddling together

kidemáski sóba *comp/nf* reception area/hall

kidemáta/kidimáta *nm/pl* **1)** assets, savings **2)** collections, gatherings **3)** arrests **4)** assemblies, meetings, rallies

kidemos/kidimos *nm* **1)** collection (*of money, etc*) **2)** assembly, congregation, convention, crowd, gathering, meet, meeting, rally, reception; **baro** ~ massive assembly/gathering **3)** **rángo** ~ police roundup, mass arrest **4)** harvest **5)** **guruvêngo** ~ roundup (*steers*)

kidiníl-pe *v/refl* assemble, be assembled/collected/gathered together, form a group: *pp/adj* **kidinime**; **Kidinisáile hai marde lês.** They ganged up and beat him up.

kíka *nf* **1)** braid (*hair*); **Si la lúngone bal phangle kikênsa.** She has long hair tied up in braids. **2)** pigtail, pony tail

kilo *nm* **1)** peg, tent peg **2)** fencepost, post, stake

kilodori *comp/nf* guy rope of a pole/tent, supporting rope: *pl* **kilodorya**

kimikálno *adj* chemical

kimikálo *nm* chemical

kimikálurya *nm/pl* chemicals, chemical compounds used in metalwork

kimísto *nm* chemist

kimistríya *nf* chemistry

kímpo *nm* grassland, hinterland, moor, plain, prairie, steppe

kimpósko *gen/adj* of the grassland/prairie; **khainí-kimpóski** prairie chicken (*Am*)

Kímpurya *nm/pl* Prairies, Prairie Provinces/States; **Phirel ánde l' Kímpurya**. He's traveling through the Prairies. (*Am*)

kíndyol *vi* be bought, purchased; *pp/adj* **kindilo**

kinel *vt* buy, purchase: *pp/adj* **kindo**

kingimos *nm* dampness, humidity

kingitóri *nm* humidifier

kingo *adj* **1)** wet **2)** slippery (*like a wet fish*) **3)** damp, humid

kingyárdyol *vi* be drenched, become soaked/sodden/wet, be made wet: *pp/adj* **kingardilo**; **Astárdilem ándo breshûn hai kingárdilem.** I got caught in the rain and became drenched.

kingyarel *vt* **1)** douse (*fire*), drench, immerse, make wet, soak: *pp/adj* **kingyardo 2)** dampen *us with* **tsîrrá**; **Kingyar lês tsîrrá!** Dampen it a little!

kingyol *vi* become/get drenched/soaked/wet: *pp/adj* **kingilo**; **Pelo ándo pai hai kingilo.** It fell in the water and got wet.

kinimos *nm* **1)** bargaining, buying **2)** purchase **3)** shopping **4)** **lasho** ~ good buy/bargain

kiníno *nm* quinine

kinitóri *nm* buyer, purchaser, shopper: *nf* **kinitórka**

kíno *nm* **1)** penalty, punishment, rap (*Am*) **2)** abuse, anguish, frustration, pain, suffering, torment, torture **3)** oppression **4)** *comp/vi* **lel o** ~ take the rap (*Am*)

kinowil/kinuwil *vt* **1)** abuse, hurt, cause pain, make to suffer: *pp/adj* **kinowime 2)** cause anguish, suffering **3)** torture, torment **4)** punish severely **5)** oppress **6)** *v/refl* **kinowíl-pe a)** be annoyed by, bothered by, concerned, torment oneself, be worried by **b)** suffer torture, undergo torture; **Kinowisáilo ánde rrobíya.** He was tortured in jail.

kinowime *pp/adj* abused, made to suffer, tormented, tortured

kinowimos *nm* **1)** anguish, physical abuse, torment, torture; **Xalem but kinowimos lêstar.** I suffered a lot of physical abuse from him. **2)** corporal punishment (*whipping, etc*)

kinowitóri *nm* 1) bugbear 2) abuser, tormentor, torturer: *nf* **kinowitórka**

kintála *nf* see **kuntári** *nm*

kipári *nm* die, form, former, jig, mold

kípo *nm* 1) figure, figurine, sculpture 2) idol, image, statue 3) scarecrow

kipútso *nm* figurine

kirádyol *vi* 1) boil, broil, cook: *pp/adj* **kiradilo** 2) be bubbling, bubble

kiral *nm* 1) cheese 2) smegma

Kirali *nm* King (*in cards*) (*Eur*)

kiralo *adj* 1) cheesy 2) exhibiting the presence of smegma

kiravel *vt* boil, cook by boiling/steaming, broil: *pp/adj* **kirado**; **So kiraves ánde gadya piri?** What are you boiling/cooking in that pot? **Kiradyas le tsáliya divliyone buriyatsênsa te xalavel o rat ánda lênde.** She boiled the clothes with wild mushrooms to remove the blood from them.

kirivimos *nm* godfathership, godmothership, godfather/godmother relationship

kirivo *nm* 1) a) godfather appointed soon after birth, b) co-godfather, the relationship between adults in two families when one couple are godparents to the child of the parental couple 2) best man 3) *nf* **kirivi** a) godmother appointed soon after birth, b) co-godmother relationship between adults in two families when couple are godparents of the child of the other 4) bridesmaid. **Note:** godparents and bridegoom and bridesmaid are often the same people at a *Kalderash* wedding.

kiríya *nf* 1) loan; **Lem la pe kiríya.** I got it on loan. 2) rental; **Lêsko mobíli si pe kiríya.** His car is on rental.

kiro *pron/poss/s* your, *var of* **tiro** *qv*; **kíro dad** your father, **kíri dey** your mother, **kire love** your money

kishai *nm* grit, sand

kishaiyalo *adj* gritty, sandy

kishlo *adj* emaciated, lean, meager, skinny, slim, thin

kishlorro *adj* 1) on the thin side 2) *nm* slim man: *nf* **kishlyorri**

kishlyol *vi* become emaciated, skinny, slim down, lose weight: *pp/adj* **kishlilo**

kishti *nf* 1) girdle 2) waist belt, garter belt

kisi *nf* inside pocket in the waist a *Kalderash* woman's skirt

Kitai *nm* China

Kitáitsa *nm* Chinese man: *nf* **Kitaitsútsa**

Kitaitsítska *nf* Chinese (*Lang*)

Kitaitsítsko *adj* Chinese; **Kitaitsítsko xabe** Chinese food

kíya *nf* 1) key (*Eur*) 2) wrench

kiyáma *nf* temple (*Anat*)

kiyátra *nf* theater

kiyáya/kyáya *nf* 1) key 2) tuning screw (*Mus*) 3) wrench

kiyósko *nm* kiosk, newspaper stand, phone booth (*Eur*)

kizligárda *nf nf* compound, immigration compound

kláfo/klávo *nm* key (*Mus*), key (*piano*), valve (*on wind instruments*)

klaksonil *vt* honk, sound automobile horn (*Eur*): *pp/adj* **klaksonime**

klaksóno *nm* automobile horn (*Eur*)

kláro *adj* 1) clear 2) *adv* clearly

klavil *vt* 1) enslave: *pp/adj* **klavime** 2) *v/refl* **klavíl-pe** enslave oneself, become enslaved

klavimos *nm* enslavement

klavitóri *nm* cnslaver, slave driver: *nf*: **klavitórka**

kláviya *nf* captivity, slavery

klaviyatúra *nf* keyboard (*of an synthesizer*) (*Eur*)

klávo *nm* captive, slave: *nf* **klaváika/klavútsa**

klédka *nf* 1) cage 2) birdcage

kledkol *vt* cage, place in a cage: *pp/adj* **kledkome**

klépovo *adj* 1) awkward, blundering, clumsy, gangling, lumbering 2) *nm* awkward/clumsy man: *nf* **klepováika** clumsy woman, klutz

kléshto *nm* 1) tongs, large tongs to lift aluminum pots and pans out of boiling water and to remove defiled objects without touching them, *us appears as pl* **kléshturya** **2)** pliars

kleshtol *vt* bend with pliars: *pp/adj* **kleshtome**

kleshtútso *nm* tweezers, pincers

kleshtútsurya *nf/pl* **1)** sugar tongs **2)** pliars, pincers

kléyo *nm* adhesive, glue

kleyol *vt* **1)** glue: *pp/adj* **kleyome 2)** post (*bills*) **3)** *v/refl* **kleyól-pe** adhere

kleyónka *nf* linoleum, linoleum tile, oilcloth

klíma *nf* clime, climate

klíniko *nm* clinic

klíno *nm* wedge (*Eur*)

klíska *nf* book

klóbo *nm* **1)** club, policeman's nighstick/truncheon **2)** nightclub **3)** social club (*Am*)

klócha *nf* clutch of an automobile (*Am*)

klónka *nf* **1)** streetcar (*Eur & prob onomatopoeic because of the sound of its brakes like like sound of a screech eagle*) *see also* **tramvíya** *nf* **2)** female screech eagle

klonkáno *nm* male eagle, screech eagle (*Eur*)

klonkil *refl/v* cry, scream, screech, shriek (*as an eagle*): *pp/adj* **klonkime** (*Eur*)

klonkimos *nm* screeching, shrieking

klonkóvo *nm* crow/raven, (*Eur*)

klóno *nm* **1)** circus clown: *nf* **klonáika 2)** prankster

klonútso *nm* clown; **Che klonútso!** What a clown! **2)** wise guy, smart ass (*Am*)

klopotil *vt* **1)** tinkle, jingle: *pp/adj* **klopotime 2)** *v/refl* **klopotíl-pe** jingle, tinkle as a cowbell

klopóto *nm* cow bell

klopotútso *nm* jingle-bell: *pl* **kopotútsurya** jingle-bells strung on curtains to advise of entry into a reader-advisor parlour or storefront

klotsil *vt* **1)** hatch, sit on: *pp/adj* **klotsime 2)** *v/refl* **klotsíl-pe a)** hatch **b)** lay (*eggs*)

klótska *nf* **1)** brood hen, clocker **2)** clunker (*Am*)

klúbo *nm* nightclub

klúch *nf* key: *pl* **klúcha**

klúchi *nf* key: *pl* **kluchya**

klyámpa *nf* clamp, vise

kníshka/kníga/knízhka *nf* book

ko *dem/adj* this *var of* **kako** *qv* (*used before mn/s*)

ko *prep* at, for, to (*Eur*) *see also* **ka** *prep*

kochai *nm* cob, stalk, stem

kochak *nf* **1)** button: *pl* **kochaka 2)** die **3)** switch

kochaka *nf/pl* **1)** dice **2)** *comp/vi* **khelén-pe pe l' ~** gamble with dice, play dice **3)** **shuden ~** roll/throw dice; **E baxt si sar peren le kochaka.** Luck is how the dice fall.

kochakári *nm* gambler at dice

kochakil *vt* button/button up (*jacket*): *pp/adj* **kochakime**

kóchi *nm* carriage, coach, stagecoach: *pl* **kóchya**

kochiyáko grast *comp/nm* coach horse

kochiyash *nm* **1)** coachman **2)** driver

kodka *adv* there, right there

kodkar *adv* from there, from right there

kodo **1)** *dem/adj/pron* that, that one, that male *psn/animal* **2)** *conj* **pála kodo** because of that, for that reason, that's why

kodola *dem/pron/adj* those, those things, those female people/animals

kodolátar *adv* **1)** like that one, like that, like her, of all that; **So gîndís sa kodolátar**? What do you think of all that? **2)** (*id expecting*) **Ashili kodolátar**; She became like that (*became with child, polite speech*). **3)** *conj* because of, for that reason, that's why, because of that woman; **Kinowí-ma kodolátar.** I'm suffering anguish because of that woman.

kodole *dem/pron/adj* those, those things, those male *psns/animals*

kodolêndar *adv* **1)** like those, like them, like those men/people?; **Mai phiravésas tsáliya kodolêndar?** Would you ever wear clothes like those? **2)** *adv/conj* because of those, those people

kodoles *mm/pron/dem* that male *psn*/thing; **Dikhlan kodoles?** Did you see that man?

kodolêstar *adv* **1)** like that one, like him **2)** because of that thing, that man; **Dilyováva kodolêstar.** I am going crazy because of that man. **3)** about that

kodóva *dem/pron* that

kodya *dem/adj/pron* **1** that, that thing, that female *psn/animal* **2)** *adv* like that, so, thus

koféri *nm* coffer, vault

koi *dem/adj* this *var of* **kakya** *qv* (*used before nf*) (*Eur*).

kokala *nm/pl* **1)** bones, skeleton, ribs (*of an old ship*). **2)** framing/standards (*of a new building*); **le kokala le kherêsko.** the framing of a (new) house **3)** remains; the remains of an old house or ribs of an old rotting ship; **Dikhlem le kokala phurane kheréstar.** I saw the remains of an ancient house. **4)** leukemia; **Naswaló-lo, le kokala, zhanes?** He is sick, the bones (*he has leukemia*), you know.

kokalêngo *gen/adj* of the bones; **kokalêngo-naswalimos** leukemia

kokalo *nm* **1)** bone: *pl* **kokala 2)** bridge bone of a stringed instrument (*Mus*) **3)** shell

kokaluno *adj* bone, resembling bone; **kokalunó-shoro** bonehead, skinhead. (*Am*)

koklyailo *pp/adj* tarnished

koklyal *vi* develop a patina with age, tarnish: *pp/adj* **koklyailo; Koklyáili murri angushtri.** My ring became tarnished.

koklyála *nf* patina, tarnish

kóko *nm* cocoa

kokorócho *nm* cockroach (*Am*)

kokósho *nm* **1)** cock of any fowl species: *pl* **kokósha 2)** breeding cock

kokostúrko *nm* crane, heron, stork: *pl* **kokostúrchi** .

kol *cont of* **kodol-** *dem/pl/obl stem of* **kodo** *dem/adj/pron*; **Kol shonêndar** (*cont of* **kodole shonêndar**) from those months/some months ago

kola *dem/adj/pron* **1)** those *var of* **kodala** *qv* (*used before nf/s*) **2)** those things, those people (*for both genders*). **Kon si kola?** Who are those people? **Kola si ánde América.** Those people are in the US. **3)** *nf/pl* assets, clobber, belongings, items, objects, stuff, things. **Si lês kola te bikinel.** He has assets/stuff to sell. **4) ke kola,** etcetera

kolaborátsiya *nf* collaboration

kol-aver *pron/adj* the other, that other one/that other, opposite number; **Káko Rrom bashavel e gitára hai kol-aver bashavel e lávuta.** This Rom plays the guitar and that other one plays the violin.

kol-ávere 1) *dem/adj/pl* those other; **kol-ávere mobílya si múrre phralêske.** Those other cars belong to my brother **2)** *nm/pl* those other ones, those other people

kolbása *nf* large sausage, type of Polish sausage

kolédjo *nm* college

kolégo *nm* associate, collegue (*Eur*): *nf* **kolegútsa**

kolektóri *nm* **1)** collector **2)** collector road (*Am*) **3)** recycler, man who collects empty bottles and other items for deposit refund or recycling (*Eur*)

koléniya *nf* **1)** era, generation **2)** dynasty, family dynasty; **zhi ka o shtárto koléniya.** to the fourth generation

kóleno *nm* regime, reign, rule

kólêra *nf* cholera

kol-gesa *adv* these days, these past days, recently; **Kol-gesa délas but breshûn.** It has been raining a lot these past few days.

kóliba *nf* hut, cabin

kolibítsa *nf* small cabin, tiny hut

koliflóra *nf* cauliflower (*Am*)

kolikíri *nm* **1)** branding iron (*for animals*) **2)** soldering iron or tool

kóliko *nm* colic

kolikósko *gen/adj* suffering from colic

kolil *vt* **1)** apply solder, solder: *pp/adj*
kolime 2) temper, harden **3)** *v/refl*
kolíl-pe a) harden, become tempered **b)**
become soldered
kolimos *nm* **1)** tempering process **2)**
soldering
kolin *nm* chest, male breast (*Anat*)
kolínda *nf* Christmas carol/song
kolinêsko-kokalo *comp/nm* sterum
kolinêsko-naswalimos *comp/nm* chest
sickness, consumption
kólitsa *nf* cart, hand cart
kolkorres *adv* all alone, lonely; **Fal ma
kolokorres ánde kakya bári lúmiya.** I
feel all alone in this big world.
kolkorrimos *nm* loneliness, solitude
kolkorro/korrkoro *adj* **1)** alone, solitary,
unique; **Me, o kólkorro símas ándo
gado fóro.** I was the only one in that
town. **2)** lonely **2)** single (*unmarried*) **3)**
only; **múrro kólkorro shav** my only son,
4) *adv* alone, by oneself, isolated, on
one's own, singly, spontaneously;
Sikilem me kólkorro. I learned on my
own. **Beshélas kólkorro.** He was sitting
all by himself. **Sluchaiyisáilo kólkorro.**
It happened spontaneously/all by itself.
Beshénas kólkorro, dur savorrêndar.
They were living alone/isolated, far from
everybody. **4)** *nm* self: *nf* **kolkorri**: pl *pl*
kolkorre/kolkorra
kólo *nm* **1)** circle-dance at a wedding, type
of hora: *pl* **kólya 2)** circle; **Zhála kruyal
ándo kólo.** He's going around in a citrcle.
3) orbit
kolóda *nf* pack; **kolóda kárti** pack of cards
kolópo *nm* fedora, dressy hat, stetson
koltrabánso *nm* **1)** contraband **2)** handler
of smuggled goods, smuggler: *nf*
koltrabansáika
koltrobansil *vt* **1)** smuggle, distribute
smuggled goods: *pp/adj* **koltrobansime**
2) handle
black-market/contraband/smuggled
goods; **Koltrobansílas but ánde l'
phurane gesa, rrûmbo, rrakíya, sya
fyálurya pimáta.** He used to handle

contraband in the old days, rum whisky,
all kinds of drinks. (*legend referring to a
Rom during Prohibition*)
koltrobánsiya *nf* contraband, handling of
black-market goods, contraband,
smuggling
koltsil *vt* **1)** corner: *pp/adj* **koltsime 2)**
v/refl **koltsíl-pe** be cornered
kóltso *nm* **1)** corner, street corner **2)** nook
kolumpíra *nf* potato *var of* **kolumpíri**; *id*
Si lês rúzho kolumpíra ánde lêste. He
is seething with anger.
kolumpíri *nf* potato: *pl* **kolumpírya**
kóma *nf/neolog* comma
kománda *nf* command (*Mil*)
komandéri *nm* commander (*Mil*)
komandil *vt* command, order: *pp/adj*
komandime
kómbo *nm* **1)** knot **2)** *vt/i* **phandel** ~ tie
(*close*) a knot
komédiya *nf* play/comedy, theatrical
production (*Eur*)
komedyash *nm* **1)** actor, comedian, joker:
nf **komedyáshka 2)** performer
komérsyo *nm* business, commerce, trade
komesáro *nm/neolog* commissioner
komisáriyo *nm* communist commissar
(*Eur*); **Kerél-pe sar komisáriyo te del
ándo gor.** He acts like a commisar to get
what he wants/uses communist tactics.
(*Eur*)
komisíya *nf/neolog* commission
komitéto *nm* committee (*Eur*)
komitíya *nf* committee (*Eur*); **komitíya
advizóriya** advisory committee
kómodo *adj* comfortable, cozy
komóra *nf* chamber, hall, room (*Eur*)
kómpak-dísko *comp/nm* CD: *pl*
kómpak-dískurya (*Eur*)
kompetítsiya *nf* competition, contest
komplétno *adj/adv* complete, completely
komporátsiya *nf* comparison
komputéri *nm* computer
komunikátsiya *nf* communication; ~ **po
Internéto** by the Internet, ~ **lilênsa** by
mail **po tilifóno** ~ by phone
Komunísmo/komunízmo *nm* communism

Komunísto 1) *adj* communist 2) *nm*
Communist: *nf* **komunísta**

komunitáto *nm* community (*Eur*)

komunitéto *nm* 1) community (*Eur*);
amáro lokálno komumitéto our local
community 2) community center/hall
(*Eur*)

komvindjil/konvindjil *vt* convince: *pp/adj*
komvindjime (*Eur*)

komvindjimásko *gen/adj* convincing

kon *pron* who, whoever; **Kon avel?** Who is
coming? **Chi zhanav kon si.** I don't
know who he/she is. **Kon si kodole
Rroma?** Who are those Roma?

kóna *nf* basket (*Eur*)

konchayil *vt* 1) complete, conclude, end,
finish, terminate: *pp/adj* **konchayime** 2)
konchayíl-pe be ended, come to an
end/conclusion

konchayimáta *nm/pl*; conclusions

konchayime *pp/adj* concluded, ended,
finished

konchayimos *nm* completion, conclusion,
end, termination

kónchina *nf* 1) completion, conclusion,
end, finality, termination 2) *adv/phr* **ánde
kónchina** finally, in the end

kóncho *nm* 1) Spanish-style hair bun or
coiffure

kondítsiya *nf* condition

konditsyonéri *nm* air conditioner, air
conditioning system (*Eur*)

konektóri *nm* connector, junction adaptor,
two-way sound system connector

konfuzátsiya *nf* confusion (*Eur*)

konfuzil *vt* confuse: *pp/adj* **konfuzime**
(*Eur*)

konfyánsa *nf* confidence, trust

kongodi *pron* whoever, whomever

kónik *pron* anybody/nobody; **Nai kónik
andre.** There's nobody inside. **Chi
dikhlem konikas.** I didn't see anybody.

konikásko *nm/pron/indef/gen* belonging to
nobody/anybody; **Wo nai konikásko
fréno.** He is nobody's friend. **Nai
konikásko.** It doesn't belong to anybody.

kónitsa *nf* basket (*Eur*)

konkréto *adj* 1) concrete 2) concrete
(*material*)

konkretósko *gen/adj* made of concrete

konosári *nm* connoisseur: *nf* **konosárka**

konsérva *nf* jam

konsêshonári *nm* concessionair: *nf*.
konseshonárka (*Am*)

konsêshono *nm* carnival/amusement-park
concession (*Am*)

kónsilo *nm/neolog* council; **Kónsilo la
Ivropáko.** Council of Europe

konstitútsiya *nf* constitution

konsuláto *nm* consulate

kónta *nf* account, bank account

kontáina *nf* 1) shipping crate/container 2)
movable dwelling for refugees or for
people rendered homeless by a
disaster.(*Eur*)

kontaktil *vt* connect (*with*), contact: *pp/adj*
kontaktime

kontákto *nm* 1) connection,
electrical/sound system connection,
contact 2) *comp/vt/i* **kerel ~** make a
connection, make contact

kontêntíl *vt* 1) make *smbdy*
content/contented: *pp/adj* **kontêntimé** 2)
v/refl **kontêntíl-pe** become
content/satisfied, be contented/satisfied

kontêntimós *nm* contentment, satisfaction

kontênto *adj* content, satisfied

kontésto *nm* competition, contest, game,
match

kontinénto *nm* continent

kóntra *prep* against, up against (*Eur*) *see
also* **prótivo**

kontrákto *nm* contract, business contract,
lease, rental agreement

kontroléri *nm* control panel, remote
controler for TV, stereo, etc

kontrolérya *nm/pl* control panel, controls

konyáko *nm* cognac

ko-operátsiya *nm/neolog* cooperation

kopach *nm* block/billet of wood, chopping
block, tree stump; **kopach kasht** block of
wood

kopáchi *nm* 1) any large, imposing tree,
giant redwood: *pl* **kopácha** 2) tree trunk

kopal *nf* carpet beater, tent-peg mallet, wooden mallet

kopérish *nm* **1)** cover, lid, top **2)** manhole cover **3)** hatch, trapdoor

kopidi *nf* **1)** chisel **2)** screwdriver *(Am)* **3) kopidí-sastrêski** chisel, cold chisel

kopílcho *nm* **1)** bastard *(us applied only to Roma)* **2)** *adj* bastard, illegitimate

kópita *nf* foot *(of a horse)*, hoof

kópiya *nf* **1)** copy **2)** *vt/i* **kerel ~** copy, make a copy

kopúto *nm* **1)** coat, jacket, over jacket, topcoat **2)** poncho *(Am)*

koráli *nm* stockyard *(Am)*

korámo *nm* coram, quorum; **Ame sam dósta te keras korámo.** We are enough to form a quorum *(at a Board meeting)*.

korbach *nm* knout, lash

korbáchi *nm* bullwhip, knout, lash

kordári *nm* device for tuning musical instruments, electric tuner *(Mus)*

kordil *vt* **1)** tune a musical instrument *(Mus)* **2)** *v/refl* **kordíl-pe** tune, be put in tune

kordime *pp/adj* tuned, in tune *(Mus)*; **Chi ashel kordime mi gitára.** My guitar won't stay tuned.

kordimos *nm* **1)** tuning **2)** accompanying rhythm *(Mus)*

kórdo *nm* **1)** chord *(Mus)* **2)** plug in cable for electrified instrument *(Mus)*

korespónso *nm* correspondent: *nf* **koresponsáika** *(Eur)*

korkodílo *nm* alligator, crocodile

korlôntso *nm* **1)** connector, trailer hitch, link **2)** pot hook, heavy hook for hanging things from the ceiling, etc. **3)** staple

kornyácha *nf* turtle

koróbo *nm* locust bean *(gleditsia triacanthos)*, carob

koróna *nf* crown *(of a king)*

koronéri *nm* coroner

koronovátsiya *nf* coronation

koronovil *vt* **1)** crown: *pp/adj* **koronovime 2) koronovíl-pe** be crowned, crown oneself

kórpo *nm* **1)** trunk *(of a tree)* **2)** body, main part of *smthg*, stem

korporátsiya *nf* corporation

korr *nf* **1)** neck *(Anat)*; **Pelo ándo pai zhi-ka korráte.** He fell up to the neck in the water **2)** neck of an instrument *(Mus)* **3)** throat; **Shindyas le balêski korr.** He cut the pig's throat. **4)** throttle; **Phuterdyas e korr.** He opened the throttle.

korradi *nf* game of hide-and-seek

korrádyol *vi* **1)** be blinded, derived of sight: *pp/adj* **korradilo 2)** be deluded, led astray, made ignorant of the truth, be misinformed; **Korrádile lêske swatonêndar.** They were misinformed of the truth by his statements.

korráte *nf/prep* to the neck/to the neck; **del pa korráte** *vi/phr* perform a sommersault; **Dyas pa korráte.** He performed a somersault.

korravel *vt* **1)** blind, dazzle, make blind**:** *pp/adj* **korrado 2)** delude, make ignorant of the truth, misinform

korrávol *vi* become dazzled, go blind, lose one's sight: *pp/adj* **korrailo**; **Korráilo kána sas térno shavorro.** He went/became blind when he was a young boy.

korrimásko *gen/adj* blinding, dazzling, flashing

korrimos *nm* **1)** blindness **2)** ignorance

korro *adj* **1)** blind **2)** ignorant of the truth, misinformed

korung *nf* crow, raven

kósho *nm* **1)** chimney **2)** funnel of a ship **3)** ventilator **4)** dormer window

koshtícha *nf* darn, seam *(of a garment)*

kostúmo *nm* attire, costume, suit

kothal *adv* from there; **Shavorrále, zhan kothal!** Kids, get away from there!

kothar *adv/conj* thence, from there, from right there, that way; **Huryárdilam ándo Târánto hai kothar telyárdilam te zhas kai Santána.** We flew into Toronto and from there, we departed to go to Saint Anne de Beaupré.

kotharutno *adj* from there, there; *nm* man from there: *nf* **kotharutni**

kothe *adv* in that direction, there. yonder (*isti*)

kotka/kothka *adv* right there, there

kotléta *nf* porkchop, cutlet

kotor *nm* **1**) morsel, piece, portion; **kotor manrro** a piece of bread **2**) patch (*on clothing*)

kotora *nm/pl* bits and pieces, debris, fragments, remains, scattered remains; **Pharradyas la ánde kotorênde.** He smashed it to fragments.

kotoráma *nf* belt buckle, cinch buckle

kotororro *nm* fragment, small piece/portion

kótso *nm* chicken coop, henhouse

kôtsiyíl *vt* **1**) sway (*in dancing*): *pp/adj* **kôtsiyime 2**) **kôtsiyíl-pe** *see var in* **kuchiyil-pe** *vi*

kotunítsa *nf* **1**) gopher **2**) prairie dog. *(Am)*

kóva *nf* bay, cove

kova *pron* **1**) that **2**) that person (of either gender) **3**) *nf* asset, belonging, item, thing: *pl* **kola**

kovántsa *nf* anvil, blacksmith's anvil

kovantsítsa *nf* jewelers's anvil, portable anvil

kovérka *nf* one of two upright tent poles forming a triangle with the ridge pole (**berand**) supported at the point where they cross: *pl* **kovérchi**

kovles *adv* gently, lightly, softly, subtly, weakly; **Kovles délas o breshûn.** The rain was gently falling.

kovlé-kokala *comp/nm* rachitis (*rickets*)

kovlé-yilêsko *gen/adj* kind, soft hearted

kovlí-dab *comp/nm* light pat/tap

kovlimos *nm* **1**) insipidity **2**) softness, subtlety **3**) gentleness tenderness

kovlo *adj* **1**) breakable, fragile, insipid, light, pliable, soft, weak **2**) kind, gentle, lenient **3**) domesticated, tame **4**) tender (*meat*) **5**) subtle **6**) comfortable (*bed*) **7**) *id* **Wo si kovlo le shavorrênsa.** He spoils the children/is soft with them.

kovlyárdyol *vi* be softened, become softened/cushioned/diluted/tenderized: *pp/adj* **kovlyardilo**

kovlyarel *vt* **1**) cushion, deaden, dilute, make soft, marinate, soften, tenderize: *pp/adj* **kovlyardo 2**) cause to relent

kovlyarimos *nm* cushioning, softening, softening up, tenderizing

kovlyol *vi* **1**) become soft, soften, waver: *pp/adj* **kovlilo 2**) relent; **Kovlilo karing pêske shaves.** He relented towards his son.

kovrígo *nm* **1**) hard tack (*Am*) **2**) pretzel

kovrígurya *nm/pl* pork cracklings (*Am*)

kowãchi *nm* blacksmith, smith

kowãchíl *vt* forge: *pp/adj* **kowãchimé**

kowãchimós *nm* art of forging, process of forging

kowãchíya *nf* forge, smithy

kowári *nm* spool

koya *pron* that *psn* (*if nf*), that thing (*if nm*): *pl* **kola**

kozácha *nf* measles

kózachek *nm* Russian dance melody (*Eur*)

kozachil *vt* **1**) infect with the measles: *pp/adj* **kozachime 2**) *v/refl* **kozachíl-pe** become infected with the measles/develop measles

kozachime *pp/adj* sick with the measles

Kozáko *nm* Cossack: *pl* **Kozácha**

kózeri *nm* trump (*card*)

kozeril *vt* **1**) trump (*in cards*): *pp/adj* **kozerime 2**) *v/refl* **kozeríl-pe** be trumped

kozhnítsa *nf* basket

krái *nm* king (*Eur*)

králitsa *nf* queen (*Eur*)

krályo *nm* king: *pl* **králya**

kránko *nm* crank starter (*for early automobiles*)**,** crank (*Am*)

kránto *nm* **1**) cock, tap, faucet **2**) fire hydrant **3**) valve

kraváta *nf* cravat, tie (*Eur*)

krécho *nm* **1**) *adj* chalk **2**) chalk (*substance*) **3**) chalk (*for blackboard*), crayon

krechol *vt* whitewash: *pp/adj* **krechome**

krechomos *nm* whitewashing

krécho-parno *nm* lime, quicklime
Krechúne *adv* at/on Christmas
Krechúno *nm* Christmas
Krechunósko *gen/adj* Christmas;
Krechunósko-kasht Christmas tree
krédito *nm* credit: *adv* **po krédito** on
credit
krepeskúla *nf* twilight (*Eur*)
kréposto *nm* barracks, base, guardhouse,
headquarters, military installation/outpost
(*Mil*)
krestavésto *nm* 1) cucumber 2) pickle; ~
guglo sweet pickle, ~ **shuklo** sour pickle
krestavésto-shuklo *comp/nm* dill pickle
krétsa *nf* curl: *pl* **krétsû/krétsi**
krétso *adj* curly; **Si la krétsi bal.** She has
curly hair. **Shukar shey si, lungone,
kretsone balênsa.** She is a pretty girl,
with long, curly hair.
kretsol *vt* 1) curl: *pp/adj* **kretsome** 2) coil;
Kretsosardem o shelo. I coiled the rope.
3) *v/refl* **kretsól-pe** a) be curled, curl b)
coil; **O sap kretsosáilo kruyal lêste.**
The smake coiled/curled around him.
kretsome *pp/adj* 1) curled 2) coiled; ~
shelo coiled rope
kreyóno *nm* colouring pencil, crayon
kríchma/kírchma *nf/arch* inn, country inn,
saloon bar of an inn, tavern
krichmári innkeeper: *nf* **krichmárka**
innkeeper, innkeeper's wife
kríma *nf* crime
kriminalil *vt* 1) criminalize, declare to be
criminal, label as criminal: *pp/adj*
kriminalime; **Le Gazhe kriminalisarde
le Rromen.** The non-Roma have
criminalized the Roma. 2) *v/refl*
kriminalíl-pe be/become criminalized
kriminalimos *nm* crime, criminality
kriminálno *adj* 1) criminal 2) *nm* criminal:
nf **kriminála**
kríno *nm* computer screen, screen
Kris *nf* Libra (*Zod*)
kris/krisi *nf* 1) court, tribunal 2) justice,
law, Romani law 3) trial, assembly of
elders/judges to hear a case 4) judgement,
sentence, verdict; **Dem lês ánde kris.** I

took him to trial/court. **Mangel kris.** He
wants justice. **Dine lês kris.** They tried
him in court. **Kris le Devlêski** Laws of
God. **Kris le Manushêngi** Laws of
Man/Men. **Kris-Rromani.** Internal
Romani (*Kalderash*) Tribunal. **5) del
ánde** ~ take *smbdy* to court, trial **6) del** ~
hold a trial
krisáki pudyáriya *comp/nf* power of the
court
krisáki-buki *comp/nf* 1) lawsuit, case 2) a
matter for the Romani tribunal
krisáki-shib *comp/nf* rhetorical Romani, a
type of flowery or formal Romani used in
trials and on solemn occasions by the
family heads and elders and not used by
children or young people.
krisáko baro *comp/nm* head of a tribunal,
head judge
krisáko *gen/adj* 1) having to do with a trial
or Romani law 2) lawful, legal, just;
krisáko bukfári lawbook, book of
statutes, **krisáko shinimos** court
decision, verdict
kris-bangi *comp/nf* a trial resulting in a
negative decision for the accused or
plaintiff
kris-chachi *comp/nf* a trial resulting in a
positive decision for the accused or
plaintiff
Kris-Gazhikani *nf* 1) Non-Romani
court/trial. (*adjudicates on crimes against
the State, murder, robbery of non-Roma,
etc*). 2) Law of the land, Provincial/State
law
krisimos *n* judgement, sentence, verdict
krisinil *vt* 1) judge, try: *pp/adj* **krisinime**;
O Del krisinil lês. God will judge him 2)
place on trial 3) condemn, sentence;
krisinisarde lês te merel. They
sentenced him to death. 4) *v/refl*
krisiníl-pe a) be judged, judge oneself 2)
have a court case, be engaged in a court
case 3) condemn/sentence oneself
krisinimásko *gen/adj* legal, of the court,
judicial
krisiminos *n* judgement, sentencing

krisinitóri *nm* 1) judge, juror on the *Kris Rromani*; **O krisinitóri o baro** The supreme judge 2) referee

krisinitórya *nm/pl* jury on a Romani tribunal, tribunal members, members of the court

Kris-Rromani *nf* 1) *Kalderash*-Romani court. Tribunal. 2) Law of the *Roma*. The Romani Tribunal deals with breaches of Romani law as understood from the *Rromanía* and interpreted by the *krisinitórya* or members of the tribunal.

kristála *nf* crystal ball; **Nai ma kristála.** I have no crystal ball/How the hell do I know?

Kristiyanitéto *nm* Christianity

Kristiyáno *adj* 1) Christian 2) *nm* **Kristiyáno** Christian: *nf* **Kristiyánka**

Krísto *nm* Christ; **O Anklimos le Kristósko** the Resurrection of Christ

Kristóso *adj* Christian, Christlike; **O Del Kristóso** Jesus Christ, Christian God

krisûngo *adj* judicious, diplomatic, wise in judicial matters, experienced in Romani law

kriyánga *nf* bough, branch, limb: *pl* **kriyênzhi**

kriyangítsa *nf* branch/twig

kriyatúra *nf* 1) creature, critter; **O Del kerdyas sa l'zhívinde kriyaturi.** God make all living creatures. **Che djúngali kriyatúra!** What an ugly creature! 2) creation, handiwork

krízhma *nf* christening clothes, swaddling clothes (*Eur*)

kroxmáliyo *nm* cornstarch, starch

kruchóko *nm* 1) large hook 2) anchor, grapnel

krutsitóri *nm* thrifty man: *nf* **krutsitórka** (*Eur*)

krútso *adj* economical, thrifty (*Eur*)

krutsól 1) cut down on (*expenses*), economize, practice thrift: *pp/adj* **krutsome** (*Eur*) 2) *v/refl* **krutsol-pe** be thrifty, economize, be thrifty

krutsomos *nm* economizing, thrift (*Eur*)

kruyal *adv/prep* around, round about; **Phirdem kruyal núma chi arakhlem la.** I walked around but I did not find it. **Beshénas kruyal e síniya.** They were sitting around the table. (*Am*)

kryámeno *nm* flint, flintstone

kryashtéto *nm* 1) withers (*of a horse*) 2) crown of the head

ku *prep* along with, with (*Eur*)

Kúba *nf* Cuba

kúbo *nm* cube

kuch *adj* 1) costly, dear, expensive; **kuch-práma** expensive item, expensive jewel, **kuch barr** gemstone (*Am*)

kúchi *adj* sexy, sexually appealing (*Am*); **kúchi státo** sexy figure/shape

kuchi *nf* cup, egg cup, small cup

kúchi-khelitórka *nf* 1) kooch dancer on a carnival, a carnival-slang term originally applied to Little Egypt and her imitators on the American carnivals as hoochy-koochy dancers 2) go-go dancer, nude dancer (*Am*)

kuchiwales *adv* lewdly, provocatively; **Khelél-pe kuchiwales.** She dances provocatively.

kuchiwalo *adj* lewd, provocative; **asamos kuchiwalo** provocative smile

kuchiyil *vt* 1) cause to shake, shake, sway: *pp/adj* **kuchiyime** 2) come onto someone sexually, arouse sexually by suggestive body contact 2) *v/refl* **kuchiyíl-pe** shake, shimmy, sway, wiggle

kuchol *vt us with* **mai** 1) hike in price, make more expensive, mark up, raise in price: *pp/adj* **kuchome**; **Mai kuchosardyas o mobíli.** He raised the price of the car. 2) *v/refl* **kuchól-pe** become more expensive; **Swáko ges mai kuchól-pe o tráyo.** Life becomes more expensive every day.

kuch-práma *nf* valuable asset/gem: *pl* **kuch-prámi**

kuchyorri *nm* phial/vial; **kuchyorri drab** phial of some drugged liquid, Mickey Finn, *sl* mickey; **Dya lês kuchorri drab**

hai zalisáilo. She slipped him a mickey and he passed out.

kui *nf* elbow (*Anat*): *pl* **kuiya**

kukar *nm* breeding cock of any fowl species

kukashtára *nf* **1)** bathroom, lavatory, toilet: *pl* **kukashtéri 2)** toilet bowl, seat. **Note:** This word should not be used in mixed company or by men in front of women. A polite way to ask for the toilet (man to man) is **Kai tumáre grasten?** Where are your horses? and for women to women, **Kai zhan le ranya?** Where do the ladies go?

kúkla *nf* puppet (*Eur*)

kuklári *nm* **1)** puppeteer: *nf* **kuklárka** (*Eur*) **2)** manipulator (*of people*)

kuko *dem/adj/pron* that, yonder, that thing, that male *psn/animal*

kukolá-sya *nf/pl* the rest of it, all the rest of it

kukudi *nf* **1)** hailstone *us pl in* **kukudya** (*Eur*) **2) Del kukudya** It is hailing

kukui *nf* **1)** bump, lump **2)** cyst, tumour

kukuriyáshka *nf* female cuckoo

kukuriyézo *nm* male cuckoo

kukurizíl-pe *v/refl* crow: *pp/adj* **kukurizime**

kukurizimos *nm* crowing

kukurúzo *nm* **1)** Indian corn; **kukurúzo po kochai** corn on the cob, North-American corn **2)** popcorn (*Am*)

kukya *dem/adj/pron* that (*far*), that thing, that female *psn/animal*

kulkui *nf* heel (*Anat*)

kúlsa *nf* flannel: *gen/adj* **kulsáko** made of flannel

kultúra *nf* culture

kulturálno *adj* cultural; **chêntro kulturálno** cultural center

kumbétsa *nf* noodle: *pl* **kumbétsi**

kumnáta *nf* husband's sister, wife's sister, sister-in-law

kumnáto *nm* husband's brother, wife's brother, brother-in-law

kumpániya/kumpaníya *nf* **1)** assembly, association, club, company, group, union **2)** local Romani community/society, community of Roma living in a town/city or section/borough/district of a city who claim this as their territory, a traveling community of Roma **3)** commercial company **4)** company (*Mil*)

kumpaniyáko/kumpanyáko 1) *gen/adj* belonging to the **Kumpaníya 2)** *nm* **Rrom ~** male member of the **kumpaníya:** *nf* **Romni kumpaniyáki**

kúna *nf* **1)** cradle **2)** *comp/vt/i* **del ~** rock (the) cradle

kúnda *nf* milking can also used as a vamping drum by Vlax-Romani musicians (*Eur*) *see also* **bragi** *nf*

kunselári *nm* alderman, councilor: *nf* **kunselárka**

kûntára/kîntála *nm/nf* **1)** scale, balance **2)** natural order or balance of the universe

kûntári *nm* counter (*in a store*)

kûnteríl *vt* **1)** balance, weigh: *pp/adj* **kûnterimé 2)** *v/refl* **kûnteríl-pe** be balanced, weighed

kûnterimós *nm* balancing, weighing

kunúna *nf* **1)** bridal crown, bridal wreath, wreath **2)** crown worn by both bride and groom at an Orthodox wedding ceremony; **kunúna-kanrrêngi**, crown of thorns. **3)** wreath

kununil *vt* **1)** crown, marry; **Konunisardyas la ánde Rumúnya.** He married her in Romania. **2)** *v/refl* **kununíl-pe** get married, marry; **Kununín-pe tehára.** They are getting married tomorrow. **Kununisáile garades.** They married secretly. **Kununisáili araki.** She got married yesterday,

kununime *pp/adj* crowned, married

kununimos *nm* crowning of the bride and groom, marriage, wedding ceremony

kûpêriwára *nf* **1)** red deer, roe deer **2)** antelope **3)** caribou (*Can*) **4)** reindeer (*Eur*)

kúpla *nf* couple of; **De lêske kúpla tiléri te kinel pêske kamféti.** Give him a couple of dollars to buy candy.

Kuráni *nm* Quran

Kuranyáko *gen/ádj* of the Quran

kurel *vt* **1)** *vt* coïre, fuck: *pp/adj* **kurado 2)** *v/refl* **kurél-pe** be engaged in sexual intercourse (*Am*) **Note:** When referring to sexual intercourse, **kurel** and its derivatives are not used in polite or mixed conversation but are reserved for private conversation between men only or women only and in vile insults uttered in anger. *see* **kamél-pe** *v/refl*

kurimos *nm* copulation, sexual intercourse

kurko *nm* **1)** week **2)** Sunday **3) Kúrkone** *adv* on Sunday, Sunday

kurkutno *adj* weekly, Sunday

kúrsa *nf* **1)** trap, snare; **Pelo ánde kúrsa.** He fell into a trap. **2)** *comp/vi* **thol ~** set a trap **3)** *nm* course

kúrso *nm* **1)** race track (*Eur*) **2)** course (*in teaching*)

kúrso-grastêngo *comp/nm* horse racing

kúrso-mobilêngo *comp/nm* auto race track

kurtalil *vt* **1)** free, rescue, save, set free: *pp/adj* **kurtalime 2)** free oneself from, get rid of *v/refl* **kurtalíl-pe a)** escape, save oneself **b)** get oneself out of, rid oneself of; **kurtalisáilem ánda e béda.** I got myself out of the jam.

kurtalimos *nm* **1)** escape, getaway, rescue

kúrva *nf* **1)** professional prostitute, call girl **2)** adultress **3)** hussy, trollop, woman considered to have loose moral conduct according to the **Rromaníya 4)** *fig* bitch (*Am*)

kurvári *nm* **1)** pimp **2)** lounge lizard, rake, swinger, womanizer **3)** whoremaster, man of unacceptable moral conduct; **Chi dav múrra sha ka êkh kurvári sar lêste.** I won't give/marry my daughter to a whoremaster like him. **3)** adulterer **4)** *fig* bastard, son-of-a-bitch

kurvaríya *nf* immorality, indecent/unacceptable sexual behaviour on the part of a man

kurvárka *nf* madame, woman who runs a bawdy house

kurvashágo *nm* **1)** any sexual relationship condemned by the **Rromaníya**, adultery,

illicit sex, incest, taboo sex: *pl* **kurvashégurya 2)** any act of adultery or incest **3) del-pe ándo ~** commit adultery or incest; **Diné-pe ándo kurvashágo.** They committed adultery.

kurvil *vt* **1)** cuckold **2)** *v/refl* **kurvíl-pe** (*be cuckolded*)

kurvimos *nm* **1)** prostitution **2)** illicit sexual relations outside the **Rromaníya 3)** act of frequenting brothels and prostitutes

kurvítsa *nf* **1)** naughty little girl. Often used as a term of endearment in North America for very young daughters and daughters of close family relations. **2)** little hussy, a teenage girl who dresses immodestly or acts flirtatiously (*Am*)

kurvíya *nf* prostitution

kúshtik *nf* **1)** garter belt, woman's waist belt for stockings **2)** sash **3)** *arch* corset, girdle

kushtiki *nf* life belt

ku-sya *prep* along with everything, with everything (*Eur*)

kutári *nm* so-and-so, what's his name, such-and-such: *nf* **kutárka; Godo Rrom, kutári, kai avilo ánda Parídji.** That Rom, what's his name, who came from Paris. **Chi zhanav o kutári kai pilas e rrakíya.** I don't know the person who drank the whisky.

kutíya *nf* tin box/metal box, biscuit/cookie box, sardine can, tin can

kutka *adv* there, over there, in that place, right there

kûtûráma/kôtôráma *nf* belt buckle. buckle

kúxniya *nf* kitchen; **Nai e mai skutsome shuri ánde kúxniya.** He/she is not she sharpest knife in the kitchen/not the brightest of people.

kuxniyári *nm* cook: *nf* **kuxniyárka**

kuxniyarítsa *nf* cook

kuya *nf/dem* thing, that thing, that person (*if feminine*); **Kon si kuya?** Who is that person? **So mangel kuya?** What does that woman want?

kuzméta *nf* beauty product: *pl* **kuzméti** beauty products, cosmetics

kúzniya *nf* kitchen

kwafóri *nm* hairdresser: *nf* **kwafórka** (*Eur*)

kwalifikátsiya *nf* qualification/qualifications

kwárda *nf* clockwork spring, clock/watch spring, generic spring

kwãsa *nf* sickle, scythe

kwãsíl *vt* mow, mow down, scythe, reap: *pp/adj* **kwãsimé**

kwãsimós *nm* harvesting, mowing, reaping

kwãsitóri *nm* **1)** reaper **2)** lawnmower

Kwíbêk *nm* Quebec Province, Quebec city

kwíbo *nm* bird nest, nest (*of insects*), hive; **birovlyángo kwíbo** bee hive

kyo *pron/poss/s* your; **Kai kyo dad?** Where is your father? *var of* **tyo** *qv*

kyúdo *nm* mood, disposition; **Astardem la ándo lásho kyúdo.** I caught her in a good mood.

KH

khai *nf* **1)** inaudible passing of wind **2)** **del ~** fart inaudibly

khaililo *adj* **1)** indolent, lazy **2)** *nm* indolent/lazy man: *nf* **khailili**

khailimos *nm* apathy, laziness

khailo *adj* apathetic, indolent, lazy

khailyarel *vt* make apathetic/ indolent/lazy: *pp/adj* **khailyardo**

khailyol *vi* become apathetic/indolent/lazy: *pp/adj* **khaililo**; **Khailili lêski Rromni.** His wife has become lazy.

khaini *nf* chicken, hen

khainí-dívliyo *comp/nf* grouse

khainya *nm/pl* poultry

khainyorri *nf* spring chicken, young chicken

khaiyarel *vt* induce flatulence: *pp/adj* **khaiyardo**

khaiyarimásko *gen/adj* condusive to flatulence, inducing flatulence

khaiyarimos *nm* induced flatulence

kham *nm* sun

khamalo *adj* sunny

khamêski-sistéma *comp/nf* solar system

khamni *adj* pregnant (*Eur*)

khamnimos *nm* conception, pregnancy

khamnyárdyol *vi* be made pregnant: *pp/adj* **khamnyardili**

khamnyarel *vt* impregnate, make pregnant: *pp/adj* **kamnyardi**

khamnyarimos *nm* impregnation, period of pregnancy.

khamnyol *vi* become pregnant: *pp/adj* **khamnili** (*Eur*); **Khamnili e grasni.** The mare has become pregnant.

khanchêsko *adj* worthless, worth nothing

khánchi *pron* nothing/anything; **Nai khánchi**. It's nothing/ It doesn't matter.

Nai ma khánchi. I don't have anything: **Note:** *Kalderash* Romani employs a double negative like Spanish *No tengo nada*. 'I don't have nothing.'

khand/khan *nf* **1)** smell, odor **2)** stench, stink

khándel *vt/i* smell, stink: *pp/adj* **khandino; Phuter e filástra, khándel thuv ándo kher.** Open the window, it smells of smoke in the house. **Khándel mánge phabarimos**. It smells to me like *smthg* is burning. **Khándel mánge xabe.** I smell food. **Khándel shukar.** It smells nice: **Note:** Two thematic verbs exist in *Kalderash* which both mean smell/stink, **khándel** and **sungal**. The meanings can vary between different groups of speakers and in different countries.There is also an athematic verb in **mirishil** *qv.*

khandimos *nm* aroma, smell, stench

khandini *nf* polecat, skunk

khandinimos *nm* laziness, sloth, uselessness

khandino **1)** *adj* malodorous, smelly, tainted (*food*) **2)** repugnant **2)** indolent, lazy, useless **3)** *nm* person who smells badly, repugnant lout (*Am*) **4)** *nm* lazy man, layabout: *nf* **khandini**

khandinol *vi* become malodorous/tainted, develop an odor/stink: *pp/adj* **khandinailo**

khangeri/khangiri *nf* **1)** church, place of worship, temple **2)** *comp/v/refl* **thol-pe ánde kangeri** place oneself under the protection of the church (*to avoid deportation*).

khangerí-Xoraxani *comp/nf* mosque

khangeriyáki-buki *comp/nf* church work (*replating of religious items*)

khangeriyáko-túrno *comp/nm* church tower/steeple

khas *nm* hay

khasêsko *gen/adj* hay, having to do with hay

khatêndar *adv* from nowhere, from anywhere, out of the blue, out of the woodwork

khatênde *adv* nowhere/anwhere; **Chi zhas khatênde kakala bukyása.** We're not going/getting anywhere with this issue. **Káko drom chi zhal khatênde.** This road goes nowhere.

khaver/kaver *adj/pron var of* **aver** *qv.* another, other, next; **Khaver Rrom sas kai kerdyas.** It was another Rom who made it. **Kon sas khaver Rrom kai avilo lêsa ándo mobíli?** Who was the other Rom who came with him in the car? **Me zhav khaver shon.** I'm going next month.

khaver-rêgáko *gen/adj* opposite, on the other side, across from; **Lêsko kher si pe khaver-rêgáko le dromêstar.** His house is on the opposite side of the street.

khelavel *vt* 1) bamboozle, get the better of, make fun of by tricking, overreach, trick 2) excel/outdo *smbdy* in dancing, outdance *smbdy*

khelel *vt* 1) dance; **Shai kheles o kólo?** Can you dance the kolo? **Shai kheles Rromanes?** Can you do Romani dancing? 2) gamble, play; **khelel kárti.** He's playing cards. 3) *v/refl* **khelél-pe a)** dance; **Kheldém-ma lása ándo báldo.** I danced with her during the ball. **b)** play; **Le shavorre khelén-pe ánde úlitsa.** The kids are playing in the street. **c)** gamble; **Khelén-pe.** They are gambling **d)** risk; **Khelél-pe la Martyása.** He's gambling with (risking) death.

khelimásko *gen/adj* 1) dancing, dance; **khelimáski gili** dance song 2) playing; **khelimáske kárti** playing cards 3)

gambling; **khelimáski sínya** gambling table

khelimos *nm* 1) dance, dancing 2) gambling, game, playing

khélindoi *v/part* dancing, gambling, playing

khelitóri *nm* 1) dancer: *nf* **khelitórka** 2) gambler, player

kher le mulêngo *nm/phr* mortuary

khêr *nf* boot, dancing boot, high boot: *pl* **khêreyá**; **zhuto khêreyá** pair of boots

kher/khêr *nm* home, house; **Kerdyas nevo wudar le kherêske.** He made a new door for the house.

kheral *adv* out (*not home*), from home; **Sóma avilem kheral.** I just came from home.

khere *adv* home, homeward; **Zhav khere.** I'm going home. **Kheré-la.** She is at home.

kherênge lasharimáta *comp/nm* house repairs

kherêngo chor *comp/nm* burglar

kherêngo *gen/adj* of homes, houses; **Rrom-kherênge** Roma who own or rent houses

kherêngo-adjênto *comp/nm* housing agent, rental agent, real-estate agent: *nf* **kherêngi-adjêntáika**

kherêsko *gen/adj* of/belonging to a house

kherêski-fátsa *comp/nf* façade of a house, frontage of a house

kher-sobódniko *comp/nm* rooming house

kher-stakláko *nm* greenhouse

kherutno *adj* 1) domestic, domesticated, home, housebound; **kherutno adréso** home address, **kherutno tráyo** home life, family life. **Ansurisáilo de trin shon hai Rrom kherutno si akana.** He got married three months ago and he's a domesticated Rom now. 2) *nm* inhabitant of a house, member of the household: *nf* **kherutni**

khetane *adv* together (*Eur*)

khetanes *adv* together (*Eur*)

khil *nm* butter

khil-xoxamno *com/nm* margarine

khinilo *pp/adj* exhausted, tired, worn out

khinimos *nm* tiredness

khino *adj* exhausted, tired, worn out

khinol *vt* **1)** jiggle, shake, wiggle: *pp//adj* **khinome 2)** *v/refl* **khinól-pe a)** shake oneself, shake **b)** waddle (*as a duck*) **c)** wiggle (*as a snake*)

khinyardilo *pp/adj* burned out, de-energized, exhausted, wasted **2)** *nm* burned out/exhausted man: *nf* **khinyardili**

khinyardo *pp/adj* **1)** tired out, exhausted. **2)** bored to death.

khinyárdyol *vi* become bored to death, burned out, depleted, de-energized, dissipated, exhausted, tired, wasted, worn out : *pp/adj* **khinyardilo**

khinyarel *vt* **1)** exasperate, exhaust, overtire, tire, wear out: *pp/adj* **khinyardo 2)** nag, pester **3)** bore, bore to death

khinyarimásko *gen/adj* **1)** exhausting, tiring **2)** boring

khinyarimos *nm* **1)** exasperation, exhaustion **2)** boredom

khinyol *vi* **1)** become exasperated/exhausted/tired: *pp/adj* **khinilo 2)** become bored/bored to death

khir *nf* ant: *pl* **khira/khirya**

khirángo kwíbo/khiryêngo kwíbo *comp/nm* ant hill/nest

Khitai/Kitai *nm* China

khoi *nf* **1)** suet **2)** tallow (*Eur*)

khoiyáko *gen/adj* **1)** suet **2)** tallow

khoro *nm* **1)** jug, pitcher, pot **2) mutrêsko khoro** chamber pot, piss pot; **Nai lês khoro te mutrél-pe.** He doesn't have a pot to piss in.

khosári *nm* **1)** wiper, wiping cloth **2)** windshield wiper

khosel *vt* **1)** wipe, wipe off/up: *pp/adj* **khoslo; Khos tyo mui!** Wipe your mouth! **Khoslas le prushuka.** She wiped off the crumbs. **2)** sponge **3)** mop

khosno *nm* **1)** rag, wiper **2)** dishcloth **3)** napkin **4)** handkerchief

khul *nf* **1)** excrement, feces, dung, shit, stool; **kotor khul** turd **2)** *comp/vt* **del ~**

bawl out, give shit (*Am*) **3)** *comp/vi* **shúdel ~** fight back, kick ass, retaliate (*Am*); **Xalem dósta xoli lender, akana shudav khul.** I've had enough aggravation from them, now I'm going to kick ass/retaliate.

khuláki-tséra *comp/nf* large defiled tent on a carnival or fairground used as a toilet area

khuláki-vîla *nf* shit fairy, bringer of misfortune (*Am*)

khuláko *gen/adj* **1)** of shit, related to shit **2)** defiled, taboo

khulalo *adj* **1)** covered with dung, defiled with shit, shitty, squalid **2)** fecal **3)** defiled (*by fecal matter*), degenerate, taboo **3)** *nm* defiled man, male adult who has been in bodily contact with excrement: *nf* **khulali** (*woman are not defiled when dealing with body waste of babies and young children*) **4)** *nm* bureaucrat, civil servant, member of a city or town administration **5)** honey dipper; **Le Rrom-Khulale** The Honey-Dippers, an apocryphal family of American Roma who allegedly worked as cesspool engineers, a taboo trade under the **Romaníya**.

khulaló-pai cesspool refuse

khulaló-vagóno *nm* cesspool tanker, 'honey-dipper wagon'

khulári *nm* septic engineer, 'honey-dipper'

khulavel *vt var of* **khulyarel** *vt qv*

khulyarel *vt* **1)** befoul, defile with excrement: *pp/adj* **khulyardo 2)** defile, desecrate, render polluted **3)** cover with excrement/fertilizer **4)** get the better of or make a monkey out of *smbdy v/refl* **5) khulyarél-pe a)** befoul oneself, defile oneself with excrement; **Khulyardyás-pe.** He betrayed/shit himself. **6)** ruin one's reputation

khulyarimos *arch/nm* defilement with excrement (*a punishment for adultery for both parties in the nomadic era in Canada/US when Kalderash traveled in* *groups, horse droppings thrown with a shovel were used for this purpose*)

khulyávol/khulyol *vi* become defiled with excrement: *pp/adj* **khulilo**; **Pelo ánde gozhni hai khulilo.** He fell in the manure and became defiled.

khur *nf* heel (*of a shoe*)

khuri *nf* **1)** filly **2)** *fig* energetic, frisky young woman

khuro *nm* colt, yearling: *nf* **khuri**

khuvári *nm* ball of yarn

khuvdo *pp/adj* **1)** braided, plaited, spun, woven **2)** coiled, twisted **3)** *nm* loom

khuvel *vt/i* **1)** braid, curl, plait, twist, weave: *pp/adj* **khuvdo**; **khúvde bal** braided hair **2)** coil (*rope*) **3)** curl, curl up **4)** ~ **le wastênsa** make hand movements (*us* while dancing) **5)** *v/refl* **kuvél-pe a)** coil (*as a snake*) **b)** curl, curl up; **E mútsa kuvdyás-pe pasha e yag.** The cat curled up near the fire.

khuvimos *nm* **1)** braiding, weaving **2)** coil (*of rope/rubber hose*); **khuvimáta shele** rope coils **3)** kink

khuvimos le wastênsa *nm/phr* hand movements made by a dancer

L

l' *pl/def/art see* **le** *def/art/pl*; **Zhav ka l' grast.** I'm going to the race track.

la *pron/acc* her, it (*if nf*); **Dikhlem la arakí.** I saw her yesterday.

la *pron/enclitic* she is, it is; **Baxtalí-la.** She/it is lucky. **Opré-la.** She's upstairs.

la woyása *adv/phr* gladly, with pleasure; **Kerav túke la woyása.** I'll do it for you with pleasure.

lába *nf* 1) paw 2) *comp/vt* **azbal labánsa** paw, touch with paws

labarínto *nm* labyrinth, maze

láda *nf* 1) chest, steamer trunk 2) trunk (*of an automobile*)

ladavel *vt* load, pack: *pp/adj* **ladado**; **Ladade le mobilárya.** They loaded the furniture.

ladimos *nm* load, loading

ladjári *nm* 1) boatman. 2) sailor (*Eur*)

ladjíya *nf* 1) rowboat. 2) small vessel. (*Eur*)

ladútsa *nf* small chest, traveling chest

lágera *nf* laager

láiboro *nm* vest, waistcoat: *pl* **láiborya**

láira *nf* harp, probably lyre originally, *see* **árpa**

láiyo *nm* lye, sodium hydroxide, used in coppersmithing work

lake *nm* butler, footman, flunky: *pl* **lakeyi**

láko *pron/poss* her, hers, its (*if nf*)

lakorro *nominalized pron* hers

lalorro *adj* 1) incoherent, mumbling 2) *nm* **lalorro** incoherent man: *nf* **lalorri**

Lamári *nm* West; **Phirdyam Lamári.** We walked West.

Lamariyêsko; *gen/adj* of the West; **lamariyêski balwal** west wind.

Lamaryêste *adv* to the West

lámpa *nf* lamp, light

lampáso *nm* braid, especially gold braid, brocade

lampítsa *nf* nightlight

Lamurátsiya *nm./pl* Algeria

Lamurátso *nm* Algerian: *nf* **Lamurátsa**

landíl-pe *v/refl* become a landed immigrant: *pp/adj* **landime** (*Can*)

lang *adj* 1) lame 2) *nf* limp

langal *vi* 1) become lame 2) limp; **O grast langal.** The horse is limping.

langalo *adj* 1) exhibiting a limp 2) *nm* human or animal with a limp: *nf* **langali**

langárdyol *vi* be lamed, made lame: *pp/adj* **langardilo**

langimos lameness

lango *adj* 1) lame 2) *nm* lame man: *nf* **langi**

langyarel *vt* cripple, lame, make lame: *pp/adj* **langyardo**

Lanorde *adv* northward, to the North

Lanórdo *nm* North; **Avilyas katar o Lanórdo.** He came from the North.

Lanordósko *gen/adj*; of the North; **E Lanordóski cheran** The North Star

Lanordóste *adv* towards the North

lantsári *nm* chain maker, maker of chain link for fences

lántso *nm* 1) chain, shackle 2) neck chain *us* with an expensive gold coin (**morokóto**) attached to it by a clasp.

lantsol *vt* 1) chain, shackle: *pp/adj* **lantsome** 2) **lantsól-pe** *v/refl* be chained, chain oneself.

lántsurya *nm/pl* chains,gyves, shackles

lapisári *nm* pencil (*Am fr Sp*)

Lasári *nm* East; **Nashléntar karing o Lasári.** They fled towards the East.

Lasariyêsko *gen/adj* of the East;
  Lasariyêski balwal East wind
Lasaryêste *adv* to the East
lashárdyol *vi* be fixed/fixed up/repaired:
  pp/adj **lashardilo**; **Meklem o mobíli
  ándo shâpo te lashárdyol.** I left the car
  in the shop to be repaired.
lasharel *vt/i* **1)** ameliorate, arrange, fix, get
  smthg repaired, repair: *pp/adj* **lashardo
  2)** fix, fix up, patch up; **Lashardem le
  ran.** I fixed it up with the cops.
  Lasharav o mobíli tehára. I'll get the
  car fixed tomorrow. **3)** organize; **Músai
  te lasharav kakale papírya.** I have to
  organize these papers/this paperwork. **4)**
  overhaul **5)** rectify
lasharimásko *gen/adj* repairable; **Nai
  lasharimásko o mobíli.** The car is not
  able to be repaired.
lasharimáta *nm/pl* repairs; **lasharimáta
  bovênge** stove maintenance and repairs
lasharimos *nm* **1)** maintenance and repairs,
  repairing **2)** correction
lashes *adv* excellently, perfectly
lashé-xamásko *gen/adj* delicious, good to
  eat
lashimos *nm* goodness, kindness
lasho *adj* **1)** excellent, good, kind, nice,
  perfect, sympathetic; **Lásho drom túke!**
  Have a nice trip/safe journey! **Lasho
  símas lása.** I was kind to her. **Lasho sas
  mánsa.** He was good to me. **Nas lasho
  lênsa.** He wasn't nice to them. **2)** *adv*
  fine, O.K., well; **Lasho sim.** I am well.
lásho kyúdo *comp/nm* good
  disposition/mood
lashyol *vi* improve (*with* **mai**): *pp/adj*
  lashilo; mai lashyol ges geséstar. He's
  improving day by day.
lástiko *nm* **1)** elastic band, elastic **2)** pull
  spring, tension spring. *(Am)*
Lasude *adv* South, to the South
Lasudêsko *gen/adj* of the South;
  Lasudêski balwal South wind
Lasudêste *adv* towards the South
Lasúdo *nm* South; **Gêlótar karing o
  Lasúdo.** He went towards the South.

láto *nm* **1)** lot, pitch *(Am)* **2)** used-car lot,
  parking lot
látsa *nf* layer, tier
lav *nm* word *(Eur)* *see more common*
  swáto *nm*
lávka *nf* **1)** shop/store: *pl* **lévchi** *(Eur)* **2)**
  booth, stall, stand *(Eur)*
lávuta *nf* violin
lavutári *nm* **1)** violinist **2)** musician *(Eur)*:
  nf **lavutárka**
lavutash *nm* **1)** violinist **2)** musician *(Eur)*:
  nf **lavutáshka**
lazéri *nm* laser, laser beam, laser surgery
lazhal *vi* be ashamed, be
  embarrassed/shy/self-
  conscioust/reticent/timid: *pp/adj*
  lazháilo; Lazhal te gilabal. She is (*too*)
  shy to sing.
lazhano *adj* **1)** bashful, embarrassed, meek,
  self-conscious, shy, timid **2)** shy person:
  nf **lazhani** *nf* wallflower
lazhav *nm* **1)** modesty **2)** disgrace,
  seduction, shame; **Dyas la po lazhav.** He
  seduced her. **3)** offence, scandal;
  Kerdyas bári lazhav ánde familíya. He
  created a great scandal in the family. **Te
  xal lês lêsko lazhav.** May his
  disgrace/shame destroy him. **Lazhav
  lêske so kerel.** It's scandalous what he is
  doing. **Nai la lazhav.** She has no
  modesty/shame. **4) del ándo ~** make to
  feel ashamed **5)** *comp/vt* **del po ~ a)** sleep
  with *smbdy* **b)** copulate, give oneself to
  smbdy sexually. **c)** insult/shame *smbdy* **6)**
  v/refl **del-pe po ~** act
  disgracefully/shamefully; **Dyas-pe po
  lazhav.** He committed a shameful act. **7)**
  comp/vt/i **lel po ~** be shamed/take offense:
  Na le lês po lazhav! Don't take it as an
  offence! **8)** *v/refl* **lel-pe/po ~** be offended,
  take offence, be shamed; **Na le-tu po
  lazhav!** Don't be offended/shamed! **9) ~**
  with dative case feel shame, be ashamed;
  Lazhav lêske te mothol o chachimos.
  He is ashamed to tell the truth. **10) ~** *with*
  avel *and accusative case*; begin/start to

feel shame; **Avel lês lazhav.** He is starting to feel shame/to be ashamed

lazhavayimos *nm* disgrace, embarrassment, scandal, shame

lazhavel *vt* **1)** make ashamed: *pp/adj* **lazhaveldo**; **2)** cause disgrace, embarrass, scandalize, shock **Lazhaveldyas pêska familíya.** He scandalized his family **3)** seduce (*a virgin*)

lazhavêsko *gen/adj* disgraceful, embarrassing, outrageous, scandalous, shameful, shameless, shocking

lazhimos *nm* shyness, timidity

le 1) *enclitic* they are; **Bokhalé-le.** They are hungry. **2)** *pron/acc* them *cont of* **lên** *qv*

le *def/art/pl* the: *nom/pl* of both genders, *obl/ms* and *obl/pl* of both genders, often elided to **l'** by native speakers; **Zhálas pa l' gava.** He was traveling around the towns/rural area.

lédje *nm* law: *pl* **lédji** (*Eur*)

ledjéri *nm* accounts ledger, minute book, ledger

legálno *adj* legal; **legálno arakhimos** legal defense

legalnones *adv* legally

lêgéno *nm* bidet, bowl, washbasin, washbowl

legíya *nf* legion; **Kali Legíya** Black Legion, Gestapo, Nazi SS

legonil *vt see* **lyagonil** *vt*

léktsiya *nf* lesson

lektúra *nf* **1)** lecture **2)** commentary

lekturash *nm* lecturer: *nf* **lekturáshka**

lel *vt/i* **1)** catch, choose, grasp, marry, sieze, take: *pp/adj* **lino/lilo 2)** accept, acquire, get, obtain; **Lem/linem but love katar e buki.** I got a lot of money from the work. **3)** arrest, capture, seize **4)** choose/take in marriage, marry **5)** occupy, possess, take possession of **6)** hold; **Le lês an tyo wast!** Hold it in your hand! **7)** ~ *with dative case,* take for oneself; **Lem mánge xabe.** I took food for myself. **Lyás pêske Rromni.** He took a wife for himself. **8)** *comps/vt/i with* **lel; 9)** ~ **ánd angáli** hug,

take in an embrace **10)** ~ **bori** take a bride **11)** ~ **búrrnex** grasp, take hold of **12)** ~ **chai** take tea, accept hospitality **13)** ~ **chánsurya** take chances/risks **14)** ~ **e dosh** accept/take the blame **15)** ~ **gyórtso** take a gulp/sip **16)** ~ **inkya** remove, take away **17)** ~ **míta** take a bribe **18)** ~ **e mom** accept the lure/take the bait **19)** ~ **nasul** take offence **20)** ~ **pa** *with prep/case* take off, remove (*clothing*); **Lem o gad pa lêste.** I removed his shirt **21)** ~ **pálpale** take back/back again **22)** *with prep*; **Lem pe mánde.** I took the blame/I held myself responsible. **23)** ~ **patréto** take a photograph **24)** ~ **pe** *with prep case* a) dress, get dressed, put on; **Lem pe mánde gad shukar.** I put on a beautiful/fancy shirt. **25)** ~ **pe kiríya** hire, rent **26)** ~ **primúta** take/get revenge **27)** ~ **rêgáte** take sides **28)** ~ **rrûmashágo** accept/take a bet/wager **29)** ~ **sáma a)** be careful/take care **b)** take care of, protect *us with abl of object*; **Lav sáma tútar.** I'll take care of you **30)** ~ **síla** take advantage of **31)** ~ **tele** take down/off **32)** ~ **trázna** catch a cold **33)** ~ **tsegótso** take aim (*with a gun*) **34)** ~ **vraz** take a weld/be welded **35)** ~ **vúna** take root **36)** ~ **wuzhile** borrow **37)** ~ **xoli** become/get angry; **Lyas xoli pe lêske dades.** He got angry at his father. **38)** ~ **yilo** cheer up, take heart

lel-pe *v/refl* **1)** get for oneself, possess for oneself, take unto oneself/for oneself, take upon oneself **2)** begin, begin to, get going, get started, start, start to, take place; **Lem-man, Dále, thai gêlèmter.** I got started/started out, Mother, and I departed. **Lyás-pe te gilabal.** He started to sing. **O abyav lel-pe ka l' trin ánde misméri.** The wedding reception will take place at three p.m. **3)** decide; **Lem-man te zhávtar.** I decided to depart. **4)** be catchy/contagious **5)** take oneself; **Lyás-pe hai gêlótar.** He took himself and departed. **6)** *comp/vbs with* **lél-pe; ~ ánde yakh** catch the attention

of; **7**) ~ **pála** annoy, bother, nag, pester;
Na mai le-tu pála mánde! Don't
bother/nag me any more!

lên *pron/acc* them

lênde *pron/prep/pl* all of them, them all;
Wo si o mai baro ánda lênde sya. He is
the biggest of them all.

lêngo *pron/poss* their, theirs

lêngorró *nominalized pron* theirs

lenívo *adj* **1**) lazy **2**) unambitious **3**) *nm*
lazy man: *nf* **lenivútsa**

lentíla *nf* lentil

leopárdo *nm* leopard: *nf* **leopardútsa**

lês *pron/acc* him, it (*if nm*)

lêsko *pron/poss* his, its (*if nm*)

lêskorró *nominalized pron* his

Lévo *nm* **1**) Leo (*Zod*) **2**) lion, pet name for
a male lion or child's stuffed lion

lewudil *vt* **1**) acclaim, compliment, extol,
laud, make famous, praise: *pp/adj*
lewudime 2) flatter, suck up to. *v/refl*
lewudíl-pe a) boast, brag, extol one's
own virtues **b**) **3**) browbeat, intimidate,
threaten; **lewudíl-pe mánde.** He's
threatening me.

lewudimos *nm* acclaim, compliment, fame,
flattery, homage, praise, reputation: *pl*
lewudimáta compliments

leznil *vt* **1**) bargain/haggle down in price,
make cheaper, cut, reduce in price: *pp/adj*
leznime 2) *v/refl* **lezníl-pe** become
cheaper/reduced in price, go on sale

lézno *adj/adv* cheap, cheaply; **mai lézno**
cheaper, more cheaply

li *art* sometimes used with numbers as
follows; **li dui** the two, the two of them, **li
pansh** the five, the five of them

libertátiya *nf* freedom, liberty

libertáto *adj* at liberty, free

libérto *adj/adv* **1**) at liberty, available, free
2) *nm* freedom, liberty **3**) free man: *nf*
libertútsa

lichil *vt* **1**) cure, heal: *pp/adj* **lichime 2**)
v/refl **lichíl-pe a**) cure oneself **b**) heal

lichimos *nm* **1**) cure, healing **2**) antidote

lichitóri *nm* healer/ herbal healer: *nf*
lichitórka

lídero *nm* leader: *pl* **lídere**; leader, used in
a restrictive sense of a leader of Roma, a
Romani representative in the
national/local government, an NGO,
political party, etc. (*Eur*); **Chi sim
prósto Rrom! Me símas lídero ánde
Rumúnya!** I am not an ordinary Rom! I
was a leader in Romania!

ligúma *nf* vegetable

líka *nf* linden (*tree*)

likh *nf* louse, nit

likhalo *adj* infested with nits

likhyárdyol *vi* become infested with nits

likhyarel *vt infect with nits: pp/adj*
likhyardo

líkido *nm* liquid

likoríso *nm* liquorice

likyarde barra *nm/pl* gravel, ground up
stone

likyardé-kolumpírya *comp/nf* mashed
potatoes

likyárdyol *vi* be/become blended/crushed/
ground/mashed/minced/powdered/
pulverized/squashed: *pp/adj* **likyardilo**

likyarel *vt* **1**) blend, crush, granulate, grind,
mash, mince, powder, pulverize, squash:
pp/adj **likyardo 2**) repress, stamp down
on, suppress

likyarimos *nm* **1**) blending, crushing,
grinding, mashing, mincing, powdering,
pulverizing, squashing **2**) repression,
suppression

lil *nm* **1**) letter **2**) newsletter, publication **3**)
letter of reference **4**) licence

lila *nm/pl* **1**) correspondence **2**) documents,
letters, papers

lilêngo *gen/adj* literate

liliyáko *nm* **1**) vampire **2**) ghoul **3**) bat,
vampire bat: *pl* **lilyácha**: *nf* **liliyakútsa**

lilorro *nm* memo, note, short letter

lim *nf* **1**) mucous, snot **2**) slime

limalo *adj* **1**) sniveling, snotty,
snotty-nosed; **límalo nakh** snotty nose **2**)
covered with slime, slimy **3**) *nm* snot,
snot face, snotty: *nf* **limali 4**) *nm* welsher
(*on debts*)

limáwol *vi* drip mucus, have a runny nose: *pp/adj* **limailo; Limáwol pêsko nakh.** His nose is running.

limbrítsa *nf* **1)** heartburn **2)** stomach disorder

limbúto *adj* **1)** suffering from a speech impediment like stammering or stuttering **2)** man who is vocally challenged: *nf* **limbutsáika**

limbutsíl-pe *v/refl* be vocally challenged, stammer, stutter: *pp/adj* **limbutsime**

limbutsomos *nm* speech impediment

limonáda *nf* lemonade

limos *nm* **1)** acceptance **2)** possession **3)** *smthg* possessed/taken **4)** taking **5)** acquisition

limos pe sîla *nf/phr* rape, violation

limpedil *vt* **1)** make to abate, make calm, clear up (*weather*), calm down, smooth, smooth out: *pp/adj* **limpedime 2)** *v/refl* **limpedíl-pe** abate, calm down, clear up

límpedo *adj* **1)** calm, clear, placid, smooth (*water*), quiet **2)** polite, unaffected **3)** bright, clear, light, lucid

limúno/limóno *nm* lemon: *pl* **limúya**

linayíl-pe *v/refl* **1)** develop palsy: *pp/adj* **linayime 2)** become paralyzed

linayimos *nm* **1)** palsy **2)** paralysis

linchil *vt* condemn without justification, lynch: *pp/adj* **linchime; Linchime símas ánde kris.** I was lynched in (my) trial/condemned by stacked false evidence. (*Am*)

linchimos *nm* kangaroo court, lynching (*Am*)

lindíko *nm* clitoris (*Anat*): *pl* **lindíchi**

lindral *vi* become drowsy/sleepy: *pp/adj* **lindrailo**

lindralo *adj* drowsy, sleepy

lindravel *vt* **1)** make drowsy/sleepy: *pp/adj* **lindrado 2)** anesthetize

lindri *nf* drowsiness, sleep; **Bi-lindráko si.** He's restlesss.

líniya *nf* line; **ánde líniya** in line, in single file

lintíya *nf* lentil: *pl* **lintíyi**

línyol *vi* be accepted, be gotten/obtained, be taken: *pp/adj* **linilo**

lipil *vt* **1)** attach, paste, seal, stick to, stick on: *pp/adj* **lipime 2)** *v/refl* **lipíl-pe** adhere, attach, stick to

lipimos *nm* **1)** attachment **2)** adhesive, goo, goop, paste

lipitári *nm* **1)** bloodsucker, leech **2)** *fig* man who drains another's money or time, sponger: *nf* **lipitárka**

lípsa *nf* deprivation, lack of, need, penury, want

lipsime *pp/adj* grasping, greedy, importuning, needy

líra *nf* **1)** unit of $50 originally based on the price of gold at $50 an ounce (*Am*) **2)** pound sterling (*Eur*)

liséyo *nm* high school (*Eur*); **Anklisto katar o liséyo.** He graduated from high school.

lísitsa *nf* **1)** fox **2)** squirrel (*Am*)

lísta *nf* list, menu

lítra *nf* liter (*Eur*)

litriwóno *nm* **1)** nitric acid **2)** sulphuric acid

livádya *nf* cow pasture, hay meadow, meadow, paddock

liyázha *nf* religion

liyondári *nm* lion: *nf* **liyondárka**

liyopárdo *nm* leopard: *nf* **liyopardáika**

lizníko *nm* forest/park ranger, game warden

liznyáka *nf* twin, twin sister: *pl* **liznyáki**

liznyáko *nm* twin, twin brother: *pl* **liznyácha**

Liznyázha *nm/pl* Gemini (*Zod*)

lo *enclitic* he is/it is; **Barvaló-lo.** He is rich.

lóbi *nm/neolog* lobby

lobóda *nf* goosefoot, lambsquarter (*chenopodium album*)

logódba *nm* **1)** proposal, proposition; **Te nashti maládyovas ánde kakya treyába musai te wazdas aver logódba.** If we can agree in this matter we must come up with/raise another proposal. **Si te shinavas logódba.** It is necessary for us to offer a proposal. **2)** proposal of marriage

logodil vt **1)** propose (*motion, solution*), propose (*bylaws, rules*), propose (*marriage*): *pp/adj* **logodime 2)** *v/refl* **logodíl-pe a)** be proposed **b)** propose marriage

logodimos *nm* motion, proposal

lokálno *adj* local

lokálo *nm* **1)** location **2)** hang out where Roma congregate such as a bar, disco, etc (*Eur*)

lokatash *nm* locksmith

lokáto *nm* **1)** padlock, lock; **Tho o lokáto!** Lock the door! **2)** oarlock

lokes *adv* **1)** cautiously, easily, gently, lightly, softly **2)** slowly

loki gili *nf* light song, song of life or hope

loko *adj* **1)** easy, gentle, light, soft, unabrasive; **loki buki** easy work/light work/soft job **2)** slow *see also* **polokorro** *adj*

lokústo *nm* locust, weevil

lokyarel *vt* lighten (*load*), make easy/easier: *pp/adj* **lokyardo; O swiyádero lokyardyas amári buki.** The (electric) drill has made our work easier.

lokyol *vi* become easy, become lighter: *pp/adj* **lokilo**

lolé-balêngo *comp/gen/adj* red-haired

lóli fárba *nf* red ink, red paint

Loli Lulugi *nf* Red Flower/Little Red Riding Hood (*Eur*)

lolichóso *adj* **1)** reddish, pink, shade of red **2)** sorrel (*colour*); **lolichóso grast** sorrel (*horse*)

lolimos *nm* **1)** redness **2)** rouge **3)** embarrassment **4)** rash

lóli-múra *nf* raspberry

lolo *adj* **1)** red **2)** sexually aroused/excited **3)** embarrassed **4)** *nm* diamonds (*in playing cards*): *pl* **lole; o zhandári lolêngo** the Jack of diamonds

lolo fanári *comp/nm* red light/stop light

lolo pe pûrr *nm/phr* **1)** Romani male *psn* unable to speak Romani (*Eur*): *nf* **loli pe pûrr**

loló-kolináko *comp/nm* male robbin: *pl* **lolé-kolinácha** *nf* **lolí-kolináki**

lolyárdyol *vi* become embarrassed: *pp/adj* **lolyardilo**

lolyarel *vt* embarrass, make to blush, make red: *pp/adj* **lolyardo**

lolyol *vi* **1)** turn red **2)** blush **3)** become embarrassed: *pp/adj* **lolilo**

lómo *nm* **1)** junk, salvage, scrap, slag, waste material **2) shúdel po ~** scrap, turn into scrap

lond thai manrro *nm/phr* **1)** bread and salt **2)** *v/phr* **lel o ~** take the bread and salt, get married/marry; **Line o lond thai o manrro.** They took the bread and salt/They married under Romani law. (*Taking of bred and salt in a ceremony officiated by an elder was the original Kalderash marriage in Canada and the US*)

lond/lon *nm* salt; **maryáko lond** sea salt

londalo *adj* saline, salty, tasting of salt; **pai londalo** salt water, **Rovélas londale aswênsa.** She was crying salty tears.

londo *adj* salty, seasoned (*food*)

lóndo pai *comp/nm* salt water/sea water

Lóndono *nm* London (*UK*)

londyárdyol *vi* be made saline/salty, be seasoned: *pp/adj* **londyardilo**

londyarel *vt* salt/season (*food*): *pp/adj* **londyardo**

londyarimos *nm* salting/seasoning (*food*) salting (*street*); **Manai londyarimos po drom.** There is no salting on the roadway.

londyol *vi* become salty/saline, be seasoned: *pp/adj* **londilo**

lopáta *nm* **1)** shovel, spade **2)** paddle

lopatári *nm* snow shovel

lopatash *nm* fireman on a train, stoker on a steamship, ditchdigger

lopatil *vt* **1)** scoop, shovel: *pp/adj* **lopatime; Lopatílas o iv kána pharrulo pêsko yilo.** He was shoveling the snow when he had his heart attack. **2)** paddle (*canoe*)

lopatimos *nm* scooping, shoveling

lopatítsa *nf* **1)** dustpan, ladle, poop scoop **2)** drumstick, thigh of a chicken leg

lopunts/lopunz *nf/s* 1) hobble (*horse*) 2) brake (*of a vehicle*): *pl* **lopunts/lopúnza**

lopuntsil *vt* 1) to hobble a horse 2) apply brakes 3) *v/refl* **lopuntsíl-pe** hobble oneself, place limitations on one's ability

lopuntsime *pp/adj* **a)** hobbled; **Me sim sar o grast lopuntsime.** I am like a hobbled horse/ restricted in every direction. **b)** with the emergency brake on

losh *nf* gladness, joy

loshal *vi* be joyful, feel joy, rejoice: *pp/adj* **loshailo; Loshayas te ashunel o nevimos.** He was overjoyed to hear the news.

loshalo *see* **loshano** *adj*

loshano *adj* glad, happy, joyful, overjoyed

loshárdyol *vi* be made glad, joyful: *pp/adj* **loshardilo**

losharel *vt* cheer up, gladden, make joyful: *pp/adj* **loshardo**

loshyol *vi* become glad/joyful: *pp/adj* **loshilo; Loshilem kána ashundem.** I became overjoyed when I heard about (it).

loteríya *nf* lottery (*Am*)

lôto/láto *nm* car lot, lot, parking lot, place where automobiles are sold by Roma (*Am*)

lovach *nm* 1) hunter 2) sniper (*Mil*)

lovalo *adj* profitable, prosperous; **Lovale Rrom si.** They are monied Roma.

Lovári *nm* male member of the **Lovara** group: *nf* **Lovarútsa**

Lovarítksko *adj* of the Lovara; **Rrom Lovarítsko si.** He's a Rom of the **Lovari** group.

Lovarítska *nf* **Lovára** dialect of Vlax-Romani

love *nm/pl* 1) money, monies 2) capital, finances

lovêngi-gazhi *comp/nf* money lady, female welfare worker (*Am*)

lovêngi-tsedúla *comp/nf* money order

lovêngo-gazho *comp/nm* male welfare worker (*Am*)

lovêngo-redjistéri *nm* cash register

lovêngo-yáshchiko *comp/nm* safe, vault

lóvo *nm* 1) hunt, hunting 2) **zhal po ~** go hunting, go on the hunt, hunt

lovorro *nm* dividing up of money. A *Kalderash* ceremony where partners, after a completed job, divide the money equally among themselves after deducting the expenses incurred on the job.

loyáko *adj* 1) law abiding, loyal 2) *nm* loyal friend/person: *nf* **loyakútsa**

loyíya *nf* loyalty

lóza *nf* grape orchard. vinyard

lubenítsa *nf* honey dew melon, muskmelon

lubni *nf* 1) prostitute 2) *fig* slut, whore

Lucháforo *nm* 1) Venus as the morning star 2) Planet Venus

lúcho *nm* kindling, tinder

Ludári *nm* member of a non-Kalderash group of Roma from Romania otherwise known as *Bayash* (*qv*): *nf* **Ludárka**

lulugi *nf* 1) flower 2) menstruation; **Si la lulugi.** She is menstruating/She has a flower 3) *id* **Woi kerdyas e shonêski lulugi.** She became pregnant while unmarried.

lulugí-kêrtitsáki *comp/nf* pansy

lulugimos *nm* bloom, flower, flowering

lulugyári *nm* 1) horticulturalist 2) florist, flower vendor: *nf* **lulugyárka**

lulugyol *vi* bloom, blossom, flower: *pp/adj* **lulugyailo**

lulyáva/luleyáva *nf* pipe (*for tobacco*)

lumína *nf* 1) light, illumination 2) break of day, early dawn

lúmiya/lúmya *nf* 1) planet earth, world: *pl* **lúmiyi** 2) people, humanity, human society, world; **ánde lúmiya le Rromêngi** in the world of the Roma, in Romani society 3) Roma from somewhere else; **Dikhlem them hai lúmiya kai sláva.** I saw local Roma and Roma from elsewhere at the feast.

lumiyáki-miriyázha *comp/nf* world-wide web, Internet

lumiyáko/lumyáko *gen/adj* global, of the world, worldwide: **lumiyáke nátsiyi** nations of the world

lungárdyol *vi* be made longer/stretched: *pp/adj* **lungardilo**

lungichóso *adj* longish, rather long

lungimos *nm* length; **Sóde si de lungimos?** How long is it?

lúngo *adj* **1)** extended, long, of long duration; **Si la lúndji bal.** She has long hair. **Lúngo drom thai lángo grast.** A long road and a lame horse, *id* It's never so bad that it couldn't be worse. **2)** *comp/nm* a long way

lúngo drom *comp/nm* extended/long trip, long road; **Phiravélas lungone dromênsa.** He has wandered far and wide.

Lúngo Támna *comp/nf* Indian Summer

lúngo tráyo *comp/nm* longevity; **Baxt, sastimus thai lúngo tráyo!** Good fortune, health and longevity! (toast)

lúngo-mannro *comp/nm* French bread, long roll of hard-crusted bread

lungones *adv* long, lengthy

lunguriyétso *adj* oblong

lungyarel *vt* **1)** extend, lengthen, stretch: *pp/adj* **lungyardo 2)** continue, go on, carry on; **Lungyaren o marimos.** They are continuing the war.

lungyarimos *nm* extension

lungyol *vi* become extended/longer: *pp/adj* **lungilo**

lúpo *nm* jeweller's loupe, magnifying glass

lutênto *nm* lieutenant

lutsári *nm* fairy guardian, guardian angel, good fairy

Luwine *adv* on Monday

Lúya *nf* Monday

lyagonil/legonil *vt* **1)** rock, sway, swing: *pp/adj* **lyagonime 2)** dangle **3)** *v/refl* **lyagoníl-pe** dangle, rock, sway, swing oneself, be dangling/rocking/swaying/swinging

lyágono *nm* **1)** basinet **2)** swing **3)** hammock

lyagonútso *nm* bassinet

lyáko *nm* antidote, cure

lyóno *nm* nothing, zero

M

ma 1) *conj cont of* **núma** *qv* 2) *pron/acc* me. myself *commonly heard cont of more formal* **man** *pron/acc qv*: **Zhanes ma?** Do you know me? 3) *imp* don't *var of* **na** *qv*

Machwanítska *nf Machwáya* dialect of Vlax-Romani spoken in the Americas

Machwanítsko *adj* of the **Machwáya**

Machwáno *nm* Male member of the **Machwáya** group: *nf* **Machwánka**

Machwanútsa *nf* girl or young woman of the **Machwáya** group

Machwáya *nm/pl* Large group of Vlax-Roma in California and elsewhere in the Americas

madjikánto *nm* performing/stage magician: *nf* **madjikantáika**

mádjiko *nm* 1) magic (*as performed on stage*); **Kerel ~** perform carnival/stage magic

madjikósko *adj* magic; **madjikóski fórma** magic trick

madjíya *nf* magic, state magic (*Eur*)

madjóre *adj/nm* major (*Mus*); **Re madjóre** D major

madjoritéto *nm* majority

madjoritetósko *gen/adj* of a majority; **vóta madjoritetóski** majority vote

magarêsto *nm* stud donkey

magári *nm* 1) ass, burro, donkey: *nf* **magarútsa** 2) jackass

magaril *vt* 1) defile, profane: *pp/adj* **magarime** 2) *v/refl* **magaríl-pe** defile/profane oneself (*Eur*)

magarimos *nm* defilement, profanity (*Eur*)

magazúno *nm* 1) magazine of a gun 2) magazine (*Am*) 3) breech, breechblock (*of trapdoor, breechloading, hunting rifles* such as the Martini-Enfield) 4) ammunition storage room, arsenal, magazine, storage room

mágla *nf* fog, mist

magláko *gen/adj* foggy

magnéto *nm* 1) electric pickup for a guitar or other stringed acoustic instrument (*Mus*) 2) magnet

magnetofóno *nm* tape recorder (*Eur*)

máhala *nf* 1) district/settlement inhabited by Roma, Romani quarter (*Eur*) 2) **mahála** suburb (*Am*)

mahálya *nf/pl* suburban areas, suburbs (*Am*)

mai *adv/pron* 1) more (*used to form comp adjs, advs, preps*); **Swáko ges mai baryol.** He grows bigger every day. **mai dur**, more far (*further*), **mai baro**, bigger, **mai andre,** more(*further*) inside. 2) more *us with* **but**; **Kames mai but te zhanes?** Do you want o know more? **Trobul man mai but baxt.** I need more luck. **Kindyas mai but mas**. He bought more meat. 3) *adv* ever; **Mai dikhlan kodya?** Have you ever seen anything like that? 4) **so mai**, what more; **So mai kerdyan?** What more have you done/What have you been up to? **So mai keres?** What more are you up to? (*calque on Romanian Ce mai faci?*) 4) *nm* more, some more *always with* **but**; **Manges mai but?** Do you want (some) more? **De mánge mai but!** Give me some more/more! **O mai but kai dikhav lês o mai xansû me kamav les.** The more I see him, the less I like him.

mai akana *id*; **Mulo mai akana trin bersh.** He died three years ago now

mai anglal *adv/prep/phr* ahead, before, first (*before*)**,** further, further ahead, more ahead, more in front, in front of; **Zha anglal!** Go in the front!/Lead on! **Tu zhas mai anglal!** You are going first! (*before anyone else*) **Wo gêlótar mai anglal mándar.** He departed before I did.

mai anglal katar *conj/phr* before; **Mai anglal katar te zhas, ker sigúro ke si tu sya le papírya.** Before you go, make sure you have all the documents/paperwork. **Gêlótar mai anglal katar dine gáta e sláva.** He departed before they ended the feast.

mai anglal yekh dáta *adv/phr* once before

mai angle *prep/phr* forward, forwards; **Zha mai angle!** Go forward/move ahead/get going!

mai anglunes *comp/adv* **1**) beforehand, early, earlier **2**) in the future, at some future time

mai angluno *comp/adj* earlier, first, former, more ahead of

mai but *comp/adv* **1**) any more, more; **Mangel mai but xabe.** He wants more food. **2**) *nm* any more, more, some more; **Chi mangav mai but.** I don't want any more. **3**) majority (*of people/animals*), the greater number of, most of, the maximum number of; **O mai but le themêstar mangel te ashel kathe.** The majority of the people (Roma) want to remain here. **O mai but le grastêndar pravárdile.** Most of the horses have been fed.

mai chorro *comparative/adj* worse; **Wo si mai chorro pêske phralêstar.** He is worse whan his brother. **O Zurka si o mai chorro kodolêndar.** Zurka is the worst of them.

mai d'anglal *adv/conj/phr* before, earlier, previously; **Areslas pansh ges mai d'anglal.** He arrived five days previously. **Areslo mai d'anglal ke gêlèmtar.** He arrived before I left.

maidáno *nm* tower

mai desar/mai but desar *comp/adv* more than

mai gorde *comparative/adv* worse; **Meyázol mai gorde ages desar araki.** He looks worse than (he did) yesterday. **Mai gorde si desar so gîndís.** It's worse than you think.

mai lasho *comparative/adj* better

mai mishto *comparative/adv* better; **Mai mishto si te zhas akana.** We had better leave now.

mai nasul *comp/adj* worse (*more evil*)

mai palal katar *conj/adv/phr* after; **Kai zhas mai palal katar e sláva?** Where are you going after the feast? **Mai palal katar avilo katar o Chikágo, phuterdyas ófisa ándo Târáno.** After he came from Chicago, he opened a parlour in Toronto.

mai palunes *comp/adv* in the past, previously

mai paluno *comp/adj* **1**) last **2**) late, latest **2**) endmost

mai phurano *comp/adj us with* **d'**, **do** *and* **de**) longer than; **Símas kathe mai phurano d'ek bersh.** I have been here longer than one year. **Na hamisáwo ka murri bori kai si kathe mai phurani de trin bersh.** Don't meddle with my daughter-in-law who is here (*for*) longer than two years.

mai xansû/mai xansi *oppositional* less, the less **1**) **O mai xansû sikyol, o mai xansû zhanel.** The less he learns, the less he knows. **2**) *adv/comparison with* **desar**; **Wo si mai xansû bokhalo desar túte.** He is less hungry than you. **3**) *adj*; **Si lês mai xansû vryámya te bashavel muzíka.** He has less time to play music. **4**) *prep*; **mai xansû; Pansh mai xansû de dui ashavel trin.** Five less two equals three. **5**) *nf* **mai xansû; Dinilo mai xansû desar wo manglas.** He got less than he asked for.

mai-do-gáta *comp/adv* almost, just about, nearly; **Mai-do-gata sam othe.** We are almost there. **Mai-do-gáta mulo.** He almost died. **Mai-do-gáta xalem dósta xoli lênder.** I've had just about enough of their aggravation.

mai-êkh-dáta *adv/phr* again, once more, one more time

maimúnka *nf* **1)** female monkey **2)** computer mouse

maimúno *nm* ape, monkey: *nm/dim* **maimunútso** little monkey, little rascal

maistoríya *nf* masterpiece

Máistoro Manóliyo *comp/nm* Master Craftsman Manolio (*fr* Rumanian *Mesterul Manole*) a master stone maker who immures his wife in a structure, a character in a Kalderash folktale

máistoro *nm* master craftsman

máistoro shibêngo *comp/nm* linguist

máistoro-barrêsko *comp/nm* stone mason

máistoro-muzikánto *comp/nm* master of music, music master

maiyónsto *nm* belongings, chattels, property, things owned, real estate

makar *adv* **1)** at least, the least: **Mek te sovel-pe makar pe ekh cháso!** Let him sleep for at least an hour! **2)** although **3)** even; **Chi ashav, makar yekh chaso.** I won't stay, even for one hour.

makar ke *conj* although, despite the fact that, even though, even if; **Makar ke aresav ánde wúrma, me zhávtar defyal.** Even though I'll get there late, I'm going anyway. **Makar ke baró-lo, chi darav lêstar.** Even though he is big, I don't fear him. **Kamav tut makar ke chi kames man.** I love you even though you don't love me. **Maker ke mothol ke barvalo si, chi pakyav lês.** Even though he says he's wealthy, I don't believe him.

makéta *nf* model (*of smthg*), mock up, stage prop

maketísta *nm/nf* model builder

makh *nf* fly, housefly

makhalo *adj* infested with flies

mákhel/makhel *vt* **1)** grease, lubricate, oil: *pp/adj* **makhlino/makhlo 2)** daub, smear, stain

makhimos *nm* **1)** grease job, lubrication, lubrication job **2)** staining

makhlino *pp/adj* daubed, greased, lubricated, smeared, stained

makhlo *adj* greasy, lubricated, slippery with grease

makh-Shpanyolítsko *comp/nf* Spanish fly

makhyorri *nf* fruit fly

máko *nm* **1)** opium, poppy seed, poppy **2)** club (*in playing cards*): *pl.* **mákurya; E Rani makuryêngi** the Queen of Clubs

makrish *nm* sheep sorrel (*rumex acetosella*)

makyárdyol *vi* be made drunk/intoxicated: *pp/adj* **makyardilo**

makyarel/matyarel *vt* **1)** intoxicate, make/get somebody drunk: *pp/adj* **makyardo 2)** *v/refl* **makyarél-pe** get hammered, make oneself drunk

makyarno *adj* **1)** alcoholic **2)** *nm* alcoholic man, drunk: *nf* **makyarni**

makyarnomos *nm* **1)** drunken debauchery, drinking spree, drunken orgy **2)** alcoholism

makyol/matyol *vi* become drunk, intoxicated: *pp/adj* **makilo; Makilo ánde sláva.** He got drunk during the feast.

mal *nf* field (*Eur*)

maladimos *nm* **1)** co-operation, joint action **2)** unification **3)** meeting

maladino *adj* allied, in agreement, together, united; **Nátsiyi-Maladine** United Nations

malado *part/adj* **1)** asinine, foolish, silly, trivial; **Xasarel pêske vryámya djelênsa maladênsa.** He wastes his time with asinine trivialities. **2)** banged, bruised, hurt **3)** fitting, suitable

maládyol/maládyovel *vi* **1)** come together, fit together, join together, match, unite: *pp/adj* **maladilo 2)** come across, encounter, find, meet, run into, *us* with *inst* of object; **Maládilem vúni Rromênsa ándo fóro**. I met with some Roma in town. **Maládilo le Babêsa ánde sláva** He met Bob during the feast. **Maládilam ándo kher le Zlatchósko.**

We met at Zlatcho's house. **3)** come to an agreement/understanding, unite; **Maládilam pe gadya buki**. We reached an greement on that issue. **4)** fit (*as clothes/shoes*); **Chi maládyon mánge le tsokólya**. The shoes don't fit me. **5)** eclipse; **Tehára si kána o shon maládyol le khamésa**. Tomorrow is when the moon eclipses the sun. **6)** co-operate, become united, unite with; **Musái te maládyos lênsa**. We have to unite with them. **7)** accommodate, contain, hold **8) maládyol mai ekh dáta** *vi/phr* meet again, become reunited

malavel mai ekh dáta *vt/phr* meet again, rejoin, restart, reunite

malavel *vt* **1)** begin, strike up, start; **Maladyas te gilabal**. He started to sing: *pp/adj* **malado 2)** bang into, crash into, collide, sideswipe; **Maladyas múrro mobíli**. He rear-ended my car. **3)** bang, hit, knock, stomp, strike, thump **4)** afflict, bruise, hit, hurt **5)** graft, bring together, bring together in agreement, unite **6)** meet by chance, run into; **Maladem lês ánde úlitsa**. I ran into/met him on the street. **7)** eclipse

malayimos le khamêsko *comp/nm* solar eclipse

malayimos *nm* **1)** contact, encounter, meeting **2)** alliance, co-operation, union, unity **3)** eclipse **4)** collision, fender-bender **5)** chance encounter/meeting

maléta *nf* **1)** suitcase, valise **2)** carrying case for musical instrument (*Am*)

malini *nf* cranberry

málo *nm* mall, shopping center (*Am*)

mamadéra *nf* pacifier, rubber nipple for a baby bottle

mamalíga *nf* corn mush, polenta

mami *nf* **1)** grandmother **2)** wet nurse

Mámo! *nf/voc* Mother!, Mom!

mámux *nm* blackthorn

mámuxar *nm* blackthorn bush

mamyáki-dey *nf* maternal great-grandmother

mamyáko-dad *comp/nm* maternal great grandfather

mamyorri *nf* **1)** little old witch, sorceress; **mamyori le wêrshèski** old witch in the forest who can bring death by plague (*Folk*) **2)** cholera

man *pron/acc* me, myself

manadjéri *nm* manager: *nf* **manadjérka**

manai *pres/predicate/negative* there is no/are no, there is not/are not; **Manai love**. There is no money. **Manai kónik ánde sóba**. There is nobody in the room. **Love manai ándo godo fóro**. There's no more money in that town.

manas *past/predicat/negative* there was no/was not, there were no/were not; **Manas love ándo bánko**. There was no money in the bank.

manáshka *nf* nun (*Am*)

manashkángi-manustíra *comp/nf* nunnery

manáxo *nm* monk (*Eur*)

mandáto *nm* mandate (*Eur*)

mandolíno *nm* mandoline

mandrágo *nm* mandrake root

mangel *vt/i* **1)** ask (*for a specific item*), desire, want, wish for: *pp/adj* **manglo**; **So manges?** What do you want? **2)** beg, bum, panhandle; **Mangélas po drom**. She was begging on the street. **3)** *vi/phr* ~ **pe sîla** insist/insist on **4)** *comp/vt/i* ~ **pai** beg for mercy; **Dem lês daba zhi-ka manglas pai**. I beat him until he begged for mercy. **5)** ~ **te phenel** imply, mean; **So manges te phenes?** What do you imply/mean?

mangimáta *nm/pl* **1)** alms, proceeds in goods or money from begging **2)** demands, needs, request, wants

mangimos *nm* **1)** claim, demand request, want; **Zhal o mangimos**. The request is going forward/being processed. **2)** begging, panhandling

mangin *nm* **1)** treasure. **2)** wealth, fortune **3)** ransom

manginalo *adj* **1)** possessing treasure/enormous wealth; **Manginale si**

kódole Rrom. Those Roma are rolling in dough/are extremely wealthy **2)** *nm* wealthy man: *nf* **manginali 3)** *nm* treasurer, *psn* who holds joint money: *nf* **manginali**

mangitóri *nm* **1)** person making a demand or request, plaintiff **2)** beggar, bum, panhandler: *nf* **mangitórka**

mangli *adj* asked for, off limits **2)** *nf* a girl who has been asked for in marriage.

manglo *pp/adj* asked for, begged, demanded, requested, wanted

manifestátsiya *nf* demonstration, manifestation, protest (*Eur*)

maníya *nf* obsession, mania

manogála *nf* love potion, philter

manrrári *nm* baker: *nf* **manrrárka,** baker's wife

manrráriya *nf* bakery

manrro *nm* **1)** bread, loaf of bread; *id* **Xalyas pêsko manrro.** He has eaten his bread/He has lived his life to the full. **Mulo bi te xal pêsko manrro.** He died without fulfilling his life's potential. **2) nakhel o ~** pass he bread (*pasing of a hollowed out loaf among male guests at a wedding in whch they place money for the newlyweds*)

manrró-peko *nm* toast

manrrorro *nm* roll, small bread

mánsiya *nf* mansion

manûsh *nf* **1)** glove: *pl* **manûsh 2)** asbestos gloves used in wipe-tinning

manush *nm* **1)** male human being **2)** man, elderly man; **Sar san, Manúsha?** How are you Sir? (*to an elderly man*) **3)** *nf/nm/pl* humanity, human beings, human race, mature adults, people in general; **Avile but them hai manush.** Many Romani people (*them*) and people in general (**manush**) attended. **O Del kerdyas le manushen.** God created humanity.**Won si manush.** They are mature adults. **Che manush si gadala?** What people are these?

Manush *nm/pl* A Romani group in France

Manushênge-Chachimáta *comp/nm* Human Rights

manushêngo *gen/adj* human; **o dúxo manushêngo,** The human psyche/soul, **manushêngo-xamári** man-eater, man-eating wild animal

manushkano/manushikano *adj* **1)** human **2)** humane

manushni *nf* **1)** female human being **2)** matriarch, elderly woman; **Sar San, manushníyo?** How are you, old lady?

manushwalimos *nm* humanity

manushwalo *adj* human, humane

manustíra *nf* convent, monastery, nunnery

mápa *nf* chart, map

Mára *nf* Mary; **Swínto Mára** Saint Mary, **Swúntunya Máriyo!** Saint Mary! (*Voc*)

mardé-anrre *nm/pl* scrambled eggs

mardino *pp/adj* beaten/punished/whipped *var of* **mardo** *qv*

mardo *pp/adj* beaten, beaten up, roughed up; **Trobul mardo.** He needs to be beaten up.

márdyol *vi* **1)** be assaulted, get beaten, beaten up/punched/slugged *pp/adj* **mardilo; Márdilo ándo bírto.** He got beaten up in the saloon. **2)** be beaten/punished/whipped **3)** bruise oneself accidentally; **Maládilem po wudar hai márdilem.** I banged into the door and bruised myself.

marel *vt/i* **1)** beat, clobber, hit, palpitate, punch, slug, stamp, strike: *pp/adj* **mardo; Mardem lês ándo mui.** I slugged him in the kisser/mouth. *id* **Te marel ma o Del!** Honest to God!/May God strike me! **Marel e tóba.** He's beating the drum/rhythm. **2)** knock, knock on; **Kon marel po wudar?** Who is knocking on the door? **3)** beat, beat up, punish, thrash, whip **4)** assault/attack (*psn*)**,** make war, wage war **5) ~ telé** knock down, floor, turf **7) ~ mui** make fun of, mock, ridicule, *see also* **muimarel** *vt* **7)** resist (*with* **prótivo); Mardyam prótivo le neve zakóya.** We resisted the new laws. **8)** *v/refl* **marél-pe** brawl, compete, feud, engage in warfare, fight; **Rromále! Na maren-tume!** Roma! Don't fight!

marfáko *nm* goods, merchandise (*Eur*); **Avilyam ánda Rumúnya ándo báro tíro mashkar o marfáko.** We came from Romania in a big transporter truck among the merchandise.

mariki *nf* cake

maril/mahril *vt* **1)** contaminate, defile, make dirty, render unclean, pollute, profane, spread contagion: *pp/adj* **marime/mahrime 2)** *v/refl* **maríl-pe** become contaminated/defiled, become a potential source of defilement to others, defile/pollute oneself

marime/mahrime *pp/adj* contagious, agent of contamination/pollution, defiled, defiling, capable of pollution, taboo, polluted, unclean

marimé-gazho *comp/nm* defiled man, usually a derelict, who comes to Kalderash houses in Canada/US to do floor cleaning and work in bathroom and elsewhere performing tasks which would be taboo for Roma.

marimé-skamin *comp/nm/arch* defiled chair, a chair kept in many *Kalderash* homes in Canada/US for non-Romani customers, detectives, landlords, etc.(*Am*)

marimé-wásurya *comp/nm/pl* defiled dishes kept apart from the family and Romani guest dishes to serve non-Romani visitors such as detectives, social workers, tradesman and menial derelicts called in to clean the house and bathroom. (*Am*)

marimé-zhukel *comp/nm* hyena

marimni *nf* female agent of pollution under the rules of the **Rromaníya** who can spread defilment to others.

marimos familiyáko *comp/nm* family violence

marimos *nm* **1)** beating, thrashing, pounding **2)** brawl, fight, fist fight, punch-up **3)** combat, violence, war, warfare **4)** feud; **Si marimos mashkar amáre vítsi.** There is a feud between our clans.

marína *nf* navy (*Mil*), merchant marine

marinári *nm* sailor, seaman, serviceman aboard ship, naval rating

maripe/maxrimos *nm* contamination, defilement, filth, pollution, sewage

mâritíl *vt see* **môritíl** *vt*

máriya *nf* ocean, sea: *pl* **méri**

Máriya-Atlántiko *comp/nf* Atlantic Ocean

mariyáki char *comp/nf* seaweed

mariyáko *gen/ádj* of the sea

mariyáko-chiriklo *comp/nm* sea bird, seagull

mariyáko-chor *comp/nm* pirate, sea hijacker/robber

mariyáko-grast *comp/nm* walrus

mariyáko-kasht *comp/nm* driftwood

mariyáko-liyondári *comp/nm* sea lion

mariyáko-zhukel *comp/nm* seal

Máriya-Pasífiko *comp/nf* Pacific Ocean

márka *nf* **1)** brand, design, label, mark, stamp, sticker **2)** target (*in shooting*); **Xasardyas e márka.** He missed the mark/target.

markéto *nm* market; **bursáko markéto** stock market *see also* **yarmáko** *nm* & **pasári** *nm*

marmaláda *nf* marmalade

mârmuríl *vt* **1)** amaze, astronish, bewilder, surprise: *pp/adj* **mârmurimé 2)** shock; **Mârmurimé símas pêske swatonêndar.** I was shocked by his words. **3)** *v/refl* **mârmuríl-pe a)** become amazed/astonished/bewildered/flabbergasted **b)** be shocked/surprised, go into shock

mârmurimós *nm* **1)** amazement, astonishment, bewilderment, surprise **2)** shock

mármuro *nm* **1)** marble **2)** enamel, tooth enamel

marmurósko *gen/adj* made of marble; **síniya-marmuróski** marble table

marózhina *nf* ice cream (*Am*)

marro *nm* bread *var of* **manrro**

marrózo/morrózo *nm* **1)** freezing weather, sub-zero weather **2)** frost

Mártsi/Marts *nm* Tuesday

Mártso *nm* March

Mártsone *adv* in March

Martsune *adv* on Tuesday

marturíya *nf* 1) evidence, testimony by a witness 2) *comp/vi* **del ~** give witness testimony

márturo *nm* witness: *nf* **marturútsa**

Mártya *nf* 1) Angel of Death; **Naswaló-lo thai e Mártya pashal.** He is on Death's doorstep/He is sick and the Angel of Death is nearby. 2) Death personified. 3) death, destruction, fate, doom, nemesis; **Le grast si lêski mártya.** Gambling on the horses is his nemesis. **Nashel pála pêski mártya.** He's courting his own nemesis/destruction. 5) addiction, destructive or negative habit or obesssion.

marzol *vt* 1) freeze: *pp/adj* **marzome** 2) refrigerate 3) *v/refl* **marzól-pe** be freezing, freeze to death, freeze/frost over, suffer from frostbite/hypothermia; **Marzosáilo.** He froze to death. **Mai do-gáta marzosáilem.** I almost died from hypothermia/almost froze to death. **Marzól-pe o réko.** The lake is feeezing over.

marzome *pp/adj* frosted, frozen, refrigerated

marzomos *nm* 1) freezing cold 2) hypothermia 3) refrigeration

mas *nm* 1) meat 2) flesh 3) *fig* hide/body; **Marav lêsko kálo mas.** I will thrash his evil hide.

mas-ánde-búlka *comp/nm* meat in a bun, hamburger

masalo *adj* 1) carnivorous, meat-eating 2) *nm* carnivore *nm*: **masali** *nf*

masári *nm* butcher, seller of meat: *nf* **masárka**, butcher's wife

masáriya *nf* butcher's shop, meat market

mas-bakrano *comp/nm* mutton

mas-balano *comp/nm* pork

másek/másak *nm* month (*Eur*) *see also* **shon** *nm*

masêngo-yarmáko *comp/nm* meat market

masêski-tórta *comp/nf* meat pie, tortière

mas-guruvano *comp/nm* beef

mashalo *adj* brawny, muscular

Mashári *nm* 1) male member of the **Mashára** Romani group in Hungary: *nf* **Masharútsa.** 2) **mashári** *nm* fisherman: *nf* **mashárka**

Masharítska *nf* Romani dialect of the **Mashára** Vlax-Roma

Masharítsko *adj* of the **Mashára** Vlax-Romani group

masharíya *nf* fishery, fishing hole

mashárka *nf* 1) fishing bird, kingfisher 2) fishing net

mashe *nm/pl* 1) fish 2) biceps

mashêngi-kózhnitsa *comp/nf* creel

mashêngi-ruvli *comp/nf* fishing rod

mashína *nf* automobile, car (*Eur*)

mashkar *nm* 1) waist (*Anat*); **sáno mashkar** slim waist 2) center, core, middle; **mashkar la ratyáko** *nm* midnight 3) *prep* among, amongst, between, in the middle; **Mashkar tu hai me, chi pakyav lês.** Between you and me, I don't believe him. **Woi si e mai shukar, mashkar le sheyánde.** She is the most beautiful among the girls. **So si o aver-fyál mashkar le dónde?** What is the difference between the two of them?

mashkaral *adv* in the middle, from the center/middle, from in among, in amongst/between; **Alosardem o mai lasho mobíli mashkaral le avrênde ánde tobolátsiya.** I chose the best car from among the rest in the auction. **Beshel pashal o réko mashkaral le playingánde.** He lives near the lake in the middle of the mountains.

mashkárdyol *vi* become/get in the middle, be placed in the middle: *pp/adj* **mashkardilo; Mashkárdilem ándo xamos.** I got into the middle of the argument.

mashkare *adv* into the middle of/center of/midst of; **Nashti thós-tu mashkar o Rrom thai e Rromni kána xan-pe.** You can't place yourself in between a man and his wife when they are arguing.

mashkarel *vt* get between, go in between, go into the middle: *pp/adj* **mashkardo**

mashkaré-themêngo *comp/gen/adj* among/between countries/States, international; **nashkaré-themêngo diwáno** intercountry conference

mashkarunes *adv* centrally

mashkaruno *adj* **1)** central, middle **2)** *nm* centerpiece, middle man: *nf* **mashkaruni**

mashkarutno *adj* **1)** central, intermediate, middle **2)** go-between, middle man

masho *nm* **1)** fish **2)** calf of the leg **3)** muscle **4)** dupe, sucker, victim *(Am)* **5)** **Masho** *nm* Pisces

mashó-buflo *comp/nm* flatfish, flounder

mashó-kanrralo *comp/nm* perch *(fish)*

mashorro *nm* **1)** minnow **2)** sprat

mashó-sumakuno *comp/nm* goldfish

mashó-zéleno *nm* mackerel

mashtíko/mashtúko *nm* cigarette holder, filter

mashtívo *adj* **1)** adopted **2)** step; **mashtívo phral** step brother **3)** foster; **mashtívo dey** foster mother

mashûna *nf* match *(to strike)*

mashûnka *nf* machine. **Note:** In North-American Kalderash this word is often combined with nouns and verbs to create compound nouns as in; **mashûnka púshka** machine gun, **mashûnka kai xalavel** machine that washes/washing machine, **mashûnka kai ramol** machine that writes/typewriter.

mashûnka-púshka *com/nf* machine gun *(Am)*

mashûnki *nf/pl* machinery

máska *nf* **1)** mask **2)** masking tape

maskaráda *nf* masquerade

mas-likyardo *comp/nm* hamburger meat, ground meat, minced meat *(as in sármi qv)*

maslína *nf* black olive, olive

maslinêngo-zetino *comp/nm* olive oil

mas-mulano *comp/nm* carrion, corpse, road kill

mas-pe-busht *comp/nf* shish kebab

mas-thulo *comp/nm* lard, fatty meat

mas-thuvlyardo *comp/nm* smoked meat

mastíko *nm* filler, filler putty, paste, putty

mastrápa/mashtrápa *nf* flagon, mug, stein, tankard

mastúko *nm* **1)** cigarette holder **2)** cigarette filter

masúra *nm* **1)** tape measure **2)** ruler **3)** measurements

masuril *vt* measure: *pp/adj* **masurime**

masúrya *nf/pl* dimensions, measurements

mas-vitsalêngo *comp/nm* veal

matadóro *nm* matador *(Am fr Sp)*

matánsiya *nf* **1)** annihilation, massacre, mass execution, slaughter *(Am)* **2)** abattoir, chopping block, slaughter house, knacker's yard, place of execution *(Am)*

matemátichi *nf/pl* calculations, mathematics

matemátiko *adj* **1)** mathematical **2)** *nm* mathematician: *nf* **matemátika**

materítsa *nf* **1)** afterbirth, placenta **2)** womb **3)** uterus **4)** *comp/vt* **shinel e ~** remove the uterus, perform a hysterectomy; **Shinde láki materítsa.** They performed a hysterectomy on her.

mato *adj* drunk, intoxicated

máto-chik *comp/adj* dead drunk, staggering drunk; **Máto chik sas o Bóyo ánde sláva.** Boyo was staggering drunk during the feast.

matomos *nm* drunkenness, intoxication

matóra *nf* **1)** automobile *(Eur)* **2)** engine, motor *(Am)*

matoráki bárka *comp/nf* motor boat

matoráko *gen/adj* motor, having an engine, motorized

matorro *adj* **1)** alcoholic, drunken, overly intoxicated **2)** *nm* alcoholic, drunkard, staggering drunk, rummy: *nf* **matorri**

matróso *nm* **1)** sailor, seaman **2)** mattress

Máyo *nm* May

Máyone *adv* in May

mazúro *nm* ruler, measure, tape measure

me *pron/nom* I; **Me sim Rrom.** I am a Romani man. **Me sim!** It's me!

-me 1) indicates the *pp/adj* of *athem* verbs in < **-il** > and < **-ol** >; **Volil** *vt* He loves, *pp/adj* **volime, farbol** *vt* he paints *pp/adj* **farbome 2)** sometimes used as a *prod*

suff with nouns to create an *athem/adj*;
Amerikanime Americanized
mêcha *nf* bit (*for a drill*)
méchka *nf* female bear
mechkári *nm* bear trainer
mechkoi *nm* male bear
medalyóno *nm* medal, medallion
medesína *nf* medication, medicine
médiya *nf* media (*Eur*)
mediyáko *gen/adj* media, of the media
mediyáko lil *comp/nm/neolog* press release
mediyángo *gen/adj* having to do with the
media; **mediyángo wusharimos** media
coverage
mêg-dáta *adv cont of* **mai-ekh-dáta**
adv/phr qv (*Am*)
Mek Zhal! *id/phr* Good riddance! (*to
smbdy or smthing*)
mekanísto *nm* machinist, mechanic
mekanízmo *nm* mechanism
mekel *vt/i* **1**) abandon, desert, leave: *pp/adj*
meklo; **Meklas pêski zhuvli.** He left his
wife. **Meklas o marimos.** He abandoned
the fight/He threw in the towel. **2**) leave,
leave up to; **Mek lês le Devlêste!** Leave
him to God/Let God deal with him. **3**)
allow, let, permit; **Mek lês lêsko!** Let
him keep it. **Mek lês mánde!** Let me
take care of it! **Mek lês te avel andre!**
Let him come inside. **Mek te avel!** Let it
happen! **Meklem la andre.** I let her
in/let her live here. **4**) make to
cease/desist, stop; **Meklem lês te na
kerel.** I stopped him from doing it. **5**)
allow to remain, leave; **Musái te mekas
dósta love ándo bánko**. We must leave
enough money in the bank **6**) *comp/vt/i* ~
te perel allow to fall, drop, let fall;
Meklem te perel. I let it fall/dropped it.
7) *comp/vt* ~ **te zhal** free, let go, unleash
(*dog*), part with; **Chi mekav la te zhal.** I
won't allow her to go. **Chi mai mekav te
zhal kakya gitára.** I will never part with
this guitar. **8**) *v/refl* **mekél-pe** allow
oneself, let oneself, stop oneslf from **9**)
v/refl **mekél-pe** leave one another,
separate; **Meklé-pe** They separated. **10**)

comp/v/refl ~ **pe fúga** escape, take flight
11) *comp/vt/i* ~ **tele** let down
mekimos/meklimos *nm* **1**) abandonment,
desertion **2**) release **3**) permission **4**)
parting
meklo pe solax *v/phr* released on parole
meklo *pp/adj* **1**) abandoned, deserted,
forsaken, separated; **Meklo sas pêska
familyátar o goro**. The poor fellow has
been abandoned by his family. **2**) allowed,
permitted; **Nai meklo te dohanis kathe.**
Smoking is not allowed here.
méklyol *vi* **1**) be abandoned/deserted:
pp/adj **meklilo 2**) be allowed/permitted
3) be left up to
Meksikanítsko *adj* Mexican
Meksikáno *nm* Mexican: *pl* **Meksikáya**:
nf **Meksikánka**
Méksiko *nm* Mexico
mel *nf* **1**) dirt, earth, soil **2**) dirt, filth,
grime, grotte
meláiso *nm* molasses, treacle
melalé-mósko *comp/adj* **1**) foul-mouthed
2) *nm* man charged with slander or verbal
obscenities by another *psn*
melalimos *nm* dirt, filth, smut
melalíya *nf* dirt, trash
melalo *adj* **1**) dirty, soiled with earth, dirt **2**)
off colour (*joke*), smutty **3**) obscene, vile;
mélalo swáto obscenity; **Dyas mánge
mélale swáturya.** He gave me dirty
words/Insulted me with obscenities.**4**) *nm*
dirty man or male animal: *nf* **melali**
mélalo pai *comp/nm* polluted water
melaxno *adj* **1**) brown **2**) dark,
brown-skinned **2**) brunette
melaxnó-manrro *comp/nm* brown bread
melaxnó-zaháro *comp/nm* brown sugar
mêlayíl/mêlíl *vt* **1**) crush, granulate, grind,
mill: *pp/adj* **mêlayimé 2**) *v/refl*
mêlayíl-pe be crushed, granulated,
ground up
mêlayimós *nm* crushing, milling
mêlcho *nm* generic snail; **Mishkíl-pe sar o
mêlcho.** He/she moves like a snail.
mêlchoi *nm* male snail: *nf* **mêlchka**

melyárdyol *vi* make dirty, caused to be covered with dirt/earth/soil: *pp/adj* **melyardilo**

melyarel *vt* **1)** make dirty with earth, oil, etc, soil : *pp/adj* **melyardo 2)** pollute (*environment*) **3)** *v/refl* **melyarél-pe** make oneself dirty.

melyarimos *nm* accumulated dirt, filthiness, dirty mess

melyol/melyávol *vi* **1)** become soiled, become/get dirty: *pp/adj* **melailo 2)** become filthy/polluted; **Meláilo gunoiyésa o réko.** The stream has become polluted with rubbish.

mêmbro *nm* member (*of an organization*): *pl* **mêmbri**: *nf* **mêmbra**

ména *nf* manna

mênshiya *nf* ball, basketball, football

mênshiyútsa *nf* little ball, marble

merásto *adj* **1)** chocolate-coloured, brownish **2)** purple

merel *vi* **1)** cease to exist, die, expire: *pp/adj* **mulo 2)** break down, cease to function, conk out, crash (*computer*), give up the ghost (*appliance/machine/vehicle, etc*), stall (*vehicle*) **3)** fail (*electricity*) **4)** go out (*fire*), run out (*luck*); **Muli lêski baxt.** His luck ran out. **5)** whither away, wilt **6)** *id* **merel ánda láte.** He misses her/longs to be with her. **Me voliv la hai ánda láte me meráva.** I love her and I miss her terribly.

meréltar *vi* depart from life, die, pass away, pass on; **Mulítar kána sovélas.** She passed on while she was sleeping. **Kam-merávtar thai kam-pharruváva.** I shall pass away and disintegrate. (*song*)

mêríl *v* **1)** ambush: *pp/adj* **mêrimé 2)** surprise

merimásko *gen/adj* dying, moribund, wilting

merimáta *nm/pl* mass death; **O póno andyas bare marimáta.** The plague brought mass death.

merimos *nm* **1)** death, dying; **pakivalo merimos** expected death allowing time to die gracefully with respect, **bi-baxtalo merimos** unespected death by accident/murder, etc. **2)** annulment (*of a contract, policy, etc*), expiration **3)** doom

mêritíl *vt* **1)** deserve: *pp/adj* **mêritimé 2)** *v/refl* **meritíl-pe** deserve, be deserving; **Dinilo so meritisáilo.** He got/was given what he deserved.

mêritimós *nm* just deserts/reward

meríya *nf* town hall

mêrmuntári *nm* grave digger

mêrmúnto *nm* **1)** burial place, crypt, grave, tomb, sepulcher. vault

mêrmúntsi *nm/pl* **1)** graves, tombs **2)** cemetery; **Dikhlas choxãnó mashkar le mêrmúntsi.** He saw a ghost among the graves/in the cemetery. **Arakhline le liliyakósko mêrmúnto mashkar le mêrmúntsi.** They found the vampire's grave among the tombs/in the cemetery.

mêrrêyíl-pe *v/refl* growl, snarl: *pp/adj* **mêrrêyimé; O zhukel mêrrêyisáilo pe mánde wórta mai anglal ke xuklo pe mánde.** The dog snarled at me right before it sprang at me.

mêrrêyimós *nm* growling, snarling

mêrza *nf* envy, jealousy; **Mêrza lêske.** He is envious/jealous; **Mêrza lêske ánda mánde.** He is envious of me.

mêrzál *vt/i* **1)** covet, envy, be envious of, be jealous of; **Mêrzál ánda mánde.** He is envious of me. **Mêrzáili ánda láko shukarimos.** She became envious of her beauty. **2)** be resentful

mêrzála *nf* envy, jealousy, resentment

mêrzaló *adj* **1)** jealous, envious, resentful **2)** *nm* jealous, envious *psn*: *nf* **mêrzalí**

merzhála *nf* pearl

mesádja/mesádjo *nf* message (*Eur*)

mêsha *nf* mood, state of mind: *pl* **mèshû; Chi lem lês ande l' mèshû lashe.** I didn't catch him in a good mood/good state of mind.

mêshùnsa *nf/pl/ins* moody, with moods: **Wo si mêshùnsa.** He is moody/is with moods.

metódo *nm* method, way of doing things (*Eur*)

métra *nf* meter

mêtrika *nf* birth certificate, certificate: *pl* **mêtrichi**

mêtro *nm* subway system, subway train: *pl* **mêtrya** (*Eur & Can*)

meyázol/myázol *def/vt/i* **1**) look like, resemble; **Pe kãste meyázol?** Whom does he look like/resemble? **2**) *with dat/case* appear to be, seem; **Meyázol mánge mishto.** It seems all right to me.

mezhára *nf* small ring/earring, small body ornament; **Si la mezhári ánde l' splincháni.** She has small rings in her eyebrows.

mezhedíya *nf* decorative coin sewn into a women's headscarf or shawl

mézo *nm* **1**) punkwood, pulpwood, soft center of a dead, rotten tree **2**) marrow **3**) dried out kindling wood **4**) pulp, soft interior of a fruit **5**) the soft interior of a loaf of hard-crusted bread

Michaléshti *nm/pl* large Kalderash clan in US and Canada

midálo/medálo *nm* medal

midjkári *nm* lesbian

míkro- *prod pref* micro (*Am*); **míkro-rrókya** micro-skirt (*Am*)

mikróbo *nm* germ: *pl* **mikróburya** disease, germs

míkro-bov *nm/neolog* microwave oven

mikroskópa *nf* microscope

mikséri *nm* cement mixer (*Am*)

Míkulash *nm* Santa Clause (*Lovari & Hungarian Kalderash*)

mil *nf* thousand: *pl* **mil** & **míli**

míla *nf* **1**) compassion, mercy, pity; **Nas láke míla ánda mánde.** She has no pity for me. **2**) sorrow/suffering; **Míla mánge ánda lêste** I'm sorry for him. **Dikh che bári míla!** Look what great sorrow! **3**) Grace; **Devlêski Míla** God's Grace. **4**) **del ~** grant compassion, mercy

milai *nm* summer: *pl* **mila**

milaiyutno *adj* summer

miláki *nm* one-thousand-dollar bill, one thousand dollars; **Dem lês miláki wuzhile.** I loaned him a thousand dollars.

milásko *gen/adj* summer; **milásko ges ~** day

miláto *nm* one thousandth

militári *nm* member of the armed forces, militiaman/paramilitary (*Eur*)

militáriya *nm/pl* military, militia; **Cháiko ánda l' Militáriya**. Chaiko of the *Militáriya*, a legendary *Kalderash* leader in Argentina around 1880-90 (*oral legend*)

milítsiya *nf* militia, para-military group (*Eur*)

militsiyáno *nm* militiaman, paramilitary soldier: *nf* **militsiyánka**

milivonovar/miloyonowar *adv* one million times

milivonári *nm* millionaire

milivonáto *nm* millionth

milivóno/miliyóno *nm* million (*Num*): *pl* **milivóya/miliyónurya**

milódiya *nf* melody

milóso *adj* **1**) pitiful **2**) merciful

miluwil *vt/i* **1**) extend mercy (to), feel compassion/pity for: *pp/adj* **miluwime**; **Miluwiv lês.** I feel sorry for him. **2**) *v/refl* **miluwíl-pe** feel pity for oneself, feel sorry for oneself

miluwimos *nm* compassion, Grace, mercy, pity

mílwar *adv* a thousand times

milwares *adv* a thousandfold

milyáko *nm* corn meal

milyáko-manrro *comp/nm* cornbread (*Am*)

milyonáki *nm* one million-dollar bill, one-million dollars

milyonáto *nm* one millionth

milyonéri *nm* millionaire: *nf* **milyonérka**

milyóno *nm* one million

milyónowar *adv* one million times

mína *nf* **1**) coal mine, mine; **sumnkáski-mína** goldmine **2**) land mine (*Mil*) *comp/vi* **3**) **thol míni** plant/lay mines

minerálo *nm* mineral: *pl* **mineráli**

minéri *nm* coal miner, miner

minil *vt* **1)** mean, signify: *pp/adj* **minime**
2) *v/refl* **miníl-pe; So minís-tu?** What do
you mean? (*Am*)
mínimo *nm* minimum
míni-rrókya *comp/nf* miniskirt (*Am*)
ministéri *nm* government minister; **O**
Pêrvo Ministéri The Prime Minister
Ministériya *nf* Government Ministry;
Ministériya la Imigratsiyáki. Ministry
of Immigration
minóre *adj/nm* minor (*Mus*); **La minóre** A
minor
minoritéto *nm* minority
minoritetósko *gen/adj* belonging to a
minority
mîntya *nf* **1)** intellect, intelligence, mind:
pl **mîntsyi 2)** mood; **Wo si mîntsyènsa.**
He is moody.
minúto minute: *pl* **minútsi**
minútsi *nm/pl* minutes (*of a meeting*)
minzhwali *adj* eager for sex, lustful
miráklo *nm* miracle; **Miráklo sas te na**
mulo. It was a miracle that he didn't die.
miriklêngi-firánga *nf comp/nf* beaded
curtain
miriklo *nm* **1)** bead. **2)** pearl. (*Eur*)
miril *vt* **1)** astonish, surprise **2)** *v/refl*
miríl-pe be astonished/surprised
mirime *pp/adj* astonished, surprised
mirimos *nm* astonishment, surprise,
wonderment
mirishil *vt* **1)** make fragrant: *pp/adj*
mirishime 2) smell **3)** deodorize **4)** *v/refl*
mirishíl-pe emit fragrance, smell
(*pleasant*)
mirishimos *nm* **1)** fragrance, smell **2)** air
freshner
mírishtya *nf* bog, swamp; **O grast tasulo**
ánde mírishtiya. The horse sank in the
bog.
mirishtyalo *adj* swampy
mirishyála *nf* fragrance, odor, smell
miriyázha *nf* spider web, web;
punzhavonéski-miriyázha, spider web,
Lumyáki-Miriyázha, World-Wide Web,
miriyazháko-than, web site

mírno *adj* **1)** calm, peaceful, quiet, silent,
tranquil; **Besh mírno!** Calm down!/Stay
quiet! **2)** *adv* calmly, peacefully, quietly,
silently; **Phirdyas mírno opre l' skéri.**
He walked quietly upstairs.
mirnomos *nm* calm, hush, peacefulness,
quiet, silence, tranquility
míro *nm* **1)** peace, silence, tranquility **2)**
myrrh
mirutno *adj* peaceful, quiet
misáli/misáyi *nf* table (*Eur*)
mishkil *vt* **1)** flap, make vibrate, move,
shake, stir, sway, wag: *pp/adj* **mishkime**
2) *v/refl* **mishkíl-pe** convulse, flap, flutter,
move, rustle, shake, shimmy, sway,
twitch, vibrate, wag (*tail*), wiggle
mishkimos *nm* flapping, movement,
shaking, shimmy, swaying, wagging,
waving, vibrating
mishto *adv* **1)** all right, great, neatly, nicely,
perfectly, well, OK; **Mishto kerdyan.**
You did well. **2)** *with dat,* not to
appreciate/approve of; **Nas lênge mishto**
so kerdyas. They didn't appreciate what
he did. **Nas lênge mishto.** They didn't
approve of it. **3)** *comparative/adv* **mai**
mishto better **4)** *adj* (*non-declinable*)
all-right; **Mishto sim.** I am all right. **5)**
Interj Perfect!
Mishto avilyan! *exp* Welcome!
mishtomáste *adv* in the best possible
way (*usually with* **pe** ~)
mishtomos/mishtimos *nm* courtesy,
favour, kindness; **Ker mánge**
mishtomos! Do me a favour!
mishyáko 1) dung beetle, dung crawler,
scarab: *nf* **mishyáka:** *pl* **mishyácha 2)**
filthy person, scumbag **3)** mouse (*Eur*)
mîskêraló *adj* foul mouthed
mîskêrícha *nf* **1)** filthy language, impolite
speech, obscenity, vulgarity **2)** *vi/phr*
del-dúma mîskêrícha. speak/use
filthy/vulgar language
mîskêríl *vt* **1)** badmouth, insult with filthy
language **2) mîskêríl-pe** *v/refl* speak in
foul language/obscenities: *pp/adj*
mîskêrimé: Rromále! Na

mîskêrín-tume ándo djuléshi! Roma! Don't use foul language during the meeting!

mîskêritóri *nm* man who uses foul language: *nf* **mîskêritórka**

mísmo/mízmo *adj/nm* the same, the same thing; **Ame das-ame borya mísmo, sar tume ánde Kanáda.** We give one another daughters in marriage, the same as you do in Canada. **Wo kerdyas o mísmo.** He did the same. (*Am fr Sp*)

mistériya *nf* mystery; *comp/nf* **bari mistériya** big mystery

misteriyóso *adj* mysterious

míta *nf* **1)** bribe **2)** payoff **3)** cut (*of the profit*) **4)** protection money **5)** *vt/i* **del ~** give bribe/ payoff/protection money **5)** *comp/vi* **lel ~** take bribe/payoff

mitáko *gen/adj* able to be bribed, on the take; **rai-mitáko** detective on the take, **gazhó-mitáko** foreman or manager who gives out work to Roma for a percentage of the profits, government member or official who accepts bribes

mitalísta *nm* metal smith, metallurgist, a man skilled in working metals

mitalêsko *gen/adj* made of metal

mitálo *nm* metal; **phurano mitálo** old/scrap metal, **shudino mitálo,** scrap metal

mitína *nf* mit, mitten

mitiriyálno *adj* material

mitiriyálo *nm* material

mitrayéta *nf* machinegun (*Eur*)

mitrayil *vt* mow down with machinegun(s), rake with machinegun fire, strafe: *pp/adj* **mitrayime**

mitrayimos *nm* machinegun fire, strafing (*Eur*)

mitrayitóri *nm* machine gunner (*Eur*)

mituwil 1) *vt* bribe, pay off; **Mituwimé-lo o formáno.** The foreman is in our pocket. **2)** *v/refl* **mituwíl-pe** be bribed, bought off; **Mituwisáilo.** He's been bribed, bought off.

mituwime *pp/adj* bribed, bought off, in *smbdy's* pocket, paid off

mituwimos *nm* bribery, payoff, take

míya *nf* **1)** mile **2)** thousand (*Num*)

miyáki *nf* one thousand dollar bill

miyáko *num* one thousandth

miyópo *adj* **1)** myopic **2)** *nm* myopic man: *nf* **miyopáika**

mizériya *nf* misery, privation (*Eur*)

mizh/minzh *nf* female genitalia, pudenda, vagina (*not used in polite conversation*) (*Anat*)

mizhári *nm* pimp (*Eur*)

mizméri *nm/adv* Noon; **pála-mizméri** afternoon

mízmo *see* **mísmo** *adj*

mo *pron/poss* my

Mo! Sir! Old man! Father! *vocative address to an elder*; **Sar san Mo?** How are you, Sir?

mobilári *nm* **1)** piece of furniture **2)** bureau

mobilárya *nm/pl* furniture, furnishings

mobilêngi-buki *comp/nf* automobile body work, automobile repairs

mobilêngo *gen/adj* belonging to automobiles; **mobilênge shûni,** automobile tires, **mobilênge lasharimáta** automobile repairs.

mobilêsko *gen/adj* belonging to an automobile

mobíli *nm* automobile, car (*Am*): *pl* **mobílya**

mobílo *nm* cell phone (*Eur*)

modélo *nm* **1)** model (*of smthg*) **2)** fashion model: *nf* **modéla**

modérno *adj* modern

módo *nm* **1)** fashion; **ándo módo** in fashion/style **2)** habit, manner, mode, way of doing

mohóro *nm* millet

mol *def vt/i* have value, be worth: *pp/adj* **molilo; Sóde mol o mobíli?** How much is the car worth? **Chi mol khanchi.** It's not worth anything. **Chi mon khánchi.** They are worth nothing. **Chi molyas but.** It wasn't worth much.

mol *nf* wine

molári *nm* vintner

mólatni *nf* celebration, party, drinking spree (**Lovaritska** *but used by Western-European Kalderash and Hungarian Vlax Roma*)

molatnil *vt/i* **1**) celebrate, live it up, throw a party, engage in a drinking spree: *pp/adj* **molatnime**; **Molatnívas sórro ryáto, tehára ánde diminyátsa.** I was living it up all night, until the following morning. (*song*). **2**) *v/refl* **molatníl-pe** go on a drinking spree, have a wild party, tie one on (*Eur*)

Moldáviya *nf* Moldavia

Moldováno *nm* Moldavian man: *nf* **Moldováika**

molébina *nf* plea, prayer, supplication

molífta *nf* holy water, blessing with holy water

moliftil *vt* **1**) sprinkle with Holy water as at a baptism: *pp/adj* **moliftime 2**) bless/consecrate with holy water (*as the lamb at the feast table of St. Ann*); **O Rashai moliftisardyas amáro bakro.** The priest has consecrated our (*cooked*) lamb.

moliftimos *nm* blessing, consecration, sprinkled with Holy water

molil *vt* **1**) beseech, implore, pray: *pp/adj* **molime**; **Molisardyas Dêvléstar te sastyarel pêske shavorres.** He beseeched God to heal his son. **2**) *v/refl* **molíl-pe** beseech, implore, request, pray

molimos *nm* imploration, prayer, request

molivêsko *gen/adj* made of lead

molivi *nm* lead, solder

mólo 1) breakwater, harbour, mole **2**) anchorage

molorri *nf* sip of wine, small glass of wine

molyol/molyovel *vt/i* have value, be worth: *pp/adj* **molyailo**; **Sóde molyólas?** How much was it worth?

môm *nm* **1**) wax, candle wax **2**) earwax **3**) bait (*for fish*) **4**) lure

mômêlári *nm* **1**) candle-stick holder **2**) candlemaker

mômêlí *nf* candle

momentálno *adj* momentary

moménto *nm* moment; **ekh moménto po mishtimos** one moment please

mômíl *vt* **1**) wax (*floor, etc*): *pp/adj* **mômimé 2**) bait; **Mômisardyám o réko.** We baited the lake. **3**) coax, lure; **O beng mômisardyá lês ka lêski mártya.** The devil lured him to his doom. **4**) humor, indulge, placate, please

môminós *nm* baiting, coaxing, indulgence, luring, waxing

monáklo *nm* monacle

Mongolítska *nf* Mongolian (*Lang*)

Mongolítsko *adj* Mongolian

Mongólo *nm* Mongol: *nf* **Mongoláika**

mônstro *nm* behemoth, monster: *nf* **monstráika**

môpa *nf* mop (*Am*)

móra *part/v/aux* **1**) be obliged to/have to/need to, *us with* **te** (*Eur*); **Móra te beshav ánde ófisa sórro ges.** I need to stay in the office all day. **Móra te zhas akana?** Must you go now? **2**) be necessary *us with* **si**; **Móra si te phérdyon kakale papírya.** It is necessary that these papers are filled out/These papers need to be filled out. **Móra te zhanav o chachimos.** I need to know the truth. **Kon si te phenel o chachimos móra te thol yekh pûnrró ánde bakháli.** Whoever is about to tell the truth needs to place one foot in the stirrup. (*proverb*)

Móre! *Voc* buddy, friend, pal; **Ashun Móre!** Listen Bro!

morfíno *nm* morphine

môritíl/mâritíl *vt* **1**) marry, marry off (*daughter*): *pp/adj* **môritimé** Used only for women. For men see **ansuril** *vt* **2**) *v/refl* marry, get married (*for women only*)

môritimásko *gen/adj* marital, marriage (*for a woman*)

môritimé *pp/adj* married (*woman*)

môritimós *nm* marriage (*woman*)

morki *nf* **1**) hide, pelt, skin (*Anat*) **2**) drum skin **3**) membrane **4**) veneer **5**) skin, outer covering of *smthg*

morkí-gurumnyáki *comp/nf* cowhide

morkoi *nm* carrot: *pl* **morkoiya**

morkói-parno *comp/nm* parsnip

morkyáko *gen/adj* skin, made of hide/skin

morkyári *nm* dealer in skins, tanner

morkyorri *nf/dim* thin skin/membrane, eardrum

mormoláko *nm* pollywog, tadpole: *pl* **mormolácha**

morokóta *nf* twenty-dollar gold piece (*Am*): *pl* **morokótsi**

morokóto *nm* gold coin, *us* worn on a heavy gold chain by Romani men

morrádyol *vi* be clipped, shaved, sheared: *pp/adj* **morradilo**

morravel *vt* clip, cut (*hair*), shave, shear: *pp/adj* **morrado; Morravel pêske bal.** He's clipping his hair.

morrayimos *nm* clipping, shaving, shearing

morrdo *nm* blender, cheese grater, coffee/meat grinder, electric shaver, graterer, grinder

morrel *vt* 1) chaff, massage, rub: *pp/adj* **morrdo** 2) buff, polish 3) sand (*with sandpaper*), scrape, scrub 4) *v/refl* **morrél-pe** massage/rub oneself, undergo a massage treatment **morrimos** *nm* 1) massage 2) rubbing down (*horse*) 3) buffing, polishing 4) chaffing, friction

morrozil *vt* 1) freeze, freeze over: *pp/adj* **morrozime** 2) *v/refl* **morrozíl-pe** freeze, be freezing, freeze to death; **Mai do-gáta morrozisáilem.** I almost froze to death.

morrozimos *nm* freezing, freezing cold, frigid weather

morrózo *nm* 1) ice 2) ice-cream

mortsol *vt* 1) make hard, stiff: *pp/adj* **mortsome** 2) make numb, numb 3) *v/refl* **mortsól-pe** become hard, stiff, numb; **Mortsosáilo múrro pûnrró.** My foot has gone to sleep.

mósa *nm/inst/adv* orally, verbally

môshkêríl *vt see* **mîskêríl** *vt*

mósko *gen/adj* oral, verbal; **móski medesína** oral medicine

Móskva *nf* Moscow

móstar *nm/abl/adv* verbally, from the mouth; **Ashundem móstar, le Babêstar.** I heard it verbally, from Bob.

motári *nm* 1) motorcycle 2) biker, motorcycle enthusiast,

motaryash *nm* biker, motorcyclist: *nf* **motaryáshka** biker's old lady, female motorcyclist

motása *nf* 1) lichen, moss 2) frog spawn

motelash *nm* motel owner, man in charge of a motel: *nf* **moteláshka**

motéli *nm* motel

mothayimos *nm* 1) announcement, bulletin, order 2) account, story, tale

mothol *vt/i* 1) announce, explain, inform, order, say, tell: *pp/adj* **mothodino**; **Motho l' Rromênge te aven kai sláva!** Tell the Roma to attend the feast. **Mothodem lês te na mai kerel.** I ordered him not to do it again. 2) *comp/vt/i* ~ **páplale** *vt/i* reply, answer 3) *v/refl* **mothól-pe** explain, mean, say; **So mothól-pe godo swáto?** What does that word mean?

motívo *nm* 1) motive 2) motif (*Eur*)

motosíklo *nm* motorcycle

motsyúne *nm* motion (*at a meeting*): *pl* **motsyúni** (*Eur*)

motúra *nf* broom; **Te del-dab e motúra, chi mai ansurís-tut.** If the broom touches you (*when a woman is sweeping*) you'll never get married.(*Can Kalderash saying*)

moxto *nm* 1) coffin 2) casket, chest, strongbox (*Eur*)

moxtorro *nm* small box, ring box

móyo *nm* moth

moyútso *nm* miller

Móise *nm* Moses

mudardo *nm* 1) murder victim: *nf* **mudardi** 2) casualty (*of war*), victim (*if fatal*)

mudárdyol *vi* 1) be killed, be murdered: *pp/adj* **mudardilo**; **Te marés-tu lêsa, mudárdyos po than.** If you fight with him, you'll be killed on the spot. 2) be

annulled, eliminated, eradicated,
extinguished, turned off
mudarel *vt* **1)** kill, slay; *pp/adj* **mudardo
2)** murder **3)** extinguish, turn off **4)** bring
down (*fever*), deaden **5)** abolish,
eradicate, finish off *smth,* put an end to,
wear out; **Mudar e rrakíya!** Kill/finish
off, the whisky! **E tréla si desya but
phari, mudarel o mobíli.** The trailer is
too heavy, it will wear out the car. **6)** pass
(*time*); **Sar mudarel pêski vryámya?**
How does he kill/pass his time? **7)** blow
away, overwhelm with emotion;
Bashaven Shavále! Mudaren amen!
Play Boys! Blow us away (*with music*) **8)**
cancel, terminate; **Mudardem o mobili
ánde hêrtíya.** I cancelled the newspaper
ad for the car. **9)** defeat, destroy;
Mudarel o gor kai manges te keres. It
will defeat the purpose of what you wish
to accomplish. **10)** drive/put out of
business; **Na phuter ófisa kadka,
mudares ma!** Don't open a parlour right
here, you'll put me out of business! **11)** *id
expressions with* **mudarel; Mudarel
pêske chánsurya.** He's blowing his
chances. **Mudardyas o buzherimos.** He
put an end to the gossip. **12)** *v/refl*
mudarél-pe commit suicide, kill oneself
mudarimásko *gen/adj* homicidal, killer,
lethal, murderous
mudarimásko/zhegáno *comp/nm* **1)** killer
beast, predator **2)** *fig* dangerous man (*Am*)
mudarimásko-mobíli *comp/nm* death car,
killer car (*car that killed somebody or in
which somebody died because of an
accident*)
mudarimos *nm* **1)** killing **2)** murder **3)**
slaughter **4)** execution
mudaritóri *nm* **1)** assassin, executioner,
killer: *nf* **mudaritórka 2)** murderer **3)**
knacker (*us as* **grastêngo mudaritóri**)
mûdríya *nf* **1)** craftiness, cunning, the
smarts **2)** cunning trick
mûdro *adj* crafty, sly, smart, tricky
múfla *nm* muffler (*of a vehicle*)

mugash *nm* derelict who picks up
cigarette/cigar butts from the street (*Am*)
múgo/múko *nm* **1)** bud: *pl* **múgurya 2)**
cigarette butt **3)** *sl* clitoris **4)** nipple **5)**
pushbutton **6)** ~ **sir** clove of garlic
múi *nm* **1)** mouth (*Anat*) **2)** mouth/jaws,
entrance (*cave, etc*), entry, intake;
Dikhlas ándo mui la martyáko. He
stared into the jaws of death. **3)** slot (*in
toaster*), slot (*coin slot for machine*),
spout (*teapot*) 4) face, surface; **o mui le
rekósko** the surface of the lake *see also*
fátsa *nf* **5)** noise, shouting, yelling **6)**
phase; **le muiya le shonêsko** the phases
of the moon, **Ándo sávo mui si o shon
akana?** In what phase is the moon now?
7) reputation **8)** order(s); Obey my orders.
Kánde múrro mui 9) *comp/vi* del ~
complain by shouting, shout, yell, yelp
10) kerel ~ make a noise
muimarel *vt/i* make fun of, mock, ridicule
us with ablative of object: *pp/adj*
muimardo; Muimarel mándar. She's
making fun of me.
muimarimos *nm* mockery, ridicule
mui-opral 1) *comp/adv* face upwards, right
side up; **Mulo mui-opral.** He died facing
upwards.
mui-ródko *id/comp/adj* loquacious,
talkative
mui-telal *comp/adv* face downwards,
upside down; **Sovélas mui-telal ándo
wêrsh.** He was lying face down in the
forest.
muiyal *adv* **1)** face down, inverted, upside
down, overturned **2)** facing, opposite
from **3)** *vt/i* del ~ roll over, turn over; **O
vôrdòn dyas muiyal.** The wagon
overturned. **De lês muiyal!** Turn it
over/Roll it over!
muiyalo *adj* **1)** impudent, mouthy **2)**
blabbermouth, indiscreet babbler: *nf*
muiyali
mukel *vt/i* **1)** allow, let, permit, release:
pp/adj **muklo 2)** abandon, desert, leave **3)**
leave out, omit; **Muklas do-pash le
chachimáta.** He left out half the facts.

mukil *vt* 1) evacuate, move, relocate, remove: *pp/adj* **mukime** 2) budge 3) shunt (*railway cars*) 4) transfer, transpose 5) *v/refl* a) **mukíl-pe** move, relocate elsewhere, be evacuated b) allow to be moved, budge

mukimos 1) evacuation, relocation 2) change of dwelling 3) movement 4) progress; **Manai mukimos mai angle.**There is no progress forward/towards the future 5) **mukimos pe sîla** eviction, ethnic cleansing

muklo *pp/adj* 1) abandoned, deserted 2) divorced, let free, set free 3) *nm* deserted husband: *nf* **mukli** abandoned/deserted wife

múko *nm* 1) pushbutton 2) bud 3) nipple (*Anat*) 4) clitoris (*Anat*) *see also* **múgo** *nm*

mulano *adj* dead (*animal*), deceased

Mulátiko *nm* 1) Mulatto: *nf* **Mulátika** 2) *adj* Mulatto

mule *nm/pl* ancestral dead, deceased ancestors of the family groups/clans who are still remembered by living descendants/relatives; **Na xolyar amare mulên!** Don't anger our ancestral dead!

mulênge-tsáliya *comp/nf* cerements

mulêngo kher *comp/nm* 1) mortuary 2) funeral parlour

mulêngo than *comp/nm* 1) mortuary 2) cemetery

mulêngo-vôrdòn *comp/nm* hearse

mulêske-kokala *comp/nm/pl* skeleton: *pl* **mulênge-kokala**

mulêski-dori *comp/nf* 1) a piece of string used to measure the body of a deceased **Rrom/Rromni** to determine the length of the coffin. 2) "dead man's measure" The piece of string used to measure the length of a dead Romani person's coffin, tied in a knot. It is used to summon the ancestral spirits or **mule** for protection.

mulêsko-lil *comp/nm* obituary (*of one psn*): *pl* **mulênge-lila** (*obituary column*)

mulêsko-shoro *nm* skull, skull of a dead man

mulikanes *adv* fatally, mortally

mulikano *adj* 1) dead, deceased, stone dead; **kasht mulikano** coffin 2) deadly, fatal, lethal, mortal; **Dya lês dab mulikani.** He struck him a fatal blow.

mulo *pp/adj* 1) dead, deceased 2) broken down, defunct, expired (*battery*), out-of-business 3) *nm* ghost, spirit of a specific male *psn*: *nf* **muli** 4) casualty (*if fatal*), corpse, dead body, victim (*if fatal*) 5) astral body after death

mulyovel/múlyol *vi* be/become dead, die, expire: *pp/adj* **mulilo**; **Kam-mulyol teharása.** He/she will be dead by tomorrow. **Mulyol akanash o zhukel.** The dog will expire soon. **Mulyovélas te na ankaladyásas lês o dóftoro.** He would have been dead if the doctor hadn't saved him.

munchil *vt* 1) amass, gain, save: *pp/adj* **munchime** 2) labour, strive, work 2) **munchíl-pe** *v/refl*, a) amass, gain, save b) labour, strike, work

mûndrimáta *nm/pl* marvels, uniqueness, wonders

mûndrimós *nm* charm, fascination, marvel, wonderful thing

mûndríya *nf* beauty, charm, fascination; **Che mûndríya!** How charming/fascinating!

mûndro/múndro *adj* beautiful, charming, fascinating, nice, one-of-a-kind, splendid, unique, wonderful

Mûndro Salamon *nm* Wonderful Solomon, a mythical wise man in *Kalderash* folk tales.

mûndronès *adv* splendidly, wonderfully

múnka *nf* effort, labour, work

mûnta *nf* mountain: *pl* **mûntsi**

munyátiko *nm* sweet potato, yam: *pl* **munyátichi**

múra *nf* berry; **káli-múra** blackberry

múra-biráki *nf* hop; **Kíden múri te peken bíra.** They are picking hops to make beer.

Mûre! *voc* My friend! Buddy! (*only to men*); **Ashun Múre!** Listen Brother/Buddy!

muril *vt* 1) alienate, isolate, make resentful; *pp/adj* **murime** 2) *v/refl* **muríl-pe** alienate oneself, isolate oneself, become resentful

murimos *nm* alienation, isolation, resentfulness

mûrmuyíl *vt* 1) mumble, murmur: *pp/adj* **mûrmuyimé** 2) *v/refl* **mûrmuyíl-pe** mumble, murmur

mûrmuyimós *nm* mumbling, murmuring

múro *nm* exterior wall, city wall, rampart: *pl* **múrya**

murro *pron/poss/nominalized pron* my, mine; **Kako si murro.** This one is mine.

mursh *nm* 1) man, fellow, guy; **Kon si kodo mursh avri ánde úlitsa?** Who is that guy outside in the street? **Savo dilo mursh rranglas múrro mobíli?** What dumb clod scratched my car? (*Am*) 2) male of a species; **So si, mursh wórka zhuli?** What is it, male or female? **Note:** *mursh* is never applied to a male Romani person in *Am* Kalderash.

murshano *adj* male, masculine

murshikano *adj* male, masculine, macho

murshimos *nm* 1) manliness, virility 2) courage

murtanêngo *comp/adj* belonging to male cats or to cats of mixed gender

murtáno *nm* tomcat: *pl* **murtáya**; **dívlyo-murtáno** feral cat, lynx, wild cat

murtsála *nf* numbness, stiffness

murtsol *vt* 1) make numb/stiff, numb 2) *v/refl* **murtsól-pe** become numb, stiff; **Murtsisáilo múrro pûnrró.** My foot has gone to sleep.

murtsome *pp/adj* numbed, stiffened

murtsomos *nm* numbness, stiffness

musai *nf* arm (*Anat*) (*Eur*): *pl* **musa**

músai *v/aux* must, have to, had to; **Músai te zhávtar akana.** I must depart right now. **Músai te das mui e probléma.** We must face the problem. **Músai sas**

mánge te lasharav o mobíli. I had to repair the car.

musaiyil *vt* 1) challenge, confront, dare: *pp/adj* **musaiyime; Kon musaiyil ma?** Who is challenging me? 2) compel, force 3) threaten 4) make necessary, necessitate 5) convince, persuade 6) *v/refl* **musaiyíl-pe a)** dare; **Chi musayíl-pe.** He wouldn't dare. **b)** become necessary; **Musaiyisáilo te akharas diwáno.** It has become necessary to call for a discussion.

musaiyime *pp/adj* 1) challenged, confronted, dared 2) compelled 3) threatened 4) necessitated, made necessary

musaiyimos *nm* 1) challenge, confrontation, dare 2) cohersion 3) threat 4) persuasion

múshitsa *nf* fruit fly, gnat

mushkerilyáva *nf* annoyance, bore, nuisance, pest

mushtíko *nm* cigarette holder

Muslimáno *nm* Muslim: *nf* **Muslimánka**

mustáka *nf* moustache *var of* **mustátsa**

mustári *nm* juice maker

mustátsa *nf* moustache: *pl* **mustétsi**

músto *nm* 1) juice. 2) raw maple syrup, sap (*of a tree*) 3) nectar

mutêlítsa *nf* mortar (*for pestle*); **mutêlítsa hai pilógo** mortar and pestle

muter *nm* pee, urine: *pl* **mutra; grastênge-mutra** horse piss

muterdo *nm* bed-wetter: *nf* **muterdi**

mutérdyol *vi* be urinated on: *pp/adj* **muterdilo**

muterimos *nm* piss, urination

muteritóri *nm* urinal

múto *adj* 1) dumb, mute (*unable to speak*) 2) *nm* male *psn* unable to speak: *nf* **mutáika**

mutol/mutosarel *vt* 1) make unable to speak, silence, strike dumb: *pp/adj* **mutome** 2) **mutól-pe** *v/refl* be struck dumb/make mute, become dumb/mute

mutomos *nm* inability to speak

mutrel *vt* 1) urinate: *pp/adj* **muterdo;** 2) *v/refl* **mutrél-pe** 2) **a)** pee, urinate; **E**

gláta muterdyás-pe pe pêste. The baby peed itself. **Naswalo si, nashti mutrél-pe.** He's sick, he can't urinate. *id* **Nashti mutrés-tu prótivo e balwal.** You can't piss against the wind/do the impossible. **b)** piss oneself; **Makilo hai muterdyás-pe.** He got drunk and pissed himself.

mútsa *nf* **1)** female cat **2)** anchor

mútsa-khandini *comp/nf* skunk (*Am*)

mutsáko *gen/adj* of a female cat; **la mutsáke púyurya** the cat's litter/kittens

mutsáko–zhútso *comp/nm* catgut

mutsalo *adj* feline

mutsángo *gen/adj* belonging to cats; **mutsánge yakha** cat's eyes, highway refectors.

mutsángi-kakadéra *comp/nf* cats' litter box

mutsashóro *nm* kitten: *pl* **mutsashórya**

mútya *nf* **1)** butt (*of rifle*) **2)** after end, end opposite the blade on a cutting tool

múvi *nm*: *pl* **múviz** film, movie (*Am*)

muzáko *nm* museum

muzéyo *nm* museum (*Eur*)

muzíka *nf* music; **Rromále! Keren tumênge muzíka!** Roma! Start playing music!

múzíka-foklóriko *comp/nf* folk music (*Eur*)

muzikánto *adj* **1)** musical **2)** *nm* musician: *nf* **muzikánta**

muzikash *nm* musician: *nf* **muzikáshka**

N

na *adv* **1)** no (*in answer to a question*) **2)** used instead of **chi** as a negative particle in the infinitive and subjunctive moods; **Te del o Del te na avel kai sláva.** I hope he doesn't come to the feast. **3)** don't. Used in commands and requests with the imperative tense; **Na zha akana!** Don't go now! **Na motho o gazho ke Rrom sam!** Don't tell the non-Romani man that we are Roma! **4)** *adv* not; **Zhas vai na?** Are you going or not?

nã *adv/conj/imp* anyhow, now, so; **Nã ashun, Ráiya!** Now, listen, Sir! **Pushlas mándar te avel, nã gêlém,** He asked me to come, so I went. **Nã ashun, phrála, so kamav te phenav túke me.** Now listen, brother, what I want to say to you. **Nã, káko Rrom, o Miláno, o Rrom ánda l' Mihaiyêshti, pushlas mándar pe múrra sha, zhanes, E Rayída...** Now, this man, Milano, the Rom from the *Mihaiyêshti*, asked me for my daughter, you know, Edith... (*Am*)

na but *pron* few, not many; **Na but zhanen godo swáto ages.** Not many (Roma) know that word today. **Avile wúni Rrom, na but.** Some Roma attended, not many.

na kámas-avel *v* wouldn't it be; **Na kámas-avel mai xarano te telyaras akana?** Wouldn't it be smarter to depart now?

na mai *adv* **1)** never; **Na mai zha kothe!** Don't ever go there/Never go there! **Na mai ker gadya!** Don't do that anymore! **Mai mishto mánge te na mai dikhav la.** It's better for me that I never see her again. **Note:** *Do not confuse with* **chai mai** *qv* **2)** any longer, any more, no longer, no more; **Na mai ánd-ékh-than-le.** They are no longer together (*married couple*).

nacháino *adv* **1)** accidentally, by accident, by chance, unexpectedly; **Arakhlem lês nacháino.** I met him accidentally/I ran into him by chance. **2)** in spite of

na-domult *adv/phr* not long ago, recently; **Dikhlem la na-domult.** I saw her not long ago.

na-domultano *comp/adj* recent

náfta *nf* crude oil, petroleum

nagráda *nf* award, present, reward, treat

nagradil *vt* **1)** award, reward, treat: *pp/adj* **nagradime 2) nagradíl-pe** reward/treat oneself

nagradimos *nm* presentation of awards/rewards

nagradóstya *nf var of* **nagráda** *nf*

nai *nm* **1)** finger (*Anat*); **báro nai** thumb. **le naiya le wastênge** the fingers of the hands **2)** toe; **báro nai** big toe, **le naiya le punrrenge** the toes of the feet

nai *pres/predicate/negative* he/she is not, they are not; **Nai dilo.** He is not stupid. **Nai gadiki de baro.** He is not *that* big. **Won nai barvale.** They are not rich.

naihíya/nahíya *nf* jurisdiction, territorial jurisdiction of a local Romani leader; **Nai ánde múrri naihíya.** He/she/it is not within my jurisdiction.

naiyarel *vt* **1)** bath, bathe: *pp/adj* **naiyardo; Naiyardyas e gláta.** She bathed the baby. **Le Rrom naiyaren le grasten.** The men are washing down the horses. **2)** *v/ref* **naiyarél-pe** take a bath, go bathing/swimming, bathe oneself

naiyarimos *nm* bathing

naiyêngi-fárba *comp/nm* nail polish

naiyimáske sostya *comp/nf* swimming suit

naiyimos *nm* 1) bathing, swimming 2) dip, short swim

naiyitóri *nm* bather, swimmer: *nf* **naiyitórka**

naiyol *vt* 1) bathe: *pp/adj* **naiyome** 2) *v/refl* **naiyól-pe** bathe, swim

naiyorro *nm* little finger/toe

nakh *nm* 1) nose (*Anat*), snout. 2) beak 3) bow (*of a ship*) 4) nozzle, spout

nakhadimos *nm* absorbing/taking point (*for tin plating of copper*)

nakhádyol *vi* 1) absorb, soak up, swallow, take (*in tin plating*): *pp/adj* **nakhadilo**

nakhalimos *nm* curiosity, inquisitiveness, nosing around, snooping

nakhalo *adj* 1) curious, nosy, overly inquisitive 2) *nm* inspector, snooper: *nf* **nakhali**

nakh-ande-bul *id/phr* **Kerdem lês te perel pêsko nakh ánde bul.** I made him feel ridiculous.

nakhavel *vt* 1) make to happen/occur: *pp/adj* **nakhado** 2) pass by/over/through, smuggle 3) absorb (*information*), swallow 4) bear, endure, stand, put up with; **Nashti nakhavav godolen.** I can't stand those people. 5) overcome, surpass 6) thread (*needle*)

nakhbango *adj* 1) having a crooked nose 2) man with a crooked nose: *nf* **nakhbangi**

nakhel *vt/i* 1) happen, pass: *pp/adj* **nakhlo**; **Nakhlem katar e Kánada ánde América.** I passed from Canada into the US. **Nakhlo o inspêkshono.** It passed inspection. **So nakhlo?** What happened? **But bersh nakhle desar avilyam kathe.** Many years have passed since we came here. 2) climb over, get through, get over, go through, pass/go through, walk over/through, surmount (*difficulties*) 3) come to an end, expire, go/pass away; **Nakhlo o milai.** Summer has ended. 4) pass, spend (*time*)

nakhêsko-naswalimos *comp/nm* sinus of the nose

nakhlo *pp/adj* 1) past 2) ago; **0 bersh nakhlo** the week past/last week. **But bersh nakhle** Many years past/ago

nakh-opre *id* nose up, contemptuously; **Dikhel pe amênda nakh opre.** He looks down on us.

nakhorro *nm* spout (*of a kettle*)

nakh-tele *id* ashamed, embarrassed; **Kerdem lês te pelo lêsko nakh tele.** I made him feel ashamed. **Pelo lêsko nakh tele.** He became embarrassed.

nanári *nm* pineapple

nangé-chuchyángo *comp/adj* bare-breasted, topless

nangé-punrrêngo *gen/adj* barefoot, bare-footed

nangí-butêlka *nf* empty bottle

nangimos *nm* 1) nudity, nakedness. 2) emptiness, void

nangitóri *nm* male exhibitionist/streaker

nangitórka *nf* stripper, female streaker

nango *adj* 1) bare, deserted, empty 2) bare, naked. 3) bare (*facts*) 4) flat (*tire*); **nángi shûna** flat tire 5) hollow; **nango manrro** hollowed out loaf of bread 6) evident, obvious, transparent; **nange xoxayimáta** transparent lies 6) bankrupt, cleaned out (*in gambling*)

nangó-buláko *comp/nm* wretchedly poor man: *pl* **nangé-bulácha:** *nf* **nangí-buláki**

nangorro *nm* exhibitionist, flasher: *nf* **nangyorri** stripper, woman who exposes herself

nangyá-buláko *gen/adj* poverty-stricken, *lit* "bare-assed"

nangyárdyol *vi* 1) be stripped naked/strip searched: *pp/adj* **nangyardilo** 2) be hollowed out/made empty/stripped bare 3) be revealed, exposed. 4) be made bankrupt, despoiled of everything; **Nangyárdilo.** He was cleand out. (*at a gambling table*)

nangyare l *vt* 1) clean out, clear out, empty, flush (*toilet*): *pp/adj* **nangyardo**; **Nangyar o hãlo!** Empty the hall/Clear everybody out of the hall! 2) strip naked, strip search, undress; **Le rai nangyarde la Mara ánde stánsiya**. The police strip-searched Mary in the station. **3)** bankrupt, clean out (*in gambline*) **4)** unload; **Nangyardyas o vôrdòn**. He unloaded the wagon. **5)** reveal, expose; **Nangyardyam lêske xoxayimáta**. We exposed his lies. **Nangyardem o chachimos**. I revealed the truth. **6)** bare, denude, empty of everything, hollow out, make hollow, plunder, strip bare; **Le charanchya nangyarde le nívi**. The locusts stripped the fields bare. **7)** *v/refl* **nangyarél-pe** disrobe, strip oneself, get undressed; **Nangyarél-pe ánde l' klúburya**. She strips herself in the clubs/She is a go-go dancer.

nangyol *vi* **1)** become naked: *pp/adj* **nangilo**. **2)** become empty **3)** flush (*toilet*) **4)** bankrupt oneself, become bankrupt, be cleaned out (*in gambling*).

náno *nm* father's brother, uncle (*Eur*)

nanúla *nf* **1)** boot: *pl* **nanúlya**

nanúlya gêrchóske 1) rubber boots **2)** overshoe, rubber (*Can - now generally obsolete rubber shoe cover to fit over leather shoes in the winter*)

narándja *nf* orange

narandjáda *nf* boxed/canned orange juice

narandjáko *gen/adj* orange; **narandjáko músto** home-made orange juice

narandjelin *nf* orange tree

narkomaníya *nf* drug addiction

narkomanyáko *nm* drug addict: *nf* **narkomanyakútsa**

naródo *nm* **1)** people, population; **Lasho naródo si**. They are nice people. **2)** ethnic population

nas *pst/predicate negative* was not, he/she/it was not, were not, they were not; **Amáro zhukel nas bokhalo**. Our dog wasn't hungry. **Nas kai sláva**. He/she was not at the feast. **O Stévo thai e Mára nas khere**. Steve and Mary were not home.

nashado *pp/adj* **1)** fugitive, refugee (*if forced to flee*), male person forced to

flee/seek refuge, refugee: *nf* **nashadi** fugitive woman/girl, female refugee **2)** abductor, man who kidnaps or forces a woman elope

nashádyol *vi* be made to bolt/elope/flee/run away/stampede: *pp/adj* **nashadilo**; **Nashadile le grast**. The horses were stampeded. **Nashádilem ándo marimos**. I was forced to flee during the war.

nashavel *vt* **1)** chase, drive away, force to flee, force into exile, make or cause to run/run away: *pp/adj* **nashado 2)** make a *psn* elope, abduct, kidnap; **Nashadyas múrra sha**. He made my daughter elope. **3)** stampede (*horses*), rustle (*cattle*) **4)** race (*horses*) **6)** overtake, pass **7)** exercise (*horses*) : *pp/adj* **nashado 8)** *v/refl* **nashavén-pe** elope, run off together

nashayimos *nm* **1)** stampede, rustling (*of cattle*) **2)** abduction, forced elopement **3)** race **4)** enforced flight **5)** exercise (*horses*)

nashayitóri *nm* rustler

nashel *vt/i* **1)** bolt, elope, flee, get away: *pp/adj* **nashlo 2)** race, run, run away **3)** desert (*Mil*) **4)** pass, pass by **5)** *v/refl* **nashél-pe** elope; **Nashlé-pe araki**. They eloped yesterday. **5) ~ pála a)** come on to *smbdy*/flirt with, pursue, run after **b)** chase, pursue

nashéltar *vi* **1)** bolt, get away, run away, run off; **Ame sámas pansh hai o grast nashlótar**. There were five of us and the horse got away. **2)** escape, flee **3)** elope **4)** jump (*bail*)

nashimásko *gen/adj* **1)** racing running **2)** fleeing **3)** eloping

nashimos *nm* **1)** racing, running **2)** escape, flight **3)** elopement **4)** race **5)** desertion (*Mil*)

nashitóri *nm* **1)** jogger, runner **2)** deserter (*Mil*)

nashlo *pp/adj* **1)** deserted, eloped, eloped; **grast nashlo** runaway horse **2)** *nm* deserter, fugitive, escapee, man who has eloped, runaway: *nf* **nashli** eloped daughter, runaway girl; **Ródel pêska sha,**

la nashlya. He's searching for his daughter, the runaway. **3)** *nm* refugee: *nf* **nashli**

nashti *v/aux* **1)** cannot/can't, could not, used with conjugated verbs to indicate impossibility; **Nashti zhav.** I can't go. **Nashti kam-zhav.** I will not be able to go. **2)** combined with verb "to be" to indicate impossibility; **Nashtí-sas mánge te zhav.** I was not able to go. **Nashtí-avel mánge te zhav.** It will not be possible for me to go.

nashtíl-pe *v/refl* be unable to, not to be able to; **Nashtíl-pe.** He can't do it/it can't be done. **Nashtisáilo.** He couldn't do it/it couldn't be done.

nashtimos *nm* impossibility

nasul *adj* **1)** bad, dangerous, harmful; **Mai nasul lêske.** It's even worse for him **2)** *adv* bad, badly, dangerously, wickedly **3)** *nf* danger, harm, evil, injury, mischief; **Keren mánge nasul.** They are doing me harm. **Chi kerav túke nasul.** I won't harm you. **3)** *comp/vt* **kerel** ~ mistreat (*with dat*); **Kerel pêska Rromnyáke nasul**. He mistreats his wife.

nasulíl-pe *v/refl,* become/get bad/worsen: *pp/adj* **nasulime**; **Swáko ges, nasulíl-pe mai but.** It gets worse every day.

nasulimos *nm nm* **1)** evil, harm, injury **2)** tribulation, trouble, woe

naswalichóso *adj* sickly, slightly sick, a little unwell, prone to sickness, weak

naswalimos *nm* ailment, disease, medical condition, sickness

naswalo ándo shoro *adj/phr* mentally unbalanced, sick in the head

naswalo yilo *comp/nm* heart problem, *lit* sick heart, *sl* bum ticker

naswalo/nasvalo *adj* **1)** ailing, infirm, sick **2)** having a menstrual period; **Naswali múrri Rromni, zhanes.** My wife is sick, you know. (*the polite way of saying she is menstruating and unable to entertain guests*) **2)** *nm* sick man, sickly man: *nf* **naswali 2)** patient

naswalyarel *vt* make sick, sicken: *pp/adj* **naswalyardo**

naswárdyol *vi* be made sick, become sick, sickened (*from/of*): *pp/adj* **naswardilo**; **Naswárdilem katar o mas.** I got sick from the meat. **Naswárdilem kodolêndar.** I got sick of those people.

naswol/naswályol *vi* get sick/fall sick: *pp/adj* **naswailo**; **Na naswáwo!** Don't get sick! **Naswáilem tsîrrá mai anglal katar o Krechúno.** I got sick a little before Christmas.

nátsiya *nf* **1)** nation, Romani nation such as *Kalderash, Lovara, Machwáya*, etc. **2)** nation state, nation (*of the world*); **Le Nátsiyi Maladine** The United Nations **3)** nationality

natúra *nf* **1)** house plants, indoor plants **2)** nature

naturálno *adj/adv* **1)** as usual, natural,naturally, real, realistic, typical; **Mangel bare love anglál o avokáto, sar naturálno.** The lawyer wants a lot of money up front, as usual. **2)** *adv* **sar naturálno** like the real thing; **E makéta meyázol sar naturálno.** The model looks like the real thing.

nav *nm* **1)** name **2)** signature **3)** identity *see also* **anav** *nm*

navála *nf* fern

navêsko ges *comp/nm* birthday, name day

nav-Gazhikano *nm* non-Romani name, name used with non-Roma like Frank Smith, whose Romani name could be **O Zlátcho le Todorósko.**

nav-Rromano *nm* name used within the Romani community **Note:** Vlax-Roma have only a given name such as **Stévo** *or* **Mara.** The equivalent of a surname is the name of the father in the genitive case. Thus; **O Stévo le Babêsko,** Steve, Bob's son or **E Mára le Babêski**, Mary. Bob's daughter.

nayisil *vt* **1)** thank **2)** *v/refl* **nayisíl-pe** thank oneself, be thanked

nayisime *pp/adj* appreciated, thanked

nayisimos *nm* gratitude, thanks

Nayís-túke Thank you. (*one psn*),
  Nayís-tumênge. (*more than one psn*)
nedezhdil *vt* **1)** hope, hope for: *pp/adj*
  nedezhdime 2) *v/refl* **nedezhdíl-pe** hope;
  Nedezhdí-ma ke avel. I hope that he
  comes/hopefully, he will come.
  Nedezhdíl-pe te aven lês love. He hopes
  to get money. **Nedezhdí-ma**. I hope so.
nedezhdimásko *gen/adj* hopeful
nedezhdimos *nm* expectation, hope
nedezhdíya/nyedázhdya *nf* hope; **Si**
  amên nedezhdíya. We have hope/We are
  hopeful
nêg/nêgo *conj* instead, instead of, rather
  than; **Wo gêló nêg mánde.** He went
  instead of me. **Pilem chái nêg káfa.** I
  drank tea instead of coffee. **Nêg te zhav**
  akana, me zhav tehára. Rather than
  going now, I'll go tomorrow.
nêgo *conj see* **nêg** *conj*
négo *nm* wart
nêkazhíl/nêkêzhíl *vt* **1)** cause
  anxiety/agitation, cause to worry, create
  mental anguish, create frustration, create
  upset, cause to worry, cause harassment:
  pp/adj **nêkazhimé; Nêkazhíl ma.** It
  worries me. **Nêkazhín ame ánda o**
  rénto. They are harassing us about the
  rent. **2)** *v/refl* **nêkazhíl-pe** become
  agitated/apprehensive, become
  upset/worried; **Nêkazhí-ma ánda lêste.** I
  am worried about him. **Na nêkazhisáwo!**
  Don't worry!
nêkazhimé *pp/adj* agitated, alarmed,
  apprehensive, stressed, upset, worried;
  Simas defyal nêkazhimé. I was really
  alarmed/worried. **Nêkazhimé-la ánda**
  páki she. She is stressed out over her
  daughter.
nêkazhimós *nm* alarm, apprehension,
  mental anguish, mental frustration, stress,
  worry
nêkazhisáwol *vi* worry *see* **nêkazhíl-pe**
  v/refl
nêkázo *nm* **1)** aggravation, alarm, anguish,
  apprehension, distress, mental frustration,
  sorrow, stress, trouble, worry **2)** hassle,

misfortune, ordeal, sorrow, suffering,
  tribulation; **Che nêkázo xalyam ándo**
  kodó kámpo! What an ordeal we went
  through in that (*refugee*) camp!
nêkêzhála *nf* alarm, apprehension, distress,
  worry
neologísmo *nm* **1** neologism/newly-coined
  word **2)** words or expression coined by
  Romani writers which are not yet widely
  used in the spoken language but which
  appear in print in publications in Romani
  ranging from political and social activism
  publications and Internet bulletins and
  reports to private email correspondence
  and translations of Biblical texts.
nepáta/nipáta *nf* **1)** niece **2)** grand
  daughter **3)** term of respect for a young
  woman by an older man
nepóto *nm* **1)** nephew **2)** grandson
neril *vt* **1)** beat, gain, vanquish, win **2)** *v/refl*
  neríl-pe be victorious, succeed, win (*Eur*
nerime *pp/adj)* beaten, gained, victorious,
  won
nerimos *nm* success, victory, winnings
neritóri *nm* conqueror, successful
  candidate, victor, winner
nêrva *nf* nerve: *pl* **nêrvi** nervous condition
nervosíya *nf* nervousness, nervous
  breakdown; **Si lês nervosíya.** He is
  suffering from nerves.
nervóso *adj* **1)** agitated, apprehensive,
  jittery, nervous, skittish (*horses*) **2)**
  impatient
nêvála *nf* **1)** fern **2)** bracken (*pteridium*
  aquilinum)
Nevé-Bershêski chinesára *nf/phr* New
  Year's Eve
nevó-biyandorro *comp/nm* newborn baby
  boy: *nf* **neví-biyandorri**
neví-fátsa *comp/nf* **1)** facial **2)** face lift **3)**
  cosmetic facial surgery
nevikanimos *nm* modernity
nevikano *adj* modern, new-fangled,
  ultra-modern, up-to-date
nevimatángo lil *comp/nm* newsletter

nevimos *nm* **1)** news; **Che nevimos amênge?** What new for us? **2)** innovation, newness, something new

nevo **1)** *adj* new, recent **2)** *nm* newcomer, new *psn*: *nf* **nevi**

nevó arakhimos *comp/nm* new discovery

nevó-avilo *comp/adj* **1)** newly-arrived **2)** *comp/nm* newly arrived male *psn*: *nf* **neví-avili; Kon si kodole nevé-avile?** Who are those newly-arrived people/new people who just arrived?

nevó-dúxo *nm* reincarnation, transmigration of soul

nevo swáto *comp/nm* new word, neologism

nevorro *adj* brand new

nevóya *nf* need, requirement(s); **Si amen bari nevóya lovêndar.** We are in desparate need of money.

nevyárdyol *vi* be reconstituted/renewed/ modernized, be re-issued, be renovated, be replaced: *pp/adj* **nevyardili**

nevyarel *vt* **1)** make new, re-issue, renew, renovate, replace: *pp/adj* **nevyardo 2)** modernize **3)** renew or change one's image **4)** regenerate

nevyarimos *nm* **1)** renewal, renovation, replacement **2)** modernization

níchi *adv/id* **1)** definitely not, no, none, not, not at all, no, not all; **Si tut love wórka níchi?** Do you have money or not? **Sa le Rrom traden hai me níchi.** All the Roma are departing and I'm not. **Aves wórka níchi?** Are you coming or not? **2)** *adv* neither, nor **3)** *pron* nothing; **Nai ma níchi.** I have nothing. **Nai tut khánchi hai í-me nai ma níchi.** You have nothing and I have nothing either.

nigerel *var of* **nikerel** *vt qv*

nikelil *vt* nickel plate: *pp/adj* **nikelime** (*Am*)

nikelime *pp/adj* nickel-plated (*Am*)

nikelimos *nm* nickel plating

nikerel *vt* **1)** bear, carry, carry off, transport: *pp/adj* **nikerdo**; **O beng nikerdya lês yadóste.** The devil carried him off to hell. **2)** brace, hold, maintain, steady, support, sustain **3)** brandish **4)**

hold, retain, restrain: **Niker lês te na marél-pe!** Restrain him so he won't get into a fight! **5)** *v/refl* **nikerél-pe** bear oneself, carry oneself, present oneself, support oneself, sustain oneself

nikerimásko *gen/adj* moveable, portable

nikerimos *nm* **1)** transporting, transportation **2)** support **3)** restraint **4)** preservation

nikeritóri *nm* holder, retainer, supporter

níklo/níkelo *nm* **1)** nickel (*coin*) (*Am*) **2)** nickel (*material*)

nikushára *nf* nutmeg

nilóno *nm* nylon string (*Mus*), nylon, nylon stocking

nilonítsko *adj* nylon

nímbo *nm* halo (*Eur*)

nípo *nm* **1)** extended family **2)** family history, lineage **3)** genealogy; **Kodo phuro, o Zlátcho, zhanel sa amáre nípurya.** That old (Rom), Zlatcho, knows all our genealogies.

Nipóna *nf* Japan

Niponsítska *nf* Japanese (*Lang*)

Niponsítsko *adv* Japanese

Nipónso *nm* Japanese man: *nf* **Niponsáika** Japanese woman

nipóto *nm* **1)** nephew: *nf* **nepáta** niece **2)** grandson: *nf* **nepáta** granddaughter

níshto *pron* no, nothing

níshte *pron* another, some, some unidentified/some nameless *psn or thing*; **níshte dokumênto** some document or other. **Níshte Rrom phendyas kadya.** Some Rom or other said that. **Níshte Rroma avile ándo fóro.** Some(*as yet unknown*) Roma came into town. **Níshte dilo phendyas kadya.** Some fool or other said that.(*Eur*)

nitála *conj* although, even if/though, not withstanding, though; **Nitála baró-lo chi darav lêstar.** Even though he is big I am not afraid of him. **Kamel tu, nitála chi zhanes.** He loves you, even if you don't know (so).

níva *nf* field (*Am*)

nivélo *nm* **1)** level: *pl* **nivélya 2)** carpenter's level

nizháko *nm* **1)** ornate staff of a *Kalderash* patriarch or leader. **2)** a custom-made or hand-made utility tool with a flexible steel shaft covered in leather rings the length of a walking stick with a pointed steel tip and a heavy copper or brass head at right angles to the staff. When swung from the tip it was used for herding, stunning or killing dangerous animals, breaking arms in self-defense if attacked by rural mobs, smashing holes in ice for fishing and then used as a fishing rod and had other practical purposes. It was used in the nomadic era in North America and a few old examples were still extant in the 1960s.

no *adv/conj/imp see* **nã**

Nórdo *nm* North (*Eur*)

Nordósko *adj* North, northern (*Eur*)

normálo *adj/adv* normal, normally, as usual, as it usually is; **Sas baro xamos ándo djuléshi, sar normálo.** There was a big argument during the business meeting, as there usually is.(*Eur*)

Nort-Amérika *comp/nf* North-America (*Am*)

Nórto *adj* North

Nortóski-Cheran *comp/nf* North Star

nosílka *nf* stretcher (*medical*)

nóta *nf* **1)** note(*Mus*) **2)** note (*written*)

notári *nm* **1)** justice of the peace **2)** notary public

notásh *nm* swimmer: *nf* **notáshka**

notil *vt* **1)** bathe, make to swim: *pp/adj* **notime**; **Notisar le grasten ándo rivéri.** Swim the horses in the river. **2)** *v/refl* **notíl-pe** bathe, swim

nôtso *nm* nut (*for a bolt*); **karfin thai nôtso,** bolt and nut

novéla *nf* novel

Novímbra *nf* November

Novímbrone *adv* in November

nóvina *nf* **1)** new-fangled gimmick, new invention **2)** novelty

Nówa *nm/neolog* Noah; **O Nówa ankaldyas sa le zhívini katar o baro tasayimos.** Noah saved all the animals from the great flood.

núla *nf* zero (*Eur*)

núma/númai *adv/conj* but, just, only, yet; **Kámas-kindem la núma nas ma dósta love.** I would have bought it but I didn't have enough money. **Nai kónik ándo hãlo, núma o Stévo.** There is nobody in the hall, just Steve. **Núma avilem d'ekh cháso.** I just/only arrived an hour ago. **Chi kerdem khánchi núma vi-me akushádilem.** I didn't do anythiny, yet I too was cussed out.

número *nm* **1)** number, phone number: *pl* **númerya 2)** id number; **Si-ma lêsko número.** I have his number/I got him pegged (*Am*)

número-poshtáko *comp/nm* zip code

númerya *nm/pl* arithmetic, numbers

nupêrka *nf* newt, water lizard

nuvaralo *adj* cloudy

nuvaril *vt* **1)** cloud, cloud over, make overcast with smoke/smog **2)** *v/refl* **nuvaríl-pe** become cloudy, cloud over

nuvarime *pp/adj* clouded, overcast

nuvarimos *nm* clouding, overcast

núvaro *nm* cloud: *pl* **núvarya**

nyáma *nf* female relative/relation

nyámo *nm* male relative, relation; **Ame sam nyámurya ka l' Minéshti.** We are relatives of the **Minéshti** clan. **Wo si nyámo mánsa.** He is related to (*with*) me.

Nyamptsítska *nf* German (*Lang*)

Nyamptsítsko *adj* German

Nyamptsíya *nf* Germany

Nyámptso *nm* **1)** Germany **2)** German man: *nf* **Nyamptsáika**

nyúrtso *nm* **1)** sandpiper (*sub-order Charadrii*) **2)** blue jay

O

o *def/art/ms* the; **o grast** the horse

obérzha *nf* inn (*Eur*)

oberzhísto *nm* innkeeper nm: **oberzhísta** *nf* (*Eur*)

obicháyo *nm* custom, habit, tradition: *pl* **obicháyurya**

oblichóso *adj* egg-shaped, oval

obligátsiya *nf* obligation, responsibility

ôblo *adj* oval, round

ôblól *vt* **1)** make round, round off: *pp/adj* **ôblomé 2)** *v/ref* **oblól-pe** become round, get round

ôblosável *vi* become round: *pp/adj* **ôblosailó** (*Eur*)

odmavinil/odbil *vt* **1)** refuse, turn down: *pp/adj* **odmavinime/odbime 2) odmaviníl-pe/odbíl-pe** *v/refl* be refused/turned down **3) odmavinisável/odbisável** *vi*

odoring *adv* in that direction, that way, over there

odoringal *adv* from over there

ófisa *nf* **1)** business office **2)** reader-advisor parlour. (*Am*); **Kerel but love ánde láki ófisa.** She makes a lot of money in her parlour. **Zéleno ófisa si sáyek mánge baxtali.** A green (*painted*) parlour is always lucky for me.

ofishiyálno/ofisiyálno *adj/adv* **1)** official, officially **2)** *nm* official

ofitsyéri *nm* officer (*Mil*)

okothar *adv* from that direction, from there

okothe *adv* at/to that place, in that direction

oktávo *nm* octave (*Mus*)

Októbra *nf* October

Októbrone *adv* in October

ombutsmáno *nm/neolog* ombudsman: *nf* **ombutsmánka**

Ontáryo *nm* Ontario (*Can*)

Ópa! *see* **Hópa!**

operatóri *nm* operator

operátsiya *nf* operation, surgery; **Trobul operátsiya.** He/she needs an operation.

operil *vt* operate (*machinery*): *pp/adj* **operime**

opínyo *nm* opinion: *pl* **opínya** *see also* **gûndo** *nm*

ópiyo *nm* opium

opral *adv/prep* **1)** above, on top of, over, upstairs, up there; **Háide opral!** Come upstairs! **Tho la opral o wudar!** Put it above the door! **So keres opral?** What are you doing up there? **2)** aboard, up on board, loaded on top, on top of **3)** above and beyond, additional, extra, over and above, spare; **Si tut shûna opral?** Do you have a spare tire? **Nai ma love opral.** I have no extra money.

opral pe *prep* **1)** as well as, besides; **Akushlas avre Rromen opral pe mánde.** He cursed out other Roma as well as me. **Opral pe lêste, kon zhanel?** Besides him, who else knows? **2)** other than

opraluno *nm* above, upper

opre *adv/prep* up, upwards, upstairs; **Opre Rróma!** Arise Rom!

opré-xaráte *adv/phr* up the hill/incline/slope, uphill; **Tradásas opré-xaráte kána mulo o mobíli.** We were driving uphill when the car stalled.

ôpríl *vt* **1)** ban, caution (*against*), forbid, prevent, prohibit **2)** impede, obstruct, thwart **3)** *v/refl* **ôpríl-pe** be/become banned/forbidden, forbid oneself (*to do*), stop doing

ôprimé *pp/adj* banned, forbidden, no-no, prevented; **Ôprimé-lo**, It is forbidden.

ôprimós *nm* ban, caution, prevention, prohibition, interdiction

opruno *adj* 1) top, upper, uppermost, upstairs; **ópruno than** upper bunk bed, **ópruwi sóba** upstairs room 2) extra, spare 3) *nm* high man on the totem pole, honcho, top dog: *nf* **opruwi**

oráit *interj* all right, alright. (*Am*)

órdina *nf* 1) order 2) *comp/vi* **del** ~ place an order

ordináriyo *adj* ordinary *see also* **prósto** *adj*

ordinil *vt* order, place/send an order: *pp/adj* **ordinime**

organaizil *vt* organize: *pp/adj* **organaizime** 2) *v/refl* **organaizíl-pe** become/get organized (*Am*)

organarizil *vt/neolog* see **organaizil** *vt*

organizátsiya *nf* organization

órgano *nm* organ (*Mus*)

oril *vt* 1) wish: *pp/adj* **orime**; **Oriv tu Lásho Krechúno**. I wish you Merry Christmas. 2) hope for 3) *v/refl* **oríl-pe a)** wish, be wished for; **Orí-ma ke símas barvalo.** I wish I were rich. **b)** be hoped for; **Gêlítar o Stánko?** Has Stanko departed? **Orí-ma!** I hope so!

originálno *adj* original

origin álo *nm* original

orimáski-xaying *nf comp/nf* wishing well

orimos *nm* 1) wish 2) hope

orkéstra *nf* orchestra

ornaménto *nm* bauble, decoration, ornament

órrla *nf* eagle (*Am*) *see* **wórrla**

-orro *prod/suffix nm/s* **–orro** *nf/s* **–orri/yorri** *mn/pl* **–orre** *nf/pl* **–orra/yorra** 1) **a)** to form a diminutive; **grastorro** little horse, **grasnyorri** little mare, **grastorre** little horses (*mixed gender*), **grasnyorra** little mares **b)** suffixed to numbers; **yekhorro** one little one/male child, **yekhorri** one little one/female child 2) *suffixed to thematic adjectives to modify basic meaning*;

adj/ms **sano** *becomes* **sanorro** on the thin side, *adj/fs* **sani** *becomes* **sanyorri** *and* *adj/pl becomes* **sanorre** *mn/pl and* **sanyorre** *nf/pl* 3) to express endearment; **rromorro** dear husband, **romnyorri** dear wife 4) to express the pejorative; **Che zhuklorro!** What a miserable mutt of a dog/What a puny runt of a dog! **Che bukyorri!** What an inferior job of work!

ortografíya *nf/neolog* orthography

órxida *nf* orchid

ósa/ósitsa *nf* wasp (*Am*)

Oshwítsa *nf* Auschwitz; **Oshwitsáte, mule but Rroma.** At Auschwits, many Roma died.

ostavkil *vt* 1) depose, force to abdicate/resign 2) *v/refl* **ostavkíl-pe** abdicate, resign, stand down

ostavkime *pp/adj* abdicted, deposed, resigned

ostavkimos *nm* abdication, resignation

Otáwa *nf* Ottawa (*Can/Am*)

otázho *nm* hostage: *nf* **otazhútsa**

oteshil *vt* 1) comfort, console, make calm, lull, pacify, quieten down, settle, smooth out, sooth: *pp/adj* **oteshime** 2) commisserate, condone 3) *v/refl* **oteshíl-pe a)** calm down, clear up, become quiet, become pacified, settle, sooth; **Oteshisáilo o réko.** The lake has calmed down. **b)** commiserate, sympathize (with); **Oteshí-ma túsa.** I sympathize with you.

oteshimos *nm* calming down, comfort, sympathy

othar *adv* from there

othar angle/othar mai angle *adv/conj* from then on, from that time forward; **Othar angle chi mai dikhlem la mai ekh dáta.** From then on, I never saw her again.

othe *adv* there (*illi*)

Otománo *nm adj* 1) Ottoman, Turkish 2) *nm* Turk: *nf* **Otománka**

ôvgín *nm* honey *see also* **âvgín**

owérish 1) *nm* The day before yesterday 2) *adv* day before yesterday; **Avilem**

owérish. I came the days before yesterday.

oxtali *nf* eight, eight in cards

oxto *num* eight

oxtopódya *nf* octopus

oxtóto *num* eighth

oxtówardesh *num* eighty

oxtowardéshto *adj* eightieth

P

pa *prep* about, by way of, concerning, from/off, through and very idiomatic; **Ashundem pa late.** I've heard about her. **Avilem pa América.** I came through the USA. **Do-pash Rrom si pa lêski dey.** He is half Romani through his mother. **Pelo pa o taváno.** He fell from/off the roof. **Den-dúma pa l' love.** They are talking about money. **Anklisto pa e filástra.** He got out through the window. **Kerdyan but love pa gadya buki.** We made a lot of money through that work. **Lyas pêske tsáliya pa pêste.** He took his clothes off.

pácha *nf* peace, safety; **Zha ánde pácha!** Travel in peace/safety!

pachása *nf/inst/adv* in peace; **Mêk te zhal pachása!** Let him go in peace!

páchka *nf* 1) package, pack, parcel; **páchka tsigéri** pack of cigarettes 2) patch

padjámi *nf/pl* pyjamas

padlidjáni *nf* 1) tomato *see more common* **peradáika** *nf* 2) eggplant *see also* **bórfa** *nf*

paduriyátsa *nf* crab apple

paganêsko *gen/adj* pagan

pagáno *nm* male pagan: *nf* **pagánika**

pagúba *nf* 1) damage, destruction, loss, vandalism 2) ceremonial prank or raid to get the better of other Roma (*like stealing a bottle of whisky from a gathering of another clan group or kumpaníya before leaving the gathering*)

pagubash *nm* victim of damage, injured party, plaintiff: *nf* **pagubáshka**

pagubil *vt* damage, commit vandalism, trash: *pp/adj* **pagubime**; **Pagubisardyas**

múrro mobíli te lel pêski primúta. He trashed my car to get his revenge.

pai *nm* 1) water, body of water 2) sweat 3) *vt/id* **mangel ~** beg for mercy; **Mardyas lês zhi-ka manglas pai.** He beat him until he begged for mercy. 4) *comp/vt* **del ~** water; **Dav pai le grasten.** I'm watering the horses. (*id* I am heeding the call of nature) 5) Aquarius (*Zod*)

pai ánde l' pulmóni *nm/phr* pleurisy

pai-shuklo *comp/nm* mineral water

paiyarel *vt* hose down, irrigate, water: *pp/adj* **paiyardo**

paiyarimos *nm* irrigation, watering

paiyaslo *adj* 1) leaking, leaky 2) watery 3) liquid 4) sweaty

paiyésa *nm/inst/adv* with the water, with the flow, along with the herd, along with the majority; **Móra te zhas le paiyésa.** We need to go with the flow.

paiyorro *nm* glass/drink of water

pakh *nf* 1) wing 2) fin (*of a fish*) 3) *comp/vi* **del pakha** take flight, take off (*aircraft*): **Pêsko aropláno dyas pakha.** His airliner took off. 4) *comp/vt* **lel pakha** take flight

pakhalo *adj* 1) winged 2) having fins

pakimos *nm* fruition, ripeness

pakiv *nf* 1) admiration, awe, dignity, honour, propriety, reverence, respect, virtue; **Godya nai bari pakiv.** That's no great honour. **Sa le Rroma den lêske pakiv.** All the Roma pay him respect. 2) trust 3) dharma, duty (*towards one's community*) 3) feast given to honour a person or persons. 4) *comp/vt/i* **kerel ~** entertain, honour (*guests*) 5) *comp/vt/i* **del ~ a)** give a feast in honour of a friend/guest **b)** honor, respect (*smbdy*); **Dav lês pakiv.** I respect him. **6) del-pe ~** throw a party; **Le Rroma den-pe bári pakiv.** The Roma are having a big party.

pakiváki gili *comp/nf* song sung to honour a person or persons

pakiváko khelimos *comp/nm* a dance done to honour a person or people

pakivales *adv* honorably, respectably, responsibly

pakivali rani *comp/nf* respectable lady

pakivalimos *nm* dignity, honour, respect

pakivalo *adj* **1)** awesome, dignified, honest, honourable, respectable, responsible, sincere, trustworthy **2)** faithful (*to Romani traditions/laws*) **3)** religious (*within the* **Romaníya**)

pakivása *adv* with honour, with respect, respectfully

pakivil *vt* **1)** admire, honour, pay honour, give homage, respect: *pp/adj* **pakivime 2)** entertain (*guests*) **3)** *v/refl* **pakivíl-pe** be respected, respect oneself

pakivime *pp/adj* honoured, given honour/respect

pakivimos *nm* honour

pákla *nf* hell; **Zha ánde pákla!** Go to hell!

pako *adj* ripe

páko *pron/poss/refl* her own (*Am*) *see* **pêsko** *pron/poss/refl*

pakorro *nominalized pron* her own

pakyádyol *vi* **1)** be made to believe: *pp/adj* **pakyadilo 2)** be/become brainwashed

pakyal *vt/i* **1)** believe, believe in, have confidence in, have faith in, rely on, respect, trust in, trust: *pp/adj* **pakyalo; Pakyas ándo Del?** Do you believe in God? **Chi pakyalyas man.** He didn't believe me. **2)** obey **3)** be believed (*to be smth*); **Pakyalo si ke chachó** It is believed to be true. **4)** doubt *id* **Chi pakyav ke wo shai kerel.** I doubt if he can do so.

pakyamos *nm* belief, confidence, faith, trust

pakyárdyol *vi* **1)** be loaded, packed, packed up *pp/adj* **pakyardilo 2)** be ripened

pakyarel *vt* **1)** load up, pack up, pack: *pp/adj* **pakyardo 2)** bundle up, wrap up **3)** make to ripen; **O kham pakyardyas le drakha.** The sun has ripened the grapes.

pakyarimos *nm* **1)** loading, packing **2)** bundling up, wrapping up **3)** ripening, season of ripening

pakyavel *vt* brainwash, make to believe in, convert: *pp/adj* **pakyado**

pakyayimáta *nm/pl* beliefs, spiritual beliefs

pakyayimos *nm* **1)** belief, faith, illusion, trust; **Kerdyas pakyayimos te sas barvalo.** He created (*an*) illusion that he was wealthy **2)** religious belief, religion **3)** brainwashing, conversion

pakyayitóri *nm* **1)** believer, disciple: *pl* **pakyayitórya** believers, converted, disciples **2)** *nm* brainwasher, dream merchant, missionary

pakyol *vi* become ripe, come to fruition, ripen: *pp/adj* **pakilo**

pála *prep* **1)** after, behind; **Phir pála mánde!** Walk behind/with me! **(2)** about, at, according to, because of, for, to, over to, with (*in a limited sense*) & very idiomatic; **Háide pála mánde!** Come over to my place! **Si lês Gazhi pála pêste.** He has a non-Romani woman (*living*) with him. **Wo beshel pála mánde.** He is staying at my place. **Avilo o gazho pála o mobíli.** The man came about the car (*to see the car for sale*). **Kerdem pála túte.** I did (it) for your sake. **Xolyáilo thai pála godya chi avilo kai sláva.** He got angry and because of that he didn't come to the feast. **Me merav pála láte.** I am dying because of her/I love her greatly. **Me avav ka l' desh pála shtar.** I will come at ten past/after four. **3)** *comp/v/refl* **lel-pe ~** bother, pester; **Na mai lé-tu pála**

mánde! Don't pester me any more/Get off my case!

pála- *prod/pref* post-; **pála-komunísto Ivrópa** post-communist Europe

pála godya *adv/conj* after that, because of that, next; **So kam-keres pála godya?** What will you do after that/next? **Avilam andré o hãlo thai pála godya pelo o marimos.** We entered the hall and after that the fight started.

pála kodya *see* **pála godya**

pála phandade wudara *adv/phr* behind closed doors/privately

palal *adv/prep* back, back again, behind. in the back, in the rear; **Háide palal,** Come on in the back (*of the house*). **E garádja si palal o kher.** The garage is behind the house.

palal kai anglal *adv/phr* back to front. backwards; **Todyas le petala palal kai anglal.** He attached the horseshoes backwards. (*Folk*)

palaluno *adj* back, behind, following, rear

pála-mizméri *nm/adv* after noon, afternoon

palaríya *nf* fedora, dress hat, Stetson

palátsiyo *nm* palace

palazhéniya *nf* situation

pále *adv* 1) afresh, again; **Pále avel.** He's coming again. **Pále zumadyam te wazdas o vôrdòn opre.** Again we tried to raise the wagon. **Pále avilem pálpale ka l' tséri.** Again, I returned to the camp. **Pále astárdilam.** We started afresh. **Arakhás-ame pále.** We'll meet again. 2) continuing to, still; **Pále badil ma.** He's continuing to annoy me. **Pále kerel.** He's still doing it/He's at it again. **Pále kames la?** Do you still love her? **Pále mangel!** He wants more! 3) later; **pále ekh kurko,** one week later.

paléta *nf* epaulette, shoulder strap: *pl* **palétsi**

pálma/pérma *nf* 1) palm of the hand (*Anat*): *pl* **pálmi/pérmi** 2) slap 3) clap 4) palm tree 5) *vt* **del** ~ slap, spank

palorral *adv* later, later on *us with* **mai**; **Zhas mai palorral.** We'll go later/later on.

pálpale *adv* 1) back, back again; **Avéltar pálpale.** He's coming back again. **Kána avilo pálpale ándo hãlo, istráilo pe l' phaleya.** When he came back again into the hall, he slipped on the (*polished*) floor. 2) *comp//vt/i* **del** ~ a) bounce back, draw back, kick back, echo, pull back, rebound b) give back, return (*smthg to smbdy*) 3) *comp/vi* **zhal** ~ go back, retreat, withdraw

pálpale-bulása *adv/phr* backwards; **O grast phirdyas pálpale-bulása.** The horse backed up/walked backwards. **Zha pálpale-bulása!** Go backwards! **Gîndíl-pe pálpale-bulása.** He thinks backwards.

palunes *adv* finally, lastly, lately

paluno *adj* 1) final, hindmost, hinter, last, latest, rearmost, ultimate, *us* with **mai**; **Tu san o mai paluno ánde línya.** You are the last in line. 2) *nm* last one, last person: *nf* **paluni**; **Símas o paluno te zhávtar.** I was the last to leave.

palyánka *nf* phony coin, coin the same on both sides, trick coin

pamfléto *nm* circular, handbill; **Si la ófisa, dikhlem láke pamfléturya pe l' mobílya.** She has a parlour, I saw her handbills on the (*parked*) cars. (*Am*)

pampúri *nm* ship (*Am*)

pampurítsa *nf* 1) gay 2) homosexual

pampuritsíya *nf* 1) gay lifestyle 2) homosexuality

pa-mui *id/adv* orally; **Lav e medesína pa-mui.** I take the medicine orally.

pamúko *nm* cotton

pamukósko *gen/adj* made of cotton

pánda *adv* still, yet (*Eur*)

panéla *nf* panel

páni *nm* water *see also more common* **pai** *nm*

pansh/panzh *num* five

panshali *nf* figure five, five in cards

panshêngi *nf* 1) five-dollar bill (*Am*) 2) *gen/adj* five years old; **Panshêngi si e tsinoni.** The little girl is five-years old.

pánshto *num* fifth

pánshwardesh *num* fifty

panshwardéshto *num* fiftieth

pantalóya *nm/pl* 1) pants, trousers 2) bloomers, pantaloons

pantéla *nf* lace

pantéra *nf* panther

pantúfla *nf* house slipper, loafer, slipper

pap *nm* grandfather *see* **pápo**

Pápa! *nm/voc* Granddad!

papagálto *nm* parrot: *nf* **papagálta**

papalam *adv* fifty-fifty; **Huladyam e dobúnda papalam.** We shared the profit fifty-fifty.

paparúga/papalúda *nf* butterfly: *pl* **paparúdji**

paparugítsa *nf* miller

Pápe! *nm/voc* Granddaddy!

papin *nf* goose

papíra *nf* 1) document, paper: *pl* **papíri** (*Eur*) 2) single piece of cigarette paper

papíri *nm* 1) paper 2) documents, papers 3) cigarette paper/rolling paper (*Am*)

papirosh/papiróshka *nf* cigarette (*Eur*)

papírya *nm/pl* paperwork

pápo *nm* grandfather

paporr *nf* 1) bulrush, reed, rush 2) reed (*of a clarinet, etc*)

paporra *nf/pl* bulrushes, reeds, rushes

paporrángo *gen/adj* made of bulrush/reeds

papóski-dey *comp/nf* paternal great-grandmother

papósko-dad *comp/nm* paternal great-grandfather

paprikash *nm* gulyas, spicy meat stew

papuchyári *nm* shoemaker

papúka *nf* 1) slipper 2) woman's fancy/dancing shoe: *pl.* **papúchi; sumnakune papúchi** golden shoes/slippers, **lole papúchi** red shoes. **Phiravel lole papúchi.** She wears red shoes.

papúsha *nf* 1) doll 2) puppet 3) mannequin 4) child's toy

papushári *nm* 1) maker of dolls/puppets 2) pupeteer

paráda *nf* parade

parafína *nf* paraffin

paralegálno *n* paralegal: *nf* **paralegála**

paramilitárno *adj/neolog* paramilitary

paramilitáro *nm/neolog* member of a paramilitary unit,

paramédiko *nm* paramedic: *pl* **paramédichi**

paramíchi *nf* 1) folktale in the gendre of Jack-and-the-Beanstalk or Little-Red-Riding- Hood. In a general sense it can include any folk tale. 2) myth

paramichyári *nm* teller of stories/folktales, raconteur: *nf* **paramichárka**

paramíshi *nf var of* **paramíchi** *qv*

Parashtune *adv* on Friday, Friday

Parashtuvi *nf* Friday

parashúta *nf* parachute

parasóla *nf* parasol

paraxódo *nm* steamship,large passenger liner

paraxódo-batalyáko *comp/nm* battleship

pardnoi *nm* tailor

parfúmo *nm* perfume

Paridjêsko *gen/adj* 1) of Paris; **Wo si Rrom Franzúzo, Paridjêsko.** He is a French Rom, from Paris.

Parídji *nm* Paris

parintêngo *gen/adj* ancestral (*for multiple ancestors*)

parintíya *nf* 1) ancestry, family lineage, parentage 2) heritage

parínto *nm* male ancestor, forefather: *pl* **parínchi**: *nf* **parintáika**

parintósko *gen/adj* ancestral (*for a single ancestor*)

párka *nf* 1) park, playground 2) parka jacket (*Am*)

parkil *vt* 1) park (*automobile*); **Parkisardem o mobíli.** I parked the car. 2) *v/refl* **parkíl-pe** park, become parked; **Kai shai parkí-ma?** Where can I park?

parkime *pp/adj* parked; **Avile thai parkimé-le palal e khangeri.** They have arrived and are parked behind the church.

parkimos *nm* parking, parking lot, place to park

párko *nm* park, recreational area

parlaménto *nm* parliament

párne bal *comp/nf/pl* grey hair

párne lulugya *comp/nf /pl* syphilis

parné-balêngo *comp/gen/adj* grey-haired

Párni Ivrópa *comp/nf* western Europe (*Eur*)

parnichóso *adj* 1) gray, whitish colour, light-grayish colour, off-white colour 2) pale, pallid

parní-lulugi *comp/nf* 1) daisy 2) syphilitic suppuration

parno *adj* 1) white 2) bright, clear 3) pale, pallid 4) innocent, unblemished 5) white-skinned, non-Romani (*Eur*) 6) *nm* White man, white European: *nf* **parni** (*Eur*)

párno golúmbo *comp/nm* white dove

párno grast *comp/nm* white horse; **O párno grast si baxtalo.** A white horse is lucky.

párno manrro *comp/nm* white bread

parno/parrno *comp/nm* 1) barium sulphate 2) cocaine, hard drugs in powdered form

párno-barr *comp/nm* barium, barium sulphate

parnomos *nm* 1) paleness, whiteness 2) bleach

Parnorro *nm* Caucasian, White man: *nf* **Parnorri**

parnyarel *vt* 1) bleach, fade, make white, make grey (*hair*)**,** whiten, whitewash; *pp/adj* **parnyardo** 2) *v/refl* **parnyarél-pe** whitewash oneself; **Nashti parnyarél-pe ánde kris.** He won't be able to whitewash himself in court.

parnyarimos *nm* bleach, whitener

parnyol *vi* 1) become/turn white, grey (*hair*): *pp/adj* **parnilo** 2) fade 3) become pale/pallid; **Parnilo darátar.** He turned white from fear.

Parnyorri *nf* Snow White; **Parnyorri thai le Hifta Gazhorre** Snow White and the Seven Dwarfs

páro/párro *nm* 1) steam, vapor: *pl* **párya** 2) steam radiator (*in a house*) 3) automobile radiator

parol *vt* cook by steaming, steam, stew: *pp/adj* **parome**

parome *pp/adj* steamed, cooked by steaming, stewed

paromos *nm* steaming, steam pressure, vaporizing

parovíko *nm* 1) steam engine, steam-driven engine, steam roller 2) pressure cooker, steam boiler

pàrrâ/pùrrû *nf* 1) flame: *pl* **pêrri/pûrri** 2) hue and cry, pursuit, warrant for arrest, APB; **Si lês pàrrâ pe lêste.** He has a warrant out for him. 3) flash; **Gêló pârrása.** He left in a flash.

párro *nm* 1) pair; **párro tsokólya** pair of shoes 2) couple, married couple 3) pair/team of two horses

parrudimos *nm* alteration, change *see also* **parruyimos** *nm*

parrúdyol 1) be bartered/changed/exchanged/traded: *pp/adj* **parrudilo** 2) be adapted, changed, changed in behaviour; **Parrúdilo desar ansurisáilo.** He changed since he got married.

parruvel *vt* 1) change. exchange, trade (*horses, etc*): *pp/adj* **parrudo**; **Parruvav múrre tsáliya.** I am changing my clothes. 2) adapt (*to new conditions*) 3) modify 4) evolve 5) *v/refl* **parruvél-pe** adapt, undergo change, change oneself 4) convert

parruwil *vt* 1) compare: *pp/adj* **parruwime** 2) *v/refl* **parruwíl-pe** compare oneself, make comparisons

parruwimos *nm* comparison

parruyimos *nm* 1) bartering, change, exchange, trade, trading 2) adaptation, change, evolution 3) alteration 4) religious conversion

partída *nf* party, political party (*Eur*); **Partída Komunísto** Communist Party, **Partída Rromani** Romani Political Party (*Eur*)

partisipánto *nm/neolog* participant: *nf*
partisipánka

partisipátsiya *nf/neolog* participation

partizáno *nm* partisan, resistance fighter:
nf **partizánka**

pártya *nf* **1)** part, share: *pl* **pêrtsi 2)**
allocation, ration **3)** comp/vi **lel ~ a)** take
part (*in*), participate (*in*); **Sa le Rroma
músai te len pártya ándo diwáno.** All
the Roma must take part in the discussion.
b) choose/take sides (*in*); **Chi lav
kanikáski pártya ándo xamos.** I won't
take anyone's part in the argument.

pasári *nm* **1)** market place **2)**
merry-go-round (*Am*)

pasaxéri *nm* passenger, person who goes
along for the ride; **Me sim férdi
pasaxéri.** I'm just going along for the
ride; *nf* **pasaxérka**

pash *nm* **1)** half *see also* **do-pash** *adv* **2)**
prep beside, by, close by, near, next to
cont of **pásha** qv

pásha *prep* beside, by, close, close to, close
by, near, near to, next to; **Besh pásha
mánde!** Sit beside me/next to me! **Wo
beshélas pásha mánde ánde sláva.** He
was sitting next to me during the feast.
Chi mai zhav pásha lêste. I always
avoid him/I never go near him.

pashal *prep/adv* close, close by, from
nearby, near, nearby *often with* **mai**;
Beshel pashal mánde. He lives near me.
Háide mai pashal! Come closer!

pashalo *adj* close, near, nearby *see also*
pashuno *adj*

pashe/pashû *adv* close; **Háide mai pashe!**
Come closer!

pashimos *nm* affinity, closeness, intimacy

pashlimos *nm* **1)** period of being
bedridden, state of being bedridden **2)**
laying out of a corpse

pashlo *adj* **1)** bedridden, confined to bed,
laid up **2)** *nm* patient in a hospital: *nf*
pashli

pashlyardo *pp/adj* bed-ridden, confined to
bed, laid up

pashlyarel *vt* **1)** confine to bed, put to bed
(*because of sickness*): *pp/adj*
**pashlyardo; Pashlyardyas lês o
dóftoro.** The doctor confined him to bed.
2) lay out a deceased *psn* in a chapel

pashlyol *vi* **1)** become bedridden, take to
one's bed (*in sickness*) : *pp/adj* **pashlilo
2)** become laid up; **Pashlilo
naswalimása.** He become bedridden
with sickness. **3)** go to bed, lie down to
rest; **Pashlilo te hodeníl-pe.** He laid
town to rest **4)** be at rest, be laid out in a
chapel

pasho *adj* close; **nyámo pasho**
close/paternal relative: *pl* **nyámurya
pashû**

pásho *nm* brother–in-law, wife's sister's
husband

pashuno *adj* **1)** adjacent, close, near,
nearby; **Nashlo ándo wêrsh o pashuno.**
He fled into the nearby forest. **2)** *nm*
close male associate: *nf* **pashuni**

pashuvel/pashol *vi* **1)** approach, come
close, draw near, skirt: *pp/adj* **pashilo**;
Mai pashol. He's coming closer.
Pashilam ka o fóro/Pashilam le forêste.
We drew near the city. **Pashilam o fóro.**
We skirted the city. **Mai pashilem lêste.**
I came closer to him. **Pashilo, pashilo, o
zhêgáno!** Closer, closer, came the wild
beast! **Mai pashuvélas amen o guruv.**
The bull was moving closer to us. **Peli
ryat kána pashuvávas le tséri.** Night
fell when I was approaching the camp. **2)**
come/get/go close (to), come.get/go near
(to); **Nashti pashúvavas lêste.** I wasn't
able to get close to him. **Na mai pashuv
lêste!** Don't go near him again!
**Pashulam te arakhas o atwéto kai
skêlchála.** We came close to solving the
riddle.

páska *nf* Easter bread *us* decorated with
dyed eggs

páso *nm* **1)** gait, footstep, step, stride **2)**
dance step **3)** pace **4)** position, rank,
status

pásta *nf* goop, grout, paste, putty any kind of paste such as woodfiller, autobody repair putty, etc.

pásta-plochángi co*mp/nf* tile grout

pastéla *nf* cake, pastry

pastóri *nm* minister, pastor of the Romani Pentecostal Church

pastúxo *nm* cowboy, herdsman

pasútso *nm* short step; **Phirel pasutsênsa.** She walks with short steps.

patakóno *nm* **1)** slug (*gastropod*); **Mishkil-pe sar o patakóno.** He moves himself like a slug. **2)** *fig* slug, false coin for coin-operated machines, plugged nickel, wooden nickel (*Am*) **3)** clunker, automobile that can only drive slowly (*Am*) **4)** foot-dragger, sluggard

patav/patavo *nm* gaiter, puttee (*Mil*), spat: *pl* **patave**

patave *nm* gaiters, leg wrappers/warmers, puttees (*Mil*), spats

páte *adv* really

patéka *nf* pharmacy

patekári *nm* pharmacist

páto *nm* bed, cot, sleeping place; **Kerdyas pêsko páto – Mek sovel pe lêste!** He's made his bed – Let him lie on it! **Note:** This word is considered impolite for use in mixed company in Canada/US and is replaced by **than** *nm qv*

Patragí *nf* **1)** Easter; **Te avel baxtali tiri Patragi!** May your Easter bring you luck! **2)** Passover

Patragyáko *gen/adj* pertaining to Easter; **Patragyáke anrre** Easter eggs

patretash *nm* photographer: *nf* **patretáshka**

patréto *nm* painting, photograph, picture, portrait

patrin *nf* **1)** leaf: *pl* **patrya; O kasht wushárdilo pateryánsa.** The tree has been covered with leaves. **2)** leaf/sheet of paper **3)** page **4)** wafer; **Devlêski-patrin** communion/consecrated wafer **5)** flake; **ivêski-patrin** snowflake

patrinalo *adj* covered with folliage/leaves, leafy

patróno *nm* **1)** contact in business: *nf* **patronáika 2)** patron, protector, sponsor

patrúla *nf* patrol; **granitsáki patrúla** border patrol

patrulil *vt* patrol: *pp/adj* **patrulime**

patrya *nf/pl* **1)** foliage leaves **2)** *Arch* cluster of leaves thrown on the road, at the crossroads or at the entrance to a cart track to indicate the route traveled to those of the group following.

pátsina *nf* skate; *us plural in* **pátsini**

patsinil *vt* **1)** glide, skate, slide: *pp/adj* **patsinime 2)** *v/refl* **patsiníl-pe a)** skate **b)** glide, slide

patsinimos *nm* **1)** skating

pátsuma *nf* account, behalf, sake; **Pe káski pátsuma keres?** On whose behalf are you doing (this)?

pátura *nm/pl* bedding, bedclothes, blankets (*Eur*)

patútso *nm* cot, crib

pavalo *adj* icy, slippery with ice

pávo *nm* ice; **Arakh tu katar o pávo!** Watch out for the ice!

pavol *vi* become ice, freeze, ice over; **Pavosáilo o réko.** The lake iced over.

pavome *pp/adj* frozen, iced over, icy; **Pavome si o drom.** The road is iced over.

pavorro *nm* icicle

pavúno *nm* male peacock: *nf* **pavúna; pavunênge pora** peacock feathers

pe 1) *prep* on, at, by, for, per, to and very idiomatic; **Khelén-pe pe lovênde.** They are gambling for money. **Tho les pe sínya!** Place it on the table. **Kerdem lês pe lêski pátsuma.** I did it for his sake. **Pe múrro Del!** By/on my God! **Kerav solax pe amáre mulênde.** I make an oath on our dead. **Kindem e gitara pe pansh shela tiléri.** I bought the guitar for five-hundred dollars. **So si pe lêste?** What is he charged with? (*by the police*) **Wo si o baro pe lênde.** He is the boss over them. **Woi si sáyek pe mánde.** She is always at me/always prodding me. **2)** *pron/refl* **a)** himself, herself, *cont of* **pês** *qv* **b)** themselves *cont of* **pên** *qv*

pe godya *adv* by that; **Na zha pe godya!** Don't go by that! **Chi mai zhávas pe godya.** I wouldn't go by that.

pe sáva rêga *adv/phr* all over the place, everywhere, on every side

pe swáko rêgá *adv/phr* all around, all over the place, everywhere; **Le shavorre rrêspisárde gunoi pe swáko rêgá.** The kids scattered trash all over the place.

pe yekháko *id* in desperation; **Pushav tútar pe yekháko.** I ask you in desperation.

pechánza *nf* aging spot, freckle, mole, splotch

pecháta *nf* **1)** badge, emblem, insignia: *pl* **pechêtsi 2)** mark, stain, splotch, spot

pechênziya *nf/pl* aging spots, freckle, speckle, splotch, spot, stain: *pl* **pechênziyi**

pechêtsèngo *gen/adj* marked with spots, sploches, piebald; **petchêtsèngo grast** piebald horse

pechètsi *nf/pl* pox, spots (such *as chicken pox, measles, etc)*; **Si la pechêtsi.** She's got the pox.

pédka *nf* blot, blotch, spot, stain

pêkatúra *nf* **1)** drip, drop, droplet **2)** small amount, spot, trifling amount

pekel *vt* **1)** bake, broil, cook, fry, roast, toast: *pp/adj* **peklo; So pekes ánde tigáiya?** What are you cooking in the skillet? **2)** brew *(beer)* **3)** *vt/i/phr* ~ **ándo bov**, bake/broil in the oven **4)** *vt/i/phr* ~ **pe busht** barbecue **5)** *vt/i/phr* ~ **ánde chik** bake in clay **6)** *vt/i/phr* ~ **ánde tigáiya** fry

pekimos *nm* **1)** cooking, cuisine; **Lashé-xamásko si láko pekimos.** Her cooking is delicious. **2)** brew, brewing

pekitóri *nm* brewer, cook: *nf* **pekitórka**

peko *adj* **1)** baked, cooked, fried, roasted, toasted **2)** brewed

pekyol *vi* **1)** be cooked, be cooking: *pp/adj* **peklo; Peklo o xabe;** The food has been cooked. **2)** be brewed, be brewing; **Pekli e bíra d'ekh bersh.** The beer was brewed a year ago.

pel *vt/i* drink *var of* **piyel** *qv*; *pres* **piyav, pes, pel, piyas, pen, pen** *(Am)*; **Pes bíra mánsa?** Will you drink a beer with me?

pele *nm/pl* testes *(Anat)*

pelêngo *gen/adj* entire, possessing testicles; **pelêngo grast** entire horse, stallion

pelivoníya *nf* wrestling, wrestling match

pelivóno *nm* wrestler: *pl* **pelivóya:** *nf* **pelivónka**

pelo *nm* testicle *(Anat)*

pelsúya *nf* hypodermic needle, syringe

pelsuyála *nf* injection, inoculation, vaccination

pelsuyil *vt* **1)** give an injection, inject, inoculate, vaccinate: *pp/adj* **pelsuyime 2)** *v/refl* **pelsuyíl-pe** be vaccinated, inject oneself

pelsuyimos *nm* **1)** injection **2)** inoculation, vaccination

pên *pron/refl* themselves *see also* **pe** *pron/refl*

penax *nm* nut in general

pendex *nf* hazel nut

pendíkso *nm* appendix *(Anat)*

pêngo *pron/poss/refl* their own

pêngorró *nominalized pron* their own; **Ashilam amarênsa thai won gêlèntar pêngorrènsa.** We stayed (there) with our people and they left with their people/entourage.

péni *nm* penny *(British)*: *pl* **péni**

pênsilo *nm* ballpoint pen *(Am)*; **An mánge pênsilo te ramov lêsko número.** Get me a ballpoint to write (down) his (phone) number.

Pentekostálno *adj* Pentecostal

Pentekostálo *nm* member of the Pentecostal religion: *nf* **Pentekostaláika**

pênziya *nf* allowance, pension, old age pension/security *(Am)*

peradáika *nf* tomato: *pl* **peradéchi**

perado *pp/adj* **1)** felled, demolished, in ruins **2)** devastated

perádyol *vi* **1)** collapse, implode: *pp/adj* **peradilo; Perádilo o pódo.** The bridge collapsed. **2)** *(aircraft)*

peravel *vi* **1)** fell, chop down, demolish, destroy, knock down, tear down: *pp/adj* **perado; E kriyánga persadyas lês katar e zûn.** The branch knocked him from the saddle. **2)** drop, let fall, reduce in price, reduce (*sentence*) **3)** deflate, reduce in importance, reduce to impotence, destroy influence **4)** make/cause to collapse, implode **5)** cause to crash, shoot down (*aeroplane*), sabotage **6)** defeat, overthrow, surmount (*difficulties*) **7)** eliminate, eradicate, get rid of; **Músai te peravas e diskriminátsiya.** We must eliminate the discrimination. **8)** shed (*hair*); **O zhukel peravel pêske bal pe ponyáva.** The dog is shedding on the carpet. **9)** break camp, dismantle temporary construction like a carnival. **10)** dismantle, undo, wreck (*plans, etc*) **11)** ~ **mútsa** *comp/vt* drop anchor

perayimos *nm* **1)** felling (*trees*), leveling (*structure*), demolition. **2)** avalanche, collapse, implosion, landslide **3)** shooting down of an aeroplane **4)** crash (*of an aeroplane*) **5)** shedding (*hair, feathers*) **6)** elimination

pêrdál *adv* across, over, opposite (*Eur*) *see more common* **inkyal** *adv for Canada/US*

perel *vi* **1)** collapse, crash (*aircraft*), fall, stumble: *pp/adj* **pelo; Pelo ánde úlitsa.** He fell in the street. **Peli naswali e glatútsa.** The baby girl fell sick. **Pelo o póno pe amênde.** The plage struck/fell upon us. **2)** engulf, start, strike; **Pelo o marimos kána sámas ánde Itáliya.** The war started when we were in Italy. **3)** attack, fall upon (*us with* **pe**); **Le chor pele pe lêste ándo párko.** The muggers fell upon him in the park. **Pelo pe láte ánde ófisa.** He attacked her in the parlour. **4)** fail; **Pelo ánde pêski buki.** He failed in his work. **5)** turn out; **Chi pelo mánge mishto.** It didn't turn out well for me. *comp/vi* ~ **rêgáte** fall aside, be overlooked **6)** *comp/vi* ~ **tele** collapse, fall down, fall in ruins **7)** *comp/vi* ~ **mulo**

drop dead, fall dead (*psn*) **8)** *comp/vi* ~ **mulano** drop/fall dead (*animal*); **Pushkisardyas le ruves hai pelo mulano.** He shot the wolf and it fell dead. **9)** *comp/vi/phr* ~ **ánde kotorênde** fall to pieces; **Kodo phúrano kher perel ánde kotorênde.** That ancient house is falling to pieces.

pêríl *vt* **1)** steam cook, cook in a pressure cooker, stew: *pp/adj* **pêrimé 2)** scald **3)** *v/refl* **pêríl-pe a)** be scalded, scald oneself **b)** be steam-cooked

perimásko-pai *comp/nm* waterfall

pêrimé *pp/adj* **1)** steam-cooked **2)** scalded, disfigured by scalding

perimos *nm* **1)** crash (*aircraft*), downfall, failure, fall, fiasco **2)** chute, disposal chute **3)** shedding (*of hair/pelt, etc*)

pêrimós *nm* **1)** steam-cooking, cooking in a pressure cooker **2)** stew **3)** scalding

périna *nf* **1)** bedspread, coverlet, eiderdown **2)** blanket

periplékso *nm* plexiglass

péritsa *nf* diced potato, *us* plural in **péritsi**

pérla *nf* pearl. (*Am*)

pêrlíl/pîrlíl *vt* scorch, singe: *pp/adj* **pêrlimé**

pêrlimós *nm* scorching, singeing

permíto *nm* permit, driving licence, licence to run a business

pêrra *nf see* **pàrrâ** *nf*

persekútsiya *nf* persecution (*Eur*)

perúka *nf* wig: *pl* **perúchi**

pêrvimáta *nm/pl* priorities (*in an agenda, etc*)

pêrvimós *nm* priority

pêrvina *nf* beginning, commencement, start; **Ánde pêrvina, O Del kerdyas vyedyáriya.** In the beginning, God created light.

pêrvo *adv/adj* first, firstly, first of all (*Am*)

Pêrvo-Marimos *comp/nm* First World War

pêrvo-nav *nm* first name

pêrvo-thud *comp/nm* colostrum

pêrvo-xamos *nm* breakfast, brunch, first meal of a day

pês *pron/refl* himself, herself *see also* **pe** *pron/refl*

pêshtíri *nf* **1)** cave, cavern **2)** den/lair (*of a wild anmal*)

pêsko *pron/poss/refl* his own, her own

pêskorró *nominalized pron* his own, her own

pêstáika *nf* pea pod, pod: *pl* **pêstéchi**

petalári *nm* blacksmith who shoes horses, farrier

petalo *nm* horseshoe: *pl* **petala**; **petalóski-karfin** *comp/nf* horseshoe nail

petalol *vt* shoe (*a horse*): *pp/adj* **petalome**

petalomos *nm* shoeing of horses, art/process of shoeing a horse

petsíl-pe *v/refl* happen, occur, take place

peyápeno *nm* **1)** cantaloupe: *pl* **peyápenya**

pidálo *nm* pedal; **pidálo gasóski** gas pedal

pífo *nm* PIF (*personal information form for refugee claim*) (*Can*)

píko *adj* **1)** little, tiny (*Eur*) **2)** *nm/nf* little one (*child*) **3)** *nm* pick, plectrum **4)** awl, ice pick, prick paunch, scriber **5)** lance, poker, stabbing device, spear

pikópo *nm* pickup attachment/needle (*for stereo*)

pikyal *vi* **1)** drip, dribble, drool, drop, leak, spring a leak (*boat*): *pp/adj* **pikyailo**; **Pikyayas e ladjíya hai tasuli.** The boat sprung a leak and sank. **Pikyálas o kránto desar d'ekh kurko.** The tap has been leaking since a week ago. **2)** ooze

pikyayimásko *adj* **1)** dripping (*tap*), leaking (*roof*) **2)** oozing

pikyayimos *nm* **1)** drip, leak **2)** ooze

píldoro/pílduro *nm* pill in general, birth control pill, sleeping pill: *pl* **píldorya**; **Woi si po píldoro.** She is on birth control pills. **Trobul lês píldurya te sovél-pe.** He needs sleeping pills to fall asleep, **sovimásko píldoro** sleeping pill

piligránto *nm* pilgrim: *nf* **piligrantútsa**

piligrántsiya *nf* pilgrimage

pílo *nm* birth control pill (*Am*); **Woi si po pílo**. She is on the pill.

pilo *pp/adj* drained, drunk, used up, worn out *see* **piyel** *vt/i*

pilógo *nm* pestle

pilóto *nm* pilot

pimásko pai *comp/nm* drinking water

pimásko/piyimásko *gen/adj* absorbing, drinking

pimos *nm* **1)** drink, liquid refreshment **2)** alcoholic beverages **3)** dose (*medicine*)

pínda *num* fifty

pindáki *nf* fifty-dollar bill (*Am*)

pindáto *num* fiftieth

pingwíno *nm* penguin

píno *nm* **1)** tie pin/clip **2)** lapel pin, lapel badge of an organization. **3)** safety pin, straight pin **4)** pine tree

pinótso *nm* peanut (*Am*)

pipárka *nf* cayenne (*Cul*)

pipéri *nm* **1)** pepper (*Cul*) **2)** bell pepper, **gálbeno**, ~ yellow pepper, **lolo** ~ red pepper, **zéleno** ~ green pepper

pipiyil *vt* **1)** feel; **Tunyáriko sas hai pipisardem múrro drom pálpale.** It was dark and I felt me way back again. **2)** fondle, feel, paw (*at*): *pp/adj* **pipiyime 3)** diddle, grope, feel up, fondle sexually

pipiyimos *nm* **1)** fondling **2)** groping, touchy-feely

pipiyitóri *nm* groper, somebody who is always hands on *nf* **pipiyitórka**

pípota *nf* craw, gizzard: *pl* **pípotsi**

pirado *pp/adj* courted, sought after, wooed; **Kána símas ternyorri, símas, Dévla, shukarni, thai buté Rromêndar piradi.** When I was a young woman, God, I was beautiful and courted by many men. (*song*)

pirádyol *vi* be courted: *pp/adj* **piradilo**

piramni *nf* girlfriend, lover, sweetheart

piramno *nm* boyfriend, lover, suitor

piráta *nm* pirate *nm/nf*

piravel *vt* **1)** court, seek hand in marriage, woo: *pp/adj* **pirado 2)** *v/refl* **piravél-pe** court, date, pay attention to each other; **Piravél-pe lása.** He is dating her.

pirayimos *nm* courting, dating

piri *nf* cooking pot, pot (*in general*), crock; **Kiravel kolumpíri ánde piri.** She is boiling potatoes in the cooking pot.

pírohi *nm* dumpling

píroska *nf* dumpling

pírostya *nf* **1)** grating, grate **2)** barbeque, gridiron, grill **3)** tripod (*for stove*) **4)** trivet

pishkíri *nm* bathroom towel, towel

pishkirítsa *nf* small cloth, facecloth, paper towel

pishom *nf* **1)** flea **2)** insect

pishomalo *adj* **1)** infested with fleas **2)** flea-bitten

pishot *nm* bellows; **do-wasténg ~** two-handed bellows (*formerly used by Kalderash metalsmiths*), sometimes as **pishota** *nm/pl*

pishtálo/pishtólo *nm* hand gun, pistol

pishtóla *nf* **1)** spray painting gun. **2)** gas torch. **3)** welding torch **4)** caulking gun

písika *nf* pussey cat (*Eur*)

pistoléri/pistoléro *nm* gunman, hit man, shooter (*Am from Sp*)

pistóno *nm* piston

pítomo *adj* cultivated, gentle, docile, domesticated, tame; **pítomo grast** docile horse

pítomo-múra *comp/nf* strawberry: *pl* **pítomi-múri**

pitsagoi *nm* **1)** finch **2)** swallow

píva *nf* **1)** pestle **2)** beer

piyáno *nm* piano

piyátso *nm* market, plaza, square (*Eur*)

piyel/pel *vt/i* **1)** drink: *pp/adj* **pilo; Kon piyel desya but, xal pêsko shoro.** He who drinks too much, destroys himself. (*proverb*) **2)** drink a toast, toast; **Ame das pakiv kai Santána hai piyas láte ángla e khangeri.** We honour Saint Anne and we drink to her/toast her in front of the church. **3)** smoke (*tobacco*) **4)** absorb, soak up **5)** consume (*gasoline*), use, use up **6)** drain, drain off, suck up/out **7)** use (*drugs*) **8)** ~ **chuchi** breastfed, be breastfeeding **9)** ~ **rat** respect; **Pyav tyo rat.** I drink your blood/I respect you enormously **10)** ~ **yakha** adore, love; **Piyav ke yakha.** I drink your eyes/I love you **11)** ~ **zor** exhaust; **E buki pilas múrri zor.** The work has exhausted me.

11) ~ **balwal** breathe **11)** *v/refl* **piyél-pe** drink; **Piyél-pe ánde phuv.** He'll drink himelf into the ground/into his grave.

piyonéri *nm* forerunner, founder, pioneer: *nf* **piyonérka**

pîzníl *vt/i* **1)** cheep **2)** squeak

pîznimós *nm* cheap, squeak

plácha *nf* pleasure

placháko *gen/adj* having to do with pleasure, pleasurable

plachal *def/v* It pleases; **Plachal ma te ashunav kadya.** It pleases me to hear that. **Chi plachal ma gadya buki.** That thing doesn't please me. **Chi plachálas lês.** He wasn't pleased with it.

plafóno *nm* ceiling (*Eur*) **Nai lên plafóno opral lêngo shoro.** They have no roof over their head.

plai *nf* hillock, low hill

plaiying *nf* mountain

plaiyingáko *gen/adj* of a mountain; **plaiyingáko-murtáno** cougar, mountain lion (*Am*)

plaiyingalo *adj* hilly, mountainous

plakáto *nm* placard/poster (*Eur*)

pláko *nm* licence plate, plate, plaque (*Eur*)

pláncha *nf* clothes iron

planchil *vt* **1)** iron: *pp/adj* **planchime 2)** *v/refl* iron, be ironed

planchimáski-phal *comp/nf* ironing board

planéta *nf* planet

pláno *nm* **1)** blueprint, diagram, plan **2)** plot **3)** scheme

plánta *nf* **1)** plant (*flower, etc*) **2)** planted evidence (*Am*)

plantil *vt* plant (*evidence*): *pp/adj* **plantime** (*Am*)

plantimos *nm* planting (*of evidence*) (*Am*)

plapóno *nm* eiderdown, quilt, sleeping bag

plapóya *nm/pl* bedclothes (*Am*)

plasháto *adj* **1)** bald, balding *2) nm* bald-headed man: *nf* **plashatútsa**

plashatyárdyol *vi* be made bald : *pp/adj* **plashatyardilo**

plashatyarel *vt* cause loss of hair, make bald: *pp/adj* **plashatyardo**

plashátyol *vi* become bald, go bald: *pp/adj*
  plashatilo

plástiko *nm* plastic: *gen/adj* **plastikósko**

plastínka *nf* phonograph record

plastisína *nf* Plasticine, modeling clay,
  modeling putty (*Am*)

plastóri *nm* plaster

pláta *nf* fee, pay, wages (*Eur*)

platfórmo *nm* platform, stage set up on the
  ground, erected scaffold for workmen

pláto *adj* flat (*Eur*)

plátso *nm* **1**) town square, square (*Eur*) **2**)
  plaza, shopping mall/plaza (*Am*)

plázha *nf* beach

plêchka *nf* **1**) shoulder blade (*Anat*) **2**)
  shank (*of an animal*)

pléteri *nm/arch* strip of ribbon with small
  silver coins attached, wound around a
  woman's braids: *pl* **pléterya**

pléto *nm* licence plate (*Am*)

plevil/plivil *vt* **1**) float, launch, sail a boat:
  pp/adj **plivime 2**) fly (*flag*) **3**) *v/refl*
  plivíl-pe a) drift, float, sail **b**) flutter, fly
  (*flag*)

plevimos *nm* **1**) launching **2**) drift

pleyíl *vt* play: *pp/adj* **pleyime** (*Am*); **Na
  pleyisar gadya gili!** Don't play that
  song!

pleznil *vt* **1**) break/fracture, burst, crack,
  wrench out of joint, smash, split: *pp/adj*
  pleznime 2) destroy, ruin; **Pleznil pêski
  familíya.** He is destroying his family **3**)
  v/refl **plezníl-pe** become
  broken/burst/cracked/fractured/wrenched
  out of joint

pleznimos *nm* break/fracture, crack,
  dislocation, split

plivimásko kasht *comp/nm* **1**) driftwood **2**)
  floating logs

plócha *nf* **1**) flagstone **2**) tile

plochil *vt* **1**) cover with tiles, tile **2**) *v/refl*
  plochíl-pe be tiled, be able to be tiled

plochime *pp/adj* tiled, covered with tiles

plochimos *nm* tiling

plondjéri *nm* plunger (*for toilet*)

plópo *nm* poplar, poplar tree

plótska *nf* bottle of whisky presented to
  the father of the bride by the father of the
  groom at a betrothal. This is saved to be
  consumed at the wedding feast by the
  married couple, their parents and others
  of the wedding party. *see also* **kapára** *nf*

plúga *nf* plug *nf*

plugári *nm* driver of a plow/snowplow

plúga-yagáki *comp/nf* sparkplug

plugil *vt* **1**) plow/plough *pp/adj* **plugime 2**)
  plug in

plugimos *nm* ploughing

plúgo *nm* plow/plough, snowplow

plûmbo *nm.* bullet, shotgun shell; **kóvlo
  plûmbo** hunting/SP bullet

plúta *nf* raft, life raft

plútka *nf* small raft

plyásha *nf* bald head, bald spot

plyasháto/plasháto *adj* bald

plyashátyol *vi* become bald: *pp/adj*
  plyashatilo; **Plyashátilo kána sas térno
  Rrom.** He became bald when he was a
  young man.

po *prep cont of* **pe o**; **Beshel po shkamin.**
  He is sitting on the chair. **O parkimos si
  oxto tiléri po cháso.** The parking (fee) is
  eight dollars per hour. **Trayin po
  mangimos.** They live by/through
  begging. **Golo po táksi.** He went by taxi.

po cháso *comp/adv* in time, on time,
  punctually; **Avilo po cháso.** He came on
  time. **Av po cháso!** Come/be on time!

po drom *adv/phr* during the journay, on the
  road, while driving/traveling

po dúito *comp/adv* for the second time;
  Ansurime sas po dúito. He was married
  for the second time.

Po k'aver wast *comp/adv/conj/phr*
  alternatively, on the other hand; **Shai dav
  túke o chêko ages, wórka, po k'aver
  wast, shai dav túke le love ándo wast
  tehára.** I can give you a cheque now, or,
  alternatively, I can give you the money in
  cash tomorrow.

po kalo *comp/adv* on the sly, underground;
  Kerel buki po kalo. He works in the
  underground economy.

po mishtimos *adv* please; **De mánge pai po mishtimos!** Give me (some) water please!

po nevo *adv* anew. once again, once more

po than *comp/adv* **1)** on the spot. right here; **Mulo po than.** He died on the spot. **Khandel po than.** It smells around here. **Ash po than!** Stay right here! **2)** around the place, in this area; **Phirél-pe wárekai po than.** He's wandering around here somewhere.

po vucho nivélo *adv/phr* at/on a high level

pochitayil *vt* **1)** esteem, honour, respect **2)** *v/refl* **pochitayíl-pe** be esteemed/honoured/respected

pochitayime *pp/adj* esteemed, respected

pochitayimos *nm* dignity, esteem, respect; **pochitayimós-Rromano** Romani respect, respect for Romani customs and traditions

podárka *nf* gift, present (*Eur*)

pódo *nm* bridge

podrómo *nm* basement, cellar, underground vault

poéta *nm/nf* poet, romantic

poétiko *adj* poetic, romantic

poezíya *nf* poetry (*Eur*)

pofída *nf* allusion, hint

pófta *nf* **1)** appetite, craving **2)** delicacy **3)** item of gourmet food

poftári *nm* glutton, gourmand: *nf* **poftárka**

poftárniko *nm* **1)** living person or deceased relative in a dream with a craving for a certain food and who must be satiated; *nf* **poftarnikútsa 2)** *adj* exhibiting an unsatiated craving for a certain food

pogácha *nf* ash bread, homemade (unleavened) Kalderash bread

pogi *nf* **1)** sanitary napkin, tampon **2)** *arch*: type of underskirt

pogya *nf/pl* **1)** woman's panties **2)** skirt (*of a tent*) **3)** outskirts (*of a town*)

pohárro *nm var of* **porráro** *qv*

pokála/pûkála *nf* **1)** disgraceful behaviour, insult, obscenity, outrage **2)** period that a person is declared outcast by the *Kalderash* Tribunal, period of banishment

from the community for an offence against the laws of the Tribunal; **Dine lêske triné-shonêski pokála.** They imposed a three-month period of banishment from the community. **3)** black mark, stigma **4)** **kerel** ~ commit an indecent act, insult indecently

pokil *vt* **1)** honor financially, make financial restitution: *pp/adj* **pokime 2)** appease, honour (*debts*), pacify, settle (*debts/obligations*) (*Am*). **Pokisardyam godole Rromen.** We patched up our differences/gave satisfaction under Romani law to those Roma.

pokin *nf* pay, money earned, pay, payment

pokíndyol *vi* be financially reimbursed, be paid, pay: *pp/adj* **pokindilo**

pokinel *vt/i* **1)** pay, reward: *pp/adj* **pokindo 2)** rent or hire; **Pokinas avtobáso te anel le ka o mítingo.** We will rent (pay for) a bus to bring them to the meeting. **2)** ~ **pálpale** repay

pokinimos *nm* **1)** pay, payment **2)** salary **3)** mortgage payment **4)** installment; **shonênge pokinimáta** monthly installments/payments **5)** alimony

pokinitóri *nm* paymaster, person who pays bills or salaries

poklátka *nf* interior covering, lining (*of a garment*)

Poláko *nm* Pole: *nf* **Poláika**

Polichítska *nf* Polish (*Lang*)

Polichítsko *adj* Polish; **Rrom-Polichítsko** Polish Rom: *nf* **Rromni-Polichítsko:** *pl* **Rrom-Polichítska** Polish Roma

polintil *vt* apply balm, cream, polish, ointment: *pp/adj* **polintime**

polínto *nm* **1)** balm **2)** lotion **3)** polish **3)** cream, ointment

polítika *nf* politics

politikáko *genádj* of poltics, political

politikálno *adj* political; **adjénda politikálno,** political agenda

polítiko *nm* **1)** politics **2)** politician: *pl* **polítichi**

pológo *nm* netting, mosquito net, window screen

polokkorrês *adv* carefully, little by little, slowly; **mai ~** more carefully/slowly

polokorril *vt* **1)** reduce speed, slow down: *pp/adj* **polokorrime 2)** *v/refl* **polokorríl-pe** slow down

polokorro *adj* **1)** careful, slow

Pólska *nf* Poland

poltítsa *nf* poultice

pomáda *nf* **1)** facial **2)** beauty product, facial cream, hair styling

pomána *nf* **1)** period of mourning and remembrance for a deceased adult which can last one year but must follow in units of three, 3, 6, 9 or 12 months. **2)** solemn funeral feast, a table or feast given in honour of a deceased adult: *pl* **poméni 3)** *id* **xal ~** die; **Xalyas pêski pomána.** He ate his pomana feast/He died.

pomenáke-tsálya *comp/nf/pl* a complete outfit of clothing given to the person chosen to represent the deceased at a **pomána** feast table

pomenáki-síniya *comp/nf* table of the **pomána**

pomenáko *gen/adj* having to to with a **pomána**

pomenil *vt* **1)** hold a **pomána** for deceased family member, honour and pray for a deceased person, remember a deceased person: *pp/adj* **pomenime 2)** awaken/wake up, bring/come to one's senses **3)** *v/refl* **pomeníl-pe** come to one's senses, come to/regain consciousness, come out of *(a coma),* wake oneself

pomozhála *nf* **1)** aid, assistance, charity, help **2)** Social Assistance, Welfare **3)** co-operation

pomozhil *vt* **1)** aid, assist, help: *pp/adj* **pomozhime 2)** *v/refl* **pomozhíl-pe** help oneself, be helped

pomozhimos *nm* aid, assistance, help

pomózhnik *nm* **1)** assistant, helper, hired man, servant: *nf* **pomozhnikútsa** baby sitter, chambermaid, domestic, nursemaid **2)** waiter

pómpa *nf* **1)** pump *(automatic)* **2)** gas pump *(Am)* **3)** pageantry, pomp

pompéri *nm* fireman *(Eur)*: *nf* **pompérka**

pompil *vt* pump, run a pump: *pp/adj* **pompime**

ponalo *adj* infected with typhus/with the plague, suffering from plague/typhus

pôncho *nm* punch *(drink)*

ponil *vt* put, place: *pp/adj* **ponime** *(Am fr Sp)*; **Ponisár la kadka!** Put it right here!

pônko *nm* **1)** disreputable man, male punk, person without honor/respect: *nf* **pônkáika** *(Am)* **2)** thug

póno *nm* **1)** epidemic, infexious disease, typhus, plague **2)** disgust**; Che póno!** How disgusting!

ponyáva *nf* **1)** carpet: *pl* **ponyévi 2)** blanket

popíko *nm* top *(toy)*

Pópo *nm* Pope

populízmo *nm/neolog* populism

por/porr *nf* **1)** feather **2)** *arch* fountain pen, pen. quill; **Mai zorali e por la sabyátar.** The pen is mightier than the sword. **3)** plume

porano *adj* feathery, downy

pôrênchíl *vt* **1)** run *(things)*: *pp/adj* **pôrênchímé; Kon pôrênchíl o foro?** Who is running the city? **2)** be in charge of, command, keep order; **Wo pôrênchíl amári organizátsiya.** He is running our organization. **2)** recommend

porêngo *gen/adj* having feathers, feathered

pori *nf* **1)** tail **2)** handle, projecting handle *(as on a frying pan)* **3)** knob **4)** hilt **5)** *vi* **shinel e ~** cut off the tail/curtail the activities of somebody/put a stop to somebody's activities; **Shindem lêski pori.** That'll put an end to his monkey business.

pôrík *nm* currant, raisin

pórma *conj/adv* afterwards, then; **Xalem, pórma gêlém khere**. I ate, then I went home. **Dikhav lês akana thai pórma.** I see him now and then. **Pharrulo lêsko yilo, pórma mulo.** He had a heart attack, then he died.

pórma mai angle *conj/adv/phr* from then on, from that time onward

porradi *pp/adj* deflowered

porrado *pp/adj* **1)** openened, wide apart, spread-eagled; **porrade punrrênsa**, with legs wide apart **2)** erect (*as in erect penis*) **3)** rent asunder, split apart, split wide open **4)** ripped off, skinned alive, swindled

porrádyol *vi* **1)** become forced apart/ripped apart/torn to shreds: *pp/adj* **porradilo 2)** be raped, ravished **3)** become opened, open (*as a bud of a flower*), become loosened/unfastened/untied, become stratched, stretch **4)** be ripped off, swindled

porráro *nm* chalice, ewer, flagon, goblet, stein: *pl* **porrári**

Porráro-Sumakuno *comp/nm* Holy Grail

porravel *vt* **1)** create a fissure, force apart/open, make to open up/wide: *pp/adj* **porrado 2)** rend asunder, rip to shreds rip up, split apart **3)** distend, extend, stretch, stretch apart **4)** deflower, rape, ravish. **5)** *fig* defraud, fleece, gouge, rip off, skin alive, swindle; **Porradya lês e tsip.** He skinned him alive.

porrayimos *nm* **1)** crevasse, fissure, opening, split, a rendering asunder **2)** rip off, swindle **3)** *neolog* The Nazi Holocaust of the Roma

pôrrùl/pôrríl *vt* **1)** accuse, betray, denounce, inform on, rat on, squeal on, tattle: *pp/adj* **pôrrûmé**; **Pôrrûsardyás ka l' rai.** He squealed to the police. **2)** frame by falsely informing on, set *smbdy* up for a fall **3)** expose, finger **Pôrrùsardyás ma falshanes thai kerdyas fakalétso ánda mánde**. He accused me falsely and made a stooge out of me/set me up for a fall. **4)** *v/refl* **pôrrùl-pe** confess; **O chor pôrrûsáilo ka l' rai.** The thief confessed to the police.

pôrrûmásko *gen/adj* having a reputation for informing on; **~ Rrom, godo.** That Rom is a tattler.

pôrrûmé *pp/adj* **1)** betrayed, denounced, exposed, informed on **2)** framed

pôrrûmós *nm* **1)** betrayal, tattling **2)** confession **3)** framing

pôrrûtóri *nm* betrayer, informer, squealer, tattler: *nf* **pôrrûtórka.**

porselína/porseslána *nf* china

porselinári *nm* potter

portash *nm* caretaker, sexton

pórto *nm* dock, harbour, port (*Eur*); **portítsko hambári** dockside shed/warehouse

Portogála *nf* Portugal

Portogezítska *nf* Portuguese (*Lang*)

Portogezítsko *adj* Portuguese

Portogézo *nm* Portuguese man: *nf* **Portogezútsa**

portsûvóno *nm* **1)** bunch, bundle **2)** ration (*Eur*)

porum/porun *nf* onion

porumorri *nf* scallion, shallot

poryáki-harávli *comp/nf* crupper (*horse harness*)

poryalo *adj* long-tailed

pósha *nf* **1)** ascot, cravat, tie **2)** bandana, neck cloth/scarf

pósha-morkyáki *comp/nf* stole

póshta/pósta *nf* **1)** mail, postal service **2)** **trádel ánde ~** send by mail

poshtádjo/postádjo *nm* postage, cost of postage

poshtári *nm* postman: *nf* **poshtárka**

poshtin *nm* coat made of hide/skin

poshum *nf* wool

poshumalo *adj* wooly, having hair like a sheep

poshumêsko *gen/adj* woolen, made of wool

postárniko *adj* **1)** avaricious, greedy, rapacious, voracious **2)** *nm* greedy man: *nf* **postarnikútsa**

postávo *nm* **1)** cloth **2)** bedsheet, sheet

postil *vi* **1)** fast: *pp/adj* **postime 2)** *v/refl* **postíl-pe** fast, undergo a fast, be on a diet

Pósto *nm* **1)** Meatless Friday, Good Friday, Lent **2)** **pósto** abstention from animal products, fast, fasting **3)** hunger strike; **Le aktivísturya si po pósto.** The activists are conducting a hunger strike.

Pósto-Patragyáko *comp/nm* Lent
posuki *nf* **1)** pocket **2)** sac
posukyáke love *nm/pl* pocket money
posukyári *nm* pickpocket: *nf* **posukyárka**
potása *nf* **1)** potash, sodium hydroxide **2)** caustic soda
potrokol/potrokólo *nm* affidavit
potrowil *vt* **1)** avenge, pay back, take revenge: *pp/adj* **potrowime 2)** **potrowíl-pe** *v/refl* avenge oneself, take one's revenge
potrowimos *nm* revenge, vengeance
póxtan *nm* **1)** linen **2)** bedsheet **3)** sail of a boat/ship **4)** **fabric 5)** cloth, tent cloth
poxtanêsko *gen/adj* linen, made of linen
poxtan-thanêsko *comp/nm* bedspread
pozhárna *nf* fire engine, fire truck
pozhárniko *nm* fireman: *pl* **pozhárnichi**
pozítsiya *nf/neolog* position (*on an issue*)
pôzlé *adv* afterwards, later, later on (*us with* **mai**); **Dikhav lês mai pôzlé.** I'll see him later/ afterwards. (*Eur*)
pôzlo/pózno *adj* late
pozunári *nm* **1)** pouch **2)** pocket
prágo *nm* **1)** sill, windowsill **2)** porch **3)** threshold; **po prágo** on the threshold **4)** doorstep
praktikil *vt* **1)** practice: *pp/adj* **praktikime 2)** *v/refl* **praktikíl-pe** practice
práksiya *nf* practice
práma *nf* item, thing, jewel; **kuch ~** expensive jewel
pramáta *nf* profession
pramátno *adj* professional *nm* professional (person): **pramatnútsa** *nf*
prápta *nf see* **prévta** *nf*
prasádyol *vi* cause to be derided, heckled, made fun of, mocked, ridiculed, taunted
prasal *vt/i* deride, hackle, make fun of, mock, ridicule, taunt: *pp/adj* **prasailo; Prasayas man.** He mocked me. **Na prasa man!** Don't mock me!
prasamos/prasayimos *nm* derision, ridicule, mockery
prasavel *vt* cause to be derided, heckled, made fun of, mocked, ridiculed, taunted:

pp/adj **prasado; Prasadyas man.** He caused me to be ridiculed.
prasayimáski-chirikli *comp/nf* mocking bird
prashav *nm* **1)** rib: *pl* **prashave** (*Anat*) **2)** sparerib (*Cul*)
práskya *nf/arch* **1)** traditional wide leather waist belt of a *Kalderash* man, usually heavily ornamented **2)** belt/belt with pouches for money **3)** heavily decorated leather belt
práso *nm* leek
praspáto *nm* fresh, newly picked
prástal/prástel *vi* **1)** canter, trot, race, run: *pp/adj* **prastailo/prastino; O grast prastayas mishto.** The horse trotted well. **2)** jog, jog along, lope along
prastári *nm* sulky horse
prastimos *nm* **1)** cantering, trotting, running **2)** sulky race
pravárdyol *vi* be nourished/fed/ provided with nourishment/sustenance: *pp/adj* **pravardilo; Dav le grastênge dósta te pravárdyon.** I give the horses enough to keep them nourished.
pravarel 1) feed (*animals*): *pp/adj* **pravardo 2)** feed, nourish, provide for, take care of needs; **Zhav te pravarav le grasten/Zhav le grastênde.** I am going out to see to the horses. *id* polite way of saying I am going to the washroom. **Baryardem la hai pravardem la.** I brought her up and provided her with all her needs.
pravarimos *nm* **1)** animal feed, fodder **2)** care, nourishment
pravarno *nm* care giver, feeder, nourisher, provider: *nf* **pravarni**
Pravoslávniko *adj* **1)** Orthodox (*Christian*) **2)** Orthodox Christian *nm*: **Pravoslávnika** *nf*
Práxa *nf* Prague
praxalo *adj* dusty
práxo *nm* **1)** ash, ashes **2)** dust, grit, floor sweepings **3)** powder
praxol *vt* reduce to ashes/dust: *pp/adj* **praxome 2)** inter **3)** *v/refl* **a) praxól-pe**

become reduced to ashes/dust, turn to ashes/dust **b)** be interred

prázniko *nm* **1)** holiday in general, vacation: *pl* **práznichi 2)** religious feast or festival, religious holiday

predikatóri *nm* preacher, minister of the Romani Pentecostal religion

preferil *vt/i* prefer: *pp/adj* **preferime**

prefíkso-tilifonósko dialing code *(Eur)*

prekáza *nf* **1)** jinx, Jonah, misfortune; **Si ma prekáza pe mánde.** I've got a jinx on me. **2)** chastisement, curse, punishment, revenge/vengeance *(from beyond)*

prekazhil *vt* **1)** jinx, place a jinx: *pp/adj* **prekazhime 2)** curse **3)** *v/refl* **prekazhíl-pe** be jinxed, jinx oneself*)*

prekazhime *pp/adj* cursed, jinxed, punished

prekazhimos *nm* punishment from the afterworld, state of being jinxed

premenil *vt* change underwear

preminimos *nm* change of underwear

preminyála *nf* singlet and shorts, underclothing, underwear: *pl* **preminyéli**

prepedil *vt* **1)** annihilate, destroy, devastate, ruin, smash, smash up, wreck: *pp/adj* **prepedime; E treséniya sa prepedisardyas ándo kher.** The earthquake smashed up everything in the house. **2)** *v/refl* **prepedíl-pe** be annihilated, be destroyed, ruined, smashed, wrecked; **Prepedisáilo o mobíli.** The car was wrecked.

prepedimos *nm* crash *(of a vehicle)*, destruction, devastation, perdition, wreck

prepeditóri *nm* annihilator, destroyer, devastator, wrecker: *nf* **prepeditórka**

prepedyála *nf* accident, debacle, destruction, ruination, wreck

presentátsiya *nf/neolog* presentation

presentil *vt* present, offer *(to)*: *pp/adj* **presentime**

preskríptsiya *nf* prescription

presyáli *nf* **1)** butt *(of a pistol/revolver)* **2)** handle *(of a knife)* **3)** haft *(of a tool)*

prévta *nf* stair, step, stoop

prévti *nf/pl* stairs, stairway

preya *adv* too, too many, very; **preyá-but** too many/much, **preya zhene** too many people

prezénto *nm* present *(Am)*

prezérva *nf* jam

prezidênto *nm* president

pêznayíl *vt* **1)** celebrate/honour/respect a religious holiday or Holy Day: *pp/adj* **prêznayimé 2)** *v/refl* be celebrated/honoured/respected

prêznayimós *nm* **1)** celebration, observance, rite, respect of /for a holiday

priboi *nm* **1)** center punch, punch: *pl* **priba 2)** splitter, wedge

prícha *nf* disgust

prichimos *nm* **1)** idle chatter **2)** preaching, sermon, spiel *(Am)*

prichol *vt/i* **1)** chat, converse, talk: *pp/adj* **prichime** *(Am)* **2)** pontificate, preach, sermonize *(Am)*

primil/primisarel *vt* get, receive: *pp/adj* **primime/primisardo** *(Eur)*

primovára *nf* spring *(season)*

primúdjka *nf* **1)** revenge, reprisal, vengeance; **Devlêski primúdjka** Vengeance of the Almighty **2)** vcndetta

primúta *nf* revenge, reprisal, vengeance; **Lav múrri primúta pe lêste.** I'll get my revenge on him.

prindjardo *pp/adj* familiar, recognized

prindjárdyol *vi* be acquainted with/known, be recognized: *pp/adj* **prindjardilo; Vêstimé sánas ánde Rumúnya núma chi prindjárdyos ánde Kanáda!** You were famous in Romania but you are unknown in Canada!

prindjarel/prinzharel *vt/i* **1)** recognize, be familiar with: *pp/adj* **prindjardo; Prindjardem lês kai sláva.** I recognized him at the feast. **2)** know, be acquainted with, be known, have met; **Prindjarel tut o Bábi?** Does Bob know you? **3)** aclnowledge

prinzhanel *vt/i var of* **prinzharel** *vt/i qv*

prishkíri *nm* **1)** hose, hosepipe **2)** sprinkler system **3)** lawn sprayer

prishkiyil *vt* **1)** hose down, spray, sprinkle, splash, wash down (*automobiles, horses*): *pp/adj* **prishkiyime 2)** *v/refl* **prishkiyíl-pe** hose oneself, shower oneself, splash oneself

prishkiyimos *nm* car wash, hosing down, spraying, sprinkling, washing down

privátno *adj* private; **privátno phuv** private land/property

priváto *nm* private (*Mil*)

priyêteno *nm* **1)** male friend **2)** boyfriend (*Eur*)

priyoritéto *nm* priority

príza *nf* electrical power source, wall plug/socket

prizonéri *nm* prisoner: *nf* **prizonérka**

próba *nf* **1)** evidence, proof **2)** example, pattern, sample **3)** test

probil *vt* **1)** prove: *pp/adj* **probime 2)** sample **3)** *v/refl* **probíl-pe** be proven, prove oneself

probléma *nf* problem; **Manai probléma!** There is no problem!

prochênto *nm* **1)** percentage **2)** interest (*on loan*)

prochéso *nm/neolog* method, process

prodjékto *nm* project

prodjektóri *nm* movie projector

proféshono *nm* profession (*Am*)

profesóri *nm* **1)** professor, scholar: *nf* **profesórka 2)** expert; Romani man who works as an advisor/consultant (*Am*) see **drabarno** *nm* **3)** **profesóri le cherángo** *nm/phr* astrologer

profúndo *adj* deep, profound, thoughtful

programil *vt* **1)** program: *pp/adj* **programime 2)** *v/refl* **programíl-pe** be programmed

prográmo *nm* program

prográmo-buflyarimásko *comp/nm* outreach program

prográmo-edukatsyálno *comp/nm* educational program

prográmo-kulturálno *comp/nm* cultural program

prográmo-sportívo *comp/nm* sports program

promotil *vt* promote: *pp/adj* **promotime**

promótsiya *nf* promotion, publicity

propagánda *nf* propaganda

propertíya *nf* property (*houses, land*)

proposítsiya *nf/neolog* **1)** proposition **2)** sentence

proséso *nm* process (*Eur*)

prósti-gazhe *comp/nm/pl* **1)** non-Romani common people/working class **2)** proletariat (*Eur*)

prostil *vt* **1)** humble *smbdy*: *pp/adj* **prostime 2)** forgive, pardon **3)** *v/refl* **prostíl-pe a)** to humble oneself, become humble; **Prostisáilo ángla le Devlêste.** He humbled himself before God. **b)** be forgiven; **Prostisáilo Devlêstar.** He was forgiven by God.

prostime *pp/adj* **1)** humbled **2)** forgiven

prósto *adj* **1)** common, modest, ordinary, run-of-the-mill, simple **2)** low-class; **Chi zhav ándo kodo bírto, si phérdo prósti gazhe.** I won't go into that bar, it's full of low-class non-Roma. **3)** low grade (*ore, etc*) **4)** contrite, humble, meek; **Te aven lênge prósto o them kai xal katar kakya síniya.** May they become humble the Romani people who eat from this table (*benediction at a* **pomána** *table*).

prósto bírto *comp/nm* dive, dump, honky-tonk, low-class bar

prósto gazho *nm* common man, nobody of importance, ordinary Joe: *nf* **prósto gazhi**

prósto kúrva *comp/nf* common whore

prósto Rrom *nm* ordinary Rom, nobody of importance: *nf* **prósto Rromni**

prósto zakóno *nm* common law; **ándo prósto zakóno** under/in common law

próstone-zakonésko *comp/gen/adj* common law

prostováno *adj* **1)** basic, simple **2)** naïve man, simpleton: *nf* **prostovánka**

prósturya *nm/pl* common people/herd, the nobodies in society

protéktsiya *nf/neolog* protection

Protestánto *nm* **1)** Protestant: *nf* **Protestánka 2)** *adj* Protestant

protestil *vt* protest: *pp/adj* **protestime**

protestimos *nm* protestation. protesting

protésto *nm* demonstration, political protest

prótivo/prótiv *prep* against, up against; **Wo ashel prótivo o zudo.** He is standing against the wall. **San tu mánsa wórka prótivo mánde?** Are you with me or against me? **Me sim prótivo o marimos.** I am against the war.

protokólo *nm* protocol

providénya *nf* providence

Provínsiya *nf* Province (*Can*)

Provinsyáko *gen/adj* Provincial (*Can*)

provyantil *vt* **1)** provision, stock, supply **2)** *v/refl* **provyantíl-pe** stock up on provisions, supply oneself, provision oneself

provyantime *pp/adj* provisioned, stocked up on, supplied with

provyantimos *nm* provisioning, stockpiling

provyánto/prevyánto *nm* provisions, stock of food/supplies, supply

provyantóri *nm* provisioner, supplier

prozhéto/prozhêkto *nm* project (*Eur*)

prúna *nf* plum

prunelin *nf* plum tree

prushûk *nf* **1)** bread crumb, crumb **2)** *fig* crumb, scraps; **Woi lyas o báro téko hai shudyas mánge le proshûká!** She took the big score/profit and threw me the crumbs! (*Am*)

prya *adv* **1)** overly, very **2)** too many, too much **3) prya mishto**, very well.

púdra *nf* **1)** powder **2)** face powder

pudril *vt* powder, reduce to powder

pudrime *pp/adj* powdered, reduced to powder

pudyáriya/pudáriya *nf* strength, power: *pl* **pudyéri**; **Le Devlêski pudyáriya** The power of God

púfa *nf* **1)** crêpe **2)** flapjack, pancake

pûkála/pokála *nf* disgrace, insult, outrage

pûkelíl *vt* **1)** damn, make a person taboo, declare *smbdy* polluted: *pp/adj* **pûkelimé 2)** act indecently, commit an obscenity, insult, profane, outrage, moon. **3)** defile, contaminate, pollute **4)** declare to be in contempt of the Romani tribunal until the court's decision in the trial has been fulfilled, for instance, unwillingness to pay a fine imposed by the Tribunal to the plaintiff in the case. **5)** *v/refl* **pûkelíl-pe a)** act indecently, bring shame on the community or on an individual **b)** become defiled/polluted, damn oneself; **Arakh te na pûkelís-tut.** Watch out you don't become polluted/defiled **c)** ~ **ándo mui;** damn oneself by uttering a verbal obscenity before other Roma or by spreading lies about *smbdy*; **Pûkelisáilo ándo mui.** He defiled himself in the mouth/He spread false rumors and has been found guilty by the Tribunal.

pûkelimé *pp/adj* **1)** taboo **2)** damned, blackballed, contaminated, defiled, polluted, disgraced, socially ostracized **3) damned** (found guilty by the *Kalderash* Tribunal of obscene public behaviour). **Note:** In Canada/US a person cannot become **marime** *qv,* the term is **pûkelimé; marime** refers to substances capable of defiling human beings. However, a person declared **pûkelimé** by the Tribunal is capable of spreading this pollution to others by contact and in in this sense, **marime** or taboo. **Pûkelimé** also covers social behaviour and respect, the breaching of which are not **marime** offences but the offender can be declared **pûkelimé.**

pûkelimé-ándo-mui *pp/adj/phr* damned in the mouth, declared defiled because of spreading false rumors or using obscene language in front of Romani females

pûkelimós *nm* **1)** damnation, unacceptable or scandalous social behaviour **2)** period of contamination, pollution **3)** behaviour resulting in banishment from the community until reinstated **4)** obscenity, obscene behaviour

pulberil *vt* 1) cover with dust, make dusty, raise dust: *pp/adj* **pulberime** 2) *v/refl* **pulberíl-pe** become dusty

pulberimos *nm* 1) covering of dust 2) dust storm

pulbériya *nf* dust, granules

pulmóna *nf* lung (*Anat*): *pl* **pulmóni**

pulmonêngo naswalimos *comp/nm* emphysema

pulmoníya *nf* pneumonia

púlpa *nf* 1) loin, thigh (*Anat*) 2) haunch; **O ruv beshélas pe l' púlpi.** The wolf was squatting on (its) haunches.

pulpáko-kokalo *comp/nm* femur

púnkta/púnkto *nf* 1) point; **Kerav púnkta.** I make a point. **So si e púnkta?** What's the point? **Chi dikhes e púnkta.** You're missing the point. 2) *nf/neolog;* full-stop, period 3) **dui púnkti** colon

punktil *vt* get to the point, be more explicit; **Punktisáilo fugása.** He quickly got to the point.

punktime *adj* explicit, to the point; **Shai phenes mai punktime?** Can you be more to the point?

pûnrránd *prep* at the foot of; **pûnrránd o than** at the foot of the bed

pûnrranél *vt* remove shoes from somebody: *pp/adj* **punrrando**

pûnrrangló *pp/adj* barefooted, barefoot

pûnrrángyol *vi* remove one's shoes: *pp/adj* **pûnrrangiló**; **Pûnrrángilem mai anglal te zhav ándo kher.** I removed my shoes before entering the house.

pûnrró *nm* 1) foot (*Anat*) 2) leg, shank (*Anat*) 3) foot (*of the bed, etc*) 4) foot (*measure*) 5) **pe l' pûnrrènde** on foot

púnto *nm* deck, back veranda, deck of a ship (*Eur*)

pûnzhavóno/pûndjavóno *nm* spider

pûnzhavonósko thav *comp/nm* cobweb: *pl* **pûnzhavonênge thava**

pûnzheníl *vt* 1) cause to mildew/mould: *pp/adj* **pûnzhenimé** 2) develop verdigris 3) *v/refl* **pûnzheníl-pe** 1) become mildewed/mouldy, mildew 2) be affected by verdigris

pûnzhenimós *nm* mildew, moulding, verdigris

pûnzhenyála *nf* 1) mildew 2) mould 3) verdigris

púpo *nm* squatting; **beshel ~** sit squatting (*Eur*)

pupóza *nf* cuckoo

pupuyil *vt* 1) badmouth, slander: *pp/adj* **pupuyime** 2) badmouth 3) inform (*on*): **Pupuyisardyas pe mánde.** He informed on me. 4) *v/refl* **pupuyíl-pe** gossip, spread gossip/rumors

pupuyimos *nm* 1) gossip, rumors, slander 2) informing. squealing (*to the authorities*), tattling

pupuyitóri *nm* gossiper, spreader of rumors: *nf* **pupuyitórka**

Purgatóriya *nf* 1) Purgatory 2) *fig* miserable, subject to deplorable conditions; **Múrro tráyo si Purgatórya.** My life is Purgatory.

pûrr/pêrr *nm* belly, gut, intestines, stomach (*Anat*): *pl* **pûrr/pûrrá** bowels, guts, entrails, intestines, innards, offal

pûrraló/pêrraló *adj* 1) intestinal 2) pot-bellied

purun *nf* onion *var of* **porum/porun** *nf*

pûrûnchíl *vt see* **pôrênchíl** *vt*

pusadi *nf* hay fork, pitchfork

pusado *pp/adj* pentrated, pierced; **púsade kan** pierced ears

pusádyol *vi* be injected/gored/pierced/pricked/stabbed/stung: *pp/adj* **pusadilo**; **Pusádilo ándo marimos.** He was stabbed during the brawl.

pusavel *vt* 1) inject, gore (*bull*), penetrate, pierce, prick, puncture, stab, stick, sting (*wasp*): *pp/adj* **pusado; Pusadya lês e birobli.** The bee stung him. 2) bayonet 3) impale 4) jab, prod 5) *v/refl* **pusavél-pe** be injected, given a needle, get oneself stung, prick/stab oneself

pusayimos *nm* 1) injection, jab, piercing, prick, prod, stab, sting 2) flat tire, puncture 3) bayonetting

pushel *vt/i* 1) ask, ask for, implore, petition, request (*us with abl of object*): *pp/adj* pushlo; **Pushlem lêstar te gilabal.** I asked him to sing. **Pushlas azílo la Kanadátar.** He requested Convention-refugee status in /from Canada. **2)** apply (*for*) **3)** interrogate; **Le rai pushen lêstar.** The police are interrogating him. **4)** invite; **Pushlem múrra da te avel.** I invited my mother to attend. **Pushlem sa le Rromen te aven.** I invited all the Roma to attend. **5)** *vt/i* ~ **pála** ask about, check on, investigate; **O Fránki pushélas pála túte.** Frank was checking up on you.

pushimásko-sámno *comp/nm* question mark

pushimáta *nm/pl* interrogation, questioning

pushimos *nm***1)** invitation, petition, question, request **2)** application, claim

pushimós-azilósko *comp/nm/neolog* request for political asylum/refugee status

púshka *nf* firearm, gun, rifle

pushkári *nm* gunman, rifleman, hit man/torpedo (*Am*)

pushkárya *nm/pl* firing squad

pushkash *nm* gunsmith

pushkil *vt* **1)** gun down, execute by firing squad, shoot: *pp/adj* **pushkime; Pushkisardya la pa o shoro.** He shot her through the head. **Pushkidardem pa lêsko shoro.** I shot above/over over his head **2)** *v/refl* **pushkíl-pe a)** discharge accidentally **b)** shoot oneself

pushkime *pp/adj* executed, shot to death; **Pushkime sas katar le shingale.** He was shot to death by the police.

pushkimos *nm* **1)** barrage of gunfire, shooting, volley **2)** death/execution by shooting, murder by shooting

pushlino *nm* invited guest: *nf* **pushlini**

pushlo **1)** *pp/adj* asked for, invited, requested **2)** *nm* supplicant: *nf* **pushli**

púshlyol *vi* be invited: *pp/adj* **pushlilo; Chi pushlilem.** I wasn't invited.

pústik *nf/neolog* book

pustil *vt* **1)** abandon, desert, neglect (*property, land*): *pp/adj* **pustime 2)** *v/refl* **pustíl-pe** become abandoned/deserted/disused; **Pustisáilo kána sas shavorro.** He was abandoned when he was a child.

pustime *pp/adj* abandoned, deserted, neglected; **phurano pustime kher** an old abandoned house

pustimos *nm* abandonment

pustíya *nf* **1)** desert, desolate region, wasteland **2)** Dust Bowl (*Am*)

pustiyála *nf* abandonment, desolation

pústo *adj* abandoned, deserted, desolate, disused

pústo–than *comp/nm* abandoned area, desert, wasteland

pustyála *nf* abandonement, desertion, desolation

putrokóla *nf* grapefruit

puxalo *adj* covered with down, downy

púxo *nm* **1)** down, fuzz **2)** lint

púya *nf* **1)** chick, young chicken **2)** *sl* chick, non-Romani girlfriend, non-Romani groupie (*Am*)

puyil *vt see* **ampuyil** *vt*

púyo *nm* a newly born or very young offspring of animals and fowls: *pl* **púyurya**: *nf* **púya**

púzho *nm* shell (*of a snail, mussel, etc*)

pwárta *nf* **1)** gate, entry wicket (*to subway, etc*) **2)** barrier

pyêrsichelín *nf* peach tree

pyêrsika *nf* peach: *pl* **pyêrsichi**

PH

phabai *nf* apple: *pl* phaba

phabardo *pp/adj* 1) burned, burned out, burnt 2) dissipated, spent, used up, wasted, worn out

phabárdyol 1) become/get burned, be consumed by fire/cremated: *pp/adj* phabardilo 2) become used up/worn out, be consumed/wasted 3) become dissipated/exhausted

phabarel *vt* 1) burn, burn up, cremate, incinerate, set alight/light, smoke up: *pp/adj* phabardo 2) finish off/up, use up, waste, wear out, overtax, exhaust; **Phabardem le sya.** I used them all up. 3) shine; **O Kham phabarel.** The sun shines/is shining: *Note: In Kalderash, transitive verbs used without an object can be considered to be transitive absolutes.* 4) consume, use up, ruin (*business*) 5) afflict, affect, hurt, scar emotionally, leave scars; **O marimos phabardyas amen.** The war left us with deep scars. **Phabardyas lêsko yilo.** She burned his heart/left him with deep, emotional scars. 6) scald, leave burning sensation. **Phabarel lês o muter**. He has gonorrhea/urine burns him. 7) excite/arouse sexually 8) excite, exacerbate, rev up; **Phabarel ma e rrakíya**. The whisky is burning me up/exacerbating my anger. **Phabarel e matóra**. He is revving up the engine. 9) cauterize 10) burn (*a C.D.*) 11) *v/refl* phabarél-pe dissipate oneself, burn oneself out, overtax oneself, waste oneself, wear oneself out.

phabarimásko *gen/adj* combustible, inflammable

phabarimáta *nm/pl* burnt remains, charred remnants, remains of a house that burned down

phabarimos *nm* 1) bonfire, conflagration, holocaust, fire, inferno 2) cremation 3) arson 4) cauterization 5) combustion

phabaritóri *nm* arsonist, firebug

phabaritóriya *nf* crematorium

phabelin *nf* apple tree

phabêngi-mol *comp/nf* apple cider

phabêngi tórta *comp/nf* apple pie. (*Eur*).

phabêngo *gen/adj* apple, made of apples

phabêngo-músto *comp/nm* apple juice

phabol *vi* 1) burn: *pp/adj* phabulo; **O kher phabol.** The house is burning. **Phabulo o bírto.** The bar burned down. 2) get burned/ripped off/tricked; **Chi mangav te phabuvav.** I don't want to get burned. (*Am*) 3) singe *with* tsîrrá; **Phabulo tsîrrá múrro gad.** My shirt got a little singed. 4) ~ choryal smoulder; **E yag phabólas choryal.** The fire was smouldering. 4) shine (*sun*)

phaborri *nf* crab apple, small apple

phabulo *pp/adj* burnt, singed

phagel *vt* 1) break, crack, fracture, snap: *pp/adj* phaglo; **Phaglas pêsko wast.** He broke his arm. **Phaglas pêsko shoro.** He cracked his skull. 2) discipline, break in, train (*horses, dogs*) 3) deflower (*a bride/lover*) 4) assuage, quench 5) ~ andre break in, burglarize 5) ~ e dar, overcome fear, gain courage 6) ~ e shib become fluent (*in a language*); **Músai te phagel e shib.** He needs to break in/train his tongue/start speaking the language to become fluent.

phagimásko *gen/adj* breakable, fragile, trainable

phagimos *nm* break, fracture, training

phagles *adv* brokenly, ungrammatically, in another dialect; **Del-duma phagles.** He speaks ungrammatically.

phaglo *pp/adj* broken, fractured, snapped

pháglyol *vi* become/get broken, break/fall apart, come apart: *pp/adj* **phagilo**; **Pakisar la mishto te na pháglyol!** Pack it well so it doesn't get broken!

phak *nf* wing (*bird or aircraft*), fin/scale (*fish*)

páko /**pheyáko** *pron/gen* belonging to a sister, sister's; **Múrro páko shav si.** He is my newphew.

phal *nf* **1**) board, plank **2**) thwart (*of a boat*) **3**) slat

phaleya *nf/pl* floor, floorboards, planking

phaleyángo *nm gen/adj* made of planks

phalorri *nf* batten, narrow plank

phandadyá-gogyáko *comp/gen/adj* closed-minded

phandádyol *vi* be arrested/detained/enclosed/imprisoned/impounded/padlocked/locked up/shut in/up: *pp/adj* **phandadilo**; **Phandádilo**. He was arrested/imprisoned/taken into custody.

phandavel *vt* **1**) enclose, corral, padlock, shut in: *pp/adj* **phandado 2**) impound **3**) arrest, detain, imprison/incarcerate, lock up, take into custody **4**) block, close off; **Phandade e úlitsa.** They blocked the street **5**) close, place off limit, shut down; **Phandade amáre ófisi.** They shut down our parlours. **6**) *comp/vt* ~ **o fóro** close a town, place a town off limits to other Roma by a local Romani leader. **7**) ~ **droma** close roads back (*of the dead*); **Te yertil lês o Del hai te phandavel lêske droma!** May God pardon him and close his roads back (so that he may not return from the dead). (*Benediction said at the graveside*)

phandayimos *nm* **1**) corral **2***)* arrest, confinement, incarceration, detention **3**) dead end

phandel *vt/i* **1**) clamp (*shut*), close, cork, fasten, plug, shut, stop, terminate (*deal*): *pp/adj* **phanglo 2**) buckle (*belt*), connect, bind up, join (*together*), tie; **Phanglem o wudar.** I closed the door. **3**) apply (*brakes*); **Phanglem le frénurya.** I applied the brakes **4**) clench (*fist*), crease, cross (*arms, legs*), fold **5**) contract **6**) hang up (*phone*) turn off (*lamp*) **6**) block, jam; **Phanglo o tázo.** The sink is blocked. **7**) ~ **kómbo** tie a knot, knot

phandimásko *gen/adj* closing; **phandimáske swáturya** closing address/words

phandimos *nm* **1**) bond **2**) fastening **3**) detention, prison **4**) gridlock **5**) enclosure, fold, pen

phangli *nf* bolt (*for a door*)

phanglilo-ándo-gi *adj/phr* **1**) constipated **2**) colicky

phanglimos **1**) arrest, confinement **2**) detention, imprisonment **3**) gridlock, traffic jam **4**) blockage

phanglimos-ándo-gi *nm/phr* **1**) constipation **2**) colic

phanglo *pp/adj* **1**) closed (*door*), bound, bound up, hogtied, tied up; **wast phanglo kai gorr** arm in a sling **2**) blocked, jammed

pánglyol *vi* **1**) become bound up/delayed/tied/tied up/restricted/stuck (*in traffic*): *pp/adj* **phanglilo 2**) **phanglyol ando gi** *vi/phr* become constipated

phanrr *nm* silk

phanrrêsko *gen/adj* made of silk

phanrruno *adj* silk, silken

pharé-yilésa *id* with a heavy heart, full of sadness

phari *adj* **1**) pregnant, heavy (*with child*). It is considered impolite to use **phari** with Roma referring to a Romani woman. The polite way to express this is **Avel la gláta akanash**, A baby is coming to her soon, or **Woi si kodolátar**. She is like that (*expecting*). It can be used for animals; **E**

grasni si phari, The mare is pregnant. **2)** *nf* pregnant women or animal

pharimása *nm/instr* with difficulty/hardship

pharimáta *nm/pl* **1)** burdens, cares, difficulties, hardships, worries **2)** emotional issues

pharimos *nm* **1)** affliction, burden, cross to bear, difficulty, hardship, heaviness, load, weight, worry: *pl* **pharimáta 2)** pregnancy **3)** melancholia

pharno *nm* baby's diaper: *pl* **pharne** diapers, swaddling clothes

pharo *adj* **1)** boring, heavy **2)** arduous, difficult, hard, strenuous; **phari buki** hard work **Pharo mánge te kerav.** It's difficult for me to accomplish. **Sas man pharo.** It wasn't easy for me. **3)** grave; **pharo strazhnimos** grave danger **4)** strict (*law*); **phare zakóya** strict laws **5)** awkward, clumsy; **Pharo si te mukis gadya láda.** That trunk is awkward to move around.

pharo pe yekh rêg *adj/phr* lopsided, overly loaded on one side

pharol *vi* **1)** become heavy: *pp/adj* **pharilo 2)** become pregnant; **Pharili.** She became pregnant.

pharradé-yilêsko *comp/gen/adj* broken-hearted

pharrado *pp/adj* **1)** broken up/apart, demolished, shattered **2)** *with* **do-pash**; **do-pash pharrado** dilapidated, half in ruins **2)** ripped to pieces/shreds

pharrádyol *vi* **1)** be blown apart, become demolished/shattered/smashed, break apart, blow up, explode into fragments, split apart/up: *pp/adj* **pharradilo 2)** be/become burst be broken apart/fissured/split; **Pelo pe l' phaleya hai pharrádilo.** It fell on the floor and burst apart. **3)** break up (*husband/wife*) **4)** be/become reduced to shreds/tatters; **Pharrádili lênge tséra ánde furtúna.** Their tent was ripped to shreds during the storm. **5)** crash; **Pharrádilo lêsko mobíli.** His car crashed.

pharravel *vt* **1)** break, break/blow apart, break into pieces, break up, demolish, destroy, explode, shatter, smash, split apart/open, tear apart, wreck: *pp/adj* **pharrado**; **Pharradyas e fénda pa pêsko mobíli.** He tore the fender off his car. **Pharradyas man o yilo.** She broke my heart. **Pharradyas e filástra.** He broke the window. **Pharradyas o mobíli.** He wrecked the car. **2)** break up (*fight*), make to cease **3)** crash, smash into; **Pharradyas aver mobíli.** He crashed (into) another car. **4)** deflower, ravish, rupture **5)** blow up, detonate **6)** cut/rip to shreds, reduce to splinters, reduce to tatters, tear apart/up

pharrayimáta *nm/pl* **1)** debris, remains, shattered remains **2)** rags and tatters

pharrayimos *nm* **1)** crash, destruction, demolition, wreck; **mobilésko ~** car crash (*single car*) **mobilêngo ~** smashup involving two or more cars, **vaporiyêsko ~** shipwreck **2)** crack, fissure **3)** debacle, disaster **4)** explosion, outburst; **pharrayimos branimáta** outburst of objectioins

pharrimos/pharromos *nm* **1)** blast, detonation, explosion **2)** volcanic eruption **3)** shock

phárruli-shûna *comp/nf* blowout, flat tire

pharruvel/pharrol *vi* **1)** burst, disintegrate, fall apart, fall to pieces, fade away, split apart: *pp/adj* **pharrulo**; **Kam-merel thai pharruvel.** He will die and disintegrate. **2)** blow up, explode, die from shock, go into shock; **Pharruli hai muli.** She had a shock and died. **Mai do gáta pharrulem.** I almost died from shock. **Pharrulo lêsko yilo.** His heart blew up/He had a heart attack. **Pharruli lêski gogi.** He has a nervous collapse/breakdown. **Pharrule lêske pendíksurya.** He had a pendicitis. **Pharrulo o bov.** The furnace blew up. **Pharruli múrri shûna.** My tire blew out. **3)** expire, decay, die, perish; **Kam-merávtar thai pharruváva.** I shall die and disintegrate. (*song*) **4**) erupt (*volcano*)

pharyárdyol *vi* become pregnant/impregnated: *pp/adj* **pharradilo**

pharyarel *vt* **1**) increase load, make heavy *pp/adj* **pharyardo 2**) make difficult/hard **3**) impregnate, make pregnant **4**) stud (*animals*)

phendino *pp/adj* admitted, said, stated, quoted

phéndyol *vi* It is said, stated: *pp/adj* **phendilo**; **Sar phéndyol.** As it is said, as they say, so it is said; **Le Rroma aven ánda Índiya, sar phéndyol.** The Roma come from India, so it is said.

phenel *vt/i* **1**) imply, narrate, relate, say, state: *pp/adj* **phendo; Chi phenes!** You don't say! **Phendem lêske me.** I told him so. **2**) announce, tell; **Phen te manges xabe.** Say/tell if you want food. **3**) declare, state **4**) *v/refl* **phenél-pe** imply, mean, signify; **So phenél-pe godo swáto?** What does that word mean? **So phenés-tu godolêstar?** What do you mean by that?

phênga/phènkê *verbal* said, quoth; **"Kai zhas?" Phendem.** "Where are you going?" I said?. **"Zhav khere," phênga-wo.** "I'm going home," said he.

phenimos *nm* adage, proverb, saying

pherdo *pp/adj* **1**) filled, full, full of, complete **2**) full of, infested with, invaded by, overgrown by; **O kámpo si phérdo shobolánya.** The (refugee) camp is infested with rats. **3**) charged, loaded, loaded with; **Pherdo love si.** He's loaded with money.**E púshka nai pherdi.** The gun is not loaded. **4**) padded, stuffed; **O sherand si pherdo poránsa.** The pillow is stuffed with feathers. **pherdo wusharimos** padded upholstery

phérdyol *vi* **1**) be filled, be fulfilled, fill: *pp/adj* **pherdilo 2**) become full of/infested with, be invaded by/overgrown with **3**) become recharged/reloaded (*battery, gun, etc*)

pherel *vt/i* **1**) fill, fill up: *pp/adj* **pherdo 2**) complete, fulfill **3**) load, charge (*battery*) **4**) pack, stuff; **Pherdyas lêsko shoro dilimatánsa.** She stuffed his head with crazy ideas. **5**) pass/spend (*time*) **6**) cover with; **Pherdem la galbênsa.** I covered her with gold coins. **7**) infest

pherimáta *nm/pl* filling, padding, stuffing

pherimos *nm* **1**) fulfillment, filling, filling of a tooth **2**) charge (*battery*) **3**) padding, stuffing; **tudkaláko-pherimos** turkey stufffing **4**) load, loading

phey *nf* **1**) sister; **Maládilem lêska phása ánde últisa.** I met his sister in the street. **2**) *fig* Romani sister

pheyimos *nm* sisterhood

Phéyo! *nf/voc* Sister!

phiko *nm* **1**) back (*Anat*) **2**) shoulder (*Eur*)

phiradi *nf* **1**) seductress, vamp **2**) flirt, man chaser

phirado *pp/adj* **1**) worldly, experienced (*in life*); **Nai dilo, phirado si.** He's not stupid, he's wise in the ways of the world **2**) *nm* **a**) man experienced in the ways of the world: *nf* **phiradi b**) flirt, woman chaser: *nf* **phiradi** flirt, man chaser

phiravdo *adj* **1**) nomadic, traveling **2**) *mn* male nomad, traveler: *nf* **phiravdi**

phiravel *vt* **1**) walk along/around, explore by taking a walk around, take a promenade: *pp/adj* **phirado 2**) show a guest around, take *sombdy* for a walk, walk, take on a tour **3**) wear (*clothes*); **Phirav lên sastimása!** Wear them with health! **4**) trample on, walk on; **Le grast phirade pe lêste.** The horses trampled on it. **5**) march **6**) *v/refl* **phiravél-pe a**) walk, walk around, travel; **Phiravél-pe po drom sórro ges.** He walks on the roads all day long **b**) hang around, prowl, slink around; **Le ruva phiravénas-pe kruyal le tsêri.** The wolves were prowling around the camp. **Phiravél-pe wárekai.** He's prowling/slinking around somewhere. **7**) amuse oneself; **Shavorrále! Zhan phiravén-tumé**

wárekai! Kids! Go amuse yourselves
somewhere!
phiravo *nm* **1)** hiker, traveler, walker: *nf*
phiravni 2) womanizer: *nf* **phiravni**
man-chaser
phirayimos *nm* hiking, roaming around,
wandering around
phirel *vt/i* **1)** journey, march, travel, walk:
pp/adj **phirdo; Phirdyas ánde but
thema.** He has travelled in many
countries. **2)** strive (*te be*); **Me phirav te
avav sar múrro dad.** I will strive to be
like my father **3)** run on, operate by;
Phirel po ilêktriko. It runs on electricity.
4) *comp/vt* ~ **pála** walk after, come on to
smbdy; **Kadya rakli phirel pála mánde.**
That girl is coming on to me. **5)** *v/refl*
phirél-pe get around, go around, lurk,
roam around, stroll around; **Kodo Rom
phirél-pe.** That Rom gets around/goes
around with many women. **Phirél-pe
ándo fóro.** He's roaming around the city.
phirimásko *gen/adj* traveling, roving,
wandering
phirimos *nm* **1)** journey, traveling, walk,
wandering **2)** outing **3)** promenade, walk;
Zhas po phirimos! Let's go for a walk!
4) *comp/vi* zhal po ~ take **a)** go for/take a
walk **b)** go on an outing
phiritóri *nm* rover, traveler, wanderer: *nf*
phiritórka
phiriyása/phiriyas *nf* **1)** amusement, fun,
joke; **Kerdyas phiriyása pe mánde.** He
played a joke on me. **Keráva mánge
phiriyása túsa.** I'm joking with you.
Amboldya lês ánde phiriyása. He
turned it into a joke. **2)** amusement,
entertainment **3)** *comp/vi* kerel ~
entertain, provide amusement; **Keras
piriyása le gostônge.** We will provide
entertainment for the guests.
phiriyasalo *adj* amusing, entertaining,
funny
phirutno *nm* traveler, voyager: *nf* **phirutni**
phivli *nf* widow
phivlimos *nm* widowhood
phivlo *nm* widower

phivlyárdyol *vi* be made a widow: *pp/adj*
**phivlyardili; Phivlyárdili de pansh
bersh.** She became a widow five years
ago.
phivlyarel *vt* widow, make *smbdy* a widow:
pp/adj **phivlyardo**
phral *nm* **1)** brother **2)** *fig* bro, fellow
Romani man
phralêsko *pron/gen* belonging to a brother,
brother's
phralikanes *adv* brotherly, fraternally
phralikano *adj* brotherly, fraternal
phralimos/phralipe *nm* brotherhood and
sisterhood, fraternity, solidarity/unity
among Roma
phub *nf* **1)** pus, suppuration **2)** cyst
phubalo *adj* infected with pus
phubilo *pp/adj* suppurated
phubimos *nm* suppuration
phubyarel *vt* cause to fester/supperate,
cause pimples
phubyarimos *nm* festering, suppuration
phúbyol *vi* become covered with zits, form
pus, suppurate: *pp/adj* **phubilo**
phugni *nf* blister, boil, pimple
phugnyalo *adj* covered with
blisters/pimples/zits, pimply
phugnyol *vi* become covered with
pimples/zits: *pp/adj* **phugnilo**
phukyal *vi* **1)** become/get bloated, become
blown up/distended, become
inflated/swollen, expand: *pp/adj*
phukyailo 2) bluff, boast **3)** exaggerate
phukyardo *adj* conceited, exaggerated,
inflated
phukyárdyol *vi* become blown up/
distended/inflated/swollen/exaggerated:
pp/adj **phukyardilo**
phukyarel *vt* **1)** blow up, inflate, make to
swell, make expand: *pp/adj* **phukyardo
2)** persuade, urge (*on*) **3)** exaggerate **4)**
cheer on, encourage **5)** *v/refl*
phukyarél-pe boast, exaggerate, show
off
phukyarimos *nm* **1)** inflation, swelling **2)**
obstentatious behaviour, self-promoting
behaviour **3)** exaggeration **4)** bluff

phúrane-sastrya *com/nm* scrap iron

phuranes *adv* as formerly, in the old way, formerly, previously

phuranimos *nm* antiquity

phúrani-práma *comp/nf* antique: *pl* **phurané-prámi**

phurano *adj* 1) ancient, antique, archaic,old (*for inanimates*), olden; **Bikinel phúrane-prámi.** He sells old things/antiques. **Phurano kher si.** It's an old (*decrepit*) house. 2) former, previous, *often with* **mai**; **le phurane thema** the old countries/previous countries of residence, **le phúrane gesa** the old days, **le phurane droma** the old ways/customs, **e phúrani shib** the older form of (Romani) speech, **e mai phurani bori** the previous/former daughter-in-law, **ánde l' phurane gesa** in former times

phurano mobíli *nm* jalopy, old car, rent-a-wreck

phurarel *vt* 1) age, make obsolete/old: *pp/adj* **phurardo** 2) make outdated, render obsolete

phurdayimos *nm* blow, strong wind force

phúrdel *vt/i* pant, breathe, blow, exhale, gasp, puff: *pp/adj* **phurdino**; **Phúrdel e balwal.** The wind is blowing.

phurdimos *nm* 1) breath, gasp, puff; **phurdimos balwal** of wind 2) breathing, respiration, respiratory system

phurdini *nf* 1) peashooter (*Am*) 2) weasel (*Eur*)

phurdino *pp/adj* blown, blown away

phúrdyol *vi* 1) be blown, blown away: *pp/adj* **phurdilo** 2) breathe

phuri *nf* elderly lady, female elder, matriarch

phurikanes *adv* formerly, in the past; **Trayil phurikanes.** He's living in the past.

phurikano *adj* ancient, erstwhile, former, old fashioned

phurimásko *gen/adj* of the old, belonging to the old, past, former; **O tráyo phurimásko.** The old way of life.

phurimáta *nm/pl* antiques, old things, old ways

phurimos 1) age, old age 2) elder status 3) maturity 4) the old ways, past

phuro *adj* 1) aged, old (*for animates*) 2) *nm* elder, old man, patriarch

phúro them *nm* elders, elderly people, senior citizens

phurt *nf* footbridge

phurya *nf/pl* elderly/older women, female elders, matriarchs

phuryárdyol *vi* be made old/aged: *pp/adj* **phuryardilo; Phuryárdili e mol.** The wine has been aged

phuryarel *vt* 1) age, cause to grow old, make old: *pp/adj* **phuryardo** 2) make dated/obsolete 3) age (*wine*)

phuryol *vi* 1) grow/become old: *pp/adj* **phurilo** 2) become dated 3) age (*wine*)

phuryóltar *vi* grow old and feeble, become helpless with old age, pass into old age; **Phurilémtar thai diláilem.** I grew old and senile.(*song*)

phus *nm* straw, thatch

phusutno *adj* straw, thatched; **phusutno taváno** thatched roof

phuterdyá-gogyáko *comp/adj* open-minded

phuterdes *adv* openly

phuterdo *pp/adj* loosened, opened, opened up, spread open, unbraided, unclogged, untied

phutérdyol *vi* 1) be opened, come ajar, open: *pp/adj* **phuterdilo; Phutérdilo o wudar.** The door opened on its own. 2) become unblocked, unclogged, untied 3) begin, start; **Chi phutérdyilo inka o ges.** The day hasn't started yet. **Kána phutérdyol o spektákulo?** When does the show start? 4) be dismantled, taken apart 5) be cut open, operation on

phuterimásko *gen/adj* opening; **phuterimáske swáturya** opening address

phuterimos *nm* 1) clearing, opening 2 *nm/phr* **phuterimos le paiyêngo le mulêngo** opening of the waters of the

dead (*ceremony to ensure that a deceased psn will have water in the afterlife*);
phuterimos ándo wêrsh, forest glade

phutrári *nm* **1)** opener, can opener, letter opener **2)** doorman

phutrel *vt/i* **1)** open: *pp/adj* **phuterdo; Phuter o wudar!** Open the door! **Te phutrel pêsko drom ángla lêste hai te avel ángla lêste pai ándo Rrayo!** May his road open before him and may he be provided with water in Heaven! (*Benediction said at the ceremony of the opening of the waters of the dead three days after death*) **2)** clear, release, undo, unlock, untie, unwrap **3)** open wide, spread (*arms, legs*) **4)** switch on, turn on, start **5)** let down, comb out, spread out **6)** unblock, unclog **7)** dismantle, take apart **8)** cut open, operate on **9)** with **hámo** *nm*, remove harness, unharness

phuv *nf* earth, country, ground, land, land holding, property

phuv-xali *comp/nf* worn out land, Dust Bowl (*Am*)

phuvyáko *gen/ádj* of the earth/ground; **gazhe phuvyáke,** men who work underground, sewer maintenance workers

R

rábeno *nm* rabbi
radéri *nm* radar, radar trap
rádiyo *nm* radio
radiyútso *nm* portable radio/tape player
rádo *adj* joyous, proud
rádosta *nf* **1)** delight, joy **2)** pride
radóstar *nf/abl/adj* gladly, happily, proudly, willingly; **Kerav radóstar.** I'll gladly do it.
rádostiya *nf* **1)** happiness, joy **2)** pride
raduyil/raduwil *vt* make to rejoice, gladden, make joyful, make proud: *pp/adj* **raduyime 2)** *v/refl* **raduyíl-pe a)** express joy, rejoice **b)** be glad **c)** be proud of/take pride in
raduyimástar *adv/nm/abl* from joy, gladly, joyfully
raduyimé *pp/adj* **1)** delighted, gladdened, overjoyed **2)** proud
raduyimos *nm* **1)** joy, rejoicing **2)** pride
rádyo *nm* radio (*Eur*)
radyográfo *nm* X-ray
radyútso *nm* portable radio
rafin *nf* spine, spinal column (*Anat*)
rafináko *gen/adj* dorsal, spinal
ragátka *nf* sling (*for throwing stones*)
rai *nm* **1)** aristocrat, gentleman, member of the nobility: *pl* **rai** *less often* **ra**; **De skamin le ras!** Offer the gentleman a chair! **2)** constable, cop on the beat, municipal police officer **3)** *nm/pl* nobility, upper class **4)** *nm/pl* police, police force
ráikane tsáliya *comp/nf/pl* formal wear
raikanes *adv* **1)** courteously, gentlemanly, nobly **2)** elegantly
raikano *adj* **1)** aristocratic, courteous, dashing, dignified, noble **2)** elegant, fancy
raikanomos *nm* dignity, elegance, noblesse

ráikano-rat *comp/nm* aristocracy, aristocratic lineage
Ráiya *voc* Sir; **So keres Ráiya?** What are you doing, Sir?
raiyi *nf var of* **rani** *qv*
raklanes *adv* like a non-Romani boy, immaturely
raklano *adj* relating to non-Romani boys/youths, immature (*if non-Romani*)
rakle *nm/pl* **1)** male children/teenagers, boys/boys and girls (*if non-Romani*) **2)** sons/sons and daughters (*if non-Romani*)
rakli *nf* **1)** girl, teenager, young unmarried woman (*if non-Romani*) **2)** daughter (*if non-Romani*) **3)** waitress **4)** barmaid **5)** salesgirl
raklikanes *adv* like a non-Romani girl; **Kerél-pe raklikanes.** She is behaving like a non-Romani girl.
raklikano *adj* like a non-Romani girl, girlish (*if non-Romani*). **tsáliya raklikane** clothes worn by non-Romani girls
raklo *nm* **1)** boy, teenager, unmarried youth (*if non-Romani*) **2)** son (*if non-Romani*); **thagarêsko raklo** prince **3)** delivery boy, waiter
raklorro *nm* **1)** male child, young boy (*if non-Romani*) **2)** baby son (*if non-Romani*)
raklya *nf/pl* girls/daughters (*if non-Romani*)
raklyorri *nf* young daughter/girl (*if non-Romani*)
rakúno *nm* raccoon
rakyol *vi* become night: *pp/adj* **rakilo**; **Rakyólas kána areslem.** Night was falling when I arrived

ram *nf* **1)** print, writing; **ánde ram** in writing/in print **2)** document, manuscript **3)** font

ráma *nf* oar, sweep: *pl* **rêmi**

ramil *vt* row (*boat*): *pp/adj* **ramime**

ramitóri *nm* **1)** writer: *nf* **ramitórka 2)** printer

ramol/xramol *vt* **1)** print, sign, write: *pp/adj* **ramome; Ramosar kyo nav wórta kathe!** Sign your name right here! **2)** draw, tattoo (*with* **sámnurya**) **3)** register, sign *smbdy* in/up **4)** *v/refl* **ramól-pe a)** be written, be in writing, be spelt **b)** sign oneself in/up, register oneself

ramome *pp/adj* established, written; **Ramomé-lo ánde amári búkfa.** It's written in our book/It's one of our laws. **Amári búkfa nai ramome.** Our Bible is unwritten/Our scriptures are not written. **Amári búkfa si ramome ándo chéri.** Our book/Bible is written in the sky.

ramosarno *nm* author, writer: *nf* **ramosarni** (*Eur*)

ranchéri *nm* rancher

ráncho *nm* ranch

rángi stánsiya *comp/nf* police station

rángo *gen/adj* belonging to the nobility/to the police

rángo/rêngo *gen/adj/pl* **1)** of the gentry, nobility **2)** of the police; **Dikhlem rángo mobíli ánde úlitsa.** I saw a police car in the street.

rángo-mobíli *comp/nm* cruiser, police car (*Am*)

rángo-tráyo *comp/nm* life of the idle rich/nobility/upper class

rángo-vôrdòn *comp/nm* paddy wagon, police patrol wagon (*Am*)

rani/raiyi *nf* **1)** gentlewoman, lady **2)** female police officer (*Am*) **3)** women's washroom/toilet, powder room (*Am*)

ranikanes *adj* like a gentlewoman/lady, ladylike

ranikané-tsáliya gentlewomen's clothing, fancy women's clothes

ranikano *adj* like a gentlewoman/lady

ráno/rano *adv* early; **Avilo ráno.** He came early; **Mulo ráno ánde diminyátsa.** He died early in the morning.

rapári *nm* rapper (*Eur*)

rapil *vi* rap, perform rap music (*Eur*): *pp/adj* **rapime**

rápo *nm* rap music (*Eur*)

rása/rrása *nf* **1)** bloodline, breed, lineage, race, species (*Eur*) **2)** clan (*Eur*)

rashai *nm* **1)** priest **2)** clergyman: *pl* **rasha**

rashángi buki *comp/nf* work of the clergy

rashángo/rashêngo *adj* belonging to the clergy

rashásko *gen/adj* belonging to a clergyman/priest; **rashásko kher** clergyman's house

rashni *nf* **1)** wife of a clergyman **2)** priestess

rasistítsko *adj* racist

rasísto *nm* racist: *nf* **rasistútsa** *nf*

rasízmo *nm* racism

ráski-pecháta *comp/nf* detective's shield/badge (*Am*)

rásko/rêsko *gen/adj/s* **1)** of the gentleman/nobleman **2)** of the policeman

raspúnso *nm* response

rat *nm* **1)** blood, gore (*Anat*) **2)** bloodline, breed; **Lásho grast si, chísto Arabítsko rat.** It's a good horse, pure Arabian bloodline. **3)** heredity, nature; **Ándo rat si.** It's hereditary. **5)** *vt/i* **del ~** give blood **4)** *comp/vi* **piyel ~** receive a blood transfusion

ratêski-goi *nf* blood pudding (*Am*)

ratêsko-pimos *comp/nm* blood transfusion

ratuno *adj* blood, bloody, having the appearance/color of blood

ratwalo *adj* **1)** bloodstained, bloody, covered with blood, gory **2)** bloodshot **3)** morbid

ratyáki-chirikli *comp/nf* nightingale

ratyáko *gen/adj* night, of the night

ratyáko-húlyo *comp/nm* night owl

ratyol *vi* become night: *pp/adj* **ratilo; Ratyol rano kála gesa.** Night falls early these days.

raváni *nm* buggy horse, sulky horse

raxámi *nf* **1**) blazer, jacket, coat, sportscoat, suit jacket **2**) car coat (*Am*) **3**) book cover

ráya *nf* beam, ray (*Am*)

razbóinik *nm* impudent little rascal, naughty boy, rascal, scallywag; **térno razbóinik** young rascal

razbóiniko *adj* cheeky, defiant, impudent, insolent, mischevious, naughty, ornery, saucy

ráziya *nf* police raid, raid (*Eur*)

razóno *nm* meaning, reason, right; **Si tu razóno.** You are right.

realitéto *nm* reality

redaktíl *vt* **1**) edit: *pp/adj* **redaktime 2**) *v/refl* **redaktíl-pe** edit, be edited (*Eur*)

redaktime *pp/adj* edite

redaktimos *nm* editing, editing process (*Eur*)

redaktíya *nf* editing

redaktóri *nm* editor: *nf* **redaktórka** (*Eur*)

redechína *nf* tap root (*of a tree*)

rédiyo *nm* radio (*Am*)

redjistéri *nm* **1**) cash register, register **2**) meter (*for gas, etc*)

redjistrátno *adj* registered

redjistrátsiya *nf* registration

refréno *nm* chorus

rêg/rig *nf* **1**) angle, aspect, edge, side; **Beshélas pe rêg le dromêski.** He was sitting by the side of the road. **2**) camp, side; **Chi sim pe lêngi rêg.** I am not on their side/in their camp.

rêgáko *gen/adj* lateral

rêgáte *nf/prep/adv* aside, at the side, sideways, to one side; **Tho lês rêgáte!** Put it aside! **De-tu rêgáte!** Move aside! **Mukisarde lês andre pe rêgáte.** They moved it inside sideways.

rêgunó *adj* on the side, marginal

réko *nm* **1**) lake **2**) creek, stream

relígiya *nf* religion

rêltsa *nf* **1**) banister, guard rail, rail, railing: *pl* **réltsi 2**) railway, railway line, rail, railway spur

rêltso *nm* rail, railway track

rêngo *gen/adj* belonging to the police/nobility

rêntíl *vt* **1**) lease, rent: *pp/adj* **rêntimé 2**) *v/refl* **rêntíl-pe** be rented, be renting (*Am*)

rênto/rênta *nm/nf* rent (*Am*)

repetóriya *nm* repertoire (*Eur*)

repitítsiya *nf* practice session, rehearsal (*Eur*)

representátsiya *nf* representation

representívo *nm* representative: *nf* **representíva** (*Eur*)

repúblika *nf* republic

republikáno *nm* republican: *nf* **republikánka**

resáko *nm* race horse

reséto *nm* receipt (*Am*)

resh *nm* sore; **zûnáko resh** saddle sore

reshalo *adj* sore

reshol *vt* **1**) make sore **2**) *v/refl* **reshól-pe** become sore

rêsko *gen/adj* belonging to a policeman; **rêske tsáliya** policeman's uniform

réso *nm* race, racetrack: *nm/pl* **grastêngo réso** horse race

resórto *nm* pull spring, tension spring (*Eur*)

resósko *gen/adj* having to do with a race/races

respondil *vt* **1**) answer, reply, respond: *pp/adj* **respondime 2**) *v/refl* **respondíl-pe** answer, reply, respond

respondimos *nm* reply, response

responsabilitáte *nm* responsibility (*Eur*)

responsabílo *adj* responsible (*Eur*)

resúrsa *nf* asset, resource

revolútsiya *nf* civil war, revolution

reyaktóri *nm* reactor

reyáktsiya *nf/neolog* reaction

rêz/rrêz *nm* **1**) arbor, grapevine arbor, vine **2**) vineyard

rezervátsiya *nf* **1**) reservation **2**) Native Reservation (*Am*)

rezolvil *vt* **1**) resolve, settle, solve: *pp/adj* **rezolvime 2**) *v/refl* **rezolvíl-pe** be resolved/settled

rezolvimos *nm* resolution, settlement, solution

rezultáto *nm* result

ríkono *nm* puppy: *pl* **ríkoya**
rikordéri *nm* recorder, tape recorder
rikórdo *nm* record
rilífo *nm* relief, Social Welfare (*Am*)
rimol *vt* **1)** damage, make soft, ruin, spoil, trash **2)** demolish, destroy, disintegrate, ruin **3)** pamper/spoil (*child*) **4)** *v/refl* **rimól-pe a)** be damaged/ruined/spoiled/ruined/wasted, spoil oneself, become/decadent/dilapidated **b)** be pampered, be spoiled **c)** waste oneself
rimome *pp/adj* **1)** demolished, destroyed, disintegrated, ruined, spoiled **2)** decadent **3)** decayed, dilapidated **4)** pampered/spoiled
rimomos *nm* **1)** damage, ruination **2)** decadence, disintegration, decay, destruction
rimóto *nm* remote control (*for TV, stereo, etc*)
rin *nm* file;
rin-baro *comp/nm* rasp
ríngo *nm* gas ring (*for a stove*), burner
rinil *vt* file, rasp: *pp/adj* **rinime**
rinimos *nm* filing, rasping
rinorro *nm* nail file, small file
riportéri *nm* media reporter: *nf* **riportérka**
ripórto *nm* media report, report (*Eur*)
rish *nm* male bear
rishalo *adj* ursine
rishári *nm* man who works with performing bears
rishêsko-chekûn *comp/nm* bear grease
rishni *nf* female bear
rishorro *nm* little bear, teddy bear: *nf* **rishnyorri**
rispektil *vt* respect: *pp/adj* **rispektime** *see also* **pakil** *vt*
rispéto/respéto *nm* respect
ristoránto *nm* restaurant
rítmo *nm* rhythm (*Mus*)
rivéri *nm* river
robinéta *nf* faucet, tap (*Eur*)
ródel *vt/i* **1)** look for, search, seek: *pp/adj* **rodino; ródav buki.** I am looking for work. **2)** investigate, look into **3)** look up

4) get; **Goló te ródel xabe.** He went to get (some) food. **5)** ~ *with dat case*; find/get for *smbdy*; **Róde mánge xabe!** Get me (some) food! **Ródav mánge shukar Rromni.** I am searching to get a beautiful wife for myself.
rodimos *nm* **1)** investigation, quest, search **2)** manhunt **3)** lawsuit
ródina *nf* county, homeland, motherland
rodínyol *vi* be looked into, searched for: *pp/adj* **rodinilo**
ródka *nf* **1)** beet, red beetroot **2)** *types of beetroot*; **ródka-loli** red beetroot, **ródka-parni** chard, Swiss chard, **ródka-zahárniko** sugar beet
rogádka *nf* **1)** highway toll booth, tollgate **2)** toll road
róida *nf* pomegranate
rokéta *nf* rocket, rocket missile
Rômichel *nm see* **Rômnichel** *nm*
Rômnichel *nm* English Romani (*Am*): *nf* **Rômnichelútsa Note:** In the US and Canada the term **Rrom-Anglézurya** means *Kalderash* from the long-established British *Kalderash* community. *Rômnichel* refers to the English Romanies or *Romanichels* whose ancestors migrated to the US and Canada in the 19th and 20th centuries.
Romúngero *nm* **1)** Hungarian Rom of the **Romúngere** group, the majority group in Hungary, most of whom do not speak Romani: *nf* **Romúngeri**
Romûngrítsko *adj* of the **Romûngero** group of Roma
Romûngro *nm* Hungarian Non-Vlax Rom: *nf* **Romûngrítsa: Note:** As a group, most Hungarian **Romûngere** do not speak Romani unless they have relearned it.
rópa *nf* sling
rósto *nm* job, employment, position, situation
rovashágo *nm* bet, wager *var of* **rrûmashágo** *qv*
rovel *vt/i* **1)** cry, shed tears, weep: *pp/adj* **ruyo; Ruyas dukhátar.** He cried from

pain. **2)** *id* miss; **Chi rovav ánda lêste. I
don't miss it.**
rovimos/ruyimos *nm* crying, lament
rovli *nf var* of **ruvli** *qv*
rovyarel *vt* bring to tears, make to cry:
pp/adj **rovyardo**; **Na rovyar e gláta!**
Don't make the baby cry!
rovyarimásko *gen/adj* tear-jerking
rovyarimos *nm* crying, weeping, state of
being brought to tears
rubíya/rúbiya *nf* ruby
rubízla/rrubízla *nf* gooseberry
rúda/rrúda *nf* pole, shaft (*cart*)
rufyáno *nm* ruffian, thug: *nf* **rufyánka**
(*Am*)
rukh *nm/neolog* tree
rulóta *nf* caravan, RV, travel trailer (*Eur*)
rumátiko *nm* rheumatism
rumatikósko *gen/adj* rheumatic
Rumunítska *nf* Romanian (*Lang*) (*Eur*)
Rumunítsko *adj* Romanian
Rumúnya *nf* Romania
rûndavo *adj* mottled, speckled
rup *nm* **1)** silver **2)** silver coins
rupêsko *gen/adj* made of silver
rupunil *vt* **1)** plate with silver: *pp/adj*
rupunime 2) turn silver (*in color*)
rupunimos *nm* silver plating
rupuno *adj* **1)** silver, colour of silver,
having the appearance/quality of silver; **O
shon si rupuno aryat.** The moon is
silver tonight. **2)** *fig* attractive, alluring; "
**Láko mui si rupuno hai o státo
sumnakuno**... He face is silver and her
body golden..." song
rup-zhivindo *comp/nm* quicksilver
Rusalíno *nm* mythical city in folk tales,
probably Jerusalem *see* **Yeruslámo** *nm*
Rusáliya *nf* Whit Sunday, Whitsun
ruv *nm* male wolf; *id* **bokhalo ruv**
ravenous wolf, *fig* very greedy man: *nf*
bokhali ruvni

ruvalo *nm* werewolf: *nf* **ruvali** (*Folk*)
ruvanes *adv* in the manner of wolves, like
wolves; **Le zhukla den mui ruvanes.**
The dogs are howling like wolves.
ruvano *adj* wolfish
ruvêsko-drab *comp/nf* aconite, wolfsbane
(*aconitum vulparia*)
ruvikano *adj* wolfish, wolflike
ruvli/rovli *nf* **1)** baton, shepherd's crook,
staff, stick, walking stick **2)** drum stick
(*Mus*) **3)** pool cue **4)** fishing rod **5) del**
ruvlyása *comp/vt/i* beat with (a) stick
ruvlí-bilyardóski *comp/nf* cue,
billiard/pool cue
ruvni *nf* wolf bitch
ruvorro *nm* coyote
ruyimos *nm* crying, grief, lamenting,
sorrow, weeping
rúyindoi *v/part* crying, lamenting
ruyitóri *nm* **1)** complainer, cry baby: *nf*
ruyitórka 2) professional mourner
rúzha *nf* rose
rúzhina/ruzhinála *nf* corrosion,
oxidization. rust
ruzhinil/ruzhenil *vt* **1)** corrode, oxidize,
rust: *pp/adj* **ruzhinime 2)** *v/refl*
ruzhiníl-pe become oxidized/rusty, rust;
Avtsûn kai chi mai ruzheníl-pe
stainless steel
ruzhinimásko *gen/adj* causing rust
ruzhinime *pp/adj* corroded, oxidized,
rusted, rusty
ruzhinimos *nm* rusting process
rúzho *adj* **1)** burning, red-hot **2)** *nm* bronze
ruzhósko *gen/adj* made of bronze
ryat *nf* **1)** late evening, night; **Avilo Marts,
e ryat.** He came on Tuesday, in the
evening. **Avav tehára, e ryat.** I'll come
tomorrow, in the evening. **So kerdyan e
ryat kai nakli?** What did you do last
night? **2) del** ~ night falls

RR

rrábosh *nf* cut, nick, notch: *pl* **rrábosha**

rráchi ánde vádra *id/exp* backbiters, dogs in the manger, losers who try to prevent others from succeeding in life, *lit* 'crabs in a bucket'; **Ages, si but Rrom kai si rráchi ánde vádra.** Today, there are many Roma who are dogs in the manger.

rrâdíka *nf* radish: *pl* **rrâdíchi**

rrai *nf* **1)** cane, rod, switch **2)** wand, willow wand **3)** branch

rraiyorri *nf* **1)** thin rod/switch **2)** branch, twig

rráka ánde vádra *nf/phr* backbiter, dog in the manger, a loser whose aim in life is to prevent others from succeeding.

rráka *nf* crab: *pl* **rráchi**

rrâkíl *vt* cause cancer: *pp/adj* **rrâkimé 2)** *v/refl* **rrâkíl-pe** develop/get cancer; **Rrâkisáilo hai mulo.** He developed cancer and died.

rrâkimé *pp/adj* cancerous, carcinogenic; **O dóftoro phendyas ke rrâkimé sas.** The doctor said it was cancerous.

rrakítsa *nf* shrimp

rrâkíya *nf* **1)** whisky **2)** hard liquor

rráko ánde l' kokala *nm/phr* bone cancer

rráko ándo rat *nm/phr* lukemia

rráko *nm* cancer; **O rráko xalyas lês.** Cancer ate him/He died from cancer. **2)** Cancer (*Zod*)

rráko-ánde-xírpa *nm/phr* cancer of the colon

rrána *nf* injury, wound

rrandári *nm* **1)** electric shaver, shaver **2)** spokeshave

rrándel *vt* **1)** scrape, scratch, scuff, shave: *pp/adj* **rranglo 2)** clip, shear **3)** sand, smooth with sandpaper **4)** shave down (*wood*) **5)** peel **6)** *v/refl* **rrandél-pe** shave oneself

rrangli *nf* scraper, pick (*tool to remove manure or other material from the hooves of shod horses to prevent hoof rot*)

rranglimos *nm* **1)** clipping, scraping, scraping, scratching, shaving, shearing **2)** scrape, scratch

rranglo *pp/adj* clipped, scraped, shaved, shaven

rranglo shorro *comp/nm* shaven head, skinhead, person with a shaven head

rrâníl *vt* **1)** injure, wound: *pp/adj* **rrânimé 2)** *v/refl* **rrâníl-pe** injure oneself

rrânimé *pp/adj* injured, wounded

rrânimós *nm* injury, wound

rrâspúnda *nf* cry baby, spoiled brat, whining tot

rrâspundíl -pe *v/refl* act like a cry baby/spoiled brat, whine

rrâspundimé *pp/adj* cry-babyish, whining

rrâspundimós *nm* childish/spoiled behaviour

rráta *nf* **1)** wheel: *pl* **rróti**; **Lóli Rráta** Red Wheel (*on the Romani flag*) **2)** steering wheel **3)** castor **4)** company (*Mil*)

rratáko fidévo *comp/nm* hub cap

rratári *nm* wheelwright

rratítsa *nf* gear, small wheel: *pl* **rrotítsi**

rrátsa *nf* female duck: *pl* **rrêtsi**

rratsoi *nm* drake

Rrayo/Rráyo *nm* **1)** Afterworld, Heaven, Romani Afterlife/Heaven; **Te avel ángla lêste/láte ándo Rrayo!** May (this) appear before him/her in Heaven! (*Benediction at a* pomána *to ensure that the deceased will have food and drink in the afterlife*) **2)** paradise

rráza *nf* 1) beam, ray, moonbeam, sunbeam 2) reflection 3) delusion, fantasy, illusion, hallucination, mirage

rrâzíl *vt* 1) reflect: *pp/adj* rrâzimé 2) v/refl rrâzíl-pe be reflected, reflect

rrâzimós *nm* reflection

rrâzitóri *nm* reflector

rrêgo *nm* blackberry

rrêguyála *nf* belch, burp

rrêguyíl/rrêgíl *vt* 1) belch, burp: *pp/adj* rrêguyimé 2) v/refl belch, burp

rrêguyimós *nm* belching, burping

rrênzál *vt/i* frown, scowl: *pp/adj* rrênzailó; Rrênzáilo pe mánde. He scowled at me.

rrênzála *nf* frown, scowl: *pl* rrênzéli

rrênzhedo *adj* bad, rancid, stale

rrênzhezíl *vt* 1) make bad/rancid/stale: *pp/adj* rrênzhezimé 2) v/refl rrênzhezíl-pe become/go bad/rancid/stale

rrêspíl *vt* 1) distribute, pass around, scatter: *pp/adj* rrêspimé 2) litter 3) v/refl rrêspíl-pe a) be distributed/scattered, be distributing scattering b) be littered, be littering; O drom rrêspisáilo perde pateriyánsa. The road became littered wih fallen leaves.

rrêspimós *nm* 1) distribution 2) litter, mess on the floor

rrêvda/rrávda endurance, patience; Nai ma rrêvda te ashunav lêste. I have no patience to listen to him.

rrêvdíl *v/tr* 1) bear, endure, put up with, stand, undergo, suffer (*changes*); Nashti rrêvdíl e dukh. He can't stand the pain: *pp/adj* rrêvdimé 2) support 3) v/refl rrêvdíl-pe a) last, endure, suffer (*changes*), survive (*Eur*); Amári kultúra rrêvdisáili desar but ginerátsiyi. Our culture has survived for many generations. b) exhibit/show patience

rrêvdimós 1) endurance, resilience 2) patience

rrêgo/rrûgo *nm* sedge

rrêz *nm* grape arbor, grapevine

rrêzgeyála *nf* caressing, fondling, pampering, stroking

rrêzgeyíl *vt* 1) caress, indulge in foreplay, pet, stroke: *pp/adj* rrêzgeyimé 2) coddle, pamper, spoil by pampering 3) v/refl rrêzgeyíl-pe a) caress, fondle b) be coddled, pampered

rrêzgeyimós *nm* caressing, fondling, foreplay, pampering, stroking

rrindiláshka *nf* swallow (*bird*)

rrîl *nf* 1) belch 2) fart, loud fart: *pl* rra 3) comp/vi shúdel ~ fart

rrîlíl-pe *v/refl* fart: *pp/adj* rrîlimé

rrîlimé *pp/adj* suffering from flatulence

rrîlimós *nm* flatulence

rrîlitóri *nm* man suffering from flatulence: *nf* rrîlitórka

rrînduyála *nf* 1) warbler. wood warbler (*family Parulidae*) 2) bluejay (*Am*)

rrînza/rrûnza *nf* chitterlings, chitlins, tripe

rrînza-búla *nf* bullshit, hogwash, propaganda, tripe; Mothodyas mánge ladimos rrînza-búla. He told me a load of bullshit.

rrobíya *nf* 1) jail, prison 2) hard labour (*Eur*)

rrobiyash *nm* convict, hostage, prison inmate: *nf* rrobiyashútsa

rrobíya-ternêngi *comp/nf* reformatory, youth correctional facility (*Am*)

rróbo *nm* 1) prisoner, slave (*Eur*)

rroiyi *nf* spoon. tablespoon

rroiyí-bari *comp/nf* large ladling spoon, ladle

rroiyorri *nf* teaspoon

rrókya *nf* skirt (*Am*), robe (*Eur*): *pl* róchi see also tsóxa *nf*

Rrom bi-krisáko *comp/nm* A Rom who does not adhere to the rules of the kris-Romani: *pl* Rroma bi-krisáke: *nf* Rromni bi-krisáki: *pl* Rromnya bi-krisáke

Rrom bi-kumpanyáko *nm* Rom not belonging to a kumpaníya: *pl* Rrom bi-kumpanyánge Roma not belonging to any kumpaníya, Roma outside any kumpaníya jurisdiction, maverick Roma: *nf* Rromni bi-kumpanyáki

Rrom bi-shibáko *nm* a Romani man who
does not speak Romani: *nf* **Romni
bi-shibáki**

Rrom *nm* **1)** Romani man: *pls*
Rrom/Rroma 2) adult/married Romani
man: *pls* **Rroma 2)** husband (*if Romani*);
Nai ma rrom. I have no husband. **3)** man
(*if Romani*); **Kon si kodo rrom?** Who is
that man?

Rromále! *nm/pl/voc* Roma! Romani men!
Romani people!

Rromanes *adv* like a Romani
person/man/woman; **Del-dúma
Rromanes.** He speaks like a Romani
person/speaks Romani. **Besh púpo,
Rromanes!** Sit squatted, like a Romani
person! **Zhanes te pekes Rromanes?**
Do you know how to cook like a Romani
person/Romani food? **Ker tut
Rromanes, na Gazhikanes!** Behave like
a Romani person, not like a non-Romani
person! **Note: Romanes** is an adverb,
not a noun, and is often used incorrectly
to mean 'the Romani language' instead of
Rrómani shib.

Rromaní-buki *comp/nf* Romani work,
internal Romani business, Romani affair

Rrómani-fórma *comp/nf* Romani
behaviour, acceptable/correct Romani
behaviour

Rromanipe *nm cognate of* **Rromaníya** *nf
qv*

Rrómani-shib/shib-Rromani *comp/nf*
Romani language/dialect; **Che fyál
Rrómani shib des-dúma?** Which
Romani dialect do you speak?

Rromaníya *nf* **1)** Romani
behaviour/culture/customs/laws **2)**
Romani environment, world or sphere of
the Roma, Romani society and its values

Rromano *adj* Romani

Rrómano chai *comp/nm* Romani
(Kalderash) tea, tea served with fruit
floating in it instead of sugar and milk

Rrom-Bibliyáko *nm* Pentecostal Rom: *nf*
Rromni-Bibliyáki

Rrom-Dasikano *comp/nm* Christian Rom
in Bulgaria: *nf* **Rromní-Daskikani**

Rrom-Gazhikanime *comp/nm* assimilated
Rom: *nf* **Romní-Gazhikanime** (*Eur*)

Rrom-Kashtalo *nm* **1)** Romani man who
does not speak Romani, *lit* "Wooden
Rom" *nf* **Rromni-Kashtali** (*Eur*)

Rromni *nf* **1)** adult, married Romani
woman **2)** wife (*if Romani*)

Rromnyále! *nf/pl/voc* Romani women!

Rromorro *nm/dim* **1)** dwarf (*if Romani*) **2)**
dear husband

Rrom-skutsome *nm* Romani dude (*Am*)

rrongyal *vi* thunder: *pp/adj* **rrongyailo**;
Rongyal dural. It is sounding thunder
far off. **Rrongyaiyas dural.** Thunder
rolled far away.

rrongyála *nf* thunder

rrongyáto crash/peal of thunder, thunder
clap

rróti *nf/pl* **1)** wheels **2)** wheelchair (*Am*);
Beshel pe l' rróti. He is in a wheelchair.

rrubízla *nf* gooseberry

rrúda/rúda *nf* pole, shaft (*of a cart*)

rrûgíl *vt* **1)** celebrate by prayer: *pp/adj*
rrûgimé; **Rrûgís e Santána.** We
celebrate Saint Anne by prayer. **2)** pray **3)**
ask (*from God*), beseech (*with abl of
object*); **Rrûgisardyás le Devlêstar**. He
beseeched God. **4)** *v/refl* **rrûgíl-pe** pray,
celebrate by prayer; **Rrûgíl-pe le
Devlêste.** He is praying to God.
**Rrûgisáilo te lel-pe yertimos le
Devlêstar.** He prayed for forgiveness
from God.

rrûgimáta *nm/pl* prayers, requests

rrûgimós *nm* act of prayer, praying,
supplication

rrûgitóri *nm* supplicant: *nf* **rrûgitórka**

rrûgûshála *nf* hoarseness, sore throat from
shouting

rrûgûshól-pe *v/refl* become hoarse: *pp/adj*
rrûgûshomé

rrûma/rrûmo *nf* dew worm, earthworm,
worm: *pls* **rrûmi/rrûmurya**

rrûmâshagári *nm* bookie

rrûmashágo *nm* **1)** bet, wager **2)** betting: *pl* **rrûmâshégurya**

rrûmbo *nm* rum

rrûmi-ánde-pûrr *nf/pl/phr* intestinal worms

rrúmo/rúmo *nm* room (*Am*)

rrûndiláshka *nf* plover (*bird*)

rrûndo *nm* **1)** order **2)** place, position, rank, status **3)** credentials, degree (*academic*)

rrûnkezhála *nf* neighing, snorting

rrûnkezhíl *vt* **1)** neigh, snort: *pp/adj* **rrûnkezhimé 2)** *v/refl* **rrûnkezhíl-pe** neigh, snort, be neighing/snorting; **Rrûnkezhín-pe l' grast.** The horses are neighing.

rrûnza/rrînza *nf* entrails, tripe

rrûnza-búla *comp/nf* **1)** bullshit, hype, tripe **2)** double talk

rrûnzaiyíl-pe *v/refl* frown, grimace: *pp/adj* **rrûnzaiyimé**

rrûnzaiyimós *nm* frowning, grimmace

rrûnzal *vi* frown, grimace: *pp/adj* **rrûnzailó**; **Rrûnzáilo pe mánde.** He frowned at me.

rrûnzála *nf* frown, grimmace

Rrusítska *nf* Russian (*Lang*)

Rrusítsko *adj* Russian

Rrusíya/Rrúsiya *nf* Russia

Rrusnyácha *nm/pl* A Russian Romani musician group many of whose descendants now live in the Americas.

Rrusnyáko *nm* **1)** member of a Russian Romani musician group: *nf* **Rrusnyáika**

Rrúso *nm* Russian: *nf* **Rrusáika**

rrûto *nm* bog, quagmire, quicksand

rrutuni/rrûtúi *nf* nostril: *pl* **rrutunya/rrûtuyá**

rruzhinil *see* **ruzhinil** *vt*

S

sa *pron/adj/adv* **1)** all, everybody, everything; **Sa avile.** They have all arrived. **Mangel sa.** He wants everything. **Sa le Rroma zhanen ke wo si dilo.** All the Roma know he is an idiot. **Mothodem saren.** I told everybody. **Xalyás-pe sare le Rromênsa.** He argued with all the Roma. **Xoxavel amênsa, sarênsa.** He lies to us, all of us. **2)** always, everywhere; **Sa phirel.** He's always traveling all over.

sábiya *nf* saber, sword

sabiyash *nm* fencer, swordsman

sabotázha *nf* sabotage

sabotazhil *vt* sabotage: *pp/adj* **sabotazhime**

sabotazhitóri *nm* saboteur

sa-de-yekh *adv/phr* all of a sudden, immediately, right away, suddenly; **Sa-de-yekh, ashundem muzíka.** All of a sudden, I heard music.

sadil/sadisarel *vt/i* cultivate (*garden*), garden, plant (*in garden*), practice market gardening//produce from gardening/market gardening: *pp/adj* **sadime/sadisardo; Sadisaren lulugya kai bikinen.** They produce flowers which they retail.

sádo *nm* **1)** garden **2)** courtyard **3)** orchard. (*Eur*); *id* **Kána sámas ándo sádo.** When we were courting.

safíra *nf* sapphire

sa-gadiki *adv* more or less, so-so, such and such

sa-gadikí-si *conj/phr* all the same, although, as if, whether, it doesn't matter; **Te zhas wórka chi zhas, sa-gadikí- si mánge.** Whether you go or you don't go,

it's all the same to me. **Í-me ahundem kodola, sa- gadiki-si, shai te aven xoxayimáta.** I heard that too, all the same, it might be lies.

sa-gadya *conj* **1)** all that, in that case, so, so-so, therefore **Sa-gáta zhanel sa-gadya.** He already knows all that. **2)** fair to middling, so-so; **Ánde shpíta-lo, sa gadya si.** He's in the hospital he is so-so.

sa-gáta *adv* all ready, already; **Sa-gáta xalem.** I already ate.

sa-vaxt *adv* all the time, always (*Eur*)

sa-yêkh-fyálo *adv/phr* all same, the same.

ságda *adv* always, continually *var of* **swágdar** *adv qv*

sa-kadya *conj* see **sa-gadya** *conj*

sákra *nf* mother-in-law

sakûz *nm* **1)** gum **2)** chewing gum. (*Am*)

saláta *nf* **1)** salad **2)** lettuce

salavári *nm* **1)** bridle **2)** rein

salaváriya *nm/pl* reins

salimándra *nf* salamander

salipátra *nf* saltpeter

Sálma *nf* Psalm

sálsa *nf* sauce

salvátiko *adj* fierce, savage, wild; *nm* savage **salvátiko** *nm*: **salvatikútsa** *nf*

salvatil *vt* **1)** make wild: *pp/adj* **salvatime 2)** **salvatíl-pe** *v/refl* (become fierce/wild)

salvatimos *nm* ferocity, savagery

sam *v* we are (*pl/v/to be*); **Rrom sam.** We are Roma (*Am*). **Rroma sam.** We are Roma (*Eur*).

sáma *nf* **1)** account, attention, care; **Le sáma so mothav!** Pay attention to what I am saying! **Le sáma kai zhas!** Take care/Be careful where you go! **Na zhátar**

pe múrri sáma! Don't go on my account! **2)** notice, heed

sámas *v* we were, used to be (*pl/v/to be*)

samása *nf/inst/adv* with care. carefully

sámicho *nm* sandwich (*Am*): *pl* **sámichez**

sámno/sûmno/sêmno *nm* **1)** cue, indicator, sign, mark, symptom **2)** trace, trail sign; **Dikhlem le sámnurya kai sas lêngo kámpo.** I saw the signs where their camp had been. **3)** badge, emblem **4)** signal, signpost; **dromêsko sámo** road sign, **sámno-naiyêsko** finger print: *pl* **sámnurya-naiyênge 5)** premonition **6)** scar **7)** tattoo **8)** *comp/vi* **thol** ~ get a tattoo

samnol *vt* **1)** denote, identify (*by marking*), mark, place a sign: *pp/adj* **samnome 2)** sign, signal **3)** see, spot **4)** *v/refl* **samnól-pe a)** be authenticated/signed, be marked **b)** be seen/spotted

samovári/samuvári *nm* samovar

samuchi *adv* almost, nearly; **Samuchi mulo ánde shpíta.** He almost died in the hospital.

san *v* you are (*s/pl/v/to be*); **San tu kathe amênsa wórka opral le chiriklênsa?** Are you here with us or up there with the birds/out of it completely? **San tume Rroma?** Are you (*people*) Roma?

sánas *v* you were/used to be (*sing & pl v/to be*)

sandála *nf* sandal

sané-ratêsko *adj* suffering from hemophilia

sanes *adv* thinly, meagerly

sángwicho *nm* sandwich (*Eur*)

sanimos *nm* daintiness, finesse, slimness

sániya *nf* bobsleigh, sleigh, sled; ~ **zhuklênsa** dogsled

saniyáko-zhukel *comp/nm* malamute

saniyútsa *nf* hand sled

sano *adj* **1)** delicate, fine, meager, slender, thin; **Saní-la sar e momeli.** She is slim, like a candle. **2)** diluted, thinned; **sani mol** diluted wine

sáno-rat *comp/nm* hemophilia

Santána *nf* **1)** Saint Ann **2)** annual pilgrimage to the shrine of *Ste Anne de Beaupré* in Quebec, Canada **3)** Saint Anne's Day, July 26th and celebrated from July 17th through 26th **4)** village of *Sainte Anne de Beaupré* in Québec. Canada

sanyárdyol *vi* be thinned down, made thinner, made to lose weight: *pp/adj* **sanyardilo; Sanyárdilo ánde shpíta,** He became much thinner in the hospital.

sanyarel *vt* **1)** make thinner, make to lose weight, reduce in weight, slenderize, trim down: *pp/adj* **sanyardo 2)** reduce in thickness, thin down, file down; **Desya but zalzáiro sanyarel e rêg la basunáki.** Too much acid will thin down the side of the mixing bowl. **3)** dilute

sanyol *vi* **1)** become thin, slim down: *pp/adj* **sanilo; Músai te xas mai xantsi te sanyos.** You need to eat less to slim down. **2)** be/become diluted

sap *nm* snake: *nf* **sapni**

sápa *nf* **1)** hoe **2)** spade

saparíko *nm* ammonium chloride, sal-ammoniac

sapêsko chiriklo *comp/nm* yellowhammer/yellow-shafted flicker (*Colaptes auratus*)

sap-izwoyênsa *nm/phr* rattlesnake

sap-mulikano *comp/nm* cobra, deadly snake

sapui *nm* soap; **dandêngo-sapui** toothpaste, **rranglimásko-sapui** shaving soap, **balêngo-sapui** hair shampoo.

sapuiyalo *adj* soapy, sudsy

sapuiyil *vt* **1)** soap: *pp/adj* **sapuiyime 2)** sponge, wash down, wash off with soap and water **3)** get the car washed (*Am*) **4)** **sapuiyíl-pe** *v/refl* sponge oneself down

sapuiyimos 1) soaping **2)** washing down **3)** car wash (*Am*)

sapuno *adj* **1)** like a snake, serpentine **2)** *fig* backbiting, vicious, vindictive

sapûsh *nf* inch

sar *adv/conj/prep* **1)** according to, as, as far as, as much as, how, like, resembling, similar to; **Ker sar mánde.** Do as/like I do. **Sar kai me zhanav.** As far as I know/to my knowledge. **Xal sar o balo.** He eats like a pig. **Nakhél-pe sar kamel o Del.** It will happen as God wills it. **Sar kamel o Del.** As God wills it. (*equivalent of Inshallah in Arabic*) **Sar me ashundem.** According to what I heard. **Chi lem tu sar san.** I misjudged you/I didn't take you as you are. **2)** *adv with* de; **Sar de baro si?** How big is it? **Sar de bokhalo san?** How hungry are you?

sar mothon *adv/phr/id* as they say; **Sar mothon: "chi perel e phabai dur katar o kasht."** As they say: " The apple doesn't fall far from the tree."

sar o pai *adv/phr* easily, fluently, like water; **Dêl-dúma Rromanes sar o pai.** He speaks fluently in Romani. **Kána kerel love, zhan sar o pai.** When he makes money, it goes like water.

sar phenen *adv/phr/id* allegedly, so they say; **Kodo Rrom xoxavel, sar phenen.** That Rom is lying, so they say.

Sarái *nm* Sarajevo (*Eur*)

saránda *num* forty *see also* **shtárwardesh**

sarandáto *num* fortieth

sardína *nf* sardine

sárekai *adv* everywhere

saré-la-lumyáko *gen/adj* belonging to the whole world, international, universal

saré-lumiyáke themêngo *gen/adj* belonging to all countries, international, universal

Saré-lumiyáko Rrómano ges *nm/phr* International Romani Day. (*April 8*)

sarêngo *pron/gen* belonging to everybody (*Eur*)

saré-themêngo *gen/adj* belonging to all countries, international

sargodi *adv/conj* **1)** however; **Sargodi kai keres, músai te kerdyol.** However you do (it), it must get done. **3)** anyhow, anyway

sárma *nf* stuffed cabbage roll

sarmále *nm* meal/serving of stuffed cabbage rolls; **Lasho sarmále kerdine**

kai sláva. They made excellent stuffed cabbage rolls at the feast.

sármi *nf/pl* stuffed cabbage rolls rice and mixed, minced pork and beef; **xóxamne sármi** false cabbage roles, spiced meat, onions and rice, served on a plate but not wrapped in cabbage leaves

sar-te-avel *id/v/phr* as it may/will be; **Mek sar te avel!** Let it be as it may!

Sar-te-na! *interj* Why not! Of course! Certainly! Why shouldn't it be so!

sas kai *v/phr* there was/were about; **Sas kai dui shela zhene kai sláva.** There were about two hundred people at the feast.

sas thai nas thai shai-vi te avel... *id/phr* once upon a time/there was and there was not and there may be again... *Often used to introduce folk tales*

sas *v/to be* he/she/it/they was/were/used to be, there was/were/used to be; **Mato sas.** He was drunk. **Vuchi sas.** She was tall. **Bokhale sas.** They were hungry.

sas-pe *id* There was once/once upon a time (*Folk*); **Sas-pe, Dévla, thai shai te avél-pe...** There was once, God, and there may be again... (*often used to begin a poem or folktale*)

sastárdyol *vi* become cured/healed/made healthy/well: *pp/adj* **sastardilo; Naswáilem núma sastárdilem.** I got sick but I was cured.

sastevésto *adj* alive and well, fit, heathy, safe, well

sastimári *nm* healer: *nf* **sastimárka**

sastimása *nm/inst/adv* with health; **Phirav len sastimása!** Wear them with health (*new clothes*)

sastimásko *gen/adj* **1)** healthy **2)** sanitary

sastimáste *nm/prep* to health; **Piyas sastimáste!** Let's drink to health! **Xa pe sastimáste!** Bon Apetit!

sastimus/sastimos *nm* fitness, health; **E buki si o sastimus**. Work is healthy/health. **Baxt, sastimus!** Luck and health! (*a toast*)

sastipe *nm* health (*Eur*)

sasto *adj* **1)** healthy, well **2)** intact, perfect, having no defects, sound. sturdy; **sásto grast** a horse without blemish **3) avel ~** become healthy; **Xa but, Dále, t'aves sasti!** Eat a lot, Mother, so you may become healthy!

sastrêsko *gen/adj* made of iron

sastri *nm* **1)** iron. **2)** crowbar, power bar, tire iron **3)** handcuff. (*us nm/pl* **sastrya**) **4)** metal rod **5)** iron bar/lever, railway switch handle

sástro *nm* father-in-law (*Eur*)

sastruno *adj* like/resembling iron

sastrya *nm/pl.* **1)** handcuffs, manacles **2)** irons, fetters, leg irons

sastyardo *pp/adj* cured, healed, made healthy/well **2)** *nm* convelescant, patient: *nf* **sastyardi**

sastyarel *vt* cure, heal, make healthy/well: *pp/adj* **sastyardo**

sastyarimos *nm* cure, healing process, recovery from sickness, medical treatment

sastyarno *nm* healer, therapist: *nf* **sastyarni**; faith ~ **Devlêsko sastyarno** *comp/nm*

sastyol *vi* **1)** be cured, become healthy/well: *pp/adj* **sastilo 2)** convalesce

satíno *nm* satin

satinósko *gen/adj* made of satin

sátso *nm* behaviour, deportment, manner, manners; **Si lês lásho sátso.** He has good deportment

satsuwil *vt* do in moderation, moderate: *pp/adj* **satsuwime 2)** *v/refl* **satsuwíl-pe** be in moderation, do in moderation

satsuwime *pp/adj* in moderation, moderate, rational

satsuwimos *nm* moderation

satsuwitóri *nm* moderator, rationalizer

sáva *pron* all, everything; **Sáva me keráva túke.** I'll do everything for you. **Peradyas sáva kai kerdem.** He destroyed/undid everything I did. **Gadya si sáva kai si.** That's all there is.

Sávato *nm* Saturday

Savatone *adv* on Saturday

savêstar *adv* from which, from which kind of, from what kind of

saviyáko *nm* rice cake, sweetcake with fruit and cheese in a pastry roll: *pl* **saviyácha**

savo *pron/adj* which, what, what kind of; **Savo mobíli si kiro?** Which car is yours? **Save basúni si te hanos?** Which mixing bowls are we supposed to be wipe tinning?

savorrángo *gen/adj* belonging to everybody, common (*if all feminine gender*)

savorrêngo *gen/adj* belonging to everybody, common (*if all masculine gender or mixed gender*); **savorrêngo-gîndo** censenus of opinion, commonly held opinion

savorro *pron/m* **1)** each male *psn*, everybody: *pron/f* **savorri:** *pron/pl* **savorre; Makilo hai akushlas savorren.** He got drunk and cussed everybody out. **2)** all, each and every; **Savorre godolêndar chi móla khánchi.** Each and every one of those people isn't worth anything.

Savotune *adj* Saturday

sa-wast *nm* arm *see* **wast** *nm*

sáyêk *adv* always, all the time, constantly, continually, usually; **Sáyek si problémi.** There are always problems. **Sáyek vakíl-pe.** He's always complaining.

sa-yêkh-fyalo *comp/adj* all identical, all the same

sázi *nm* saz (*Mus*): *pl* **sázya** (*Eur*)

sebóvo *nm* tailor

sebovútsa *nf* dressmaker

segúndo *nm* **1)** second (*time*) **2)** second, second in command or control

sehaiyil *vt* **1)** say hello: *pp/adj* **sehaiyime 2)** *v/refl* **sehaiyíl-pe** say hello; **Chi sehaiyisáilo.** He didn't (even) say Hello. (*Am*)

sekretáriyo *nm* male secretary: *nf* **sekretáriya**

sekuritéto *nm* security (*Eur*)

seliýa *nf* **1)** veil **2)** christening/wedding veil **3)** lace

sêlka *nf* willow tree (*salix alba*)

sêlkáko *gen/adj* made of willow wood; **sêlkáki-rrai** willow divining rod

sêlo *nm* cell phone

sêmána *nf* **1)** seed **2)** sperm **3)** pollen **4)** *comp/vt/i* del ~ seed, insert sperm, pollinate

sêmésto *nm* people, family, relations (*Eur*)

seméstra *nf* semester

semestrálno *adj* semestral, sessional

seminári *nm* seminar

semnifikáto *adj* significant

semnifikátsiya *nf* significance

senatóri *nm* senator (*Am*)

sénda *nf* corridor, hallway, passageway

sênséri/sênsóri *nm* censor, incense burner/tray

sênto *nm* cent (*coin*) (*Am*)

sênúro *nm* potassium cyanide

sênzéro *nm* ashtray: *pl* **sênzérya**

Sêrbíya *nf* Serbia

Sêrbo *nm* Serb: *nf* **Sêrbáika**

Sêrbyanítska Serbian (*Lang*)

Sêrbyanítsko *adj* Serbian

Sêrbyánka *nf* Serbian woman

sérdyol *vi* **1)** be remembered: *pp/adj* **serdilo 2)** be reminded

serel *vt/i* **1)** recall, recollect, remember: *pp/adj* **serdo 2)** remind **3)** *v/refl* **serél-pe** bring to mind, recollect, remember

serimáta *nm/pl* **1)** recollections, memories, remembrances, souvenirs **2)** memorabilia

serimos *nm* **1)** recollection, remembrance, reminder **2)** memory **3)** memento, souvenir

seriyóso *adj* serious

sersámo *nm* equipment, implements, tools, utensils

serviséto *nm* **1)** NGO, community organization **2)** office of an organization (*Eur*)

sérviso *nm* service (*Am*)

servíso *nm* service (*Eur*)

sésiya *nf/neolog* session

sezóna *nf* season

sfériya *nf* **1)** area of influence **2)** globe, sphere **3)** realm, region

si *s/pl/v/to be*; he/she/it is, there is/are, they are; **Bokhalo si.** He is hungry. **Murri phey si.** She is my sister. **Rroma si.** They are Roma.(*Eur*) **Rrom si.** They are Roma.(*Am*)

si kai *v/phr* there is/are about/around; **Si kai shel zhene ándo párko.** There are about a hundred people in the park.

Sibériya *nf* Siberia

sída *nf* AIDs (*Eur*)

sideyil *vt* **1)** infect with AIDs **2) sidiyíl-pe** become infectefd with AIDs (*Eur*)

sideyime *pp/adj* infected with AIDs (*Eur*)

sidi *nm* CD

sídra *nf* cider

siflátiko *nf* **1)** syphilis, VD **2)** *nm* man infected with syphilis: *nf* **siflatikútsa**

sig *adv* shortly, soon

sígno *adv* soon; **mai sígno** sooner

sígo *adj/adv* fast, quick, quickly; **Nashlo sar sígo vi grastêste.** He ran off as fast as a horse. **Tíro mobíli chi zhal sar sígo vi murrêste.** Your car doesn't go as fast as mine (does). **Zha mai sígo!** Go faster!

sigurántsiya *nf* **1)** security, safety **2)** insurance, insurance policy **3)** guarantee

sigurimos *nm* confidence, safety, security, surety

sigúrno *adj* **1)** guaranteed, locked up, safe, secure **2)** reliable, trustworthy

sigúro *adj* **1)** confident, guaranteed, positive, safe, secure; **Sigúro sim ke wo phenel o chachimos.** I am confident he will tell the truth. **2)** *adv* by all means, certainly, of course, sure **3)** *comp/vt/i* **kerel** ~ determine, make sure

sigyárdyol *vi* to be hurried/rushed/speeded up: *pp/adj* **sigyardilo**

sigyarel *vt* **1)** accelerate, make to go fast, rush, speed up, speed up: *pp/adj* **sigyardo 2)** *v/refl* **sigyarél-pe** hurry oneself along, rush; **Sigyár-tut!** Hurry up!

sigyarimos *nm* **1)** acceleration, increased tempo **2)** hurry, rush **3)** urgency

sikadi *nf* omen, portent, sign

sikado *pp/adj* **1**) acquainted with, educated, experienced, trained, worldly wise **2**) displayed, exhibited, exposed **3**) *nm* educated man: *nf* **sikadi; Trobul amen mai but Rroma sikade.** We need more educated Roma.

sikádyol vi **1**) appear/show oneself, be displayed, be revealed: *pp/adj* **sikadilo 2**) be acquainted with/educated, be experienced

si-kai *v/phr* there is/are about/around; **Si-kai shel zhene ándo párko.** There are about a hundred people in the park.

sikamúra *nf* sycamore, sycamore tree

sikavel *vt* **1**) advise, educate, guide, teach, show (*how to*), point the way: *pp/adj* **sikado 2**) reveal/expose (*to be*) **3**) advise, train **4**) convince **5**) *id* **sikadem lês o drom.** I showed him the road/I sent him about his business. **6**) ~ **wása** put hands up (*at a meeting*), show hands, wave to *smbdy* **7**) *v/refl* **sikavél-pe a**) teach oneself **b**) introduce oneself, reveal oneself to be, turn out to be **c**) commit indecent exposure; **Phuro gazho sikadyás-pe nango ánde úlitsa hai le rai shudine les ándo mobíli.** An old guy exposed himself on the street and the cops threw him in the (police) car. **d**) make an appearance, make one's presence felt, show oneself

sikavno *adj* **1**) instructive, instructional **2**) *nm* instructor, teacher: *nf* **sikavni**

sikayimáski sóba *comp/nf* classroom

sikayimos/sikayvimos *nm* **1**) advice, education, erudition, experience, teaching **2**) revelation **3**) demonstration, display, exhibition **4**) exposure **5**) flashing, indecent exposure

sikimáta *nm/pl* studies

sikimos *nm* learning, study

sikiyil *vt* **1**) lure, tease, tempt: *pp/adj* **sikiyime 2**) annoy, irritate

sikiyimos *nm* allure, allurement, teasing, temptation, tempting by teasing

sikiyitóri *nm* teaser, tempter: *nf* **sikiyitórka**

síkla *nf* bicycle (*Eur*)

síklo *nm* **1**) cycle **2**) bicycle

sikréto *nm* **1**) secret **2**) moral (*to a story*) **2**) *adj* confidential, secret

sikyarel *vt* see **sikavel**

sikyayitóri *nm* **1**) male *psn* who instructs/shows/teaches: *nf* **sikyayitórka 2**) guide **3**) flasher, streaker (*Am*)

síkyol/síklyol *vi* **1**) learn, be shown, get used to, become familiar with, be taught: *pp/adj* **sikilo; Sikilem látar pa l' draba.** I learned about herbs from her. **2**) practice, study, teach oneself; **Mangav te sikyovav Franzuzítska.** I want to learn French. **Sikilem kólkorro.** I learned on my own.

sîla *nf* **1**) force, power, occult/spiritual power, strength **2**) *vt/i* **lel pe** ~ overpower, take by force, rape, violate **3**) *comp/vi* **mangel pe** ~ insist; **Manglem pe sîla ke zhal.** I insisted that he go.

sîlno *adj* **1**) all mighty, forceful, powerful, strong **2**) omnipotent

sîlowíl *vt* **1**) despoil, loot, plunder, ravage, sack, take by force **2**) deflower, ravish, rape, violate

sîlowimé *pp/adj* **1**) looted/plundered, taken by force **2**) deflowered, ravished, raped, violated

sîlowimós *nm* **1**) looting, sack **2**) defloration, rape, rapine, violation **3**) sexual molestation, violation

sîlowitóri *nm* **1**) looter, plunderer **2**) rapist, violator

sim *v* I am; **Rrom sim.** I am (a) Romani man.

símas *v* I was/used to be/have been (*v/s/to be*)

simil *vt* seed, sow seeds: *pp/adj* **simime**

simimos *nm* seeding time

siminériya *nf* seminary

sîmîníl/sêmîníl *vt* **1**) plant/sow (*seeds*) **2**) *v/refl* **sîmîníl-pe** become seeded, take seed

sîmînimé *pp/adj* planted, seeded, sown

sîmînimós *nm* sowing, sowing time

sîmìnsa/sîmìntsa/sêmínsa/sêmúnsa *nf* **1)** grain, kernel, seed (*wheat*) **2)** semen **3)** ancestry, pedigree (*of an animal*), stock

simitériya *nf* cemetery

simpátiko *adj* friendly, nice, pleasant (*Eur*)

Sim-Pétre/Sim-Pétri Saint Peter

Sim-Pétri Saint Peter

Sim-Petrína *nm/voc* Saint Peter

sinagóga *nf* synagogue

sinematúra *nf* **1)** portable film projection equipment **2)** trade of itinerant cinema presentations (*in villages in Mexico by Mexican and American Roma*)

sini *nf* tray

síniya/siníya *nf* table

siniyítsa *nf* meager table, small table

síno *nm* **1)** film, movie **2)** cinema, movie threatre

Sintiyítska *nf* a Romani dialect of the Sinti group

Sintiyítsko *adj* Sinti, of the Sinti

Sínto *nm* male member of the Sinti group: *nf* **Sintáika**

sinyáko *gen/adj* of the table, table; **sinyáki-gili** table song, **sinyáki fátsa** table top

sinzizáto *nm* electric synthesizer (*Mus*)

Siptímbra *nf* September

Siptímbrone *adv* in September

sir *nf* garlic; **siráko-manrro** garlic bread

siréna *nf* mermaid, siren

siríngo *nm* syringe

sírma *nf* **1)** metallic brocade, strand, thread; **sáni sírma** slender thread **2)** lace (*shoe*)

sirmorro *nm* small string/thread

sistéma *nf* system; **sistéma-sonóri** sound system

sîta *nf* **1)** dipper, filter, sieve, siphon, strainer; **E Bári Síta** The Big Dipper **2)** coffe percolator

sîtíl *vt* filter, sift, strain, siphon: *pp/adj* **sitime**

sîtimós *nm* filtering, sifting, straining, syphoning

sitizáno *nm* male citizen *nf.* **sitizáika** (*Am*)

síto *nm* site

situwátsiya *nf* situation

sívo *adj* grey (*Eur*)

Siyas! *interj* Cheers!

siyasil *v* propose a toast: *pp/adj* **siyasime 2)** **siyasíl-pe** *v/refl* be toasting

siyasimos *nm* toasting

sîyíl *vt* **1)** plant, seed, sow **2)** be planted, sowed, seeded

sîyimé *pp/adj* planted, sowed, seeded

sîyimós *nm* planting, seeding, sowing

sîyitóri *nm* planter, sower of seeds: *nf* **sîyitórka**

skába *nf* stitch

skála *nf* **1)** scale (*Mus*): *pl* **skéli 2)** step of a ladder or stairway

skamin *nm* **1)** chair, bench; **baro skamin** easy chair **2)** bridge of a stringed instrument (*Mus*)

skamin pe rróti *nm/phr* chair on castors

skaminári *nm* maker or repairer of chairs/rattan chairs

skaminash *nm* maker/repairer of chairs

skaminorro *nm* footstool, small chair

skandálo *nm* **1)** scandal, skeleton in the closet **2)** rumor

skára *nf* step of a ladder or stairway: *pl* **skéri**

skarlatína *nf* scarlet fever

skatérka *nf* tablecloth

skayétso/skayéto *nm* **1)** burdock **2)** burr

skéla *nf* **1)** stair, step **2)** ferry, ferryboat

skêlchála *nf* conundrum, jig-saw puzzle, puzzle: *pl* **skêlchéli; swatêngi-skêlchála** crossword puzzle

skêlchelíl *vt* confuse, puzzle **2)** **skêlchelíl-pe** become confused/puzzled

skêlchelimós *nm* **1)** consternation **2)** conundrum, puzzle, riddle

skêlchimé *pp/adj* puzzled

skéli *nf/pl* steps, stairs

skéma *nf* scheme

skêpíl *vt* **1)** free, protect (from), rescue, save: *pp/adj* **skêpimé 2)** dispose of, get rid of, rid oneself of **3)** *v/refl* **skêpíl-pe a)** escape, escape (from), be saved, save oneself **b)** rid oneself of, be disposed of, get free from; **Skêpisáilem múrre**

pharimatándar. I rid myself of my worries.

skêpimós nm 1) escape 2) rescue 3) Salvation 4) pl skêpimáta disposable clutter/materials/junk

skêpisávol vi be rescued/saved (Eur) see skêpil-pe v/refl

skéri nf ladder, stairway

skéritsa nf stepladder

skini nm skinhead: pl skiní (Eur); Marde lês le skini. The skinheads assaulted him.

skinteyíl-pe v/refl 1) sparkle 2) spark, throw off sparks: pp/adj skinteyime

skinteyimos nm shooting of sparks, sparking

skintíya nf spark: pl skintíyi/skinteyi

skintomos nm dislocation, sprain

sklintol vt 1) dislocate, sprain: pp/adj sklintome 2) v/refl sklintól-pe become dislocated/sprained

skóika nf 1) oyster: pl skoitsi 2) shelfishl (clam, mussel, etc) 3) limpit

SKOKRA; nf/abbreviation of Sóveto Katar le Organizátsiyi hai Kumpaníyi Rromane ánda l' Américhi. Council of the Organizations and Romani Communities of the Americas. A united front of Romani organizations and communities in Latin America, Central America and North America.

Skokráko gen/adj belonging to SKOKRA qv

skópíl vt 1) castrate, geld 2) make impotent, neuter 3) sterilize 4) v/refl skopíl-pe become impotent

skopime pp/adj 1) castrated, gelded 2) made impotent 3) neutered, sterilized

skopimos nm 1) castration, gelding 2) impotence 3) sterilization

skópitsa nf 1) eunuch 2) sterilized woman or female animal

skorbúto nm scurvy

skorrushelin nf persimmon tree

skorrush nm persimmon

Skotishmáno nm Scotsman: nf Skotishmánka (Am)

Skotlandítsko adj Scottish

Skotlándiya nf Scotland

skótya nf tablecloth

skráma nf 1) knickknack, trinket 2) id Chi muklas chi yekh skráma. He left without a trace/He didn't leave a trace/one thing behind. (Am)

skrípta nf script

skriptúra nf scripture

skrivil/skriyil vt 1) inscribe, write: pp/adj skrivime (Eur) 2) v/refl skrivíl-pe be inscribed

skrivimáski-shib comp/nf/neolog literary language, language as written

skrivimásko/skriyimásko gen/adj having to do with writing, literary, writing

skrivimos/skriyimos nm inscription, transcript/transcription

skriyipe nm inscription, transcription (Eur)

skrúma nf 1) cigarette/cigar/pipe ash 2) ash from burnt incense

skrumára nf ash tray (Eur)

skrúmo nf ashes, cigar/cigarette/pipe ash (Eur)

skrumol vi burn by droping hot ashes, singe: pp/adj skrumome (Eur)

skulptúra nf sculpture

skúpo adj costly, expensive (Eur)

skúrto adj short (in length); skúrtsi bal short hair

skúrto drom comp/nm shortcut, short way round

skurtol vt 1) make shorter, shorten: pp/adj skurtome 2) v/refl skurtól-pe become shorter

skurtomos nm brevity, shortness

skúrto-rrókya nf short skirt, miniskirt (Am)

skúrturya nm/pl Bermuda shorts, shorts (Am)

skurtyarel vt shorten: pp/adj skurtyardo

skurtyarimos nm reduction in length, shortening

skútso adj honed to a fine edge, sharp

skutsol vt 1) hone, sharpen, make sharp, whet 2) v/refl skutsól-pe a) be sharpened, take an edge b) dress sharply, dress to kill

(Am): **Skutsól-pe o Stévo.** Steve dresses sharply/like a dude.

skutsome *pp/adj* **1)** acute, astute, sharp, sharpened, whetted **2)** cool, dapper, neat, sharp *(Am)*; **skútsome tsáliya** sharp clothes. **Skutsome meyázos.**You look sharp.*(Am)*

skutsomos *nm* **1)** edge, sharpness *(of a cutting tool)* **2)** astuteness *(Am)*

skwártsa *nf* bark *(of a tree)*

skwartsáko *gen/adj* of bark, bark

slaiyúxa *nf* **1)** messy woman, slattern **2)** slut

slaiyúxo *nm* bottom feeder, dissolute wretch, scumbag, sot

slapavítsa *nf* **1)** sleet **2)** slush **3)** *comp/vt/i* **del ~** sleet is falling

sláta *nf* sleet

slâto *nm* slot *(Am)*

sláva *nf* **1)** banquet, celebration, feast *(usually in honour of a Saint)* **2)** Saint's day

slavil *vt* **1)** celebrate, feast, honour by feasting: *pp/adj* **slavime; Ame slavis e Santána.** We feast Saint Ann's Day. **Ame slavis amáre mai bare gesa.** We celebrate our most important days. **2)** *v/refl* **slavíl-pe** celebrate, be celebrating by preparing a feast table; **Slavín-pe ándo hâlo.** They are celebrating the feast in the hall. **Slavíl-pe o gazho.** The man is celebrating himself *(said of a drunk singer passing in the street)*.

Slavóko *nm* Slav: *nf* **Sláváika**

slavorro *nm* host of a feast, man giving a feast

sléto *nm* slate, slate for an election; **Kon si po sléto?** Who is on the slate? *(Am)*

slobezhil *vt* **1)** emancipate, free, liberate, set free: *pp/adj* **slobezhime 2)** *v/refl* **slobezhíl-pe** become free, emancipated, liberated, unfettered

slobóda/slóboda *nf* freedom, liberty

slobodil *vt* **1)** free, set free: *pp/adj* **slobodime 2)** *v/refl* **solobozhíl-pe** become free, free oneself

slobodítsko-lil *comp/nm* letter of pardon, parole, release form

slóbodno *adj* free, at liberty

slóbodo *adj* **1)** allowed, permitted **2)** at liberty, available, emancipated, free, loose, untied **2)** *nm* freedom, liberty, permission, right; **Nai tut slóbodo te zhas.** You don't have the right to go.

slobozhimos *nm* freedom, liberty

Slobuzhéniya *nf* Emancipation of Romani slaves in Romania in 1864.

slucháino *adv* accidentally, by chance

sluchayíl-pe *v/refl* happen, take place, occur; **So sluchayisáilo?** What happened? **Zhanes tu so sluchayisáilo le grastênsa?** Do you know what happened to (with) the horses? **Nai lêske so sluchayíl-pe.** He doesn't care what happens.

sluchayimos *nm* event, happening, occurance; **sluchayimáta te aven** forthcoming events.

slúga *nf* domestic, servant, *fig* slave: *pl* **slúzhi; Sim ki Rromni, chi sim ki slúga!** I am your wife, I am not your slave!

slugíl *vt* **1)** draft, make to serve, serve: *pp/adj* **slugime; Slugisardyas pansh bersh ánde kataníya.** He served five years in the armed forces. **Nashti slugis do-xulan.** You can't serve two masters. **2)** *v/refl* **slugíl-pe** serve, be drafted; **Slugisáilo.** He was drafted *(Am)*

slúgo *nm* domestic, servant: *pl* **slúzha/slúgurya**

slúzhba *nf* **1)** daily grind, drudgery, grunt work, menial work **2)** monotonous, time-consuming work for little recompense, soul-sucking drudgery **3)** domestic service

sluzhbáika *nf* charwoman, drudge

smêntána *nf* cream

smêrkíl *vt* pump *(by hand)*: *pp/adj* **smêrkimé**

smêrkimós *nm* pumping

smêrko/smîrko *nm* hand-operated pump, crank pump, shadoof, well pump

smokína *nf* fig
smokinelin *nf* fig tree
snat *nf* 1) warning 2) *comp/vt/vi* **lel ~** take warning, be warned 3) *comp/vt/vi* **del ~** give warning
snatáko sámno *comp/nm* danger signal, warning sign
snopil *vt* bind/tie up in bunches/bundles/sheaves: *pp/adj* **snopime**
snopimos *n* binding sheaves of wheat, bundling, making bunches
snópo *nm* 1) bail, bouquet, bunch, cluster 2) sheaf 3) **~ khas** bail of hay
so *pron* 1) what; **So keres?** What are you doing? **Chi zhanel so kerel.** He doesn't know what he is doing. **So gîndís?** What do you think? **Chi hakyarel so del duma.** He doesn't understand what he's talking about. 2) *idiom* **Nai ma so te kerav.** I have not what to do/I don't have anything to do. **Nai lês so te kerel.** He's got nothing to do. **Dévla! So si te keras?** God! What can we do about it/what can be done about it?
sóba *nf* room; **shukar sóba** living room, **sóba opral** attic, **sovimáski sóba** bedroom
sóba-gasóski *comp/nf* gas chamber
sobódniko *nm* 1) roomer: *pl* **sobódnichi**: *nf* **sobódnika** 2) **kher-sobódniko** rooming house
soboláko *nm* male rat: *pl* **sobolácha**: *nf* **soboláika** (*Am*)
soboláko-paiyêsko *comp/nm* muskrat (*Am*)
soborrála *nf* hernia, rupture
soborril *vt* 1) rupture: *pp/adj* **soborrime** 2) *v/refl* **soborríl-pe** become herniated/ruptured
soborrime *pp/adj* herniated, ruptured
soborrimos *nm* 1) rupture 2) hernia
sóda *nf* soft drink, pop
sóde *adv* as much, how much; **Sóde vrámya sánas tu kai sláva?** How long were you at the feast? **Chi zhanav sóde koshtíl-pe.** I don't know how much it

costs. **Kam-azhutiv tu sóde kai dashtiv.** I'll help you as much as I can.
sóde de dur *adv* how far; **Sóde de dur ka Toronto?** How far to Toronto? **Sóde de dur si?** How far is it?
sodêngo *adv* how old; **Sodêngo san?** How old are you?
sodéto *adv* 1) what date; **Sodéto si ages?** What date/day of the month is it? 2) what/which number; **Sodéto san pe lísta?** What number are you on the list?
sódevar *adv* how many times
sodya *pron/adv* how many, how many people; **Sodya shave si tut?** How many children do you have? **Sodya sas ándo hãlo?** How many people were in the hall?
sófta *nf* couch, sofa
sogodi *pron* whatever, whichever, in as far as, in as much as; **Sogodi kai keres, arakhel tut ánde wúrma.** Whatever you do, he'll find you in the end. **Sogodi mothól te kerel, kerel po sigúro.** Whatever he says he will do, he is sure to do.
sogodil *vt* 1) *figure out*, reckon *var of* **sokotil** *qv* 2) *v/refl* **sogodíl-pe** reckon to oneself, figure out for oneself
sogodimos *nm* account, reckoning
sohóro *nm* bridal veil, christening veil
sokotíl *vt* 1) decide, decide in council/group decision: *pp/adj* **sokotime** 2) calculate, deduce, figure out, reason, reckon 3) estimate 4) *v/refl* **sokotíl-pe a)** deduce, introspect oneself, reckon for oneself, reason out for onself; **Gîndisáilem pe so sokotisáilem.** I contemplated on what I had figured out. **b)** estimate
sokotimos *nm* 1) addition, bill, count, reckoning 2) accounting, financial report 3) estimate 4) calculation, deduction
sókra *nf* mother-in-law
sókro *nm* father-in-law: *pl* **sókrya**
soláriya *nf* monstrance, gold candalebras and other gold or gold-plated items used in Catholic churches.

soláriyo *nm* ostensorium, monstrance: *pl* **soláriya**

solax *nf* 1) affirmation, assurance, guarantee, oath, promise, vow, word of honour 2) parole; **Mekle lês te zhal pe solax.** They released him on parole. 3) *comp/vi* **lel ~** swear/take an oath, vow; **Les tu solax pe túte te mothos o chachimos?** Will you swear an oath to tell the truth? 3) *comp/vi* **del ~** give a guarantee/oath/promise 4) **kerel ~** make a promise/vow 5) *vt/ph* **Mekel te zhal pe ~** release on parole

solaxal *vi* assure, guarantee, promise, swear an oath: *pp/adj* **solaxado**; **solaxadyas ánde kris.** He swore an oath at the trial.

soldáta *nm/nf* fighter, soldier, trooper, veteran/survivor of life

soldatsíya *nf* army, soldiery, troops

soldui *pron* both, both of the; **Soldui avile.** They both came. **Dikhlem le solden.** I saw both of them (*if male*). **Dem-dúma le soldánsa.** I spoke with both of them. (*if female*)

sólfa-yagáki *comp/nf* fire extinguisher

solidaritéto *nm* solidarity

solum *nf* piece of straw *us plural in* **soluma**

soluma *nf/pl* straw

solumítsa *nf* drinking straw

solútsiya *nf* solution

sólza *nf* scale; **mashêske sólzi**, scales of a fish

sóma *adv* just, only now; **Sóma dikhlem lês araki.** I just saw him yesterday. **Sóma avilo ándo hãlo.** He just came into the hall. **Sóma akhardem te phenav túke ánda e sláva.** I just called to tell you about the feast.

sómo *nm* 1) tuna 2) catfish (*Am*)

sonóri *nm* sound: *pl* **sonóriya** (*Eur*)

sorr *adj/adv* all; **sorr o ges** all day, **Xalyas sórr o mas.** He ate all the meat.

sórro *pron/adj* all, every, the whole

sórrone-gesêsko *comp/adj* all-day, day-long

sórrono *pron* all, each one, everybody

sórro-ryáto *adv/phr* all night, all night long, throughout the night

sórta *nf* 1) formula, recipe 2) kind, ilk, sort (*Am*) 3) method, process

sósa *pron/inst* with what; **Sósa kinel? Nai lês love.** With what will he buy (it)? He has no money.

sosetátiya *nf* surrounding society (*Eur*)

soséto *adj* affable, cordial, easy-going, friendly, genial, sociable

sóska *nf* baby bottle

sóske *pron* why (*Eur*), *see also* **sóstar** *pron*

sósko *pron* what kind of, of what

sospíno *nm see* **suspíno** *nm*

sóstar *adv/conj/pron/interj/nm* 1) why; **Sóstar avilan?** Why have you come? **Sóstar dar túke?** Why are you afraid? **Chi zhanav sóstar.** I don't know why. 2) *nm* explanation, motive, provocation, reason; **Nai lês sóstar.** He has no motive/reason.

sóste 1) *adv* why (*Eur*) 2) *nm/prep* what (*Am*); **Pe sóste thos tyo gîndo?** On what do you place (base) your theory? **Ánda sóste si gadya?** What's that about?

sostin *nf* singlet, T-shirt, undershirt

sostya *nf/pl* 1) underwear 2) long johns, male underwear

Sosyalísmo *nm* Socialism

Socialísto *adj* 1) Socialist 2) Socialist *nm*: **Sosyalísta** *nf*

sosyálno *adj* social (*Eur*)

sosyetáto *nm* surrounding society (*Eur*)

sovel *vi* 1) sleep, be asleep, be sleeping: *pp/adj* **suto**; **Sovel e gláta?** Is the baby sleeping? **Sovélas sórro ges.** He's been sleeping all day. 2) go off to sleep; **Zhav mánge te sovav.** I am going to sleep. 3) **~** *with instrumental case*; sleep with, make love to. **Mangel te sovel lása.** He wants to sleep with her. 4) go to eternal rest, be at eternal rest; **Te sovel mishto!** May he/she be at eternal rest! 5) be dormant; **Ándo ivênd, le lulugya soven.** In the winter, the flowers are dormant. 6) lie, be lying; **Sovel pe l' phaleya.** He is lying on the floor. 7) act lost, be in a daze 8) **~**

tele lie down; **Sov tele po than**! Lie down on the bed! **9)** *v/refl* **sovél-pe a)** go to bed, fall asleep, go to sleep, put oneself to sleep; **Khino san, trobul te sovés-tu.** You are tired, you need to sleep. **Zhá-ma te sová-man.** I'm going away to sleep/I'm going to bed. **Mangel te sovél-pe**. He wants to go to sleep. **Nashti sová-ma, trobul ma píldurya,** I can't sleep, I need sleeping pills. **Sutyás-pe pe'l phaleya.** She fell asleep on the floor. **b)** hibernate; **Le risha sovén-pe ándo ivend.** Bears hibernate during the winter.

sóveto *nm* **1)** Council. **2)** office, NGO, organization **3)** advice, counsel

Sovimáski Shukarni *comp/nf* Sleeping Beauty (*Folk*)

sovimásko *gen/adj* **1)** sleep-inducing **2)** boring **3)** sleeping

sovimos *nm* sleep, sleeping

sovyardo *pp/adj* **1)** put to sleep (*as a baby*). **2)** euthanized **3)** hypnotized

sovyárdyol *vi* **1)** to be put to sleep: *pp/adj* **sovyardilo**; **E gláta tobul te sovyárdyol**, The baby girl needs to be put to bed **2)** euthanize, put down; **Kodo phuro zhukel trobul te sovyárdyol.** That old dog needs to be euthensized. **3)** be bored **4)** become hypnotized

sovyarel *vt* **1)** cause/make to sleep, put to bed/sleep: *pp/adj* **sovyardo 2)** put to sleep, euthanize **3)** bore to death **4)** hypnotize

sovyarimásko *gen/adj* boring, sleep-inducing

sovyarimos *nm* **1)** act of putting to sleep/bed **2)** euthanasia

spândja *nf* sponge (*Am*)

sparadrápo *nm* adhesive bandage, Band-Aid (*Eur*)

spasénya *nf* good deed, favour

spáta *nf* spade (*Eur*)

spátsiya/spásiya *nf* room, space

spátso *nm* sparrow, nickname for a very small man (*Eur*)

spektákulo *nm* show, presentation: *pl* **spektákulya** (*Eur*)

spektatóri *nm* spectator: *nf* **spektatórka**

spektatóriya *nm/pl* audience, spectators

spesyálno *adj* special (*Eur*)

spídel *vt* **1)** jostle, push, shove, urge: *pp/adj* **spidino**; **Spíde e sínya prótivo o zudo!** Push the table against the wall! **Spídem lês te zhal**. I urged him to go. **Spidem lês te na kerel.** I urged him not to do it. **2) spídél-pe** push oneself, exert oneself to do

spidemos *nm* **1)** jostling, push, pushing, urging **2)** onrush, surge forward

spíko *nm* railway spike

spína *nf* thorn, plant or bush having thorns: *pl* **spíni** thorn-bush patch

spináka *nf* spinach

spítsa *nf* spoke (*of a wheel*)

splinchána *nf* **1)** eyebrow **2)** eyelash

splínta *nm* chock, wedge

spônxa *nf* sponge (*Eur*)

sporil *vt* **1)** fight. quarrel **2) sporíl-pe** *v/refl* fight, quarrel

sporimos *nm* fighting, quarreling

spóro *nm* bet, wager; **Thodem spóro po marimos**. I made a bet on the fight/boxing match.

sportívo *adj* sportive, having to do with athletics/sports; **gazho sportívo** sportsman

spórto *nm* sport, sports

sportsmáno athlete, sportsman: *nf* **sportsmánka**

spreyil *vt* **1)** spray, spray paint; **Spreyisardem o mobíli**. I spray painted the car. **2)** *v/refl* **spreyíl-pe** spray, be sprayed (*Am*)

spreyime *pp/adj* sprayed, spray painted.

spreyimos *nm* spray painting, spraying

sprúsa *nf* spruce, spruce wood

sprusáko *gen/adj* spruce

spruselin *nf* spruce tree

spúma *nf* **1)** froth, lather, foam, spume, suds **2)** frog spittle **3)** saliva

spumalo *adj* frothy, sudsy

spumól-pe *vi* foam: pp/*adl* **spumome**; **Spumólas-pe pêske móstar.** He was foaming from the mouth.

spûnzo *nm* Mayapple (*podophyllum peltatum*)

stádiya *nf* grandstand, stadium

stáfi *nm/neolog* employees, staff (*Eur*)

stafída *nf* currant, raisin

stagi *nm* hat; **kali stagi** black hat (*traditionally worn by Romani family heads and elders, esp in Europe*)

stagyári *nm* millener

stagyorri *nf* baby bonnet

stakatáto *nm* staccato, double-beat on drums (*Mus*)

stákla/shtákla *nf* 1) glass 2) monacle 3) glass bottle/jar 4) hourglass

stakláki-mênshiya *com/nf* crystal ball

stakláko *gen/adj* glass, made of glass; **stakláki yakh** glass eye

staklalo *adj var of* **stakluno** *adj qv*

stákli/shtákli *nf/pl* eyeglasses; **kále stákli** sunglasses

stáklitsa *nf* 1) glass bead, mica glass, rhinestone 2) glass marble 3) lens

stakluní-patrin *comp/nf/neolog* transparency

stakluno *adj* having the qulality of glass, smooth like glass, transparent

stála *see* **shtála** *nf*

Stalinísmo *nm* hard-line communism, Stalinism (*Eur*)

Stalíno *nm* Joseph Stalin (*Eur*)

stámena *nf* 1) rock, stone 2) cairn

stámpa *nf* postage stamp (*Am*)

stampil *vt* stamp, place a stamp: *pp/adj* **stampime**

stampíla *nf* corporate stamp, rubber stamp

standardaizil *vt/neolog* 1) standardize: *pp/adj* **standardaizime** 2) *v/refl* **standardaizíl-pe** become standardized

standárdo 1) *adj* standard 2) *nm* standard

stánlitsa *nf* 1) bedbug 2) tick 3) chigger (*Am*)

stánsiya *nm* bus/railway station, station; **rêngi stánsiya** police station, **stánsiya gasóski** gas station

starluchal *vi* gleam, glimnmer, glisten, glitter, reflect light, shimmer, shine, sparkle: *pp/adj* **starluchailo**;

Starluchánas le chera ándo chéri. The stars were shining in the sky. **Starluchálas o phérdo shon.** The full moon was shining.

starluchála *nf* 1) reflection, shine 2) starlight

starluchimos *nm* glistening, glittering, shimmering shining, sparkling

startuwil *vt* 1) begin, start, turn on: *pp/adj* **startuwime** 2) *v/refl* **startuwíl-pe** start, be started

státo *nm* 1) body 2) bearing, figure, shape, stature; **Shukar státo kai zhuli.** The girl has a nice figure. 3) **Státo** State

Státurya Maladine *nm/pl* United States

status *nm* status (*as a refugee, claimant, etc*)

statútso *nm* figurine

sténa *nf* stage

stêngál *adv* from the left/left side; **Maladyas múrro mobíli stêngál.** He crashed into my car from the left side.

stêngásh *nm* left-handed person: *nf* **stêngáshka**

stêngo *adj* 1) left; **stêngo wast** left hand, *id* **Si lês dui stênzhi punrre.** He has two left feet. 2) *nm* left; **Bangyar ka o stêngo!** Turn to the left!

stêngonés *adv/prep* left, on the left side of, to the left of; **O bírto si stêngonés la khangeryátar pe stêngo rêg le dromêski te zhas ka o Lanórdo.** The bar is to the left of the church on the left side of the road if you are going North.

stêngoné-wastêsko *comp/adj* left-handed

stêpêníl *vt* 1) govern, have dominion over, rule: *pp/adj* **stêpênimé; Kodo emperáto chi stêpênílas mishto.** That king didn't rule well. 2) enforce discipline, discipline 3) *v/refl* **stêpêníl-pe a)** be governed/ruled **b)** rule oneself **c)** have discipline over oneself

stêpênimós *nm* 1) domination, rule 2) discipline

Stéto *nm* State of the USA (*Am*)

Stetósko *gen/adj* State, belonging to the State (*Am*)

Stéturya Kidine *nm/pl/comp/nm* United
States (of America)
steyágo/stiyágo *nm* 1) banner, flag 2)
bridal standard (*pole adorned with
ribbons or head scarves carried around
at a Kalderash wedding*). 3) The first
bandana (**diklo**) given to a Romani bride
on betrothal and worn for the first time at
her wedding before the guests to show
her new status as a **bori**
stíko *nm* bayonet (*Mil*)
stîlpo/shtîlpo *nm* 1) style 2) pillar, pole,
post 3) brace, prop, support
stipénda *nf* allowance, stipend (*Eur*)
stíriyo *nm* stereo player
stokáto *nm* 1) investor 2) stock broker 3)
shareholder
stôko *nm* stock, stockmarket (*Am*); **po
stôko** on the stockmarket
stóla *nf* stole; **vizonéski stóla** mink stole
stómago *nm* stomach
stóriyo *nf* report, magazine/newspaper
story (*Am*): *pl* **stóriya**
stóro *nm* store (*Am*): *pl* **stórya**
stráfo *nm* fine, penalty
strafyal/shtrafyal *vt/i* 1) flash lightning;
Strafyáilo. Lightning flashed 2) be
struck by lightning 3) light up
strafyarel *vt* strike by lightning: *pp/adj*
strafyardo
strafyarimos *nm* act of being struck by
lightning
strafyayimásko *gen/adj* flashing
strafyayimos *nm* lightning, flash of
lightning, flash of light
stramil *vt* 1) abuse, illtreat, mistreat:
pp/adj **stramime** 2) **stramíl-pe** *v/refl* be
abused/mistreated
stramimos *nm* abuse, illtreatment,
mistreatment
strána *nf* beach
strangil *vt* 1) filter, strain, wring (*washing*):
pp/adj **strangime** 2) squeeze 3) *v/refl*
strangíl-pe be filtered, squeezed out,
wrung out
strangimos *nm* filtering, straining,
wringing

stranxéro *nm* stranger: *nf* **stranxerútsa**
(*probably Am from Sp*)
strázha *nf* 1) deportation 2) guard,
surveillance; **pe strázha** under guard,
under surveillance 3) deportation; **Gêló
pe strázha.** He was deported. 4) custody;
ánde strázha, in custody
strazhánya *nf* banishment, deportation
strazhári *nm* bodyguard, escort, guard
strazhil *vt* 1) expel, deport 2) guard, keep
watch 3) *v/refl* **strazhíl-pe** be
deported/expelled
strazhime *pp/adj* banished, deported,
expelled
strazhnimos *nm* 1) danger, risk;
Chungerdel po strazhnimos. He has
contempt for danger 2) menace
strázhno *adj* 1) dangerous, hazardous,
risky; **Na tho tu kathe ke si strázhno!**
Don't hang around here because it's
dangerous! 2) menacing 3) *nm* danger,
hazard, risk, menace
strazhnones *adv* dangerously, hazardously,
menacingly
strázo *adv* 1) right away, immediately 2)
soon, *cont of* **izdrázo** *adv qv*
strékya/shtrékya *nf* bonanza, killing,
lucky strike, strike; **Mardem bári
shtrékya.** I hit a big strike/had a run of
success in business/ struck a big business
deal.
streyinil *vt* 1) estrange, make *smbdy* a
stranger: *pp/adj* **streyinime** 2)
streyiníl-pe a) become estranged **b)**
estrange oneself
streyinimos *nm* estrangement, separation
(*from a spouse*)
streyíno *adj* 1) alien, foreign, strange 2)
nm male stranger: *nf* **streyinútsa**
strítsa *nf* pouch
stropíl *vt* 1) splash 2) **stropíl-pe** *v/refl*
stropimos *nm* splashing
strugála *nf* plane (*tool*) (*Eur*)
strugelil *vt* plane, shave down: *pp/adj*
strugelime (*Eur*)
strúguro *nm* grape (*Am*)
struktúra *nf/neolog* structure

strumênto *nm* instrument (*Mus*)

stúdiya *nf/neolog* study: *pl* **stúdiyi**; **Rrómane stúdiyi.** Romani studies

studiyil *vt/neolog* 1) study: *pp/adj* **studiyime** 2) *v/refl* be studied

stúdiyo *nm* studio: *pl* **stúdya**

stugil *vt* 1) pile, stack: *pp/adj* **stugime** 2) *v/refl* **stugíl-pe** be piled, stacked

stúgo/stúko *nm* haystack, stack, pile; **stúgo gozhni** pile of manure

stugol/stukol *vt* 1) stack (*hay*): *pp/adj* **stugome** 2) stoke (*coal*)

stugomos *nm* stacking, stoking

stúko *nm* pike (*fish*)

stûmpo *nm* blind, butt

stúrko *nm* stork

subdjékto *nm* subject

Súdo *nm* South

Sudósko *adj* South, southern

sukalétso *nm* draw-string bag/purse

súko/sóko 1) juice 2) tree sap 3) semen, sperm (*Eur*)

súlitsa *nf* 1) arrow 2) *id* bow and arrow; **Lyas pêski súlitsa hai mudardyas le shoshes.** He took his bow and arrow and killed/shot the rabbit. (*Folk*)

Sultáno *nm* Sultan

súma *nf* bill, sum, sum of, total

sumagi *nf* 1) bail, pledge, parole 2) *comp/adv* **pe sumagi** on bail; **Anklisto pe sumagi.** He got out on bail. 3) *comp/vi* **thol ~ a)** post bail **b)** pawn, place in hock 4) *vt* **dav pe ~** pawn

sumagyári *nm* 1) pawnbroker 2) bail bondsman

sumagyáriya *nf* pawn shop

súmnakai *nm* gold

sumnakári *nm* goldsmith

sumnakásko *gen/adj* made of gold

sumnakunil *vt* 1) plate with gold 2) *v/refl* **sumnakuníl-pe** be plated with gold; **Shai sumnakuníl-pe kako?** Can this be plated with gold?

sumnakunime *pp/adj* gold-plated

sumnakunimos *nm* gold plating

sumnakuno *adj* 1) gold, having the colour/quality of gold 2) *fig* alluring, attractive, charming, persuasive; **Sumnakunó-lo núma strázhno si.** It looks alluring but it's dangerous. **Xoxadyas la sumnakune swatonênsa.** He deceived her with smooth talk/impressive bullshit. **Si lês shib sumnakuni.** He has a golden tongue/He is a master conman.

Sumnakuno Fluyeritóri *comp/nm/fig* Pied Piper, person who leads others astray with smooth talk

sumnakunó-gazho *comp/nm* Sugar Daddy, very wealthy man

sung *nf* aroma, odor, scent, smell

sungal *vt/i* 1) scent, smell: *pp/adj* **sungailo; O zhukel sungyayas lêski wúlma.** The dog scented his trail.

sungalo 1) *adj* exuding an odor/smell

sungyarel/sungavel *vt* create an odor/smell: *pp/adj* **sungyardo**

sungyarimásko *gen/adj* able to create an odor

sunitóri *nm* dreamer: *nf* **sunitórka**

suno *nm* 1) dream, imagination; **Motho mánge pa tyo suno!** Tell me about your dream? 2) ambition 3) vision 4) fantasy; **Si lês suno kai nashti anklel.** He has a dream that cannot be realized/an impossible dream. 5) *vt/i/phr* **dikhel ándo ~** dream. see in a dream, imagine

suntsokréto *nm* sunflower

superstítsiya *nf* superstition

supíka *nf* 1) icepick, pick, toothpick 2) broach pin, pin, safety pin, tie pin 3) splinter 4) icicle 5) spike

supozil *vt/i* 1) assume, suppose; **Suposiv ke wo avel tehára.** I suppose he is coming tomorrow. 2) *v/refl* **supozíl-pe** be assumed to be, suppose to be, be supposed to; **Supozíl-pe te avel tehára.** It is assumed/supposed that he is coming tomorrow.

supozime *pp/adj* supposed to, supposed to be

supozimos *nm* assumption. supposition

supózo *id* let's suppose, suppose

supríza *nf* surprise; **bari supríza** a big surprise

surogáto *nm* substitute, surrogate: *nf* **surogáta** (*Eur*)

sûrruchíl *vt/i* decide to, determine, have intent to, intend, plan to: *pp/adj* **sûrruchimé**

sûrruchimós *nm* decision, intent, intention, plan

susédo *nm* neighbour: *nf* **sesedútsa**

suspiníl-pe *vi* 1) sigh, sob, whimper 2) breathe asthmatically 3) gasp; **Suspinílas-pe te piyel balwal**. He was gasping for air.

suspíno *nm* 1) gasp, sigh, sob 2) cry, lament 3) asthma

suto *nm* 1) sleep 2) *pp/adj* asleep, sleeping; **do-pash suto** half asleep 3) **ashel suto** *comp/vi* fall asleep

súto *nm* 1) suit (*clothing*). (*Am*) 2) suit in cards (*Am*) 3) lawsuit (*Am*)

suv le dumêski *comp/nf* collar bone

suv *nf* 1) needle: *pl* **suvya** 2) key to a mystery 3) sign of the cross 4) hand on a watch or clock, indicator on a speedometer, mileage indicator, etc 5) secret society 6) **kerel ~** make the sign of the cross

suvárka *nm* dressmaker, seamstress

súvel *vt/i* 1) embroider, do needlework, sew, sew together: *pp/adj* **suvdo/suvlo**; **Súva mánge gad shukar**. Sew/embroider me a beautiful shirt. 2) bind together by stitching

suvimos *nm* 1) embroidery, needlework, sewing 2) binding 3) closing of a cloth package by sewing around all the edges.

suvyáko kan *comp/nm* eye of a needle

swágdar *adv* always, all the time, constantly, eternally, forever

Swagyárya *nf* The original name of the fast traditional dance melody often called **Báso** by Canadian/American *Kalderash*. It is played all over the Americas at weddings and other occasions as a solo or group dance.

swáko/sáko *pron* each, each one, each person, every, every person; **Swáko lyás pe dui**. Each person got two. **Swáko mursh si lês pêski baxt**. Every man has his own destiny. **swáko buki** each thing, everything

swakorráko *gen/pron* belonging to each *psn if nf*

swakorro *pron* each *psn*/thing, each and every *psn*/thing.

swakorrrêsko *gen/pron* belonging to each *psn if nm*

swatash *nm* 1) speaker, spokesman; **Kerdine le Stevos, pêngo swatash**. They made Steve their spokesman. 2) envoy, representative 3) go-between: *nf* **swatáshka**

swáto *nm* 1) word & *id*; **Kodo si o chácho Rrómano swáto**. That's the real Romani word. **E Rrómani shib si la but swáturya avre shibándar**. Romani has many words from other languages. **Manai swáto Rromanes godolêska**. There is no word in Romani for that. **Che djúngalo swáto!** What an obscenity! (*obscene word*) **Dyam-ame wúni swáturya**. We exchanged a few words/ had a brief conversation. **swáto po swáto** word by word. **Tu dyan man tyo swáto**. You gave me your word/promise. 2) statement/proposal; **Me sim túsa pe godo swáto**. I am with you/agree with you on that statement/proposal. 3) approval, promise; **Dav túke múrro swáto**. I give you my word/promise. 4) fairy tale usually dealing with supernatural, magical or divine myths such as the creation of the world or the origin of man and woman 5) lecture, speech; **Na de mánge swáto!** Don't lecture me! 6) pact 7) remark 8) say; **Phendem múrro swáto**. I have had my say. 9) *comp/vt* **del ~** speak for, represent (*us with dative of object*); **Trobul tu avokáto te del túke swáto**. You need a lawyer to represent you. **Kam-des swáto**

mánge? Will you speak on my behalf?
10) *comp/vi* **kerel ~** make a remark
swáto-garado *comp/nm* password
swatol *vi* make/keep one's promise/word:
pp/adj **swatome; Nai Rrom te swatol.**
He's not a man likely to keep his word.
swáto-po-swáto *adv/phr* word by word,
word for word
swatósko *gen/adj* of word; **Wo si Rrom**
pêske swatósko. He is a man of his
word.
swáturya *nm/pl* **1)** conversation, dialogue,
discourse; **Dyam-ame swáturya.** We
had a conversation. **Ashundem lênge**
swáturya. I overhead their conversation.
Dyas mánge swáturya Rromanes ánde
avré-themêski Rrómani shib. He had a
conversation with me in Romany in a
foreign dialect. **2)** deposition, testimony
3) address, announcement, speech
Swîntáika/Swûntáika *nf* **1)** female saint
2) woman who has passed menopause
swînto/swûnto *adj* **1)** consecrated, holy,
sacred, sanctified, saintly **2)** male Saint

Swînto Mára *nf* Saint Mary: *Voc*
Swíntonya Máro
swîntól/swûntól *vt* **1)** consecrate, sanctify:
pp/adj **swintome 2)** *v/refl* **swîntól-pe** be
consecrated, pass through menopause
swîntomé *pp/adj* **1)** consecrated, sanctified
2) passed through menopause, undergone
a change of life
swîntomós/swûntomós *nm* **1)** sainthood **2)**
sanctity **3)** menopause
swiráika *nf* **1)** rattle **2)** tambourine
swiyaderil *vt* bore, drill, ream: *pp/adj*
swiyaderime
swiyaderimos *nm* boring, drilling. reaming
swiyádero *nm* auger, drill
swiyádero-balwaláko *comp/nm* pneumatic
drill/jack hammer
swiyaderútso *nm* auger, Dremel tool,
minidrill, rotary tool
Swûnto Dúxo *nm* Holy Ghost
Swûnto Níkolai *nm* Saint Nicholas, Santa
Clause
sya *adj/pron* all, all of it, it all, them all *var*
of **sa** *qv*

SH

shádel/shadel *vt/i* **1)** spew, vomit, *sl* puke: *pp/adj* **shaglo 2) shadél-pe** throw up/vomit on oneself; **E gláta shaglás-pe.** The baby threw up on itself.

shadyarel *vt* make disgusted, make to vomit/induce vomiting: *pp/adj* **shadyardo**

shaglimos *nm* vomit, *sl* puke

shai *v/aux* **1)** can, may, might. used with verbs as follows; **Shai zhas?** Can you go/Are you able to go? **2)** I can/Yes, I can. (*in answer to a question asking if smbdy can do smth*)

shaimáta *nm/pl* possibilities

shaimos *nm* **1)** likelihood, opportunity, possibility **2)** capability

shai-vi *adv* maybe, perhaps; **Shai-vi me avav tehára, chi zhanav inka.** Maybe I can go tomorrow, I don't know yet.

shaiyutno *adj* possible

sháko *gen/adj* **1)** of a daughter, daughter's; **Múrra sháki gláta si.** She is my daughter's baby. **2)** belonging to a girl, girlish; **sháko státo** girlish figure

shalimo *nm* cigarette lighter, small gas blowtorch: *pl* **shalima** (*Eur*)

shalvárya *nm/pl* harem pants, ankle-length puffy pants worn by Muslim Romani women

shampána *nf* champagne

shandilériya *nf* chandelier

shangíra *nf* canker, canker sore

shantíra *nf* **1)** building/construction site **2)** scaffolding (*Eur*)

shantsári *nm* ditch digger

shántso *nm* **1)** ditch, moat, trench **2)** gutter **3)** channel, drainage ditch, irrigation ditch, open conduit

shantsútso *nm* small channel, ditch

shâpo *nm* **1)** atelier, auto-body shop, workshop **2)** work location where nomadic *Kalderash* do plating and other work which could be an open field behind a bakery or confectionary factory when working in situ.

sharlatáno *nm* charlatan: *pl* **sharlatáya:** *nf* **sharlatánka**

sharol *vi* **1)** zig-zag **2)** *v/refl* **sharól-pe** move erratically, stagger, zig-zag, be zig-zagged

sharome *pp/adj* zig-zagged (*stitches*)

sharomos *nm* zig-zagging, zig-zag pattern

shásha *nf* chaff, corn husks

shási *nm* chassis (*Am*)

shásto *nm* party

shâtáika *nf* **1)** wife of a Romani territorial boss (*Am*) **2)** *Kalderash* widow who has replaced her husband as the local leader and runs a town through her sons (*Am*)

shâto *nm* local leader, big man, influential Romani leader, fixer, honcho, Romani territorial boss (*Am*); **báro shâto.** big shot, leader of a **kumpaníya** (*Am*); **Kon si lêngo shâto?** Who is their local leader? (*Am.*). **Me sim o mai báro shâto ándo fóro.** I am the most important honcho in the city. (*Am*). (*Said by a Romani leader in Los Angeles where there are many shâturya each with his own kumpaníya, the Valley, Santa Monica, Beverly Hills, etc.*) **Gîndíl-pe shâto.** He thinks of himself as a big shot. **O Fránki si lêngo shâto.** Frank is their big shot.

shâto/shôto *nm* **1)** shot glass, shot of (*whisky, etc*) **2)** gunshot (*Am*)

shátra *nf* **1)** Romani rural settlement, camp: *pl* **shêtri** (*Eur*) **2)** awning, canopy, open tent (*Am*)

shatráko *gen/adj* belonging to the settlement, local (*Eur*)

shatrash *nm* representative for a Romani settlement, camp leader (*Eur*)

shav/shaw *nm* **1)** Romani boy, young man, unmarried youth **2)** son (*if Romani*): *pl* **shave**

Shavále ! *nm/voc/pl* Boys! Youth! (*referring to either young or adult Romani men*)

shavêsko *gen/adj* **1)** boyish **2)** of a son, son's; **Múrre shavêsko mobíli.** My son's car.

shavimos *nm* boyhood, youth (*of Roma*)

shávo *nm European variant of* **shav** *qv*

Shavorrále ! *nm/pl/voc* Kids!; **Shavorrále! Na keren mui!** Kids! Don't make a noise!

shavorrêngo -dóftoro *comp/nm* pediatrician

shavorrimos *nm* boyhood, male childhood (*of Roma*)

shavorro/shaworre *nm* **1)** pre-adolescent Romani boy, little boy **2)** pre-adolescent son, dear son, male child; **Le shavorre khelén-pe avri.** The children are playing outside.

shax *nm* cabbage; **shax-parno** cauliflower

shax-shuklo *comp/nf* sauerkraut

shaxorre *nm/pl* Brussel(s) sprouts

sheftári *nm* businessman, tradesman

sheftimos *nm* buying and selling, dealing in commodities and goods

shêfto *nm* business, commerce, trade; **Zhanel but shêfturya.** He knows many trades.

shel *nm* one hundred; *pl* **shela**

sheláki *nf* one hundred-dollar bill

sheláko *nm* **1)** shellac (*Am*) **2)** *gen/adj* belonging to one hundred; **Sheláko si o phuro.** The old man is one-hundred years old.

shelo *nm* **1)** rope (*generic*), hangman's rope **2)** clothesline **3)** lariat, lasso **4)** leash, tether

sheló-tsaliyángo *nm* clothesline

sheltéri *nm* shelter, refugee shelter (*Can*)

shélto *num* one hundredth

shêlyá *nf/pl* **1)** dandruff **2)** flakes, shavings **3)** bran flakes, breakfast cereal **4)** freckles **5)** floor sweepings **6)** remains, residue

sheptézo *nm* **1)** blunder, error, mistake **2)** *comp/vi* **kerel ~** blunder, make a mistake

sherand *nm* **1)** cushion, pillow **2)** *prep* at the head of; **sherand o than** at the head of the bed

sherano *adj* **1)** head **2)** *nm* head person, *psn* in charge: *nf* **sherani**; **Kon si o sherano ándo prográmo?** Who is the head *psn* in the program?

shêrèngo-dóftoro *comp/nm* psychiatrist

sherêste *adv/nm/prep* **1)** ahead, forward; **Zha sherêste!** Go ahead!/Move on! **2)** *comp/vi* **del ~** get ahead, make progress

sherífo *nm* sheriff (*Am*)

shêrkáno *nm* **1)** dragon, fire dragon **2)** sea monster

shêrnangó *adj* bare-headed, hatless

shêró/shero *nm* head *var of* **shoro** *qv*

sheró-sherêste *prep* head on, head to head; **Diné-pe sheró-sherêste.** They crashed head on.

sherúto *nm* cheroot (*Am*)

shêryádya *nf* **1)** rear end of a cart or wagon **2)** cratch (*of a horse-drawn caravan*)

shetévo *nm* screw

shevril *vt* **1)** appoint godparent(s): *pp/adj* **shevrime** **2)** **shevríl-pe** be appointed as a godparent

shevrimos *nm* **1)** ceremony of appointing a godparent(s) **2)** godparentship

shey *nf* **1)** Romani girl/teenager/young woman, unmarried Romani woman **2)** daughter (*if Romani*); **Dya lês pêska sháke.** He gave it to his daughter. **3)** *fig* wife (*term of endearment*)

Sheyále! *nf/pl/voc* Girls!

shey-bari *nf* **1)** eldest/oldest daughter **2)** spinster

sheyimos *nm* girlhood, youth (*of Romani girls*)

shey-lashi *nf* **1)** virgin **2)** Virgo (*Zod*)

shey-mangli *nf* a girl who has been asked for in marriage but is not yet formally engaged *see* **tumnime; Chorri, Rósa, chi-mai manglí-la**. Poor Rosie, she has never had a proposal of marriage/never been asked for in marriage.

Shéyo *voc* **1)** Girl!; **Shéyo! Kheré-lo tyo dad?** Girl! Is your father home? **2)** Often used by a Romani man to address his wife; **Shéyo! Akhardyas wárekon?** Wife! Did anyone telephone?

sheyorri/shyorri *nf* **1)** pre-adolescent Romani girl, little girl **2)** daughter, little daughter, female child, dear daughter (*if Romani*) **3)** dear girl, sweet girl

sheyorrimos *nm* girlhood

Sheyorríyo *voc* **1)** Dear girl! **2)** Dear little wife!

shib/ship *nf* **1)** tongue (*Anat*) **2)** tongue, language, speech **3)** jet (*of flame*) **4)** snap-up catch on a beer or soft drink can **5)** blade (*of a knife, etc*) **6)** sting, prick

shîba *nf* **1)** flagellation, whipping **2)** *comp/vt/i* **del ~** flaggelate, punish by whipping **3)** scourge **4) dél-pe ~** *v/refl;* flaggelate oneself, scourge oneself

shibalo **1)** *adj* talkative, fluent (*in a language*), loquacious **2)** *nm* spokesman: *nf* **shibali,** chatterbox

shibash *nm* linguist: *nf* **shibáshka**

shib-dili *nf* carnival slang (*ex; Ixnay atay uckerslay!* Leave that sucker alone!), pig Latin, slang in general (*Am*)

shíka *nf* fig

shîl *nm* cold, fever, flue

shîlaló *adj* **1)** aloof, cold, frigid, reserved, unemotional

shîl-gurumnyáki *comp/nf* cowpox

shîl-khainyángi *nf/pl* chicken pox

shîl-tsinó *comp/nm* smallpox

shîló **1)** cold **2)** aloof, cool, cold, reserved

shi-mai *oppositional construction* the more; **Shi mai xal, shi mai baryol.** The more he eats, the more he grows. **Shi mai sikyovav, shi mai zhanav.** The more I learn, the more I know.

shimyáko *nm* dung-beetle, scarab beetle, *fig* person suggesting a dung-beetle: *nf* **shimyáka**

shinado *pp/adj* **1)** offered, proposed, suggested **2)** promised

shinádyol *vi* **1)** be offered/promised/proposed/suggested: *pp/adj* **shinadilo 2)** come to terms

shinali *nf* cutting tool, chisel, drawknife, spokeshave

shinavel *vt* **1)** make/propose/suggest an offer, offer, profer: *pp/adj* **shinado 2)** promise **3)** offer mediation/negotiation **4)** allot/award by majority decision of the *Kalderash* Tribunal **5)** agree on, award, determine, decide on/determine a fine, recompense, etc, by the *Kalderash* tribunal **6)** predict, prophesy

shinayimos *nm* **1)** agreement/decision to offer, bid, offer, promise **2)** suggestion **3)** prophecy

shindo *pp/adj* **1)** circumsized, cut/deleted/removed **2)** ripped, slashed, torn **3)** butchered, slaughtered/sacrificed **4)** decided in court

shíndra *nf* roof

shíndyol *vi* **1)** be cut/deleted, be circumcised: *pp/adj* **shindilo 2)** be carved/cut/sliced **3)** be butchered, be sacrificed/slaughtered; **Shindili e bakri.** The lamb has been butchered. **4)** become ripped/slashed/torn **5)** be cut out/excluded, be cut off from **6)** break free of/from, cut oneself off from; **Shindilo hai nashlótar.** He broke free and fled/He cut and ran. **7)** be chopped/hewed (*wood*) **8)** reach a decision in court, be judged, be condemned, be sentenced

shinel *vt/i* **1)** cut, cut off/up/out, delete, chop (*vegetables, wood*), hew (*wood*): *pp/adj* **shindo 2)** pare, peel **3)** butcher, sacrifice/slaughter (*animals*) **4**) carve, slash, slice **5**) rip, tear **6**) decide, reach a verdict in a trial/judgement, condemn, sentence, dispense justice; **Mek te shinel e kris!** Let the court decide! **7**) ease (*pain*) **8**) operate, perform surgery, perform an autopsy **9**) circumsize **10**) engrave **11**) exclude *with* **katar; Shinde lês katar e kumpaníya.** They excluded him from the community. **12**) cut into, interrupt; **Shindyas múrro swáto.** He interrupted my conversation. **13** *comp/vt/i* ~ **o shorro** behead, decapitate **14**) *comp/vt* ~ **o trúpo** perform an autopsy **15**) *comp/vt* ~ **po yilo** hurt deeply/cut to the heart; *id* **Shindyas lês po yilo.** She cut him to the heart/hurt him deeply.

shing *nm* **1**) antler, horn **2**) *arch* powder horn (*Folk*) **3**) saddle horn/pommel **4**) shoe horn **5**) *comp/vt/i* **del** ~ **gore; O guruv dya lês shing.** The bull gored him.

shingalo *nm* **1**) horned one, Satan **2**) border policeman, immigration policeman, policeman **3**) cuckold **4**) rhinoceros

shingêngo *gen/adj* antlered, possessing horns

shingérdyol *vi* **1**) to be rent/ripped/torn to pieces: *pp/adj* **shingerdilo 2**) to be cut to pieces

shingerel *vt* **1**) lacerate, rip/tear to shreds, reduce to rags and tatters: *pp/adj* **shingerdo 2**) cut/hack to pieces, tear apart, tear to pieces

shingerimos *nm* destruction by ripping to pieces or hacking to splinters

shingêsko-grast *nm* unicorn

shîngorró *nm* carob pod, locust fruit

shinimáta *nm/pl* **1**) charcuterie, cold cuts **2**) slices

shinimos *nm* **1**) break, cut, incision, slice **2**) sacrifice/slaughter (*of animals*) **3**) laceration, rip, tear **4**) decision in a trial, judgement/penalty/sentence, verdict **5**) surgery; **Daral o shinimos.** He is afraid of surgery.

shinitóri *nm* can opener, cutter, slicer

shinyorri *nf* buttonhole

shípka *nf* lathe (*Eur*)

shkáfa *nf* **1**) shelf, storage shelf

shkafidi *nf* coffee table, low table

shkáfo *nm* **1**) drawer, bureau, chest of drawers **2**) closet, cupboard, storage cabinet **3**) desk

shkála *nf* school *see also* **wushkála; shkaláki-buki** school work

shkamin *nm* chair *var of* **skamin** *qv*

shkatérka *nf* tablecloth

shkóla *nf* school

shkolári *nm* schoolboy: *nf* **shkolarítsa**

shkoláriko 1) *adj* scholarly, studious; **Rrom shkoláriko** scholarly Rom *nf* **Rromni shkoláriko 2**) *nm* scholar

shlangónto *nm* brazing compound, brass solder, used with Borax for brazing copper

shlívo/shlíva *nm* plum, prune (*Eur*)

shlivovítsa *nf* slivovitz (*Eur*)

shlobóko/zlaibóko *nm* billfold, wallet

Shlúzhla *nf* Mass; **Shlúzhla-Bari** High Mass

shobódniko *nm* shoemaker: *pl* **shobódnichi**

shobolána *nf* female rat: *pl* **shoboláni** (*Eur*)

shoboláno *nm* male rat: *pl* **shobolánya** (*Eur*)

shófto *num* fourth

shógora *nf* wife's sister, sister in law

shogorítsa *nf* wife's sister, sister in law

shógoro *nm* wife's brother, brother-in-law: *pl* **shógorya**

shóha *adv* never (*Eur*) *see* **chi mai** *and* **na mai** *advs*

shol *nf* **1**) whistle **2**) *comp/vi* **del** ~ whistle

sholíl-pe *v/refl* hiss, whistle: *pp/adj* **sholime; Sholíl-pe e kakyavi.** The electric tea kettle is whistling.

shon *nm* **1**) moon; **phérdo shon** full moon **2**) month: *pl* **shon**

shon-dino *comp/adj* **1**) moonstruck **2**) *nm* lunatic: *nf* **shon-dini**

shondríla/shandríla *nf* shingle (*for a roof*)

shonêngo *gen/adj* of months, monthly;
Shove shonêngo si o glatútso. The baby
boy is six months old.

shonêsko *gen/adj* of a month/moon,
monthly; **Yeke shonêski si, e gláta.** The
baby girl is one month old. **Sonêsko dilo
si.** He suffers from moon madness (is
moonstruck).

shonkéri *nm* grocer who also sells meat or
delicatessen products

shônkèriya *nf* delicatessen

shônko *nm* 1) ham 2) roast of ham. 3) leg
of pork

Shonúto *nm* New Moon

shopêrka *nf* sand lizard

shoperláno *nm* 1) large lizard. 2) gila
monster. 3) iguana

shoperláno-baro *nm* dinosaur

shopotil *vi* 1) whisper: *pp/adj* **shopotime**
2) *v/refl* **shopotíl-pe** whisper, be
whispering

shopotimos *nm* whispering

shopotyála *nf* whisper, whispering

shorêngo-dóftoro *comp/nm* psychiatrist

shorêsko -naswalimos *com/nm* sinus head
cold

shornango *adj* bareheaded

shoro/shêró *nm* 1) head, skull (*Anat*), bust;
baro ~ big head, swellhead, ostentatious
person **~ balano** blockhead 2) *fig* brain,
head (*of an organization, etc*) 3) crest,
summit, top; **o shoro la playingáko** the
top/summit of the mountain

shoró-balano *comp/nm*
pig-headed/obdurate man: *nf*
shoró-balani

shorofil *vt* screw (*in*): *pp/adj* **shorofime**

shorófo *nm* screw (*Eur*)

shorr *nf* 1) beard 2) whisker

shorra *nf/pl* whiskers

shorrádyol *vi* 1) be poured/shed
(*blood*)/spilled

shorravel *vt* 1) pour, pour out, spill
out/over: *pp/adj* **shorrado** 2) shed
(*blood*)

shorrayimos *nm* outpouring, overflow,
spill

shorrdyol *vi* become poured out/spilt,
overflow, spill: *pp/adj* **shorrdilo**; **O tázo
shorrdilo**. The wash basin overlowed.
Shorrdilo o thud pe síniya. The milk
spilled on the table.

shorrel *vt* 1) pour, scatter by
spilling/tipping over, spill: *pp/adj*
shorrdo; **O tróko shorrdyas poruma
ánde úlitsa.** The truck scattered/spilled
onions in the street. **O gáso shorrel
katar o tánko.** The gasoline is flowing
from the tank. 2) shed (*blood/tears*) 3)
ejaculate 4) *v/refl* **shorrél-pe** spill
out/over

shorrimos *nm* 1) outpouring 2) ejaculation

shorrowali *nf* bearded lady on a carnival

shorrwalo *adj* 1) bearded, bewhiskered 2)
in need of a shave, unshaven, unkempt;
shórrwalo trámpo unshaven/unkempt
bum 3) *nm* derelict, unshaven bum (*Am*)

shortíl-pe *vi* short, short out (*electric
circuit*)

shórto *nm* electrical short

shoshênge grópi *comp/nf* rabbit warren

shoshni *nf* 1) female rabbit

shoshoi *nm* rabbit: *pl* **shosha**

shôto *nm* shot, shot of (*whisky, etc*) (*Am*)

shov *num* six

shovali *nf* number six, six in cards

shovardesh *num* sixty

shovardéshto *num* sixtieth

shóyo *nm* movie show, show (*Am*): *pl*
shóya

Shpániya/Spániya *nf* Spain

Shpanyáko *adj* Spanish (*of Spain*)

Shpanyolítska *nf* Spanish (*Lang*)

Shpanyolítsko *adj* Spanish (*by nationality*)

Shpanyólo *nm* Spaniard: *nf* **Shpanyoláika**

Shpanyolútsa *nf* young Hispanic/Spanish
woman

shparadrápo *nm* adhesive bandage

shpídel/spídel *vt/i* 1) push, shove, force,
press, propel, urge: *pp/adj*
shpidino/spidino 2) induce, motivate 3)
impel 4) *v/refl* **shpídel-pe** exert oneself,
motivate oneself, be motivated; **Na
shpíde tut!** Take it easy/Relax! **Trobul**

lês yag ánde bul te sphídel-pe. He needs fire in his rear end to motivate him.

shpidemos *nm* 1) pushing, shoving 2) propulsion 3) inspiration, motivation 4) urging

shpílka *nf* hat ornament, safety pin, pin on broach (*Eur*) *see also var in* **supíka**

shpináka *nf* spinach

shpírto *nm* alcohol, spirits

shpíta *nf* hospital

shpitáli *nm* hospital: *pl* **shpitálya**

shpítsa nf spoke (*of a wheel*)

shpiwonil *vt* snoop, spy: *pp/adj* **shpiwonime**

shpiwoníya *nf* 1) espionage, spying, snooping 2) Secret Service

shpiyáltero *nm* zinc, zinc plates/sheets

shpiyalterósko *gen/adj* made of zinc

shpiyóno *nm* spy: *nf* **shpiyonútsa**

shrínko *nm/sl* shrink (*psychiatrist*) (*Am*)

shtákla/stákla *nf* 1) glass 2) hourglass 3) monacle 4) glass bottle/jar 5) **shtákla-farbome** stained glass 6) window pane, glass frame for a photograph

shtakláki-fátsa *nf* glass facing, glass top

shtakláko/stakláko *gen/adj* 1) made of glass 2) transparent

shtákli/stákli *nf/pl* eyeglasses, spectacles

shtakluno/stakluno *adj* having the quality of glass, smooth like glass; **Shtakluno o réko.** The lake (is) smooth like glass.

shtála/stála *nf* 1) horse stall, stall 2) shed for farm animals such as chickens, cows, pigs, etc 3) booth, pitch, stand (*at a fair*)

shtampimáta *nm/pl* printed documents/materials

shtampimos *nm* printed document/sheet

shtar *num* four

shtarali *nm* number four, four in cards

shtaré-rêgèngo *gen/adj* four-sided, square

shtárto *num* fourth

shtárwardesh *num* forty

shtarwardéshto *num* fortieth

shtáviya *nf* cowslip (*primula veris*)

shtíkla *nf* heel of a boot/shoe, high heel of a woman's shoe

shtíriya *nf* information, knowledge, news

shtóla *nf* barstool., bench, stool

shtólitsa *nf* footstool, stool

shtrafil *vt* 1) fine, impose a fine 2) **shtrafíl-pe** be fined

shtrafime *pp/adj* fined, penalized, punished by a fine

shtráfo/stráfo *nm* fine, penalty

shtrafyal/strafyal *vi* 1) lighten/flash lightning 2) be struck by lightning; **Bari furtúna sas, rrongyálas hai shtrafyálas.** It was a big storm, it was thundering and flashing lightning. **Shtrafyáili lêski tséra.** His tent was struck by lightning. 3) flash light, sparkle

shtrafyayimos *nm* 1) lightning, flash of lightning 2) bolt of lightning 3) flash

shtrangil *vt* 1) string a musical instrument 2) hog-tie, rope

shtrangime *pp/adj* 1) fitted with strings, strung (*instrument*); **Mi gitára nai shtrangime.** My guitar is not fitted with strings. 2) roped, hog-tied

shtrangimos *nm* stringing/fitting of strings to an instrument (*Mus*)

shtrángo *nm* 1) thick rope 2) cable, power cord 3) string for a musical instrument 4) hangman's rope 5) lariat, lasso

shtrékya *nf* 1) lucky strike, run of good luck, especially in business, *var of* **strékya** 2) bonanza, jackpot

shtrélitsa *nf* bolt from the blue, lightning bolt

shtrímfa *nf* woman's stocking

shtrímfi *nf/pl* female stockings, pantyhose, tights; **kézhlane-shtrímfi** nylons, silk stockings

shtudênto/studênto *nm* male student: *nf* **shtudentáika**

shtúdero *nm* expert, student of *smth*

shtyúko/styúko *nm* pike (*fish*)

shúdel *vt* 1) bounce, cast (*in fishing*), eject, evict, exile, hurl, juggle, fling, propel, puff, throw, throw down, toss: *pp/adj* **shudino; Shudélas ánde mánde dural.** He was throwing (things) at me from a distance. 2) dispose of, get rid of, throw away/out; **Shudya lês ánda o kher.** She threw him out of the house. **3)** belch, emit (*smoke*) **4)** miscarry; **Shudyas láki gláta.** She miscarried her baby. **5)** pass around (*handbills*) **6)** dump **7)** sow (*seeds*) **8)** *comp/vt/i* ~ **khul** kick ass (*Am*) **9)** *comp/vt/i* ~ **grenádi** shell; **Shudine grenádi ánde máhala Rromani ándo kodo marimos.** They shelled the Romani quarter during that war (*in Saravejo*). **10)** *comp/vt/i* ~ **pálpale** send back, throw back **11)** *comp/vt/i* ~ **pe rêgáte** bar, exclude, reject **12)** *comp/vi* ~ **yag** emit fire, shoot out flames **13)** *comp/vi* ~ **yakha** look around/check out visually **14)** *comp/vi* ~ **fléchki** play darts/throw darts **15)** *comp/vi* ~ **plûmbo** fire a bullet **16)** *comp/vt/i* ~ **inkya, a)** throw away **b)** reject **17)** *comp/vi* ~ **rat** bleed **18)** *comp/vi* ~ **rrîl** fart **19)** *comp/vt/i* ~ **tele** get the better off, throw down, overpower **20)** *comp/vi* ~ **wushalin** cast a shadow **21)** *comp/vi* ~ **yakh** look around, take a look around **22** *comp/vt* ~ **ka l' zhuklênde** throw *smbdy* to the dogs; **Shúdine lês ka l' zhuklênde.** They threw him to the dogs. **23)** *v/refl* **shúdel-pe a)** wrestle **b)** throw oneself down; **Shudyás-pe telé pe sófta.** He threw himself down on the couch. **c)** thresh around, toss and turn.

shudemásko *adj* dispensable, disposable, expendable, throwaway

shudemáta *nm/pl* cast-offs, disposable material, junk, scrap, scrap materials

shudemos *nm* **1)** cast/casting, throwing, throw, puff (*of smoke from an engine*) **2)** miscarriage **3)** juggling **4)** eviction **5)** wrestling

shudemós-khuláko *comp/nm/arch* **1)** manure tossing, old punishment for adultery between two married Romani adults **2)** ass-kicking, retaliation; **Zhas Rromále! Shudas khul!** Let's go Roma! Time to kick ass! (*Am*)

shudemós-pe-rêgáte *noun/phr* shunting/throwing aside, exclusion

shudini *nf* projectile, something fired/thrown

shudino *pp/adj* **1)** exiled **2)** discarded, ejected, rejected, thrown away/out **3)** evicted **4)** *nm* reject, rejected man: *nf* **shudini 5)** exile, outcast, pariah

shudinó-mitálo *comp/nm* discarded/scrap metal, scrap metal

shudinó-regáte *adj/phr* excluded, marginalized, rejected, shunted aside

shudínyol *vi* be discarded/ cast out/evicted/rejected/ostracized/thrown away/ thrown out: *pp/adj* **shudinilo**

shuditóri *nm* **1)** bouncer (*in a nightclub/discoteque*) **2)** juggler **3)** pitcher (*baseball*)

shudres *adv* coldly, chilly

shudrilo *pp/adj* **1)** frigid, bitter cold, numbed with cold **2)** frostbitten

shudrimos *nm* chill, cold, coldness

shudro *adj* cold (*temperature*)

shudrol *vi* **1)** become cool, cool, cool down/off, refrigerate: *pp/adj* **shudrilo**; **Phuter le filástri te shudrol o kher!** Open the windows to cool down the house! **2)** cool oneself, cool down/off; **Gêló avri te shudról.** He went outside to cool off.

shudryarel *vt* chill, cool off, cool down: *pp/adj* **shudryardo**

shuk *nf* beauty, niceness

shukar *adj/adv* **1)** beautiful, handsome, nice, pretty, well; **shukar sheyorri** pretty little girl, **Wo si shukar mursh.** He is a handsome fellow. **Vorbisardyas la shukar swáturya.** He told her sweet nothings. **2)** *nm* handsome man: *nf* **shukarni 3) shukar fistáno** best, dress; **shukar gad** dress shirt, **mai shukár tsáliya** best outfit, **mai shukar stagi** best dress hat

shukárdyol *vi* become beautified/beautiful, renovated: *pp/adj* **shukardilo**; **Mai shukárdyos swáko ges.** You become more beautiful each day.

shukarel *vt* **1)** adorn, apply cosmetics, beautify, decorate make beautiful, make oneself over: *pp/adj* **shukardo 2)** renovate, spruce up **3)** *v/refl* **shukarél-pe** make oneself over, beautify oneself, tart oneself up

shukares *adv* attractively, nicely, politely; **Pushlem lêstar shukares**. I asked him nicely.

shukarimáta *nm/pl* attractions, beauties, beautiful things; **Dikhlas le nevikane mobílya, le shukarimáta**. He saw the cars, the attractive ones.

shukarimos *nm* attraction, beauty, beautiful thing, wondrous thing; **Woi sas shey le desh-u-dónsa shukarimatánsa.** She was a girl possessed of the twelve beauties/stunningly beautiful.

shukarni *nf* beautiful girl/woman; **E Shukarni thai o Djungalo** Beauty and the Beast (*Folk*)

shukarníyo! *nf/voc* **Sar san, Shukarníyo?** How are you, Beautiful? (*address to little girl*)

shukarnyorri *nf* beautiful child/pretty little girl

shukimos *nm* dryness, sarcasm

shukles *adv* bitterly, sarcastically

shuklimos *nm* bitterness, sarcasm, sourness

shuklo *adj* **1)** bad (*beer*), bitter, pickled, sarcastic, sour **2)** curdled **3)** in a sour/bad mood; **Shuklo si, defyal**. He's really pissed off.

shúklo-bózo *nm* rhubarb

shukló-pipéri *comp/nm* pickle: *pl* **shuklé pipérya**

shuklyarde anrre *comp/nm* pickled eggs

shuklyardo *pp/adj* pickled

shuklyárdyol *vi* **1)** be made bitter/sour, be made sarcastic: *pp/adj* **shuklyardilo 2)** become pickled

shuklyarel *vt* **1)** make bitter/sour, create sarcasm: *pp/adj* **shuklyardo 2)** pickle

shuklyol *vi* **1)** become bitter, sarcastic: *pp/adj* **shuklilo; Shuklilo o réko.** The lake dried up. **2)** become pickled **3)** ferment

shuko *adj* **1)** empty (*bottle*), dry. **2)** dry, stale, tasteless **3)** caustic, dry (*humor*) **4)**

hollow (*as an old, felled tree*) **5)** hoarse (*voice*) **6)** whithered **7)** fermented

shúko-réko *comp/nm* arroyo, wash (*Am*)

shukyárdyol *vi* **1)** become dried up/out, evaporated: *pp/adj* **shukyardilo 2)** be fermented

shukyarel *vt* to **1)** dry (*after washing*): *pp/adj* **shukyardo 2)** dry out, evaporate **3)** make arid **4)** make whithered, whither **5)** cause to ferment **6)** make curdle

shukyaritóri *nm* dryer, hair dryer

shukyol *vi* **1)** become bland, become dry, dry up/out: *pp/adj* **shukilo; Shukilo o réko**. The stream dried up. **2)** become whithered, whither; **Le drakha shukile po rez.** The grapes whithered on the arbor. **3)** ferment **4)** curdle

shuladitóri *nm* **1)** cleaner, janitor, sweeper: *nf* **shuladitórka** charwoman **2)** leaf sucker, mechanical leaf sweeper

shuládyol *vi* be swept, vacuumed: *pp/adj* **shuladilo**

shulavel *vt* **1)** sweep, sweep up, vacuum, dust bust: *pp/adj* **shulado 2)** clear up leaves with a mechanical leafsucker

shulávka *nf* broom (*Eur*)

shulayimos *nm* sweeping, vacuuming

shûma *nf* strange/weird noise, unfamiliar sound; **Ashundem shûma ándo wêrsh.** I heard a strange noise in the forest.

shûna *nf* tire/tyre; ~ **opral** spare tire

shurano *nm* carp

shuri *nf* **1)** carving knife, kitchen knife, knife **2)** dagger, hunting knife **3)** scalpel, surgery; **Daral e shuri.** He is afraid of surgery/the knife.**3)** *id* **Le e shuri ándo wast!** Draw/take out your knife!

shuril *vt* **1)** knife, stab: *pp/adj* **shurime 2)** attack with a knife **3)** slash with a knife **4)** **shuríl-pe** be stabbed with a knife; **Shurisáilo hai chorádilo ánde úlitsa.** He was stabbed and robbed in the street.

shurimos *nm* **1)** assault with a knife, attempted stabbing **2)** knife fight **3)** stabbing

shuritóri *nm* knife thrower (*on a carnival*)

shuriyári *nm* knife sharpener

shuriyash *nm* **1)** slasher, stabber; **O Djak o Shuriyash.** Jack the Ripper. **2)** knife thrower on a carnival

shuriyorri *nf* pocket knife, small penknife

shurya *nf/pl* cutlery

shut *nm* vinegar

shutlo *adj* having the taste or quality of vinegar

shuvlimos *nm* **1)** inflation **2)** swelling

shuvlo *adj* inflated, swollen

shuvlo masho *comp/nm* puffer

shuvlyarel *vt* cause/make to swell, inflate: *pp/adj* **shuvlyardo**

shuvlyol *vi* swell, become inflated/swollen; *pp/adj* **shuvlilo**

Shvaitsári *nm* Swiss man: *nf* **Shvaitsarútsa**

Shváitsi *nm* Switzerland

Shvaitsítsko *adj* Swiss; **Shvaitsítsko kiral** Swiss cheese

shwãrtsa/shôrtsa *nf* apron, pinafore (*Eur*)

Shwedáika *nf* Swedish woman

Shwedítska *nf* Swedish (*Lang*)

Shwedítsko *adj* Swedish

Shwédo *nm* **1)** Sweden **2)** male Swede

shwézo *adj* fresh

T

t' *cont of* **te** *qv as part.* Usually before a word beginning with a vowel; **Pushlem lêstar t'avel.** I invited him to come. **T'aves baxtalo/baxtali!** May you be fortunate! (*usual modern greeting*)

-ta suffixed to imperative commands; **Ashúnta!** Listen! *from* **ashun!** (*imp/sing*)**; Beshénta, Rromále!** Be seated, Gentlemen! (*Eur*) This seems to be *non-prod* in Canada/US.

tabazhnítsa *nf* tobacco pouch for pipe smoker

tábera *nf* blackboard

táblitsa *nf* **1)** billboard, bulletin board **2)** plaque, large brass/copper plaque **3)** large sign on a carnival **4)** large poster

tablo *adj/neolog* warm

tablyárdyol *vi/neolog* be warmed up: *pp/adj* **tablyardilo**

tablyarel *vt/neolog* warm, warm up: *pp/adj* **tablyardo**

tablyol *vi/neolog* become/get warm: *pp/adj* **tablilo**

tábora *nf* **1)** army camp, camp, encampment **2)** Romani camp (*Eur*)

taboránka *nf/arch* camp woman, camp following prostitute (*Eur*)

Táika *voc* Lad! (*address to a young boy*)

táimo *nm* time (*Am*); **Sar nakhel pêsko táimo?** How does he pass his time?

táina *nf* secret

takh *nf* armpit

takimos/tatimos *nm* **1)** heat, humidity **2)** fever **3)** passion **4)** temperature

takyárdyol *vi* become heated/ warmed up: *pp/adj* **takyardilo**

takyarel/tatyarel *vt* **1)** heat up, make hot, warm up: *pp/adj* **takyardo 2)** incubate **3)** *v/refl* **takyarél-pe** heat/warm oneself

takyári *nm* heater

takyarimos *nm* **1)** heating/warming up process **2)** incubation

takyol/tatyol 1) become hot/warm, get warm, warm oneself: *pp/adj* **takilo; O gês takilo.** The day grew warm. **Gelem andre te takyuváv.** I went inside to get warm. **Takyuv angla e yag!** Warm yourself in fromt of the fire! **2)** become humid **3)** burn with fever

talakráno *nm* **1)** scorpion, tarantula: *pp/adj* **talakráya**, *var of* **yalakráno** *qv* **2)** tumbleweed

talénto *nm* **1)** business acumen, expertise **2)** finesse, talent

taloi *nm* palate, roof of the mouth (*Anat*)

táma/ta *conj* but (*Eur*)

tamboríno *nm* tambourine (*Mus*)

tambúra *nf* **1)** musical instrument resembling a flat-backed mandola with four sets of double strings which is popular among Vlax-Roma in Hungary (*Mus*) **2)** two-double-string, long-necked lute of the saz family played by Roma in Bulgaria and elsewhere in the South Balkans

támna *nf* autumn, fall (*season*); **Lúngo támna** Indian summer

tamnáko *gen/adj* fall, of the autumn; **tamnáki vryámya** Fall weather

tamne *adv* during the autumn, in the fall; **Mulo tamne.** He died during the fall.

tampóno *nm* **1)** plug, tompion (*Mil*) **2)** sanitary napkin, tampon

tang *adj* **1)** confined, tight **2)** narrow

tangimos *nm* **1**) constraint, constriction, tightness **2**) narrowness

tango **1**) tight **2**) narrow **3**) confined, constrained, constricted

tangyárdyol *vi* **1**) become constricted/tightened: *pp/adj* **tangyardilo 2**) become narrowed down

tangyarel *vt* **1**) constrict, tighten, tighten up, make tight: *pp/adj* **tandgardo 2**) make narrow, narrow **3**) ~ **ándo wast** squeeze in the hand

tangyarimos *nm* **1**) constriction **2**) tightening, narrowing

tangyol *vi* **1**) constrict, tighten **2**) become narrow: *pp/adj* **tangilo**

tánko *nm* **1**) gas tank **2**) water tank **3**) oxygen tank **4**) tank (*Mil*) **5**) nickname for an oversized teenager

tapestíra *nf* tapestry

-tar *ablative suff attached to verbs of motion or state of being*; **Gêló.** He went. **Gêlótar** he departed/went away. **Phurili.** She grew old. **Phurilítar.** She passed into old age.

tar *prep/cont of* **katar** *prep qv*

tarakáno *nm* **1**) beetle, cockroach (*Eur*) **2**) tumbleweed (*Am*)

taráno *nm* tarantula

Târáno *nm* Toronto (*Am*)

Târánto *nm* Toronto (*Eur*)

Târantósko *gen/adj* of Toronto; **amári Târantóski kumpaníya** our Toronto community

tárdyulash *nm/neolog* immigration hearing/inquiry (*Can fr Lovarítska*)

targéto *nm/neolog* target

taróchi *nf/pl* tarot cards; **kolóda taróchi** deck of tarot cards (*Eur*)

taróka *nf* tarot card (*Eur*)

tasádyol *vi* **1**) be asphyxiated/choked/ smothered/strangled/suffocated: *pp/adj* **tasadilo 2**) be drowned **3**) sink, founder, be pulled down/under **4**) be flooded/inundated/swamped **5**) be gassed **6**) be killed (*gossip*)/muffled/stifled/suppressed

tasavel *vt* **1**) asphyxiate, choke, clog, smother, strangle, suffocate, throttle: *pp/adj* **tasado 2**) drown **3**) engulf (*tidal wave, avalanche*), flood, inundate, **4**) cause to founder, scuttle, sink, torpedo (*ship*) **5**) suck under (*quicksand*), pull under **6**) gas **7**) kill (*gossip/rumors*), muffle (*sound*), stifle, suppress **8**) endure, stand, put up with, submit to; **Nasthti tasavav kodolen.** I can't put up with those people. **Chi mai tasavav gadya.** I will never submit to that.

tasayimos *nm* **1**) asphyxiation **2**) flood, inundation **3**) suffocation **4**) drowning **5**) gassing **6**) swallowing **7**) strangulation **8**) suppression **9**) submission

tasayitóri *nm* strangler

taslo/tasulo *pp/adj* asphyxiated, choked, clogged up, drowned, flooded, smothered

tasol *vi* **1**) choke (*on smthg*): *pp/adj* **tasulo 2**) become smothered, suffocate **3**) be drowned, drown **4**) swallow **5**) be asphyxiated/gassed **6**) flood; **Tasuli e karburéta.** The carburetor has flooded.

táta *nm* daddy

Táte! *nm/voc* Daddy!

tato *adj* hot, warm

Tatradjine/Tatradjune *adv* on Wednesday

Tatrági *nf* Wednesday

tavalil *vt* **1**) bounce, roll, roll over: *pp/adj* **tavalime 2**) bounce/roll along **3**) *comp/v i* ~ **pálpale** bounce back, roll back **4**) **tavalíl-pe** *v/refl* **a**) roll oneself along, roll oneself along, let *smth* roll **b**) bounce along, roll along **c**) wallow

tavalimásko-bózo *nm* tumblweed

tavalimos *nm* **1**) bounce, bouncing **2**) somersault **3**) wallowing

tavalitóri *nm* **1**) roller, something that bounces or rolls; **Devlêsko Tavalitóri** Holy Roller: *nf* **Devlêski Tavalitórka** (*Am*) **2**) steamroller (*Am*) **3**) high roller (*Am*)

taváno *nm* **1**) ceiling **2**) roof: *pl* **taváya te avel** *part* forthcoming, next (*week, etc*), to come; **Me zhav o kurko te avel.** I'll go next week/during the coming week.

tavérna *nf* tavern
taxtai/taxdai *nm* **1)** glass: *pl* **taxta**; **taxtai pai** glass of water **2)** cup
taxtáno *nm* glass, stein, tumbler
tázo *nm* **1)** washbasin, washtub **2)** sink
te avel *part* forthcoming, next (*week, etc*), to come; **Me zhav o kurko te avel.** I'll go next week/during the coming week.
te *conj* **1)** if; **Te dikhes les, motho lêske te akharel ma po tilifóno.** If you see him, tell him to call me on the phone. **Te símas te zhav, trobúlas man neve tsáliya.** If I were to go, I would need some new clothes. **2)** whether; **Chi zhanav te avel wórka chi avel.** I don't know whether he's coming or not. **Kam-zhanav te mothos ma wórka na.** I'll find out whether you tell me or not. **3) te** *part* that/to/*id* **a)** used to express the English infinitive of the verb; **Mangav te zhav** I want to go/that I go., *often cont to* **t'** *as in* **Mangel t'avel.** He wants to attend. **b)** used to introduce optative statements; **Te del o Del láke hódina!** May God give her rest! **Te merav!** That I were dead! **c)** used to express verbals; **Ashundem la te gilabal.** I heard her singing. **Dikhélas man te kerav buki.** He was watching me working. **Dikhlem lês te ginel le love.** I saw him counting the money.
te na *conj/id* in order not to, lest, unless, so that, so that not, so not to, not to; **Chi dikhel la te na avel.** He won't see it unless he comes. **Motho lêske te na kerel**, Tell him not to do it. **Garav lês te na dikhen!** Hide it lest they see it!
te si kadya *conj* in this case, if this be so, this being the case; **Te si kadya me chi zhav.** If that is so, I won't go.
tehára 1 *) nf* tomorrow **2)** future; **amári tehára** our future; **Keras buki ages te dikhas amári mai lashi tehára.** Let's work today in order to see/have a better tomorrow. **3)** *adv* tomorrow; **Zhav tehára.** I'll go tomorrow.

teharáko *gen/adj* **1)** tomorrow's **2)** belonging to the future
teharása *nf/inst/adv* by tomorrow; **Kam-zhanav teharása.** I shall know by tomorrow.
teharin *nf* **1)** the morrow, the following day, day after tomorrow **2)** *adv* tomorrow morning, the following day in the morning
teharinása *nf/inst/adv* with the morrow, early tomorrow morning; **Tradav la teharinása.** I will depart early tomorrow morning.
teharuno *adj* tomorrow's
teknikálno *adj* technical
tékniko *nm* technician: *pl* **téknichi**
teknologíya/teknolodjíya *nf* technology
téko *nm* score, profit, take (*in gambling, etc*); **báro téko** big grab/take (*Am*)
têktso *nm/neolog* text
tela *prep* under, underneath
telal *prep/adv* **1)** below, under, underneath; **telal o pódo.** under the bridge, **Dikh telal!** Look underneath! **2)** *id* **Si telal múrro wast.** It's at my disposal/I am in control of it.
telaluno *adj* below, lower, under
telázo *nm* **1)** wave **2)** *pl* **telázurya** waves/tide; **Avile l' telázurya.** The tide came in.
tele *adv* **1)** down, downstairs; **Besh tele!** Sit down! **2)** down, as deposit, as a retainer **3)** *comp/vt* **del ~** demolish, knock down/over, turf; **Dem lês tele.** I knocked him down. **O mobíli dya lês tele.** The car knocked him down. **Den tele e phurani khangeri.** They are knocking down/demolishing the old church.
telefonísta *nf* telephone operator
telé-skêrènde *adv/phr* downstairs, down the stairs; **Pelo telé-skêrènde.** He fell downstairs.
televízhono *nm* television, television set (*Am*)
televizíya *nf* television, television set (*Eur*)
televizóri *nm* television (*Eur*)

telé-xaráte *adv/phr* downhill, down the incline/slope

téliga *nf* 1) cart 2) calèche, horse-drawn buggy

teluno *adj* 1) bottom, low, lower, nether, under:*adj/nf/s* **teluvi** 2) lowest man in order of rank, underling, low man on the totem pole: *nf* **teluvi**

téluve-kalts *comp/nf/pl* shorts, underpants

téluvi-lúmya *comp/nf* netherworld, subterranean world in mythology

téluvi-rrókya *comp/nf* petticoat, underskirt

telyárdyol *vi* be beginning (*a journey*), be getting started, be departing, be leaving: *pp/adj* **telyardilo**; **Telyárdyovav tehára ráno ánde diminyátsa.** I will be departing early tomorrow morning. **Telyárdyos, Rromále!** Let's get going, Roma! **Katar telyárdilan?** From where did you depart?

telyarel *vt/i* 1) go, go away, depart: *pp/adj,* **telyardo** 2) begin a journey, exit, get going, get started, get rolling, leave, move ass, start off; **Telyardyan pe buki?** Did you get started on the job yet? 3) make to get going, cause to start, flush (*toilet*)

telyarimos *nm* departure, exodus, start (*of a journey*)

telyol *vi* 1) descend, go down, flush: *pp/adj* **telilo** 2) sink

téma *nf* theme; **téma lekturáki** theme of lecture (*Eur*)

têmnitsa *nf* 1) dungeon 2) solitary confinement cell

têmnitsári *nm* jailer *nm*

têmno *adj* 1) dark, dim, dismal, gloomy, morbid 2) obscure, overcast (*sky*) 3) dangerously alluring/enchanting

têmnól *vt* 1) make dark/dismal/gloomy/obscure: *pp/adj* **têmnomé** 2) make dangerously enchanting or mysterious 3) *v/refl* **têmnól-pe a)** become dark/dismal.gloomy/obscure **b)** become dangerously enchanting or mysterious

têmnomós *nm* 1) darkness, gloom, obscurity 2) eclipse 3) **têmnomós le**

khamêsko *comp/nm* solar eclipse 4) **têmnomós le shonêsko** *comp/nm* lunar eclipse

têmplo *nm* temple (*room in a house or flat used for readings*) (*Am*)

tenásurya *nm/pl* long, large tongs used by Kalderash metalsmiths for lifting pots and pans out of boiling water

terapísto *nm* therapist: **terapísta** *nf*

terapíya *nf* therapy

têrdimós/tôrdimós *nm* halt, delay, stoppage

têrdyarél/tôrdyarél *vt* halt, make to stay, make or cause to stop: *pp/adj* **têrdyardó; Têrdyardé o tréno ánda o pharrayimos mai dur anglal.** They stopped the train because of the wreck further ahead,

têrdyol/tórdyol *vi* halt, stay, stop; *pp/adj* **têrdiló; Têrdilam trin ges ándo fóro.** We stayed three days in the town. **Nashti têrdyovav but.** I can't stay long.

térgo *nm* 1) aggreement, business deal/transaction, deal 2) bargain, *us with* **lasho; lásho térgo** bargain, good deal. 3) **phandel ~** *comp/vt/i* close a business deal

tergol *vt* 1) deal in; **Tergol tsólurya.** He deals in rugs. 2) make a deal, haggle over a deal 3) *v/refl* **tergól-pe a)** be a dealer/trader **b)** bargain/haggle with: **Tergosáilem lêsa.** I bargained/haggled with him to get a good deal.

tergótso *nm* dealer, handler of commodity goods, middle-man, trader

tergotsomos *nm* commerce, dealing, handling of goods, trading

têrminálo *nm* terminal (*airline*, *railway or bus*)

ternimos *nm* youth

terno 1) *adj* young, youthful 2) *nm* bridegroom 3) *nm* young boy/man, youth: *nf* **terni**

ternorre *nm/nmn/pl* young people, just-married couple

ternorro *nm* 1) young lad: *nf* **ternyorri** young girl 2) bridegroom: *nf* **ternyorri** bride

térno-them *comp/nm* young Romani people, young Romani adults

ternyárdyol *vi* be made young, be rejuvenated; *pp/adj* **ternyardilo**; **Ternyárdilo.** He has been rejuvenated.

ternyarel *vt* make younger, rejuvenate, restore youthful vigor: *pp/adj* **ternyardo**

ternyarimos *nm* rejuvenation, youthful vigor

terorísmo *nm* terrorism (*Eur*)

terorísto *nm* terrorist (*Eur*)

têrtitsa *nf* parson's nose (*rump of a cooked fowl*)

Testaménto *nm* Testament

têstéri *nm* branding iron

têsterîl *vt* brand (*animals*): *pp/adj* **têsterimé**

têsterimós *nm* brand, branding

tetéisha *nf* sister-in-law, husband's sister, wife's sister, relationship between husband's sister and wife's sister as sisters-in-law

têxdere/têxderi *nm* male detective: *pl* **têxderya**: *nf* **têxderútsa/têxderítsa** (*Am*)

teyáka *nm* **1)** sheath **2)** holster **3)** scabbard **4)** quiver **5)** pod **6)** cocoon

teyáka-dumêski *nf* shoulder holster

teyátro *nm* theater (*Eur*)

téyo *nm* elm, elm tree

têzhúla *nf* small pouch; **dohanóski-têzhúla** tobacco pouch

tiburóno *nm* shark: *pl* **tiburóya**

tigáiya *nf* frying pan, skillet

tigáno *nm* **1)** frying pan, skillet, wok *var of* **tigáiya** which is actually the plural used as a singular noun by many speakers.

tígra *nf* female tiger, generic tiger

tigráno *nm* male tiger: *nf* **tigráika**, female tiger, tiger's wife (*in folktales*)

tigrítsa *nf* tiger cub, child's stuffed tiger

tikno/tsikno *adj* little, small (*Eur*)

tilára *nf* dollar (*Can/Am*): *pl* **tiléri**

tilifonil *vt* telephone: *pp/adj* **tilifonime**

tilifóno *nm* telephone

tíliga/téliga *nf* **1)** buggy, horse-drawn cab, calèche **2)** cart

tinikíya *nf* can, tin can; **tinikíya fusui** can of beans

tínta *nf* **1)** ink **2)** dye

tinzhíri *nm* **1)** cooking pot. **2)** wok, saucepan, deep frying pan. **3)** bean pot (*with lid and very long handle*)

típo *nm* sort, type

típsa *nf* alum, aloe root, alum; **e vúna tipsáki** root of alum

tipsíya *nf* **1)** large, round or square, shallow pan or tray as used for cooking baklava or pizza **2)** griddle pan, skillet **3)** hotplate, tray under samovar

tirabushóno *nm* corkscrew (*Eur*)

tiraníya *nf* tyranny

tiránto *nm* tyrant: *nf* **tirantáika** domineering women; **Woi si tirantáika ánde familíya.** *id* She wears the pants in the family.

tirax/tirex *nm* boot, high leather boot (*Eur*)

tirázho *nm* circulation (*of an issue*), printing, printing run

tíro *nm* tractor-trailer truck, transporter truck: *pl* **tírya** (*Eur*); **báro tíro** big, twelve-wheeler truck; **Avilyam ánda Rumúniya ándo báro tíro.** We came from Romania (*to Italy*) in a huge truck.

tiro *pron/poss/nominalized pron/s* your. Yours; **Savo si tiro?** Which one is yours.

tirrúmo/tirúmo *nm* tea room, reader-advisor parlour (*Am*)

tísta *adv* completely, quite, very/very much; **Me sim tísta d'akórdo túsa.** I am very much in agreement with you.

tistára *adv* a lot, altogether, completely, quite, thoroughly, to the nth degree, utterly; **Tistára diferénto si.** It's a lot different. **Tistára mato sas.** He was completely drunk.

tivil *vt* **1)** hem (*garment*), take in cuffs, sleeves **2)** *v/refl* **tivíl-pe** be cuffed/hemmed/quilted

tivime *pp/adj* cuffed, hemmed, quilted

tivimos *nm* act of heming, cuffing, quilting

tivitúra *nf* cuff of trousers, duvet, hem, quilt

tívo/tsívo *adj* able, capable, clever

tiyára *nf* **1)** dinner plate, flat plate, plate **2)** platter: *pl* **tyári/tyéri**

tiyátra *nf* see **kiyátra** *nf*

tiyúdo *adj* square (*in shape*) (*Am*)

tóba *nf* drum (*Mus*)

tobásh *nm* drummer (*Mus*): *nf* **tobáshka**

tobil *vt* **1)** drum: *pp/adj* **tobime; Tobil pêske nai pe síniya.** He's drumming his fingers on the table. **2)** *v/refl* **tobíl-pe** play the drum(s), drum, be drumming (*Mus*)

tobimos *nm* drumming (*Mus*)

tobolátsiya *nf* auction; **O kher si pe tobolátsiya.** The house is up for auction/sale.

tobolatsyáno *nm* auctioneer, broker: *pl* **tobolatsyáya**

tochíla *nf* grindstone, whetstone

tochilári *nm* knife grinder/sharpener

tokáto *nm* cooking pot, saucepan, *fig* family pot/larder

tolmach *nm* interpretor, translator: *nf* **tolmáchka**

tolmachil *vt* **1)** interpret, translate **2)** *v/refl* **tolmachíl-pe** be interpreted, be translated, interpret, translate

tolmachime *pp/adj* interpreted/translated

tolmachimos *nm* process of translation, translation

tolmachíya *nf* translation

tómbola *nf* lottery, draw, raffle (*Eur*)

tomúya *nf* incense in general, frankincense

tomuyil *vt* **1)** purify with incense, sanctify or make spiritually cleansed with incense: *pp/adj* **tomuyime; Tomuyin le pomenáke tsáliya.** They are spiritually cleansing the **pomána** clothes. **2)** **tomuyíl-pe** be purified/cleansed with incense

tomuyime *pp/adj* perfumed/purified with incense, spiritually cleansed with incense

tomuyimos *nm* purification, passing of incense to purify a room, an object or **pomenáke-tsáliya** for a **pomána** ceremony

tóno *nm* sound, tone (*Mus*)

tonomáto *nm* jukebox (*Eur*)

tópo *nm* cannon, field gun (*Mil*)

tópurya *nm/pl* artillery (*Mil*)

topzhívo *nm* gunner, gunman, machine gunner (*Mil*)

tórcha *nf* flashlight

tôrdimós *nm* cessation, deadlock/gridlock, delay. stoppage

tôrdyarél *vt* bring to a halt, hold in check, pull up/over, prevent from doing, restrain, stop; *pp/adj* **tôrdyardo; Tôrdyardém lês po drom.** I stopped him on the road/way here.

tôrdyól *vi* **1)** cease, stop (*working*), come to a stop, take a break/rest: *pp/adj* **tordilo 2)** endure, stay, stand, remain **3)** stand, stand still **4)** come to a halt, halt **5)** encamp; **Tôrdilé pashal o fóro.** They camped near town **6)** maintain a a penile erection, remain erect, stand erect

tórfa *nf* **1)** turf **2)** peat **3)** thatch

tórta *nf* cake, pie (*Eur*)

tortúga *nf* tortoise/turtle (*Eur*)

tósta *nf* toast *see also* **manrró-peko** *comp/nm*

tostéri *nm* electric toaster

továrro *nm* goods, stock, material: *pl* **továrrurya**; materials, metals, stock of items

tover *nm* axe, chopper, cleaver

tóyo *nm* **1)** abundance, a lot of **2)** collection, flock, gathering, horde, mass, shoal (*fish*)

trabáko *nm* cargo vessel/ship, freighter (*Eur*)

trad *nf* **1)** admonition, warning **2) del ~** admonish, warn

trádel/tradel *vt/i* **1)** drive, fly (*aircraft*): *pp/adj* **tradino; Trádav tut ándo mobíli.** I'll drive you in the car. **2)** roam, travel, wander; **Tradásas sa l' droma ánde Kánada.** We used to travel all the roads in Canada. **3)** break camp, depart, leave **4)** transport **5)** send/send away, ship **6)** banish, chase away/out, deport, expel, exile **7)** chair/run (*meeting*) **8)** *comp/vt/i ~* **pe ilêktrolil** send by email

tradimásko *gen/adj* having to do with delivering/departing/driving/transporting;

Permíto-tradimásko Driving
licence/permit

tradimos *nm* 1) transportation 2)
drive/outing/trip, journey shipment 3)
breaking of camp, departure; **Avilem po
tradimos.** I arrived just as they were
breaking up camp. 3) chase, drive, pursuit

tradino *pp/adj* banished, chased away/out,
driven away, expelled, sent away

tradítsiya *nf* tradition (*Eur*)

trádyol *vi* 1) drive, travel: *pp/adj* **tradilo**;
2) depart, leave; **Trádilam araki.** We left
yesterday. 3) be sent/transported

tráfiko *nm* traffic; **Astárdilem ándo
tráfiko.** I got stuck in the traffic.

traktóri *nm* 1) tractor 2) tractor driver

traktóri-tréla *comp/nm* tractor trailer

trákula *nf* railway track

trambúli/tramvúli *nf* trolley bus

trámpa *nf* change, evolution

trampáika *nf* 1) female bum, drifter, hobo
2) tramp

trámpo *nm* bum, hobo, drifter, male tramp:
nf **trampáika** (*Am*); **De o xabe bi-xalo
ka ekh trámpo ánde úlitsa.** Give the
uneaten food to some bum in the street.

tramvíya/tramváli *nf* streetcar, tramcar

trankílo *adj* 1) quiet, tranquil 2) *adv*
peacefully, quietly (*Eur*)

tránsa *nf* trance

transmítsiya *nf* transmission (*Eur*)

transportátsiya *nf* transportation; **prósto
transportátsiya** public transportation

trash *nf* alarm, apprehension, fear, horror,
terror

trashado *adj* frightened, horrified, terrified,
terror-stricken 2) *nm* panic-stricken
fugitive: *nf* **trashadi**; **Nashlam le
forêstar le trashadênsa.** We fled the city
with the panic-stricken fugitives.

trashádyol *vi* 1) be intimidated, made to
fear: *pp/adj* **trashadilo** 2) be horrified

trashal *vi* be afraid, fear; **Trasháilem
ánda lêski xoli.** I became afraid because
of his anger.

trashalo *adj* afraid, horrified, scared,
terrified

trashása *nf/inst/adv* with fear, in a state of
fear, fearfully; **Mai palorral ke pelo o
marimos, trayísas trashása.** After the
war started, we lived in a state of fear.

trashavel *vt* 1) inspire fear, intimidate,
frighten, terrify: *pp/adj* **trashado** 2)
horrify

trashayimásko *gen/adj* alarming,
intimidating, frightenin, terrifying

trashayimos *nm* 1) intimidation 2) fear,
terror

trástiya *nf* 1) begging bag, leather bag,
shoulder bag, large purse 2) booster bag

traxterítsa *nf* small/cozy restaurant

traxtíri *nm* restaurant

trayil *vi* 1) be alive, exist, live; *pp/adj*
trayime; **Te trayis shel bersh!** May you
live a hundred years! **Trayin ándo
chorromós.** They live in poverty. **Trayin
po drabarimos.** They live through
fortune-telling. **Trayin po welféri.** They
live on welfare. **Trayil o Gyórgi?** Is
George still alive? 2) survive;
Naswaló-lo núma trayil. He's sick but
he'll survive. 3) come into existence

trayimásko *gen/adj* having to do with life,
liveable; **Pushkisáilo hai na mai
trayimásko.** He was shot and he is not
expected to live.

tráyo *nm* 1) life 2) existence; **Tsirdyam
chórro tráyo ándo kodo kámpo.** We
led a miserable existence in that (refugee)
camp. 3) **del ~** behave towards, treat; **Del
ma tráyo sar o zhukel.** He treats me like
a dog. **Dyas pêska Rromnyáke chórro
tráyo.** He treated his wife very
badly/gave her a miserable life.

trázna *nf* nasal infection, head cold, flu

traznalo *adj* suffering from a nasal
infection

traznol *vt* 1) cause a head cold/nasal
infection: *pp/adj* **traznome** 2) *sl* infect
with VD 3) *v/refl* **traznól-pe a)** catch a
head cold/nasal infection **b)** *sl* catch VD

tréla *nm* travel trailer

tréno *nm* train

tréno-bagazhósko *comp/nm* freight train (*Am*)

treséniya *nf* earthquake; **E treséniya peradyas o gav.** The earthquake demolished the town.

tresnéto/treznéto *nm* tremor, shock wave from an earthquake

tresol *vt* **1)** cause tremors: *pp/adj* **tresome 2)** *v/refl* **tresól-pe** shake, quake

tréstiya *nf* bamboo, cane, reed, wind instrument reed (*Mus*)

trestyáko *gen/adj* **1)** made of bamboo/cane/reed **2)** wicker

treyázo *adj* sober

treyázol *vt* **1)** make sober, sober up: *pp/adj* **treyazome 2)** *v/refl* **treyázol-pe** become sober, sober oneself up. **Treyazosáilo.** He sobered up.

treyazomos *nm* sobriety

tribunálo *nm* court, tribunal (*Eur*)

tribuyála/tribuyára *nf* necessity, need, requirement, want: *pl* **tribuyéli**

trifoi *nm* clover (*Eur*)

trigántsiya *nf* trigger

trin 1) *num* three **2)** *pron* three people

trinali *nf* number three, three in cards

trinen *pron/pl/obl* three of them; **Dikhlem le trinen.** I saw the three of them

triné-rêgèngo *adj* three-sided, triangular

tripíya *nf* diphtheria

trisikléta *nf* tricycle

trísto *adj* **1)** dejected, depressed, forlorn, sad **2)** lonely **3)** pathetic

trísto gili *comp/nf* lament, sad song

tristol *vt* **1)** depress, make sad, sadden: *pp/adj* **tristome 2)** **tristól-pe** become dejected, become, become depressed, become sad, grow sad

tristomása *nm/inst/adv* sadly, with sadness; **Gilabadyas tristomása.** She sang sadly.

tristomos *nm* dejection, depression, gloom, sadness

tríto *num* third

trivardesh/triwardesh *adv* thirty

trivares/triwares *adv* three times, thrice; **Tsipisáilo triwares.** He yelled three times.

tríwar *adv* three times; **Si tríwar mai baro.** It is three times bigger

triyánda *num/nm* thirty

triyandafírya *nf* **1)** rose (*thirty petals*) **2)** rose bush **3)** Rosie

triyandáto *num/adj* thirtieth

triyandawares *adv* thirty times

triyungalo *adj* triangular

triyúngi *nf* triangle: *pl* **triyúngya**

trobul/trebul *def/v* **1)** need, need to, ought to have, should have: *pp/adj* **trobulo**; **Trobul ma xabe.** I need food. **Trobun ma love.** I need money. **Trobúlas te avel.** He ought to have come. **Músai sas túke te kindyan le vêska trobúnas.** You must have bought them because they were needed. **Trobúl te avel kerdo/Trobul te kérdyol.** It needs to be done. **Músai te keras so trobul.** We must do what needs to be done. **Trobúlas te zhav.** I should have gone. **2)** be necessary; **Chi trobul.** It's not necessary. **3)** deserve; **Trobul mardo.** He deserves to be beaten up. **Trobul gadya.** He deserves that. **4)** *v/refl* **trobúl-pe** be needed; **Kána trobúl-pe, sáyek bilal wárekai.** When he is needed, he always disappears somewhere. **5)** be required

trobutno *adj* necessary, needed, required

trokash *nm* truckdriver: *nf* **trokáshka** female truck driver

trokashítska *nf* CB truckers' radio talk (*Am*)

tróko *nm* truck (*Am*)

trokútso *nm* pickup truck (*Am*)

tróma *nf* audacity, bravery, courage, daring

tromádyol *vi* **1)** challenged, dared, defied: *pp/adj* **tromadilo 2)** be risked, ventured

tromal *vi* have the audacity to, dare: *pp/adj* **tromailo**; **Chi tromálas te kerel.** He wouldn't dare do that. **Chi tromáilo te del-fátsa le Yonos.** He didn't dare face Yono.

tromavel *vt* **1)** challenge, dare, defy; *pp/adj* **tromado 2)** risk, venture

tromayimos *nm* **1)** challenge, dare, defiance **2)** risk, venture

trómfa *nf* trump
tromfil *vt* **1)** trump (*in cards*): *pp/adj*
  tromfime 2) tromfíl-pe be trumped
tromimos *nm* audacity, daring
trompéta *nf* bugle, trumpet
trompetash *nm* bugler, trumpet player
tronil *vt* enthrone, place on the throne:
  pp/adj **tronime**
tronimos *nm* enthroning
tróno *nm* throne
trotwári *nm* sidewalk (*Eur*)
trózna/trázna *nf* bad cold, flu
troznalo *adj* suffering from a bad cold, flu
troznyarel *vt* infect with a bad cold, flu:
  pp/adj **troznyardo**
troznyol *vi* catch/develop a bad cold, flu:
  pp/adj **troznailo; Troznailem.** I caught a
  bad cold.
trúba *nf* **1)** flue, funnel, pipe, ventilator,
  vent **2)** roll, tube; **trúba kleyónka** roll of
  linoleum **3)** drainpipe, pipe
trúba-bovêski *comp/nf* stove
  canopy/chimney
trúbitsa *nf* funnel
trúblo *nm* trouble; **Na ker mánge trúblo!**
  Don't make trouble for me!
trúdno *adj* complicated, difficult, involved
  (*Eur*)
Trukomanítska *nf* Turkish (*Lang*)
Trukomanitsko *adj* Tukish
Trukománo *nm* Turk: *nf* **Trukománka**
trúpa *nf* gang, mob, troop (*Mil*)
trupêski-khand *comp/nf* body odor
trúpo *nm* **1)** body (*Anat*) **2)** carcass, mortal
  remains **3) múlo-trúpo** dead body,
  corpse **4)** content
trush *nf* **1)** thirst **2)** drought; **Peli êkh bári
  trush po them.** A great drought struck
  the land.
trushádyol *vi* be made thirsty: *pp/adj*
  trushadilo
trushalimos *nm* **1)** thirst **2)** drought
trushalo *adj* **1)** thirsty **2)** gas-guzzling
  (*automobile*) **2)** *nm* gas guzzler
  (*automobile*) (*Am*)

trushávol *vi* become thirsty: *pp/adj*
  trushailo; Trusháilam ándo mobíli. We
  got thirsty in the car.
trushni *nf* water bottle/flask
trushul *nf* **1)** cross, crucifix; **Lóli Trushul**
  Red Cross **2)** crossroads, intersection; **e
  trushul le dromêngi** the crossroads **3)**
  evidence, imprint, marking, spoor,
  trace/traces; **Meklas trushul.** He left
  evidence. **Biláili bi te mekel trushul.**
  She vanished without leaving a trace. **4)**
  linchpin
trushul wozyáki *comp/nf* axle linchpin of
  a wagon
trushula *nf/pl* **1)** crosses **2)** cemetery;
  Angropasarde lês mashkar le trushula.
  They buried him among the crosses (*in
  the cemetery*). **Beshel o rashai ándo
  párno kher pashal le trushula.** The
  minister lives in a white house near the
  cemetery.
Trusháko *gen/adj* of the cross, Christian
trushulalo *adj* cruciform
trushulardo *pp/adj* crucified
trushulárdyol *vi* be crucified, get oneself
  crucified: *pp/adj* **trushulardilo**
trushularel *vt* crucify: *pp/adj* **trushulardo**
trushulimos *nm* crucifixion
trushyarel *vt* make thirsty: *pp/adj*
  trushyardo
truyal *prep* around, round about (*Eur*) *see
  also* **kruyal** *prep*
tryába/treyába *nf* **1)** thing, matter, object,
  subject **2)** affair, business
tu **1)** *pron/nom/s* you; **Tu gîndís?** You
  think so? **2)** *pron/acc/s* you, yourself;
  Yóshkane! Tu san! Yóshka! Is that you?
túbo *nm* inner tube
túdka *nf* female turkey
tudkála *nf* coal tar, tar
tudkalil *vt* do blacktopping, pave, tar:
  pp/adj **tudkalime**
tudkalimos *nm* blacktopping, paving,
  tarring
tudkáno *nm* male turkey
tulévo *nm* cornstalk, stalk in general
tulipána *nf* tulip

túlso *nm* tool. *(Am)*: *pl* **túlsurya** tools. *(Am)*

túma *nf* tumour

tumaro *pron/poss/nominalized pron/pl* your, yours

tume *pron/nom/pl* you **2)** *pron/acc/pl* you, yourselves

tumên *pron/pl/acc* you, yourselves

tumên sya/tume sya *pron/pl/acc* all of you; **Zhanel tumên sya.** He knows all of you.

tumnil *vt* **1)** betroth **2)** ask for in marriage **3)** *v/refl* **tumníl-pe, 1)** be promised in marriage **2)** become formally engaged.

tumnime *pp/adj* betrothed, formally engaged, promised in marriage

tumnimos *nm* **1)** betrothal **2)** betrothal ceremony

tumnyála *nf* betrothal, engagement

tûmpo *adj* **1)** blunt, dull **2)** obtuse

tûmpól *vt* **1)** blunt, dull **2)** *v/refl* **tûmpól-pe** become blunt, dull

tûmpomé *nm* blunted

tunéla *nf* mine shaft, subway tunnel, tunnel

tunerichil *vt* **1)** make dark/gloomy: *pp/adj* **tunerichime 2)** *v/refl* **tunerichíl-pe a)** become dark/gloomy/overcast, could over **b)** become twilight **c)** become clouded over/overshadowed

tunerichimos *nm* clouding over, dusk, gloom, twilight

tunyáriko *adj* **1)** dark, foreboding, gloomy **2)** *nm* darkness. gloom

túpo *nm* toupée

turbáno *nm* **1)** turban **2)** headdress

turbarichil *vt* **1)** enrage, madden **2)** drive insane **3)** *v/refl* **turbarichíl-pe** go stark, raving mad

turbarichime *pp/adj* **1)** enraged, maniacal, raving mad **2)** rabid

turbarichimos *nm* **1)** madness, raging insanity **2)** rabies

turbatil *vt* **1)** drive mad, make mad/insane: *pp/adj* **turbatime 2)** arouse, excite **3)** make rabid **4)** *v/refl* **turbatíl-pe a)** become demented, go mad, run amok; **Turbatisáilo.** He went berserk/postal. **b)** become rabid; **Turbatisáilo o zhukel.** The dog became rabid.

turbáto *adj* **1)** berserk, furious, crazy, demented, insane, mad, postal, wild **2)** rabid **3)** abandoned, exuberant, excited, stormy, tumultuous; **turbáto tsipimos** tumultuous cheering or shouting. **4)** *adv* amok **5)** *nm* madman, raving lunatic: *nf* **turbáika**

turbáto gazho *comp/nm* lunatic, madman: *nf* **turbáto gazhi**

turbáto máriya *comp/nf* stormy sea

turbáto-bózo *nm* locoweed (*astragalus melissimus*) *(Am)*

turbyála *nf* **1)** dementia, insanity, madness, rage **2)** rabies

Turkítska *nf* Turkish (*Lang*)

Turkítsko *adj* Turkish

Turkíya *nf* Turkey

Túrko *nm* Turk: *nf* **Turkáika**

turnavísa *nf* screwdriver (*Eur*)

túrno *nm* bell tower, spire, steeple, tower, turret, watchtower

turpentáimo *nm* turpentine

Túrsko *adj* Turkish (*Eur*); **Túrsko ponyáva** Turkish carpet

tut *pron/acc/s* you, yourself

túzo *nm* ace (*in cards*)

tyo *pron/poss/s* your

tyúdo *nm* cube; ~ **pavósko** ice cube

TH

tha *conj* and *us with numerals*;
bish-tha-dui twenty and two/twenty-two
thagar *nm* **1)** king (*Eur*). **2)** chieftain,
headman, ruler (*Eur*)
thagarêski rakli *comp/nm* princess (*Eur*)
thagarêsko raklo *comp/nm* prince (*Eur*)
thagarimos *nm* **1)** kingship, rule **2)**
kingdom (*Eur*)
thagarni *nf* **1)** queen **2)** female ruler, wife
of a chieftain/ruler (*Eur*)
thagaruno *adj* monarchial, royal
thai *conj* and, also
thai-vi *conj* and also, as well as, along
with; **Akushlas man thai-vi murra
rromnya.** He insulted me and also my
wife. **Zhanav lês thai-vi zhanav i-lêske
phrales.** I know him as well as his
brother.
than *nm* **1)** haunt, lair, location, place,
scene, site, spot **2)** area, region, vicinity
3) *fig* bed, sleeping place **4)** stead, place
(*as in the following*); **Wo zhal ándo
múrro than.** He will go in my
stead/place. **5)** room, space; **Manai
dósta than savorrênge.** There is not
enough room/space for everybody.
thanêsko *gen/adj* of the place, local;
thanêske gazhe local people
than-po-Internéto *nm/phr* web site: *pl*
thana-po-Internéto
thar *nf* **1)** eyetooth, molar tooth **2)** fang **3)**
tusk **4)** jaw of an animal
thav *nm* thread; **suv hai ~** needle and
thread: *pl* **thava** spider threads in a web
them *nm* **1)** people, Romani
people/community, our people; **Motho l’
themêske te avel kai sláva.**Tell the
(Romani) people to come to the feast.

Avile but them hai lúmiya. Many local
Roma and Roma from out of town
attended. **Ame sam o Rrómano them.**
We are the Romani nation/people.
Meklas pêske themes. He left his own
people. **2)** country, homeland, land,
national state, region **3)** foreign, *esp*
European country (*Am*); **Rrom ánda l’
thema.** Roma from (European) countries.
themêngo *gen/adj* belonging to the
countries, i.e. European *(Am)*; **themêngo
Rrom** a Rom from Europe, European
Rom
themêski-gili *comp/nf* national anthem; **e
themêski-gili la Kanadáko** the national
anthem of Canada.
themêski-shib *com/nf* **1)** European
Romani dialect (*Am*) **2)** national language
of a country
themêski-zastáva *comp/nf* national flag of
a country
themêsko *gen/adj* belonging to a country,
national
themuno *adj* **1)** foreign, from another
country **2)** European (*Am*) **3)** belonging
to a country, national **4)** *nm* foreigner **5)**
national of a country **6)** fellow
countryman
themutno *nm* citizen/national of a country:
nf **themutni**
thodimos *nm* **1)** inducement **2)** placement
3) setting of a table
thodino *pp/adj* appointed, placed, put
thóila *nf* toilet (*Am*)
thol *vt* **1)** cast, lay, portray, put, put on,
place, set: *pp/adj* **thodino**; **Thodyas e
sínya.** She set the table. **Thodyas pêski
stagi.** He put his hat on. **2)** to turn on, put

on; **Tho le ilêktrichi**! Turn on the
headlights! **3)** convince, induce; **Thodine
lês te xoxavel**. They induced him to lie.
4) plant, install; **Le gazhe thodine o
ilêktriko**. The men installed the
electricity. **Thodyas poruma ándo
djardíno**. She planted onions in the
garden. **Kai manges te tháva**? Where do
you want me to set it up? **5)** appoint **6)**
v/phr ~ **ánde hârtíya** *v/phr* advertise in
the newspaper **7)** *comp/vt/i* ~ **ándo shoro**
put into (somebody's) head, influence **8)**
comp/vt/i ~ **anglal** place before, present
(*an issue at a meeting, etc*) **9)** *comp/vt* ~
gogi be considerate of *smbdy/think about*
10) *comp/vt* ~ **o lokáto** bolt, lock (*door*)
11) *comp/vt/i* ~ **sáma a)** notice, pay
attention to **b)** *with negative part* **chi** *and*
pe *vt/i* ignore; **Chi thodem sáma pe
lêste.** I ignored him. **Chi mai thol sáma
pe mánde.** He always ignores me. **12)**
comp/vt ~ **tele** lay down, put down **13)**
comp/vt/i ~ **yakh** watch, keep an eye on;
Tho ki yak pe láte. Watch her/Keep your
eye on her. **14)** *comp/vt/i* ~ **zêfto** lay
ashphalt/blacktop **15)** *comp/vt/i* ~ **zûn**
saddle **16)** *v/refl* **thol-pe, a)** join, enlist,
place oneself, put oneself; **Thodyás-pe
pe l' chângènde te rrugíl-pe.** He got
down on his knees to pray. **Thodyás-pe
katána.** He became a soldier/joined the
army. **b)** begin, start, get to doing, set
oneself to do; **Thodyás-pe te akushel
ma ánde sláva.** He started to cuss me out

during the feast. **Thodyas-pe te gilabal.**
She started singing. **c)** get involved in,
interfere; **Thodyás-pe ánde múrri buki.**
He got involved in my business.

thud *nm* milk
thudalo *adj* milky, resembling milk
thudári *nm* milkman
thudárnitsa *nf* **1)** dairy **2)** milk churn
thudêsko *gen/adj* containing milk, of milk
thud-shuklo *comp/nm* buttermilk
thulimos *nm* corpulence, obesity
thulo *adj* **1)** corpulent, fat, obese, stout **2)**
    thick **3)** *nm* fat man: *nf* **thuli**
thulyarel *vt* fatten/fatten up, thicken:
    pp/adj **thulyardo 2)** *v/refl* **thulyarél-pe**
    fatten oneself up, gain wight, thicken
    itself
thulyarimos *nm* fattening process,
    thickening process
thulyol *vi* grow/become fat, thicken: *pp/adj*
    thulilo; **Thulili desar me dikhlem la
    mai anglal.** She got fat since I last saw
    her.
thuv *nm* **1)** smoke, cloud of smoke **2) del** ~
    emit smoke, smoke **2) shúdel** ~ belch
    smoke
thuvalo *adj* smoky
thuvli/thuvali *nf* cigarette (*Eur*)
thuvlyardo *pp/adj* cured, smoked
thuvlyarel *vt* cure, smoke (*fish, meat*),
    smoke out (*wasps*): *pp/adj* **thuvlyardo**
thuvlyol *vi* **1)** emit smoke, smoke,
    smoulder **2)** be curred/smoked (*meat, etc*)
thuv-tsigarêngo *comp/nm* cigarette smoke

TS

tsála *nf* article of clothing, garment

tsáliya *nf/pl* garments, clothes, clothing

tsálpa *nf* 1) sole of a boot/shoe 2) sole of the foot (*Anat*)

tsav *nm* cord, thread, twine *var* of **thav** *nm*

tsáva *nf* 1) pipe, smokestack, stove pipe 2) barrel/muzzle of a rifle/shotgun 3) drain pipe, eaves trough

tsávi *nf/pl* roof gutter and water runoff pipe

tsávitsa *nf* gas pipe, small pipe, tube, water pipe

tsedúla *nf* bank note, letter of credit, ticket from a pawnbroker

tsegásh *nm* marksman, sniper

tsêgátsa *nf* 1) hiccup 2) burp

tsêgêtsíl *vt* 1) cause or induce hiccups: *pp/adj* tsêgêtsimé 2) *v/refl* tsêgêtsíl-pe have the hiccups, be hiccupping 3) belch, burp

tsêgêtsimé *pp/adj* afflicted with hiccups; **Tsêgêtsimé-lo.** He's got the hiccups.

tsêgêtsomos *nm* burping, eructation

tsêgêtsyála *nf* hiccups

tsegomos *nm* aim, act of aiming, pointing, training a weapon

tsegosarel/tsegol *vt* 1) aim (*a weapon*), take aim: *pp/adj* tsegosardo/tsegome 2) point, point at 3) *v/refl* tsegól-pe be aiming, pointing

tseléra/seléra *nf* one stick of celery: *pl* teleléri

tsélo/chélo *adj* entire, whole (*Eur*) *see also* **ântrégo** *adj*

tsênída/tsûnída *nf* nettle

tsêpêníl *vt* 1) make numb, make to become hard/stiff, stiffen: *pp/adj* tsêpênimé 2) *v/refl* tsêpêníl-pe become hard/stiff, become numb

tsêpênimós *nm* 1) numbness, stiffness 2) deadlock, impass, stalemate 3) blockage; **Si baro tsêpênimós ándo tázo.** There is a serious blockage in the sink.

tséra *nf* 1) tent 2) extended family, family members in the tent; **Sodya zhene si ánde tumári tséra?** How many people are in your extended family? 3) family unit, household; **Si lês bori ánde tséra.** He has a daughter-in-law in the household. 4) lel ánde ~ take into the tent/ family, adopt; **Lyam la ánde tséra hai barisardyam la sar yekha amara familyátar.** We adopted her into the home and raised her like one of our family.

tseráda *nf* canvas awning, roof of a tent, tent cover

tserakano 1) *adj* having to do with a tent, camping 2) *nm* tent dweller: *nf* tserakani

tserépo *nm* 1) awning; **Wazde o tserépo!** Raise the awning! 2) canvas ceiling/roof

tséri *nf.pl* 1) tents, camp; **Kai si lêngi tséri?** Where is their camp? 2) extended families; **Chi zhanav sodya tséri si ánde amári vítsa, bari, barí-la.** I don't know how many extended families there are in our clan, it is really big.

tserkol *vt* 1) wean: *pp/adj* tserkome 2) kick/withdraw (*get rid of a habit*)

tserkome *pp/adj* weaned; **Tserkome e gláta?** Is the baby weaned?

tserkomos *nm* weaning, withdrawal

tsêrkulo *nm* compass (*for drawing*)

tserúla *nf* pump, slipper, soft indoor slipper

tserútsa *nf* pup-tent, light, smallish tent that can be backpacked

tsigára *nf* **1)** cigarette: *pl* **tsigéri; tsigára chepósa** filter-tipped cigarette **2)** cigar

tsigaréta *nm* cigarette (*Eur*)

tsígênó/tsigno *adj* little, small

tsígla *nf* brick

tsiglángo *gen/adj* brick, made of bricks

tsiglári *nm* bricklayer

tsîmbála *nf* cymbalom

tsímburo *nm* **1)** seed (*of a plant/tree*) **2)** kernel, pip, stone **3)** bulb

tsímparo *nm* sulphur

tsimptsára *nf* **1)** mosquito: *pl* **tsimptséri 2)** helicopter (*Am*)

tsîna *nf* estimate, cost, price, value; **Shai des mánge tsîna?** Can you quote me a price?

tsino *adj* **1)** little, small, tiny **2)** *nm* small male child: *nf* **tsini**

tsinono *nm* baby boy: *nf* **tsinoni**

tsíno-réko *comp/nm* creek, stream

tsinorro *adj* **1)** tiny, minuscule, very small **2)** *nm* baby boy: *nf* **tsinyorri**

tsînowíl *vt* **1)** appraise, assess, determine the price/value of, evaluate, price, estimate/set a price; **Tsînowisardém o mobíli.** I had the car appraised/estimated/evaluated//priced. **2)** *v/refl* **tsînowíl-pe** have a set price, be appraised/evaluated

tsînowimé *pp/adj* assessed, established/set (*price*)

tsînowimós *nm* appraisal, assessment, estimation, evaluation

tsinyarél *vt* contract, diminish, make smaller, reduce in size, shrink: *pp/adj* **tsinyardo**

tsinyol *vi* **1)** become reduced in size, grow smaller, shrink: *pp/adj* **tsinilo 2)** wane (*moon*)

tsip *nf* coins, poke, wad of money

tsípa *nf* **1)** shout, scream, yell **2)** coin, piece of money

tsipil *vt* **1)** bawl out, cheer, scream, shout/shout at, yell at: *pp/adj* **tsipime**; **Tsipisardyas mánde te zhávtar.** He yelled at me to depart. **Tsipíl pe láte.** He's yelling at her. **Na tsipisar pe**

mánde! Get off my case! **2)** call to, hail **3)** howl **4)** squawk **5)** *v/refl* **tsipíl-pe** cry out, scream, howl; **Tsipisáilo dukhátar.** He cried out in/from pain.

tsipimos *nm* **1)** clamour, howling, screaming, shouting, uproar, verbal din, yelling; **Ashundem lêngo tsipimos.** I heard their clamour. **2)** cheering, round of applause, ovation; **Dinilo baro tsipimos.** He was given a great round of applause/standing ovation

tsiplíga *nf* chip, splinter

tsirdári *nm* drawer (*of bureau/desk*)

tsírdel *vt* **1)** draw, haul, pull, row (*boat*), tow: *pp/adj* **tsirdino 2)** endure, enjoy, undergo, pass; **Tsirdyam lásho tráyo ándo fóro.** We enjoyed a good life in the city. **Tsirdyam but nekázo ándo marimos.** We endured much suffering during the war. **3)** solder **4)** draw in, lure in, influence, pull into sphere of influence **5)** breathe in, draw, inhale **6)** *vt* **tsirdéltar** pull off, tear off; **E balwal tsirdyástar e fundánya.** The wind tore off the tent cover. **7)** attract, draw toward **8)** draw, pull (*bow*) **9)** *v/refl* **tsírdel-pe a)** crawl, creep, pull oneself along, schlep along **b)** be attracted to/pulled towards

tsirdimásko-grast *comp/nm* cart horse

tsirdimásko-tróko *comp/nm* tow truck

tsirdimos *nm* load, weight (*of a cart*), act of drawing, pulling

tsirdínyol *vi* become/be soldered: *pp/adj* **tsirdinilo; Chi mai tsirdínyol, hamime hárkoma si.** It will never take solder, it's alloyed copper (*copper alloy*).

tsirditóri *nm* **1)** soldering iron. **2)** electric or gas soldering torch

tsirkash *nm* circus performer *nf* **tsirkáshka**

tsírko *nm* circus

tsírkulo *nm* compass (*for drawing*)

tsîrlígo *nm see* **kêrlígo** *nm*

tsîrrá 1) *pron/nf* a little, small amount, tad, speck, spot; **Si tut but, si lês tsîrrá.** You have much, he has little. **2)** *adv* a little, slightly, somewhat; **Dikhlem lês ánde**

sláva, tsîrrá mato sas. I saw him during the feast, he was a little drunk.

tsîrrá xabe *comp/nm* snack (*a little food*); **Las tsîrrá xabe!** Let's have a snack!

tsîrratsítsa *pron* dash, speck, tad, pinch, trifling amount; **tsîrratsítsa lond** a dash of salt

tsivîlno *adj* civil (*administration*)

tsokóla/tsokóli *nf* shoe in general, dress shoe, leather shoe: *pl* **tsokóli/tsokólya**

tsokolári *nm* shoe maker

tsokólya *nf/pl* footwear, shoes, pair of shoes; **Kai múrre tsokólya?** Where are my shoes?

Tsolári *nm* **1)** carpet dealer **2)** male member of the **Tsolára** group in Hungary: *nf* **Tsolarítsa**

Tsolarítska *nf* dialect of the **Tsolára**

Tsolarítsko *adj* of the **Tsolára,** a Vlax-Romani group

tsólo *nm* **1)** area rug, carpet, mat **2)** horse blanket

tsolútso *nm* doormat

tsóxa *nf* skirt (*Eur*); **Nai ma tsóxa nai ma gad, na kinéla múrro dad.** I have no skirt, I have no blouse, my father won't buy them for me. (*Romani song*)

tsûmpo/chûmpo *nm* **1)** drumstick (*of a fowl*) **2)** leg (*of an animal/fowl*) **3)** junctioin of a branch to a tree

tsúrkulo *nm* circle; **Ramosardyas tsírkulo ándo kishai.** She drew a circle in the sand.

tsyapenil/tsyepenil *vt* **1)** make hard, numb, stiff: *pp/adj* **tsyapinime 2)** block (*an issue*) **3)** cause a deadlock create a stalemate: *pp/adj* **tsyapenime 4)** *v/refl* **tsyapenil-pe** become/grow hard, numb, stiff

tsyapenimos/tsyepenimos *nm* deadlock, stalemate

tsyápeno/tsyépeno *adj* hard, numb, stiff

U

u *conj* and *with numbers fom 11 to 19;*
  desh-u-trin ten-and-three/thirteen
Uf! *interj* Oh! **Áve-uf!** Oh God!
úlitsa/wúlitsa *nf* street; **e mai bari úlitsa**
  main street
umidimos *nm* humidity (*Eur*)
úmido *adj* humid; **Takyová-ma ke úmido.**
  I'm getting hot because it's humid. (*Eur*)
umidóra *nf* humidifier (*Eur*)
Ungarítska *nf* Hungarian (*Lang*),
  Modyarítska (*Lang*)
Ungarítsko *adj* Hungarian
Ungáriya *nf* Hungary
Úngaro *nm* **1)** Hungarian, Magyar: *nf*
  Ungarútsa 2) Hungary
universálno *adj* universal: *adv*
  universalnones
universitáriyo *nm* university (*Am*)
universitéto *nm* university (*Eur*)
univérso *nm* universe

úniya *nf* ethnic/political union, labour
  union, union
Úniya-Ivropanóski *comp/nf* European
  Union (*Eur*)
Úniya-Rromani *comp/nf* Romani Union
uril *vt* **1)** wish: *pp/adj* **urime**; **Uriv túke**
  but baxt. I wish you much good fortune.
  (*Eur*) **2)** *v/refl* **uríl-pe** be wished for, wish,
  hope, hope for; **Uri-ma.** I hope so/I wish
urimáski-xaying *nf* wishing well (*Eur*)
urimos *nm* wish (*Eur*)
Ursitóri *nm see* **Wursitóri** *nm*
utílno *adj* useful (*Eur*)
uzil *vt* **1)** exploit, make use of, use, use up:
  pp/adj **uzime** (*Eur*) **2)** *v/refl* **uzíl-pe** be
  used for

V

va *adv* yes (*in answer to a question*)

va nichi/vad níchi *conj* or not; **Aves mánsa va níchi?** Are you coming with me or not?

va/vad *conj* or

vádna *nf* bath, washing tub

vádra *nf* 1) bucket, pail; **vádra pai** pail of water 2) trash bucket, waistbasket

vága *nf* cart, wagon

vagóno *nm* 1) wagon, coach on a train. 2) station wagon (*Am*)

vagóno-bagazhósko *comp/nm* boxcar of a freight train

vagzála/vuksála *nf* depot, station, terminus, train station

vai *conj* either, or; **Aves vai zhas?** Are you coming or going? **Chachó-lo vai na?** Is he right or not?

váida *nm arch* chieftain, headman, honcho, leader (*Eur*)

vái-ke *conj* either, or, or that; **So phenes, ke xoxavel vái-ke chi zhanel?** What are you saying, that he's lying or that he doesn't know?

vakil *vt* 1) criticize, find fault, groan, moan: *pp/adj* **vakime** 2) *v/refl* **vakíl-pe** bitch, complain, grouch, grumble, harp on

vakimos *nm* complaint, criticism, grievance, groaning, grouching, grumbling , moaning

vakitóri *nm* complainer, critic, groucher, grumbler, moaner, whiner: *nf*: **vakitórka**

vakt *nm* time (*Eur*)

vákto *nm* time *var of* **vákt** (*Eur*); **Nai ma vákto te xasarav kodolênsa.** I have no time to waste with those people.

valádriya *nf* reed/wicker basket

valentíya *nf* gallantry, valor (*Eur*)

valíso *nm* suitcase

valóvo *nm* trough, horse trough, water trough, water tank; **balêngo ~** pig trough

válso *nm* waltz

valuv *nm* tent flap

válvo *nm* valve

vangeli *nf* religious ornament, Saint's medallion

vangilíya *nf/pl* church mementos, holy ornaments, Saints' medallions

vánisho *nm* varnish (*Am*)

vapóri *nm* steamer, steamhip. (*Eur*)

vára *nf* female cousin: *pl* **várya/véri**

várga *nf* chevron, stripe: *pl* **vêrzhi**

várro *nm* 1) chalk 2) lime, quicklime 3) guano, birdlime (as *used as fertilizer*)

várro/wárro *nm* flour, grain *see also* **árro** *nm*

vash *prep/neolog* for, for the sake of (*Eur*) Note: While this preposition is not technically core vocabulary in Vlax-Romani dialects, it has been adopted more and more in writing and publications in Vlax- Romani dialects and in email communication; **Kerav lês vash le Rromênde.** I'm doing it for the Roma. **Kindyas káfa vash o djuléshi.** He bought coffee for the meeting.

vashári *nm* horse auction, horse fair

vátra *nf* 1) abode, camp, camping place/spot, settlement, shelter 2) fireside, hearth, home 3) aegis, auspices, sponsorship

vatrári *nm see* **vatrash** *nm*

vatrash *nm* 1) (*Arch in Am*) Rom elected to represent a camp/settlement of Roma to the authorities, camp representative: *nf*

vatráshka wife of the camp representative **2)** patron, sponsor

vechíno *nm* neighbour: *nf* **vechinútsa** *nf*

vedyárya *nf var of* **vyedyárya**

véko *nm* **1)** life, lifetime, time (*of*): *pl* **véchi; Tradásas ándo véko múrre papósko.** We used to travel during the time of my grandfather. **2)** age, eon, era, eternity, long period of time

véla *nf* sail of a boat/ship (*Eur*)

velinil *vt* **1)** make venomous, poison with slander/venomous talk: *pp/adj* **velenime 2) veliníl-pe** *v/refl* become spiteful/venonmous/ vindictive

velinime *pp/adj* **1)** poisonous, venemous **2)** spiteful, vindictive

velinimos *nm* venomous talk, vicious slander, vindictiveness

vélino *nm* **1)** venom **2)** bile **3)** spite **4)** malicious gossip **5) sapésko ~** snake venom

velinósko *gen/adj* possessing venom, malicious, spiteful, venemous; **velenóski shib** venomous tongue, **velinênge sapa** venomous snakes, vindictive people

velinóso *adj* malicious, spiteful, venomous

vêlo *nm* will (*of deceased psn*)

véna *nf see* **vûna** *nf*

ventilatóri *nm* fan, ventilator (*Eur*)

veríga *nf* chain link, eyebolt/ringbolt, link, metal ring: *pl* **verízhi**

véro *nm* male cousin: *pl* **vérya**

vêrzhimé *pp/adj* marked with chevrons, striped; **verzhime padjámi** striped pyjamas

vêrzjènsa *nf/pl/inst* with stripes, striped; **mútsa vêrzhènsa** tabby cat, tiger cat

veshtári *nm* jeweler *nm*

véshto *nm* jewel. piece of jewellery, valuable object: *pl* **véshturya**

véska *conj* because

vesolil *vt* **1)** cheer up, encourage, gladden, make happy: *pp/adj* **vesolime 2)** *v/refl* **vesolíl-pe** become happy/encouraged

vesolimos *nm* happiness, joy

vesolíya *nf* happiness, joy

vésolo/véselo *adj* **1)** cheerful, content, contented, glad, happy **2)** happily excited (*about smthg*)

vesolones *adv* cheerfully, happily

vêstíl *vi* **1)** glorify, laud, lionize, make famous: *pp/adj* **vêstimé 2)** *v/refl* **vêstíl-pe** blow one's own horn, glorify oneself, laud oneself, sing one's own praises

vêstimé *pp/adj* fabled, fabulous, famous, glorious

vêstimós *nm* **1)** fame, lionization **2)** glory

veterinári /veterinéri *nm* veterinary surgeon: *nf* **veterinárka**

vi *adv/prep/conj* **1)** as; (*often used with* **sar** *in comparison of adjectives and adverbs with prep case of object*); **Wo si sar bokhalo vi mánde.** He is as hungry as I am. **Sar xarane sam vi le avre Rromênde.** We are as smart as the other Roma. **Wo nai sar baro vi mánde.** He is not as big as I am. **Wo nashel sar zurales vi mánde.** He runs as quickly as I do.(*It is also used to express "less than"*); **Wo nashel mai xansû zurales vi mánde.** He runs less quickly than I do. **Wo si mai xansû sikado vi mánde.** He is less educated than me. (*To express "more than"*); **Tu san mai shukar vi láte.** You are more beautiful than her/she is. **2)** also, even, too; **Vi me shai zhav.** I too can attend. **Vi tu músai te zhanes gadya.** Even you must know that. **Wo gêlótar thai-vi o Geórgi.** He departed, and also George. **Vi-wo xálas-pe mánsa.** He was also arguing with me. **Vi-tu shai keres.** You too can do it/Even you can do it.

vi-akana *adv* still, until now; **Vi-akana san tu kathe?** Are you still here? **Vi-akana ashukerávas.** I have been waiting until now. **So kerdyan aryat te vi-akana soves?** What did you do last night so that you are still sleeping until now?

víchera *nf* dinner, evening meal, supper

vídra *nf* beaver

víla *nf* elf, fairy, gnome

viláko *adj* fairy; ~ ring, **vilángo kólo** *comp/nm*

vína *nf* excuse, justification

vínto *nm* screw (*Am*)

vintol *vt* screw, screw in: *pp/adj* **vintome** (*Am*)

víra *nf* **1)** block and tackle, hoisting device **2)** crane, derrick

viram *nm/neolog* full stop, period

virítsa *nf* davit, hoist

vi-si/vi-sû *id* just, exactly; **Si ma trin tiléri vi-si.** I have exactly three dollars. **Avile gadiki zhene vi-si.** Just that many people came.

víso/váiso *nm* vice (*tool*)

Visóki Stévan *nm* Mighty Steven, hero in folktales

vis -presidênto *nm* vice president

vitamíno *nm* vitamin

vitéza *nf* **1)** speed (*Eur*); **Si la trin vitézi.** It has three speeds. (*bicycle*), **mai sígo vitéza** maximum speed, **2)** velocity

vitiyazáika/vityazáika *nf* **1)** giantess **2)** heroic woman, heroine

vitiyazítsko *adj* brave, heroic

vitiyazíya *nf* bravery, courage. heroism

vitiyázo/vityázo *nm* **1)** physical giant **2)** giant among men, great man, hero, living legend **3)** champion (*in sports*); **Wo si vitiyázo mashkar le Rromênde.** He is a living legend among the Roma. **Múrro dad sas chácho vitiyázo an lêske bersh.** My father was a great man during his lifetime.

vitrína *nf* **1)** large window, showroom window **2)** showcase (*Eur*)

vítsa *nf* clan, extended group of families sharing patrilineal descent

vitsáko *gen/adj* belonging to the clan; **Wo si o phuro amare vitsáko.** He is the elder of our clan.

vitsálo *nm* **1)** bull calf, young steer: *nf* **vitsála** female calf **2)** veal

viyátsa *nf* **1)** life, lifetime, time; **Chi mai dikhlem ánde múrri viyátsa.** I never saw it during my lifetime. **2)** living, livlihood, susbsistence, survival, way of life; **Sar kerel pêski viyátsa?** How does he survive/How does he gain his livlihood? **3)** existence

viyatsayil *vt* **1)** earn a living, live: *pp/adj* **viyatsayime 2)** *v/refl* **viyatsayíl-pe** earn a living, get by, live

viyáxo *nm* voyage

viyoléntsiya *nf* violence

víza *nf* **1)** visa **2)** *vt* **del ~** issue a viza

vizáko *gen/adj* possessing a visa

Vizántiya *nf* Byzantium

Vizantyáko *gen/adj* Byzantine

vizása *adv* by visa, with a visa

vizíta *nf* appointment, visit; **kerel ~** make an appointment, pay a visit

vizitil *vt* pay a visit, visit: *pp/adj* **vizitime**

vizitóri *nm* visitor: *nf* **vizitórka**

vízlo *nm* weasel (*Am*)

vízlo-baro *comp/nm* wolverine (*Am*)

vízlo-shoshoiyêngo *nm* ferret (*Am*)

vizonésko *gen/adj* mink; **vizonêngi búnda** mink coat

vizóno *nm* mink

Vlaxítska *nf* Romanian (*Lang*)

Vlaxítsko *adj* Romanian, Wallachian

Vlaxíya *nf* Romania, Wallachia

vláxo *nm* **1)** clod-hopper, peasant: *pl* **vláxurya**: *nf* **vlaxútsa 2)** Romanian: *nf* **Vlaxáika/Vlaxútsa**

vokyáno *nm* telescope

vokyáya *nm/pl* binoculars

volil *vt* **1)** care for, hold in high esteem, love (*us in the agapic sense*): *pp/adj* **volime**; **Voliv tut.** I love you. **Voliv tu sar múrro phral**. I love you like my brother. **Voliv tu sar múrri phey**. I love you like my sister. **2)** *v/refl* **volíl-pe** love oneself, think highly of oneself; **Volíl-pe, kodo baro shoro**. He really loves himself, that ostentatrious person/swell head.

volime *pp/adj* beloved, loved

volimos *nm* love (*usually agapic*)

voltádji *nf/pl* voltage (*Eur*)

vólto *nm* volt

vólturya *nm/pl* volts, voltage (*Am*)

voluntéri *nm* volunteer: *nf* **voluntérka**

voluv *nm* **1)** flap, tent flap **2)** blinker (*for a horse*) **3)** tab **4)** screen, wind screen/shelter

vórba *nf* **1)** word **2)** conversation, discourse, oration, rhetoric, speech, talk, verbal exchange, words; **cháchi Rrómani vórba** rhetorical speech, honest Romani speech/talk. **Dósta vórbi, Rromále, muzíka, khelimáta, xabe, pimáta!** Enough babbling, Roma, music, dancing, food, drinks! **3) del ~** converse, speak, talk

vorbáko *gen/adj* of words, loquacious; **Rrom vorbáko** orator

vórbi *mf/pl* conversation, talk, verbal exchange

vorbil *vt/i* **1)** address: *pp/adj* **vorbime**; **Rromále! Me sim o Wáso kai vorbiv tumênde!** Roma! This is Wáso who is addressing you! **2)** converse, have a discussion, speak **3)** *v/refl* **vorbíl-pe** be in a discussion, be speaking

vorbimos *nm* oration

vorbitóri *nm* orator, speaker (*at a meeting*): *nf* **vorbitórka**

vôrdòn le mulêngo *nm* hearse

vôrdòn *nm* **1)** horse-drawn caravan, wagon, vehicle **2)** station wagon **3)** van

vordonári *nm* cooper, maker of wagons

vordonútso *nm* shopping cart, small cart, wheelbarrow

vorrûchóso *adj* abominable, awful, contemptible, despicable, disgusting, hateful

vorrúto *adj* **1)** abominable, awful, contemptible, despicable, disgusting, hateful, terrible; **Che vorrúto gazho!** What a despicable man! **Che vorrútsi gazhe!** What despicable men! **2)** *exp of disgust* Yuck!

vorrûtsíl *vt* **1)** detest, find despicable, hate, loath, resent: *pp/adj* **vorrûtsimé 2)** *v/refl* **vorûtsíl-pe** become hated, become detestable/detested

vorrûtsimé *pp/adj* detested, hated, loathed, resented; **Kérdilo vorrûtsimé.** He made himself detested.

vorrûtsimós *nm* **1)** disgust **2)** abomination

vorrûtsíya *nf* contempt. disgust, hatred, loathing, resentment

vorrûtsyála *nf* digust

vórrzo *nm* rye grass

vóta *nf* ballot, vote; **pe vóta** by ballot/vote

votári *nm* voter: **votárka** *nf;* **le votárya,** the electorate

votil *vt* **1)** vote: *pp/adj* **votime 2)** *v/refl* **votíl-pe** be voting/holding an election

vóto *nm* vote

vóya *nf* see **wóya** *nf*

voyága *nf* **1)** carafe, glass container, glass jug: *pl* **voyézhi 2)** glass (*material*)

voyagáko *gen/adj* made of glass

vrágnitsa *nf* **1)** gate (*Eur*) **2)** door frame, doorpost

vramyása *nf/inst/adv* eventually (*with time*); **Vramyása, kam-zhanes o chachimos.** Eventually, you will know the truth.**Vramyása, ame dás-ame lása.** Eventually, we'll get used to it.

vraz/vras *nf* **1)** weld **2)** *vt/i* **del ~** weld

vrazitóri *nm* welder

vryámya/vráma *nf* **1)** time: *pl* **vryémi/vrémi; Nai ma vryámya te xasarav kakale dilimáta.** I have no time to waste with this stupidity. **2)** weather **3)** climate

vrêzhitóri *nm* sorcerer, warlock, wizard

vrêzhitórka *nf* sorceress, witch

vuchimos *nm* altitude, height

vucho *adj* **1)** elevated, high. tall **2)** loud

vucho bíldingo *nm* hi-rise, skyscraper

vúcho rat *comp/nm* high blood pressure

vuchyárdyol *vi* become elevated/raised, be made taller: *pp/adj* **vuchyardilo**

vuchyarel *vt* raise/make higher/taller: *pp/adj* **vuchyardo**

vuchyarimos *nm* elevation

vuchyol/vuchol *vi* become higher/more elevated/taller, grow taller: *pp/adj* **vuchilo; Mai vuchyol ges-gêsèstar.** He grows taller from day to day.

vududi *nf* **1)** pupil (*of the eye*): *pl* **vududya 2)** flash, light **3)** will-o-the-wisp **4)** eyelash (*Am*)

vuksála *nf* depot, station *var of* **vagzála** *qv*

vulil/vuluwil *vt* **1**) furl, roll up, wrap, wrap up **2**) engulf, enshroud, entwine, envelop, smother **3**) *v/refl* **1**) **vulíl-pe** be furled/rolled up/wrapped up **2**) be engulfed/entwined/enveloped.

vulime/vuluwime *pp/adj* enveloped, furled, rolled up, wrapped up

vulimos *nm* **1**) furling, rolling up, wrapping up **2**) envelopment

vulisarel *vt* entwine, envelop: *pp/adj* **vulisardo** (*Eur*) *see also* **vulil** *vt*

vulkáno *nm* volcano

vúlma/wúlma *nf* path, pathway, trail

vúlpa/húlpa *nf* fox

vultúra *nf* vulture

vûna/wûna *nf* **1**) root **2**) blood vessel, vein (*Anat*); **vûna bari** artery

vûndji *nf/pl* fingernails, toenails; **vûndji le wastênge** fingernails, **vûndji le punrrênge** toenails

vûnga/vûngiya *nf* **1**) fingernal, nail, toenail: *pl* **vûndji** **2**) claw of a smallish animal (*cat/dog, etc*) *see* **zgyárra** *nf for large, wild animals and birds of prey.*

vúrvo *nm* crest, peak, summit

vûngitsa *nf* fish hook, small hook

vusht/wusht *nm* lip: *pl* **vusht**

vúzhe *adv* already (*Eur*); **Si vúzhe kerdo.** It's already done. **Kána gêlèm khere mo phral sas vúzhe kothe.** When I went home, my brother was already there. **Manai xabe, vúzhe xale.** There's no food, it's already eaten.

vuzheyil *vt* **1**) buzz, ring, wail: *pp/adj* **vuzheyime** **2**) *v/refl* **vuzheyíl-pe** buzz, ring (*in ears*), wail (*as the wind*)

vuzheyimos *nm* buzzing, ringing, wailing; **o wuzheyimos la balvaláko** the wailing of the wind

vyástya *nf* **1**) bulletin, news, report, rumor: *pl* **vêsti** **2**) hearsay, rumor

vyaverítsa *nf* **1**) squirrel **2**) chipmunk

vyedyaril *vt* **1**) illuminate, light up: *pp/adj* **vyedyarime** **2**) *v/refl* **vyedyariyiíl-pe** become illuminated

vyedyárya *nf* illumination, light

W

wagzála *nf* depot, station, terminus (*Eur*) var of **vagzála** *qv*

waksári *nm* shoe-shine boy

waksil *vt* polish, wax: *pp/adj* **waksime**

waksimos *nm* shining of boots/shoes, trade of shining shoes

wákso *nm* shoe polish

wála *nf* canyon, valley

war *prod/suff* **1)** time; *used mainly with the formation of numbers*; **shtárwardesh** four times ten/forty **2)** *augmentative/suff* **butwar mai baro** many times bigger (**but** + **war**), **pánshwar mai baro** five times bigger

wára *nf* female cousin: *pl* **wárya**

wárekai *adv/conj* **1)** somewhere, wherever; **Wárekai kai zhal, zhanglél-pe xoxamno.** Wherever he goes, he's known to be a double-crosser. **2)** recently, as in the following; **Dikhlan le Yankos wárekai?** Have you seen Yanko somewhere/recently? *Answer* **Na, chi dikhlem lês, na do-mult.** I haven't seen him, not for a long time/not recently.

wárekana *adv/conj* whenever, whensoever; **Av ka múrro kher wárekana kai kames!** Come to my home anytime you want to!

warekásko *pron/gen* belonging to somebody

wárekon *pron* anybody, somebody, someone, somebody or other

warekongodi *pron* anybody, somebody, whoever, whomever

wáresar *adv* in any way, in some way; **Músai te keres wáresar kai dashtís-tu.** You must do (it) anyway that you can.

wáresavo *pron* some, whichever, whichever one; **Le wáresavi stagi kai kames!** Take whichever hat that you want!

wáreso *pron* anything, something

waresogodi *pron* anything, something

waresóstar *adv* for some reason or other, for whatever reason

wáro *nm* male cousin: *pl* **wérya**

wása/wãsa *nm/pl* **1)** hands **2)** arms; **Beshélas pêske wása tele pe síniya.** He was sitting with his arms resting on the table. **3)** *id* clutch/clutches. **Skêpisáilo le bengêske wãsa.** He escaped the clutches of the devil.

wásdel *vt* assist, give a hand, help: *pp/adj* **wasdino**

wasdimos *nm* assistance, hand, help

wásha *nf* fair, fairground

washári *nm* **1)** horse fair **2)** pitchman at a fair

wash-bába *nf* old woman in the forest, witch

wáso/váso *nm* **1)** dish in general, bowl, container, pot, vessel **2)** dinner plate: *pl* **wásurya** dishes; **Xalavel le wásurya.** She is washing the dishes.

wast/was *nm* **1)** hand: *pl* **wast/wãsa** (*Anat*) **2)** grasp, grip; **Wo si an le bengêsko wast.** He is in the grip of Satan. **3)** arm (*Anat*) *see also* **sa-wast** *nm* **4)** *comp/vi* **del ~** give a hand, help, help out **5)** *comp/vt* **del ándo ~** surrender, turn in **6)** *v/refl* **del-pe ándo ~** surrender oneself, turn oneself in

wastári *nm* **1)** handle (*as on suitcase*) **2)** crank **3)** haft, hilt

wásurya *nm/pl* **1)** household dishes **2)** pottery

wáto *nm* watt

wáturya *nm/pl* wattage, watts

wazdári *nm* lifting device, block-and-tackle purchase, crane, davit, gantry

wázdel *vt* **1)** crank up, lift, pick up, raise up: *pp/adj* **wazdino 2)** build, construct, erect **3)** cause, instigate, raise, present (*motion at a meeting*); **Sáyek wázdel buntuyimos.** He's always causing trouble. **Wazdyas buntuyimos.** He instigated agitation **4)** boost **5)** declare (*war*), start (*a war*); **Wazdine marimos pe amênde.** They declared war on us. **6)** cock; **Wazdas o bashno la pushkáko.** He cocked the hammer of the gun. **7)** *v/refl* **wázdel-pe a)** get built; **Amáro chêntro chi mai wázdel-pe.** Our center will never get built. **b)** lift/raise oneself up; **Nashti wázden-pe katar lêngo chorromos.** They can't raise themselves from their poverty.

wazdimos *nm* **1)** construction, erection, lifting, raising **2)** instigation, presentation **3)** ~ **marimásko** declaration of war

wazdinil -pe *v/refl* **1)** be brewing (*storm*); **Wazdiníl-pe furtúna.** A storm is brewing ; *pp/adj* **wazdinime 2)** be instigated/introduced/raised/presented/proposed; **Wazdinisáile but xamáta ándo djuléshi.** Many arguments were raised during the meeting.

welféri *nm* social assistance, welfare. (*Am*); **Trayin po welféri.** They live on welfare.

wêrsh/wûrsh *nm* bush, forest, woods

wêrshaló *adj* covered with trees, wooded

wêrshorró *nm* cluster of trees, copse

wêsh *nm see* **wêrsh** *nm*

wéspa *nf* wasp (*Eur*); **wespêngo kwíbo** wasp nest

westutno/vestutno *adj* **1)** west, western **2)** westerner: *nf* **westutni**

wo *pron/nom/s* he, it (*if nm*)

wôchíl *vt* **1)** keep under surveillance, watch: *pp/adj* **wôchimé** (*Am*); **Le rai wôchín o kher.** The police have the house under surveillance. **2)** *v/refl* **wôchíl-pe** watch out for oneself; **Wôchisar tu, Brey!** Watch yourself, Man!

wodil *vt* **1)** guide, lead, lead to: *pp/adj* **wodime**; **Wodisardem le grastês le paiyêste.** I led the horse to the water **2)** *v/refl* **wodíl-pe** find one's way, lead oneself

wodimos *nm* act of leading, leadership

woi *pron/nom/s* she, it (*if nf*)

wóinsto *nm* arrest warrant, search warrant, warrant

wólno *adj* content, satisfied; **San tu wólno akana?** Are you satisfied now? **Chi mai si wólni le Rrom godole.** Those Roma are never satisified.

wolnome *pp/adj* appeased, contented, satisfied

wolnomos *nm* **1)** appeasement **2)** contentment **3)** satisfaction

wolnosarel/wolnol *vt* **1)** appease, assuage, content, satisfy: *pp/adj* **wolnosardo/wolnome 2)** *v/refl* **wolnól-pe** be appeased, contented, satisfied

won de won *pron* each another; **Volin won de won.** They love each other.

won *pron/pl* they; **Won avile araki.** They came yesterday.

wor *conj* or, *cont of* **wórka** *qv*; **Manges chai wor káfa?** Do you want tea or coffee? **Wor tu wórka me músai te zhas.** Either you or I must go.

wordal *adv cont of* **awordal** *qv*

worde *adv* here, over here, this way, *more often* **aworde** *qv*

wórka *conj* either, or; **Kames te zhas wórka níchi?** Do you want to go or not? **Wórka tu zhas, wórka tu chi zhas, nai mánge khánchi.** Either you go or you don't go, I couldn't care less.

woroslásno *nm* male elephant (*Am.*): *nf* **woroslánka**

worraníya *nf* ploughed field, cultivated area

worril *vt* **1)** make furrows, plough: *pp/adj* **worrime 2)** *v/refl* be ploughed

worrimos *nm* furrow

wórrlo *nm* male eagle/vulture: *pl* **wórrlya**: *nf* **wórrla**

wórrona *nf* female cousin

wórrono *nm* male cousin: *pl* **wórroya**

wórrzo *nm* barley

wórta *adj/ádv* **1)** correct, distinctly, just, exact, exactly, right, straight; **Dem lês wórta pínda tiléri.** I gave him exactly fifty dollars. **Kerdem lês túke wórta.** I did it just for you. **Nai wórta.** It's not right. **Símas wórta ándo mashkar.** I was right in the middle. **2)** normally, in the normal way; **Lélas balwal wórta.** He was breathing normally. **3)** straight head, straight; **Zha wórta!** Go straight ahead! **4)** agreed, for sure, sure, right **5)** steady; **Niker lês wórta!** Hold it steady!

wortachíya *nf* close relationship, partnership

wortáko *nm* buddy, business partner, close friend, sidekick: *pl* **wortácha/wortáika**

wortakútsa *nf* female friend/colleague/partner

wórto *adj* aligned, even, flat, level, right, straight

wortol *vt* **1)** align, amend, correct, level/make level, make right, sort out, straighten, straighten out: *pp/adj* **wortome 2)** reform, change a person's behaviour **3)** *v/refl* **wortól-pe a)** clean up one's act, to straighten oneself out, be amended/sorted out **b)** compose oneself, regain one's composure

wortome *pp/adj* aligned, corrected, flattened, leveled, sorted out, straightened

wortomos *nm* alignment, amendment, correction, solution

wotráva *nf* poison, pollution

wotrayil *vt* **1)** poison *pp/adj* **wotrayime 2)** pollute (*environment*) **3)** *v/refl* **wotrayíl-pe** become poisoned/ **a)** poison oneself; **Wotrayisáilo nacháino.** He poisoned himself by accident. **b)** become polluted (*environment*)

wotrayime *pp/adj* poisoned, polluted

wotrayimos *nm* poisoning, pollution

wotrayitóri *nm* poisoner, polluter: *nf* **wotrayitórka**

wóya *nf* **1)** freedom/liberty (*to do*), permission, prerogative, privilege, right; **Si ma wóya te parkí-ma kathe?** Do I have the right to park here? **2)** copyright, patent. **O Del kerel pêski wóya**, God does as he wills. **3)** delight, ecstasy, gladness, joy, pleasure; **Wóya mánge ke tu san mánsa.** I am glad that you are with me. **4)** desire, free will, will, wish; **Devlêski wóya si.** It is God's will/wish. **Tíri wóya túte!** Your will/wish be done! **Kerav lês pe múrri wóya.** I will do it of my my own free will. **5)** duty, obligation; **Si múrri wóya te kerav.** It's my duty/obligation to do (so). **Kerdyas pêski wóya.** He did his duty. **6)** glory; **Wo sas an wóya.** He was in (his) glory.

woyága *nf* **1)** glass (*material*) **2)** glass container, punch bowl

woyáko *gen/adj* cheerful, glad, joyful

woyása *nf/inst/adv* willingly, with permission; **Te chi des mánge la woyása, lav la mánge la zorása.** If you don't give it to me willingly, I'll take it by force.

wóziya *nf* **1)** axle, axle shaft/tree **2)** pivot

wuchitéli *nm* **1)** schoolteacher, teacher **2)** instructor, mentor: *nf* **wuchitélka**

wudar *nm* entrance, entry point, door, doorway, portal; **o wudar ka del ándo Rrayo** the entrance to Heaven/St. Peter's Gate

wudar angluno *comp/nm* front door

wudar paluno *comp/nm* back door

wudarorro *nm* trap door

wúlitsa/úlitsa *nf* street

wulitsári *nm* **1)** male street person, street urchin/kid: *nf* **wulitsárka**

wúlma/wúrma *nf* path, track, trail; **Wushardyas pêski wúlma.** He has covered his tracks. **Phiravel ánde pêske dadêski wúlma.** He is traveling in his father's path.

wuloi *nm* **1)** crude oil, heating oil, fuel oil **2)** kerosene **3)** varsol, paint thinner **4)** lubricating oil, motor oil

wuloiyóso *adj* oily, covered with fuel oil

wultáriya *nf* **1)** whirlpool, vortex **2)** current **3)** maelstrom

wunádyol *vi* be dug up/excavated/exhumed: *pp/adj* **wunadilo**

wunatil/wunatsil *vt* **1)** apply gun blue, dye blue, make blue: *pp/adj* **wunatime/wunatsime 2)** bruise **3)** *v/refl* **wunatíl-pe** turn blue (*with cold*), turn blue (*from a blow or bruise*)

wúnato *adj* **1)** blue **2)** iron-grey; **wúnetsi grast** iron-gray horses

wúnato-maryáko *comp/adj* azure, sea blue

wúnato-múra *comp/nf* blueberry: *pl* **wúnatsi-múri**

wúnatone-yakhêngo *comp/gen/adj* blue-eyed

wúnato-vélino *comp/nm* blue venom (*person or people seen as a dangerous menace, referring to the deadly venom of a poisonous snake*), deadly poison

wunavel *vt* **1)** dig, dig up, excavate, exhume: *pp/adj* **wunado 2)** burrow, burrow under, mine **3)** undermine **4)** rake (*ashes*)

wunayimos *nm* **1)** burrow **2)** excavation **3)** exhumation

wunetsyála *nf* bruise (*blue mark from a bruise*)

wúni *pron/indef* some; **Wúni Rrom avile katar o Chikágo.** Some Roma came from Chicago.

wúni ges *adv* any day, one day, someday, somedays

wunívar *adv* anytime, occasionally, sometime, sometimes, whenever

wúrma/wúlma *nf* **1)** end, hindmost, last **2)** stern (*boat*) **2)** path, track, trail

wurmaril *vt* **1)** sniff out (*with dogs*), track, track down, trail: *pp/adj* **wurmarime 2)** *v/refl* **wurmaríl-pe** be **tracked**, trailed, retrace one's tracks

wurmaríya *nf* endmost, last in line, last, leftover, remainder, remains

wursitára *nf* destiny, fate, lot in life

Wursitóri *nm* **1)** any one of the Three Fates or fate fairies (*Folk*) **2) wursitóri** *nm* fairy

Wursitórya *nm/pl* the three Fates (*Folk*). These are three Fates who appear at the birth of a child who can only be seen by the child's mother or the midwife if present. They plot the destiny of the child and if the mother overhears this, she can take steps to prevent it, a common thread in Kalderash foklktales.

wûrtsa/wêrtsa *nf* **1)** paint brush, scrubbing brush, small brush **2)** clothes brush

wûrtsíl *vt* **1)** brush, buff, scrub: *pp/adj* **wurtsime 2)** groom (*horses*)

wûrtsimós *nm* **1)** buffing, scrubbing, scrubbing down **2)** grooming

wûsh/wêsh *nm* forest

wushal *nf* **1)** shade **2)** lamp shade

wushalin *nf* **1)** shadow **2)** *comp/vi* **shúdel** ~ cast a shadow **3)** *comp/vt* **thol ánde** ~ overshadow

wushandi *nf* colander, pannier, sieve, sifter, strainer

wushandimos *nm* panning, sifting, straining

wushándyol *vi* be panned/sifted/strained: *pp/adj* **wushandilo**

wushanel *vt* pan, sift, strain, winnow: *pp/adj* **wushando**

wushar *nm* ash, ashes, ashes of a fire, cremation ashes

wusharádyol *vi* **1)** become covered/covered over/covered up/engulfed/hidden by covering over **2)** become overcast, cloud over

wusharalo *adj* covered with ashes

wusharavel *vt* cover over, engulf, smother: *pp/adj* **wusharado**; **E mágla wusharadyas o drom.** The fog engulfed the road.

wusharel *vt* **1)** cover, hide by covering, cover over, cover up: *pp/adj* **wushardo 2)** *comp/vt* ~ **yakha**, blindfold; **Wusharde lêske yakha.** They blindfolded him.

wusharimáta *nm/pl* **1)** coverings, cushion covers, slip covers **2)** coats of paint

wusharimos *nm* **1)** covering, slip cover, upholstery **2)** coat of paint

wushkóla/wushkála *nf* school

wushkolári *nm* school teacher: *nf* **wushkolárka**

wushoril *vt* **1)** ease (*pain*), facilitate, lighten, make easy, simplify: *pp/adj* **wushorime 2)** *v/refl* **wushoríl-pe** be eased, lightened, reduced in intensity, get something off one's chest, lighten one's load

wushorime *pp/adj* lightened, simplified

wushorimos *nm* easing, lightning, simplification

wushóro *adj* **1)** easy, easy-going, patient; **Wushóro Rrom si.** He's an easy-going/patient man. **2)** freedom to do, permission to do **3)** faint, fragile, lean, light, slight

wusht *nm* lip: *pl* **wusht** lips (*Anat*), chops (*animal*); **O ruv charrélas pêske wusht.** The wolf was licking his chops.

wushtalo *adj* abusive, impudent, lippy

wushtavel *vt see* **wushtyavel** *vt*

wúshtel *vt/i* arise, get up, rise: *pp/adj* **wúshtino** *var of* **wushtyal** *qv*

wushtêngi-fárba *nf* lipstick

wushtimos *nm* lifting, rising, uprising

wushtyal *vi* **1)** arise, get up, rise, rise up, stand up, raise, rise/arise, wake up: *pp/adj* **wushtilo**; **Wúshte!** Stand up!/Get up! **Wushtilem le khamêsa.** I arose with the sun/at dawn. **Wushtili kána ruyas e glatútsa.** She woke up when the baby cried. **2)** be disturbed

wushtyavel *vt* **1)** arouse, make to get up/wake up/rise, raise, make to stand up: *pp/adj* **wushtyado 2)** cause an upheaval **3)** disturb **3)** *vt/phr* ~ **le mulêndar** raise from the dead

wushtyayimos *nm* disturbance, upheaval

wutsil *vt* sting (*as a nettle*): *pp/adj* **wutsime 2)** *v/refl* **wutsíl-pe** hurt, smart, sting

wutsimos *nm* smarting

wuzdála *nf* confidence

wuzdil *vt* **1)** confide in, trust: *pp/adj* **wuzdime 2)** *v/refl* **wuzdíl-pe a)** confide in, trust *us with* **an/and** & *prep/case of object*; **Wuzdí-ma an lêste.** I trust him. **Nashti wuzdí-ma an lêste.** I can't trust him. **b)** rely on; **Nashti wuzdís-tu an lêste.** You can't rely on him.

wuzdimásko *gen/adj* reliable, trustworthy

wuzdimos confidence, dependability, reliance, trust; **Nai ma wuzdimos an lêste.** I have no confidence in him.

wuzhes *adv* cleanly, immaculately, neatly, perfectly

wuzhi *nf* chaste girl, respectable girl, virgin, Virgo *nm (Zod)*

wuzhile *adv* **1)** in debt, on loan; **Si ma pansh shela wuzhile pe lêste.** I have five hundred owing on it/still outstanding on it. **Lem o mobíli wuzhile.** I bought the car on time. **2)** *comp/vt* **del** ~ lend; **Dem lês shel tiléri wuzhile.** I loaned him a thundred dollars. **3)** *comp/vi* **lel** ~ borrow; **Lem pansh shela tiléri wuzhile lêstar.** I borrowed five-hundred dollars from him.

wuzhilimos *nm* **1)** advance, loan **2)** debt, outstanding payment **3)** borrowing, lending **4)** **del-pe ándo** ~ get into debt

wuzhilitóri *nm* **1)** money lender **2)** loan shark

wuzhimos *nm* **1)** cleanliness, innocence, spiritual purity, non-contamination **2)** chastity **3)** virginity

wuzhitóri *nm* **1)** cleaner **2)** cleanser

wuzho *adj* **1)** clean, immaculate, neat, perfect **2)** chaste **3)** free of contamination, pure **4)** innocent, spiritually pure, virgin **5)** *nm* innocent youth, virgin young man

wúzho pai *comp/nm* drinking water, uncontaminated water

wuzhol *vi* **1)** be cleaned/cleansed of contamination/purified: *pp/adj* **wuzhilo 2)** clear, clear up; **Wuzhol e vryámya.** The weather is clearing.

wuzhulil *vt* **1)** place in debt, drive into debt: *pp/adj* **wuzhulime 2)** **wuzhilíl-pe** fall/get into debt

wuzhulimos *nm* borrowing, credit, debt, loan, trust: *pl* **wuzhulimáta** accumulated debts

wuzhulutno *adj* **1)** in debt, indebted **2)** *nm* debtor: *nf* **wuzhulutni**

wuzhyárdyol *vi* **1)** become cleansed: *pp/adj* **wuzhardilo 2)** become cleansed spiritually from accusations of pollution **3)** be cleansed of contamination **4)** be made spiritually pure

wuzhyarel *vt* **1)** clean, cleanse, cleanse/regenerate spiritually, make free of contamination: *pp/adj* **wuzhyardo 2)** clean (*a chicken*), gut (*remove entrails of an animal or fish*) **3)** exorcise

wuzharitóri *nm* spiritual cleanser, decontaminator, exorcist, regenerator: *nf* **wuzharitórka**

X

xabe *nm* food, meal: *pl* **xabenáta**

xabenáta *nm/pl* food, foods, foodstuffs, order of food from the supermarket, provisions, food provided for a feast

xabenêngo *gen/adj/pl* of foods

xabenésko *gen/adj* of food

xabo *nm* food (*Eur*)

xal *vt/i* **1)** eat: *pp/adj* **xalo; Bokhalo sim, mangav te xav wáreso.** I am hungry, I want to eat something. **2)** consume, devour, eat up, use up/waste; **O ruv xalyas le bakres.** The wolf devoured the sheep. **Xalyas lês e mêrzála.** Jealousy consumed him. **Xal la e xoli.** She is being consumed by anger. **Xalem sórro ges te kerav khánchi.** I wasted the whole day to do nothing. **3)** use up, wear out; **Xalyas sa pêske tsáliya.** He has worn out all his clothes. **4)** corrode, destroy, dissolve, eat away at, erode, wear down; **Le kerme xale e fundátsiya le kherêsko.** Termites have eaten away the foundation of the house. **Xan amári kultúra.** They are destroying/eroding our culture. **Xalyas pêski baxt.** He has destroyed his own luck/ruined his chances to receive good karma. **5)** burn, irritate; **E thuv xal ma le yakha.** The smoke is irritating my eyes. **6)** bear, undergo, endure, suffer; **Nashti xav e dukh.** I can't bear the pain. **Xalyas but daba ándo marimos.** He suffered a lot of blows during the fight. **Xalyam but kíno.** We have endured a lot of suffering. **Xalem dui operátsiyi.** I underwent two operations. **7)** itch; **Xal ma o wast.** My hand itches **8)** gobble up, claim as exclusive, take control of, take over; **O Stévo xalyas káko gav.** Steve has taken control of this town/made it his exclusive territory. **9)** make a fool of, deceive **10)** *v/refl* **xal-pe** agitate, argue, fight verbally; **Rromále, na xan-tume!** Roma, don't argue! **Xalém-ma lêsa ándo djuléshi.** I argued with him during the meeting. **Chi mangav te xá-ma túsa.** I don't want to argue with you. **11)** Compound verbs with **xal. 1)** ~ **baxt** ruin chances for luck or success; **Xal pêski baxt.** He is ruining his chances for success. **Xal múrri baxt.** He is destroying my good karma/chances for success. **2)** ~ **kokala** consume the bones, wear oneself out, become worn out; **Xalem múrre kokala kána kerávas gadya buki.** I worked myself to the bone/wore myself out, on that job. **3)** ~ **pomana** die; **Te xal pêski pomána!** May he eat his funeral feast! (*curse*) **4)** ~ **shoro** destroy; **Xav lêsko shoro.** I will eat his head/ destroy him. **5)** ~ **swáturya** rue one's words; **Te xal pêske swáturya!** May he eat his own words/rue what he said. **6)** ~ **le yakkhênsa** ogle **7)** ~ **yilo a)** eat the heart, love/respect very much **Xav kyo yilo.** I love/respect you very much. **b)** used as a form of English "please." **Ker mánge mishtomos, xav tyo yilo.** Do me a favor, please.. **8)** ~ **xoli** bear a grudge; **Xal xoli pe mánde.** He bears a grudge against me.

xaládyol *vi* be cleansed, washed: *pp/adj* **xaladilo**

xalavel *vt* **1)** cleanse, launder, wash **2)** *v/refl* **xalavél-pe** wash, wash oneself

xalávurya *mm/pl* gargling, phlegm

xalayimáski-mashûnka *comp/nf* washing machine

xalayimos *nm* 1) cleansing, washingm 2) laundry, washing

xalayitóri *nm* 1) laundryman, launderer: *nf* **xalayitórka** 2) washing machine

xalayitóriya *nm/pl* laundromat, laundry

xalestoi *nm* bachelor

xalibúto *nm* halibut

xalo 1) *pp/adj* consumed, corroded, eaten, eaten away, endured, moth-eaten, used up, worn out 2) *nm* agent of destruction, consumer, destroyer, scourge: *nf* **xali**

xalyarel *vt* 1) consume, use up, wear out 2) devour, eat away, gnaw away 3) corrode away

xályol *vi* 1) become consumed, eaten, devoured, eaten away, eroded, corroded, used up, wasted, worn out: *pp/adj* **xalilo; Sa xalile pêske tsáliya.** All his clothes have been worn out. **Xalilem.** I've shot my bolt/I've done all I can.

xamári *nm* 1) eater: *nf* **xamárka; Baro xamári, o Fránki.** Frank is a big eater. 2) arguer, argumentative *psn* 3) corrosive substance

xamásko *gen/adj* 1) related to food, edible 2) argumentative, belligerent

xamásko-naswalimos *comp/nm* leprosy

xamáta *nm/pl* 1) foods, meals 2) arguments

xamos *nm* 1) food 2) meal 3) dining 4) argument, verbal fight 5) corrosion, erosion

xanro/xandro *nm* sword

xantsardo *pp/adj* 1) diminished, made less, minimized, reduced 2) *nm* man reduced in status: *nf* woman reduced in status

xantsárdyol *vi* be diminished, reduced, made less, minimized: *pp/adj* **xantsardilo**

xantsarel *vt* 1) diminish, make less, minimize, play down, reduce: *pp/adj* **xantsardo** 2) cut down to size, put in one's place 3) *v/refl* diminish oneself, play down oneself, reduce oneself

xantsarimos *nm* diminuation, reduction

xantsi/xantsû *nf* 1) a few, few, a little; **Si ma xantsû.** I have a little/a few. 2) *adv* a little, small amount of; **Si lês xantsi love.** He has a little money, **desya xantsi** very little/too little 3) *adv with* **mai; mai xantsi** less; **Si lês mai xantsi love vi mánde.** He has less money than I do.

xantsol *vt* 1) diminish, limit, make less, reduce (*amount of/number*), restrict (*amount/number*): *pp/adj* **xantsilo** 2) *vi* become reduced/restricted/diminished/less

xanzh *nf* 1) itch, irritant, irritation 2) greed; **Kána dikhel love, lel lês e xanzh.** When he sees money, he is seized with greed. 3) heat, lust, sexual arousal/passion; **E grasni si ánde xanzh.** The mare is in heat. 4) impulse, urge; **Zhal wárekai, kai lel lês e xanzh.** He goes wherever the urge takes him. 5) *comp/vi* **perel ánde xanzh.** come into heat (*female animal*)

xanzhal *vi* 1) itch: *pp/adj* **xanzhailo** 2) have an itch for, lust after

xanzháli *nm* dagger, hanger, poniard

xanzharel *vt* cause to itch, make itchy: *pp/adj* **xanzhardo** 2) excite sexually 3) arouse greed (*in sombdy*), make excited

xanzhwalé-lovêngo *gen/adj* 1) avaricious, money-grubbing 2) miserly, stingy, mean

xanzhwales *adv* 1) avariciously, greedily 2) lecherously, lustfully

xanzhwalimáski-patrin *comp/nf* poison ivy

xanzhwalimos *nm* 1) itching 2) avarice, greed, greediness, rapacity 3) sexual arousal/passion

xanzhwalo *adj* 1) itchy 2) avaricious, greedy, rapacious 2) lecherous, lustful, sexually, passionate, sexually aroused; 3) *nm* miser

xanzhwaló-pûnrró *comp/nm* athlete's foot

xanzhwárdyol *vi* 1) be made itchy: *pp/adj* **xanzhwardilo** 2) be made greedy 3) be aroused sexually

xanzhwarel *vt* 1) make itchy: *pp/adj* **xanzhwardo** 2) make greedy 3) arouse sexually

xanzhwarimásko *gen/adj* **1)** greedy **2)** sexually aroused

xanzhwarimos *nm* frenzy of greed or sexual arousal

xar *nf* **1)** abyss, gorge **2)** hillock, knoll, low hill **3)** incline, slope **4)** dip (*in a road*)

xarano *adj* **1)** astute, capable, confident, intelligent, sensible, smart **2)** sane, on the ball; **Nai xarano.** He's not smart/He has a few bricks missing.

xaranomos *nm* astuteness, confidence, intelligence

Xarápo/Harápo *nm* cannibal ogre in folk tales: *nf* **Xarapáika** wife of the **Xarápo**

xarné-nakhêsko *comp/gen/adj* snub-nosed

xarno *adj* **1)** short **2)** abrupt **3)** low **4)** snub

xarno nakh *comp/nm* snub nose

xarnomos *nm* brevity, shortness

xarnyardo *pp/adj* belittled, humiliated, put down

xarnyárdyol *vi* **1)** be made short, shorter, be condensed, truncated: *pp/adj* **xarnyardo 2)** be belittled/humiliated/put down; **Xarnyádyovav.** I am being belittled/humiliated.

xarnyarel *vt* **1)** condense, encapsulate, make short, shorten, truncate: *pp/adj* **xarnyardo 2)** belittle, humiliate, put down **3)** *v/refl* **xarnyarél-pe a)** become condensed, shortened, truncated **b)** belittle oneself, put oneself down, sell oneself short **c)** be belittled, put down.

xarnyarimos *nm* **1)** truncation **2)** belittling, humiliation

xarnyol *vi* **1)** become short/shorter: *pp/adj* **xarnilo**; **Xarnilo o phirimos xarnilo.** The journey became shorter **2)** be humiliated/put down

xartóna *nf* carton, cardboard: *gen/ádj* **xartonáko** made of cardboard

xarúndel/xarundel *vt/i* **1)** scratch: pp/adj **xarrundino; Na xarúnde te na xanzhal!** Don't scratch if it doesn't itch!/If it works, don't mess with it! (*proverb*) **2)** *v/refl* **xarrúndel-pe** scratch oneself

xas *nm* cough

xasádyol *vi* be coughing: **xasadilo; Xasadyovávas sórro ges katar e grípa.** I have been coughing all day from the grippe.

xasal *vt/i* cough: *pp/adj* **xasado; Xasayas zorales.** He coughed loudly

xasalo *adj* **1)** congested, suffering from a cough **2)** *nm* man suffering from congestion/a cough: *nf* **xasali**

xasamos *nm* coughing**; baro xasamos** whooping cough

xasardí-buki *comp/nf* lost cause

xasardo *pp/adj* **1)** lost, ruined, spent (*bullet*)**,** wasted **2)** *nm* lost male person or animal**:** *nf* **xasardi**

xasárdyol *vi* be/become lost/ruined/wasted: *pp/adj* **xasardilo**

xasarel *vt* **1)** lose: *pp/adj* **xasardo 2)** miss (*bus, train*) **3)** waste (*time*) **4)** ~ **rat** bleed, lose blood; **Xasarel but rat.** He's bleeding profusely.

xasarimos *nm* loss, waste

xasavel *vt* cause a coughing spell, induce coughing, make to cough: *pp/adj* **xasado**

xasávol *vi* **1)** become lost, go astray: *pp/adj* **xasailo; Xasáilo an pêske vórbi.** He got lost in his words/lost his train of thought. **Xasáilem ándo wêrsh.** I got lost in the forest. **2)** disappear, vanish from sight.

xasayimos *nm* disappearance, loss

xasel *vt/i* cough: *pp/adj* **xaslo** *var of* **xasal** *vt/i*

xashtíl-pe *vi* yawn: *pp/adj* **xashtime**

xashtimos *nm* yawning

xayil *vt/i* **1)** cause to expire/perish/wilt, cause to pass away/come to an end, destroy, ruin: *pp/adj* **xayime 2)** *v/refl* **xayíl-pe** come to an end, expire, pass away, perish, wilt

xayimásko *gen/adj* perishable, vulnerable

xayimos *nm* destruction, demise, doom, ruin

xaying *nf* **1)** well **2)** water fountain

xer *nm* ass, donkey (*Eur*): *nf* **xerni**

xeranes *adj* asininely, silly

xérani-shib *comp/nf/neolog* braying of an ass/bureaucratic or political gobbledygook, language used in governmental reports, political cant, type of overly verbose, political, rhetorical double-talk used in governmental reports about Roma

xerano *adj* asinine (*Eur*)

xeroi *nm* 1) leg (*Anat*): *pl* **xera** (*Eur*) 2) leg of a garmnent

xêrtíya/hârtíya *nf* 1) paper 2) newspaper 3) toilet paper *see* **hêrtíya**

xêrtiyáko *gen/adj* made of paper, paper

xêtelíl *vt* tickle: *pp/adj* **xêtelimé**

xêtelimásko *gen/adj* ticklish

xêtilimós *nm* tickling

xêv *nf* 1) hole (*Eur*) 2) *vlg/sl* anus (*Am*) 3) *vlg/sl* vagina (*Am*). **Note:** do not use **xêv** for hole in general in Kalderash, especially in Canada and the US, even though it does have this meaning in some European dialects. *see* **grápa** *nf*

xevítsa *nf* 1) porridge 2) grits 3) polenta

xêvyarél *vt* bore, make a hole (*Eur*); **E barr xêvyardyás o bero**. The rock made a hole in the canoe.

xindalo *adj* covered with excrement, defiled, filthy

xindi buki *comp/nf* filthy business

xindi *nf* toilet bowl

xindi/xindali *nf* outdoor chemical toilet booth/Johnny on the spot, outdoor latrine, latrine tent

xindo *pp/adj* filthy, lousy, shitty, squalid; **Kodo si xíndo them**. That's a lousy country.

xinel *vt* 1) defecate, shit: *pp/adj* **xindo**; **Chi sim o grast kai xinel súmnakai**. I am not Mister Moneybags/not the horse that voids gold. 2) *v/refl* **xinél-pe** defecate, disgrace oneself; **E gláta xindyás-pe**. The baby dirtied its diapers. **Arak o zhukel te na xinél-pe pe ponyáva!** Watch out for the dog so that he doesn't defecate on the carpet!

xindorro *nm* "little shitty" (*affectionate name for a male toddler*): *nf* **xindorri**

xinimos *nm* defecation, stool, turd: *pl* **xinimáta** animal droppings/turds,

grastênge **xinimáta** horse buns/droppings; **O grast peradyas pêske xinimáta ánde úlitsa**. The horse dumped its load in the street.

xípi *nm* hippie: *pl* **xípiz**: *nf* **xipútsa** (*Am*)

xírpa *nf* 1) anus, rectum (*Anat*)

Xitáno *nm* Spanish *Gitano*: *pl* **Xitánurya**: *nf* **Xitánka** (*Eur*)

xlel *vt* 1) defecate; **Xlel rat**. he/she is defecating blood *var of* **xinel** *qv* 2) *v/refl* **xlél-pe** defecate; (*curse*); **O grast xlás-pe ánde úlitsa**. The horse defecated in the street.

xlimáta *nm/pl* animal droppings, cow flaps, horse buns, turds

xlimos *nm* 1) defecation, elimination, 2) act of elimination

xlop/xlópo *nm* clodhopper, hick, peasant, rube, rural bumpkin: *pl* **xlópurya**: *nf* **xlópka**

Xlupêshti *nm/pl see* **Xulupêshti**

xlúpo *nm* 1) killer wolf. 2) leader of a wolf pack 3) reputed to be the name of the founder/leader of the clan known as **Xulupêshti** *qv*

xlûtríya *nf* craftiness, cunning, the smarts

xlûtro *adj* cunning, smart, streetwise; **Xlûtro Rrom godo**. That Rom is a slippery customer.

xolyáriko *adj* 1) angry, annoyed, enraged, riled up 2) grumpy, irascible, short-fused 3) *nm* angry/irascible man: *nf* **xolarikútsa**

xolyarikones *adv* angrily

xoli *nf* 1) anger, rage, wrath; **e xoli Devlêski** the wrath of God. **Si les but xoli pe túte**. He's really pissed off at you. 2) grudge 3) spite; **Kerdyas xolyátar**. She did it out of spite. 4) aggravation; **Xalyam dósta xoli godolênder**. We have suffered enough aggravation from those people. 5) temper 6) *comp/vt/i* **lel ~** become angry, get angry; **Lem xoli pe múrre dades**. I got angry at my father. 7) *comp/vt/i* **del ~** make *sombdy* angry, give cause to be angry, provoke; **Na mai de la xoli!** Don't provoke her any more!

xolyardo 1) *pp/adj* 1) angry, enraged, *sl*
pissed off 2) *nm* angry man: *nf* xolyardi
xolyárdyol *vi* be made angry/enraged:
pp/adj xolyardilo
xolyarel *vt* 1) aggravate, anger, enrage,
incite, make angry, piss off: *pp/adj*
xolyardo 2) arouse (*to anger/violence*)
3) *v/refl* xolyarél-pe become/get angry/
enrage; Xolyarél-pe o Stánko. Stanko is
becoming really angry.
xolyávol *vi* become aggravated, angry,
enraged, pissed off: *pp/adj* xolyailo;
Xolyáilem pe lêste. I got really angry at
him. Xolyáilo. He became angry. Na
xoláwo! Don't be angry!
Xóraxai *nm* Muslim, Turk: *pl* Xoraxa;
Dikhlem le Xoraxás. I saw the Turk: *nf*
Xoraxni
Xoraxanítska *nf* 1) Turkish (*Lang*) 2)
Turkish-Romani dialect
Xoraxanítsko *adj* 1) Turkish 2)
Turkish-Romani
Xoraxano *adj* Muslim, Turkish, Turkish
Rom; Rrom-Xoraxano Muslim/Turkish
Rom: *pl* Rrom-Xoraxane: *nf*
Rromni-Xoraxani
xordo *adj* little, small; xorde love small
change, xorde shave small children
xordorro *adj* 1) little, tiny, puny, very
small 2) *nm* puny or little man: *nf*
xordorri
xóro *nm* 1) choir, chorus: *pl* xórya 2) band,
entertainment group of singers, dancers
and musicians, music group
xoxádyol *vi* 1) be exaggerated/twisted:
pp/adj xoxadilo; Xoxádile pêske
swáturya. His testimony was
exaggerated 2) be deluded/deceived/lied
to
xoxamné-kashtêsko *comp/adj* made of
imitation wood
xoxamné-love *comp/nm/pl*
phony/counterfeit money, play money
xoxamno *adj* 1) false, phoney 2) artificial,
imitation 3) deceitful 4) not pure/alloyed
(*metals*), diluted (*substances, liquids*) 5)
counterfeit 6) *nm* 1) falsehood, imitation,

lie 2) bullshitter, charlatan,
double-crosser, imposter, liar, phoney: *nf*
xoxamni
xoxavel *vt/i* 1) exaggerate, lie, spread
lies/bullshit, twist the truth: *pp/adj*
xoxado 2) deceive, delude, double-cross,
lie to, take advantage of, use; Xoxadyas
ma. He double-crossed me. 3) *v/refl*
xoxavél-pe a) be in denial, deceive
oneself, delude oneself, lie to oneself
xoxáwol/xoxávol *vi* 1) be lying, lie: *pp/adj*
xoxailo 2) contradict oneself; Xoxáwol
ánde l' swáturya. He contradicts
himself in his statements.
xoxayimáta *nm/pl* bullshit, falsehoods, lies,
untruths; bare xoxayimáta a great
collection of lies
xoxayimos *nm* delusion, deceit, falsehood,
lie
xulai *nm* 1) boss, host, master, owner: *pl*
xula 2) landlord
xulángo *gen/adj* belonging to owners,
owned; Manai ekh grast do-xulángo. *id*
There is no such thing as a horse with two
masters.
xulani/xulayi *nf* 1) mistress, owner 2)
landlady
xulásko *gen/adj* belonging to an owner,
owned; Bi-xulásko si. It doesn't belong
to anybody.
xúlpa *nf* fox *see also* vúlpa *nf*
Xulupêshti *nm/pl* Killer Wolves, a
formerly Mexican Kalderash clan
reputedly descended from a founder
called Xlúpo and driven out of Mexico
after a vendetta to relocate elsewhere in
the America since the 1950s. They often
appear in Kalderash legends (hírya).
Variant form in Xlupêshti *qv*
xumer *nf* dough
xurdimos *nm* triviality; *pl* xurdimáta
trivialities, vanities
xurdo *adj* little, paltry, small; xurde love
cash, small change, xurde shave small
children
xurdyárdyol *vi* cause to become
gratered/minced: *pp/adj* xudyardilo

xurdyarel *vt* chop up, grate, grater, mince: *pp/adj* **xurdyardo**

xurdyol *vi* become smaller, become of lesser importance, crumble/dwindle away: *pp/adj* **xurdilo**

xûrtso *nm* **1)** hamster **2)** mouse **3) rodent 4)** vole

xûrtsóski-kúrsa *com/nf* mousetrap

xûruyíl-pe *v/refl* snore: *pp/adj* **xûruyimé**

xûruyimós *nm* snore, snoring

xutavel *vt* cause to hop/jump/skip: *pp/adj* **xutado**. *see* **xutyarel/xutyavel** *vt*

xútel *vt/i* **1)** attack, jump, jump at/on, jump up, pounce on, spring at/up: *pp/adj* **xuklo; O zhukel xuklo pe lêste.** The dog sprang at him. **Xukle pe mánde ándo diwáno.** They attacked me (*verbally*) during the discussion. **Zhukléya! Xúte lês!** Dog! Attack him! **2)** rise up, succeed **3)** *v/rfl* **a)** **xutél-pe**, play jump rope, skip; **Le sheyorra xutén-pe.** The little girls are skipping/playing jump rope. **b)** bound, hop **c)** pop (*as popcorn*); **Xutél-pe o kukurúzo.** The corn is popping.

xutíldyol *vi* be abducted/grabbed/seized/snatched: *pp/adj* **xutildilo**

xutilel *vt/i* **1)** abduct, catch, clutch, grab, seize, snatch: *pp/adj* **xutildo; Xutile lês!** Grab it! **2)** *v/refl* **xutilél-pe** catch/grab/seize for oneself

xutilimos *nm* catch, clutch, grab, seizing, snatching

xutimos *nm* **1)** jumping, skipping **2)** popping (*popcorn*)

xutyado *pp/adj* erect, erected, inflated, rigid

xutyádyol *vi* be made to jump up, rise up. spring up **2)** be sexually aroused (*man or male animal*): *pp/adj* **xutiyadilo**

xutyal *var of* **xutel** *vt/i*

xutyamno *nm* acrobat, jumper

xutyarel/xutyavel *vt* **1)** inflate, make to jump up/rise up/spring up: *pp/adj* **xutyardo/xutyado 2)** make to become erect **3)** instigate an attack, make to attack

xutyávol *vi* come to full size, inflate, jump up, rise up, unfurl: *pp/adj* **xutyailo; E shûna xutyáili.** The tire has become inflated.

xutyayimos/xutyarimos *nm* **1)** a jumping up/springing up, skipping **2)** erection

Y

yába/aba already, yet

yabuchítsa *nf* Adam's apple

Yádo *nm* 1) Hades, hell, a place of suffering and pollution 2) netherworld, underworld 3) non-Romani environment 3) *fig* damnation, grief, hell, misery; **Múrro tráyo si yádo pe phuv.** My life is hell on earth.

yag *nf* 1) fire, light; **De mánge yag!** Give me a light! **bári yag** inferno, serious fire 2) ignition 3) enthusiasm, zeal. zest; **De yag ánde muzíka!** Put some zest in the music! 4) passion; **Nai lês yag ánde l' vórbi.** He has no passion in his speeches. 5) enthusiasm 6) *vt/i* **del ~ a)** start the ignition; **De yag o mobíli!** Start the car. **b)** fire (*gun*); **Ankaladyas pêski púshka hai dyas yag.** He dcrew his gun and fired. 7) **astarel ~** *comp/vi* catch fire 8) **id ánde yag; So si tut ánde yag?** What do you have in the fire/What are your plans/What's on your agenda?

yagáki-púshka *comp/nf* flamethrower

yagáki-skára *comp/nf* fire escape

yagalimos *nm* 1) impetuosity 2) eagerness, enthusiasm, zeal 3) vehemence 4) morale

yagalo *adj* 1) ardent, fiery, hot-tempeered, impetuous, passionate, short-fused, touchy, vehement 2) eager, enthusiastic, excited, fired up, revved up, zealous 3) inspiring (*speech, etc*)

yagánto *nm* agent: *nf* **yagánta/yagantútsa**

yagántsiya *nf* 1) agency 2) box office

yagári *nm* arsonist, firebug

yag-dino *comp/pp/adj* aflame, on fire, set on fire

yágniya *nf* 1) gravy, sauce 2) stew

yagorri *nf* 1) flicker of fire, flame 2) glow worm

yái *interj* oh! alas! used mainly in songs

yakh/yak *nf* 1) eye (*Anat*); **e dikhimáski ~** the seeing eye. **Dav-dúma ka l' yakha, chi dav-dúma palal e zéya.** I speak face to face, I don't speak behind the back. 2) glance 3) wink; **Kerélas mánge ánda e yakh.** She was winking at me.

yakhaládyol *vi* become/get struck by the evil eye: *pp/adj* **yakhaladilo**

yakhaldel *vt* strike with the evil eye: *pp/adj* **yakhaldino**

yakhalel *vt* 1) give the evil eye, curse by the evil eye: *pp/adj* **yakhalado**

yakhalimos *nm* bewitching by the evil eye, casting of the evil eye

yakhalo 1) *nm* evil eye 2) *nm* victim of the evil eye: *nf* **yakhali** 3) *comp/vt* **shúdel ~** cast the evil eye

yakhbango *adj* cross-eyed

yakhêngo-dóftoro *comp/nm* eye doctor, optometrist

yakhorri *nf* 1) eyelet 2) grommet 3) eye of a needle

yakh-yakháte *adv* eye-to-eye/face-to-face; **Phendem lêske yakh-yakháte.** I told him eye to eye/straight to his face.

yalakráno *nm* 1) black widow spider, scorpion; **O Yalakráno e zhuvli xal o Yalakráno o mursh** . The female black widow eats the male. 2) **Yalakráno** Scorpio.(*Zod*)

yalovítsa *nf* 1) sterile woman 2) sterile female animal

yalovitsíya *nm* infertility, female sterility

yánkala *nf/arch* Kalderash woman's bolero vest

yánkalo *nm/arch* Romani man's vest, usually heavily embroidered or decorated with coins, gold/silver buttons, etc.

yar *nf* **1)** ice pick **2)** awl **3)** bodkin

yárba *nf* **1)** herb, plant **2)** maple

yarbáki-patrin *comp/nf* maple leaf

yarbáko-drab *comp/nm* herbal medicine

yarbáko-músto *comp/nm* maple syrup

yarbári *nm* male herbalist: *nf* **yarbárka**

yarbáto *nm* herbal tea

yarbelin *nf* maple tree

yárdo *nm* backyard, yard (*Am*)

yarmáko *nm* market, market place; **yarmáko-masêngo** meat market

Yásha ! *interj* Let's go! Come on! (*Eur*)

yáshchiko *nm* bin, box, container; **lovêngo-yáshchiko** safe, strongbox

yaver *when* **aver** (*pron/adj*) *follows a vowel, it usually becomes* **yaver;** in another (*electrical*) outlet, **ánde yaver grápa**

yázla *nf* manger

yázno *adj/adv* **1)** clear, clearly coherent, coherently, comprehensive, frank, frankly, lucid, lucidly; **do-pash yázno** garbled, indistinct, partially incomprehensible, murky, opaque **2)** obvious, obviously

yázo *nm* dam, levee

yazumína *nf* jasmine

yeftíka *nf* **1)** tuberculosis **2)** consumption

yeftikalo *adj* **1)** tubercular **2)** consumptive

yéftino *adj/adv* **1)** cheap, cheaply, inexpensive, paltry **2)** cheap-looking, junk, tawdry

yegúla *nf* eel; *id* **Kingó-lo sar e yegúla.** He is as slippery as an eel. **Khelél-pe sar e yegúla.** She dances like an eel/twists and elusively turns in every dirction.

yekh *num/pron* **1)** one (*num*) **2)** one male *psn* **3)** *indef/art see* **êkh** *for gloss*

yekh-mai-xansû *adv/phr* & *nm* one less

yekh -po-yekh *adv/phr* one by one, one on one

yekha *nf* one woman; **1) Yekha si la trin shave, yekha si la pansh, sa amáre Rromnya si len but shave.** One woman has five (children), one has three, all our women have many children. **2)** *adj/obl* **Dyas-dúma yekha le Rromnyánsa** He spoke with one of the woman.

yekhá-avrya *pron/f/acc* **Akushen yekhá-avrya.** They are cussing each other (*two women*).

yekháko *adj* frantic, desperate

yekhali *nf* number one

yekhátar *adv* all of a sudden, at once, immediately, right away, unexpectedly

yekh-avrêsa *pron/s/inst/adv* with each other, mutually

yekh-avrêsko *gen/adj* belonging to one another, mutual

yekhá-yekháte *comp/adv* one to one(*if two women*); **Le dui deya dine-dúma yekhá-yekháte.** The two mothers spoke one to one.

yekh-dáta *comp/adv* once, one time; **mai yekh dáta** once again/one more time **yekh mai but** *comp/adv* & *nm* one more

yekh-dáta mai anglal *adv/phr* once before

yekhé-avres *pron/m/obl* each other, one another; **Amrandine yekhé-avres.** They cursed each other (*two men*)

yekhé-gêrbêski gumíla *comp/nf* one-humped (*Arabian*) camel

yekhé-rêgáko *comp/adj* one-sided; **yekhé-rêgáko xamos** one-sided argument

yekhêsko *gen/adj* belonging to one; **Yekhêski si e gláta.** The baby is one-year-old.

yekhé-yakháko *gen/adj* one-eyed

yekhé-yekhéste *comp/adv* one to one (*if two men*); **Mardé-pe yekhé-yekhêste.** They fought one to one.(*if two men*)

yekh-fyálo *adj/phr* just the same

yekh-fyálo *nm* **1)** the same **2)** *adv* the same as; **Tume keren yekh-fyálo buki sar amênde.** You do the same thing as us/we do. **Sa yekh-fyálo si.** It makes no difference.

yekhimos *nm* oneness, solidarity, unity; brotherhood and unity under our flag, **phralimos thai yekhimos telal amári zastáva.**

yekhorro *adj* alone, lone, only, single; **Yekhorro sas, xasardo ándo wêrsh.** He was alone, lost in the forest. **Wo si múrro shav, o yekkhorro.** He is my son, the only one.

yekhorro *nm* **1)** man alone, single *psn*, lone *psn*; **Me sim núma yekhorro, so shai kerav?** I am only one man alone, what can I do?: *nf* **yekhorri 2)** one little one/little child: *nf* **yekhorri**

yekh-pála-yekh *adv/phr* in single file, one-after-the-other, one behind the other, one by one

yékhto 1) *adj* first, primary **2)** *nm* number one; **Me sim o yékhto ánde líniya.** I am number one in line.

yekhwar *num* once

yekhwares *adv* once

yélma *nf* elm

yelmáko *gen/adj* made of elm wood

yelmalin *nf* elm tree

yertil *vt* **1)** absolve, excuse, forgive, pardon: *pp/adj* **yertime**; **Yertisar ma!** Excuse me! Pardon me! **Te yertil lês o Del!** May God absolve/forgive him! **2)** *v/refl* **yertíl-pe a)** be absolved, be excused/forgiven/pardoned **b)** reach menopause, go through change of life; **Yertisáili katar o Del.** She has passed through menopause/She has ben pardoned/exonerated by God.

yertime *pp/adj* absolved, excused/forgiven/pardoned

yertimos *nm* **1)** apology, excuse, forgiveness, pardon **2)** **mangel ~** apologize, beg for forgiveness/mercy **3)** mercy

yérto *adj* **1)** absolved/excused/forgiven/pardoned; **Te avel yérto!** May he be forgiven! **2)** late (*recently-deceased*)

Yeruslámo *nm* Jerusalem (*Folk*)

Yésu Krísto *nm* Jesus Christ (*Am*)

Yesus/Isus *nm* Jesus

Yesusêsko *gen/adj* belonging to Jesus, of Jesus

Yéva *nf* Eve

yilêngo-dóftoro *nm* cardiologist

yiléstar *nm/abl/adv* from the heart, gladly, willingly

yilo *nm* **1)** heart (*Anat*); **Chordyan múrro yilo.** You stole my heart/*id* You made me fall in love with you. **2)** *fig* conscience; **Lêsko yilo phendya lêske ke nas wórta so kerénas.** His conscience told him what they were doing was not right. **3)** core, pit, stone (*fruit*) **4)** center (*flower*) **5)** heart (*in playing cards*)

yízula *nf* island

yódo *nm* iodine

Yoi *interj* Gee! Oh! Ouch!

yonáko *nm* giant (*Am*)

yorgáno *nm* patchwork quilt

yorgováno *nm* lilac

yorgutáno *nm* **1)** orangutan **2)** lout, ignorant person: *nf* **yorgutánka**

yówtra *nf* yoghurt

yugil *vt* yoke (*oxen*): *pp/adj* **yugime**

yúgo *nm* neck yoke, yoke (*for an ox*)

yuházi *nm* herdsman, shepherd

Yúro *nm* Euro Dollar: *pl* **Yúrya** (*Eur*)

yúshto *nm* pressure cooker, steam-kettle, cauldron

yústo *nm* yeast

yuzil *vt* **1)** handle, make use of, use: *pp/adj* **yuzime** (*Am*); **Zhanes sar te yuzis o blastéri?** Do you know how to use/handle a sand blaster? **2)** *v/refl* **yuzíl-pe** be used, used for; **Pe sóste yuzíl-pe kodo?** What's that used for?

yuzimos *nm* function, purpose, use

Z

zabastólka *nf* civil disobedience/disturbance, riot, uprising

zabála *nf* bit, snaffle

zabayil *vt* **1)** delay, detain, hinder, hold up, make late: *pp/adj* **zabayime 2)** *v/refl* **zabayíl-pe a)** be delayed, be late **b)** be lingering/malingering, **c)** be loafing, loaf, be wasting time on *smthg* **d)** falter, **e)** lag behind, straggle

zabayimásko *gen/adj* delaying, lingering, loafing, straggling

zabayime *pp//adj* delayed, held up, late

zabayimos *nm* delay, hindrance, hold up

zabayitóri *nm* **1)** *psn* who impedes *smthg* **2)** loafer, laggard, malingerer **4)** straggler

zabúno *nm* leather bomber jacket, car coat, leather jacket

zahárniko *adj* **1)** sugar, sugared **2)** sweetened with sugar

zaharnítsa *nf* sugar bowl

zaháro *nm* **1)** sugar **2)** lump/spoonful of sugar: *pl* **zahárya 3)** sugar diabetes

zaháro -yarbáko *nm* maple sugar

zaklótso *nm* cap, cover, lid, pot lid, top

zakoníya *nf* laws, statutes, by laws; **Bordôski zakoníya** statutes/by laws of a Board of Directors

zakóno 1) law, rule of law, statute: *pl* **zakóya/zakónurya; Amáro zakóno Rromano nai ramome.** Our Romani law is not written down. **2)** justice, human justice; **Kai si amáro zakóno?** Where is our justice? **3)** human rights, rights under the law

zakónurya *nm/pl* laws, rights, rules of behaviour

zalil *vt* **1)** knock out, render unconscious: *pp/adj* **zalime 2)** cause to be in a coma, cause to faint/swoon; **Zalisardyas lês o barrudimos**. The explosion rendered him unconscious. **2)** *v/refl* **zalíl-pe a)** suffer a concussion, become dazed/semi-conscious **b)** collapse, faint, swoon; **Zalisáili e Rromni kána ashundyás godo swáto**. The (*Romani*) woman fainted when she heard that word (*news*). **Mardyas lês o gazho thai pelo zalime**. The (non-Romani) man hit him and he fell unconscious. **Zalisáili ándo hãlo**. She collapsed in the hall.

zalime *pp/adj* faint, dizzy, in a coma, knocked/rendered unconscious; **Tsîrrá zalime sas la rrakyátar**. He was slightly dizzy from the whisky.

zalimos *nm* **1)** knockout blow **2)** collapse, fainting spell **3)** concussion **4)** daze, dizziness

zaloga *adv* **1)** slightly, a little **2)** small amount of **3)** *id* **Zaloga so chi mulem**. I almost died/A little more and I would have been a goner.

zalogítsa *adv* a little, a trifle; **Shéyo, grizhosar zalogítsa!** Girl, tidy up a little!

zalzáiro *nm* acid, muriatic acid: *pl* **zalzáirya; zalzáiro-boriyátiko** boric acid

zar *nm* pubic hair

zaralo *adj* exhibiting prominent pubic hair

zastáva/zastávo *nf* ensign, flag (*Eur*)

zástrya *nf* dowry: *pl* **zástri; zástrya-sumnakuni** golden dowry

zebáva *nf* amusement, fun

zêbavíl 1) *vt* entertain, provide amusement/fun: *pp/adj* **zêbavimé 2) zêbavíl-pe** *v/refl* amuse oneself, have fun

zêbravimásko *adj* amusing, entertaining
zêfto *nm* 1) asphalt, black topping, pavement, tarmac 2) *vt* thol ~ lay asphalt/paving, blacktop
zêftomós *nm* asphalting, paving of driveways, laying tarmac
zelenil *vt* 1) make green/verdant: *pp/adj* zelenime 2) *v/refl* zeleníl-pe become green/verdant
zelenimos *nm* 1) greening, greenness 2) landscaping, planting of trees/shrubs for non-Roma
zeleníya *nf* 1) greenery 2) verdigris 3) watercress
zéleno *adj* 1) green 2) inexperienced, young and inexperienced 3) *nm* amateur, greenhorn, neophyte: *nf* zéleni inexperienced/innocent young woman
zélenone-yakhêngo *comp/gen/adj* green-eyed
zêmliya *nf* earth
zêmlyáko *gen/adj* of the earth
zêmlyáko izdramos *comp/nm* earth tremor
zetenil *vt* anoint (*with oil*): *pp/adj* zetenime
zetinalo *adj* oily, covered with cooking oil/olive oil
zetinimos *nm* anointing
zétino *nm* 1) oil: *pl* zetina/zétina 2) cooking oil, olive oil 3) anointing oil 4) lamp oil
zéya *nf* back (*Anat*); Dukhal ma múrri zéya. My back is aching.
zeyáko *gen/adj* back, of the back, dorsal; zeyáko naswalimos back problems
zgúrra *nf* 1) cinder, railway cinders/coke 2) ember, smouldering ember: *pl* zgúrri cinders
zgyárra *nf* claw, talon: *pl* zgyérri; Mudardyas lês o zhêgáno pêske zgyarênsa. The beast mauled him to death/killed him with its claws.
zgyarril/zgyarrûl *vt* 1) claw, maul, scratch: *pp/adj* zgyarrime 2) *v/refl* zgyarríl-pe be clawed, scratched, mauled
zgyarrimos *nm* scratching, clawing, mauling

zíbra *nf* zebra
zídra *nf* dulcimer, zither (*Mus*)
zíngo *nm* zinc compound made from muriatic acid and zinc photo plates and used as a temper in wipe-tinning/tin plating.
zípra 1) zipper. 2) fly (*of trousers*); O gazho avilo ánde ófisa thai phuterdyas pêski zípra. The man came into the parlour and exposed himself/opened his zipper/fly. (*Am*)
zirópo *nm* syrup
zlag *nf* 1) earring: *pl.* zlaga pair of earrings 2) key ring 3) handle of a key
zlaibóko *nm* billfold, purse, wallet
zlatári *nm* gold panner
znachime *part* supposed to (*Eur*); Znachime sim te zhav lêsa. I am supposed to go with him.
Zodyáko *nm* Zodiac; Le Sámnurya le Zodyakóske The Signs of the Zodiac
zor *nf* 1) defense, power, strength 2) energy, pep, vigor 3) violence
zoralé-glasósko *comp/adj* heated (*argument*)
zorales *adv* hard, loudly, strongly, vigorously, with effort; Mardya lês zorales. He hit him hard.
zoralimos *nm* temper
zórali-stákla *comp/nf* plate glass
zórali-vórba *comp/nf* pep talk, strong talk
zoralo/zuralo *adj* 1) brawny, dense, durable, hard, powerful, solid, stable, strong; o mai zoralo the strongest/most striking, the most important 2) energetic, vigorous 3) bright (*light*) 4) loud (*sound*) 5) sorely, strikingly 6) compelling
zorása *nf/inst/adv* 1) by force; Nashadyas la zorása. He kidnapped her by force. 2) effectively, convincingly, with power; Del-dúma zorása. He speaks convincingly/with power. 3) energetically
zóri *nf* dawn, daybreak, sunrise; ángla zóri before dawn
zorimos *nm* 1) force, energy, strength, vigor 2) durability, endurance, stability, strength,

zoryárdyol *vi* **1)** be made harder/stronger/sturdier, be made more durable/resistant,/stable: *pp/adj* **zoryardilo 2)** be bolstered/reinforced **3)** be energized

zoryarel *vt* **1)** energize, harden, strengthen, make strong, reinforce: *pp/adj* **zoryardo 2)** bolster, reinforce

zoryávol/zoryol *vi* become energized, grow stronger, become reinforced/powerful, often with **mai:** *pp/adj* **zorailo; Swáko ges mai zoryol godo Rrom.** That Rom becomes more powerful every day.

zûdári *nm* stone mason, builder of walls

zûdó/zûdo/zîdo *nm* wall

zûduwíl/zîdowíl *v/tr* brick up, immure, wall in: *pp/adj* **zuduwime**

zûduwimós *nm* immurement

zumado *pp/adj* tried out, tested

zumádyol *vi* to have been attempted/assayed/tested/tried/tried out: *pp/adj* **zumadilo; Zumádilo. Chísto súmnakai si.** It has been tested. It's pure gold.

zumavel *vt* **1)** attempt, test drive, test, try, try out, try to prove: *pp/adj* **zumado 2)** assay **3)** dare (*to try*) **4)** *v/refl* **zumavél-pe** test oneself, put oneself to the test

zumayimos *nm* **1)** attempt **2)** try **3)** test, test drive, try out **4)** assessment

zumbil *vt* **1)** buzz, drone: *pp/adj* **zumbime 2)** *v/refl* be buzzing/droning

zumbimos *nm* agitation (*in a beehive*), buzzing, droning

zumi *nf* broth, soup

zumyáko *gen/adj* for/of soup; **charo zumyáko** soup bowl

zûn/zîn *nf* **1)** saddle; **Trádel o grast bi-zûnáko.** He rides the horse bareback **2) thol zûn** (*with* **pe**) *vt* saddle; **Thodyas zûn pe pêske grastes.** He saddled his horse.

zûnáko-sapui *nm* saddle soap

zurales *adv* **1)** in a flash, quickly; **Xoxadyas lês zurales.** She quickly deceived him. **2)** forcefully, loudly, vigorously **3)** sorely; **Zurales dorime sas pála pêsko merimos.** He was sorely missed after his death.

zuralimos *nm* temper (*for steel*)

zuralo *adj* **1)** fast, quick **2)** forceful, loud, hard, mighty, strong, vigorous, with force

zurayimásko *gen/adj* strengthening, condusive to strength

zurayimos *nm* **1)** strength **2)** exercise, exertion

zúrka *nf* zircon

zúrna *nf* **1)** elf, fairy, goblin **2)** South-Balkan double-reed shawm (*Mus*) (*Eur*)

zuryal *vi* **1)** become stronger, become bolstered: *pp/adj* **zuryailo 2)** exercise oneself, improve one's health by excercising/exerting oneself

zuryarel/zuravel *vt* **1)** brace, bolster, consolidate, fortify, make stronger, reinforce, strengthen: *pp/adj* **zuryardo 2)** drop forge, harden by forging, temper **3)** press (point); **Zuryarel pêsko swáto.** He's pressing his point.

zuryarimos *nm* **1)** forging, drop forging, tempering **2)** bracing, bolstering, consolidation, fortification, reinforcement.

ZH

zhal *vi* **1)** flow, go, run, run on/operated on/by, be ongoing/in progress: *pp/adj* **gêló/golo**; **Zha sastimása!** Go with health! **Nashlam kána zhálas o marimos.** We fled when the war was going on. **2)** travel **3)** happen, take place, be scheduled; **So zhal?** What's happening/ What's up? **So gêló?** What happened? **4)** date, go out; **Zhal kadya rakli?** Does that girl go out, go on dates? **5)** *v/refl* **zhal-pe a)** be going/make oneself go. **Zha-ma te dav yag o mobíli.** I'm going out to start the car. **b)** get started, happen, take place; **O kidimos zhal-pe ka l' trin ándo mizméri.** The meeting is taking place at 3 p.m. **Kána zhal-pe o spektákulo?** When does the peformance start? **6) ~ kruyal** go around; **Zhal kruyal ánde kólya.** He's going around in circles **7) ~ pála** follow, go after **8) ~** *with* **pai; Zhal o pai ánda lêste.** He is sweating. **9) ~** *with* **rat; Zhal o rat ánda lêste.** His blood is flowing out of him/He is bleeding to death. **10) ~** *with* **breshun; O breshun zhal pa o taváno.** The rain is flowing off the roof. **11) zhal te avel pálpale** *vi/phr* leave and return/go outside, cool off and come back

zhalil/zhalowil *vt* **1)** lament, mourn (*deceased*): *pp/adj* **zhalime, zhalowime**; **Zhalin pênge papos.** They are mourning their grandfather. **2)** deplore **3)** commisserate **3)** *v/refl* **zhalíl-pe** be in mourning, be lamenting

zhalimos *nm* bereavement, grief, mourning

zhálniko *adj* **1)** lugubrious, melancholy, mournful, sorrowful **2)** mourner: *pl* **zhálnichi:** *nf* **zhálnika**

zhalowimáta *nf/pl* womens' mourning clothes

zhalowime *nm* bereaved, lamented, mourned

zhalowimos *nm* **1)** bereavement, grief, mourning, period of mourning **2)** womens'clothes worn during mourning **3)** mourning ceremony in the funeral parlour

zháltar *vi* depart, leave, go away/get lost, take off; **Zhátar!** Get lost! **Zháltar o djédjesh.** The train is leaving. **Zhátar, Na badisar ma!** Get lost, don't bother me! **Lem-man thai gêlèmtar.** I made up my mind and I departed.

zhálya *nf* **1)** mourning; **Ánde zhálya si.** They are in mourning **2)** grief, sadness, sorrow **3)** compassion, sympathy

zhalyáko *gen/adj* grieving, lugubrious, mourning, sorrowful

zhambash *nm* horse trader, animal/cattle dealer

zhámbo *nm* toad: *nf* **zhámba**

zhámena/zhámeya 1) *nm/nf/pl* twins (*Eur*); **Dui phrala zhámena si.** They are two twin brothers. **2) Zhámena** Gemini (*Zod*)

zhámeno *nm* **1)** twin brother: *nf* **zhámenútsa** twin sister

zhamutro *nm* **1)** son-in-law **2)** brother-in-law

zhandári *nm* **1)** gendarme, federal/national policeman: *nf* **zhandárka** (*Eur*) **2)** any police officer (*Am*) **3)** RCMP officer (*Can*) **4)** Jack (*in cards*)

zhandarítsko *adj* police; **kréposto ~,** police headquarters

zhandaríya *nf* federal/national police headquarters

zhandáriya *nf* federal/national polic force

zhándoi *v/part* going, in motion; **Xálas zhándoi.** He/she was eating while walking.

zhanel *vt* **1)** know, know how: *pp/adj* **zhanglo: Chi zhanav te kerav.** I don't know how to do (it). **2)** come to know, find out **3)** have had sexual relations with *smbdy;* **Zhanglas la de trin bersh.** He knew her three years ago. **4)** *v/refl* **zhanél-pe** be aware/conscious, know oneself, be aware of oneself, be in control of one's memory/senses; **Chi zhanél-pe.** He's suffering from amnesia.

zhanglél-pe *v/refl* be known/known to be, be known as; **Sárekai kai zhála, zhanglél-pe dilo.** Everywhere he goes, he's known to be a fool.

zhanglimos 1) information, knowledge **2)** fame, recognition, status

zhanglo *pp/adj* **1)** informed **2)** known

zhanglyárdyol *vi* be awakened: *pp/adj* **zhanglyardilo**

zhanglyarel *vt* awaken, bring to consciousness, wake up: *pp/adj* **zhangyardo**

zhanglyarimos *nm* awakening

zhanglyávol *vi* awaken, wake up: *pp/adj* **zhanglailo; Zhangláilem ráno ánde diminyátsa.** I awoke early in the morning.

zhanimos *nm* fact, knowledge, understanding (of): *pl* **zhanimáta** facts, knowledge, knowhow

zhapúnka *nf* **1)** cuff link, stud **2)** broach

zhávo *nm* regret, sorrow; **Zhávo mánge ánda túte.** I empathize with you. **Zhávo mánge ke nai kathe.** I miss her. **Zhávo mánge te ashunav kodya.** I'm very sorry to hear that. **Zhávo mánge ke nai ma.** I regret that I don't have it. **Zhávo lêske ánda so kerdyas.** He feels remorse for what he did. **Manai túke zhávo ánda so kerdyan?** Aren't you sorry about what you did? **Báro zhávo mánge te phenav tumênge ke mulo o Fránki.** I am very sorry to tell you that Frank died.

id **Xalyas pêski baxt ai nai mánge zhávo ánda lêste.** He brought it on himself and I'm not at all sorry for him.

zêbáva *nf* amusement, fun

zêbavíl *vt* **1)** entertain, provide amusement/fun: *pp/adj* **zêbavimé 2) zêvabíl-pe** *v/refl* amuse oneself, have fun

zêbavimásko *adj* amusing, entertaining

zhegáno *nm* **1)** carnivore, wild animal/beast, man-eating beast, predatory animal: *nf* **zhegáni:** *nm/nf/pl* **zhegáya 2)** predator

zhêkùn *adv/conj/prep* until, so long as/as long as

zheno *nm* person: *pl* **zhene:** *nf* **zheni.** This word is used mainly with numbers & quantities but can also refer to a generic person who could be either Romani or non-Romani; **Dikhlem pansh zhene.** I saw five people. **But zhene avile kai sláva.** Many people came to the feast. **Hifta zhene mule ándo pharrayimos.** Seven people died in the crash.

zhêro *nm* acorn: *pl* **zhêrya**

zhêrtva *nf* **1)** sacrifice **2)** martyre, victim of expediency/fall guy/woman. **3)** *vt/i* **Kerel ~** make a sacrifice

zhi *adv/prep* as far as, till, until

zhi akana/zhyakana *adv/phr* until now, up to the present; **Chi mai dikhlem lês zhi-akana.** I never saw him until now.

zhi atunchára *ad/phr* until then

zhi kána? *ad/phr* until when?

zhi kothe *ad/phr* as far as there, there, to that point/place; **Areslem zhi kothe kána perélas e ryát.** I got there just as night was falling. **Zhi-kothe símas.** This was as far as I got.

zhi-ka *conj/prep/adv* until, till, up to, as far as; **Azhuker kathe zhi ka me avav pálpale!** Wait here till I return! **Pelo ándo pai zhi ka buláte.** He fell in the water up to his backside. **Phirdyas zhi ka o fóro.** He walked as far as the city.

zhí-ka-buláte *adv/phr* up to the arse; **Phirásas ándo iv zhi-ka-buláte.** We were walking up to the arse walking in snow.

zhi-kai *conj/prep* till, until, up to, as far as, while **Note:** use only when directly before before feminine nouns; **O drom zhal zhi-kai playing.** The road goes as far as the mountain.

zhí-ka-korráte *adv/phr* up to the neck; **Pelo ándo pai zhi-ka korráte.** He fell into the water up to his neck.

zhîla *nf* 1) sinew, tendon 2) vein

zhinzhíya *nf* gum (*Anat*)

zhipûn *conj* unless, if, in the event that; **Zhipûn chi pokinen man, chi kerav e buki.** If they don't pay me, I won't do the work/unless they pay me I won't do the work. **Chi kerel zhipûn chi mothav lêske me.** He won't do (it) unless (if) I don't tell him. **Note:** These types of sentences with **zhipûn** contain a double negative which is common in Kalderash dialects; **Chi keráv zhipûn wo chi avél.** I won't do it unless he doesn't come/I won't do it unless he comes.

zhiráfa *nf* giraffe

zhivel *vi* be animate, be alive, live: *pp/adj* **zhivdino** (*Eur*)

zhivimos *nm* animation, life (*Eur*)

zhívina *nf* herbivore, domesticated animal, tame animal: *pl* **zhívini** domesticated animals, farm animals

zhívindi yag *comp/nf* living fire, spark of life

zhivindil *vt* 1) awaken, wake up, revitalize, revive, bring alive, bring to life, regenerate, rejuvenate: *pp/adj* **zhivindime** 2) resurrect, raise from the dead 3) liven up 4) *v/refl* **zhivindíl-pe a)** come to life, come alive, wake up, regain consciousness **b)** become resurrected, return from the dead; **Mulo o Yesus pe trushul hai zhivindisáilo.** Jesus died on the cross and was resurrected. **c)** be regenerated

zhivindime *pp/adj* 1) awakened, conscious, revived, revitalized; **Zhivindimé-lo akana.** He's conscious now. 2)

resurrected 3) recycled; **Nai neve shûni, zhivindime si.** They are not new tires, they are retreads.

zhivindimos *nm* 1) animation 2) incarnation 3) **nevo zhivindimos** *comp/nm.* reincarnation

zhivinditóri *nm* battery charger, rejuvenator, reanimator, revitalizer

zhívindo *adj* 1) active, alive, living; **Kodo nai zhívindo swáto.** That's not a word used anymore /not a living word. 2) incarnate 3) *nm* living man: *nf* **zhívindi** 3) **zhívindo mulo** living dead man, zombie: *nf* **zhívindi muli**

zhívutro *nm* animal, creature: *nf* **zhívutrya**

zhóla *nf* 1) pulse 2) **azbal ~** *comp/vt* feel somebody's pulse; **Azba lêski zhóla!** Feel his pulse!

zhov *nf* oats; **Na de le grastêske desya but zhov, xan pêske pûrr!** Don't give the horse too much oats, they will eat out his stomach!

Zhowine *adv* on Thursday

Zhóya *nf* Thursday

Zhudovísmo *nm* Judaism

Zhudovítska *nf* Yiddish (*Lang*)

Zhudovítsko *adj* Jewish

Zhúdovo/Zhìdovo *nm* Jew: *pl* **Zhudováya:** *nf* **Zhudováika**

zhukel/zhukûl *nm* 1) male dog: *pl* **zhukla; De l' zhukles te xal!** Feed the dog! 2) hound dog, womanizer 3) **phuro zhukel** old dog/wise old man

zhuklanes *adv* like a dog; **Merel zhuklanes, bi-lovêngo, ánde úlitsa.** He will die like a dog, without money, in the street.

zhuklano *adj* canine

zhuklêsko *gen/adj* belonging to a dog; **zhuklêsko-shelo** dog leash

zhukli *nf* 1) bitch (*female dog*) 2) *fig* bitch, shrew (*Eur*)

zhuklikanes *adv* like a bitch/shrew

zhuklikano *adj* like a bitch

zhuklyáko *gen/adj* belonging to a bitch; **la zhuklyáko ríkono** the bitch's puppy

zhuli/zhuvli *nf* **1)** female, young woman (*Am*) **2)** wife, woman (*Eur*) **3)** female of a species

zhulimos *nm* mourning

zhulowil *vt* **1)** mourn: *pp/adj* **zhulowime 2)** *v/refl* **zhulowíl-pe** be mourning

Zhune *adv* On Christmas Eve

zhungalo *see* **djungalo**

Zhúno *nm* **1)** Christmas Eve

zhuto *nm* pair: *pl* **zhute**; **zhuto kalts** pair of trousers

zhutóri *nm* **1)** lawyer **2)** assistant, helper (*Eur*)

zhútso *nm* **1)** wire **2)** steel string (*Mus*) **3)** wire service, newswire **4)** antenna (*of automobile*)

zhutsol *vt* wire: *pp/adj* **zhutsome**

zhutsomos *nm* electricial wiring

zhutsóski bar *comp/nf* wire fence

zhutsósko *gen/adj* made of wire

zhútso-skutsome *comp/nm* barbed wire

zhuv *nf* louse: *pl* **zhuvya**

zhuvalo *adj* infested with lice, lousy

zhuvli *nf* **1)** female; **Si mursh wórka zhuvli?** Is it male or female? **2)** spouse, wife, woman

zhuvlikanes *adv* like a woman; **Rovélas zhuvlikanes**. He was weeping like a woman.

zhuvlikano *adj* **1)** female, feminine **2)** effete, wimpish

zhuvlimos *nm* **1)** womankind **2)** femininity

zhuvlyángo *gen/adj* relating to females/women; **zhuvlyánge drépturya/hatáya** women's rights

zhuvlyárdyol *vi* become infected with lice

zhuvlyarel *vt* infect with lice: *pp/adj* **zhuvlyardo**

Also from
MAGORIA BOOKS

E ZHIVINDI YAG
THE LIVING FIRE

BY RONALD LEE

Ronald Lee's autobiographical novel, formerly published as "Goddam Gypsy", is an intense, fast moving, and brutally honest affair.

Yanko—a Canadian Rom who 'took the non-Romani way but didn't go far'—seeks his fortunes both among and apart from the Roma, never quite finding his place. His story exposes the out of sight, out of mind world of Canada's Roma in 1970's Montréal: Parties, rackets, bar brawls, weddings, desperate poverty, and intermittent police raids fuel in Yanko the passion, creativity, and rebellious defiance that is The Living Fire.

MAGORIA BOOKS
www.MagoriaBooks.com

Also from
MAGORIA BOOKS

DUKH — PAIN

BY HEDINA SIJERČIĆ

Hedina Sijerčić's collection of richly evocative poems weave together the author's fleeting joys and enduring tragedies with traditional Romani folklore.

Hedina's poetry is enlightening in its candidness, which shatters the fanciful myth of the mysterious and ever-carefree Roma, replacing it with lyric images of a people living, loving, and dying, not immune to the caprice of the world that surrounds them. It is through such tragedies that the lingering message of these poems has become simply dukh, pain.

MAGORIA BOOKS
www.MagoriaBooks.com

RROMANE PARAMICHA:
Stories and Legends of the Gurbeti Roma

BY HEDINA SIJERČIĆ

Rromane Paramicha is a unique collection of folktales and legends that bring alive the rich cultural and religious traditions of the Roma. Hedina Sijerčić, internationally published Romani poet and author, offers us the stories from her childhood with the authenticity of a direct inheritor of oral tradition. This special bilingual edition contains both faithful English translations, as well as the Gurbeti Romani originals of each story, with a selection of Doris Greven's beautiful watercolour illustrations.

Visit www.RomaniFolktales.com for more information.

MAGORIA BOOKS
www.MagoriaBooks.com

ROMANI FOLKTALES
(illustrated children's books)

BY HEDINA SIJERČIĆ

A series of beautifully illustrated children's books featuring excerpted Romani folktales from "Rromane Paramicha: Stories and Legends of the Gurbeti Roma".

In each book, Hedina Sijerčić, internationally published Romani Poet and Author, brings us the stories from her childhood with the vivid watercolour painted illustrations of Doris Greven. These special bilingual editions contain both the English versions and the Romani originals of each story.

Visit www.RomaniFolktales.com for more information.

MAGORIA BOOKS
www.MagoriaBooks.com

Coming in 2011 from
MAGORIA BOOKS

ROMANI DICTIONARY
(English – Kalderash)

BY RONALD LEE

Ronald Lee—internationally renowned author, Romani activist, and Sessional Instructor of the University of Toronto's "The Romani Diaspora" course—brings us the most detailed and accurate English–Romani dictionary ever to be published.

Intended to be a tool for both native speakers and language learners, the dictionaries provide both grammatical classification and examples through real world phrases, making them the ideal companion volumes to the author's earlier "Learn Romani" and to Ian Hancock's "Handbook of Vlax Romani".

MAGORIA BOOKS
www.MagoriaBooks.com

ROMANI DICTIONARY
(Gurbeti – English / English – Gurbeti)

BY HEDINA SIJERČIĆ

The first comprehensive bi-directional dictionary of the compiler's native Gurbeti Romani dialect, with both grammatical classification and many examples of real-world usage. Ideal for both practical use by native speakers and language learners, as well as for academics interested in lexical comparisons of Romani dialects.

Spoken by large groups of Roma still living in the successor states of the former Yugoslavia, as well as the widely emigrated diaspora created by the turbulent history of the region; Gurbeti Romani is the native language of many a Romani artist and writer, and thus the dialect used in several notable books, Hedina Sijerčić's numerous titles among them.

MAGORIA BOOKS
www.MagoriaBooks.com

ME NI DŽANAV TE KAMAV
(tentative title)

BY RUŽDIJA SEJDOVIĆ

Ruždija Sejdović's intimate and symbolically charged love poems bring into keen focus the passion and suffering of both the poet and his people. The delicately crafted verses shift imperceptably from speaking with the voice of one man to echoing the cries of a rising Romani nation still haunted by European demons.

Containing the author's poems in English and Hungarian in addition to the original Romani; this book aims to be a mirror for and a bridge between peoples both kindred and other.

MAGORIA BOOKS
www.MagoriaBooks.com

Coming in 2011 from
MAGORIA BOOKS

ROMANI EBOOKS
(The Living Fire, Romani Folktales, etc.)

Magoria Books will soon begin a pilot project of publishing eBook Reader customized ePUB and PDF editions of our existing and upcoming titles. The first two books planned for digital distribution will be Ronald Lee's autobiographical novel "E Zhivindi Yag—The Living Fire" and Hedina Sijerčić's "Rromane Paramicha: Stories and Legends of the Gurbeti Roma", with other titles to follow.

MAGORIA BOOKS
www.MagoriaBooks.com

About Magoria Books

Magoria Books is an independent international publisher of Romani books. Our aim is to provide Romani authors with opportunities to continue to develop and enrich the ever-growing body of Romani literature.

We therefore encourage Romani poets, writers, and activists to approach us with their ideas and proposals. We are particularly interested in folktales, poetry, and other culturally focused manuscripts, including those written in Romani or Central/East European languages.

We are also interested in partnerships with translators, community organizations, and foreign publishers to find ways to increase distribution, availability, and impact of existing and upcoming titles.

Write to us at:

Magoria Books
720 Bathurst Street, 2nd Floor
Toronto, ON   M5S 2R5
Canada

CPSIA information can be obtained
at www.ICGtesting.com
Printed in the USA
BVHW01s1741070518
515484BV00013B/17/P